Names, Names, and More Names

Locating Your Dutch Ancestors in Colonial America

Names, Names, and More Names

Locating Your Dutch Ancestors in Colonial America

Arthur C.M. Kelly

Ancestry.

Table of Contents

DEDICATION

Of the many books that I've authored, compiled, or edited, I have yet to dedicate any. This was perhaps an oversight since my wife, Nancy Ann Vogel, has generally supported me in all of my genealogical ventures and has been a source of encouragement when assistance was needed. Add to that the fact that she also had been bitten by the genealogy bug at an early age and the two of us have shared family history enthusiasm.

The nature of this book, names and naming, lends itself also to my dedicating it to the memory of my parents, Arthur Maurice Kelly and Marie Caroline Geitz. My mother told me that fate had been good to her in that she always wanted a son and a daughter. My sister and I fulfilled her wishes and she, although she hadn't dabbled very much in genealogy, provided us with names that could be described as modified patronymic. For me, her son, she chose to honor my father by giving me his Christian name, Arthur, and this was followed with two middle names, one for each grandfather, Charles Geitz and Maurice Kelly so that I became Arthur Charles Maurice Kelly (and now the world knows the answer to the mystery of "What does C. M. stand for?")

Incidentally, my sister was treated the same way – Marie, for my mother, and the middle names of Imogene Clare. Now, Clara was Grandma Kelly's name but since our maternal grandmother was also a Marie, the Imogene came from the great-grandparent generation. So now you know the "rest of the story."

ACKNOWLEDGMENT

Many thanks to Henry Hoff and Harry Macy for alerting the author to sources not considered in the first draft of this book. Also, while it is intended that this book be as complete as possible, it is obvious that readers will be able to provide additional examples of patronymics/surname equivalents as well as information for the other sections of this book. If so, they are encouraged to forward that information to the author at:

Arthur C. M. Kelly
60 Cedar Heights Road
Rhinebeck, NY 12572-2200
kinship@compuserve.com

so that it may be included in future editions of the book.

Names, Names and More Names

INTRODUCTION

Through the years, meeting genealogists in various stages of involvement, from beginners to professionals, it would seem that the common element in those who are really bitten by the genealogy bug is the sense of solving a mystery and putting one more piece into the puzzle. It satisfies some need and keeps the process on going. There is always more to learn. And, of course, it is never ending, since each new discovery opens new paths to follow.

The puzzle is particularly difficult in the New York area for a variety of reasons. At one time, there were no state regulations that required the local government to keep vital records. Therefore there is no consistent body of records such as may be found in the New England states. The Dutch influence continued in the colonies although the actual control of the government was English. Major nationalities found here beside the Dutch included the Germans, French Huguenots and English as well as Irish, Scottish, Flemish, Walloon, and Scandinavian. The names written down for these people in surviving records depended to a large extent on how they were pronounced by the individual and the background and training of the person writing the information. As we might expect, the degree of Anglicization (converting the name to English) and the educational background of the participants also had its effect on the resulting entry in the record. Phonetic spelling and poor calligraphy combine to create many variations of first and last names.

Successfully accomplishing genealogy in the New York-New Jersey area requires that one be aware of a large number of factors useful in identifying individuals. These include the patronymic system of naming, the use of synonym names, name equivalents, naming customs, and significant names.

Family history research is always challenging, but the unique situation that exists in New York and New Jersey research makes the identification of individuals and the extension of family lines particularly difficult. The early settlement of these regions by the Dutch and their almost exclusive use of the patronymic system of naming provides the researcher with a real challenge when searching for family members in the period prior to about 1720. Once that hurdle is breached, New York State presents an additional barrier to family research. The state did not require the recording of vital records, i.e. birth, death, marriage, until 1880. As a result of these challenging conditions, when success in this area of the country is realized, it is particularly satisfying.

Over thirty years ago, the author began the transcription of church records under the name "Palatine Transcripts." These records focused on the early baptisms and marriages of churches which served the large 1708-1710 German Palatine settlement in New York and New Jersey. The work evolved into the Kinship transcripts which include many of the early Dutch churches of New York and New Jersey and a variety of other types of records totaling over 150 publications. This work has provided an opportunity to study naming customs used in a wide area settled by a diverse ethnic mix.

In the process of indexing the KiNSHiP books, an attempt was made to group names together if they were likely to be the same family or individual. This method of grouping did not exclude the original spellings but did help to point out to the researcher other possible names to explore. The procedure has proved helpful in highlighting families whose names were spelled in many diverse ways. Often a name had to be pronounced aloud to understand its identity. For example, looking at Twettweick, one would hardly realize that the name is probably Chadwick or Sedgewick but pronouncing the name highlights the similarity.

It is important to realize that the way in which a name was recorded depended upon the education and the native language of the scribe. These factors, combined with the accent with which the name was spoken resulted in many interesting variations on names. An interesting example occurs when German ministers attempted to write names of Scots-Irish immigrants who had settled on the Livingston Manor in what is now Columbia County, New York. "Human Gomry" is written for Hugh Montgomery. The McIntires and McDonalds were written as the name sounded to the German or Dutch minister. How many would recognize that Makentews and Markendiss are McIntosh and that Ackly and Oculi are Oakley? The researcher must realize that these names were unfamiliar to the ministers and therefore, we must be imaginative in recognizing the true identity of the individuals. We have discovered many examples of a surname being recorded in many diverse ways during a person's lifetime and then finding that the individual in preparing his last Will and Testament signs it with a flourishing "X." Obviously, if he wasn't aware of the spelling of his family name, how can we hold the scribes more accountable?

The transcription of the church baptism and marriage records includes hundreds of thousands of entries and has provided the knowledge that suggested the production of this book. Previously written articles authored by other genealogists seemed to only touch on some of the naming problems and the difficulties involved in sorting and grouping. There was very little written in the way of solutions. This book is an attempt to bring together as much helpful naming information as possible in one location and to provide the family historian with tools for becoming more successful in the search.

A study of the work of present day genealogists such as Rosalie Fellows Bailey and George Olin Zabriskie and other earlier genealogists such as Dr. S. S. Purple and William J. Hoffman were the impetus that stirred the curiosity and encouraged further study of the problem. Mr. Hoffman, who was born in the Netherlands studied many early Dutch families in New Amsterdam. His work is summarized in a typescript entitled, *Settlers from the Netherlands in America before 1700: A Compendium of Genealogical Information.* This typescript may be found at the New York Genealogical and Biographical Society's library. (NYGandB Newsletter "Settlers from The Netherlands in America Before 1700" Fall 1994, p. 19). Other author's contributions will be mentioned later in this book.

Perhaps the best advice in identifying individuals and their name variants is that the family group must be studied in its entirety in order to work out the true relationships. This is particularly true because the naming customs, which will be explained in more detail later, resulted in many cousins of approximately the same age having exactly the same name and living in the same locality. The best clue to these persons identity becomes the name of their wife. They are identified with this spouse in various places such as in the marriage and baptism records. Even records in which they are not the major participants may identify them as husband and wife and help to provide clues. For this reason close attention must be paid to the sponsors of baptisms since the ministers were very diligent in writing down if a couple were husband and wife even if he used only the abbreviation h.v. signifying his "vrouw" or the Latin "uxor".

However, it is necessary to realize that even if the wife's name is known, there may be identically named couples and therefore it is possible to find two families with the same names having children in the same region. This confusion results in family groups which are difficult to identify unless a will or bible record can be found to confirm the relationships.

Increasing the difficulty of achieving success in New York research is the lack of land records. Many of the areas of early settlement in New York were owned by landlords who held large parcels which they did not sell outright. A sale would have resulted in a recorded deed. But the land was held in a lease hold arrangement which was recorded in private papers and required annual rent payments. A more detailed description of this system may be found in Sung Bok Kim's, *Landlord and Tenant in Colonial New York,* which describes the use of leasing well into the nineteenth century. The advantage of the system to the tenant was that the large landholder provided some amenities such as a dock and mill and the tenant did not have to provide a large sum of money to obtain it. The disadvantage of the system was that the arrangement prevented the leaseholder from fully profiting from the improvements which he made to the property and that he was unable to gain full title to the property. The term of leases varied but some leases were in perpetuity and others were for the extent of three lives.

Wills and probate records are often used to confirm relationships and add detail to a family relationship. As would be expected when a lease arrangement provided for the succession of tenants on the land, a will was not necessary and as a consequence, many generations of families lived in New Amsterdam and New York without leaving a will. It is apparent why genealogy in that state is so very challenging.

EVOLUTION OF NAMES AND NAMING

From a talk delivered by George Rogers Howell in May 1894 to the Albany Institute entitled, "The Origin and Meaning of English and Dutch Surnames of New York State Families" we extract the following:

"All proper names mean something, whether family names, Christian or surnames, or geographical names of land or water. We may not always be able to give their significance. They may have been so worn down by corruption in the lapse of ages, in passing from one race to another, or in any of a number of other ways beyond the power of man to trace. But the fact remains that most names, on analysis, yield a definite meaning, which leads us to the conclusion that the same is true of all. When speaking of the family or surname, we may say that in England, surnames began to be used about the time of the Conquest, 1066. Naturally the nobility would use the name of their estate as the family name. Previous to the Conquest the Anglo-Saxons used but one name. But they, as well as the earlier Britons, the Scots, the Welsh and the Irish, frequently used an explanatory epithet or phrase following the name to designate and describe the owner. Thus we find Athelstane the Unready, Donald the Blue; Ririd the Wolf, etc. This method afforded some relief in designating individuals, but as communities grew larger the necessity of some better method became more and more urgent. The flexible and exuberant manner of obtaining names in vogue among the North American Indians was unknown in Europe.

"The stock of personal names was very limited, and each conquering race brought its own. During the Saxon occupation, Saxon names prevailed. After the Conquest, those of Norman origin grew rapidly into favor until the 12th and 13th centuries, when scarcely any other was heard among high or low, noble, middle class or peasant. This limited stock of personal Christian names led to the use of a family or surname in England as ... after the Conquest. In a typical English village of a thousand inhabitants, we can realize the difficulty that they encountered in the way of doing business with the men of the community. Along one street within a half mile of each other there may have been 12 Williams, 10 Johns, eight Roberts and eight Henrys. Out in the suburbs and the outlying farms and about the brooks and hills there were other Johns, Williams, Roberts and Henrys. How would they distinguish one John from another? The most natural way would be to add the father's name (patronymic) and thus the difficulty would be partially relieved, and only partially, because it would often happen that the fathers also would have the same name. So that several John Johnsons and William Williamsons would still involve confusion. A second process of differentiation would then come into play. One John might be a baker and thus become John Baker and in many cases the surname would become permanent in the family no matter what occupation his sons or grandsons adopted. Another John might be a miller and a third a blacksmith giving rise to the Miller and Smith families in that village. Even occupations, however, might not be sufficiently numerous to go around. Some other process had to be found. There might be a Flemish weaver leading to John Fleming or a John may have a grove of oaks about his homestead and cause him to be differentiated from other Johns by calling him John Oaks or John Oakland. If there were a single tree there, he could be known as John-at-an-oak and eventually shortened to John Nokes. If it was an ash tree, the name may have become Nash. A family at the foot of a hill would have become Underhill; in a valley, Vail or Vale; or near a brook, Brooks.

"But as a matter of fact, and quite as naturally, other circumstances would give rise to other classes of names. The office that a man held would easily designate him. The generic term for a professional man in the church or the law was clerk – then pronounced clark. Hence the great number of Clark families among the English-speaking peoples. The Beadles, Biddles, and Bedells all had for a ancestor a church beadle. A shire or county executive officer was called a reeve. Hence the word sheriff (shire-reeve) and hence also the Reeves family.

"Nicknames and pet names also gave rise to permanent surnames. For example: Alexander not only became a family name itself, but its nickname, Sandy, gave us Sanders, Saunders, and Sanderson. Elias gives Ellis, Elliot, Elkins, and Ellicott. Gilbert gives Gibbs, Gibson, Gibbons, and Gilson. Henry gives Harrison, Harris, Hallett, Halket, Hawkins, and Harriot. Hugh gives Hughes, Hutchins, Hutchinson, Hewlett, Hewet, Howlet, Howitt, Howson, Hewson, Huggins, and Higgins as well as the Welsh Pugh and the Scots Hoey and Mackey, short for MacHugh. John gives Johnson, Jonson, Johns, Jones, Johncock, Jenkins, Jenks, Jenkinson, Jennings, and Jackson. Ralph and the French form Raoul, gives Rawes, Rawson, Rawley, Rawlins, Rawlings, Rawlinson, Rollins, Rollinson, Rawkins, Rapkins, and Rapson. Richard and the nickname Dick gives

Richards, Richardson, Rix, Rixon, Ritson, Rickards, Ricketts, Dickson, Dixon, Dix, Dickens, Dickenson, Hitchins, and Hitchcock. Robert gives Roberts, Robart, Robertson, Robbins, Robinson, Robison, Robson, Dobbs, Dobson, Dobbins, Dobbinson, Hobbs, Hobson, Hobbins, Hopkins, and Hopkinson. Roger gives Rogers, Rogerson, Hodge, Hodges, Hodgkin, Hoskins, Hodgson, Hodson, and Hudson. Walter gives Watts, Watkins, Walters, Waters, Watson, Waterson, Watkins, and Watcock. William gives Williamson, Williams, Wills, Willis, Wilson, Guillemot, Guillot, Gillott, Gillett, Williamot, Wilmot, Willett, Willetts, Willert, Wilkins, Wilkes, Wilkinson, Wilcox, Wicks, Wickens, Weeks, Bill, and Bilson.

"It is not at all necessary to hold that names derived from female Christian names indicated illegitimacy, as some have supposed, for there would be many a widow left to rear young children who would naturally take the name of the mother or have it bestowed on them by the community.

"Another source from which surnames was chosen was physical attributes. If one of two Johns in a village was of light complexion from indoor work and the other swarthy from labor in the sun, it would be natural to call the first John White and the latter John Black. Physical peculiarity gives us surnames of Longshanks or Cruikshanks (tall or crooked). Names of Stark, Sharp, or Smart indicating strong, keen, or bright.

"A final source of surnames particularly for the traveler is the name of the town from which the person came. A John coming into a village would naturally be designated by his former residence providing us with a wealth of surnames.

"An entire new realm of surname possibilities exists when we consider a variation from the patronymic method before noticed. The Irish used two prefixes to the ancestor's name to designate children and remote descendants. 'Mac' and 'Mc' signified the son and 'O' the grandson or a more remote descendant. Thus, if a Donald should have a son he would be called MacDonald and a grandson of Donald would be O'Donald and so on with the added Christian name. The Scots also used this system but a son was more apt to accept his father's 'Mac' surname especially if the name was made illustrious in war or otherwise thus leading to tartans and clans. The Welsh used the prefix 'ap' to indicate lineal descent so that a son might be named Robert ap John ap William ap Owen ap Reese thus providing five generations of lineage in one name. Later the 'ap' coalesced with the second name and ap Hugh became Pugh; ap Howell became Powell; and ap Richard became Prichard.

Names, Names and More Names

"The Dutch for many years had a singular fashion of their own in the matter of family names. The process of assuming unchanged family names was not accomplished at one stroke and at one definite time. It was a gradual process though it became quite general after the English conquest of the colony in 1664. It would seem that the surname used by the first comer was never lost sight of, but was remembered and used on formal occasions. But the every-day name used by their neighbors for the surname was the name of the father with a suffix of 'se' or 'sen'. Thus, a Jan Van Antwerp would have sons Arent and Wouter. These would be known as Arent Jansen and Wouter Jansen. Arent Jansen's sons would be known as Willem Arentsen and Hendrick Arentsen, or Arentse. While Wouter Jansen's sons would take the surname of Wouterse or Wouters. All of them would occasionally add the first surname of the original emigrant ancestor, Van Antwerp, and when the time came for the adoption of a permanent family name, like the English people about them, this would be the name generally selected.

"Most of the original Dutch settlers in New York, as their names indicate, came from small villages in Holland or Gelderland, or another of the United States of the Netherlands. This is indicated by the prefix van or vander signifying of or of the. Vander was often contracted to ver and this latter suffix, vander or ver, was applied usually to a place smaller than a village, as Vander Veer, from the ferry or marsh; Vander Poel, from the pool.

"For the most part from small villages of the same name in the Netherlands are derived the names of 'Van' Antwerp, Arnhem, Benthuysen, Bergen, Blarcom, Bockelem, Burgh, Buren, Bunschooten, Cleef, Cott, Dam, Deventer, Doesen, Dorn, Duyne, Eps, Esselstein/Ysselstein, Etten, Gansevoort, Giesen, Gysbeeck/Gasbeeck, Hatten, Horn, Hoesen, Houten, Ingen, Linden, Olinda, Loon, Ness, Patten, Stantvoort, Schaick, Schoonhoven, Tassel, Tiel, Tienhoven, Valkenburg, Vechten, Vliet, Voorst, Voort, Wie, Winkel, Woerden, Wormer, Wort, and Wyck.

"Some families quite early dropped the prefix van, such as the Gansevoorrts, Couwenhovens, Schermerhorns, and Tienhovens all from villages of the same name."To complete the names of Dutch origin which are more or less familiar, we have the following which are of various etymologies:

Ackerman - farmer

Bancker - banker

Barheit - lived on the barrens

Barkalo -village of Barculo, Gelderland

Beekman - by the brook

Blauvelt - of the blue field

Bleecker - bleacher of cloth

Bloomingdale/Bloemendael - flowery valley

Bogart/latin Bogardus - orchardist

Bratt - dealer in fine silk/wool
Brevoort - village name
Brouwer - brewer
Bruyn - brown, dark complexion
Clute/Kloet - boatman's pole
Coeyman - herdsman
Covert - village in Brabant
Coster - sexton
Cryger - soldier
Cuyler - cave man
DeBoer - peasant
Decker - roof slater
DeFries - from Friesland
DeHaas - hare, swift footed
DeVolger - follower
DeVos - fox, cunning
DeWitt - white, light complexion
Douw - village name
Dret - from Utrecht/Dordrecht
Dyckman - ditcher, dike digger
Engles - Englishman
Groesbbeck - town name
Groot - tall
Hagedorn - thorn hedge
Hageman - hedger, makes hedges
Hallenbeck - town on Rhine
Hasbrouck - town of Hazebrouck, in Artois
Heemstraat/Hemstreet - town in Holland
Hoffman - man of the court
Hoogeboom - high tree
Hooghteeling - high birth; head accountant; money collector
Hoogland - high land
Huyk - cloak
Klein - short
Knickerbacker - marble baker
Kooper - merchant, buyer

Lansing - village name
Loockermans - leeks
Magapolensis - latin for Mecklenberg
Metselaer - mason
Meyer - sheriff, town mayor
Middagh - midday
Onderdonk - below Donk, Brabant village
Oostehout - east woods
Oostrander - east shore
Oothout - east woods
Opdyke - on the dike
Ouderkerke - old church
Peltz - fur trader
Pruyn - plum
Quackenbush - mountain ash
Roseboom - rose tree
Roosevelt - rose field
Ryckman - rich man
Schaats - skater
Schenck - inn
Schoonmaker - shoemaker
Schuyler - lurk or skulk
Snediker - sharper
Snow - sly, crafty
Snyder - tailor
Staats - United Provinces resident
Steenhuysen - stone house
Stoutenberg - town name
Stopplebean - short-legged
Stuyvesant - quick sand
Swartwout - "swarthy Walter" Black Forest man
Ten Broeck - marsh
Ten Eyck - oak
Van Alstyne - village name
Van Broeckhoeven - goat farm
Van Buskirk - wooden church; church in woods

Van Cortland - shor lane

Vandenberg - of the hill

Vanderbilt - of the elevation (Gelderland)

Vander Heyden - Heyden, Holstein and Westphalia

Vanderlinden/Olinda - linden trees

Vanderlippe - Lippe, Germany

Vander Mark - district in Holland

Vander Poel - of the pool

Vanderzee - of the sea

Van Vranken - of France

Vanzandt - village in Holland

Visscher - fisherman

Voorhies - Town of Hess, Gelderland

Vos - fox

Vosburgh - where foxes live

Vrooman - honest

Wagenaar - wagoner

Wyngaart - wine maker

Wynkoop - wine merchant

Wyckoff - parish court

Finally, we present here a listing of place names with their probable meaning:

Arnheim - town from the old Roman Arenacum

Benthuysen - frame houses

Brugh - town of Bruges, Belgium; bridges

Cott - cottage

Dam - by the dam

Dom/Doom - thorn tree

Eps - wild parsley

Horn/Hoorn - curved street

Hout/Houten - forest

Linden - linden tree

Schoonhoven - shoe court

Tienhoven - ten gardens/courts

Valkenburg - raising hawks/falcons

Vechten - on river Vecht

Vliet - brook; running water

Winkel - market town

Wyck - refuge/sanctuary"

SURNAMES

Patronymics – What They Are

When first confronted with the term patronymics, many family researchers are apprehensive about what lies ahead. In reality, if they've been dabbling in genealogy for a while, they've already been exposed to a modified form of patronymics, namely, the system generally known as the Record or Report format with "generation numbering" or "back referencing" which would produce an item, for example, such as: John[4] Smith (James[3], John[2], Richard[1]). Many scholarly genealogies published in the past 100 years have used this system to show, at a glance, the direct line of the person whose vital statistics are being recorded. The major differences between back referencing and patronymics is that back referencing:

1. provides the given names for all direct line male ancestors and not just the previous generation,
2. does not add the suffixes "s", "se", "sz", etc to the given name as the patronymic usually does, and
3. uses a superscript to indicate the level of the generation

During the period of Dutch settlement, encompassing most of the seventeenth century, patronymics were commonly used. Many of the early Dutch settlers arrived in New Amsterdam without an established surname. Individuals were identified by adding their father's name to their given name with an attached suffix to indicate child of such as "-s", "-se", "-zen", etc. For example, an individual named Jacob might be further identified as the son of Jan by calling him Jacob Jans or Jansen. This use of the father's name or patronymic, meant that in the next generation, the child would use his father's name so that Jacob's children would be called by a first name, followed by the name Jacobse to indicate his parentage. The patronymic was used to identify both male and female children and is especially evident in early colonial records.

In a region where only one individual of a particular given name was living, the patronymic system provided a clear indication of descent. But where several persons in a region who carried the same given name were fathering children, it became increasingly difficult to identify families.

The Patronymic system is much easier to follow if you begin with the immigrant and work through his children and his children's children. The riddle occurs when you search backward, reaching the point when the surname the family assumed in later generations had not yet been established and you are trying to find the name of the father of an individual. Many genealogies end at this point because the researcher may not have learned how to extend the line and assumed that the emigrant was the earliest person identified, when actually records exist with the individual identified by his patronymic rather than by the surname which was assumed later on.

Several techniques will help to identify the patronymic and allow extension of the family line. The first method is to consult the works of family historians and genealogists who have published books on given families. Consulting books such as *Genealogies in the Library of Congress* by Marion Kaminkow; the family records section of *Index to Genealogical Periodicals* by Donald Lines Jacobus; *Index to American Genealogies* compiled by Joel Munsell's Sons; and *Genealogical and Local History Books in Print, Family History Volume*, 5th edition, by Marian Hoffman (as well as the previous four editions compiled by Netti Schreiner-Yantis) all can provide valuable information. A second method is to refer to lists of patronymics associated with corresponding family surnames. Prof. Jonathan Pearson published such a list in 1872 but his work involved only the families found in the Reformed Church record and primarily of the Albany, New York area.

The lists found in the current book are the results of combining previously existing lists together with all known church records that were kept prior to about 1700 together with those civil records that could be consulted. The end result should be helpful in identifying surnames adopted by a family where the given names of the couple are known. After about 1700-1710, use of patronymics declined as families were encouraged to acquire a surname, which would extend from one generation to the next. There are obviously some exceptions and some families seem to have refrained from establishing a surname until well into the 18th century. Also, some families, because their surname was so abundant in a region, used a combination of patronymic/surname so that a child was baptized with a single name but became known in later life as a patronymic together with the family surname.

We find the following quote from the NEHG Register, volume 27, Jan 1873: "But while many individuals had no surnames whatever, apparently, a few families had two or more. Marcelis Janse Van Bommel was farmer of the burger and tapster's excise of liquors in Beverwyck many years. Some of his children took Marcelis as their surname, others Van Iveren [Van Everen]; without knowledge of this fact it would be quite impossible for his descendants to trace back their pedigree to him. A similar case occurred in the Albany branch of the Bratts. In the passage over from Holland, one child was born at sea in a storm, and he was named Storm Van Der Zee, which epithet he and his descendants have since used as a surname.

"It was not uncommon for the same individual to have two or more surnames, and to use them indifferently. Jan Barentse Wemp [Wemple] was sometimes called Poest; he had a mill on Poesten-kil, which perhaps derived its name from him rather than from the Dutch word poesten. After his death, in 1663, his widow Marietie Myndertse married Sweer Teunise. He had two surnames, Van Velsen and Van Westbroeck. Jan Fort, of Niskayuna, had the following aliases: Jan LaFort, Jan Vandervort and Jan Libbertee."

Patronymic as a Surname:

In many cases the Patronymic of one generation was assumed as the family surname and continued into the following generation without maintaining the patronymic meaning. Thus surnames such as Williams, Williamson, Jans, Johnson, etc. were established. The patronymic got "stuck" and was continued as the family name.

Names, Names and More Names

In Scotland, the patronymic became a surname much earlier than in Holland and we find Scots immigrants with surnames which may be identified with the same meaning as the Dutch but using the Scottish form. Thus Mac is Gaelic for "son of" and "Lean" is derived from "Ian" or John so that MacLean may be interpreted "son of John."

Variations of Patronymic Suffix:

The suffix used to designate a patronymic varied. A single letter "s" or "z" might be used or the suffix expanded to "-sen" or "-zen" Thus a father, Jan, might have children, Jans, Janz, Jansen, or Janzen. The suffix "-sse" and "-sz" also had the same meaning. It is important to be aware of these name forms and to realize that they are likely to indicate the name of the father of the individual well into the eighteenth century.

An example of a family adopting both the patronymic surname and a place identifying surname is given in the July 1944 issue of de Halve Maen Newsletter of the Dutch Settlers Society from Albany, NY(#15 Vol XIX No. # p. 4.) showing the Van Reypen/Van Riper family. The immigrant ancestor was Jurian Tonassen. He sailed to New Netherland in De Bonte Koe, a ship whose name is translated "The Spotted Cow" and which brought many settlers to New Amsterdam. Jurian arrived April 16, 1663. He probably came from De Ryp in North Holland although the ship sailed from Amsterdam. He is recorded as a member of the Bergen, New Jersey Reformed Dutch Church in 1667 and on May 25, 1667, married Reycke Hermens. Through the will of Guert Coerten dated 1671 he received property within the old stockade and among the "Out Gardens" in Bergen (Jersey City). Jurian and Reycke had ten children including five sons. They adopted a patronymic surname which extended into future generations and included various spellings of Juranse and Jurijaense which in later generations was frequently spelled Jurriaen and Yearance.

The second son, Gerrit (1670-1748) and his descendants occupied the old family place for generations. This portion of the family assumed the surname, Van Repen. The place identifying surname is first noticed in an October 1671 baptismal record at the Bergen Reformed Church. The sponsors of the baptism are listed as Daniel Van Reype and Beeletze Van Reype. At present Van Riper seems to be the most common form of the name. Today Van Repen, a street in Jersey City intersects with Academy Street at the place where he acquired a plot of land.

The point to remember is that various branches of a family may have adopted different surnames and descend from a common ancestor whose patronymic was yet another name. Rosalie Fellows Bailey, in her valuable book, *Dutch System in Family Naming* gives an excellent discussion of a real life situation involving the New York/New Jersey families and how surnames evolved. Of particular interest is the way that one ancestor became the progenitor of the Rutgers, Rutsen, and Van Woert families living in New York City and upstate New York. She gives many examples from her vast research knowledge including changes from patronymic to surname and also other derivations of present day family names. Readers are urged to consult her book.

Name forms that could be considered to be "double patronymics" seem to be occasionally used. For example, a father named Jan Dominicus could have sons named Peter Jans Dominicus and Willem Jans Dominicus thus indicating the use of a double patronymic. These double patronymics should not be confused, however, with double Christian names given at the time of a baptism, such as John Baptist. It is for this reason that when abstracting the Albany-Rensselaer County area records, the name John Baptist Van Rensselaer was not considered for inclusion in TABLE 1A and TABLE 1B which follows, the assumption being that John Baptist is a doubled given name and not a patronymic indicating that John Baptist's father was Baptist (_____).

Patronymics/Surname Tables:
The names in the following two tables (1A and 1B) were selected from those that appeared in published records with both a patronymic (given as a middle name) and a surname (given as a family name). The published records that were consulted are (together with the abbreviations used in these tables):
Alb Ref - Albany Reformed Church, 1683-1710
Anjou Prb - Anjou "Ulster County Probate Records, 1663-1710"
Atns Lth - Zion Lutheran Church, Athens, 1704-1710
Berg Ref - Bergen, NJ Reformed Church, 1666-1710
Bkln Ref - Brooklyn Reformed Church, 1660-1710
Brgr Frm - Burghers of New Amsterdam and Freemen of New York, 1648-1702
Crt Assz - New York Historic Manuscripts, Court of Assizes, 1665-1682
Evjen Scn - Evjen "Scandinavian Immigrants in New York, 1630-1674"
Fern Wills - Fernow "New York Wills, 1626-1710"
Fltb Ref - Flatbush Reformed Church, 1677-1710
Gen Entr-1 - New York Historic Manuscripts, General Entries, 1664-1673
Gen Entr-2 - New York Historic Manuscripts, General Entries, 1674-1688
Hack Ref - Hackensack, NJ Reformed Church, 1686-1721
Jam Ref - Jamaica Reformed Church, 1707-1717
King Co - Bergen "Early Settlers of Kings Co" to 1700
King NYGB - Kingston Reformed Church Marriages, 1667-1672 (The Record v106)
King Pap - New York Historic Manuscripts, Kingston Papers, 1661-1675
King Ref - Kingston Reformed Church, 1660-1710

LI Fam-1 - Hoff "Genealogies of Long Island Families", vol 1
LI Fam-2 - Hoff "Genealogies of Long Island Families", vol 2
LI Sources - Hoff "Long Island Source Records"
Nicl Lvl - New York Historic Manuscripts, Nicolls-Lovelace Papers, 1664-1673
NY Luth - New York Lutheran Church, 1704-1710
NY Ref - New York Reformed Church, 1639-1710
NYC Court - Scott "New York City Court Records, 1684-1760"
NYC Wills - New York Historical Society "Abstracts of Wills, 1665-1707, vol 1
Nycol Doc 1 - Colonial History of New York State, vol 1, 1614-1656
Nycol Doc 2 - Colonial History of New York State, vol 2, 1657-1678
Nycol Doc 3 - Colonial History of New York State, vol 3, 1614-1692
Nycol Doc 4 - Colonial History of New York State, vol 4, 1693-1706
Nycol Doc 5 - Colonial History of New York State, vol 5, 1707-1710
Orphan Mst - O'Callaghan "Minutes of the Orphanmasters of New Amsterdam"
Pearson - Pearson "First Settlers of Albany Co"
PRch Ref - Port Richmond Reformed Church, Staten Island, NY, 1696-1719
Rcrd Nam 1-7 - Records of New Amsterdam, 1653-1674
Rens Crsp-1 - Van Laer - Correspondence of Jeremias Van Rensselaer, 1651-1674"
Rens Crsp-2 - Van Laer "Correspondence of Maria Van Rensselaer, 1669-1689"
Rens Court - Van Laer "Minutes of Court of Albany, etc, 1668-1673"
Schn Ref - Schenectady Reformed Church, 1694-1710
Ship Lists - Boyer "Ship Passenger Lists, NY and NJ"
Tap Ref - Tappan Reformed Church, 1694-1710
Tary Ref - Tarrytown Reformed Church, 1697-1710
West Wills - Pelletreau "Early Wills of Westchester Co, 1720-1735"

Hints in Using the Patronymic Tables:

Names in the following Tables were selected from the 43 references listed above based on the criteria that the name appeared in the original source in three parts, namely:

1. Given first name
2. Given middle name with "s", etc suffix, and
3. A surname (even though it may have been intended as a "from" designation only).

Each entry is arranged in Table 1A by:

1. Surname
2. Middle Name (patronymic)
3. Reference where name was found
4. Year of occurrence

Names, Names and More Names

With this information the researcher can establish what possible patronymics were used in conjunction with a particular surname and the period of time and geographic region associated with the name. Also, the family historian should remember to consider to search this table for the surname in several ways:

1. Without a prefix particle as well as
2. With a prefix particle before the family name, such as:

> D'
> De
> DeLa
> Des
> Du
> Nyt
> Op
> Ouy
> Ten
> Ter
> Uyt
> Uyt De
> Van
> Van De
> Van Den
> Van Der
> Ver
> Wyt

The entries in Table 1B are presented alphabetically in the sequence:
Middle name (patronymic)
> Surname
>> Reference
>>> Year of occurrence

This table will be of use when exploring the possible surnames that a family assumed once patronymics had gone out of favor. Be aware that many of the names listed as a surname may never have been adopted as such but are simply "from" designations.

Table 1A
Surname/Patronymic Combinations

A

Aaten
 Hendricks
  Ship Lists, 1687
Abeel
 Christophs
  Pearson, 1682
 Jans
  Fern Wlls, 1678
  King Co, 1664
  NYC Wills, 1678
  Pearson, 1659
  Ship Lists, no date
Ackerman
 Abrams
  Hack Ref bp, 1711, 1718, 1719, 1720
  Hack Ref mm, 1710
  Hack Ref mr, 1712
 Davids
  NY Ref bp, 1673
  NY Ref mr, 1668
 Lawrence
  Bkln Ref bp, 1709
  Hack Ref bp, 1711, 1719, 1721
  Hack Ref mr, 1707, 1710
Aemilius
 Jans
  Rens Crsp 1, 1656
Alberson
 Rose
  King Ref bp, 1687
Alberto
 Pedro
  NY Ref bp, 1643
 Peter d'Italian
  NY Ref bp, 1645
Albertus
 Caesars
  LI Source, 1687
Alcmaer
 Jans
  Nycol Doc 1, 1625
Alst
 Joris
  NY Ref mr, 1689

Amack
 Jans
  King Co, 1673
Ameland
 Jans
  King Co, 1699
Amerman
 Dirks
  Ship Lists, no date
 Jans
  Fltb Ref bp, 1685
Amersfort
 Barents
  King Pap, 1662
 Jans
  King Pap, 1663
Amerstede
 Jans
  King Pap, 1662
Amertman
 Jans
  LI Source, 1694, 1695
Ameshoff
 Barents
  Ship Lists, 1658
Ammerman
 Jans
  Ship Lists, 1687
Ammermarc
 Dirks
  King Co, 1693
Anderson
 Christians
  Evjen, 1660
Antwerp
 Melyn
  Nycol Doc 1, 1650
Appel
 Jans
  Pearson, 1656
  Rens Crsp 1, 1664
  Ship Lists, 1649
 Lawrence
  Rcrd Nam 2, 1656
  Ship Lists, 1648
Artopejus
 Adolfs
  NY Lth bp, 1710

Asdalen
 Jans
  Rcrd Nam 4, 1663
Aten
 Hendricks
  King Co, 1680
  LI Source, 1696

B

Backer
 Alberts
  King Pap, 1664
 Claas
  Gen Entr 1, 1664
 Conrads
  Pearson, 1674
 Dirks
  NY Ref bp, 1641
 Gerrits
  Pearson, 1670
 Hermans
  Fern Wlls, 1683
  Pearson, 1658
 Jacobs
  Rcrd Nam 1, 1655
 Jans
  NY Ref bp, 1652, 1675, 1676
  Nycol Doc 2, 1664
  Rcrd Nam 6, 1668
 Jurians
  Ship Lists, 1639
 Lucas
  Pearson, 1677
 Teunis
  NY Ref bp, 1648
 Wessels
  Pearson, 1633
 Willems
  Nycol Doc 2, 1674
  Pearson, 1657
Baddie
 Thomas
  LI Source, 1670
Baech
 Ludwichs
  Rcrd Nam 1, 1654

Baker
Jans
Rcrd Nam 1, 1654
Teunis
LI Source, 1691
Bakker
Claas
Pearson, 1658
Jans
Pearson, 1665
Jurians
Ship Lists, 1637
Willems
Rcrd Nam 1, 1654
Bal
Jans
Pearson, 1660
Ship Lists, 1652
Ball
Jans
King Co, 1652
Baltes
Claas
King Co, 1659
Bamboes
Jacobs
Rcrd Nam 2, 1658
Rens Court, 1669
Rens Crsp 1, 1658
Bambus
Jacobs
Pearson, 1657
Banckert
Mathys
Tary Ref mm, 1699?
Bant
Jans
Berg Ref mr, 1697
NY Ref mr, 1697
Peters
NY Ref bp, 1679, 1690,
1697
Banta
Cornelis
Hack Ref bp, 1700, 1708,
1709, 1710, 1711, 1713,
1715, 1717, 1718, 1719,
1720

Hack Ref mr, 1696, 1708
NY Lth mr, 1707
Dirks
Berg Ref mr, 1701
Hack Ref bp, 1710, 1714,
1715, 1718, 1719, 1720
Hack Ref mm, 1702
Hack Ref mr, 1702, 1709
Edwards
Hack Ref mr, 1715
Egberts
Hack Ref bp, 1707, 1708,
1709, 1712, 1713, 1718,
1720
Hack Ref mm, page xx
Hack Ref mr, 1699, 1719
Hendricks
Hack Ref bp, 1699, 1706,
1708, 1709, 1710, 1712,
1714, 1715, 1716, 1718
Hack Ref mm, 1709
Hack Ref mr, 1703, 1705,
1708
NY Lth mr, 1705
Jacobs
Ship Lists, no date
Siberse
Hack Ref bp, 1703, 1705,
1706, 1708, 1709, 1711,
1712, 1714, 1715, 1716,
1717, 1718, 1719, 1720,
1721
Hack Ref mm, 1698
Hack Ref mr, 1699, 1703,
1705
Wiertse
Hack Ref bp, 1715, 1716,
1717, 1718, 1719, 1720
Bardt
Andries
Ship Lists, 1637
Barhyte
Hans
Alb Ref bp, 1701
Pearson, 1692
Ship Lists, 1684
Jeromes
Pearson, 1713

Barkelo
Hermans
King Co, 1662
Jans
King Co, 1672
Willems
King Co, 1680
Barns
Davis
Nicl Lvl, 1672
Barroquier
Peters
Pearson, 1654
Simons
Pearson, 1653
Bas
Hendricks
King Co, 1682
NY Ref mr, 1681
Bastians
Jans
King Ref bp, 1694
Rcrd Nam 5, 1664
Bayard
Claas
NY Ref bp, 1701
Becker
Jurians
Gen Entr 1, 1669
NY Ref bp, 1660
Pearson, 1669
Rcrd Nam 3, 1660
Rens Court, 1668, 1669
Wessels
Fern Wlls, 1681
Beek
Peters
NY Ref bp, 1687
Beekman
Hendricks
Pearson, 1661
Ship Lists, 1638, no date
Jacobs
Pearson, 1746
Martins
Pearson, 1673
Willems
King Co, 1647

Surname/Patronymic Combinations

Been
  Jans
    Bkln Ref bp, 1662
    Rcrd Nam 6, 1666

Beer
  Willems
    Rcrd Nam 2, 1658

Beeregat
  Teunis
    Nycol Doc 1, 1649

Beergen
  Hans
    Fltb Ref bp, 1681

Bennet
  Adrians
    Bkln Ref mr, 1685, 1696
    Fltb Ref bp, 1683
    Fltb Ref mr, 1685
    King Co, 1702
    LI Fam 1, 1620
  Jans
    King Co, 1696
  Willems
    Bkln Ref bp, 1682, 1687
    Bkln Ref mm, 1677
    Fltb Ref bp, 1680, 1681,
    1682, 1683, 1685
    King Co, 1662
    LI Fam 1, 1636
    LI Source, 1686, 1689,
    1698
    NY Ref bp, 1685, 1686,
    1705
    NY Ref mr, 1686, 1690
    Ship Lists, 1687

Benson
  Jans
    Hack Ref bp, 1720

Benthem
  Hermans
    NY Ref mr, 1673

Berckelson
  Jans
    Rcrd Nam 7, 1673

Bergen
  Dirks
    Nycol Doc 2, 1662

Hans
    Bkln Ref bp, 1681, 1697,
    1701, 1702, 1708
    Fltb Ref bp, 1678, 1679,
    1680, 1681, 1682, 1684,
    1685, 1688
    Fltb Ref mr, 1678
    King Co, 1633
    LI Source, 1677
    NY Ref bp, 1704
    Ship Lists, 1687, no date
  Jacobs
    King Co, 1681
  Jans
    Fltb Ref bp, 1681
  Joris
    King Co, 1684
  Michels
    King Co, 1689

Berghoorn
  Cornelis
    Ship Lists, 1638

Berrien
  Cornelis
    King Co, 1707
  Jans
    Bkln Ref bp, 1681
    Fltb Ref bp, 1678, 1681,
    1683, 1685
    King Co, 1670
    LI Source, 1684

Berrow
  Thomas
    Brgr Frm, 1688

Berry
  Jans
    LI Source, 1683

Bes
  Cornelis
    Nycol Doc 2, 1663
    Rens Crsp 1, 1663

Besems
  Jans
    NY Ref bp, 1660

Bestevaer
  Jans
    Gen Entr 1, 1669
    Nycol Doc 2, 1658

    Rcrd Nam 1, 1655
    Rens Crsp 1, 1655, 1656,
    1657, 1658, 1660, 1662,
    1664, 1668
    Ship Lists, 1657

Bet
  Simons
    Pearson, 1661

Bielefeld
  Peters
    Ship Lists, 1626

Bierdrager
  Jacobs
    Pearson, 1661

Biscop
  Everts
    NY Ref bp, 1648

Blaeck
  Jans
    NY Ref bp, 1668

Blau
  Dirks
    Nycol Doc 1, 1643
  Fredericks
    NY Ref bp, 1698
  Hendricks
    Rcrd Nam 7, 1674

Blauvelt
  Abrams
    Hack Ref bp, 1718
  Gerrits
    Tap Ref bp, 1703
  Hendricks
    Ship Lists, no date
    Tap Ref bp, 1708
  Huberts
    Hack Ref bp, 1719
    Hack Ref mr, 1709
    Tap Ref bp, 1706, 1708

Blauw
  Jans
    King Co, no date

Bleecker
  Jans
    Alb Ref bp, 1692, 1696,
    1699, 1703
    Alb Ref mm, 1683
    Gen Entr 2, 1684

Surname/Patronymic Combinations

Bleecker (cont.)
Jans (cont.)
King Pap, 1665
King Ref bp, 1678
Nycol Doc 2, 1674
Pearson, 1666
Rens Court, 1668, 1669, 1671
Rens Crsp 2, 1683
Ship Lists, 1658, no date
Rogers
Pearson, 1749
Block
Simons
NY Ref mr, 1674, 1697
Bloodgood
Frans
Fltb Ref mr, 1677
Jans
NY Ref bp, 1662
Ship Lists, no date
Bloom
Arents
NY Ref bp, 1681
Barents
Bkln Ref bp, 1694, 1699
Fltb Ref mr, 1685
King Co, 1662
LI Source, 1687, 1694, 1696
Ship Lists, 1687
Fredericks
NY Ref mr, 1697
Jans
Evjen, 1641
King Co, 1665
NY Ref mr, 1705
Ship Lists, 1637
Bloomenthal
Thomas
Alb Ref bp, 1709
Blycker
Jans
Rens Court, 1669
Boch
Christians
Ship Lists, 1661

Bock
Peters
Nycol Doc 1, 1652
Bockqui
Jeromes
Bkln Ref bp, 1678
Boeckhout
Jans
NY Ref bp, 1679, 1683, 1688
NY Ref mr, 1699
Boeg
Hendricks
NY Ref mr, 1678
Boelhont
Krynes
Ship Lists, 1663
Boer
Simons
Pearson, 1661
Boerhol
Jans
Fltb Ref mr, 1690
King Co, 1690
Boertgens
Hermans
Ship Lists, no date
Boerum
Jacobs
King Co, 1617
Willems
King Co, 1642
Ship Lists, no date
Bogardus
Jans
Fern Wlls, 1663
Bogart
Cornelis
Berg Ref mm, 1676
Bkln Ref bp, 1677
Fltb Ref bp, 1677, 1682, 1685
Hack Ref bp, 1700, 1703, 1705, 1706, 1712
Hack Ref mm, 1686
King Ref bp, 1692
LI Source, 1694
Pearson, 1660

Gilberts
Bkln Ref bp, 1662, 1663, 1678
Bkln Ref mm, 1664
Fltb Ref bp, 1678, 1680, 1681
Fltb Ref mr, 1687
King Co, 1711
Nicl Lvl, 1671
NY Ref bp, 1655, 1661, 1671, 1688, 1691
Nycol Doc 2, 1665
Pearson, 1658
Rcrd Nam 4, 1662
Ship Lists, 1687, no date
Jans
Berg Ref mm, 1676
Brgr Frm, 1702
Gen Entr 1, 1670
Hack Ref bp, 1719
Hack Ref mm, 1687
Hack Ref mr, 1718
LI Source, 1687
NY Ref bp, 1687, 1688, 1689, 1705
NY Ref mr, 1686, 1695
Pearson, 1699
Ship Lists, no date
Lawrence
Bkln Ref bp, 1663
NY Ref bp, 1679
Ship Lists, no date
Tap Ref bp, 1696
Mynderts
Pearson, 1647
Peters
Hack Ref mr, 1713
Roelofs
Hack Ref bp, 1718, 1720, 1721
Hack Ref mr, 1717
Teunis
Berg Ref bp, 1689, 1700
Berg Ref mm, 1682
Bkln Ref bp, 1693
Fltb Ref bp, 1679, 1680, 1682, 1684, 1685
Fltb Ref mr, 1677, 1679,

1681, 1689
King Co, 1685
NY Ref bp, 1691
Bol
Claas
Nycol Doc 1, 1647
Rcrd Nam 1, 1647
Bommel
Hendricks
King Co, 1662
Bond
Hendricks
King Ref bp, 1696
Schn Ref bp, 1704
Bongart
Cornelis
Berg Ref bp, 1679, 1680,
1681, 1682
Fltb Ref bp, 1684
Bont
Capito
Evjen, 1650
Lamberts
Pearson, no date
Boodt
Claas
Rens Crsp 1, 1655
Boogh
Fredericks
Alb Ref bp, 1689
Alb Ref mm, 1683
Alb Ref mr, 1686
Hendricks
NY Ref bp, 1677, 1681
NY Ref mr, 1663
Rcrd Nam 5, 1665
Boomgart
Cornelis
Fltb Ref bp, 1677, 1679,
1685
King Co, 1694
LI Source, 1690
Jans
King Co, 1684
LI Source, 1690, 1700
Boon
Capito
Evjen, 1650

Boot
Claas
Rcrd Nam 1, 1654
Ship Lists, no date
Bootsen
Jans
Brgr Frm, 1659
Willems
Pearson, 1684
Bor
Dirks
Ship Lists, 1662
Bording
Claas
NY Ref bp, 1662
Boreklo
Willems
Ship Lists, 1687
Borsboom
Jacobs
NYC Wills, 1686
Pearson, 1662
Rens Court, 1668, 1670,
1671
Peters
Alb Ref mr, 1692
Pearson, 1693
Bos
Jans
Pearson, 1666
Peters
Berg Ref bp, 1688
NY Ref bp, 1691, 1699,
1700, 1703
Teunis
Pearson, 1631
Rens Court, 1668
Ship Lists, 1631, 1637
Bosch
Conrads
NY Ref bp, 1681, 1704,
1706, 1707, 1708, 1709
NY Ref mr, 1703
Cornelis
Pearson, 1690
Fredericks
Pearson, 1689

Jans
Alb Ref bp, 1689, 1691
Alb Ref mr, 1688
NY Ref bp, 1664, 1689,
1690, 1691, 1693, 1697
NY Ref mr, 1690, 1694,
1697
Pearson, 1689
Rcrd Nam 5, 1664
Peters
NY Ref bp, 1671, 1676,
1678, 1685, 1687, 1695,
1697
Teunis
Pearson, 1631
Boschieter
Peters
Nycol Doc 2, 1660
Bout
Claas
Pearson, 1659
Everts
Brgr Frm, 1657
Fern Wlls, 1649
King Co, 1634
LI Source, 1668, 1695,
1698, 1700, 1703
NY Ref bp, 1641, 1644,
1645, 1647, 1649, 1650,
1653, 1654, 1656, 1669
NYC Wills, 1671
Nycol Doc 1, 1643
Orphan Mst, 1663
Rcrd Nam 1, 1654
Ship Lists, 1634, 1651,
1653, 1654
Fredericks
Pearson, 1654
Rens Court, 1670, 1671
Rens Crsp 2, 1675
Ship Lists, 1642
Hendricks
Alb Ref bp, 1704, 1706
Pearson, 1706
Maurits
Rcrd Nam 4, 1663
Peters
Rens Court, 1671

Surname/Patronymic Combinations

Bouw
  Fredericks
    Pearson, 1689
Bowman
  Joris
    King Co, 1693
Braack
  Claas
    Berg Ref bp, 1675, 1677,
    1682
    Berg Ref dt, 1668, 1692
    Rcrd Nam 2, 1656
  Dirks
    Berg Ref bp, 1680, 1682,
    1683, 1685, 1686, 1693,
    1695, 1698, 1707
    Berg Ref mr, 1681, 1682
Brabander
  Jans
    King Pap, 1662
    Nicl Lvl, 1667
Bradt
  Alberts
    Rens Crsp 1, 1657
  Andries
    Rens Crsp 1, 1658, 1659
Brandt
  Jans
    Nycol Doc 2, 1630
  Willems
    King Ref bp, 1681
Brasser
  Hendricks
    Fltb Ref mr, 1689
    King Ref bp, 1690
    NY Ref mr, 1689
Bratt
  Alberts
    Alb Ref bp, 1684, 1686,
    1687, 1694
    Alb Ref mr, 1684
    Pearson, 1674
    Rens Court, 1673
  Andries
    Pearson, 1630
    Rens Court, 1669, 1670
    Ship Lists, 1630, no date

Arents
  Alb Ref bp, 1686
  Pearson, 1695
  Schn Ref bp, 1700
Barents
  Alb Ref mm, 1683
  Alb Ref mr, 1686, 1693
  Pearson, 1682
  Dirks
    Pearson, 1727
  Egberts
    Pearson, 1753
  Jans
    Pearson, 1681
  Storms
    Pearson, 1699
  Teunis
    Pearson, 1701
Breested
  Jans
    NY Ref bp, 1654, 1667,
    1674
Bresse
  Hendricks
    King Co, 1689
    Ship Lists, 1687
Brevoort
  Hendricks
    King Co, 1644
    LI Source, 1695
    NY Ref bp, 1695, 1701,
    1703, 1706
  Jans
    King Co, 1630
    Ship Lists, no date
Breyandt
  Cornelis
    Hack Ref bp, 1686
    Ship Lists, 1663
Bries
  Hendricks
    Alb Ref mr, 1686
    Bkln Ref bp, 1698
    King Co, 1680
    LI Source, 1695
  Volkerts
    Ship Lists, 1655

Brimes
  Hendricks
    King Co, 1692
Brinase
  Brimasson
    LI Source, 1692
Brinckerhoff
  Abrams
    Fltb Ref bp, 1685
    King Co, 1677
  Dirks
    King Co, 1638
    Ship Lists, no date   ·
  Hendricks
    Berg Ref bp, 1709
    Berg Ref mm, 1707, 1709
    Berg Ref mr, 1682, 1708
    Hack Ref bp, 1703, 1705,
    1709, 1710, 1716
    Hack Ref mm, 1699
    Hack Ref mr, 1702, 1708
    NY Ref mr, 1708
  Joris
    Fltb Ref bp, 1684, 1685
    Hack Ref bp, 1705, 1706
    King Co, 1632
Brink
  Huberts
    Ship Lists, no date
Brisse
  Hendricks
    LI Source, 1692
Broeck
  Cornelis
    Ship Lists, 1653
Broer
  Jans
    Ship Lists, 1655
Broersen
  Jacobs
    King Pap, 1663
Bronck
  Jans
    Pearson, 1738
  Peters
    Pearson, 1669

Bronckhorst
Hendricks
Berg Ref mr, 1682
Broughton
Sheltons
NYC Wills, 1705
Brower
Adams
Fltb Ref bp, 1678, 1680, 1681
King Co, 1692
Alderts
Evjen, 1656
Clements
Nycol Doc 1, 1614
Gerrits
NY Ref bp, 1656
Pearson, 1676
Rcrd Nam 1, 1655
Hendricks
Pearson, 1660
Hermans
King Pap, 1668
Ship Lists, 1662, no date
Jacobs
King Co, 1689
Jans
Fltb Ref bp, 1678
King Co, 1683
Mathys
Ship Lists, 1663
Peters
Hack Ref bp, 1714
Hack Ref mr, 1708
Willems
Alb Ref mr, 1692
Browne
Hendricks
Gen Entr 2, 1684
Bruman
Wariverts
King Co, 1677
Bruyenburgh
Hans
King Co, 1639
Bruyn
Aerts
NY Ref bp, 1674

Hendricks
NY Ref bp, 1678
Rens Court, 1668, 1670
Ship Lists, 1677
Jans
Nycol Doc 2, 1661
Joost
NY Ref bp, 1663
Bruynen
Jans
Rcrd Nam 3, 1660
Bruynenburgh
Hans
Ship Lists, 1687
Bruyns
Hendricks
Gen Entr 1, 1664
King Co, 1685
NY Ref bp, 1697
Nycol Doc 2, 1673
Pearson, 1662
Rens Court, 1671, 1672
Rens Crsp 1, 1667
Buitenhuis
Gerrits
Brgr Frm, 1658
Burger
Hendricks
Alb Ref bp, 1706
Pearson, 1700, 1706
Burgh
Conrads
Nycol Doc 1, 1634, 1650
Burgtem
Teunis
NY Ref bp, 1657
Burhans
Jacobs
Nicl Lvl, 1667
Bussing
Hermans
Ship Lists, 1673
Buys
Cornelis
Berg Ref bp, 1678, 1686
Bkln Ref bp, 1678
Bkln Ref mr, 1663, 1690
Brgr Frm, 1657

Fltb Ref bp, 1678, 1679, 1683, 1684
King Co, 1648
LI Fam 1, 1629
LI Source, 1667, 1668, 1698
Nicl Lvl, 1672
NY Ref bp, 1654, 1656, 1674
Pearson, 1634
Rcrd Nam 2, 1656
Hendricks
King Pap, 1665
Jacobs
Brgr Frm, 1657
King Co, 1653
Rcrd Nam 1, 1655
Jans
Berg Ref bp, 1685, 1699
Berg Ref mr, 1684
Bkln Ref bp, 1683, 1691, 1694
Bkln Ref mr, 1690
Brgr Frm, 1698
Fltb Ref bp, 1682
King Co, 1684
LI Fam 1, 1652
Mathys
NY Ref bp, 1684, 1693
Peters
Berg Ref bp, 1678, 1679, 1682, 1684, 1686, 1689, 1691
Berg Ref mr, 1672
Rcrd Nam 5, 1665
Ship Lists, 1661, 1663
Buytenhuys
Gerrits
Ship Lists, 1658
Bye
Dirks
Alb Ref bp, 1704
Pearson, 1704
Hendricks
Pearson, 1675
Jacobs
Pearson, 1659

Surname/Patronymic Combinations

C

Cadmus
  Cornelis
    Hack Ref mr, 1713
Calebuys
  Jacobs
    Rcrd Nam 1, 1654
Calff
  Jans
    Ship Lists, 1647
Cam
  Aries
    King Ref bp, 1683
Cammega
  Jans
    Fltb Ref bp, 1686, 1688
    King Co, 1679
CanCommel
  Jans
    Rcrd Nam 1, 1665
Cant
  Peters
    LI Source, 1687
Cap
  Jans
    Hack Ref bp, 1704
Capteyn
  Jans
    Hack Ref bp, 1698
Carpenel
  Jacobs
    Brgr Frm, 1657
    NY Ref bp, 1642
    NY Ref mr, 1641
    Rcrd Nam 7, 1657
Carpyn
  Peters
    Rcrd Nam 3, 1661
Caspars
  Jans
    Alb Ref bp, 1705
Casparus
  Andries
    Pearson, 1700
Cavalier
  Gerrits
    NY Ref mr, 1693

Chambers
  Gaasbeek
    Alb Ref bp, 1706
    King Ref bp, 1697, 1707, 1710
    NY Ref bp, 1708
Christians
  Hendricks
    NY Ref mr, 1659
Claarbout
  Jans
    Rcrd Nam 3, 1660
Claerhout
  Peters
    Pearson, 1659
Clapper
  Jans
    Brgr Frm, 1657
    Nicl Lvl, 1672
    NY Ref bp, 1658, 1659, 1660, 1663, 1669
    NY Ref mr, 1657
    Nycol Doc 3, 1664
    Orphan Mst, 1664
    Rcrd Nam 1, 1655
    Ship Lists, 1655
Cleer
  Teunis
    LI Source, 1695
Cleermaecker
  Jans
    Ship Lists, 1648
Clere
  Teunis
    LI Source, 1692, 1694, 1696
Clockluyer
  Jacobs
    Pearson, 1661
Cloef
  Jans
    Fltb Ref bp, 1687
Cloppenburg
  Jans
    NY Ref mr, 1659
    Rcrd Nam 1, 1655

Clow
  Frans
    Alb Ref bp, 1686, 1700, 1703, 1705
    Alb Ref mm, 1683
    Alb Ref mr, 1693
    Atns Lth bp, 1705
    NY Lth bp, 1705
    Pearson, 1683
  Peters
    Alb Ref mm, 1683
    Pearson, 1662
Clum
  Simons
    Pearson, 1653
    Rcrd Nam 1, 1654
    Rens Crsp 1, 1657
    Ship Lists, 1651
Cock
  Abrams
    NY Ref mr, 1682
  Cornelis
    Evjen, 1676
    NY Ref bp, 1691
  Ernests
    Gen Entr 2, 1676
  Gerrits
    King Co, 1656
  Giles
    NY Ref bp, 1658, 1660, 1661
    Nycol Doc 3, 1664
    Rcrd Nam 3, 1659
  Jans
    NY Ref bp, 1688, 1689
  Lamberts
    Rens Crsp 1, 1654, 1656
  Lawrence
    NY Ref mr, 1657
Cocquyt
  Jans
    NY Ref mr, 1662
Codwise
  Conrads
    Hack Ref bp, 1705

Coerten
  Hermans
    LI Fam 1, 1665
Coevers
  Jans
    Bkln Ref bp, 1663, 1680
    Fltb Ref bp, 1683
    NY Ref bp, 1680, 1684
  Teunis
    Bkln Ref bp, 1690
    Fltb Ref bp, 1683
    Fltb Ref mr, 1682
    NY Ref bp, 1687
    NY Ref mr, 1680
Coeyman
  Barents
    Pearson, 1695
  Lucas
    Alb Ref mm, 1683, 1692
    Pearson, 1683
  Peters
    Alb Ref bp, 1686
    Gen Entr 1, no date
    Pearson, 1636
    Rens Court, 1673
    Rens Crsp 1, 1660
    Rens Crsp 2, 1675, 1683
    Ship Lists, 1636, 1639,
      1640, 1650
Cole
  Barents
    Alb Ref bp, 1687
    King Pap, 1666
    King Ref bp, 1665, 1666,
      1678, 1679, 1681, 1683,
    · 1687, 1695
    NY Ref bp, 1668
    NY Ref mr, 1660, 1675,
      1680
    Pearson, 1687
    Rcrd Nam 6, 1669
  Bastians
    Ship Lists, 1663
  Dirks
    NY Ref mr, 1679
  Jacobs
    Brgr Frm, 1657
    King Ref bp, 1681

    King Ref mr, 1683
    Nycol Doc 2, 1663
    Rcrd Nam 1, 1654
  Jans
    Nycol Doc 1, 1656
    Rcrd Nam 1, 1653
  Lamberts
    King Co, 1639
    LI Source, 1642
    NY Ref bp, 1639
    Nycol Doc 1, 1644
  Teunis
    King Ref bp, 1683
Collier
  Jochems
    Rens Court, 1671
Compaen
  Gerrits
    Rens Crsp 1, 1660
Coninck
  Jans
    Pearson, 1654
    Rens Court, 1670
Conine
  Caspars
    Pearson, 1703
  Lennerts
    Alb Ref bp, 1687, 1689,
      1703, 1705
    Pearson, 1683
  Philips
    Alb Ref bp, 1687, 1706,
      1707, 1708
    Berg Ref mr, 1707
    NY Ref mr, 1707
    Pearson, 1708
Constapel
  Cornelis
    Rcrd Nam 4, 1663
  Gerrits
    King Ref bp, 1707
  Herberts
    Pearson, 1640
    Rens Crsp 1, 1661
    Ship Lists, 1642
Contesse
  Bartholomeus
    Ship Lists, 1691

Cook
  Cornelis
    LI Source, 1694
  Giles
    Orphan Mst, 1664, 1665
Coon
  Dirks
    Nycol Doc 1, 1656
    Rcrd Nam 1, 1653
Coopal
  Hendricks
    Rcrd Nam 1, 1654
    Rens Crsp 1, 1661
Cooper
  Abrams
    Pearson, 1665
  Andries
    Pearson, 1646
  Claas
    Berg Ref dt, 1692
    Hack Ref bp, 1709
    Hack Ref mm, 1709
    Hack Ref mr, 1706
    NY Ref mr, 1708
    Tap Ref bp, 1695, 1700,
      1703, 1704, 1705, 1706,
      1707, 1708, 1710
  Cornelis
    Tap Ref bp, 1706
  Everts
    Pearson, 1725
  Hendricks
    Evjen, 1659
    NY Ref mr, 1659
    Rcrd Nam 5, 1664
    Ship Lists, 1659
  Jans
    Berg Ref dt, 1688, 1692
    Hack Ref bp, 1718
    Hack Ref mr, 1718
    King Co, 1655, 1675
    Nicl Lvl, 1667
    NY Ref bp, 1649
    Pearson, 1634
    Rcrd Nam 1, 1653
    Rcrd Nam 5, 1665
    Ship Lists, 1634, 1640,
      1652

Surname/Patronymic Combinations

Cooper (cont.)
  Krynes
    Ship Lists, 1657, no date
  Mathys
    NY Ref bp, 1661
    Tap Ref bp, 1706
  Peters
    Rcrd Nam 1, 1653
  Stephens
    Ship Lists, 1654

Cooperslaeger
  Willems
    King Pap, 1671

Coort
  Hermans
    Brgr Frm, 1658
    Rcrd Nam 3, 1658

Coos
  Arents
    NY Ref bp, 1647
  Peters
    Berg Ref dt, 1704
    Brgr Frm, 1657
    NY Ref mr, 1656
    Rcrd Nam 2, 1656, 1658

Coppe
  Claas
    Brgr Frm, 1657

Coppen
  Claas
    Rcrd Nam 7, 1657

Corbyn
  Jans
    Rcrd Nam 4, 1662
  Peters
    Rcrd Nam 3, 1661

Cornell
  Cornelis
    King Co, 1666
  Willems
    King Co, 1681
    LI Fam 1, 1688
    LI Source, 1679

Cort
  Hermans
    King Pap, 1665

Cortelyou
  Jacques
    King Co, 1662

Cortlandt
  Stephens
    Rens Crsp 1, 1668

Coster
  Cornelis
    Pearson, 1643

Couwenhoven
  Gerrits
    Bkln Ref bp, 1699
    Bkln Ref mr, 1695
    Fltb Ref bp, 1678, 1679,
    1680, 1681, 1682
    King Co, 1639
    Ship Lists, 1630
  Gilberts
    Ship Lists, no date
  Jacobs
    King Co, 1641
  Jans
    Bkln Ref mr, 1695
    Fltb Ref mr, 1691
    King Co, 1693
  Olivers
    King Ref bp, 1663
  Peters
    King Co, no date
  Willems
    King Co, 1676
  Wolferts
    King Co, 1631
    NY Ref bp, 1655
    NYC Wills, 1670
    Nycol Doc 1, 1643

Covert
  Jans
    Fltb Ref bp, 1680
    LI Source, 1694, 1698,
    1700
    NY Ref bp, 1691
    Ship Lists, 1687, no date
  Teunis
    Fltb Ref mr, 1679, 1682
    King Co, 1677

Cram
  Willems
    LI Source, 1679

Cray
  Geurts
    NY Ref bp, 1653
  Teunis
    NY Ref bp, 1664
    NY Ref mr, 1658
    Rcrd Nam 1, 1655

Cregier
  Martins
    Pearson, 1734

Cressens
  Claas
    NYC Wills, 1679

Cristman
  Jans
    Rcrd Nam 1, 1653

Croat
  Stephens
    Pearson, 1637
    Ship Lists, 1638

Croesen
  Claas
    LI Source, 1689, 1695
    Rcrd Nam 4, 1662
  Dirks
    Bkln Ref mr, 1661
    King Co, 1661
  Gerrits
    Fltb Ref mr, 1681

Crol
  Jans
    Pearson, 1630

Croom
  Jans
    Pearson, 1660

Croon
  Frans
    Nycol Doc 1, 1652
  Jans
    Fern Wlls, 1694
    Nicl Lvl, 1667
    Nycol Doc 1, 1652
    Ship Lists, 1649, 1654
  Willems
    NYC Court, 1693

Surname/Patronymic Combinations

Cruyf
  Gerberts
    Pearson, 1654
    Rens Court, 1668, 1669,
    1670, 1671,1672
    Rens Crsp 1, 1659, 1668
    Ship Lists, 1654
  Gerbrants
    Fern Wlls, 1663
  Herberts
    Rcrd Nam 1, 1655
Cruytdop
  Christophs
    NY Ref mr, 1660
Crynen
  Cornelis
    Gen Entr 1, 1665
Cuey
  Claas
    Rcrd Nam 1, 1655
Curtius
  Carls
    Rcrd Nam 3, 1660
Cuyter
  Peters
    LI Source, 1693
    NY Ref bp, 1642
    Nycol Doc 1, 1643
    Rcrd Nam 1, 1654
    Rcrd Nam 7, 1658

D

Daas
  Elias
    Fltb Ref bp, 1681
Dam
  Jans
    NY Ref bp, 1642, 1646,
    1660
  Teunis
    LI Source, 1695
Damen
  Claas
    NY Ref bp, 1648
  Cornelis
    Bkln Ref bp, 1674, 1678,
    1680

    Fltb Ref bp, 1683
    King Co, 1655
    LI Source, 1650
    Nicl Lvl, 1672
    NYC Wills, 1680
    Pearson, 1634
  Jans
    Berg Ref mr, 1697
    Bkln Ref bp, 1680, 1681
    Bkln Ref mr, 1695
    Fern Wlls, 1649
    Fltb Ref bp, 1680, 1681
    Fltb Ref mr, 1679, 1681
    King Co, 1677
    NY Ref bp, 1649
    NY Ref mr, 1679
    Nycol Doc 1, 1644
    Pearson, 1634
    Ship Lists, 1634, 1651
  Martins
    Bkln Ref bp, 1680
    Fltb Ref bp, 1680
Davids
  Christophs
    King Ref bp, 1697
    Pearson, no date
DBevoise
  Carls
    King Co, 1678
DeBakker
  Volkerts
    Pearson, 1654
DeBeer
  Willems
    Rens Crsp 1, 1658
    Ship Lists, 1657
DeBoer
  Cornelis
    Pearson, 1659
  Jans
    Gen Entr 2, 1675
    Pearson, 1661
    Ship Lists, 1648
DeBoogh
  Hendricks
    Nicl Lvl, 1672
    NY Ref bp, 1658
    NYC Wills, 1687

DeBrabander
  Jans
    King Pap, 1662
    Ship Lists, 1651
DeBruyn
  Adrians
    Ship Lists, 1663
  Hendricks
    Fern Wlls, 1702
    NY Ref bp, 1688
  Jacobs
    Ship Lists, 1649
DeCamp
  Jans
    King Co, 1664
    Ship Lists, 1664, 1687
Decker
  Broers
    King Ref bp, 1679
    King Ref mr, 1679
  Gerrits
    King Ref bp, 1688, 1697,
    1701, 1710
    King Ref mr, 1704, 1709
  Jacobs
    King Ref mr, 1704
  Jans
    King Ref bp, 1679, 1681,
    1684, 1687, 1688, 1695,
    1700, 1702
    King Ref mr, 1678, 1684,
    1685
DeCley
  Huygens
    NY Ref mr, 1683
DeCromp
  Hendricks
    Rcrd Nam 3, 1661
DeCuyper
  Jans
    Rcrd Nam 1, 1653
DeDrayer
  Andries
    Rcrd Nam 2, 1656
  Jans
    NY Ref bp, 1659

Surname/Patronymic Combinations

Deenmarken
  Jans
    NY Ref mr, 1659
DeGarmo
  Jans
    Pearson, 1753
DeGoyer
  Everts
    Pearson, 1664
  Hendricks
    Ship Lists, 1644
  Roelofs
    Pearson, no date
    Rens Court, 1669
DeGraef
  Anderson
    King Co, 1660
  Andries
    Pearson, 1682
    Rcrd Nam 3, 1659
    Rens Court, 1668
  Claas
    Pearson, 1699
DeGraw
  Alberts
    NY Ref bp, 1682, 1699
    NY Ref mr, 1683
  Ar.
    NY Ref bp, 1688
  Arents
    NY Ref bp, 1699, 1701
  Lennerts
    King Co, 1672
    NY Ref bp, 1684
    NY Ref mr, 1679
DeGroot
  Adolfs
    NYC Wills, 1696
  Jacobs
    NY Ref bp, 1688, 1690
  Jans
    Evjen, 1661
    Hack Ref bp, 1717, 1718, 1720
    Hack Ref mr, 1716
    King Co, 1677
    NY Ref bp, 1678, 1679, 1682, 1688

    NY Ref mr, 1677
    Rcrd Nam 7, 1674
  Peters
    Brgr Frm, 1657
    Hack Ref bp, 1716, 1718, 1719, 1720, 1721
    Hack Ref mr, 1716
    NY Ref bp, 1650, 1688
    Orphan Mst, 1665
    Rcrd Nam 7, 1674
    Ship Lists, 1662, no date
  Staats
    Hack Ref bp, 1715
DeGuyt
  Jans
    Rens Crsp 1, 1663
DeHaas
  Gerrits
    NY Ref bp, 1678
  Hendricks
    Alb Ref mm, 1683
    Pearson, 1683
  Peters
    NY Ref bp, 1652, 1655
DeHart
  Aesen
    King Co, 1664
  Jacobs
    NY Ref bp, 1683
DeHeer
  Lamberts
    Rcrd Nam 4, 1662
DeHeest
  Lamberts
    Bkln Ref mr, 1663
    King Co, 1663
DeHonneur
  Gerrits
    Pearson, 1679
DeHubert
  Teunis
    NY Ref mr, 1674
DeJones
  Jans
    Gen Entr 1, 1670
DeJonge
  Jans
    Rens Crsp 1, 1661, 1664

DeKaarl
  Elias
    Ship Lists, 1662
DeKaerl
  Elias
    Ship Lists, 1662
DeKey
  Teunis
    Crt Assz, 1676
    Fern Wlls, 1668
    NY Ref bp, 1659, 1663, 1664, 1665, 1672, 1674, 1675, 1677, 1678, 1679, 1681
DeKlein
  Barents
    NY Ref bp, 1663, 1680, 1684
    Ship Lists, 1661
  Cornelis
    King Co, 1660
  Huygens
    Bkln Ref bp, 1698
    King Co, 1683
    LI Source, 1693
    NY Ref bp, 1684, 1688, 1698, 1702, 1704, 1706
    NY Ref mr, 1670, 1680, 1704
    NYC Wills, 1695
    Rcrd Nam 6, 1670
    West Wills, 1735
DeLaa
  Cornelis
    King Ref bp, 1683
DeLaMontagne
  Monjeur
    King Ref bp, 1674, 1678, 1682
DeLange
  Jans
    King Ref bp, 1663
DeLaSalle
  Renatus
    Rens Court, 1671
DeLascher
  Peters
    Rcrd Nam 1, 1655

Surname/Patronymic Combinations

DeLeeuw
Jans
LI Fam 2, no date
Delmont
Jacobs
Alb Ref bp, 1702
DeLooper
Teunis
Pearson, 1656
Rcrd Nam 6, 1667
DeMandeville
Giles
King Co, 1680
NY Ref mr, 1680
Jans
Ship Lists, 1649
DeMare
Jans
LI Source, 1694
DeMaree
Davids
Hack Ref bp, 1717, 1718,
1719
Hack Ref mr, 1717
Sam
Hack Ref mr, 1717
Samuels
Hack Ref bp, 1708, 1710,
1715, 1717, 1718, 1719,
1720
Hack Ref mr, 1718
DeMetzelaer
Teunis
Ship Lists, 1642
Demoer
Philips
Pearson, 1693
DeMoulinars
Brumeau
Ship Lists, 1683
Joost
Ship Lists, 1683
DenHagenaer
Jans
NY Ref bp, 1659

DeNoorman
Andries
Pearson, 1630
Dirks
Bkln Ref bp, 1670
NY Ref bp, 1659
Hans
NY Ref bp, 1644
Lawrence
NY Ref bp, 1646
Peters
NY Ref bp, 1646
DeNys
Teunis
Fltb Ref bp, 1681, 1682,
1685, 1687
King Co, 1667
DePaep
Teunis
Pearson, 1660
DePaul
Michels
Gen Entr 2, 1683
DePoitiere
Baptist
King Ref bp, 1693, 1698
DePottebacker
Claas
Rcrd Nam 2, 1656
DeRaedt
Hermans
NY Ref bp, 1663
DeRapalye
Joris
Bkln Ref bp, 1662
DeReus
Mathys
Ship Lists, 1633
Teunis
Pearson, 1631
Ship Lists, 1631
DeRoode
Peters
Rens Court, 1669

DeRuyter
Adrians
Gen Entr 1, 1665
Nicl Lvl, 1665
Nycol Doc 2, 1664
Jans
Ship Lists, 1636
DeRyck
Cornelis
LI Fam 2, 1664
NY Ref bp, 1661, 1662,
1663, 1665, 1667
Rcrd Nam 6, 1671
DeRyp
Claas
Ship Lists, 1675
DesChamps
Broussard
Ship Lists, 1668
DeSee
Jans
King Co, 1660
DeSeeuw
Jans
LI Fam 2, no date
DeSweedt
Alberts
Pearson, 1674
Hendricks
Pearson, 1675
Deucht
Claas
Nycol Doc 2, 1662
Rcrd Nam 4, 1662
Rens Crsp 1, 1662
DeVass
Dirks
Rcrd Nam 3, 1661
DeVisscher
Jans
Nicl Lvl, 1672
DeVos
Andries
Pearson, 1664
Cornelis
Pearson, 1653

Surname/Patronymic Combinations

DeVos (cont.)
  Jans
    NY Ref mr, 1675
DeVries
  Dirks
    Pearson, 1654
    Rens Court, 1669
  Gerrits
    Rcrd Nam 4, 1662
  Jacobs
    King Co, 1667
    King Pap, 1664
    Nycol Doc 2, 1662
    Orphan Mst, 1666
    Rens Crsp 1, 1663
  Jans
    Pearson, 1656
  Peters
    Nycol Doc 1, 1642
  Rudolphs
    NY Ref mr, 1659
  Serix
    Nicl Lvl, 1672
  Syrachs
    King Co, 1660
  Titus
    Fltb Ref bp, 1682
  Zacharias
    Fltb Ref bp, 1682
DeVyselaer
  Bastians
    Pearson, 1675
DeWeaver
  Martins
    Pearson, 1689
DeWees
  Hendricks
    Ship Lists, 1690
DeWitt
  Alberts
    NY Ref bp, 1662, 1663
  Bastians
    Alb Ref bp, 1700
    Alb Ref mr, 1695
    Pearson, 1700
  Claas
    Anjou Prb, 1687, 1699
    Gen Entr 1, 1669

King Pap, 1662, 1666
King Ref bp, 1662, 1664,
1666, 1667, 1683, 1698, 1700
Nicl Lvl, 1667
NY Ref bp, 1665
NY Ref mr, 1656
Pearson, 1663
Ship Lists, no date
  Jans
    King Co, 1652
    Rens Crsp 1, 1660
    Ship Lists, 1687
Dey
  Jans
    NYC Wills, 1693
DeYoung
  Adrians
    King Ref bp, 1682
  Cornelis
    Pearson, 1659
  Gerrits
    NY Ref bp, 1681
  Giles
    Rcrd Nam 3, 1660
  Jans
    NY Ref bp, 1660, 1662,
    1664
    NY Ref mr, 1659
    Rcrd Nam 1, 1653
    Ship Lists, 1652
  Wessels
    NY Ref bp, 1670
DeZeeuw
  Jans
    Bkln Ref bp, 1682
    Fltb Ref bp, 1682
Diesvelt
  Arents
    Ship Lists, 1659
Diffoer
  Jans
    Alb Ref bp, 1705
Dingman
  Adams
    Pearson, 1700
Dirks
  Reyners
    Berg Ref mm, 1678

Ditmars
  Barents
    Pearson, 1692
  Jans
    Evjen, 1643
    King Co, 1647
    Ship Lists, no date
Dominicus
  Jans
    LI Fam 2, no date
Dommelaer
  Jans
    Pearson, 1657
Doorn
  Martins
    Anjou Prb, 1671
    King Pap, 1664
    King Ref bp, 1678
    King Ref mr, 1661, 1684
    Nicl Lvl, 1667
    Pearson, 1686
    Rcrd Nam 4, 1663
Doremus
  Cornelis
    Berg Ref mr, 1710
    Ship Lists, no date
Dorland
  Gerrits
    Bkln Ref bp, 1674, 1692,
    1694
    Fltb Ref bp, 1680, 1684
    Fltb Ref mr, 1682, 1683
    King Co, 1656
    LI Source, 1689, 1690,
    1693, 1701
    Ship Lists, 1687
  Jans
    Bkln Ref bp, 1696
    Bkln Ref mr, 1695
    Bogart, 1672
    Fltb Ref bp, 1681
    Fltb Ref mr, 1692
    Gen Entr 2, 1676
    King Co, 1675
    Nicl Lvl, 1672
    Ship Lists, 1663

Dorn
  Martins
    King Pap, 1664
Douw
  Andries
    Alb Ref bp, 1684, 1686,
     1689
    Pearson, 1646
    Rens Crsp 1, 1659
  Hans
    Ship Lists, no date
  Hendricks
    Rens Crsp 2, 1684
  Jans
    Evjen, 1638
    Pearson, 1681
    Rens Crsp 1, 1658, 1659,
     1661, 1662
    Rens Crsp 2, 1683
    Ship Lists, 1638, no date
  Jonas
    Alb Ref bp, 1709
  Jonasse
    Pearson, 1709
  Volkerts
    Alb Ref mm, 1683
    Alb Ref mr, 1683, 1684
    Pearson, 1690
    Ship Lists, 1642
Draeck
  Claas
    NY Ref bp, 1659
Drats
  Jans
    Fltb Ref bp, 1682
    Fltb Ref mr, 1682
    King Co, 1661
    NY Ref mr, 1682
    Rcrd Nam 2, 1658
Dreeper
  Hans
    Pearson, 1694
Druger
  Fredericks
    Gen Entr 2, 1688
Druyn
  Jans
    LI Source, 1689

Dubois
  Louis
    King Ref bp, 1664
  Willems
    King Ref bp, 1664
Dufoert
  Jans
    NY Ref mr, 1698
Dujon
  Gerrits
    NY Ref bp, 1689
Dulleman
  Barents
    Pearson, 1661
Dumont
  Baptist
    King Ref bp, 1694, 1701
  Lamberts
    Gen Entr 2, 1686
DuRues
  Pauls
    Ship Lists, 1663
Duryee
  Joost
    King Co, 1685
    LI Fam 1, 1686
DuTuffeau
  Bertrands
    Ship Lists, 1687
Duycking
  Everts
    NY Ref mr, 1666
Duyster
  Cornelis
    Pearson, 1626
Duyts
  Lawrence
    King Co, 1642
    NY Ref bp, 1671
    NY Ref mr, 1667, 1673
    Ship Lists, 1668
Duyvelant
  Arents
    Rcrd Nam 3, 1660
Dye
  Jans
    NY Ref bp, 1677

Dykehuys
  Teunis
    LI Source, 1693

E

Eeckelen
  Jans
    Rens Crsp 1, 1659
Eencluys
  Jans
    Rens Court, 1670
    Ship Lists, 1641
Egberts
  Huberts
    King Co, 1675
Eggert
  Jans
    NYC Wills, 1678
Egmont
  Claas
    Alb Ref bp, 1684
    Pearson, 1683
Elbins
  Jacobs
    Nycol Doc 1, 1633
Elkens
  Jacobs
    Pearson, 1618
Elting
  Roelofs
    Berg Ref mr, 1672
Emans
  Andries
    King Co, 1693
Emilius
  Jans
    Nycol Doc 2, 1661
Engel
  Jans
    Nycol Doc 1, 1618
Engelbert
  Peters
    Hack Ref bp, 1712
    Hack Ref mr, 1718
Engelsman
  Dirks
    Pearson, 1638
    Ship Lists, 1638

Surname/Patronymic Combinations

Engsinck
  Jans
    Ship Lists, 1660, no date

Esselstine
  Martins
    King Ref mr, 1702
  Willems
    King Co, 1661
    NY Ref bp, 1650, 1669
    Rcrd Nam 1, 1654

Ester
  Willems
    Rcrd Nam 2, 1658

Everson
  Jacobs
    Pearson, 1744

Exveen
  Cornelis
    NY Ref mr, 1693

F

Fabricius
  Cornelis
    Rcrd Nam 6, 1670

Factor
  Martins
    Rcrd Nam 1, 1655

Fenn
  Jans
    Gen Entr 2, 1684

Fesselet
  Hermans
    King Pap, 1664

Flansburgh
  Jans
    Brgr Frm, 1683
    Gen Entr 2, 1684
    NY Ref bp, 1691

Flodder
  Jacobs
    Pearson, 1685
  Jans
    Nicl Lvl, 1665
    Pearson, 1638
    Rcrd
    Rens Court, 1668, 1669,
    1670, 1671, 1672

Rens Crsp 1, 1661, 1664
Ship Lists, 1638, 1642

Floid
  Everts
    Rcrd Nam 7, 1674

Fonda
  Douws
    Pearson, 1654
    Rens Court, 1670
  Giles
    Pearson, 1674
  Isaacs
    Pearson, 1732

Fort
  Daniels
    Pearson, 1736

Fouchard
  James
    Brgr Frm, 1704

Fradell
  Simons
    Ship Lists, 1652

Fransman
  Labaties
    Ship Lists, 1637

Frelinghuysen
  Jacobs
    Ship Lists, 1720, no date

Fuyck
  Cornelis
    Nycol Doc 2, 1657

Fyn
  Jans
    King Co, 1666

Fynhoudt
  Aerts
    King Pap, 1667

G

Galma
  Jans
    Brgr Frm, 1657
    Nycol Doc 3, 1664
    Rcrd Nam 1, 1653

1655

Rens Crsp 2, 1684
Ship Lists, no date

Gardner
  Andries
    Pearson, no date
  Jacobs
    Alb Ref bp, 1685, 1689
    Alb Ref mr, 1692, 1695
    Fern Wlls, 1689, 1710
    Pearson, 1683
    Rens Court, 1672
  Jans
    Alb Ref bp, 1701
    Pearson, 1702
    Rens Court, 1672
    Ship Lists, 1638

Geelgieter
  Lennerts
    Ship Lists, 1647

Gemakelyck
  Adrians
    Pearson, 1681

Gerritsen
  Claas
    NY Ref bp, 1691

Gesscher
  Willems
    Berg Ref dt, 1696

Gilde
  Cornelis
    Gen Entr 1, 1664
    Rens Crsp 1, 1657

Glaser
  Alberts
    NY Ref mr, 1659

Glazemaecker
  Teunis
    Pearson, 1658

Glenn
  Jacobs
    Pearson, 1699
  Lennerts
    Crt Assz, 1675
    Nicl Lvl, 1669
    Nycol Doc 1, 1656
    Pearson, 1639

Rens Court, 1670, 1672
Rens Crsp 1, 1656
Ship Lists, 1639
Sanders
Alb Ref bp, 1683, 1685
Alb Ref mm, 1683
Alb Ref mr, 1696, 1699
Fern Wlls, 1685
Gen Entr 2, 1685
Nicl Lvl, 1669
NYC Wills, 1686
Nycol Doc 3, 1688
Pearson, 1695
Rens Court, 1668, 1669,
1670, 1671, 1672
Rens Crsp 1, 1658, 1659,
1662, 1670, 1672
Rens Crsp 2, 1682, 1683,
1687
Schn Ref bp, 1694, 1700,
1701, 1702, 1703, 1704, 1706
Goddard
Dirks
Rcrd Nam 1, 1653
Goemonepa
Michels
NY Ref mr, 1665
Goes
Dirks
Pearson, 1732
Jans
Alb Ref bp, 1687, 1700,
1702
Pearson, 1697
Mathys
Alb Ref mm, 1683
Fern Wlls, 1697, 1705
Gen Entr 1, 1669
Pearson, 1683
Goewey
Abels
Ship Lists, no date
Jacobs
NY Ref bp, 1706
Jans
Alb Ref bp, 1701, 1702,
1704
Pearson, 1702

Solomons
Alb Ref bp, 1701, 1702,
1707, 1708
NY Ref mr, 1707
Pearson, 1683
Gojer
Andries
Ship Lists, 1644
Gouw
Cornelis
Pearson, 1660
Rens Court, 1669, 1673
Rens Crsp 2, 1678
Gradus
Philips
NY Ref bp, 1642
Graef
Hendricks
King Pap, 1661
Pearson, 1684
Graer
Hans
Ship Lists, 1660
Grauw
Arents
Alb Ref bp, 1689
Pearson, 1689
Lennerts
NY Ref bp, 1690
Gravenhage
Jans
NY Ref mr, 1671
Greeff
Gerrits
Pearson, 1661
Grever
Jans
Rcrd Nam 2, 1658
Groen
Alderts
NY Ref mr, 1665
Marius
Alb Ref bp, 1709
King Ref bp, 1703
NY Ref bp, 1701, 1702,
1703, 1704, 1706, 1709
NY Ref mr, 1701

NYC Court, 1706
Pearson, 1709
Groenvelt
Arents
Ship Lists, 1659
Peters
NY Ref bp, 1685
Groenewout
Jans
Rens Court, 1669, 1670,
1671
Groenvis
Claas
King Pap, 1671
NY Ref mr, 1658
Groenwoet
Jans
Pearson, 1662
Groesbeek
Claas
Alb Ref bp, 1688, 1701,
1702, 1703, 1707
Alb Ref mm, 1683
Alb Ref mr, 1699
NY Ref bp, 1690
Pearson, 1695, 1707
Jacobs
Alb Ref bp, 1700, 1701
Fern Wlls, 1707
Pearson, 1661
Ship Lists, no date
Van Rotterdam
Alb Ref mm, 1683
Willems
Pearson, 1746
Groll
Gerrits
Rcrd Nam 3, 1661
Groot
Simons
Pearson, 1654
Grootvelt
Hendricks
NY Ref mr, 1706
Gruis
Jans
NY Ref bp, 1668

H

Haen
Hendricks
Brgr Frm, 1659
Ship Lists, 1657

Haas
Gerrits
Fltb Ref bp, 1680
King Co, 1680

Haeswout
Peters
Berg Ref mr, 1683

Haff
Jurians
King Co, 1679

Hafte
Hendricks
King Co, 1664

Hagel
Gerrits
Ship Lists, 1660

Hagenaar
Jans
Brgr Frm, 1657
Nycol Doc 3, 1664
Orphan Mst, 1663, 1665
Rcrd Nam 4, 1663

Hallenbeck
Caspars
Alb Ref bp, 1706
Atns Lth bp, 1705, 1708
Atns Lth mr, 1709
NY Lth bp, 1708
NY Ref bp, 1705
Pearson, 1706
Rens Crsp 2, 1683
Jacobs
NY Lth bp, 1708
Pearson, no date
Rens Crsp 1, 1674
Rens Crsp 2, 1687
Ship Lists, no date
Jans
Alb Ref bp, 1707, 1709
Atns Lth mr, 1709
NY Lth bp, 1709
NY Lth mr, 1709
Pearson, 1707

Halsyn
Cornelis
Fltb Ref mr, 1692

Hamelward
Hendricks
Pearson, 1638

Hap
Jans
King Pap, 1661
NY Ref bp, 1657
Pearson, 1630
Rens Crsp 2, 1685
Ship Lists, 1645

Harberding
Jacobs
NY Ref bp, 1671

Hardenburgh
Jans
LI Fam 1, 1670
Ship Lists, 1667

Harder
Peters
Rcrd Nam 4, 1663

Harderwyck
Hendricks
Orphan Mst, 1664

Hardick
Frans
King Ref bp, 1697
Pearson, 1737

Harding
Hans
Hack Ref mm, page xx

Haring
Jans
NY Ref bp, 1688
NY Ref mr, 1687
Tap Ref bp, 1704
Peters
NY Ref bp, 1669, 1679
NY Ref mr, 1685
Rcrd Nam 7, 1674

Hartmann
Jans
Ship Lists, no date

Harty
Hans
Hack Ref mm, page xx

Jacobs
NY Ref mr, 1668
Ship Lists, 1663, 1685

Harung
Hendricks
NY Lth bp, 1709

Haughwout
Jans
LI Fam 1, 1660
Lefferts
LI Fam 1, no date
Peters
LI Fam 1, 1675

Heemstraat
Dirks
Rens Court, 1671
Takels
Alb Ref bp, 1701, 1702
Pearson, 1701

Heerings
Cornelis
Hack Ref mr, 1717
Cosines
Hack Ref bp, 1720
Hack Ref mr, 1719
Jans
Hack Ref bp, 1694, 1711
Peters
Hack Ref bp, 1715, 1717,
1719

Hegeman
Adrians
King Co, 1688
Dennis
Jam Ref bp, 1717
Joost
King Co, 1687

Helling
Hendricks
Berg Ref mr, 1695
Teunis
Berg Ref dt, 1685, 1697
Berg Ref mr,, 1700
Hack Ref mr, 1700
Ship Lists, 1659

Helmer
Jans
Alb Ref mr, 1686

Surname/Patronymic Combinations

Hendricksen
  Selyns
    NY Ref bp, 1663
Henypot
  Jans
    Ship Lists, 1639
Herculan
  Claas
    Nycol Doc 1, 1653
Hermans
  Fockens
    Ship Lists, no date
  Volkerts
    NY Ref bp, 1694
Herttenbergh
  Jans
    Pearson, 1664
Hesse
  Jans
    Nycol Doc 1, 1633
Heyman
  Barents
    Rcrd Nam 1, 1653
  Jans
    NY Ref bp, 1652
Heyn
  Peters
    Rens Crsp 1, 1656
Heyning
  Jans
    NY Ref mr, 1667
Heyvelt
  Willems
    Rens Crsp 1, 1660
Hillebrant
  Gregors
    Pearson, 1658
    Ship Lists, 1658
Hoen
  Teunis
    NY Ref bp, 1662
Hoes- see Goes
Hoff
  Jurians
    Fltb Ref bp, 1681

Hoffman
  Hermans
    Bkln Ref mr, 1663
    King Co, 1663
Hogan
  Jurians
    Pearson, 1730
Hogeboom
  Bartholomeus
    Alb Ref bp, 1701, 1708
    Pearson, 1701
  Peters
    King Pap, 1665
    Pearson, 1661
    Rens Court, 1669
    Rens Crsp 2, 1683
  Teunis
    Pearson, 1661
Hols
  Mathys
    Ship Lists, no date
Honing
  Cornelis
    Nycol Doc 2, 1656
Hoochsaet
  Jans
    Nycol Doc 2, 1657
Hoog
  Jans
    LI Source, 1701
Hoogkerk
  Lucas
    Alb Ref bp, 1701, 1709
Hoogland
  Andries
    NY Ref mr, 1661
    Ship Lists, 1658, no date
  Cornelis
    King Co, 1645
    LI Source, 1689, 1696
    NY Ref bp, 1687
  Dirks
    Fltb Ref mr, 1689
    King Co, 1638
    LI Source, 1660
    Nycol Doc 1, 1644
    Ship Lists, 1645, 1687

Jans
  Bkln Ref mr, 1662
  Crt Assz, 1679
  Fltb Ref bp, 1681, 1686
  King Co, 1657
  LI Source, 1689, 1694,
    1695, 1697, 1698
  Ship Lists, 1662, no date
Hoogstraten
  Jans
    NY Ref bp, 1680
Hoorn
  Adolfs
    NY Ref mr, 1689
  Jans
    NY Ref bp, 1671
    Nycol Doc 2, 1659
    Pearson, 1659
    Rcrd Nam 3, 1659
Hoppe
  Adolfs
    Berg Ref bp, 1684
    Berg Ref mr, 1683
    NY Ref mr, 1683
  Hendricks
    Hack Ref bp, 1710, 1716,
      1718, 1719, 1720
    Hack Ref mm, 1710
    Hack Ref mr, 1706, 1707
  Mathys
    Hack Ref bp, 1711, 1714
    Hack Ref mm, 1708
Hortman
  Jurians
    NY Ref bp, 1710
Hotaling
  Jans
    King Ref bp, 1679
  Mathys
    Alb Ref mr, 1688
    Pearson, 1688
  Willems
    Anjou Prb, 1671, 1702
    Gen Entr 1, 1668
    King Pap, 1664
    King Ref bp, 1664, 1665,
      1679, 1697, 1699

Surname/Patronymic Combinations

Houten
Jans
    Nycol Doc 1, 1621
Joris
    Nycol Doc 1, 1621
    Pearson, 1633
Houtsager
Jans
    King Pap, 1662
Peters
    Pearson, 1660
Hovenier
Jacobs
    King Ref bp, 1683
Hoyer
Dirks
    NY Ref bp, 1700, 1706
    NY Ref mr, 1688
Hues
Martins
    Pearson, 1658
    Rens Court, 1670
Huisman
Cornelis
    King Co, 1663
Hulft
Everts
    Nycol Doc 1, 1617
Hun
Hermans
    Alb Ref bp, 1702, 1704,
    1705, 1707, 1709
    Pearson, 1662
Thomas
    Rens Crsp 1, 1660
    Ship Lists, no date
Huyck
Andries
    Pearson, 1705
Hans
    Alb Ref bp, 1700
    Alb Ref mm, 1683
    Fern Wlls, 1705
    Pearson, 1679
Huys
Jans
    Nycol Doc 1, 1656
    Rcrd Nam 1, 1654
    Rens Crsp 1, 1664

Huysman
Teunis
    Gen Entr 1, 1670

I

Iersman
Andries
    Pearson, no date
Israel
Bens
    Nycol Doc 1, 1656

J

Jacobs
Hans
    Berg Ref bp, 1688, 1691
    Berg Ref mm, 1690
    Berg Ref mr, 1687
Jacobsen
Aerts
    King Pap, 1663
Jacquet
Pauls
    Gen Entr 2, 1676
    NY Ref bp, 1655
    Nycol Doc 2, 1657
    Rcrd Nam 1, 1655
    Ship Lists, 1685
JanDenHans
Jans
    NY Ref bp, 1660
Jans
Broers
    King Ref bp, 1688
Lucas
    NY Ref bp, 1703
Jansen
Arents
    NY Ref bp, 1677
Jacobs
    King Pap, 1663
Jean
Blans
    King Ref bp, 1681, 1682,
    1683
Jeralemon
Hans
    Hack Ref mr, 1701

Jans
    Alb Ref bp, 1702
    Pearson, 1702
Jochems
Jans
    King Pap, 1662
Joerissen
Joris
    Bkln Ref mr, 1695
Jongen
Claas
    Ship Lists, 1637
Pauls
    Ship Lists, 1642
Peters
    Ship Lists, 1637
Stephens
    Ship Lists, 1638
Jongerman
Roelofs
    Ship Lists, 1658
Jonker
Jans
    Alb Ref mr, 1699
Jurianse
Jans
    King Co, 1688

K

Kamminga
Jans
    Ship Lists, 1687
Kap
Jans
    Hack Ref bp, 1702,
    1703
Karreman
Frans
    Orphan Mst, 1664, 1665
Kat
Cornelis
    Ship Lists, 1687
Kay
Teunis
    NYC Wills, 1671
    Pearson, 1676
Kaye
Claas
    Pearson, 1661

Keert
 Cornelis
  Hack Ref mm, 1686
Keet
 Melchiors
  King Ref bp, 1701, 1725
Kenne
 Peters
  King Co, 1660
Kerckoven
 Adams
  Fltb Ref mr, 1690
Kerseboom
 Everts
  Berg Ref bp, 1667, 1669, 1673
  Berg Ref dt, 1668
  Berg Ref mm, 1665
  NY Ref bp, 1678, 1681
Ketelhuyn
 Jochems
  Pearson, 1690
Keteltas
 Everts
  NY Ref bp, 1669, 1670, 1671, 1673, 1674, 1680, 1683
  NY Ref mr, 1687
  Rcrd Nam 7, 1673
  Ship Lists, no date
 Peters
  NY Ref bp, 1667, 1669, 1670, 1671, 1672, 1673, 1674, 1676, 1677
 Willems
  Ship Lists, no date
Key
 Teunis
  Gen Entr 2, 1676
  King Co, 1664
  Nycol Doc 2, 1674
  Rcrd Nam 1, 1661
Keyser
 Cornelis
  King Pap, 1668, 1669
 Dirks
  Pearson, 1658

Kidney
 Roelofs
  Alb Ref mm, 1698
Kieft
 Alberts
  Nycol Doc 2, 1661
Kies
 Clements
  Nycol Doc 1, 1614
Kieste
 Jacobs
  King Co, 1691
Kikebel
 Davids
  Pearson, 1682
Kinne
 Peters
  Fltb Ref bp, 1678, 1680, 1683
Kip
 Hendricks
  Brgr Frm, 1657
  NY Ref bp, 1647, 1662, 1668
  NY Ref mr, 1654
  Nycol Doc 1, 1644
  Rcrd Nam 5, 1664
  Ship Lists, 1637, no date
Kitser
 Jans
  Rcrd Nam 6, 1666
Kleermaker
 Jans
  Pearson, 1683
 Peters
  Pearson, 1660
Klein
 Barents
  NY Ref bp, 1664, 1671
  Rcrd Nam 4, 1662
 Cornelis
  King Co, 1660
  Pearson, 1660
  Rcrd Nam 1, 1653
 Gerrits
  Pearson, 1671

 Huygens
  NY Ref bp, 1671
Kleumpje
 Jans
  Berg Ref dt, 1688
Klinckhamer
 Jans
  Rcrd Nam 1, 1654
  Ship Lists, no date
Klock
 Abrams
  Fltb Ref bp, 1679, 1681
  NY Ref mr, 1682
Klug
 Jurians
  NY Lth bp, 1710
Knevelaar
 Adrians
  Nycol Doc 2, 1661
Knickerbacker
 Hermans
  Alb Ref bp, 1701
  Pearson, 1708
 Jans
  Alb Ref bmm, 1683
  Fern Wlls, 1708
  Pearson, 1682
  Rens Crsp 2, 1683
  Ship Lists, 1700, no date
Kocherthal
 Joshua
  Nycol Doc 5, 1708
Kock
 Giles
  Pearson, 1657
  Ship Lists, 1656
Koningh
 Jans
  NY Ref bp, 1665
  Rens Court, 1671
  Ship Lists, 1663
Koorenbeurs
 Jans
  Alb Ref bp, 1683
Koperslager
 Cornelis
  Pearson, 1675

Kortright
Hendricks
King Ref bp, 1702
Koster
Cornelis
NY Ref bp, 1662
Nycol Doc 2, 1656
Pearson, 1643
Kranckheyt
Herricks
Tary Ref bp, 1697, 1699,
1702, 1703, 1706, 1708
Tary Ref mm, 1700?
Tary Ref mr, 1708
Krast
Wolferts
Fltb Ref bp, 1680
Krol
Jans
Ship Lists, 13630
Kromenborch
Jans
Pearson, 1657
Kroock
Peters
Nycol Doc 2, 1662
Kruis
Dents
King Ref bp, 1708
Krum
Floris
Hack Ref mr, 1699
Willems
Fern Wlls, 1699
King Co, 1677
King Pap, 1668
King Ref bp, 1678, 1681
King Ref mr, 1668
LI Fam 2, no date
NY Ref bp, 1685
NYC Wills, 1699
Kulerman
Claas
Pearson, 1670
Kume
Peters
Bkln Ref bp, 1686
Ship Lists, 1663

Kunst
Barents
King Pap, 1664
King Ref bp, 1664, 1667
King Ref mr, 1668
Nicl Lvl, 1669
Pearson, 1662
Jans
King Ref bp, 1683, 1689
King Ref mr, 1684
Kuykendaal
Lawrence
Ship Lists, no date
Kuyter
Peters
Ship Lists, 1637
Kyckebul
Davis
Rens Court, 1672

L

Laenen
Jans
LI Source, 1687
Mathys
Ship Lists, 1687
Lamaker
Jans
Pearson, 1659
Lan
Cornelis
King Ref bp, 1681
Lane
Mathys
King Co, 1657
LI Source, 1693
NYC Wills, 1694
Lanen
Aerts
LI Source, 1696
Mathys
Fltb Ref mr, 1679, 1690
Teunis
Fltb Ref mr, 1686
LI Source, 1687
NY Ref mr, 1686
Lange
Frans
King Ref bp, 1696

Langedyck
Jans
Brgr Frm, 1657
King Ref bp, 1668
NY Ref bp, 1698
NY Ref mr, 1691
NYC Wills, 1698
Langelaan
Philips
Fltb Ref bp, 1679
Langerth
Frans
King Ref bp, 1688
Langestraat
Christophs
Fltb Ref bp, 1684
King Co, 1657
Dirks
King Co, 1698
Jans
NY Ref bp, 1664, 1668,
1670, 1679
Orphan Mst, 1665
Romeyns
NY Ref bp, 1697
Langet
Frans
King Ref bp, 1683
Langhaar
Jans
NY Ref bp, 1705
NY Ref mr, 1704
Lansing
Abrams
Pearson, 1728
Fredericks
Ship Lists, no date
Gerrits
Pearson, 1694
Isaacs
Pearson, 1747
Jacobs
Pearson, 1734
Jans
Pearson, 1695, 1748
Peters
Pearson, 1736

Reyers
  Pearson, 1693
Lantsman
  Jurians
    Crt Assz, 1667
    NY Ref bp, 1661, 1666
    NY Ref mr, 1685
    Rcrd Nam 3, 1659
Lanwaer
  Giles
    Rcrd Nam 7, 1674
Larzelere
  Jacobs
    King Co, 1677
Lasse
  Peters
    Ship Lists, 1659
Lassen
  Peters
    King Ref bp, 1684
    NY Lth bp, 1709
    Pearson, 1659
Lay
  Jans
    King Co, 1683
Leick
  Jans
    King Co, 1696
Lent
  Abrams
    West Wills, 1720
  Fredericks
    LI Fam 2, 1638
Lery
  Hendricks
    Pearson, 1663
Lesenter
  Claas
    Nycol Doc 2, 1662
Letelier
  Ganitzee
    King Co, 1664
Letten
  Claas
    Jam Ref bp, 1715
Levy
  Etiel
    NYC Court, 1712

Samuels
  NYC Court, 1691
Lievens
  Hermans
    Alb Ref mm, 1683
Lieversen
  Hermans
    Pearson, 1683
Lock
  Hendricks
    NY Ref bp, 1671, 1672
    NY Ref mr, 1671
    Rens Crsp 1, 1668
  Peters
    King Co, 1643
Loisen
  Jans
    Fltb Ref bp, 1681
    Fltb Ref mr, 1680
Loockermans
  Jacobs
    Rcrd Nam 3, 1661
  Jans
    Pearson, 1659
  Lamberts
    Pearson, 1682
  Peters
    Pearson, 1677
Looman
  Jans
    Anjou Prb, 1663
    King Pap, 1665
    Pearson, 1661
Looper
  Teunis
    Rcrd Nam 1, 1655
Loosdrecht
  Willems
    Berg Ref mm, 1667
Losericht
  Jans
    Berg Ref bp, 1677
    Nicl Lvl, 1672
Lott
  Engelberts
    King Co, 1684
    NY Ref mr, 1662

Hendricks
  King Co, 1692
Peters
  King Co, 1654
Louw
  Bastians
    Ship Lists, no date
  Cornelis
    Anjou Prb, 1690
    Evjen, 1659
    King Ref bp, 1683
    Ship Lists, 1659, no date
Loy
  Cornelis
    King Co, 1683
  Jans
    King Co, 1683
Loysen
  Jans
    LI Source, 1690
Lozier
  Jans
    King Co, 1680
Lubberts
  Fredericks
    Fltb Ref bp, 1680, 1687, 1688,
    1689
Luyster
  Cornelis
    Fltb Ref bp, 1681, 1683,
    1685
    King Co, 1693
    LI Source, 1687, 1690
    NYC Wills, 1695
    Ship Lists, 1687
  Mathys
    King Co, 1719
  Peters
    King Co, 1697
    LI Source, 1693, 1695
    Ship Lists, 1687
Lyndrayer
  Cornelis
    Nicl Lvl, 1666
  Jans
    Pearson, 1681

Surname/Patronymic Combinations

M

Maasen
Cornelis
Pearson, 1663
Mackelyck
Adrians
Rens Court, 1670
Ship Lists, 1655
Peters
Fltb Ref bp, 1681
King Co, 1664
LI Source, 1685,
1687,1693
Maet
Hendricks
Pearson, 1654
Maeter
Everts
King Pap, 1671
Mandeville
Giles
Fltb Ref bp, 1681
Fltb Ref mr, 1680
Hack Ref mm, 1686
NY Ref mr, 1681
Hendricks
Hack Ref mr, 1708
Marcelis
Jacobs
Rcrd Nam 6, 1668
Marinus
Jans
Ship Lists, no date
Marius
Jacobs
Brgr Frm, 1657, 1683
Crt Assz, 1668
Gen Entr 2, 1677
King Ref bp, 1681
NY Ref bp, 1650, 1651,
1657, 1659, 1661, 1664,
1665, 1666, 1667, 1668,
1674, 1676, 1677, 1678,
1679, 1680, 1681, 1682,
1684, 1686, 1687, 1688,
1689, 1690, 1691, 1693,
1695, 1696, 1702
NY Ref mr, 1655

NYC Court, 1693
NYC Wills, 1701, 1706
Nycol Doc 2, 1674
Pearson, 1663
Rcrd Nam 1, 1654
Peters
NY Ref bp, 1671
Marris
Jans
Hack Ref mm, page xx
Marshall
Giles
Brgr Frm, 1659
Ship Lists, 1658
Wartons
Rcrd Nam 5, 1665
Mathys
Cornelis
Gen Entr 1, 1672
Maul
Abrams
NY Ref mr, 1682
Hendricks
Rcrd Nam 3, 1661
Huberts
Brgr Frm, 1657
King Co, 1641
LI Source, 1693
NY Ref bp, 1648, 1658
Nycol Doc 1, 1650
Rcrd Nam 1, 1653
Jans
NY Ref bp, 1677, 1680,
1682, 1686, 1690, 1692
NY Ref mr, 1675
Ship Lists, no date
Lamberts
Gen Entr 2, 1682
King Co, 1646
NY Ref bp, 1677, 1678
NY Ref mr, 1660, 1662,
1668, 1686
Rcrd Nam 3, 1661
Ship Lists, no date
Mauritz
Peters
King Pap, 1669, 1670
Rcrd Nam 6, 1669

Mayer
Dirks
Rens Court, 1670
Jans
Ship Lists, 1662
Mebie
Peters
Alb Ref bp, 1693
Pearson, 1683
Schn Ref bp, 1695
Meed
Peters
NY Ref bp, 1700
NY Ref mr, 1676
Meerman
Dirks
King Pap, 1671
Frans
Nycol Doc 2, 1668
Meet
Jans
King Co, 1667
Megapolensis
Willems
Nycol Doc 2, 1674
Meinderts
Wemp
Schn Ref bp, 1701
Mellott
Peters
NYC Wills, 1707
Melott
Peters
Brgr Frm, 1691, 1694
NYC Court, 1697
Menevert
Josiahs
Gen Entr 2, 1685
Menist
Peters
NY Ref bp, 1660, 1665
Rcrd Nam 3, 1659
Mentelaer
Cornelis
King Co, 1645
LI Source, 1645

Meppel
  Dirks
    Ship Lists, 1698
Merie
  Jans
    Pearson, 1716
Mesier
  Jans
    Nicl Lvl, 1672
    NY Ref bp, 1661, 1686,
    1687, 1689, 1698
    Nycol Doc 2, 1673
    Rcrd Nam 6, 1673
Messcher
  Michels
    King Co, 1647
    Ship Lists, 1687
Metselaer
  Adams
    NY Ref bp, 1658, 1661,
    1674, 1691
    NYC Wills, 1695
  Giles
    Pearson, 1657
  Jans
    Pearson, 1718
  Solomons
    King Ref mr, 1683
    NY Ref bp, 1708
  Teunis
    Fern Wlls, 1685
    Pearson, 1685
    Rens Crsp 2, 1681
    Ship Lists, 1641
  Thomas
    NY Ref bp, 1644, 1645
Meulenmaecker
  Cornelis
    Ship Lists, 1636
Mevi
  Peters
    NY Ref bp, 1689
Mey
  Jacobs
    Nycol Doc 1, 1620
Meyer
  Arnouts
    NY Ref bp, 1702

Dirks
    Fltb Ref bp, 1682
    Nicl Lvl, 1672
    NY Ref bp, 1657, 1662,
    1663, 1671, 1672, 1678,
    1679, 1684, 1689
    NY Ref mr, 1677
    Nycol Doc 2, 1664
    Orphan Mst, 1665
    Rcrd Nam 5, 1664
  Giles
    NY Ref bp, 1704
    Pearson, 1676
  Jans
    Crt Assz, 1675
    Fern Wlls, 1693
    Gen Entr 2, 1685
    NY Ref bp, 1663, 1668,
    1678, 1689
    NY Ref mr, 1662
    NYC Court, 1697
    Nycol Doc 2, 1673
    Rcrd Nam 4, 1663
  Peters
    Pearson, 1660
Meyn
  Peters
    Nycol Doc 2, 1661
Michiels
  Simons
    Pearson, 1661
    Rens Crsp 1, 1663
Middagh
  Aerts
    Fltb Ref mr, 1691
    King Co, 1685
    King Ref bp, 1696
    Ship Lists, 1687
  Gerrits
    King Co, 1693
  Gilberts
    Rcrd Nam 3, 1658
  Jans
    King Co, 1681
  Teunis
    Bkln Ref bp, 1662
    Bkln Ref mm, 1664
    King Co, 1657

    NY Ref bp, 1660, 1661
    Ship Lists, 1661, no date
Miller
  Conrads
    NY Ref bp, 1710
Mingaal
  Cornelis
    Pearson, 1666
  Jans
    Alb Ref mm, 1683
    Pearson, 1656
    Rcrd Nam 4, 1662
  Teunis
    Pearson, 1685
  Thomas
    Alb Ref bp, 1701
    Alb Ref mm, 1683
    Alb Ref mr, 1685
    Rens Court, 1669, 1670
Minnelia
  Jans
    Fltb Ref mr, 1689
Minville
  James
    Brgr Frm, 1702
Mitelaer
  Cornelis
    King Co, 1671
Mitspatskille
  Engelberts
    NY Ref mr, 1680
Moer
  Martins
    Pearson, 1665
    Rens Court, 1669, 1670
Moesman
  Jans
    Nicl Lvl, 1667
    NY Ref bp, 1661, 1664
    Nycol Doc 2, 1662
    Rcrd Nam 2, 1658
    Rens Crsp 1, 1655, 1663,
    1664
Molegh
  Everts
    Hack Ref bp, 1713, 1714,
    1718
    Hack Ref mr, 1711

Molenaer
Adrians
LI Fam 2, 1660
NY Ref mr, 1681
Cornelis
King Pap, 1664
Everts
NY Ref bp, 1664
Rcrd Nam 6, 1667
Ship Lists, no date
Jans
Pearson, 1695
Peters
NY Ref bp, 1644
Monfort
Peters
Fltb Ref bp, 1678, 1679, 1683
King Co, 1648
LI Fam 1, 1646
Mooy
Jacobs
Nycol Doc 2, 1677
Moreau
Andries
Rcrd Nam 5, 1665
Rogers
Rcrd Nam 4, 1663
Mousman
Jans
Gen Entr 1, 1664
Moy
Jacobs
Rens Crsp 2, 1684
Mulder
Peters
Pearson, 1660
Stephens
Pearson, 1682
Ship Lists, 1660
Teunis
Pearson, 1703
Muller
Cornelis
Alb Ref bp, 1702
Pearson, 1702
Mathys
Alb Ref bp, 1703, 1704, 1706, 1709

Peters
King Pap, 1664
Philips
Pearson, 1663
Stephens
Alb Ref bp, 1683
Rens Court, 1670
Munnick
Willems
King Pap, 1663
Nycol Doc 2, 1663
Mynderts
Jans
Pearson, 1629
Reinerse
Pearson, 1706
Mythousen
Simons
LI Source, 1695

N

Naerden
Jans
Ship Lists, 1636
Nagel
Jans
King Co, 1683
Jurians
King Co, 1697
Neby
Peters
NY Ref mr, 1687
Neringh
Willems
LI Source, 1694
NY Ref bp, 1681, 1687, 1691
NY Ref mr, 1680
Nes
Jans
Rcrd Nam 1, 1654
Nienghs
Jans
Rcrd Nam 3, 1659
Nieuwhoff
Aerts
Rcrd Nam 3, 1658

Noll
Jans
NY Ref mr, 1692
Noorman
Andries
Evjen, 1644
Rcrd Nam 1, 1655
Rens Crsp 1, 1658
Ship Lists, 1637
Carls
Evjen, 1644
Pearson, 1673
Christians
Pearson, 16336, 1658
Rcrd Nam 1, 1655
Ship Lists, 1636, 1637
Hans
NY Ref bp, 1642
Holgers
Evjen, 1632
Jans
Evjen, 1641, 1644, 1673
Fern Wlls, 1673
NY Lth bp, 1710
NY Ref bp, 1646, 1647
NY Ref mr, 1662
Pearson, 1673
Rcrd Nam 2, 1658
Ship Lists, 1648
Lawrence
Evjen, 1631, 1639
Ship Lists, 1631, 1658
Odwaels
Nycol Doc 2, 1661
Pauls
King Pap, 1662
Peters
Evjen, 1639, 1660
King Pap, 1665
NY Ref bp, 1642, 1647
Teunis
Evjen, 1650
King Co, 1657
Noorthbrook
Jacobs
King Co, 1667

Surname/Patronymic Combinations

Noortryck
Willems
King Pap, 1671
Nostrand
Jans
Rens Court, 1668
Ship Lists, 1638
Gerrits
LI Source, 1712
Peters
King Ref bp, 1699
Norden
Peters
NY Ref bp, 1699
Norman
Jans
LI Source, 1695
Notelman
Conrads
Rens Crsp 1, 1658
Nucella
Peters
King Ref bp, 1696, 1700,
1701, 1703
Nuys
Augusts
NY Ref mr, 1673
Nykerk
Jans
Pearson, 1634
Nyssen
Teunis
Fltb Ref bp, 1678
Fltb Ref mr, 1682, 1685
Nyt Spangien
Andries
NY Ref mr, 1685

O

Obee
Hendricks
NY Ref bp, 1658, 1659
Orphan Mst, 1663, 1664
Rcrd Nam 3, 1658
Oly
Volkerts
Rcrd Nam 5, 1664

Onderdonk
Adrians
Fltb Ref bp, 1684
Fltb Ref mr, 1683
Andries
King Co, 1672
Onnosel
Jacobs
Rcrd Nam 3, 1661
Oortstraet
Jans
King Pap, 1687
Oost
Jans
Rcrd Nam 6, 1671
Oosterum
Willems
Pearson, 1631
Oothout
Aries
Pearson, 1756
OpBergen
Jans
NY Ref bp, 1688
OpHoboken
Dirks
NY Ref bp, 1687
Osterhout
Jans
King Pap, 1664
King Ref bp, 1683
Ship Lists, no date
Ostrander
Peters
Ship Lists, no date
Ostrom
Hendricks
Berg Ref bp, 1684
Berg Ref mr, 1672, 1678
Fltb Ref mr, 1683
Jans
Berg Ref bp, 1684
Berg Ref mr, 1666
King Co, 1660
LI Source, 1666
Willems
Ship Lists, 1631

Otten
Willems
Pearson, 1703
Otterspoor
Aerts
Anjou Prb, 1678
King Pap, 1662
Arents
Ship Lists, 1649
Jacobs
King Pap, 1663
Ouderkerk
Cornelis
Ship Lists, 1663
Jans
Pearson, 1681
Oudewater
Frans
NY Ref mr, 1686
Oudtlandt
Jans
Rcrd Nam 3, 1658
Outewaael
Claas
Rcrd Nam 1, 1653
Outhousen
Simons
LI Source, 1695
Outhout
Jans
Alb Ref bp, 1685
Gen Entr 1, 1664
Pearson, 1683
Rcrd Nam 2, 1656
Outwater
Frans
Berg Ref mr, 1706
Jacobs
Ship Lists, no date
OuyVriesland
Jacobs
NY Ref mr, 1666
Oylensplegel
Teunis
Pearson, 1645

Surname/Patronymic Combinations

P

Palmatier
Michels
King Co, 1680
Peters
Fltb Ref bp, 1680
King Co, 1654

Papendorp
Gerrits
Alb Ref bp, 1687
Alb Ref mm, 1683
Fern Wlls, 1689
Fltb Ref bp, 1682
Pearson, 1682

Paradys
Alderts
NY Ref bp, 1655
NY Ref mr, 1655

Pastoor
Barents
King Co, 1651
King Pap, 1668
Pearson, 1654
Rcrd Nam 4, 1663
Ship Lists, 1652

Pastoren
Barents
King Pap, 1667

Pataddes
Claas
Rcrd Nam 1, 1654

Patervaer
Jacobs
Rcrd Nam 1, 1654

Paulus
Jurians
Hack Ref mm, page xx
Peters
Hack Ref bp, 1720

Paus
Gerrits
Pearson, 1683

Pells
Everts
King Ref bp, 1687
King Ref mr, 1676
NY Ref bp, 1671, 1673
NY Ref mr, 1670

Pelt
Teunis
Nycol Doc 4, 1701

Petronellitie
Rombouts
NY Ref bp, 1673

Pier
Arents
King Ref mr, 1682, 1685
Jans
King Ref bp, 1683, 1696
NY Ref bp, 1701
Teunis
Hack Ref mr, 1708
King Ref bp, 1683, 1700

Planck
Alberts
Pearson, 1634
Rens Crsp 1, 1659
Ship Lists, 1634
Isaacs
NY Ref bp, 1639, 1640,
1641, 1642, 1643, 1644,
1646, 1648

Ploeg
Hendricks
King Ref mr, 1699

Plugiet
Cornelis
Gen Entr 1, 1669
King Co, 1626

Pluyvier
Jans
King Co, 1626
Rcrd Nam 3, 1659

Pointie
Cornelis
Rens Court, 1668, 1670,
1672
Dirks
Rcrd Nam 1, 1654
Ship Lists, 1638

Poest
Barents
Pearson, 1664
Rens Crsp 1, 1659, 1668

Polhemus
Theodurus
King Co, 1662
LI Source, 1685, 1702

Poppen
Jans
NY Ref mr, 1669

Poppinga
Lawrence
NY Ref bp, 1702
NY Ref mr, 1689, 1691,
1692
Thomas
NY Ref mr, 1695

Pos
Claas
Nycol Doc 2, 1656
Dirks
NY Ref bp, 1646, 1647
Nycol Doc 1, 1630
Pearson, 1630
Ship Lists, 1624

Post
Barents
King Pap, 1664
Cornelis
Ship Lists, no date
Everts
NYC Court, 1693
Jans
Alb Ref mm, 1683
Alb Ref mr, 1692
Pearson, 1683
Jurians
Pearson, 1667

Postma
Jans
King Pap, 1684

Pott
Jacobs
Rcrd Nam 3, 1660

Pottebacker
Claas
NYC Wills, 1679
Rcrd Nam 1, 1655
Roelofs
NY Ref mr, 1663

Potter
  Martins
    Pearson, 1659
Poy
  Jans
    Rcrd Nam 2, 1658
Prall
  Jans
    King Ref bp, 1674
    Ship Lists, no date
Prast
  Jans
    King Pap, 1671
Pratt
  Andries
    Rens Crsp 2, 1682
  Jans
    King Pap, 1671
Probasco
  Christophs
    King Co, 1685
  Jurians
    King Co, 1654
    LI Source, 1654
Provoost
  Andries
    NY Ref bp, 1671
  Jans
    Nycol Doc 3, 1690
Pruis
  Cornelis
    Berg Ref bp, 1686
Pruyn
  Frans
    Alb Ref mm, 1683
    Pearson, 1683
  Hendricks
    Hack Ref mr, 1710
  Jans
    Alb Ref bp, 1683
    Pearson, 1661
    Rens Court, 1671
    Ship Lists, no date
  Samuels
    Pearson, 1752
Prys
  Jeremiahs
    NY Ref bp, 1697

Pulman
  Hendricks
    King Co, 1664
Purmerendt
  Jans
    NY Ref bp, 1672
Pyer
  Jans
    King Ref bp, 1681

Q

Quackenbush
  Peters
    Alb Ref bp, 1685, 1688,
    1689, 1690
    Alb Ref mm, 1683
    Alb Ref mr, 1683
    Pearson, 1685
    Rens Court, 1669
Quick
  Jacobs
    NY Ref bp, 1682, 1687
    NY Ref mr, 1682, 1683,
    1685
  Teunis
    King NYGB, 1672
    King Pap, 1665
    King Ref bp, 1679, 1683,
    1688
    NY Ref bp, 1659, 1680
    Pearson, 1661
    Rcrd Nam 6, 1667
  Thomas
    Nycol Doc 3, 1664
    Rcrd Nam 1, 1654
Quisthout
  Jans
    Alb Ref mr, 1684

R

Rademacker
  Adrians
    Pearson, 1653
    Ship Lists, 1644
  Claas
    NY Ref bp, 1655

Jans
  King Pap, 1670
Raeff
  Jans
    Nycol Doc 2, 1656
Ralemon
  Jans
    Berg Ref mr, 1696
Ralewyn
  Jans
    Berg Ref dt, 1694, 1696
Rapalye
  Huygens
    Nycol Doc 1, 1652
  Jans
    King Co, 1623
    NY Ref bp, 1653, 1658
    Rcrd Nam 3, 16659
    Ship Lists, 1623
  Jeromes
    Bkln Ref bp, 1678
    Bkln Ref mr, 1695
    King Co, 1690
  Joris
    Fltb Ref bp, 1678, 1679,
    1680, 1681, 1682
    King Co, 1650
    NY Ref bp, 1655
  Teunis
    King Co, 1699
Ravenstine
  Gerrits
    NY Ref bp, 1698, 1703
Rees
  Andries
    King Pap, 1663
    Pearson, 1672
Reinerse
  Lennerts
    Fltb Ref mr, 1691
Remsen
  Joris
    King Co, 1685
Reur
  Jans
    Pearson, 1658
    Rens Crsp 1, 1659, 1662
    Ship Lists, 1651

Reuth
Frans
  NY Ref bp, 1707
Ribbide
Jans
  Pearson, 1664
Richard
Daniels
  Fltb Ref mr, 1689
Piere
  King Ref bp, 1693
Richards
Pauls
  NYC Court, 1686
Rickhout
Daniels
  King Co, 1694
Riddenhaas
Abels
  Alb Ref bp, 1684
  Alb Ref mr, 1692
  Pearson, 1680
  Ship Lists, no date
Hendricks
  Ship Lists, 1646
Ridder
Joost
  Ship Lists, 1687
Riddershalve
Abels
  Pearson, 1680
Rinckhout
Daniels
  Fltb Ref mr, 1694
Jurians
  Pearson, 1704
Ringo
Jans
  Brgr Frm, 1657
  Fern Wlls, 1646
  NY Ref bp, 1648
  Rcrd Nam 4, 1662
Philips
  Rcrd Nam 7, 1674
Rips
Claas
  Alb Ref mm, 1683
  Nycol Doc 3, 1690
  Pearson, 1683

Robert
Teunis
  Berg Ref mr, 1686
Rochel
Jans
  Ship Lists, 1634
Rochen
Hendricks
  Nycol Doc 2, 1661
Roebel
Jans
  Brgr Frm, 1657
Roelofsen
Jochems
  NY Lth bp, 1708
Peters
  NY Ref bp, 1653
Sybrants
  King Pap, 1663
Roll
Jans
  NY Ref bp, 1697, 1700,
  1702, 1706, 1709, 1710
Rome
Jans
  NY Ref bp, 1690, 1702
Willems
  Brgr Frm, 1698
  NY Ref bp, 1687, 1689,
  1692, 1702, 1703, 1707
  NY Ref mr, 1684
Romer
Jans
  NY Ref bp, 1665
Willems
  NY Ref bp, 1699
  Nycol Doc 4, 1698
Romeyn
Claas
  Hack Ref bp, 1702, 1703,
  1708, 1710, 1714, 1716,
  1718, 1720
  Hack Ref mm, 1702, page xx
  Hack Ref mr, 1699, 1703
  King Co, 1686
Jans
  Bkln Ref bp, 1686
  Crt Assz, 1680
  Fltb Ref bp, 1678, 1680,

  1681, 1682, 1683, 1684
  Fltb Ref mr, 1678
  Gen Entr 2, 1676
  Hack Ref bp, 1695, 1700
  King Co, 1653
  King Pap, 1662
  Nicl Lvl, 1672
  NY Ref bp, 1676
  NY Ref mr, 1671, 1676
  NYC Wills, 1702
  Nycol Doc 2, 1664
  Pearson, 1658
  Rcrd Nam 3, 1659
  Rens Court, 1672
  Ship Lists, 1687
Willems
  NY Ref bp, 1694, 1695,
  1697, 1699, 1700, 1701,
  1702, 1704, 1708, 1709
  NY Ref mr, 1684
Witt
  NY Ref bp, 1696
Romme
Jans
  NY Ref mr, 1705
Romp
Bartholomeus
  King Pap, 1666
Claas
  Evjen, 1657
  King Pap, 1661
  Ship Lists, 1657
Jans
  Nicl Lvl, 1667
Roome
Willems
  NYC Court, 1702
  NYC Wills, 1706
Roos
Gerrits
  Pearson, 1695
Jacobs
  Hack Ref mr, 1718
Jans
  NYC Wills, 1697, 1698
  Pearson, 1695
Roosa
Alberts
  King Pap, 1665

King Ref bp, 1679, 1682
NY Ref bp, 1678
Alderts
King Ref bp, 1679, 1692
Heymans
Gen Entr 1, 1669
King Pap, 1661, 1664
King Ref bp, 1664, 1679,
1705
Nicl Lvl, 1667
Ship Lists, no date
Jans
Brgr Frm, 1657, 1698
King Ref bp, 1699
King Ref mr, 1701
NY Ref bp, 1656, 1660, 1661,
1662, 1663, 1664, 1665,
1667, 1673, 1679, 1681,
1686, 1689
Nycol Doc 2, 1673
Rcrd Nam 1, 1654
Peters
NY Ref bp, 1642
Roosevelt
Claas
King Ref bp, 1682
Martins
Ship Lists, 1649, no date
Root
Cornelis
Pearson, 1670
Rcrd Nam 4, 1662
Rens Court, 1670, 1671,
1672
Hendricks
Pearson, 1662
Peters
Pearson, 1661
Rens Court, 1669
Rosebloom
Olivers
King Pap, 1661
Roseboom
Ahasueruse
Pearson, 1749
Hendricks
Pearson, 1704

Jans
Pearson, 1662
Rens Court, 1672
Ship Lists, 1657, no date
Mynderts
Pearson, 1728
Rosekrans
Dirks
Ship Lists, 1687
Hendricks
Evjen, 1657
NY Ref bp, 1659
Rouse
Hendricks
NY Ref bp, 1641
Roy
Jacobs
Fern Wlls, 1643
Jans
Rcrd Nam 2, 1658
Ruyn
Jans
Rcrd Nam 7, 1658
Ruysh
Bartels
Ship Lists, 1660
Ruyter
Claas
NY Ref mr, 1679
Rcrd Nam 3, 1661
Jans
Brgr Frm, 1657
King Co, 1639
LI Source, 1642, 1660
NY Ref bp, 1644, 1662
Nycol Doc 1, 1644
Pearson, 1638
Rcrd Nam 1, 1653
Ship Lists, 1638
Wooderts
NY Ref bp, 1678
Ruyting
Jans
Alb Ref bp, 1690
Pearson, 1690
Rycke
Abrams
NY Ref mr, 1681

Cornelis
NY Ref bp, 1674
Ryckman
Jans
Pearson, 1671
Rens Court, 1672
Rykskocht
Jans
NY Ref bp, 1704
Rynerman
Caspars
NYC Wills, 1683

S

Salsbergen
Hendricks
Rens Court, 1672
Jans
Pearson, 1706
Salsburg
Jans
Atns Lth bp, 1710
NY Lth bp, 1710
Sam
Jans
Rcrd Nam 3, 1660
Santvoort
Abrams
NY Ref bp, 1672
NY Ref mr, 1677
Rcrd Nam 7, 1674
Ship Lists, 1661
Sardam
Peters
Alb Ref bp, 1705
Sardingh
Jacobs
Ship Lists, 1663
Sassian
Lamberts
Pearson, no date
Schaats
Wollewevers
Alb Ref mm, 1683
Schaes
Christophs
LI Source, 1678

Schaets
  Davids
    Ship Lists, 1660
Schagen
  Jans
    Nycol Doc 1, 1626
  Willems
    Nycol Doc 2, 1657
Schars
  Christophs
    Fltb Ref bp, 1678, 1681,
    1683
    King Co, 1675
    LI Source, 1695
  Jans
    Bkln Ref bp, 1690
    Fltb Ref mr, 1686
    King Co, 1687
    LI Source, 1695
Schay
  Teunis
    NY Ref bp, 1647
Scheel
  Jans
    Pearson, 1658
Schellinger
  Tiepkesz
    Rens Crsp 1, 1657, 1658,
    1659
Schenck
  Jans
    King Co, 1675
  Martins
    Bkln Ref bp, 1682
    Fltb Ref bp, 1678, 1679,
    1680, 1682, 1683, 1684,
    1685, 1688
    Fltb Ref mr, 1690
    King Co, 1689
    LI Fam 1, no date
    LI Source, 1687, 1693,
    1694, 1696
    NYC Wills, 1688
    Ship Lists, 1650, 1687, no
    date
  Roelofs
    Fltb Ref bp, 1681, 1682,
    1683, 1684, 1685

Fltb Ref mr, 1683, 1684,
1687
    King Co, 1661
    Ship Lists, 1687
  Rudolphs
    Fltb Ref bp, 1682
Schepmoes
  Jans
    Anjou Prb, 1682
    King Pap, 1667
    King Ref bp, 1678, 1680,
    1690, 1695, 1701, 1702
    King Ref mr, 1703
    NY Ref bp, 1643, 1645,
    1647, 1648, 1654
    NY Ref mr, 1656
    NYC Wills, 1691
    Rcrd Nam 1, 1648
  Peters
    King Pap, 1661
Schermerhorn
  Cornelis
    Pearson, 1742
  Jacobs
    Alb Ref bp, 1684, 1685
    Fern Wlls, 1678
    Pearson, 1678
  Jans
    Fern Wlls, 1688
    Pearson, 1636
    Ship Lists, 1636, 1645,
    1650, no date
Scherp
  Andries
    Pearson, 1695, 1699
  Hans
    Pearson, 1674
Scheuwen
  Alberts
    NY Ref bp, 1658
Schilder
  Dirks
    Rcrd Nam 3, 1661
Schipper
  Jacobs
    NY Ref bp, 1680
    NY Ref mr, 1678

Jans
  Pearson, 1660
Peters
  King Pap, 1663
Schluter
  Claas
    Ship Lists, 1679
Schnett
  Jacobs
    NY Lth bp, 1710
Schoders
  Dirks
    Nycol Doc 1, 1621
Scholl
  Jans
    LI Source, 1667
    NY Ref bp, 1662, 1664,
    1666, 1671
    Ship Lists, 1659
  Peters
    Fltb Ref mr, 1680
    NY Ref mr, 1680
Scholt
  Jans
    NY Ref mr, 1661
Schooff
  Jacobs
    NY Ref mr, 1658
School
  Jans
    King Co, 1668
Schoon
  Willems
    King Pap, 1664
    Pearson, 1661
Schoonhoven
  Claas
    King Ref bp, 1696
  Gerrits
    Alb Ref bp, 1701
  Hendricks
    Fern Wlls, 1692
    Pearson, 1654
Schoonmaker
  Barents
    Pearson, 1636
    Ship Lists, 1636

Everts
  Pearson, 1661
Hendricks
  King Ref bp, 1698, 1699,
  1700, 1702
  King Ref mr, 1689
Jans
  NY Ref bp, 1644
Jochems
  Ship Lists, 1654, no date
Schotzina
  Walters
    NY Ref mr, 1663
Schout
  Jacobs
    Pearson, 1697
Schouten
  Cornelis
    Nycol Doc 1, 1651
  Lucas
    Ship Lists, 1657
Schryver
  Willems
    King Ref bp, 1682
Schumacher
  Arents
    Pearson, 1679
  Hendricks
    King Ref mr, 1688
Schuts
  Michels
    NY Lth bp, 1706, 1708,
    1709, 1710
    NY Ref mr, 1703
Schutt
  Hermans
    NY Ref bp, 1651
    Ship Lists, 1649
  Jans
    Anjou Prb, 1706
    King Pap, 1663, 1672
    King Ref bp, 1664, 1682,
    1683, 1684
    Pearson, 1657
    Rens Court, 1670
    Rens Crsp 1, 1659, 1668

Willems
  King Ref bp, 1696
  Ship Lists, 1646
Schuyler
  Abrams
    Pearson, 1709
  Davids
    Alb Ref mm, 1683
    Pearson, 1683
  Peters
    Crt Assz, 1674
    Gen Entr 1, 1667
    King Ref bp, 1663
    Nicl Lvl, 1665
    NY Ref bp, 1674
    NY Ref mr, 1657
    Nycol Doc 3, 1664
    Pearson, 1660
    Rcrd Nam 4, 1663
    Rens Court, 1669, 1670,
    1671
    Rens Crsp 1, 1657, 1659,
    1660, 1661, 1664, 1668,
    1672
    Rens Crsp 2, 1681, 1683,
    1687
    Ship Lists, 1650, no date
Schyf
  Cornelis
    NY Ref mr, 1707
Schyven
  Willems
    King Ref bp, 1682
Scuth
  Willems
    Pearson, 1646
    Ship Lists, 1646
Seba
  Jans
    Anjou Prb, 1663
    King Pap, 1665
Sebring
  Cornelis
    King Co, 1693
  Jans
    Bkln Ref bp1682, 1663

Roelofs
  Berg Ref mm, 1682
  Bkln Ref bp, 1687
  Crt Assz, 1672
  Fltb Ref bp, 1682
  King Co, 1631
  Nicl Lvl, 1671
  Rcrd Nam 6, 1671
  Ship Lists, no date
Seen
  Cornelis
    King Co, no date
  Jans
    King Co, 1663
Seeuw
  Cornelis
    Nycol Doc 2, 1673
  Jans
    Bkln Ref bp, 1679, 1691
    Fltb Ref bp, 1679
    Ship Lists, 1687
Selenave
  Peters
    Brgr Frm, 1702
Servis
  Dirks
    NY Ref mr, 1661
    Rcrd Nam 3, 1661
Sharp
  Andries
    Alb Ref bp, 1695, 1700,
    1701, 1702
    Alb Ref mr, 1697
  Gerrits
    Rcrd Nam 4, 1663
  Peters
    Nycol Doc 1, 1650
Sibinck
  Hendricks
    Pearson, 1655
Skerendregt
  Arents
    NY Ref bp, 1707
    NY Ref mr, 1706
Slackboom
  Teunis
    NYC Wills, 1677

Surname/Patronymic Combinations

Slecht
  Barents
    Anjou Prb, 1684
    King Co, 1661
    King Pap, 1661, 1664
    King Ref bp, 1671, 1674
    King Ref mr, 1684
    Nicl Lvl, 1667
    Rcrd Nam 4, 1662
    Rens Crsp 1, 1667
  Cornelis
    Anjou Prb, 1677
    King Co, 1652
    King Pap, 1663, 1664
    King Ref bp, 1679, 1680, 1681
    King Ref mr, 1666
    LI Source, 1652
    Ship Lists, 1661
  Hendricks
    Fltb Ref mr, 1692
    King Co, 1687
Slicoten
  Jacobs
    King Pap, 1667
  Jans
    King Pap, 1666
Slingerland
  Alberts
    Pearson, 1725
  Arents
    Pearson, 1713
  Cornelis
    Pearson, 1658
    Rcrd Nam 4, 1662
    Ship Lists, no date
  Teunis
    Pearson, 1705
Slot
  Jans
    Berg Ref bp, 1666, 1669
    King Ref bp, 1681
    NY Ref bp, 1660, 1687
    NY Ref mr, 1672
    Nycol Doc 2, 1673
    Rcrd Nam 6, 1669
    Rcrd Nam 7, 1674

Peters
  Berg Ref bp, 1690
  King Co, 1662
  NY Ref bp, 1688, 1694
  Rcrd Nam 1665, 1681
  Ship Lists, 1650
Sloth
  Peters
    Hack Ref bp, 1699
Sluys
  Jans
    Rcrd Nam 4, 1662
  Lawrence
    NY Ref mr, 1686
  Zacharias
    NYC Wills, 1686
    Nycol Doc 2, 1674
    Rcrd Nam 6, 1671
Sluyswachter
  Mauritz
    NY Ref bp, 1672, 1673, 1678
Sluyter
  Claas
    King Ref bp, 1682, 1684, 1687, 1692, 1698, 1703
    King Ref mr, 1679
  Jans
    NY Ref bp, 1657
    Rcrd Nam 1, 1655
Slyck
  Cornelis
    Pearson, 1659
  Peters
    Pearson, 1685
    Rens Court, 1669, 1671, 1672
  Teunis
    Rens Court, 1671, 1672
Slyckotem
  Jans
    Pearson, 1661
Smack
  Hendricks
    Fltb Ref bp, 1687
    Fltb Ref mr, 1685
    King Co, 1693

Mathys
  Fltb Ref bp, 1681, 1685
  King Co, 1654
  LI Source, 1687, no date
  Nycol Doc 2, 1674
  Ship Lists, 1687
Smith
  Adrians
    Tap Ref bp, 1703, 1706, 1709
  Barents
    Crt Assz, 1668
    King Co, 1663
    LI Source, 1687, 1690
    NY Ref mr, 1663
    Nycol Doc 2, 1673
    Orphan Mst, 1664
    Rcrd Nam 3, 1660
  Claas
    King Co, 1653
    NY Ref mr, 1653
  Cleyn
    NY Ref bp, 1657
  Cornelis
    King Co, 1639
    Nicl Lvl, 1667
    NY Ref bp, 1671
  Douws
    Ship Lists, 1655
  Fredericks
    Fern Wlls, 1689
  Gerrits
    Rcrd Nam 1, 1653
  Jans
    Gen Entr 1, 1665
    LI Source, 1694
    NY Ref bp, 1642, 1662, 1667
    Pearson, 1660
    Rcrd Nam 2, 1658
  Joris
    NY Ref bp, 1639
  Lamberts
    Hack Ref bp, 1716, 1719, 1720
    Tap Ref bp, 1706, 1710

50

Martins
  Pearson, 1683
Mynderts
  Pearson, 1703
Peters
  NY Ref bp, 1656
  Rcrd Nam 3, 1661
Reinerse
  Pearson, 1645
Wessels
  Nycol Doc 2, 1674
Smithing
  Aerts
    King Pap, 1662
  Snedeker
  Gerrits
    King Co, 1687
  Jans
    Fltb Ref bp, 1685
    King Co, 1660
Sneeding
  Jans
    NY Ref bp, 1668
Snyder
  Hendricks
    NY Ref mr, 1653
  Jans
    NY Ref bp, 1644, 1647,
    1680
Soestberger
  Cornelis
    Pearson, 1660
    Rcrd Nam 4, 1662
Solomons
  Jans
    Alb Ref mm, 1683
Somerindink
  Jacobs
    NY Ref bp, 1709
Soogemakelyck
  Adrians
    Pearson, 1638
    Rens Crsp 1, 1664, 1668
    Ship Lists, 1655
Sperling
  Michels
    Hack Ref mr, 1709

Spiegel
  Dirks
    Nycol Doc 2, 1662
Spier
  Hans
    Hack Ref mr, 1708
  Hendricks
    Berg Ref bp, 1687, 1692
    Berg Ref mr, 1698
    NY Ref bp, 1703
    NY Ref mr, 1683
  Jans
    Berg Ref bp, 1686, 1688
    Berg Ref mr, 1684
    Hack Ref mr, 1704, 1705,
    1709, 1710
    Nycol Doc 2, 1674
    Ship Lists, 1660
Spiering
  Jans
    NY Ref bp, 1663, 1667
  Jeremiahs
    Brgr Frm, 1659
    Rcrd Nam 3, 1659
Spiers
  Jans
    Rcrd Nam 3, 1659
Spits
  Reyners
    Nycol Doc 2, 1664
Spitsenberg
  Cornelis
    Nycol Doc 3, 1666
    Pearson, 1663
    Rens Court, 1672
    Rens Crsp 1, 1666, 1671
    Ship Lists, 1654
Splinter
  Hendricks
    Nycol Doc 2, 1673
Spoor
  Gerrits
    Pearson, 1719
  Wybrechts
    Pearson, 1685
Springsteen
  Caspars
    Brgr Frm, 1696

    King Co, 1652
    LI Source, 1652
    Rcrd Nam 2, 1658
    Ship Lists, no date
Sprong
  Jacobs
    NY Ref mr, 1670
  Jans
    King Co, 1694
Staats
  Jans
    Bkln Ref bp, 1691, 1696
    Bkln Ref mr, 1695
    King Co, 1682
    LI Source, 1689, 1693,
    1694
    NY Ref bp, 1706
    Nycol Doc 2, 1661
    Rcrd Nam 3, 1659
    Rens Crsp 1, 1657, 1661
    Ship Lists, 1687
  Peters
    Bkln Ref bp, 1697
    King Co, 1689
    LI Source, 1694
  Willems
    LI Source, 1700
Staeck
  Peters
    Evjen, 1660
Stam
  Corsen
    Ship Lists, 1641
Stanson
  Cornelis
    King Co, 1676
Stavast
  Gerrits
    Gen Entr 2, 1677
  Jans
    Crt Assz, 1668
    Gen Entr 1, 1668
    Nicl Lvl, 1673
    NY Ref bp, 1687
    Pearson, 1672, 1673
    Rcrd Nam 6, 1666
    Rens Court, 1670, 1671,
    1672

Steelman
Hendricks
King Co, 1651
Orphan Mst, 1664
Rcrd Nam 1, 1653
Rens Crsp 1, 1661
Steenhalder
Jans
Berg Ref bp, 1667
Rcrd Nam 3, 1659
Steenwyck
Jacobs
Rcrd Nam 1, 1653
Jans
King Ref bp, 1681, 1683
Sterrenvelt
Huberts
NY Ref bp, 1662
Orphan Mst, 1665
Rcrd Nam 3, 1661
Ship Lists, 1660
Stevens
Hans
Fltb Ref bp, 1685
Stille
Cornelis
NY Ref bp, 1680, 1689,
1690, 1692, 1700, 1704,
1706
NY Ref mr, 1671
Rcrd Nam 6, 1671
Jacobs
King Co, 1639
NY Ref bp, 1646, 1660,
1672
NY Ref mr, 1659
Nycol Doc 1, 1644
Rcrd Nam 1, 1653
Stock
Jans
King Co, 1657
Stoerck
Jans
Rcrd Nam 2, 1656
Stoff
Jurians
Fltb Ref bp, 1681

Stoll
Jacobs
King Pap, 1670
King Ref bp, 1685, 1689,
1695
King Ref mr, 1684
Jans
King Pap, 1661, 1665
King Ref mr, 1661, 1664
Nycol Doc 3, 1664
Pearson, 1630
Rcrd Nam 3, 1660
Rens Crsp 1, 1659, 1660
Rens Crsp 2, 1685
Ship Lists, 1630, 1645,
1650
Stoltin
Warners
Ship Lists, 1659
Stoothoff
Alberts
Bkln Ref bp, 1677
Fltb Ref bp, 1678, 1679,
1680, 1681, 1682, 1683,
1684, 1686
King Co, 1620
LI Fam 1, 1686
LI Source, 1695
Rens Crsp 2, 1683
Ship Lists, 1632, 1687
Gerrits
King Co, 1698
Stoutenburgh
Jans
King Pap, 1663, 1665
Pearson, 1646
Ship Lists, no date
Straatenmacker
Dirks
Berg Ref dt, 1686
Berg Ref mm, 1665
Berg Ref mr, 1666
NY Ref bp, 1674, 1680,
1683, 1684
Jans
NY Ref bp, 1705

Striddles
Thompsons
Rens Crsp 2, 1681
Stridler
Thomas
Alb Ref bp, 1686
Struddles
Thompsons
NYC Wills, 1702
Strycker
Gerrits
Brgr Frm, 1657
King Co, 1651
Rcrd Nam 1, 1653
Ship Lists, no date
Jacobs
Bkln Ref bp, 1687
King Co, 1673
Jans
King Co, 1677
Ship Lists, 1687
Peters
Fltb Ref bp, 1684
King Co, 1688
Stuyvesant
Lazarus
NY Ref bp, 1672
Willems
Gen Entr 1, 1665
King Pap, 1673
King Ref mr, 1681
NY Ref bp, 1678, 1679,
1683, 1685, 1687, 1691
NY Ref mr, 1672, 1681
Rcrd Nam 7, 1674
Stymets
Christophs
Hack Ref mr, 1720
Sutphin
Dirks
King Co, 1693
Jacobs
Fltb Ref bp, 1684
Jans
Fltb Ref bp, 1681
King Co, 1651
Ship Lists, no date

Suydam
Fredericks
King Co, 1663
LI Fam 2, 1663
Ship Lists, 1663, no date
Hendricks
King Co, 1684
LI Source, 1698
Jacobs
King Co, 1696
Peters
Pearson, 1705
Suyder
Jans
NY Ref bp, 1643
Swaeg
Claas
Nycol Doc 2, 1657
Swanevelt
Jacobs
Ship Lists, 1652
Swart
Cornelis
Gen Entr 2, 1676
Pearson, 1661
Ship Lists, 1641
Jans
NY Ref bp, 1647
Peters
NY Ref bp, 1654
Rcrd Nam 5, 1665

Teunis
Alb Ref bp, 1691
Pearson, 1680, 1690
Swede
Cornelis
Orphan Mst, 1666
Swits
Claas
NY Ref mr, 1656
Rcrd Nam 1, 1653
Cornelis
Nycol Doc 1, 1644
Pearson, 1663
Ship Lists, 1642

Switzer
Claas
NY Ref bp, 1642, 1643,
1647, 1653
Sybinck
Hendricks
Rcrd Nam 5, 1664

T

Tack
Aerts
King Ref bp, 1682, 1683
Arents
King Ref bp, 1688
Peters
King Pap, 1662, 1664
King Ref bp, 1663
King Ref mr, 1665
Pearson, 1661
Ship Lists, 1652, no date
Tallman
Douws
Berg Ref mm, 1685
NY Ref mr, 1686
Tap Ref bp, 1709
Hermans
Berg Ref dt, 1674, 1687
Tap Ref bp, 1706, 1710
Tappan
Jan Teunis
Ship Lists, 1652
Jans
Ship Lists, 1652
Teunis
Pearson, 1671
Rens Court, 1671
Rens Crsp 1, 1661
Rens Crsp 2, 1683
Ship Lists, 1652, 1662
Tempel
Peters
Rcrd Nam 1, 1654
Rens Crsp 1, 1655
Temper
Peters
Pearson, 1657
Rens Crsp 1, 1655, 1659

TenBroeck
Dirks
NY Ref bp, 1684
Pearson, no date
Hendricks
NY Ref bp, 1689
Wessels
Alb Ref bp, 1700, 1704
Alb Ref mm, 1683
King Pap, 1673
King Ref bp, 1678, 1682
Nicl Lvl, 1672
NY Ref bp, 1671, 1674,
1678, 1679, 1680, 1682,
1684, 1686, 1688, 1690
Pearson, 1663
Rens Crsp 2, 1678
Ship Lists, no date
TenEyck
Conrads
Pearson, 1732
Hendricks
Pearson, 1733
Teunis
NY Ref mr, 1689
Terbush
Jans
Rens Court, 1669
TerHaert
Aerts
Fltb Ref mr, 1691
Terhune
Alberts
Berg Ref bp, 1690
Fltb Ref bp, 1681, 1683,
1685, 1686
Fltb Ref mr, 1691
Gen Entr 2, 1681
Hack Ref bp, 1706
Hack Ref mm, 1689
Hack Ref mr, 1699
King Co, 1662
LI Fam 2, 1654
LI Source, 1651, 1687,
1694, 1696, 1697
Rcrd Nam 5, 1664
Ship Lists, 1687, no date

Surname/Patronymic Combinations

Terhune (cont.)
Jans
  King Co, 1684
Tery
Hendricks
  Rens Court, 1670
Tiebout
Jans
  Ship Lists, no date
Tienpoint
Joris
  Nycol Doc 1, 1644
Tietsoort
Abrams
  Pearson, 1686
Timmer
Cornelis
  NY Ref bp, 1680
  NY Ref mr, 1678
Ysbrants
  Pearson, 1662
Timmerman
Adrians
  NY Ref bp, 1662
Andries
  NY Ref mr, 1660
Barents
  Pearson, 1660
Claas
  Pearson, 1658
Cornelis
  Pearson, 1660
  Ship Lists, 1639
Gerrits
  Ship Lists, 1644
Jans
  King Pap, 1674
  Pearson, 1654
  Ship Lists, 1649
Peters
  Pearson, 1660
Toers
Arents
  Berg Ref bp, 1674, 1679,
  1682, 1685, 1687, 1688,
  1689, 1692, 1694, 1696,
  1699, 1703, 1707, 1710
  Berg Ref dt, 1673, 1682,
  1686, 1694, 1702, 1707

Berg Ref mm, 1667, 1677,
  1682
  Berg Ref mr, 1672, 1684
Lawrence
  Berg Ref dt, 1674, 1682
  Berg Ref mm, 1672
  Hack Ref mr, 1703, 1704,
  1710
Toffle
Gerrits
  Gen Entr 2, 1675
Tolier
Jacobs
  Bogamr, 1677
  King Co, 1677
Tolk
Claas
  Pearson, 1702
Toll
Hans
  Pearson, 1720
  Schn Ref bp, 1707, 1708
TonsonVanRitfort
Joris
  Brgr Frm, 1659
Toonson
Joris
  Ship Lists, 1658
Torenburg
Gerrits
  Ship Lists, 1681
Torner
Arents
  Nicl Lvl, 1672
Tours
Arents
  Fltb Ref mr, 1684
  NY Ref bp, 1694
Claas
  Berg Ref bp, 1694
Traphagen
Jans
  King Co, 1658
  NY Ref mr, 1658
  Ship Lists, no date
Trimbel
Jans
  King Co, 1662

Trommels
Cornelis
  NY Ref mr, 1656
Trynenburgh
Jans
  Evjen, 1660
  Rcrd Nam 3, 1660
Tubbing
Jans
  NY Ref bp, 1650
Tull
Peters
  King Co, 1657
  Ship Lists, 1687
Turck
Claas
  Crt Assz, 1668
  Pearson, 1664
  Rcrd Nam 3, 1659
Jacobs
  Ship Lists, 1661
Jans
  Pearson, 1659
Turkyen
Jans
  Pearson, 1681
Tuynier
Jans
  NY Ref bp, 1666, 1684
Tymesen
Cornelis
  Pearson, 1709
Tysen
Roelofs
  Fltb Ref bp, 1682
Tysvelt
Arents
  Gen Entr 1, 1669

U

Utenes
Barents
  Fltb Ref bp, 1680
Uylenspiegel
Teunis
  Ship Lists, 1642

Surname/Patronymic Combinations

UytBohemen
Hermans
NY Ref mr, 1651
UytBrabant
Arents
NY Ref mr, 1669
UytDeBeemster
Lubberts
NY Ref mr, 1655
UytDeKuyndert
Claas
NY Ref mr, 1667, 1671
UytDenemarken
Cornelis
NY Ref mr, 1676
Jans
NY Ref mr, 1677
UytDenHage
Fredericks
NY Ref mr, 1660
Jans
NY Ref mr, 1660
UytDeWalebocht
Martins
NY Ref mr, 1696
UytenBogart
Gilberts
NY Lth bp, 1704
UytHessen
Jans
NY Ref mr, 1650
UytHolstein
Andries
NY Ref mr, 1658
Jans
NY Ref mr, 1653
Peters
NY Ref mr, 1652
Uythuysen
Simons
King Co, 1695
LI Source, 1695
UytOldenburger
Willems
NY Ref mr, 1660
UytOostVrieslant
Wessels
NY Ref mr, 1658

UytSaxenlant
Claas
NY Ref mr, 1662
UytVrieslandt
Hendricks
NY Ref mr, 1698

V

Valentine
Jans
Berg Ref bp, 1701
VanAbcoude
Cornelis
Pearson, 1660
VanAchterkol
Adrians
NY Ref mr, 1695
VanAecken
Coster
Rens Court, 1669
VanAelokman
Jans
King Co, 1668
VanAelst
Gaius
Brgr Frm, 1657
Joost
NY Ref mr, 1647
Joris
NY Ref mr, 1678, 1685
VanAeltemaer
Jans
King Co, 1668
VanAken
Coster
Pearson, 1659
Martins
NY Ref mr, 1658
VanAkes
Coster
Gen Entr 1, 1664
VanAlcmaer
Hendricks
NY Ref mr, 1662
Hermans
NY Ref mr, 1664

Peters
NY Ref bp, 1641, 1643
NY Ref mr, 1643
Pearson, 1653
VanAllen
Gerrits
Hack Ref bp, 1712, 1716, 1721
Lawrence
Alb Ref bp, 1707, 1709
Pearson, 1706
Peters
Alb Ref bp, 1707
Pearson, 1689
VanAlstede
Jans
Alb Ref bp, 1705
VanAlstine
Frans
Pearson, 1700
Jans
Alb Ref mr, 1689, 1694, 1698
Pearson, 1700
Martins
Alb Ref bp, 1703
Pearson, 1703
Ship Lists, no date
VanAmach
Jans
Ship Lists, 1687
VanAmersfort
Brants
Pearson, no date
Dirks
Pearson, 1638
Ship Lists, 1638
Gerrits
LI Fam 2, 1630
Hendricks
NY Ref mr, 1668
Hermans
Pearson, 1662
Ship Lists, 1687
Jans
King Pap, 1662, 1664
King Ref bp, 1663, 1665
NY Ref mr, 1681

Surname/Patronymic Combinations

VanAmersfort (cont.)
Rogers
NY Ref mr, 1666
Wolferts
NY Ref mr, 1640
VanAmeshof
Barents
King Pap, 1662
VanAmsterd
Dirks
NY Ref bp, 1648
Willems
NY Ref bp, 1648
NY Ref mr, 1685
VanAmsterdam
Claas
Pearson, 1636
Ship Lists, 1636
Cornelis
NY Ref mr, 1655
Gerrits
NY Ref mr, 1653
Jacobs
NY Ref mr, 1655
Jans
Pearson, 1642
Ship Lists, 1636
Mathys
Brgr Frm, 1657
Pearson, 1654
Michels
NY Ref mr, 1657
Peters
Brgr Frm, 1657
King Co, 1647
Rembrants
NY Ref mr, 1655
Willems
NY Ref mr, 1660
VanAngola
Simons
NY Ref bp, 1642
Swagers
NY Ref bp, 1642, 1644
Teunis
NY Ref bp, 1641, 1643, 1645

VanAntwerp
Jans
Alb Ref bp, 1692
Pearson, 1660
Ship Lists, no date
VanArbon
Peters
NY Ref mr, 1663
VanArnhem
Coert
NY Ref mr, 1660
Davids
NY Ref mr, 1656
Dirks
NY Ref bp, 1671
NY Ref mr, 1664
Jans
Alb Ref bp, 1700, 1702, 1704, 1706, 1708
Alb Ref mm, 1699
Alb Ref mr, 1696
NY Ref bp, 1701
Pearson, 1699
Rcrd Nam 4, 1662
Wessels
NY Ref mr, 1655, 1667, 1668
VanArsdalen
Jans
Fltb Ref bp, 1678, 1681, 1683
King Co, 1656
LI Source, 1688
Ship Lists, 1653, 1687
Simons
Fltb Ref bp, 1680, 1681, 1683, 1684
Fltb Ref mr, 1678, 1687
King Co, 1687
Ship Lists, 1687
VanAs
Dirks
King Co, 1661
VanAschwoert
Jans
NY Ref mr, 1652

VanAurick
Jans
Brgr Frm, 1658
NY Ref mr, 1658
Rcrd Nam 3, 1660
VanBaasle
Willems
Pearson, 1642
Ship Lists, 1642
VanBaden
Vos
Ship Lists, 1642
VanBael
Hendricks
Gen Entr 1, 1670
Nicl Lvl, 1670
NY Ref mr, 1683
Nycol Doc 2, 1677
Pearson, 1659
Rcrd Nam 4, 1663
Rens Court, 1669, 1670, 1671, 1672
Rens Crsp 2, 1682
Ship Lists, 1653, 1657
VanBaes
Melchiors
King Co, 1680
VanBaren
Claas
Rcrd Nam 4, 1663
Jans
Pearson, 1663
VanBarnevelt
Gilberts
NY Ref mr, 1658
Thomas
NY Ref mr, 1659
VanBarsingerwout
Cornelis
Ship Lists, 1638
VanBaston
Martins
NY Ref mr, 1678
VanBatavia
Jans
NY Ref mr, 1663

Surname/Patronymic Combinations

VanBedford
  Abrams
    NY Ref mr, 1705
VanBeeck
  Isaacs
    NY Ref bp, 1655
VanBeest
  Jacobs
    NY Ref mr, 1662
VanBenschoten
  Elias
    Ship Lists, 1662, no date
VanBenthuysen
  Baltus
    Pearson, 1720
  Gerrits
    Rcrd Nam 3, 1659
  Martins
    Alb Ref mm, 1683
    Pearson, 1666
    Ship Lists, no date
  Pauls
    Pearson, 1697
VanBerckels
  Jans
    Rcrd Nam 3, 1660
VanBergen
  Aerts
    Pearson, 1677
  Gerrits
    Alb Ref bp, 1687
    Alb Ref mr, 1686
    Fern Wlls, 1701
    Pearson, 1630
    Rens Crsp 2, 1683
    Ship Lists, 1630, no date
  Hans
    Nicl Lvl, 1671
    Ship Lists, 1633
  Hendricks
    NY Ref mr, 1650, 1657,
    1683
  Jurians
    NY Ref mr, 1672, 1695
  Martins
    Alb Ref mm, 1683
    Pearson, 1683

  Mathys
    NY Ref mr, 1695
  Peters
    NY Ref bp, 1645
VanBergh
  Claas
    NY Ref bp, 1697
  Dirks
    Gen Entr 1, 1670
VanBerkome
  Jans
    NY Ref mr, 1703
VanBersingeren
  Cornelis
    Pearson, 1642
    Ship Lists, 1642
VanBeukelaer
  Everts
    Berg Ref mr, 1707
VanBlercom
  Jans
    Berg Ref mr, 1693, 1706
    Fltb Ref mr, 1693
    Hack Ref bp, 1707, 1708,
    1711, 1712, 1715, 1716,
    1717, 1719, 1720, 1721
    Hack Ref mr, 1710
    King Co, 1693
    NY Ref bp, 1704
  Kapts
    Hack Ref mm, page xx
  Peters
    Hack Ref bp, 1719
VanBlumenthal
  Bartholomeus
    Alb Ref bp, 1707
    Pearson, 1706
  Reyers
    NY Ref mr, 1688
VanBlydenstein
  Peters
    Fltb Ref mr, 1682, 1684
    King Co, 1684
VanBockhoven
  Jans
    Fern Wlls, 1689

VanBocksel
  Gerrits
    Rcrd Nam 1, 1655
VanBoekhoven
  Jans
    Pearson, 1662
VanBoertang
  Jans
    NY Ref bp, 1654
VanBoerum
  Jacobs
    LI Source, 1670, 1671,
    1675, 1687, no date
    Nycol Doc 2, 1664, 1665
    Ship Lists, 1687
  Willems
    Fltb Ref mr, 1684
    LI Source, 1649, 1687,
    1689
VanBohemen
  Bruyns
    Gen Entr 1, 1664
    King Pap, 1663
VanBolsart
  Peters
    Brgr Frm, 1657
    Orphan Mst, 1664, 1665
    Rcrd Nam 3, 1660
  Philips
    NY Ref mr, 1662
  Reinerse
    Nycol Doc 3, 1664
VanBom
  Conrads
    Pearson, 1660
VanBommel
  Claas
    NY Ref bp, 1664
  Hendricks
    Crt Assz, 1676
    Nicl Lvl, 1672
    NY Ref bp, 1658, 1660,
    1662, 1677
    NY Ref mr, 1662, 1682
    NYC Wills, 1693
    Nycol Doc 2, 1674
    Rcrd Nam 5, 1664

VanBommel (cont.)
Jans
Alb Ref bp, 1686
Pearson, 1685
VanBoren
Abrams
NY Ref mr, 1666
VanBorkelo
Hermans
Berg Ref mr, 1697
Fltb Ref bp, 1681
Jans
Ship Lists, 1662
Willems
Fltb Ref bp, 1680, 1681
Fltb Ref mr, 1679
Ship Lists, 1687
VanBosch
Walters
King Co, 1659
Ship Lists, 1687
VanBoskirk
Andries
Brgr Frm, 1657
Evjen, 1655
Hack Ref bp, 1720
NY Lth bp, 1710
Rcrd Nam 2, 1656
Ship Lists, no date
Lawrence
Hack Ref bp, 1696, 1697,
1699, 1712, 1716
Hack Ref mr, 1711
VanBoswyck
Andries
NY Ref mr, 1695
Hendricks
NY Ref mr, 1692
VanBoxtel
Gerrits
NY Ref bp, 1656, 1659
NY Ref mr, 1655
VanBrakel
Gerrits
Fern Wlls, 1709
Pearson, 1699

Gilberts
Alb Ref mr, 1693
Pearson, 1699
VanBrasiel
Fredericks
NY Ref mr, 1671
VanBreda
Adrians
NY Ref mr, 1673
Jans
Pearson, 1639
Ship Lists, 1639
Peters
NY Ref mr, 1656
VanBreestede
Jans
Brgr Frm, 1657
NY Ref bp, 1648, 1650,
1652, 1656, 1658, 1659,
1660, 1663, 1668
NY Ref mr, 1643, 1646,
1650, 16467
Nycol Doc 3, 1664
Rcrd Nam 2, 1656
Ship Lists, 1636
VanBrefoort
Jans
NY Ref mr, 1693
VanBremen
Claas
NY Ref mr, 1650
Dirks
Brgr Frm, 1657
King Pap, 1662, 1667
NY Ref bp, 1644
Pearson, 1648
Rens Court, 1668
Jans
Gen Entr 2, 1676
NY Ref mr, 1643
Pearson, 1646
Ship Lists, 1646
Lamberts
Pearson, 1661
Lawrence
NY Ref mr, 1669
Peters
NY Ref bp, 1663

VanBrent
Rogers
Ship Lists, 1687
VanBrest
Jans
NY Ref mr, 1665
Orphan Mst, 1665
VanBrestede
Jans
Pearson, 1636
VanBreuckelen
Andries
NY Ref mr, 1696
Cornelis
Rens Crsp 2, 1678
Hassens
NY Ref mr, 1669
Jans
King Co, 1656
Reyers
NY Ref mr, 1665
Teunis
Pearson, 1631
Rens Court, 1670
Ship Lists, 1631
Wynants
NY Ref mr, 1690
VanBrevoort
Hendricks
NY Ref mr, 1670, 1673
Jans
Brgr Frm, 1695
LI Source, 1695
NY Ref bp, 1693
VanBriel
Hendricks
Rcrd Nam 1, 1655
VanBriston
Frans
NY Ref mr, 1656
VanBroekhuysen
Jans
Pearson, 1636
Ship Lists, 1636, 1637
VanBronswyck
Teunis
Pearson, 1684

VanBroutangie
Jans
Rcrd Nam 1, 1654
VanBrugh
Giles
Brgr Frm, 1657
Nicl Lvl, 1667
NY Ref bp, 1652, 1653
Jacobs
NY Ref mr, 1670
Lennerts
NY Ref bp, 1653
Peters
Brgr Frm, 1657
Nicl Lvl, 1667
NY Ref bp, 1653, 1654, 1660
Nycol Doc 2, 1662
Rcrd Nam 1, 1665
Ship Lists, no date
VanBrunt
Joost
Ship Lists, 1653, 1687, no
date
Justin
King Co, 1653
Rogers
Fltb Ref bp, 1683, 1684,
1689
Fltb Ref mr, 1683, 1685,
1687
King Co, 1685
LI Fam 2, 1653
Ship Lists, 1687
VanBrutsteen
Peters
NY Ref mr, 1641
VanBunick
Adrians
Pearson, 1638
Ship Lists, 1638
Claas
NY Ref mr, 1658
Jans
Ship Lists, 1636
VanBuren
Bartholomeus
Pearson, 1733
Rens Court, 1668

Cornelis
Fern Wlls, 1703
Pearson, 1662
Ship Lists, 1683
Hendricks
Alb Ref bp, 1702
Alb Ref mr, 1699
Pearson, 1701
Ship Lists, no date
Martins
Alb Ref bp, 1701
Alb Ref mr, 1693
Pearson, 1742
Mathys
NY Ref mr, 1673
Willems
King Ref bp, 1698
VanBuytenhuys
Gerrits
NY Ref bp, 1661, 1667
Nycol Doc 2, 1664
Jans
NY Ref bp, 1686
VanCamp
Herberts
NY Ref bp, 1647
VanCampen
Claas
Nycol Doc 1, 1642
Hendricks
NY Ref bp, 1661
Nycol Doc 3, 1664
Rcrd Nam 5, 1665
Jans
King Co, 1668
NY Ref mr, 1659
Pearson, 1649
Ship Lists, 1640
Martins
NY Ref bp, 1660
VanCartagena
Augusts
NY Ref mr, 1647
VanCatalyn
Peters
NY Ref bp, 1672

VanChristianstadt
Jans
NY Ref mr, 1661
VanCleef
Dirks
NY Ref bp, 1673
Jans
King Co, 1683
NY Ref bp, 1664, 1666,
1669
Lawrence
Fltb Ref bp, 1687
VanCoetwyck
Gerrits
NY Ref mr, 1662
VanColen
Dirks
NY Ref mr, 1661
Wessels
NY Ref mr, 1654
Wygands
NY Ref mr, 1662
VanCollumer Zyll
Michels
NY Ref mr, 1654
VanCopenhagen
Jurians
NY Ref mr, 1657
Martins
NY Ref mr, 1660
Pearson, 1659
Peters
NY Ref mr, 1641, 1657
VanCoppernol
Willems
Pearson, 1676
VanCortlandt
Hendricks
Rens Crsp 2, 1681
Stephens
Brgr Frm, 1659
Evjen, 1637
Gen Entr 1, 1664
Nicl Lvl, 1667
NY Ref bp, 1641, 1642,
1643, 1644, 1645, 1646,
1648, 1649, 1650, 1651,
1653, 1655, 1656, 1657,

VanCortlandt (cont.)
Stephens (cont.)
1658, 1660, 1661, 1662,
1666, 1672, 1675, 1677,
1679, 1683, 16460
Nycol Doc 1, 1649
Orphan Mst, 1664
Rcrd Nam 1, 1653
Rens Crsp 1, 1655, 1657,
1658, 1659, 1661, 1662,
1663, 1664, 1665, 1666,
1667, 1668, 1670, 1671,
1673, 1674, no date
Rens Crsp 2, 1669, 1678,
1680, 1682, 1683, 1684
Ship Lists, 1638, no date
VanCortright
Cornelis
NYC Wills, 1706
VanCott
Cornelis
King Co, 1652
Ship Lists, 1652
VanCouverden
Teunis
NY Ref mr, 1679
VanCouwenhoven
Gerrits
Bkln Ref bp, 1677, 1678
Bkln Ref mm, 1664
Gen Entr 1, 1664
LI Fam 1, 1665
LI Fam 2, 1630
LI Source, 1676, 1687, 1688,
1689, 1693, 1695, 1697
NY Ref bp, 1651
Rcrd Nam 5, 1664
Ship Lists, 1687
Jacobs
LI Fam 2, 1639
Willems
LI Fam 2, 1662
Ship Lists, 1687
Wolferts
Gen Entr 1, 1664
LI Fam 2, 1630
NY Ref bp, 1655
NY Ref mr, 1655
Rcrd Nam 1, 1653

VanCovelens
Joost
Pearson, 1662
VanCovert
Jans
King Co, 1676
Teunis
King Co, 1679
VanCremyn
Kettelhuys
Ship Lists, 1642
VanCuylenburg
Bastians
NY Ref mr, 1673, 1684,
1685
VanDam
Claas
Pearson, 1683
Jans
Nycol Doc 2, 1661
Rips
Alb Ref bp, 1684, 1700
Nycol Doc 3, 1690
Pearson, 1658
Ship Lists, no date
VanDanswyck
Jans
King Ref bp, 1696, 1697
VanDanzig
Jurians
NY Ref mr, 1699
Stephens
NY Ref mr, 1699
VanDeBeets
Reyers
Rcrd Nam 6, 1669
VanDeBroeck
Claas
Ship Lists, 1651
VanDeCaep
Mathys
NY Ref bp, 1651
Vandecuyl
Barents
King Ref bp, 1667
VanDeGrift
Jacobs
King Co, 1667

Lennerts
King Co, 1648
VanDeGujanes
Peters
NY Ref mr, 1695
VanDeKuyl
Barents
Ship Lists, 1657, 1658
VanDeLangestraat
Jans
NY Ref mr, 1657
Rcrd Nam 3, 1659
VanDelf
Michels
NY Ref mr, 1665
VanDenBerg
Claas
Alb Ref bp, 1694, 1702
Pearson, 1651
Cornelis
Pearson, 1660
Rens Crsp 2, 1678
Ship Lists, 1645
Gerrits
Alb Ref bp, 1702, 1708
Alb Ref mm, 1699
Pearson, 1700
Rens Crsp 1, 1658, 1659
Gilberts
Alb Ref bp, 1701, 1706
Alb Ref mm, 1683
Nicl Lvl, 1672
NY Ref mr, 1663
Nycol Doc 3, 1664
Pearson, 1683
Rcrd Nam 4, 1662
Hendricks
Alb Ref bp, 1688
Pearson, 1683
Jans
Alb Ref bp, 1702
King Ref bp, 1703
NY Ref bp, 1647
NY Ref mr, 1688, 1694
Pearson, 1702
Willems
Alb Ref bp, 1700, 1708
Fern Wlls, 1706
Pearson, 1670

Wynants
  Pearson, 1749
VanDenBollch
  Claas
    Nycol Doc 2, 1660
VanDenBos
  Teunis
    Ship Lists, 1637
VanDenBosch
  Jans
    Berg Ref mr, 1685
    King Ref bp, 1688, 1702
    Ship Lists, 1657
  Jurians
    NY Ref mr, 1667
  Martins
    Nycol Doc 2, 1666
    Rcrd Nam 5, 1664
  Walters
    Fltb Ref bp, 1678, 1680,
    1682, 1683, 1684
  Willems
    Brgr Frm, 1657
    NY Ref mr, 1665
    Rcrd Nam 1, 1655
VanDenBriel
  Hendricks
    NY Ref bp, 1658, 1662
VanDenEnden
  Jans
    NY Ref bp, 1647
VanDenHam
  Jans
    Ship Lists, 1650
VanDenHoogenberch
  Cornelis
    Ship Lists, 1648
VanDenNiyen
  Jacobs
    Fltb Ref bp, 1680
VanDenUythoff
  Alberts
    Pearson, 1663
    Rens Crsp 1, 1660, 1661
VanDerArck
  Jans
    NY Ref bp, 1655

VanDerBaest
  Aerts
    Pearson, 1670
  Aries
    Pearson, 1670
VanDerBeek
  Barents
    Fltb Ref bp, 1683
  Conine
    King Co, 1682
  Jans
    Fltb Ref bp, 1678
    King Co, 1642
    Ship Lists, 1642
  Pauls
    Fltb Ref bp, 1681, 1683,
    1686
    King Co, 1647
  Teunis
    Alb Ref bp, 1683
VanDerBeer
  Reyers
    Nycol Doc 2, 1661
VanDerBeets
  Reyers
    Rens Crsp 1, 1658, 1659,
    1663
Vanderbilt
  Aerts
    Berg Ref bp, 1685, 1686
    Berg Ref dt, 1705
    Berg Ref mm, 1682
    Berg Ref mr, 1681
    King Co, 1693
    Rcrd Nam 1, 1653
    Ship Lists, 1640, no date
  Arents
    Berg Ref bp, 1683
    NY Ref mr, 1650
  Aries
    Fltb Ref mr, 1681
  Hendricks
    Rcrd Nam 1, 1653
  Jans
    Berg Ref bp, 1678, 1681,
    1682, 1686, 1693
    Fltb Ref bp, 1677, 1678,
    1681

Fltb Ref mr, 1687
    Jam Ref bp, 1707
    King Co, 1677
  Teunis
    Pearson, 1640
    Ship Lists, 1640
  Walings
    Ship Lists, 1636
VanDerBlass
  Herberts
    Pearson, 1640
VanDerBogart
  Claas
    Pearson, 1724
  Cornelis
    Alb Ref bp, 1685
    King Ref mr, 1679
  Frans
    Pearson, 1699
  Hermans
    Alb Ref bp, 1684, 1685,
    1686, 1688
    Pearson, 1683
    Rens Crsp 2, 1683
  Mynderts
    Fern Wlls, 1638
    Pearson, 1647
    Ship Lists, 1646
VanDerBorden
  Abrams
    Nycol Doc 3, 1664
    Rcrd Nam 4, 1662
VanDerBosch
  Walters
    King Co, 1677
VanDerBreets
  Hendricks
    King Co, 1687
VanDerCleef
  Jans
    NY Ref bp, 1668
    NY Ref mr, 1667
VanDerEyck
  Mathys
    Rcrd Nam 4, 1663
VanDerGoes
  Peters
    Rcrd Nam 4, 1662

Surname/Patronymic Combinations

VanDerGouw
Alberts
Ship Lists, 1651
Ferlyn
Ship Lists, 1631
Peters
King Co, 1639
VanDerGraft
Claas
Rens Crsp 1, 1657, 1658
VanDerGrift
Adolfs
NY Ref bp, 1681
Everts
Ship Lists, 1657
Jacobs
Bkln Ref bp, 1681
Lennerts
NYC Wlls, 1670
Orphan Mst, 1664, 1665
Rcrd Nam 1, 1657
Rens Crsp 1, 1659
Ship Lists, 1657
Peters
NY Ref bp, 1679
VanDerGrist
Fredericks
Fltb Ref mr, 1682
Gerrits
NY Ref bp, 1660
Jacobs
Fltb Ref bp, 1680, 1681
NY Ref mr, 1666
Lennerts
Brgr Frm, 1659
Gen Entr 1, 1664
LI Source, 1648
NY Ref bp, 1648, 1655,
1657, 1658, 1661, 1683,
1685, 1687, 1691
Nycol Doc 1, 1650
Orphan Mst, 1664, 1665
Pearson, 1658
Lubberts
Fltb Ref mr, 1682
Peters
NY Ref bp, 1657

VanDerHam
Jans
NY Ref bp, 1653, 1655,
1657
NY Ref mr, 1650
Rcrd Nam 2, 1657
VanDerHard
Aerts
Fltb Ref bp, 1682
Fltb Ref mr, 1680
King Co, 1680
VanDerHeul
Abrams
NY Ref mr, 1682
Jans
NY Ref bp, 1689
VanDerHeyden
Cornelis
Fern Wlls, 1663
Gen Entr 1, 1664
King Pap, 1664
Pearson, 1660
Dirks
Pearson, 1729
Jans
Pearson, 1755
Mathys
Pearson, 1700
Rens Court, 1670
Ship Lists, no date
Teunis
Nicl Lvl, 1669
VanDerHoeven
Cornelis
Alb Ref bp, 1686
Pearson, 1676
Rens Court, 1670
Frans
Alb Ref bp, 1686
Vanderhorst
Aerts
NY Ref bp, 1686
VanDerHout
Sybrants
King Pap, 1662
Vanderick
Jans
King Co, 1676

VanDeRip
Lubberts
NY Ref mr, 1655
VanDerKarr
Dirks
Pearson, 1694
VanDerKell
Jans
Nycol Doc 3, 1666
VanDerKleeck
Barents
NY Ref bp, 1690
VanDerKley
Jans
Nycol Doc 2, 1657
VanDerKreeft
Fredericks
Bkln Ref mr, 1677
VanDerKuyl
Barents
Nycol Doc 3, 1664
Rcrd Nam 4, 1663
VanDerLaen
Jans
Pearson, 1661
VanDerlipstradt
Roos
NY Ref bp, 1654
VanDerMeer
Jans
NY Ref mr, 1701
Peters
NY Ref bp, 1697
Vandermeulen
Adrians
Anjou Prb, 1665
Frans
Brgr Frm, 1698
VanDerMeyen
Jacobs
Fltb Ref bp, 1680
Fltb Ref mr, 1678
King Co, 1678
VanDermonde
Pauls
NY Ref mr, 1640

Surname/Patronymic Combinations

VanDerMulen
Frans
NY Ref bp, 1705
VanDerPerke
Bastians
Crt Assz, 1666
Rcrd Nam 6, 1666
Ship Lists, 1663
VanDerPoel
Cornelis
Fern Wlls, 1687, 1694
Gen Entr 1, 1670
Pearson, 1661
Rens Court, 1670
Rens Crsp 1, 1660
Rens Crsp 2, 1675, 1678, 1684
Gerrits
Alb Ref bp, 1683
Gen Entr 1, 1669
Pearson, 1654
Ship Lists, 1647, no date
Melchiors
Pearson, 1710
Wynants
Alb Ref bp, 1683, 1685, 1689, 1691, 1703
Alb Ref mm, 1683
NY Ref bp, 1690
Pearson, 1683
VanDerRee
Cornelis
Rcrd Nam 3, 1660
VanDerSchuere
Michels
NY Ref bp, 1669
Willems
NY Ref bp, 1689
VanDerVechte
Teunis
Alb Ref bp, 1701
VanDerVeen
Cornelis
Brgr Frm, 1657
NY Ref bp, 1652, 1657, 1658, 1683
Rcrd Nam 1, 1653

Jans
King Co, 1661
NY Ref bp, 1658, 1662, 1679
Nycol Doc 2, 1657
Pearson, 1654
Rcrd Nam 1, 1665
VanDerVeer
Cornelis
Fltb Ref bp, 1687
Fltb Ref mr, 1685
King Co, 1679
LI Fam 2, 1685
NY Ref bp, 1659
Ship Lists, 1687, no date
Jans
Fltb Ref bp, 1679, 1682, 1684
King Co, 1659
LI Fam 2, no date
Ship Lists, 1659, no date
Joris
NY Ref mr, 1650
VanDerVenter
Jans
Fltb Ref bp, 1687, 1688
VanDerVin
Jans
Orphan Mst, 1663
VanDerVliet
Adrians
King Ref bp, 1663, 1681
Barents
King Co, 1668
Dirks
Bkln Ref bp, 1684
King Co, 1699
Jans
Bkln Ref bp, 1678, 1696
King Co, 1660
LI Source, 1660, 1680
VanDerVolgen
Claas
Pearson, 1720
Lawrence
Pearson, no date
Ship Lists, no date

VanDerVoort
Jans
King Co, 1680
Michels
King Co, 1655
Pauls
King Co, 1640
Ship Lists, no date
VanDerVorst
Cornelis
Berg Ref bp, 1696
Berg Ref dt, 1683
Berg Ref mm, 1667
NY Ref bp, 1653, 1654
Ides
Berg Ref mm, 1672, 1682
Gen Entr 1, 1671
NY Ref mr, 1671
VanDerWel
Cornelis
NY Ref bp, 1646
Nycol Doc 2, 1662
Rcrd Nam 1, 1654
VanDerWerf
Jans
Hack Ref mm, 1686
VanDerWerken
Gerrits
Pearson, 1700
Ship Lists, 1663
Roelofs
Alb Ref bp, 1702, 1704, 1705, 1706, 1708
Pearson, 1700
VanDerWey
Cornelis
NY Ref bp, 1672
VanDerWoert
Pauls
NY Ref bp, 1650, 1653
VanDerWyck
Barents
Bkln Ref bp, 1694
VanDerZee
Alberts
Pearson, 1663
Rens Court, 1670

VanDerZee (cont.)
Storms
Pearson, 1699
VanDeSchuyven
Willems
King Ref bp, 1703, 1704
VanDeusen
Abrams
Alb Ref bp, 1685, 1708
NY Ref bp, 1667, 1669,
1672, 1677, 1678, 1684,
1695
NY Ref mr, 1666
Pearson, 1700
Ship Lists, 1657, 1663
Herberts
Pearson, 1736
Isaacs
Brgr Frm, 1698
NY Ref bp, 1700
Pearson, 1740
Jacobs
Alb Ref bp, 1700, 1701,
1702, 1703, 1706, 1709
Alb Ref mm, 1683
Pearson, 1683
Mathys
Alb Ref bp, 1700, 1702,
1708
Alb Ref mm, 1694
Alb Ref mr, 1695
NY Ref bp, 1699
Pearson, 1696
Melchiors
Alb Ref bp, 1702, 1707
Pearson, 1691
Peters
Ship Lists, 1632, no date
Teunis
Pearson, 1700
VanDeventer
Barents
NY Ref mr, 1664
Hendricks
Brgr Frm, 1657
NY Ref mr, 1646
Jacobs
King Co, 1719

Jans
Fltb Ref mr, 1686
King Co, 1695
King Pap, 1670
NY Ref mr, 1660
NYC Wills, 1686
Nycol Doc 2, 1674
Rcrd Nam 4, 1662
Ship Lists, 1687
Peters
King Co, 1662
Ship Lists, no date
Willems
Berg Ref bp, 1693
VanDeWalebocht
Martins
NY Ref mr, 1691, 1692,
1696
VanDeWater
Jacobs
King Co, 1669
Peters
Fltb Ref bp, 1682
VanDeyl
Abrams
NY Ref mr, 1665
Vandiegrist
Lennerts
Brgr Frm, 1657
VanDien
Gerrits
Ship Lists, 1660
VanDinter
Jans
Nycol Doc 1, 1651
VanDitmars
Claas
Gen Entr 1, 1664
Jans
Evjen, 1664
Fltb Ref bp, 1679, 1680
LI Source, no date
NY Ref mr, 1650, 1652
Pearson, 1685
VanDockum
Jans
NY Ref mr, 1647

Peters
Nycol Doc 2, 1665
VanDoesburg
Andries
Pearson, 1661
Rens Crsp 1, 1661
Rens Crsp 2, 1684
Hendricks
King Co, 1654
NY Ref mr, 1655
Pearson, 1698
Rcrd Nam 7, 1658
VanDolsen
Gerrits
Ship Lists, no date
VanDoorn
Claas
Rcrd Nam 4, 1662
Lamberts
Pearson, 1642
Ship Lists, 1642
Martins
King Ref mr, 1682
Mynderts
NY Ref mr, 1654
VanDorland
Lamberts
Ship Lists, 1644
VanDort
Hendricks
NY Ref mr, 1652
VanDortrecht
Wessels
NY Ref mr, 1675
VanDost
Jans
King Pap, 1662
VanDouveren
Stephens
NY Ref mr, 1692
VanDriesbergen
Dries
Ship Lists, 1642
VanDriest
Barents
Fltb Ref bp, 1680, 1681, 1684
Fltb Ref mr, 1679
King Co, 1658

Surname/Patronymic Combinations

VanDublin
  Andries
    Ship Lists, 1646
VanDuisberg
  Hendricks
    NY Ref bp, 1656
VanDurgerdam
  Cornelis
    NY Ref mr, 1657
VanDuyckhuysen
  Hillebrants
    Gen Entr 1, 1669
  Teunis
    Bkln Ref bp, 1677
    Fltb Ref bp, 1681, 1684
VanDuyn
  Cornelis
    Bkln Ref mr, 1691
    King Co, 1649
    LI Fam 2, 1649
    Ship Lists, 1649, 1687, no date
  Dennis
    King Co, 1695
  Gerrits
    Fltb Ref mr, 1691
    King Co, 1696
    LI Fam 2, 1664
    LI Source, 1699
    Ship Lists, 1687, no date
  Jacobs
    NY Ref bp, 1687
VanDuynkerken
  Jans
    Pearson, 1660
VanDuyvelandt
  Adrians
    NY Ref bp, 1658, 1662, 1664
    Ship Lists, 1658
VanDwingeloo
  Barents
    Pearson, 1662
VanDyck
  Cornelis
    Rens Court, 1668

Frans
    NY Ref bp, 1689, 1697, 1701, 1704
    NY Ref mr, 1677, 1681, 1686
  Jans
    Bkln Ref bp, 1681, 1682, 1684, 1688
    Fltb Ref bp, 1677, 1679, 1680, 1681, 1682, 1683, 1684
    Fltb Ref mr, 1680, 1694
    King Co, 1651
    NY Ref bp, 1674, 1675, 1685, 1686, 1688
    NY Ref mr, 1673, 1674
    Ship Lists, 1687, no date
  Jurians
    King Co, 1701
  Teunis
    LI Source, 1687
  Thomas
    Bkln Ref bp, 1690, 1695
    Fltb Ref mr, 1678, 1679, 1689, 1692
    King Co, 1689
    Ship Lists, 1652, 1687
VanDyckhuys
  Hillebrants
    King Co, 1661
  Teunis
    King Co, 1643
    Ship Lists, 1687
VanDyckhuysen
  Teunis
    LI Source, 1687
VanEbel
  Jans
    Rcrd Nam 1, 1653
VanEchtsveen
  Cornelis
    NY Ref mr, 1680
VanEck
  Peters
    King Co, 1632
  Wynants
    King Co, 1663

VanEdam
  Barents
    Pearson, 1636
  Jans
    Pearson, 1636
    Ship Lists, 1636
  Lubberts
    NY Ref mr, 1659
  Michels
    Pearson, 1637
    Ship Lists, 1637
  Timothys
    Ship Lists, 1636
VanEeckelen
  Jans
    Pearson, 1661
    Rens Crsp 1, 1659
VanEens
  Hendricks
    King Co, 1661
VanEgmont
  Cornelis
    NY Ref mr, 1670, 1678
VanEkel
  Jans
    Rcrd Nam 1, 1653
VanEland
  Engelberts
    NY Ref mr, 1656
VanElmendorf
  Conrads
    King NYGB, 1668
    King Pap, 1667
VanElpendam
  Jans
    NY Ref bp, 1649, 1659, 16467
VanElslant
  Jans
    Ship Lists, no date
  Joost
    Tap Ref bp, 1700
  Joris
    Hack Ref bp, 1695
VanEmbden
  Jacobs
    NY Ref mr, 1660

VanEmbden (cont.)
Jans
   NY Ref mr, 1644, 1662
VanEmbderlant
Alberts
   NY Ref mr, 1657
VanEmmenes
Jacobs
   NY Ref mr, 1643
VanEngen
Willems
   King Co, 1657
VanEps
Dirks
   Pearson, 1664
   Rens Court, 1672
   Rens Crsp 2, 1683
VanErlanger
Hendricks
   Gen Entr 1, 1664
VanEs
Hendricks
   Ship Lists, 1642
VanEsselstine
Cornelis
   King Ref bp, 1687
   Pearson, 1661
Jans
   NY Ref mr, 1676
Lawrence
   NY Ref mr, 1646, 1649
Martins
   Alb Ref bp, 1707
   King Ref bp, 1687
   Pearson, 1705
Teunis
   NY Ref mr, 1661
Walters
   NY Ref bp, 1655
   NY Ref mr, 1641
Willems
   NY Ref bp, 1658, 1661
   Rcrd Nam 2, 1658
VanEtten
Jacobs
   King Ref mr, 1685
Jans
   King Pap, 1664

   King Ref bp, 1670, 1679,
    1681, 1683, 1684, 1688
   Nicl Lvl, 1667
   Ship Lists, 1652, no date
Peters
   Pearson, 1658
VanEuchuysen
Abrams
   NY Ref bp, 1644
VanEveren
Cornelis
   NY Ref bp, 1687
Fredericks
   Pearson, 1663
Jans
   NY Ref mr, 1642
Mynderts
   Alb Ref bp, 1707, 1708
   Pearson, 1707
VanEvery
Fredericks
   Ship Lists, no date
VanExween
Cornelis
   NYC Wills, 1690
VanEyckelen
Jans
   King Pap, 1661
Joost
   King Pap, 1661
VanFeurden
Hendricks
   NY Ref mr, 1693
Jans
   NY Ref bp, 1685, 1690
   Nycol Doc 3, 1690
VanFewide
Jans
   Pearson, 1685
VanFiesvelt
Arents
   King Pap, 1664
VanFlansburg
Cornelis
   Brgr Frm, 1657
   NY Ref mr, 1659
   Pearson, 1671
   Rcrd Nam 7, 1660

Jans
   NY Ref bp, 1680, 1682,
    1683, 1684, 1688, 1689
   NY Ref mr, 1680, 1687
VanFraniker
Mathys
   Pearson, 1635
Terss
   Ship Lists, 1635
VanFrank
Fredericks
   Alb Ref bp, 1708, 1709
Gerrits
   Alb Ref bp, 1705, 1708
   Schn Ref mr, 1701, 1704
VanFrederickstadt
Andries
   Pearson, 1636
   Ship Lists, 1636
Jans
   NY Ref mr, 1650
VanFrederikfort
Jans
   Pearson, 1662
VanFrurde
Jans
   King Co, 1664
VanGansevoort
Hermans
   Pearson, 1664
VanGarder
Jans
   Ship Lists, 1658
VanGeescher
Willems
   King Co, 1696
VanGelder
Everts
   Hack Ref mr, 1706
VanGemoenepau
Gerbrants
   NY Ref mr, 1707
VanGertruydenburgh
Jans
   Pearson, 1642
   Ship Lists, 1642

Surname/Patronymic Combinations

VanGerwen
  Jans
    NY Ref bp, 1656
VanGesel
  Gerrits
    Nycol Doc 2, 1659
    Ship Lists, no date
VanGesscher
  Jans
    LI Source, 1696
  Willems
    LI Source, 1696
VanGiesen
  Bastians
    Berg Ref dt, 1707
    King Co, 1660
    Ship Lists, no date
  Reyners
    Berg Ref mm, 1677
VanGoestorp
  Peters
    NY Ref mr, 1663
VanGottenburgh
  Cornelis
    King Pap, 1664
  Hendricks
    Pearson, 1663
VanGouda
  Jans
    Fltb Ref mr, 1679
VanGraft
  Bergen
    Rens Crsp 1, 1661
  Dirks
    Gen Entr 1, 1664
    ⸳ Rens Crsp 1, 1665
VanGrist
  Hendricks
    NY Ref bp, 1681
VanGroeningen
  Claas
    NY Ref mr, 1655
  Hendricks
    NY Ref mr, 1659
  Jans
    NY Ref bp, 1647
    NY Ref mr, 1652

Lawrence
    NY Ref mr, 1663
  Wynants
    NY Ref mr, 1683
  Zacharias
    NY Ref mr, 1655
VanGroenland
  Cornelis
    Hack Ref mr, 1699
VanGroetenbaecken
  Jans
    Rcrd Nam 1, 1654
VanGrootSchermer
  Claas
    NY Ref mr, 1681
VanGrummen
  Davids
    NY Ref mr, 1705
VanGudsenhoven
  Bastians
    Pearson, 1658
VanGunst
  Hendricks
    Brgr Frm, 1657
    Gen Entr 1, 1668
    King Co, 1655
    Nicl Lvl, 1669
    NY Ref bp, 1665, 1668,
    1672, 1679, 1683
    NY Ref mr, 1685
    Rcrd Nam 3, 1659
VanGutsenhoven
  Bastians
    Rens Court, 1668, 1669,
    1670
    Rens Crsp 1, 1655, 1657,
    1658, 1661, 1662, 1666,
    1667, 1668
    Ship Lists, 1652
  Jans
    Rens Court, 1669
    Rens Crsp 1, 1659, 1662
VanHaert
  Jans
    NY Ref mr, 1677
VanHalen
  Gerrits
    Hack Ref bp, 1707, 1709,
    1710, 1714

Jans
    NY Ref bp, 1667
VanHam
  Jans
    Brgr Frm, 1657
    Rcrd Nam 1, 1655
VanHamburg
  Peters
    NY Ref mr, 1641, 1701
VanHamelwaard
  Hendricks
    Ship Lists, 1638
  Roelofs
    Pearson, 1638
    Ship Lists, 1639
VanHarderwyck
  Hendricks
    Orphan Mst, 1663, 1664,
    1665
    Rcrd Nam 3, 1659
VanHarlem
  Barents
    NY Ref mr, 1659, 1667,
    1670
  Carpenel
    NY Ref bp, 1645, 1647
  Frans
    NY Ref mr, 1664
  Gerrits
    Hack Ref mr, 1706
    NY Ref mr, 1642
  Gothards
    NY Ref bp, 1661
    NY Ref mr, 1650
  Hendricks
    NY Ref mr, 1655
  Huberts
    NY Ref mr, 1652
  Jacobs
    NY Ref mr, 1641
  Jans
    Alb Ref bp, 1697
    NY Ref bp, 1646
    NY Ref mr, 1651, 1660
    Pearson, 1697
  Joost
    NY Ref mr, 1660
  Lubberts
    NY Ref mr, 1651

VanHarlem (cont.)
Peters
NY Ref mr, 1695
VanHarlingen
Jans
NY Ref bp, 1682
Wybrechts
Pearson, 1662
VanHarstenhorst
Hendricks
Pearson, 1662
VanHartenburgh
Jans
Rens Crsp 2, 1675
VanHartevelt
Isaacs
NY Ref bp, 1662
Rcrd Nam 5, 1664
VanHasselt
Peters
Brgr Frm, 1657
Rcrd Nam 3, 1660
VanHasymes
Claas
King Co, 1687
Jans
Bkln Ref bp, 1687
VanHaughwout
Peters
Ship Lists, 1660
VanHeemst
Jans
King Co, 1661
VanHeemstraat
Dirks
Pearson, 1700
Rens Court, 1670
Rens Crsp 1, 1671
Takels
Alb Ref bp, 1704, 1706
VanHeemstwaart
Jans
Rcrd Nam 4, 1662, 1663
VanHeerd
Jans
NY Ref mr, 1654

VanHeerden
Gerrits
King Pap, 1664
Jans
NY Ref mr, 1677
Willems
Pearson, 1662
VanHersberg
Joris
NY Ref mr, 1639
VanHertogenbosch
Jacobs
NY Ref mr, 1650
VanHeyningen
Jans
King Co, 1672
NY Ref bp, 1686, 1688,
1691
NY Ref mr, 1672
Rcrd Nam 6, 1671
Ship Lists, 1662
VanHoeck
Arents
Pearson, 1700
Isaacs
NY Ref bp, 1690, 1692
NY Ref mr, 1695
Pearson, 1658
VanHoesen
Claas
Bkln Ref bp, 1674
NY Ref bp, 1668
Cornelis
Pearson, 1681
Frans
Fern Wlls, 1703
King Pap, 1666
NY Ref bp, 1640
Pearson, 1659
Ship Lists, 1646, no date
Hermans
NY Ref mr, 1641
Jacobs
Atns Lth bp, 1708, 1710
NY Lth bp, 1708, 1710
Jans
Atns Lth bp, 1708
King Ref bp, 1698

NY Lth bp, 1705, 1708
Pearson, 1694
Rens Court, 1671, 1672
Jurians
Atns Lth bp, 1708, 1710
NY Lth bp, 1708, 1710
Pearson, 1699
Peters
NY Ref bp, 1640, 1643,
1646
NY Ref mr, 1652, 1657
Volkerts
Alb Ref bp, 1700
Atns Lth bp, 1707
Atns Lth mr, 1705, 1708
NY Lth bp, 1709
NY Lth mr, 1705, 1707
VanHolstein
Christians
NY Ref mr, 1659
Jacobs
King Pap, 1664
Peters
Rcrd Nam 3, 1659
VanHolte
Jans
Gen Entr 1, 1669
VanHoochten
Jans
King Co, 1662
Rcrd Nam 1, 1655
VanHoogharsteen
Jacobs
NY Ref mr, 1658
VanHoogkerk
Lucas
Alb Ref bp, 1704, 1705
Alb Ref mr, 1686
Pearson, 1686
VanHoorstrant
Jans
LI Source, no date
VanHorn
Barents
Evjen, 1657
Hack Ref bp, 1718

Christians
    NY Lth bp, 1704, 1705,
    1708
Claas
    NY Ref mr, 1645
Cornelis
    Brgr Frm, 1657
    Hack Ref bp, 1718
    NY Lth bp, 1708, 1709
    NY Lth mr, 1705, 1707
    Nycol Doc 2, 1664
    Rcrd Nam 3, 1659
    Ship Lists, no date
Dirks
    NY Ref mr, 1655, 1660
Jacobs
    NY Ref mr, 1663
Jans
    King Pap, 1665
    NY Ref bp, 1659, 1663,
    1673, 1679, 1681, 1687
    NY Ref mr, 1659, 1666
    NYC Wills, 1689
    Pearson, 1661
    Rcrd Nam 3, 1660
Joris
    NY Ref bp, 1705, 1710
Peters
    NY Ref mr, 1672
VanHouten
Cornelis
    Hack Ref mr, 1712
    NY Ref bp, 1648
    Pearson, 1640
    Ship Lists, 1638, 1640
Jans
    NY Ref bp, 1669
    Nycol Doc 3, 1664
Krynes
    Ship Lists, 1640, 1642
Roelofs
    Ship Lists, no date
    Tary Ref bp, 1703
Teunis
    Hack Ref bp, 1719
Willems
    Hack Ref mm, page xx
    Hack Ref mr, 1712

VanHun
    Hermans
        Pearson, 1681
VanHusum
    Volkerts
        Evjen, 1705
VanHuysen
    Gerrits
        Hack Ref bp, 1694
VanIckemsburgh
    Smith
        Ship Lists, 1642
VanIlpendam
    Jans
        NY Ref bp, 1647
        Pearson, 1656
        Rens Court, 1669, 1672
VanIselstein
    Teunis
        Ship Lists, 1658
VanIsleven
    Dirks
        NY Ref mr, 1664
VanJevern
    Barents
        NY Ref mr, 1659
    Fredericks
        NY Ref mr, 1656
    Mynderts
        Gen Entr 1, 1664
        NY Ref mr, 1660
    Volkerts
        NY Ref mr, 1655
VanKalcker
    Everts
        Nycol Doc 2, 1659
VanKeulen
    Hendricks
        Brgr Frm, 1657
VanKeuren
    Jans
        Ship Lists, no date
VanKleeck
    Barents
        Berg Ref bp, 1685, 1688,
        1689
        Berg Ref dt, 1688
        King Ref bp, 1697

LI Fam 1, 1660
        NY Ref bp, 1687, 1690
VanKulenbergh
    Jans
        Pearson, 1681
VanKuyk
    Jans
        Ship Lists, 1662
VanKuykenthal
    Jacobs
        King Ref bp, 1706
VanLaer
    Gerrits
        Fern Wlls, 1684
        NY Ref bp, 1662
        NY Ref mr, 1660
        Pearson, 1670
        Ship Lists, 1658, 1659
VanLaeren
    Mathys
        Ship Lists, 1660
VanLangendyck
    Jacobs
        NY Ref mr, 1649
    Jans
        NY Ref bp, 1680, 1689,
        1691
        NY Ref mr, 1688
        Rcrd Nam 5, 1665
    Siebolds
        NY Ref mr, 1642
VanLangesout
    Carls
        King Pap, 1662
VanLangestraat
    Christophs
        Fltb Ref bp, 1677
    Jans
        NY Ref bp, 1661, 1666
        NY Ref mr, 1659, 1672
VanLansmeer
    Everts
        NY Ref mr, 1669
VanLauven
    Hendricks
        Rens Crsp 2, 1681

Surname/Patronymic Combinations

VanLeendersloot
Claas
Bkln Ref bp, 1680
VanLeerd.
Barents
NY Ref bp, 1661
VanLeeuwarden
Dominics
NY Ref mr, 1665
VanLeeuwen
Fredericks
Fltb Ref bp, 1682
King Co, 1652
Gerrits
LI Source, 1652
Hendricks
Fltb Ref bp, 1681
Fltb Ref mr, 1681
LI Source, 1670
Ship Lists, no date
Jacobs
Ship Lists, 1660
Peters
King Pap, 1664
King Ref bp, 1688
Nicl Lvl, 1667
VanLenneps
Jans
NY Ref bp, 1658
VanLemmet
Hermans
NY Ref mr, 1641
VanLent
Abrams
Tary Ref bp, 1699
VanLexmond
Cornelis
NY Ref mr, 1658
VanLeyden
Fredericks
Pearson, 1642
Ship Lists, 1642
Jans
NY Ref bp, 1659, 1660
NY Ref mr, 1659, 1675
Pearson, 1656
Rcrd Nam 1, 1655
Ship Lists, 1649

Peters
NY Ref mr, 1652, 1664
Pearson, 1661
Teunis
NY Ref mr, 1649
Pearson, 1642
Willems
NY Ref bp, 1664
VanLinden
Joost
Berg Ref mm, 1681
VanLipstadt
Rees
NY Ref bp, 1656
VanLith
Claas
Ship Lists, 1653
VanLochem
Smit
NY Ref bp, 1655
VanLoendersloot
Claas
Fltb Ref bp, 1680
VanLoenen
Teunis
Rens Crsp 1, 1659
VanLonden
Alberts
Evjen, 1639
VanLoockere
Gerrits
NY Ref mr, 1675
VanLoon
Gerrits
NY Ref mr, 1652
VanLoonen
Martins
NY Ref mr, 1659
VanLoosereght
Hendricks
Pearson, 1654
VanLuane
Jans
Fltb Ref mr, 1685
King Co, 1654
VanLubeck
Barents
NY Ref mr, 1685, 1694

Peters
NY Ref mr, 1676
VanLuisthout
Jans
NY Ref bp, 1689
VanLuyderdorp
Bestvals
Ship Lists, 1642
VanLuyten
Teunis
Ship Lists, 1642
VanMaerden
Caspars
Rcrd Nam 1, 1653
Jans
King Pap, 1670
VanMaerzen
Dirks
NY Ref mr, 1645
VanMaesterlandt
Jans
Ship Lists, 1630
VanMalmuyden
Roelofs
NY Ref mr, 1673
VanMarck
Gerrits
King Co, 1654
Nicl Lvl, 1672
Nycol Doc 2, 1673
Pearson, 1661
Rcrd Nam 5, 1665
Rens Court, 1668, 1669, 1672
VanMeckelen
Jans
Fltb Ref mr, 1690
King Co, 1690
VanMeerbeek
Joost
NY Ref mr, 1649
VanMeeuwis
Willems
NY Ref mr, 1693
VanMeppel
Dirks
NY Ref mr, 1661

Hendricks
  King Ref bp, 1663
  NY Ref mr, 1663, 1681
Jans
  NY Ref bp, 1667
  NY Ref mr, 1682
  Rcrd Nam 3, 1659
Willems
  NY Ref mr, 1662
VanMerkerk
Teunis
  Pearson, 1637
  Ship Lists, 1637
VanMerven
Peters
  NY Ref mr, 1658
VanMeteren
Gilberts
  King Co, 1663
  Nycol Doc 2, 1673
  Ship Lists, no date
Jans
  Fltb Ref bp, 1683, 1687
  Fltb Ref mr, 1683
  King Co, 1663
  LI Source, 1683, 1695
  Ship Lists, 1687
Joost
  King Pap, 1664
  Ship Lists, no date
VanMeulen
Gerrits
  Pearson, 1671
VanMiddleburg
Cornelis
  NY Ref mr, 1685
Hendricks
  NY Ref mr, 1683
Jacobs
  NY Ref mr, 1657
VanMidwout
Jans
  NY Ref mr, 1686
Jochems
  NY Ref mr, 1683, 1693
VanMispadt
Lawrence
  NY Ref mr, 1667

VanMispadtkill
Davids
  NY Ref mr, 1690
Hendricks
  NY Ref mr, 1693
Jans
  NY Ref mr, 1695
VanMunichendam
Alberts
  Pearson, 1654
Cornelis
  Pearson, 1636
  Ship Lists, 1636
VanMuyden
Claas
  NY Ref mr, 1664
Philips
  NY Ref mr, 1662
VanMydrecht
Gerrits
  NY Ref mr, 1667
VanName
Engelberts
  King Ref bp, 1682, 1683
  Ship Lists, no date
VanNarden
Jans
  King Co, 1645
VanNas
Dirks
  King Co, 1661
VanNeck
Alberts
  King Ref bp, 1663
  Nicl Lvl, 1669
  Pearson, 1659
  Rcrd Nam 4, 1662
VanNef
Dirks
  King Co, 1661
VanNess
Cornelis
  Berg Ref dt, 1689
  King Ref mr, 1663
  Pearson, 1697
  Rens Crsp 2, 1684
Dirks
  Rcrd Nam 3, 1660
  Rcrd Nam 6, 1666

Gerrits
  NY Ref mr, 1654
  Pearson, 1736
  Ship Lists, 1645
Hendricks
  Fern Wlls, 1725
  Fltb Ref bp, 1679, 1680
  Pearson, 1643
  Ship Lists, 1641, no date
Jans
  NY Ref bp, 1682
Peters
  Fltb Ref bp, 1681, 1683
  King Co, 1677
  Rcrd Nam 7, 1672, 1673
VanNeuerstrait
Jans
  NYC Wills, 1679
VanNeurenburgh
Conrads
  Pearson, 1660
VanNewkirk
Aerts
  Pearson, 1660
Alberts
  NY Ref mr, 1645
Brants
  Pearson, 1664
  Ship Lists, 1640
Claas
  Pearson, 1662
Cornelis
  Berg Ref dt, 1705
  Berg Ref mr, 1670, 1686
  King Co, 1665
Hessels
  NY Ref mr, 1667
Jans
  Ship Lists, 1636
Peelens
  Ship Lists, 1630
Peters
  King Co, no date
Ulrichs
  NY Ref mr, 1664
Willems
  NY Ref mr, 1663

VanNieuwenhuysen
  Egberts
    Rcrd Nam 7, 1659
  Teunis
    NY Ref mr, 1707
VanNieuwhof
  Aerts
    Rcrd Nam 2, 1658
VanNimmegen
  Jans
    NY Ref mr, 1657
VanNimweeg
  Barents
    King Ref bp, 1702
VanNoorden
  Claas
    Ship Lists, no date
VanNoorstrant
  Jacobs
    Pearson, 1677
  Jans
    Pearson, 1638
    Rens Court, 1672, 1668
    LI Source, 1679
    Ship Lists, no date
VanNoort
  Jacobs
    King Co, 1667
  Jans
    Ship Lists, 1661, no date
  Peters
    King Co, 1647
VanNorden
  Caspars
    Brgr Frm, 1657
    NY Ref bp, 1662
  Dirks
    Fern Wlls, 1642
  Everts
    NY Ref mr, 1643
  Gerbrants
    NY Ref mr, 1657
  Hendricks
    Evjen, 1656
    NY Ref mr, 1656
  Jacobs
    NY Ref bp, 1644

Jans
  Hack Ref bp, 1712
  Hack Ref mr, 1717
  King NYGB, 1770
  King Pap, 1670
  NY Lth bp, 1704
  NY Lth mr, 1707
  NY Ref bp, 1648
  NY Ref mr, 1647
Lamberts
  NY Ref mr, 1654
Teunis
  NY Ref mr, 1642, 1655
  Rcrd Nam 1, 1654
  Ship Lists, 1650
Wessels
  NY Ref mr, 1669
VanNordinge
  Claas
    Pearson, 1683
    Ship Lists, 1637
VanNordthorn
  Simons
    NY Ref mr, 1646
VanNorthuysen
  Coert
    NY Ref mr, 1647
VanNortwyck
  Jacobs
    King Co, 1662
VanNorwegen
  Christians
    Pearson, 1658
VanNostrand
  Gerrits
    King Co, 1687
  Hans
    Hack Ref mm, page xx
    King Co, 1685
    Ship Lists, 1639
  Jacobs
    King Ref bp, 1702
  Jans
    King Co, 1685
    NY Ref bp, 1641
    NY Ref mr, 1652
    Ship Lists, no date

Simons
  King Co, 1687
Volkerts
  King Co, 1687
VanNuxon
  Jans
    NY Ref bp, 1660
VanNuys
  Augusts
    Fltb Ref bp, 1679, 1682,
    1684, 1685
    Fltb Ref mr, 1680, 1685
    King Co, 1685
  Jacobs
    King Co, 1695
  Jans
    Fltb Ref bp, 1684, 1685,
    1687
    King Co, 1651
    Ship Lists, 1687
  Willems
    Fltb Ref bp, 1685
VanObyn
  Jans
    NY Ref bp, 1657
VanOetmarsen
  Hermans
    NY Ref mr, 1663
VanOldenburg
  Gerrits
    Pearson, 1662
  Jans
    Brgr Frm, 1659
    NY Ref bp, 1639, 1642,
    1643, 1646
    NY Ref mr, 1652
VanOldenzeel
  Jurians
    NY Ref mr, 1660
VanOlinda
  Daniels
    Pearson, 1669
  Peters
    Pearson, 1693
VanOogsten
  Dirks
    Berg Ref mr, 1693

Jans
  Berg Ref mr, 1672
VanOort
  Jans
    King Pap, 1671
VanOosanen
  Claas
    Pearson, 1658
VanOoscen
  Simons
    Gen Entr 1, 1664
VanOost
  Jans
    NY Ref bp, 1659
VanOosten
  Cornelis
    Fltb Ref mr, 1682
    LI Source, 1690
  Jans
    King Pap, 1666
    NY Ref mr, 1666, 1672
VanOosthuysen
  Claas
    NY Ref mr, 1686
VanOostsanen
  Claas
    Pearson, 1661
  Jacobs
    Pearson, 1661
  Simons
    Pearson, 1661
VanOsterhout
  Jans
    King Pap, 1663, 1665
    King Ref bp, 1663, 1665,
    1666, 1667, 1674, 1679,
    1681
    King Ref mr, 1682
    Nicl Lvl, 1667
    NY Ref bp, 1654, 1656
    NY Ref mr, 1653
VanOstrand
  Claas
    Pearson, 1658
  Jacobs
    Alb Ref bp, 1687, 1688
    Alb Ref mm, 1683

    Alb Ref mr, 1688
    King Ref bp, 1689, 1699
VanOstrander
  Peters
    King Ref bp, 1706
VanOstrom
  Hendricks
    Berg Ref bp, 1706
  Jans
    Rcrd Nam 4, 1662
    Ship Lists, 1651
VanOtten
  Jans
    Pearson, 1657
VanOtterspoor
  Arnouts
    Ship Lists, 1649
  Jans
    Pearson, 1658
VanPatten
  Fredericks
    Pearson, 1664
    Ship Lists, no date
  Jans
    Fltb Ref bp, 1678
    King Ref bp, 1678
VanPelt
  Aerts
    King Co, 1696
    LI Source, 1696
  Gilberts
    King Co, 1685
  Jans
    Fltb Ref bp, 1681
    King Co, 1700
    LI Source, 1687
    NY Ref bp, 1700
    Ship Lists, 1687, no date
  Laanen
    Bkln Ref bp, 1688
  Mathys
    Fltb Ref bp, 1679, 1681,
    1683, 1684, 1685, 1689,
    1690
    Fltb Ref mr, 1679
    King Co, 1646
  Teunis
    Bkln Ref bp, 1687

    Fltb Ref bp, 1681, 1685,
    1689, 1690
    King Co, 1686
    LI Source, 1687, 1697
    Ship Lists, 1687
  Walters
    King Co, 1687
VanPharnabuck
  Corsen
    NY Ref bp, 1687
VanPopersdorf
  Gerrits
    NYC Wills, 1680
VanPurmerent
  Jans
    King Co, 1656
    NY Ref mr, 1656
  Lawrence
    Pearson, no date
VanPutten
  Hendricks
    NY Ref mr, 1655
VanPynacker
  Adrians
    NY Ref mr, 1663
VanQuackenbush
  Peters
    NY Ref mr, 1674
VanRavenstyn
  Gerrits
    LI Fam 1, 1660
    NY Ref mr, 1681
VanRavox
  Claas
    NY Ref mr, 1649
VanReis
  Hendricks
    Pearson, 1663
VanRensselaer
  Baptist
    Ship Lists, 1651
VanReynerwout
  Barents
    NY Ref mr, 1662
VanRhenen
  Coert
    NY Ref mr, 1664
  Jacobs
    Bkln Ref mr, 1661

VanRhuyne
Fockens
NY Ref mr, 1671
VanRidding
Edsels
NY Ref mr, 1655
VanRinsburgh
Jacobs
Pearson, 1663
VanRipen
Thomas
Ship Lists, no date
VanRochel
Peters
NY Ref mr, 1680
Richard
NY Ref mr, 1664
VanRodenkirk
Hendricks
NY Ref mr, 1656
VanRoen
Josiahs
Berg Ref bp, 1686
VanRoermondt
Beeren
NY Ref mr, 1659
VanRollegom
Joost
LI Fam 1, 1640
NY Ref bp, 1685, 1688, 1689
NYC Wills, 1692
Rens Crsp 2, 1675
VanRomen
Fockens
NY Ref mr, 1667, 1676
Jans
NY Ref bp, 1658, 1700
NY Ref mr, 1691, 1699
VanRoosevelt
Martins
NY Ref bp, 1652, 1654
VanRootsisil
Lawrence
NY Ref mr, 1656
VanRosenthal
Jans
NY Ref bp, 1662

VanRossem
Aerts
King Co, 1643
Cornelis
Pearson, 1662
Rens Crsp 1, 1652
VanRotmers
Barents
Pearson, 1662
VanRotterdam
Cornelis
King Co, 1639
NY Ref bp, 1641, 1643
NY Ref mr, 1643
Jacobs
NY Ref mr, 1699
Pearson, 1661
Jans
Alb Ref bp, 1690
Pearson, 1654
Ship Lists, 1639, 1640
Teunis
NY Ref mr, 1664
VanRovenstein
Gerrits
NYC Wills, 1692
VanRuth
Jans
Ship Lists, 1641
VanRuynderwolt
Jans
NY Ref mr, 1674
VanRynsburgh
Martins
Pearson, 1662
VanRyp
Lubberts
LI Source, 1693
VanRys
Hendricks
Rcrd Nam 5, 1664
VanSale
Frans
Tap Ref bp, 1709
Jans
Nicl Lvl, 1672
Rcrd Nam 2, 166

VanSalee
Jans
Ship Lists, 1652
VanSalsbergen
Hendricks
Alb Ref mr, 1693
Nicl Lvl, 1671
Pearson, 1673
Rens Court, 1672
Jans
Alb Ref bp, 1693, 1705, 1707
Alb Ref mr, 1689, 1698
Pearson, 1699
VanSant
Hendricks
King Ref mr, 1701
VanSardam
Adrians
NY Ref mr, 1657
VanSartervelt
Isaacs
LI Source, 1667
VanSchaick
Claas
Alb Ref mm, 1696
Alb Ref mr, 1698
Pearson, 1695, 1696
Cornelis
NYC Court, 1698
Pearson, 1703
Gerrits
Fern Wlls, 1668
Pearson, 1637
Rens Crsp 2, 1661
Ship Lists, 1637, 1652, 1658, no date
Goosens
Pearson, 1681
Sybrants
Pearson, 1686
VanSchalckwyck
Jans
Brgr Frm, 1657
NY Ref bp, 1652, 1657
NY Ref mr, 1652

Surname/Patronymic Combinations

VanSchermer
Claas
NY Ref mr, 1678
Jacobs
Rcrd Nam 3, 1661
VanSchlick
Teunis
Rens Crsp 2, 1683
Ship Lists, 1634
VanSchoenderwoert
Cornelis
Pearson, no date
Gerrits
Pearson, 1642
Jacobs
Pearson, 1636
Ship Lists, 1640
Teunis
Pearson, 1709
VanSchonevelt
Warners
NY Ref mr, 1656
VanSchoondervooert
Cornelis
Ship Lists, 1641
Gerrits
Ship Lists, 1642
Jacobs
NY Ref mr, 1650
Rens Crsp 1, 1661
Ship Lists, 1636
Lawrence
LI Source, 1689
NY Ref bp, 1675
Louwens
King Co, 1670
Michels
NY Ref mr, 1673, 1686, 1689
Teunis
Alb Ref bp, 1709
Alb Ref mm, 1683
VanSchoonhoven
Claas
King Ref bp, 1699
King Ref mr, 1679

Cornelis
NY Ref mr, 1670
Gerrits
Pearson, 1701
Geurts
Pearson, 1700
Hendricks
Pearson, 1681
Ship Lists, 1658
VanSchorel
Jans
Rcrd Nam 1, 1655
VanSchouw
Cornelis
King Co, 1642
VanSchuildert
Goosens
Rcrd Nam 4, 1663
VanSchuttorp
Egberts
NY Ref mr, 1657
VanSchyven
Walters
Hack Ref bp, 1715
VanSechten
Jans
King Co, 1660
VanSevenhuysen
Claas
NY Ref mr, 1659
VanSeventer
Peters
Pearson, 1659
VanSeyl
Stephens
Hack Ref bp, 1695
VanSicklen
Ferdinands
King Co, 1694
Reyners
King Co, 1695
VanSlichtenhorst
Aerts
Pearson, no date
Rens Crsp 1, 1652, 1655
Ship Lists, 1646

VanSluys
Peters
NY Ref mr, 1665
VanSlyck
Claas
Alb Ref mr, 1696
Cornelis
Fern Wlls, 1690
Pearson, 1663
Rens Court, 1668
Peters
Alb Ref mm, 1683
Ship Lists, no date
Teunis
Pearson, 1641, 1661
Rens Crsp 2, 1683
Ship Lists, 1641
Willems
Alb Ref bp, 1688, 1689
Alb Ref mr, 1688, 1690, 1696
Pearson, 1687
VanSoest
Hendricks
Pearson, 1630
VanSoestbergen
Cornelis
Rcrd Nam 4, 1662
VanSpare
Claas
NY Ref bp, 1709
VanSpecherhorn
Jans
Rcrd Nam 1, 1655
VanStarrevelt
Cornelis
King Pap, 1666
VanStAubin
Jans
Rens Crsp 1, 1659
VanStavast
Jans
Rens Court, 1672
VanStavoren
Lennerts
NY Ref mr, 1648

Surname/Patronymic Combinations

VanStBenen
 Wanshaer
  NY Ref bp, 1662
VanSteenberg
 Jans
  King Ref bp, 1699, 1700,
  1701, 1702, 1703, 1704
  King Ref mr, 1683
  Ship Lists, no date
VanSteenwyck
 Alberts
  King Pap, 1663, 1665
 Cornelis
  Berg Ref bp, 1692
 Jacobs
  NY Ref mr, 1642
 Jans
  King Pap, 1664
  King Ref bp, 1689
  Nicl Lvl, 1667
  NY Ref mr, 1654
VanStelyn
 Pels
  Ship Lists, 1642
VanSterrevelt
 Cornelis
  King Pap, 1666
  Pearson, 1657
 Walters
  King Pap, 1666
VanStMarten
 Jans
  NY Ref mr, 1672
VanStObyn
 Jans
  Brgr Frm, 1657
  NY Ref bp, 1658, 1659
  Pearson, 1657
  Rcrd Nam 1, 1654
VanStockholm
 Barents
  NY Ref mr, 1666
 Jans
  Pearson, 1658
 Mathys
  NY Ref mr, 1661

VanStoutenburgh
 Jans
  Anjou Prb, 1671
  King Pap, 1668
  Ship Lists, 1646
VanStrabroeck
 Thomas
  Alb Ref mr, 1658
VanStraetkirk
 Jans
  Brgr Frm, 1657
VanStrapelholm
 Jans
  Gen Entr 1, 1667
VanStruckhausen
 Peters
  Brgr Frm, 1657
VanStTobin
 Jans
  Rens Crsp 1, 1659
VanStuyvesant
 Gerrits
  NY Ref mr, 1699
VanSuermarter
 Jans
  Brgr Frm, 1657
VanSutphin
 Arents
  NY Ref mr, 1659, 1684
 Barents
  Ship Lists, 1687
 Gerrits
  NY Ref mr, 1652, 1664,
  1668
 Hendricks
  NY Ref mr, 1657, 1664
 Jans
  Ship Lists, 1687
VanSwartensluys
 Arents
  NY Ref mr, 1656
VanSweden
 Hans
  Pearson, 1663
VanSwoll
 Andries
  NY Ref mr, 1659

Gerrits
  Bkln Ref bp, 1661
  NY Ref mr, 1658, 1671
  Rcrd Nam 6, 1671
 Jans
  NY Ref mr, 1652
VanTappan
 Roelofs
  Gen Entr 1, 1670
VanTassel
 Cornelis
  King Co, 1670
  NY Ref bp, 1678
  Ship Lists, no date
  Tary Ref bp, 1697
  Tary Ref mm, 1700
VanTeelickhuysen
 Lamberts
  NY Ref mr, 1661
VanTerGoes
 Jans
  Rcrd Nam 3, 1660
VanTerGoude
 Peters
  NY Ref mr, 16462
VanTerIeverlant
 Jans
  Brgr Frm, 1657
VanThresonie
 Andries
  NY Ref mr, 1661
VanThuyl
 Adrians
  NY Ref mr, 1679, 1680
 Aerts
  NY Ref mr, 1682
 Caspars
  NY Ref mr, 1664
 Gerrits
  NY Ref mr, 1667
 Hermans
  Nycol Doc 2, 1661
 Jans
  Fltb Ref bp, 1687, 1688
  LI Source, 1686
  NY Ref mr, 1686
  NYC Wills, 1696

Ottos
  Rcrd Nam 6, 1672
Sanders
  Gen Entr 1, 1664
  Nycol Doc 3, 1664
Teunis
  NY Ref bp, 1661
  NY Ref mr, 1658
VanTilburg
  Jans
    Berg Ref bp, 1691, 1694
    NY Ref bp, 1690, 1692
  Teunis
    Brgr Frm, 1695
    NY Ref bp, 1689, 1694
    NY Ref mr, 1655, 1691
VanTolhuys
  Wessels
    NY Ref mr, 1679
VanToll
  Hans
    Pearson, 1697
VanTonsbergen
  Peters
    NY Ref mr, 1641
VanTricht
  Gerrits
    NY Ref mr, 1660
    Rcrd Nam 3, 1660
VanTserooskerck
  Jans
    NY Ref mr, 1660
VanTurick
  Hermans
    Pearson, 1664
VanTuyl
  Ottos
    Ship Lists, 1663
VanTwerpen
  Daniels
    Pearson, 1720
VanTwiller
  Goosens
    Pearson, 1661
    Ship Lists, no date
VanTyne
  Jans
    NYC Court, 1685

VanUtrecht
  Adrians
    Pearson, 1630
    Ship Lists, 1639
  Hendricks
    Pearson, 1654
  Jacobs
    NY Ref mr, 1662
  Jans
    Brgr Frm, 1657
    NY Ref bp, 1651, 1656,
    1658
    NY Ref mr, 1650
  Lamberts
    NY Ref mr, 1651
  Thomas
    NY Ref mr, 1669
  Wessels
    NY Ref mr, 1656, 1664
VaNuyse
  Jans
    NYC Wills, 1694
VanUytdam
  Jacobs
    NY Ref mr, 1689
VanUythuysen
  Simons
    Bkln Ref mr, 1685
VanUytrecht
  Jans
    NY Ref mr, 1653
  Roelofs
    NY Ref mr, 1653
VanVaerden
  Peters
    Brgr Frm, 1702
VanValkenburgh
  Jochems
    Alb Ref bp, 1693, 1708
    Alb Ref mr, 1693, 1698
    Pearson, 1693
    Ship Lists, no date
  Lamberts
    Alb Ref bp, 1702
    Pearson, 1683
VanVechten
  Arents
    Fltb Ref bp, 1680

    King Co, 1660
    Ship Lists, 1660, no date
  Claas
    King Co, 1682
  Cornelis
    Alb Ref bp, 1709
    Alb Ref mm, 1698
    Pearson, 1709
    Rens Court, 1669
    Ship Lists, 1637, 1638, no
    date
  Dirks
    Alb Ref bp, 1690, 1701,
    1703, 1704, 1705
    Alb Ref mm, 1683
    Berg Ref bp, 1707
    Pearson, 1699
    Rens Court, 1668
    Rens Crsp 1, 1659, 1660
    Rens Crsp 2, 1683
    Ship Lists, 1638, 1640
  Gerrits
    Alb Ref mm, 1683, 1692
    Pearson, 1683
  Teunis
    Alb Ref bp, 1690, 1692,
    1701
    Alb Ref mm, 1683
    Alb Ref mr, 1689
    Fern Wlls, 1687, 1701
    Pearson, 1669
    Rens Court, 1668, 1670
    Rens Crsp 1, 1668
    Rens Crsp 2, 1680, 1683,
    1687, 1688
  Volkerts
    Pearson, 1747
VanVee
  Hertgers
    Ship Lists, 1645

  Hertgerts
    Pearson, 1645
VanVeere
  Adrians
    Ship Lists, 1631

Surname/Patronymic Combinations

VanVees
  Jans
    Rcrd Nam 1, 1654
VanVelde
  Teunis
    Ship Lists, 1645
VanVelsen
  Philips
    Rens Crsp 1, 1659
  Teunis
    Pearson, 1664
VanVelthuysen
  Philips
    Rens Crsp 1, 1654
VanVenlo
  Dirks
    Rcrd Nam 5, 1664
VanVerduym
  Latyns
    Ship Lists, 1636
VanVespen
  Cornelis
    Pearson, 1671
VanVessen
  Teunis
    King Pap, 1664, 1665
VanVianen
  Abrams
    NY Ref mr, 1666
VanVlecher
  Roelofs
    NY Ref mr, 1665
VanVlecheren
  Lawrence
    Rcrd Nam 4, 1663
VanVleckburgh
  Christians
    Pearson, 1636
VanVleckenstine
  Jacobs
    NY Ref bp, 1673
VanVliet
  Adrians
    King Ref bp, 1679
  Aerts
    King Ref bp, 1695
  Dirks
    Fltb Ref bp, 1684

    Fltb Ref mr, 1683, 1687
    LI Source, no date
    Ship Lists, 1687
  Gerrits
    King Pap, 1663
  Jans
    Fltb Ref bp, 1678
    Ship Lists, 1687
VanVlissingen
  Adrians
    NY Ref mr, 1703
  Cornelis
    NY Ref mr, 1687
  Huberts
    NY Ref mr, 1690
  Jans
    NY Ref bp, 1644
    NY Ref mr, 1640, 1664,
    1674, 1679, 1684, 1696
VanVogsten
  Jans
    Berg Ref bp, 1673
VanVollenhoo
  Jans
    King Pap, 1667
VanVollenhoven
  Jans
    NY Ref bp, 1668
VanVoorden
  Jans
    NY Ref mr, 1654
VanVoorhees
  Alberts
    Hack Ref mm, page xx
    Hack Ref mr, 1721
  Coert
    Fltb Ref bp, 1690
  Coerts
    Ship Lists, 1660, no date
  Court
    Ship Lists, 1687
  Courts
    Ship Lists, 1687
  Lucas
    Fltb Ref bp, 1680
  Mynderts
    Fltb Ref bp, 1690

  Stephens
    Fltb Ref bp, 1678, 1680,
    1681, 1682, 1683, 1684,
    1685, 1687
    Fltb Ref mr, 1678, 1680,
    1681
    LI Source, no date
    Ship Lists, 1687
VanVoorhout
  Cornelis
    NY Ref mr, 1649
    Pearson, 1642
    Rens Court, 1658
    Rens Crsp 1, 1659, 1660,
    1664, 1668
    Rens Crsp 2, 1683
    Ship Lists, 1644
  Segers
    Fern Wlls, 1663
    Pearson, 1642
    Rens Court, 1670
    Rens Crsp 1, 1656
    Rens Crsp 2, 1683
    Ship Lists, 1642, 1644, no
    date
VanVoorn
  Peters
    NY Ref mr, 1706
VanVoorsthuysen
  Hermans
    NY Ref mr, 1660
  Teunis
    NY Ref mr, 1659
VanVoren
  Jans
    NY Ref bp, 1671
VanVorst
  Cornelis
    NY Ref bp, 1670, 1684
    NY Ref mr, 1652, 1656
    Nycol Doc 2, 1663
    Rcrd Nam 1, 1653
  Gerrits
    Alb Ref bp, 1689
    NY Ref bp, 1662
    NY Ref mr, 1662
    Pearson, 1671
    Rcrd Nam 4, 1662

Surname/Patronymic Combinations

Ides
  NY Ref bp, 1687, 1689
  Tap Ref bp, 1705
VanVranken
  Claas
    Pearson, 1684
  Gerrits
    Pearson, 1705
  Richards
    Pearson, no date
VanVredenburgh
  Isaacs
    NY Ref bp, 1667
    Ship Lists, no date
VanVreeland
  Jacobs
    NY Ref mr, 1642
VanVrieslant
  Gerrits
    Brgr Frm, 1657
VanWaalwyck
  Jans
    Ship Lists, 1642
VanWaerdenbroeck
  Hendricks
    NY Ref mr, 1654
VanWagenen
  Aerts
    King Ref bp, 1702
  Gerrits
    Berg Ref bp, 1710
    Berg Ref mr, 1710
    Hack Ref bp, 1718
  Hendricks
    Hack Ref mr, 1721
  Jacobs
    King Ref bp, 1710
    Ship Lists, no date
VanWarbeer
  Cornelis
    NY Ref mr, 1656
VanWarlwyck
  Jans
    Pearson, 16462
VanWayen
  Hendricks
    King Ref mr, 1684

VanWeeckendam
  Jans
    Rcrd Nam 3, 1659
VanWeely
  Thomas
    Rens Crsp 1, 1657
VanWeenen
  Sickels
    Pearson, 1659
VanWel
  Cornelis
    Brgr Frm, 1657
VanWely
  Thomas
    Rens Crsp 1, 1654
VanWensveen
  Cornelis
    NY Ref mr, 1646
VanWerckendam
  Bastians
    NY Ref mr, 1668
  Jans
    NY Ref bp, 1666
    NY Ref mr, 1653
VanWeryen
  Barents
    NY Ref mr, 1661
VanWesepe
  Cornelis
    Ship Lists, 1645
VanWesop
  Rogers
    NY Ref mr, 1672, 1673
  Teunis
    NY Ref mr, 1661
VanWesp
  Cornelis
    Pearson, 1645
VanWessel
  Lubberts
    Orphan Mst, 1664, 1665
VanWessen
  Wessels
    NY Ref mr, 1670
VanWestbroeck
  Teunis
    Pearson, 1663

    Rens Court, 1668
    Ship Lists, 1631
VanWesten
  Cornelis
    LI Source, 1690
VanWesterhout
  Jans
    King Co, 1664
    NY Ref mr, 1664
VanWestervelt
  Jans
    King Co, 1664
  Willems
    King Co, 1697
    LI Source, 1697
VanWestroos
  Andries
    NY Ref mr, 1655
VanWestveen
  Cornelis
    NY Ref bp, 1681
  Dirks
    Nycol Doc 2, 1674
    Rcrd Nam 6, 1672
VanWey
  Gerrits
    Pearson, 1689
  Hendricks
    King Pap, 1665
    Pearson, 1700, 1704
  Jans
    Pearson, 1682
VanWickelen
  Jans
    King Co, 1664
    Ship Lists, 1687
  Willems
    Fltb Ref bp, 1709
VanWien
  Jans
    Rcrd Nam 6, 1671
VanWinckel
  Jacobs
    Berg Ref bp, 1686, 1688,
    1689, 1690, 1692, 1696
    Berg Ref dt, 1692, 1708
    Berg Ref mm, 1676, 1677,
    1704

Surname/Patronymic Combinations

VanWinckel (cont.)
Jacobs (cont.)
Berg Ref mr, 1671, 1675,
1676, 1695, 1699, 1703,
1710
Hack Ref bp, 1702, 1705,
1718
Hack Ref mm, 1696
Hack Ref mr, 1703, 1712
NY Ref bp, 1686
NY Ref mr, 1676, 1707
Simons
Berg Ref mr, 1701
Hack Ref bp, 1702, 1709,
1711, 1712, 1714
Hack Ref mr, 1697, 1700,
1704, 1705, 1706, 1708, 1721
Walings
Berg Ref mr, 1710
Hack Ref bp, 1699
Hack Ref mr, 1710
Ship Lists, no date
VanWitmont
Hermans
NY Ref mr, 1652
Jans
NY Ref mr, 1674
Joost
NY Ref mr, 1658
VanWoert
Claas
Pearson, 1736
Jacobs
Pearson, 1636
Ship Lists, no date
Teunis
Alb Ref bp, 1704
VanWoggelom
Peters
Fern Wlls, 1682
Pearson, 1671, 1682
VanWoggeum
Adrians
Pearson, 1638
VanWolphen
Martins
Rens Crsp 1, 1663, 1664,
1668

VanWorcum
Gerrits
NY Ref mr, 1660
VanWorden
Jans
Hack Ref bp, 1712
VanWormer
Jans
NY Ref mr, 1666
VanWoutbergh
Willems
Pearson, 1677
VanWreede
Andries
NY Ref mr, 1654
VanWurmdrink
Lawrence
Pearson, 1709
VanWyck
Barents
Fltb Ref bp, 1679, 1682,
1688
King Co, 1660
LI Source, 1660, 1684
Ship Lists, 1687, no date
Stephens
NY Ref mr, 1642
VanWytert
Jans
Pearson, 1657
VanYsendyck
Jans
NY Ref mr, 1654
VanZant
Jans
Pearson, 1753
Wenzels
Ship Lists, no date
VanZeeland
Jans
Gen Entr 1, 1670
VanZell
Teunis
NY Ref mr, 1654
VanZuydtlandt
Jans
NY Ref mr, 1659

VanZyl
Stephens
NY Ref bp, 1692
Varvanger
Hendricks
Brgr Frm, 1657
Nycol Doc 2, 1664
Pearson, 1661
Rcrd Nam 1, 1653
Rens Court, 1670
Vechten
Arents
Fltb Ref bp, 1684
LI Source, 1660, no date
Ship Lists, 1687
Claas
Bkln Ref bp, 1687, 1693,
1694, 1697
Fltb Ref bp, 1684
Fltb Ref mr, 1680, 1682
LI Source, 1680, 1689,
1693, 1696
Vedam
Timothys
Pearson, 1636
Vedder
Alberts
Pearson, 1659
Rens Crsp 1, 1658
Ship Lists, 1657
Arents
Pearson, 1715
Gerrits
Schn Ref mr, 1715
Simons
Alb Ref bp, 1709
Pearson, 1699
Schn Ref bp, 1704, 1706
Schn Ref mr, 1704
Volkerts
Fern Wlls, 1697
Pearson, 1654
Veeltje
Peters
Ship Lists, 1637

Surname/Patronymic Combinations

Veerman
  Jans
    Fltb Ref bp, 1681, 1682,
      1687
    NY Ref bp, 1677
Velthuysen
  Philips
    King Co, 1655
    Pearson, 1654
    Rens Crsp 1, 1654
Verbeeck
  Christophs
    Nycol Doc 2, 1657
  Jans
    Ship Lists, 1663
Verbraeck
  Hendricks
    Pearson, 1668
VerBrugh
  Andries
    King Pap, 1666
  Giles
    Rcrd Nam 1, 1653
  Jans
    NY Ref bp, 1691
  Peters
    NY Ref mr, 1658
    Rcrd Nam 1, 1653
    Rens Crsp 1, 1657, 1658
Verdon
  Jacobs
    King Co, 1682
Verdonck
  Andries
    NY Ref bp, 1667
VerDuyn
  Jacobs
    NY Ref bp, 1689, 1691,
      1694
  Latyns
    Pearson, 1636
Verhulst
  Peters
    King Co, 1676

VerKerck
  Jans
    Bkln Ref bp, 1682
    Fltb Ref bp, 1682
    Fltb Ref mr, 1681
    LI Source, 1663
Verkerken
  Jans
    King Co, 1655
  Roelofs
    King Co, 1680
Vermeulen
  Arents
    King Pap, 1665
  Teunis
    Ship Lists, 1659
Vernoy
  Cornelis
    King Pap, 1664
    King Ref bp, 1665, 1666,
      1667
    Pearson, 1667
    Ship Lists, 1663
VerPlanck
  Isaacs
    Pearson, 1667
    Ship Lists, 1633
Verryn
  Jans
    Crt Assz, 1665
    Gen Entr 1, 1664
    King Co, 1659
    Nicl Lvl, 1672
    Rcrd Nam 3, 1659
VerSchieur
  Gilberts
    Fltb Ref bp, 1682
    King Co, 1649
    NY Ref bp, 1688
    Ship Lists, 1687
  Walters
    Bkln Ref bp, 1688
Vertein
  Willems
    King Co, 1661
Verwen
  Gerrits
    Ship Lists, 1663

  Jans
    Ship Lists, 1663
Verwey
  Cornelis
    Hack Ref mr, 1707
    Ship Lists, no date
  Gerrits
    Alb Ref bp, 1689
    Alb Ref mr, 1692
    Pearson, 1689
  Hendricks
    Alb Ref mr, 1698
    King Pap, 1665
    Rcrd Nam 6, 1670
  Teunis
    Alb Ref bp, 1694
    Pearson, 1694
Viele
  Arents
    NY Ref mr, 1688
  Arnouts
    Alb Ref bp, 1699
    Alb Ref mm, 1699
    Pearson, 1699
  Cornelis
    Alb Ref bp, 1689
    Alb Ref mm, 1683
    Gen Entr 1, 1671
    Nycol Doc 3, 1682
    Pearson, 1661
    Rens Court, 1668, 1669,
      1671, 1672
    Ship Lists, no date
  Gerrits
    Alb Ref bp, 1684
Vielen
  Cornelis
    Rens Court, 1670
Viervant
  Arents
    King Ref mr, 1668
Villet
  Gangeloffe
    King Co, no date
Vin
  Jans
    NY Ref bp, 1679

Surname/Patronymic Combinations

Vinhagen
  Dirks
    Pearson, 1663
    Ship Lists, 1653, 1669
Vis
  Jacobs
    King Co, 1689
Vischer
  Bastians
    Alb Ref bp, 1703
    Alb Ref mm, 1683
    Pearson, 1675
    Ship Lists, 1644
  Everts
    Rcrd Nam 6, 1670
  Gangolfs
    Nicl Lvl, 1664
    NY Ref mr, 1659
    Orphan Mst, 1664
    Rcrd Nam 2, 1658
  Hermans
    Alb Ref bp, 1689, 1696,
      1699, 1700, 1701, 1702,
      1703, 1704, 1705, 1706,
      1708
    Alb Ref mm, 1683
    Alb Ref mr, 1686, 1692
    King Ref mr, 1695
    Pearson, 1701
  Jans
    Rcrd Nam 3, 1660
Vissenburg
  Damens
    Ship Lists, 1641
Viveren
  Barents
    Pearson, no date
Vlas
  Cornelis
    Pearson, 1681
Vlierboom
  Mathys
    Tap Ref bp, 1706
Voe
  Louis
    Fltb Ref mr, 1689

Vogel
  Arents
    King Pap, 1667
  Cornelis
    King Pap, 1665, 1666
    Rcrd Nam 3, 1661
Vogelsang
  Hendricks
    Rcrd Nam 1, 1655
Volck
  Hendricks
    Berg Ref bp, 1692
  Hieronymus
    Nycol Doc 5, 1708
Volckert
  Jans
    NY Ref mr, 1682
Vonck
  Jans
    Rcrd Nam 1, 1653
Voorhees
  Coertes
    King Co, 1687
  Gerrits
    King Co, 1695
  Jans
    King Co, 1679
  Lucas
    King Co, 1698
  Stephens
    Hack Ref mm, 1686
    King Co, 1660
Vosburgh
  Abrams
    Pearson, 1665
  Cornelis
    Pearson, 1683
  Jacobs
    Pearson, 1657
  Peters
    Alb Ref mm, 1683
    King Pap, 1665
    Pearson, 1653
    Rens Crsp 1, 1659
    Ship Lists, 1649
Vosje
  Cornelis
    Pearson, no date

Voss
  Barents
    King Pap, 1664
    King Pap, 1661
  Cornelis
    Alb Ref bp, 1683
    Rens Crsp 1, 1652
    Ship Lists, 1640
  Dirks
    Ship Lists, 1661
  Jans
    NY Ref mr, 1671
  Thomas
    Evjen, 1711
Vredenburg
  Isaacs
    NY Ref mr, 1664
  Jans
    NY Ref bp, 1665
Vreeland
  Cornelis
    Berg Ref bp, 1704
    Berg Ref mr, 1701, 1709
    Hack Ref mr, 1712
    NY Ref mr, 1709
  Elias
    Berg Ref bp, 1701
    Hack Ref mr, 1700, 1703
    NY Ref mr, 1689
  Enochs
    Hack Ref bp, 1696
  Enoyse
    Hack Ref mr, 1706
  Hartmans
    Berg Ref bp, 1710
    Berg Ref dt, 1692, 1697
    Berg Ref mr, 1697, 1699,
      1701, 1708
    Hack Ref bp, 1711
  Hermans
    Berg Ref bp, 1698, 1709
  Jacobs
    Ship Lists, 1633
  Jans
    Berg Ref dt, 1697
    Ship Lists, no date

Michels
  Berg Ref bp, 1685, 1686,
  1687, 1690, 1691, 1692,
  1693, 1694, 1698, 1705,
  1707, 1708, 1710
  Berg Ref dt, 1668, 1675,
  1682, 1683, 1688, 1690,
  1692, 1697, 1707, 1708,
  1710
  Berg Ref mr, 1670, 1681,
  1682, 1691
  Hack Ref bp, 1702, 1710
  NY Ref bp, 1677, 1678
  NY Ref mr, 1691
Vries
  Dirks
    Rens Court, 1669
  Gerrits
    Brgr Frm, 1657
  Jacobs
    Rcrd Nam 4, 1662
    Rens Crsp 1, 1663, 1664
Vroom
  Cornelis
    Fltb Ref bp, 1681
    King Co, 1645
  Corsen
    Bkln Ref bp, 1681
    Fltb Ref bp, 1680
    LI Source, 1689
  Jacobs
    Bkln Ref bp, 1681
  Peters
    King Co, 1645
    LI Source, no date
    Ship Lists, 1645
Vrooman
  Bartholomeus
    Alb Ref bp, 1686
    Alb Ref mm, 1683
    Alb Ref mr, 1685, 1690
    Fern Wlls, 1691
    Gen Entr 2, 1686
    Pearson, 1670
    Rens Court, 1669, 1670, 1672
  Claas
    Alb Ref bp, 1686

Hendricks
  Alb Ref mr, 1686
  Fltb Ref bp, 1683
  King Co, 1677
  Pearson, 1683
Jans
  Pearson, 1706
  Schn Ref mr, 1716
Peters
  Fern Wlls, 1684
  Pearson, 1684
Vryman
  Claas
    Pearson, 1654
Vyselaer
  Cornelis
    Pearson, 1660
    Rens Court, 1669, 1670,
    1671, 1672, 1673
    Rens Crsp 2, 1678

W

Waert
  Cornelis
    Ship Lists, 1639
  Ides
    NY Ref bp, 1657
Wageman
  Giles
    Rcrd Nam 1, 1654
Wagenaar
  Aerts
    Pearson, 1642
    Ship Lists, 1639, 1642
Waltman
  Philips
    NY Ref mr, 1674
Wanshaer
  Jans
    NY Ref bp, 1659
Want
  Peters
    NY Ref bp, 1688

Wantenaar
  Cornelis
    King Co, 1662
    NY Ref bp, 1651, 1653,
    1654
    Nycol Doc 2, 1665
    Rcrd Nam 1, 1655
Waterhout
  Dirks
    Rcrd Nam 1, 1655
Weaver
  Hermans
    Pearson, 1678
  Jans
    Rcrd Nam 6, 1667
  Martins
    Pearson, 1689
Wee
  Willems
    NYC Wills, 1667
Weendorp
  Hermans
    Pearson, 1663
Weesp
  Jacobs
    Rcrd Nam 2, 1658
Welckinghoff
  Jans
    Ship Lists, 1650
Weltman
  Peters
    Gen Entr 2, 1676
Wemp
  Barents
    King Pap, 1664
    Pearson, 1645
    Rcrd Nam 3, 1660
    Rens Court, 1669
    Rens Crsp 1, 1659, 1660,
    1661, 1664, 1668
    Ship Lists, 1643, 1645,
    1660
  Jans
    Pearson, 1663
    Mynderts

Surname/Patronymic Combinations

Wemp
 Jans
  Fern Wlls, 1664
  Pearson, 1699
Wendel
 Everts
  Pearson, 1690
 Jacobs
  Pearson, 1749
 Jans
  Pearson, 1658, 1691
  Ship Lists, 1642, 1644
Werckhoven
 Bastians
  NY Ref mr, 1665
Wesop
 Cornelis
  Pearson, 1667
Westbroeck
 Jans
  King Co, 1661
  Rens Court, 1668
Westercamp
 Alberts
  Rcrd Nam 1, 1653
 Hendricks
  King Pap, 1662, 1665
  King Ref bp, 1662
  King Ref mr, 1664
 Jans
  Pearson, 1667
  Ship Lists, 1648
Westerhout
 Jans
  Nycol Doc 2, 1673
  West Wills, 1723
 Thompsons
  NYC Wills, 1694
Westervelt
 Jurians
  Hack Ref bp, 1719, 1720
  Hack Ref mr, 1718
 Lubberts
  Berg Ref mr, 1688
  Hack Ref bp, 1709, 1712,
   1718, 1720
  Hack Ref mm, 1687

 Hack Ref mr, 1704, 1707,
  1709
 NY Ref mr, 1688
 Ship Lists, no date
 Roelofs
  Hack Ref bp, 1715, 1718,
   1719, 1720
  Hack Ref mr, 1710
Westfall
 Jurians
  King Pap, 1673, 1674
  King Ref mr, 1683
Weyt
 Barents
  Ship Lists, 1649
Whitbeck
 Andries
  Alb Ref bp, 1706
  Alb Ref mm, 1683
  Pearson, 1683
 Jans
  Alb Ref bp, 1700, 1702,
   1703, 1707
  Alb Ref mm, 1692
  Pearson, 1683
 Thomas
  Rens Court, 1669
  Rens Crsp 1, 1658
  Ship Lists, no date
Wielen
 Adrians
  Nycol Doc 1, 1645
Williams
 Abrams
  Fltb Ref bp, 1683
Wils
 Hendricks
  Bkln Ref bp, 1693
Wiltbank
 Fredericks
  Gen Entr 1, 1669
Wiltkock
 Peters
  Rcrd Nam 2, 1658
Wiltse
 Hendricks
  Fltb Ref mr, 1690

Martins
 Evjen, 1660
 NY Ref bp, 1701
Wimp
 Jans
  Alb Ref bp, 1684
Winckelhoek
 Jans
  Rcrd Nam 2, 1656
Winne
 Caspars
  Pearson, 1783
 Peters
  Rens Court, 1671, 1672
Winnen
 Peters
  Pearson, 1684
 Schermerhorn
  Alb Ref mm, 1683
Wipp
 Claas
  NY Ref mr, 1675
 Cornelis
  Rens Crsp 1, 1660
Wisselpenny
 Reinerse
  Hack Ref mm, 1686
 Reyners
  Fltb Ref bp, 1679, 1681
  Fltb Ref mr, 1678, 1680,
   1681
  LI Source, 1680
Witt
 Alberts
  NY Ref bp, 1661
 Jans
  NY Ref bp, 1652
  Nycol Doc 2, 1665
  Rcrd Nam 2, 1656
Witzen
 Jacobs
  Nycol Doc 1, 1614
 Jans
  Nycol Doc 2, 1657
Woertendyke
 Jacobs
  NY Ref mr, 1709, 1710

84

Woertman
  Dirks
    Berg Ref bp, 1691
    Bkln Ref bp, 1710
    King Co, 1678
    LI Source, 1695
  Hans
    LI Source, 1685
  Jans
    Bkln Ref bp, 1684, 1686,
      1693, 1696
    Bkln Ref mr, 1691
    Fltb Ref bp, 1684
    King Co, 1647
    LI Source, 1671, 1679,
      1684, 1687, 1689, 1691,
      1692, 1694, 1695
    Nicl Lvl, 1672
    Ship Lists, 1687
Wolf
  Jacobs
    Bkln Ref bp, 1678
    Fltb Ref bp, 1678
    King Co, 1666
Wolffenbuttel
  Christians
    NY Ref mr, 1660
Wolwesen
  Jans
    King Co, 1680
Wyckoff
  Claas
    Fltb Ref bp, 1679, 1680,
      1681, 1683, 1684
    King Co, 1679
    Ship Lists, 1636, 1687
  Cornelis
    King Co, 1685
  Peters
    Fltb Ref bp, 1679, 1680,
      1681, 1682, 1683, 1684,
      1685, 1688
    Fltb Ref mr, 1678, 1683
    King Co, 1677
    LI Fam 1, 1679
    LI Source, 1678
    NYC Wills, 1697
    Ship Lists, 1687

Wyngaerden
  Jacobs
    NY Ref mr, 1665
Wyngart
  Gerrits
    Alb Ref bp, 1703
    Pearson, 1670
    Rens Crsp 2, 1689
  Jans
    Pearson, 1726
  Lucas
    Alb Ref bp, 1695, 1700,
      1701, 1703, 1704, 1705,
      1706, 1708, 1710
    Alb Ref mr, 1694, 1695
    Fern Wlls, 1690
    Pearson, 1700
Wynhard
  Hendricks
    Fltb Ref bp, 1684
Wynkoop
  Everts
    Ship Lists, 1651, no date
Wytenhoff
  Alberts
    Pearson, 1663
WytStraat
  Jans
    Rcrd Nam 4, 1662

Y

Yansz
  Hendricks
    Rens Crsp 1, 1658
Yanzen
  Stavast
    Nycol Doc 3, 1664
Yolcx
  Hendricks
    King Co, 1692
    NY Ref mr, 1692
Yoncker
  Jans
    Pearson, 1703

Z

Zabriskie
  Jacobs
    Hack Ref bp, 1718
Zeeuw
  Cornelis
    LI Source, 1695
Zeewis
  Horns
    King Co, 1661
Zerbe
  Philips
    NY Lth mr, 1710
Zip
  Adrians
    Berg Ref bp, 1678, 1680,
      1681, 1682, 1683, 1684,
      1685, 1686, 1689, 1691,
      1694, 1695, 1708
    Berg Ref dt, 1691
    Berg Ref mm, 1666
    Berg Ref mr, 1675, 1678,
      1684
    Hack Ref bp, 1696
    NY Ref bp, 1686, 1687,
      1690, 1693, 1694, 1697
    NY Ref mr, 1684
  Hendricks
    NY Ref mr, 1656
Zuyck
  Arents
    Nycol Doc 1, 1650
Zwollang
  Emmens
    Nycol Doc 1, 1655

Table 1B
Patronymic/Surname Combinations

A

Abels
  Goewey
    Ship Lists, no date
  Riddenhaas
    Alb Ref bp, 1684
    Alb Ref mr, 1692
    Pearson, 1680
    Ship Lists, no date
  Riddershalve
    Pearson, 1680
Abrams
  Ackerman
    Hack Ref bp, 1711, 1718, 1719, 1720
    Hack Ref mm, 1710
    Hack Ref mr, 1712
  Blauvelt
    Hack Ref bp, 1718
  Brinckerhoff
    Fltb Ref bp, 1685
    King Co, 1677
  Cock
    NY Ref mr, 1682
  Cooper
    Pearson, 1665
  Klock
    Fltb Ref bp, 1679, 1681
    NY Ref mr, 1682
  Lansing
    Pearson, 1728
  Lent
    West Wills, 1720
  Maul
    NY Ref mr, 1682
  Rycke
    NY Ref mr, 1681
  Sandfort
    Ship Lists, 1661

  Santvoort
    NY Ref bp, 1672
    NY Ref mr, 1677
    Rcrd Nam 7, 1674
    Ship Lists, 1661
  Schuyler
    Pearson, 1709
  Tietsoort
    Pearson, 1686
  VanBedford
    NY Ref mr, 1705
  VanBoren
    NY Ref mr, 1666
  VanDerBorden
    Nycol Doc 3, 1664
    Rcrd Nam 4, 1662
  Vanderheul
    NY Ref mr, 1682
  VanDeusen
    Alb Ref bp, 1685, 1708
    NY Ref bp, 1667, 1669, 1672, 1677, 1678, 1684, 1695
    NY Ref mr, 1666
    Pearson, 1700
    Ship Lists, 1657, 1663
  VanDeyl
    NY Ref mr, 1665
  VanEuchuysen
    NY Ref bp, 1644
  VanLent
    Tary Ref bp, 1699
  VanVianen
    NY Ref mr, 1666
  Vosburgh
    Pearson, 1665
  Williams
    Fltb Ref bp, 1683

Adams
  Brower
    Fltb Ref bp, 1678, 1680, 1681
    King Co, 1692
  Dingman
    Pearson, 1700
  Kerckoven
    Fltb Ref mr, 1690
  Metselaer
    NY Ref bp, 1658, 1661, 1674, 1691
    NYC Wills, 1695
Adolfs
  Artopejus
    NY Lth bp, 1710
  DeGroot
    NYC Wills, 1696
  Hoorn
    NY Ref mr, 1689
  Hoppe
    Berg Ref bp, 1684
    Berg Ref mr, 1683
    NY Ref mr, 1683
  VanDerGrift
    NY Ref bp, 1681
Adrians
  Bennet
    Bkln Ref mr, 1685, 1696
    Fltb Ref bp, 1683
    Fltb Ref mr, 1685
    King Co, 1702
    LI Fam 1, 1620
  DeBruyn
    Ship Lists, 1663
  DeRuyter
    Gen Entr 1, 1665
    Nicl Lvl, 1665
    Nycol Doc 2, 1664

Adrians (cont.)
  DeYoung
    King Ref bp, 1682
  Gemakelyck
    Pearson, 1681
  Hegeman
    King Co, 1688
  Knevelaar
    Nycol Doc 2, 1661
  Mackelyck
    Rens Court, 1670
    Ship Lists, 1655
  Molenaer
    LI Fam 2, 1660
    NY Ref mr, 1681
  Onderdonk
    Fltb Ref bp, 1684
    Fltb Ref mr, 1683
  Rademacker
    Ship Lists, 1644
  Raedemacker
    Pearson, 1653
  Smith
    Tap Ref bp, 1703, 1706, 1709
  Soogemakelyck
    Pearson, 1638
    Rens Crsp 1, 1664, 1668
    Ship Lists, 1655
  Timmerman
    NY Ref bp, 1662
  VanAchterkol
    NY Ref mr, 1695
  VanBreda
    NY Ref mr, 1673
  VanBunick
    Pearson, 1638
    Ship Lists, 1638
  Vandermeulen
    Anjou Prb, 1665
  VanDerVliet
    King Ref bp, 1663, 1681
  VanDuyvelandt
    NY Ref bp, 1658, 1662, 1664
  VanDuyvelant
    Ship Lists, 1658
  VanPynacker
    NY Ref mr, 1663

VanSardam
    NY Ref mr, 1657
VanThuyl
    NY Ref mr, 1679, 1680
VanUtrecht
    Pearson, 1630
    Ship Lists, 1639
VanVeere
    Ship Lists, 1631
VanVliet
    King Ref bp, 1679
VanVlissingen
    NY Ref mr, 1703
VanWoggeum
    Pearson, 1638
Wielen
    Nycol Doc 1, 1645
Zip
    Berg Ref bp, 1678, 1680, 1681, 1682, 1683, 1684, 1685, 1686, 1689, 1691, 1694, 1695, 1708
    Berg Ref dt, 1691
    Berg Ref mm, 1666
    Berg Ref mr, 1675, 1678, 1684
    Hack Ref bp, 1696
    NY Ref bp, 1686, 1687, 1690, 1693, 1694, 1697
    NY Ref mr, 1684

Aerts
  Bruyn
    NY Ref bp, 1674
  Fynhoudt
    King Pap, 1667
  Fynhout
    King Pap, 1667
  Jacobsen
    King Pap, 1663
  Lanen
    LI Source, 1696
  Middagh
    Fltb Ref mr, 1691
    King Co, 1685
    King Ref bp, 1696
    Ship Lists, 1687
  Nieuwhoff
    Rcrd Nam 3, 1658

Otterspoor
    Anjou Prb, 1678
Arents
    King Pap, 1662
    Ship Lists, 1649
Smithing
Gerrits
    King Co, 1687
    King Pap, 1662
Snedeker
Tack
    King Ref bp, 1682, 1683
TerHaert
    Fltb Ref mr, 1691
Van Pelt
    LI Source, 1696
VanBergen
    Pearson, 1677
VanDerBaest
    Pearson, 1670
Vanderbilt
    Berg Ref bp, 1685, 1686
    Berg Ref dt, 1705
    Berg Ref mm, 1682
    Berg Ref mr, 1681
    King Co, 1693
    Rcrd Nam 1, 1653
    Ship Lists, 1640, no date
VanDerHard
    Fltb Ref bp, 1682
    Fltb Ref mr, 1680
    King Co, 1680
Vanderhorst
    NY Ref bp, 1686
VanNewkirk
    Pearson, 1660
VanNieuwhof
    Rcrd Nam 2, 1658
VanPelt
    King Co, 1696
VanRossem
    King Co, 1643
VanSlichtenhorst
    Pearson, no date
    Rens Crsp 1, 1652, 1655
    Ship Lists, 1646, no date
VanThuyl
    NY Ref mr, 1682

Patronymic/Surname Combinations

VanVliet
  King Ref bp, 1695
VanWagenen
  King Ref bp, 1702
Wagenaar
  Ship Lists, 1639, 1642
Wagennaar
  Pearson, 1642
Aesen
  DeHart
    King Co, 1664
Ahasueruse
  Roseboom
    Pearson, 1749
Alberts
  Backer
    King Pap, 1664
  Bradt
    Rens Crsp 1, 1657
  Bratt
    Alb Ref bp, 1684, 1686,
    1687, 1694
    Alb Ref mr, 1684
    Pearson, 1674
    Rens Court, 1673
  DeGraw
    NY Ref bp, 1682, 1699
    NY Ref mr, 1683
  DeSweedt
    Pearson, 1674
  DeWitt
    NY Ref bp, 1662, 1663
  Glaser
    NY Ref mr, 1659
  Kieft
    Nycol Doc 2, 1661
  Planck
    Pearson, 1634
    Rens Crsp 1, 1659
    Ship Lists, 1634
  Roosa
    King Pap, 1665
    King Ref bp, 1679, 1682
    NY Ref bp, 1678
  Scheuwen
    NY Ref bp, 1658
  Slingerland
    Pearson, 1725

Stoothoff
  Bkln Ref bp, 1677
  Fltb Ref bp, 1678, 1679,
  1680, 1681, 1682, 1683,
  1684, 1686
  King Co, 1620
  LI Fam 1, 1686
  LI Source, 1695
  Rens Crsp 2, 1683
  Ship Lists, 1632, 1687
Terhune
  Berg Ref bp, 1690
  Fltb Ref bp, 1681, 1683,
  1685, 1686
  Fltb Ref mr, 1691
  Gen Entr 2, 1681
  Hack Ref bp, 1706
  Hack Ref mm, 1689
  Hack Ref mr, 1699
  King Co, 1662
  LI Fam 2, 1654
  LI Source, 1651, 1687,
  1694, 1696, 1697
  Rcrd Nam 5, 1664
  Ship Lists, 1687, no date
Van Londen
  Evjen, 1639
VanDenUythoff
  Pearson, 1663
  Rens Crsp 1, 1660, 1661
VanDerGouw
  Ship Lists, 1651
VanDerZee
  Pearson, 1663
  Rens Court, 1670
VanEmbderlant
  NY Ref mr, 1657
VanMunichendam
  Pearson, 1654
VanNeck
  King Ref bp, 1663
  Nicl Lvl, 1669
  Pearson, 1659
  Rcrd Nam 4, 1662
VanNewkirk
  NY Ref mr, 1645
VanSteenwyck
  King Pap, 1663, 1665

VanVoorhees
  Hack Ref mm, page xx
  Hack Ref mr, 1721
Vedder
  Pearson, 1659
  Rens Crsp 1, 1658
  Ship Lists, 1657
Westercamp
  Rcrd Nam 1, 1653
Witt
  NY Ref bp, 1661
Wytenhoff
  Pearson, 1663
Alderts
  Brower
    Evjen, 1656
  Groen
    NY Ref mr, 1665
  Paradys
    NY Ref bp, 1655
    NY Ref mr, 1655
  Roosa
    King Ref bp, 1679, 1692
Anderson
  DeGraef
    King Co, 1660
Andries
  Bardt
    Ship Lists, 1637
  Bradt
    Rens Crsp 1, 1658, 1659
  Bratt
    Pearson, 1630
    Rens Court, 1669, 1670
    Ship Lists, 1630, no date
  Casparus
    Pearson, 1700
  Cooper
    Pearson, 1646
  DeDrayer
    Rcrd Nam 2, 1656
  DeGraaf
    Pearson, 1682
  DeGraef
    Rens Court, 1668
  DeGraff
    Rcrd Nam 3, 1659

Patronymic/Surname Combinations

Andries (cont.)
DeNoorman
  Pearson, 1630
DeVos
  Pearson, 1664
Douw
  Alb Ref bp, 1684, 1686,
  1689
  Pearson, 1646
  Rens Crsp 1, 1659
Emans
  King Co, 1693
Gardenier
  Pearson, no date
Gojer
  Ship Lists, 1644
Hoogland
  NY Ref mr, 1661
  Ship Lists, 1658, no date
Huych
  Pearson, 1705
Iersman
  Pearson, no date
Moreau
  Rcrd Nam 5, 1665
Noorman
  Evjen, 1644
  Rcrd Nam 1, 1655
  Rens Crsp 1, 1658
  Ship Lists, 1637
Nyt Spangien
  NY Ref mr, 1685
Onderdonk
  King Co, 1672
Pratt
  Rens Crsp 2, 1682
Provoost
  NY Ref bp, 1671
Rees
  King Pap, 1663
  Pearson, 1672
Schaap
  Pearson, 1695
Scherp
  Pearson, 1699
Sharp
  Alb Ref bp, 1695, 1700,
  1701, 1702
  Alb Ref mr, 1697

Timmerman
  NY Ref mr, 1660
UytHolstein
  NY Ref mr, 1658
VanBoskirk
  Brgr Frm, 1657
  Evjen, 1655
  Hack Ref bp, 1720
  NY Lth bp, 1710
  Rcrd Nam 2, 1656
  Ship Lists, no date
VanBoswyck
  NY Ref mr, 1695
VanBreuckelen
  NY Ref mr, 1696
VanDoesburgh
Gerrits
  Pearson, 1661
  Ship Lists, no date
VanDolsen
VanDoesburg
  Rens Crsp 1, 1661
  Rens Crsp 2, 1684
VanDublin
  Ship Lists, 1646
VanFrederickstadt
  Pearson, 1636
  Ship Lists, 1636
VanSwoll
  NY Ref mr, 1659
VanThresonie
  NY Ref mr, 1661
VanWestroos
  NY Ref mr, 1655
VanWreede
  NY Ref mr, 1654
VerBrugh
  King Pap, 1666
  King Pap, 1666
Verdonck
  NY Ref bp, 1667
Whitbeck
  Alb Ref bp, 1706
  Alb Ref mm, 1683
  Pearson, 1683

Ar.
DeGraw
  NY Ref bp, 1688

Arents
Bloom
  NY Ref bp, 1681
Bratt
  Alb Ref bp, 1686
  Pearson, 1695
  Schn Ref bp, 1700
Coos
  NY Ref bp, 1647
DeGraw
  NY Ref bp, 1699, 1701
Diesvelt
  Ship Lists, 1659
Duyvelant
  Rcrd Nam 3, 1660
Grauw
  Alb Ref bp, 1689
Graw
  Pearson, 1689
Groenevelt
  Ship Lists, 1659
Jansen
  NY Ref bp, 1677
Pier
  King Ref mr, 1682, 1685
Schumacher
  Pearson, 1679
Skerendregt
  NY Ref bp, 1707
  NY Ref mr, 1706
Slingerland
  Pearson, 1713
Tack
  King Ref bp, 1688
Toers
  Berg Ref bp, 1674, 1679,
  1682, 1685, 1687, 1688,
  1689, 1692, 1694, 1696,
  1699, 1703, 1707, 1710
  Berg Ref dt, 1673, 1682,
  1686, 1694, 1702, 1707
  Berg Ref mm, 1667, 1677,
  1682
  Berg Ref mr, 1672, 1684
Torner
  Nicl Lvl, 1672

Tours
 Fltb Ref mr, 1684
 NY Ref bp, 1694
Tysvelt
 Gen Entr 1, 1669
UytBrabant
 NY Ref mr, 1669
Vanderbilt
 Berg Ref bp, 1683
 NY Ref mr, 1650
VanFiesvelt
 King Pap, 1664
VanHoeck
 Pearson, 1700
VanSutphin
 NY Ref mr, 1659, 1684
VanSwartensluys
 NY Ref mr, 1656
VanVechten
 Fltb Ref bp, 1680
 King Co, 1660
 Ship Lists, 1660, no date
Vechten
 Fltb Ref bp, 1684
 LI Source, 1660, no date
 Ship Lists, 1687
Vedder
 Pearson, 1715
Vermeulen
 King Pap, 1665
Viele
 NY Ref mr, 1688
Viervant
 King Ref mr, 1668
Vogel
 King Pap, 1667
Zuyck
 Nycol Doc 1, 1650
Aries
Cam
 King Ref bp, 1683
Oothout
 Pearson, 1756
VanDerBaest
 Pearson, 1670
Vanderbilt
 Fltb Ref mr, 1681

Arnouts
Meyer
 NY Ref bp, 1702
VanOtterspoor
 Ship Lists, 1649
Viele
 Alb Ref bp, 1699
 Alb Ref mm, 1699
 Pearson, 1699
Augusts
Nuys
 NY Ref mr, 1673
VanCartagena
 NY Ref mr, 1647
VanNuyse
 King Co, 1685
VanNuys
 Fltb Ref bp, 1679, 1682,
 1684, 1685
 Fltb Ref mr, 1680, 1685

B

Baltus
VanBenthuysen
 Pearson, 1720
Baptist
DePoitiere
 King Ref bp, 1693, 1698
Dumont
 King Ref bp, 1694, 1701
VanRensselaer
 Ship Lists, 1651
Barents
Amersfort
 King Pap, 1662
Ameshoff
 Ship Lists, 1658
Bloom
 Bkln Ref bp, 1694, 1699
 Fltb Ref mr, 1685
 King Co, 1662
 LI Source, 1687, 1694,
 1696
 Ship Lists, 1687

Bratt
 Alb Ref mm, 1683
 Alb Ref mr, 1686, 1693
 Pearson, 1682
Coeymans
 Pearson, 1695
Cole
 Alb Ref bp, 1687
 King Pap, 1666
 King Ref bp, 1665, 1666,
 1678, 1679, 1681, 1683,
 1687, 1695
 NY Ref bp, 1668
 NY Ref mr, 1660, 1675,
 1680
 Pearson, 1687
 Rcrd Nam 6, 1669
DeKlein
 NY Ref bp, 1663, 1680,
 1684
 Ship Lists, 1661
Ditmars
 Pearson, 1692
Dulleman
 Pearson, 1661
Heyman
 Rcrd Nam 1, 1653
Klein
 NY Ref bp, 1664, 1671
 Rcrd Nam 4, 1662
Kunst
 King Pap, 1664
 King Ref bp, 1664, 1667
 King Ref mr, 1668
 Nicl Lvl, 1669
 Pearson, 1662
Pastoor
 King Co, 1651
 King Pap, 1668
 Pearson, 1654
 Rcrd Nam 4, 1663
 Ship Lists, 1652
Pastoren
 King Pap, 1667
Poest
 Pearson, 1664
 Rens Crsp 1, 1659, 1668

Barents (cont.)
Post
King Pap, 1664
Schoonmaker
Pearson, 1636
Ship Lists, 1636
Slecht
Anjou Prb, 1684
King Co, 1661
King Pap, 1661, 1664
King Ref bp, 1671, 1674
King Ref mr, 1684
Nicl Lvl, 1667
Rcrd Nam 4, 1662
Rens Crsp 1, 1667
Smith
Crt Assz, 1668
King Co, 1663
LI Source, 1687, 1690
NY Ref mr, 1663
Nycol Doc 2, 1673
Orphan Mst, 1664
Rcrd Nam 3, 1660
Timmerman
Pearson, 1660
Utenes
Fltb Ref bp, 1680
VanAmeshof
King Pap, 1662
Vandecuyl
King Ref bp, 1667
VanDeKuyl
Ship Lists, 1657, 1658
VanDerBeek
Fltb Ref bp, 1683
VanDerKleeck
NY Ref bp, 1690
VanDerKuyl
Nycol Doc 3, 1664
Rcrd Nam 4, 1663
VanDerVliet
King Co, 1668
VanDerWyck
Bkln Ref bp, 1694
VanDeventer
NY Ref mr, 1664

VanDriest
Fltb Ref bp, 1680, 1681, 1684
Fltb Ref mr, 1679
King Co, 1658
VanDwingeloo
Pearson, 1662
VanEdam
Pearson, 1636
VanHarlem
NY Ref mr, 1659, 1667, 1670
VanHorn
Evjen, 1657
Hack Ref bp, 1718
VanJevern
NY Ref mr, 1659
VanKleeck
Berg Ref bp, 1685, 1688, 1689
Berg Ref dt, 1688
King Ref bp, 1697
LI Fam 1, 1660
NY Ref bp, 1687, 1690
VanLeerd.
NY Ref bp, 1661
VanLubeck
NY Ref mr, 1685, 1694
VanNimweeg
King Ref bp, 1702
VanReynerwout
NY Ref mr, 1662
VanRotmers
Pearson, 1662
VanStockholm
NY Ref mr, 1666
VanSutphin
Ship Lists, 1687
VanWeryen
NY Ref mr, 1661
VanWyck
Fltb Ref bp, 1679, 1682, 1688
King Co, 1660
LI Source, 1660, 1684
Ship Lists, 1687, no date

Viveren
Pearson, no date
Vos
King Pap, 1664
Wemp
King Pap, 1664
Pearson, 1645
Rcrd Nam 3, 1660
Rens Court, 1669
Rens Crsp 1, 1659, 1660, 1661, 1664, 1668
Ship Lists, 1643, 1645, 1660
Weyt
Ship Lists, 1649
Bartels
Ruysh
Ship Lists, 1660
Bartholomeus
Contesse
Ship Lists, 1691
Hogeboom
Alb Ref bp, 1701, 1708
Pearson, 1701
Romp
King Pap, 1666
VanBloomenthal
Pearson, 1706
VanBlumenthal
Alb Ref bp, 1707
VanBuren
Pearson, 1733
Rens Court, 1668
Vrooman
Alb Ref bp, 1686
Alb Ref mm, 1683
Alb Ref mr, 1685, 1690
Fern Wlls, 1691
Gen Entr 2, 1686
Pearson, 1670
Rens Court, 1669, 1670, 1672
Bastians
Cole
Ship Lists, 1663
DeVyselaer
Pearson, 1675

Patronymic/Surname Combinations

DeWitt
  Alb Ref bp, 1700
  Alb Ref mr, 1695
  Pearson, 1700
Louw
  Ship Lists, no date
VanCuylenburg
  NY Ref mr, 1673, 1684,
  1685
VanDerPerck
  Ship Lists, 1663
VanDerPerke
  Crt Assz, 1666
  Rcrd Nam 6, 1666
VanGiesen
  Berg Ref dt, 1707
  King Co, 1660
  Ship Lists, no date
VanGudsenhoven
  Pearson, 1658
VanGutsenhoven
  Rens Court, 1668, 1669,
  1670
  Rens Crsp 1, 1655, 1657,
  1658, 1661, 1662, 1666,
  1667, 1668
  Ship Lists, 1652
VanWerckendam
  NY Ref mr, 1668
Vischer
  Alb Ref bp, 1703
  Alb Ref mm, 1683
  Pearson, 1675
  Ship Lists, 1644, no date
Visscher
  Ship Lists, no date
Werckhoven
  NY Ref mr, 1665
Beeren
VanRoermondt
  NY Ref mr, 1659
Bens
Israel
  Nycol Doc 1, 1656
Bergen
VanGraft
  Rens Crsp 1, 1661

Bertrands
  DuTuffeau
    Ship Lists, 1687
Bestvals
VanLuyderdorp
    Ship Lists, 1642
Blans
Jean
    King Ref bp, 1681, 1682,
    1683
Brants
VanAmersfort
    Pearson, no date
VanNewkirk
    Pearson, 1664
    Ship Lists, 1640
Voss
    King Pap, 1661
Brimasson
Brinase
    LI Source, 1692
Broers
Decker
    King Ref bp, 1679
    King Ref mr, 1679
Jans
    King Ref bp, 1688
Broussard
DesChamps
    Ship Lists, 1668
Brumeau
DeMoulinars
    Ship Lists, 1683
Bruyns
VanBohemen
    Gen Entr 1, 1664
    King Pap, 1663

C

Caesars
Albertus
    LI Source, 1687
Capito
Bont
    Evjen, 1650
Boon
    Evjen, 1650

Carls
  Curtius
    Rcrd Nam 3, 1660
  DBevoise
    King Co, 1678
  Noorman
    Evjen, 1644
    Pearson, 1673
  VanLangesout
    King Pap, 1662
Carpenel
VanHarlem
    NY Ref bp, 1645, 1647
Caspars
Conine
    Pearson, 1703
  Hallenbeck
    Alb Ref bp, 1706
    Atns Lth bp, 1705, 1708
    Atns Lth mr, 1709
    NY Lth bp, 1708
    NY Ref bp, 1705
    Pearson, 1706
    Rens Crsp 2, 1683
  Rynerman
    NYC Wills, 1683
  Springsteen
    Brgr Frm, 1696
    King Co, 1652
    LI Source, 1652
    Rcrd Nam 2, 1658
    Ship Lists, no date
  VanMaerden
    Rcrd Nam 1, 1653
  VanNorden
    Brgr Frm, 1657
    NY Ref bp, 1662
  VanThuyl
    NY Ref mr, 1664
  Winne
    Pearson, 1783
Christians
Anderson
    Evjen, 1660
  Boch
    Ship Lists, 1661
  Noorman
    Pearson, 16336, 1658

Patronymic/Surname Combinations

Christians (cont.)
  Noorman (cont.)
    Rcrd Nam 1, 1655
    Ship Lists, 1636, 1637
  VanHolstein
    NY Ref mr, 1659
  VanHorn
    NY Lth bp, 1704, 1705,
    1708
  VanNorwegen
    Pearson, 1658
  VanVleckburgh
    Pearson, 1636
  Wolffenbuttel
    NY Ref mr, 1660
Christophs
  Abeel
    Pearson, 1682
  Cruytdop
    NY Ref mr, 1660
  Davids
    King Ref bp, 1697
  Davidts
    Pearson, no date
  Langestraat
    Fltb Ref bp, 1684
    King Co, 1657
  Probasco
    King Co, 1685
  Schaers
    King Co, 1675
    LI Source, 1695
  Schaes
    LI Source, 1678
  Schars
    Fltb Ref bp, 1678, 1681,
    1683
  Stymets
    Hack Ref mr, 1720
  VanLangestraat
    Fltb Ref bp, 1677
  Verbeeck
    Nycol Doc 2, 1657
Claas
  Backer
    Gen Entr 1, 1664
  Bakker
    Pearson, 1658

Baltes
  King Co, 1659
Bayard
  NY Ref bp, 1701
Bol
  Nycol Doc 1, 1647
  Rcrd Nam 1, 1647
Boodt
  Rens Crsp 1, 1655
Boot
  Rcrd Nam 1, 1654
  Ship Lists, no date
Bording
  NY Ref bp, 1662
Bout
  Pearson, 1659
Braack
  Berg Ref bp, 1675, 1677,
  1682
  Berg Ref dt, 1668, 1692
  Rcrd Nam 2, 1656
Cooper
  Berg Ref dt, 1692
  Hack Ref bp, 1709
  Hack Ref mm, 1709
  Hack Ref mr, 1706
  NY Ref mr, 1708
  Tap Ref bp, 1695, 1700,
  1703, 1704, 1705, 1706,
  1707, 1708, 1710
Coppen
  Rcrd Nam 7, 1657
Coppe
  Brgr Frm, 1657
Cressens
  NYC Wills, 1679
Croesen
  LI Source, 1689, 1695
Croezen
  Rcrd Nam 4, 1662
Cuey
  Rcrd Nam 1, 1655
Damen
  NY Ref bp, 1648
DeGraff
  Pearson, 1699
DePottebacker
  Rcrd Nam 2, 1656

DeRyp
  Ship Lists, 1675
Deucht
  Nycol Doc 2, 1662
  Rcrd Nam 4, 1662
  Rens Crsp 1, 1662
DeWitt
  Anjou Prb, 1687, 1699
  Gen Entr 1, 1669
  King Pap, 1662, 1666
  King Ref bp, 1662, 1664,
  1666, 1667, 1683, 1698,
  1700
  Nicl Lvl, 1667
  NY Ref bp, 1665
  NY Ref mr, 1656
  Pearson, 1663
  Ship Lists, no date
Draeck
  NY Ref bp, 1659
Egmont
  Alb Ref bp, 1684
  Pearson, 1683
Gerritsen
  NY Ref bp, 1691
Groenvis
  King Pap, 1671
  NY Ref mr, 1658
Groesbeek
  Alb Ref bp, 1688, 1701,
  1702, 1703, 1707
  Alb Ref mm, 1683
  Alb Ref mr, 1699
  NY Ref bp, 1690
  Pearson, 1695, 1707
Herculan
  Nycol Doc 1, 1653
Jongen
  Ship Lists, 1637
Kaye
  Pearson, 1661
Kulerman
  Pearson, 1670
Lesenter
  Nycol Doc 2, 1662
Letten
  Jam Ref bp, 1715
Outewaael
  Rcrd Nam 1, 1653

Patronymic/Surname Combinations

Pataddes
    Rcrd Nam 1, 1654
Pos
    Nycol Doc 2, 1656
Pottbacker
    NYC Wills, 1679
Pottebacker
    Rcrd Nam 1, 1655
Rademacker
    NY Ref bp, 1655
Ripse
    Pearson, 1683
Rips
    Alb Ref mm, 1683
    Nycol Doc 3, 1690
Romeyn
    Hack Ref bp, 1702, 1703,
    1708, 1710, 1714, 1716,
    1718, 1720
    Hack Ref mm, 1702, page xx
    Hack Ref mr, 1699, 1703
    King Co, 1686
Romp
    Evjen, 1657
    King Pap, 1661
    Ship Lists, 1657
Roosevelt
    King Ref bp, 1682
Ruyter
    NY Ref mr, 1679
    Rcrd Nam 3, 1661
Schluter
    Ship Lists, 1679
Schoonhoven
    King Ref bp, 1696
Sluyter
    King Ref bp, 1682, 1684,
    1687, 1692, 1698, 1703
    King Ref mr, 1679
Smith
    King Co, 1653
    NY Ref mr, 1653
Swaeg
    Nycol Doc 2, 1657
Swits
    NY Ref mr, 1656
    Rcrd Nam 1, 1653

Switzer
    NY Ref bp, 1642, 1643,
    1647, 1653
Timmerman
    Pearson, 1658
Tolk
    Pearson, 1702
Tours
    Berg Ref bp, 1694
Turck
    Crt Assz, 1668
    Pearson, 1664
    Rcrd Nam 3, 1659
UytDeKuyndert
    NY Ref mr, 1667, 1671
UytSaxenlant
    NY Ref mr, 1662
VanAmsterdam
    Pearson, 1636
    Ship Lists, 1636
VanBaren
    Rcrd Nam 4, 1663
VanBergh
    NY Ref bp, 1697
VanBommel
    NY Ref bp, 1664
VanBremen
    NY Ref mr, 1650
VanBunnick
    NY Ref mr, 1658
VanCampen
    Nycol Doc 1, 1642
VanDam
    Pearson, 1683
VanDeBroeck
    Ship Lists, 1651
VanDenBerg
    Alb Ref bp, 1694, 1702
    Pearson, 1651
VanDenBollch
    Nycol Doc 2, 1660
VanDerBogart
    Pearson, 1724
VanDerGraft
    Rens Crsp 1, 1657, 1658
VanDerVolgen
    Pearson, 1720

VanDitmars
    Gen Entr 1, 1664
VanDoorn
    Rcrd Nam 4, 1662
VanGroeningen
    NY Ref mr, 1655
VanGrootSchermer
    NY Ref mr, 1681
VanHasymes
    King Co, 1687
VanHoesen
    Bkln Ref bp, 1674
    NY Ref bp, 1668
VanHorn
    NY Ref mr, 1645
VanLeendersloot
    Bkln Ref bp, 1680
VanLith
    Ship Lists, 1653
VanLoendersloot
    Fltb Ref bp, 1680
VanMuyden
    NY Ref mr, 1664
VanNewkirk
    Pearson, 1662
VanNoorden
    Ship Lists, no date
VanNordinge
    Pearson, 1683
    Ship Lists, 1637
VanOosanen
    Pearson, 1658
VanOosthuysen
    NY Ref mr, 1686
VanOostrand
    Pearson, 1658
VanOostzanen
    Pearson, 1661
VanRavox
    NY Ref mr, 1649
VanSchaick
    Alb Ref mm, 1696
    Alb Ref mr, 1698
    Pearson, 1695, 1696
VanSchermer
    NY Ref mr, 1678

Claas (cont.)
VanSchoonhoven
King Ref bp, 1699
King Ref mr, 1679
VanSevenhuysen
NY Ref mr, 1659
VanSluyck
Alb Ref mr, 1696
VanSpare
NY Ref bp, 1709
VanVechten
King Co, 1682
VanVranken
Pearson, 1684
VanWoert
Pearson, 1736
Vechten
Bkln Ref bp, 1687, 1693,
1694, 1697
Fltb Ref bp, 1684
Fltb Ref mr, 1680, 1682
LI Source, 1680, 1689,
1693, 1696
Vrooman
Alb Ref bp, 1686
Vryman
Pearson, 1654
Wipp
NY Ref mr, 1675
Wyckoff
Fltb Ref bp, 1679, 1680,
1681, 1683, 1684
King Co, 1679
Ship Lists, 1636, 1687

Clements
Brower
Nycol Doc 1, 1614
Kies
Nycol Doc 1, 1614

Cleyn
Smith
NY Ref bp, 1657

Coertes
Voorhees
King Co, 1687

Coerts
VanVoorhees
Ship Lists, 1660, no date

Coert
VanArnhem
NY Ref mr, 1660
VanNorthuysen
NY Ref mr, 1647
VanRhenen
NY Ref mr, 1664
VanVoorhees
Fltb Ref bp, 1690

Conine
VanDerBeek
King Co, 1682

Conrads
Backer
Pearson, 1674
Bosch
NY Ref bp, 1681, 1704,
1706, 1707, 1708, 1709
NY Ref mr, 1703
Burgh
Nycol Doc 1, 1634, 1650
Codwise
Hack Ref bp, 1705
Miller
NY Ref bp, 1710
Notelman
Rens Crsp 1, 1658
TenEyck
Pearson, 1732
VanBom
Pearson, 1660
VanElmendorf
King NYGB, 1668
King Pap, 1667
VanNeurenburgh
Pearson, 1660

Cornelis
Banta
Hack Ref bp, 1700, 1708,
1709, 1710, 1711, 1713,
1715, 1717, 1718, 1719,
1720
Hack Ref mr, 1696, 1708
NY Lth mr, 1707
Berghoorn
Ship Lists, 1638
Berrien
King Co, 1707

Bes
Nycol Doc 2, 1663
Rens Crsp 1, 1663
Bogart
Berg Ref mm, 1676
Bkln Ref bp, 1677
Fltb Ref bp, 1677, 1682,
1685
Hack Ref bp, 1700, 1703,
1705, 1706, 1712
Hack Ref mm, 1686
King Ref bp, 1692
LI Source, 1694
Pearson, 1660
Bongart
Berg Ref bp, 1679, 1680,
1681, 1682
Fltb Ref bp, 1684
Boomgart
Fltb Ref bp, 1677, 1679,
1685
King Co, 1694
LI Source, 1690
Bosch
Pearson, 1690
Breyandt
Hack Ref bp, 1686
Ship Lists, 1663
Broeck
Ship Lists, 1653
Buys
Berg Ref bp, 1678, 1686
Bkln Ref bp, 1678
Bkln Ref mr, 1663, 1690
Brgr Frm, 1657
Fltb Ref bp, 1678, 1679,
1683, 1684
King Co, 1648
LI Fam 1, 1629
LI Source, 1667, 1668,
1698
Nicl Lvl, 1672
NY Ref bp, 1654, 1656,
1674
Pearson, 1634
Rcrd Nam 2, 1656
Cadmus
Hack Ref mr, 1713

Patronymic/Surname Combinations

Cock
Evjen, 1676
NY Ref bp, 1691
Constapel
Rcrd Nam 4, 1663
Cook
LI Source, 1694
Cooper
Tap Ref bp, 1706
Cornell
King Co, 1666
Coster
Pearson, 1643
Crynen
Gen Entr 1, 1665
Damen
Bkln Ref bp, 1674, 1678, 1680
Fltb Ref bp, 1683
King Co, 1655
LI Source, 1650
Nicl Lvl, 1672
NYC Wills, 1680
Pearson, 1634
DeBoer
Pearson, 1659
DeKlein
King Co, 1660
DeLaa
King Ref bp, 1683
DeRycke
LI Fam 2, 1664
DeRyck
NY Ref bp, 1661, 1662, 1663, 1665, 1667
Rcrd Nam 6, 1671
DeVos
Pearson, 1653
DeYoung
Pearson, 1659
Doremus
Berg Ref mr, 1710
Ship Lists, no date
Duyster
Pearson, 1626
Exveen
NY Ref mr, 1693

Fabricius
Rcrd Nam 6, 1670
Fuyck
Nycol Doc 2, 1657
Gilde
Gen Entr 1, 1664
Rens Crsp 1, 1657
Gouw
Rens Crsp 2, 1678
Gou
Rens Court, 1669, 1673
Gow
Pearson, 1660
Halsyn
Fltb Ref mr, 1692
Heerings
Hack Ref mr, 1717
Honing
Nycol Doc 2, 1656
Hoogland
King Co, 1645
LI Source, 1689, 1696
NY Ref bp, 1687
Huisman
King Co, 1663
Kat
Ship Lists, 1687
Keert
Hack Ref mm, 1686
Keyser
King Pap, 1668, 1669
Klein
King Co, 1660
Pearson, 1660
Rcrd Nam 1, 1653
Koperslager
Pearson, 1675
Koster
NY Ref bp, 1662
Nycol Doc 2, 1656
Pearson, 1643
Lan
King Ref bp, 1681
Louw
Anjou Prb, 1690
Evjen, 1659
King Ref bp, 1683
Ship Lists, 1659, no date

Loy
King Co, 1683
Luyster
Fltb Ref bp, 1681, 1683, 1685
King Co, 1693
LI Source, 1687, 1690
NYC Wills, 1695
Ship Lists, 1687
Lyndrayer
Nicl Lvl, 1666
Maasen
Pearson, 1663
Mathys
Gen Entr 1, 1672
Mentelaer
King Co, 1645
LI Source, 1645
Meulenmaecker
Ship Lists, 1636
Mingaal
Pearson, 1666
Mitelaer
King Co, 1671
Molenaer
King Pap, 1664
Muller
Alb Ref bp, 1702
Pearson, 1702
Ouderkerk
Ship Lists, 1663
Plugiet
Gen Entr 1, 1669
Pointie
Rens Court, 1670, 1672
Post
Ship Lists, no date
Pounties
Rens Court, 1668
Pruis
Berg Ref bp, 1686
Roodt
Pearson, 1670
Root
Rcrd Nam 4, 1662
Rens Court, 1670, 1671, 1672

Cornelis (cont.)
Rycke
NY Ref bp, 1674
Schermerhorn
Pearson, 1742
Schouten
Nycol Doc 1, 1651
Schyf
NY Ref mr, 1707
Sebring
King Co, 1693
Seen
King Co, no date
Seeuw
Nycol Doc 2, 1673
Slecht
Anjou Prb, 1677
King Co, 1652
King Pap, 1663, 1664
King Ref bp, 1679, 1680, 1681
King Ref mr, 1666
LI Source, 1652
Ship Lists, 1661
Slingerland
Pearson, 1658
Rcrd Nam 4, 1662
Ship Lists, no date
Slyck
Pearson, 1659
Smith
King Co, 1639
Nicl Lvl, 1667
NY Ref bp, 1671
Soesbergen
Pearson, 1660
Soestberger
Rcrd Nam 4, 1662
Spitsbergen
Pearson, 1663
Rens Court, 1672
Spitsenbergh
Ship Lists, 1654
Spitsenberg
Nycol Doc 3, 1666
Rens Crsp 1, 1666, 1671
Stanson
King Co, 1676

Stille
NY Ref bp, 1680, 1689, 1690, 1692, 1700, 1704, 1706
NY Ref mr, 1671
Rcrd Nam 6, 1671
Swart
Gen Entr 2, 1676
Pearson, 1661
Ship Lists, 1641
Swede
Orphan Mst, 1666
Swits
Nycol Doc 1, 1644
Pearson, 1663
Ship Lists, 1642
Timmerman
Pearson, 1660
Ship Lists, 1639
Timmer
NY Ref bp, 1680
NY Ref mr, 1678
Trommels
NY Ref mr, 1656
Tymesen
Pearson, 1709
UytDenemarken
NY Ref mr, 1676
VanAbcoude
Pearson, 1660
VanAmsterdam
NY Ref mr, 1655
VanBarsingerwout
Ship Lists, 1638
VanBersingerem
Pearson, 1642
VanBersingeren
Ship Lists, 1642
VanBreuckelen
Rens Crsp 2, 1678
VanBuren
Fern Wlls, 1703
Pearson, 1662
Ship Lists, 1683
VanCortright
NYC Wills, 1706

VanCott
King Co, 1652
Ship Lists, 1652
VanDenBerg
Pearson, 1660
Rens Crsp 2, 1678
Ship Lists, 1645
VanDenHoogenberch
Ship Lists, 1648
VanDerBogart
Alb Ref bp, 1685
King Ref mr, 1679
VanDerHeyden
Fern Wlls, 1663
Gen Entr 1, 1664
King Pap, 1664
Pearson, 1660
VanDerHoeven
Alb Ref bp, 1686
Pearson, 1676
Rens Court, 1670
VanDerPoel
Fern Wlls, 1687, 1694
Gen Entr 1, 1670
Pearson, 1661
Rens Court, 1670
Rens Crsp 1, 1660
Rens Crsp 2, 1675, 1678, 1684
VanDerRee
Rcrd Nam 3, 1660
VanDerVeen
Brgr Frm, 1657
NY Ref bp, 1652, 1657, 1658, 1683
Rcrd Nam 1, 1653
VanDerVeer
Fltb Ref bp, 1687
Fltb Ref mr, 1685
King Co, 1679
LI Fam 2, 1685
NY Ref bp, 1659
Ship Lists, 1687, no date
VanDerVorst
Berg Ref bp, 1696
Berg Ref dt, 1683
Berg Ref mm, 1667
NY Ref bp, 1653, 1654

VanDerWel
  NY Ref bp, 1646
  Nycol Doc 2, 1662
  Rcrd Nam 1, 1654
VanDerWey
  NY Ref bp, 1672
VanDurgerdam
  NY Ref mr, 1657
VanDuyn
  Bkln Ref mr, 1691
  King Co, 1649
  LI Fam 2, 1649
  Ship Lists, 1649, 1687, no
    date
VanDyck
  Rens Court, 1668
VanEchtsveen
  NY Ref mr, 1680
VanEgmont
  NY Ref mr, 1670, 1678
VanEsselstine
  King Ref bp, 1687
  Pearson, 1661
VanEveren
  NY Ref bp, 1687
VanExween
  NYC Wills, 1690
VanFlansburg
  Brgr Frm, 1657
  NY Ref mr, 1659
  Pearson, 1671
  Rcrd Nam 7, 1660
VanGottenburgh
  King Pap, 1664
VanGroenland
  Hack Ref mr, 1699
VanHoesen
  Pearson, 1681
VanHorn
  Brgr Frm, 1657
  Hack Ref bp, 1718
  NY Lth bp, 1708, 1709
  NY Lth mr, 1705, 1707
  Nycol Doc 2, 1664
  Rcrd Nam 3, 1659
  Ship Lists, no date
VanHouten
  Hack Ref mr, 1712

  NY Ref bp, 1648
  Pearson, 1640
  Ship Lists, 1638, 1640
VanLexmond
  NY Ref mr, 1658
VanMiddleburg
  NY Ref mr, 1685
VanMunichendam
  Pearson, 1636
VanMunnichendam
  Ship Lists, 1636
VanNess
  Berg Ref dt, 1689
  King Ref mr, 1663
  Pearson, 1697
  Rens Crsp 2, 1684
VanNewkirk
  Berg Ref dt, 1705
  Berg Ref mr, 1670, 1686
  King Co, 1665
VanOosten
  Fltb Ref mr, 1682
  LI Source, 1690
VanRossem
  Rens Crsp 1, 1652
VanRossum
  Pearson, 1662
VanRotterdam
  King Co, 1639
  NY Ref bp, 1641, 1643
  NY Ref mr, 1643
VanSchaick
  NYC Court, 1698
  Pearson, 1703
VanSchoenderwoert
  Pearson, no date
VanSchoonderwoerdt
  Ship Lists, 1641
VanSchoonhoven
  NY Ref mr, 1670
VanSchouw
  King Co, 1642
VanSluyck
  Fern Wlls, 1690
VanSlyck
  Pearson, 1663
  Rens Court, 1668

VanSoestbergen
  Rcrd Nam 4, 1662
VanStarrevelt
  King Pap, 1666
VanSteenwyck
  Berg Ref bp, 1692
VanSterrevelt
  King Pap, 1666
  Pearson, 1657
VanTassel
  King Co, 1670
  NY Ref bp, 1678
  Ship Lists, no date
  Tary Ref bp, 1697
  Tary Ref mm, 1700
VanVechten
  Alb Ref bp, 1709
  Alb Ref mm, 1698
  Pearson, 1709
  Rens Court, 1669
  Ship Lists, 1637, 1638, no
    date
VanVespen
  Pearson, 1671
VanVlissingen
  NY Ref mr, 1687
VanVoorhout
  NY Ref mr, 1649
  Pearson, 1642
  Rens Court, 1658
  Rens Crsp 1, 1659, 1660,
    1664, 1668
  Rens Crsp 2, 1683
  Ship Lists, 1644
VanVoorst
  NY Ref mr, 1652
VanVorst
  NY Ref bp, 1670, 1684
  NY Ref mr, 1656
  Nycol Doc 2, 1663
  Rcrd Nam 1, 1653
VanWarbeer
  NY Ref mr, 1656
VanWel
  Brgr Frm, 1657
VanWensveen
  NY Ref mr, 1646

Claas (cont.)
VanWesepe
Ship Lists, 1645
VanWesp
Pearson, 1645
VanWesten
LI Source, 1690
VanWestveen
NY Ref bp, 1681
Vernoy
King Pap, 1664
King Ref bp, 1665, 1666, 1667
Pearson, 1667
Ship Lists, 1663
Verwey
Hack Ref mr, 1707
Ship Lists, no date
Vielen
Rens Court, 1670
Viele
Alb Ref bp, 1689
Alb Ref mm, 1683
Gen Entr 1, 1671
Nycol Doc 3, 1682
Pearson, 1661
Rens Court, 1668, 1669, 1671, 1672
Ship Lists, no date
Vlas
Pearson, 1681
Vogel
King Pap, 1665, 1666
Rcrd Nam 3, 1661
Vosburgh
Pearson, 1683
Vosje
Pearson, no date
Voss
Alb Ref bp, 1683
Vos
Rens Crsp 1, 1652
Ship Lists, 1640
Vreeland
Berg Ref bp, 1704
Berg Ref mr, 1701, 1709
Hack Ref mr, 1712
NY Ref mr, 1709

Vroom
Fltb Ref bp, 1681
King Co, 1645
Vyselaer
Pearson, 1660
Rens Court, 1669, 1670, 1671, 1672, 1673
Rens Crsp 2, 1678
Waert
Ship Lists, 1639
Wantenaar
NY Ref bp, 1651, 1653, 1654
Nycol Doc 2, 1665
Rcrd Nam 1, 1655
Wantenaer
King Co, 16462
Wesop
Pearson, 1667
Wip
Rens Crsp 1, 1660
Wyckoff
King Co, 1685
Zeeuw
LI Source, 1695
Corsen
Stam
Ship Lists, 1641
VanPharnabuck
NY Ref bp, 1687
Vroom
Bkln Ref bp, 1681
Fltb Ref bp, 1680
LI Source, 1689
Cosines
Heerings
Hack Ref bp, 1720
Hack Ref mr, 1719
Coster
VanAecken
Rens Court, 1669
VanAken
Pearson, 1659
VanAkes
Gen Entr 1, 1664
Courts
VanVoorhees
Ship Lists, 1687

Court
VanVoorhees
Ship Lists, 1687

D
Damens
Vissenburg
Ship Lists, 1641
Daniels
Fort
Pearson, 1736
Richard
Fltb Ref mr, 1689
Rickhout
King Co, 1694
Rinckhout
Fltb Ref mr, 1694
VanOlinda
Pearson, 1669
VanTwerpen
Pearson, 1720
Davids
Ackerman
NY Ref bp, 1673
NY Ref mr, 1668
DeMaree
Hack Ref bp, 1717, 1718, 1719
Hack Ref mr, 1717
Kikebel
Pearson, 1682
Schaets
Ship Lists, 1660
Schuyler
Alb Ref mm, 1683
Pearson, 1683
VanArnhem
NY Ref mr, 1656
VanGrummen
NY Ref mr, 1705
VanMispadtkill
NY Ref mr, 1690
Davis
Barns
Nicl Lvl, 1672
Kyckebul
Rens Court, 1672

Patronymic/Surname Combinations

Dennis
  Hegeman
    Jam Ref bp, 1717
  VanDuyn
    King Co, 1695
Dents
  Kruis
    King Ref bp, 1708
Dirks
  Amerman
    Ship Lists, no date
  Ammermarc
    King Co, 1693
  Backer
    NY Ref bp, 1641
  Banta
    Berg Ref mr, 1701
    Hack Ref bp, 1710, 1714,
    1715, 1718, 1719, 1720
    Hack Ref mm, 1702
    Hack Ref mr, 1702, 1709
  Bergen
    Nycol Doc 2, 1662
  Blau
    Nycol Doc 1, 1643
  Bor
    Ship Lists, 1662
  Braack
    Berg Ref bp, 1680, 1682,
    1683, 1685, 1686, 1693,
    1695, 1698, 1707
    Berg Ref mr, 1681, 1682
  Bratt
    Pearson, 1727
  Brinckerhoff
    King Co, 1638
    Ship Lists, no date
  Bye
    Alb Ref bp, 1704
    Pearson, 1704
  Cole
    NY Ref mr, 1679
  Coon
    Nycol Doc 1, 1656
    Rcrd Nam 1, 1653
  Croesen
    King Co, 1661

Croezen
  Bkln Ref mr, 1661
DeNoorman
  Bkln Ref bp, 1670
  NY Ref bp, 1659
DeVass
  Rcrd Nam 3, 1661
DeVries
  Pearson, 1654
  Rens Court, 1669
Engelsman
  Pearson, 1638
  Ship Lists, 1638
Goddard
  Rcrd Nam 1, 1653
Goes
  Pearson, 1732
Heemstraat
  Rens Court, 1671
Hoogland
  Fltb Ref mr, 1689
  King Co, 1638
  LI Source, 1660
  Nycol Doc 1, 1644
  Ship Lists, 1645, 1687
Hoyer
  NY Ref bp, 1700, 1706
  NY Ref mr, 1688
Keyser
  Pearson, 1658
Langestraat
  King Co, 1698
Mayer
  Rens Court, 1670
Meerman
  King Pap, 1671
Meppel
  Ship Lists, 1698
Meyer
  Fltb Ref bp, 1682
  Nicl Lvl, 1672
  NY Ref bp, 1657, 1662,
  1663, 1671, 1672, 1678,
  1679, 1684, 1689
  NY Ref mr, 1677
  Nycol Doc 2, 1664
  Orphan Mst, 1665
  Rcrd Nam 5, 1664

OpHoboken
  NY Ref bp, 1687
Poentie
  Rcrd Nam 1, 1654
  Ship Lists, 1638
Pos
  NY Ref bp, 1646, 1647
  Nycol Doc 1, 1630
  Pearson, 1630
  Ship Lists, 1624
Rosekrans
  Ship Lists, 1687
Schilder
  Rcrd Nam 3, 1661
Schoders
  Nycol Doc 1, 1621
Servis
  NY Ref mr, 1661
  Rcrd Nam 3, 1661
Spiegel
  Nycol Doc 2, 1662
Straatenmacker
  Berg Ref dt, 1686
  Berg Ref mm, 1665
  Berg Ref mr, 1666
  NY Ref bp, 1674, 1680,
  1683, 1684
Sutphin
  King Co, 1693
TenBroeck
  NY Ref bp, 1684
  Pearson, no date
VanAmersfort
  Pearson, 1638
  Ship Lists, 1638
VanAmsterd
  NY Ref bp, 1648
VanArnhem
  NY Ref bp, 1671
  NY Ref mr, 1664
VanAs
  King Co, 1661
VanBergh
  Gen Entr 1, 1670
VanBremen
  Brgr Frm, 1657
  King Pap, 1662, 1667
  NY Ref bp, 1644

Dirks (cont.)
  VanBremen
    Pearson, 1648
    Rens Court, 1668
  VanCleef
    NY Ref bp, 1673
  VanColen
    NY Ref mr, 1661
  VanDerHeyden
    Pearson, 1729
  VanDerKarr
    Pearson, 1694
  VanDerVliet
    Bkln Ref bp, 1684
    King Co, 1699
  VanEps
    Pearson, 1664
    Rens Court, 1672
    Rens Crsp 2, 1683
  VanGraft
    Gen Entr 1, 1664
    Rens Crsp 1, 1665
  VanHeemstraat
    Pearson, 1700
    Rens Court, 1670
    Rens Crsp 1, 1671
  VanHorn
    NY Ref mr, 1655, 1660
  VanIsleven
    NY Ref mr, 1664
  VanMaerzen
    NY Ref mr, 1645
  VanMeppel
    NY Ref mr, 1661
  VanNas
    King Co, 1661
  VanNef
    King Co, 1661
  VanNess
    Rcrd Nam 3, 1660
    Rcrd Nam 6, 1666
  VanNorden
    Fern Wlls, 1642
  VanOogsten
    Berg Ref mr, 1693
  VanVechten
    Alb Ref bp, 1690, 1701,
    1703, 1704, 1705

    Alb Ref mm, 1683
    Berg Ref bp, 1707
    Pearson, 1699
    Rens Court, 1668
    Rens Crsp 1, 1659, 1660
    Rens Crsp 2, 1683
    Ship Lists, 1638, 1640
  VanVenlo
    Rcrd Nam 5, 1664
  VanVliet
    Fltb Ref bp, 1684
    Fltb Ref mr, 1683, 1687
    LI Source, no date
    Ship Lists, 1687
  VanWestveen
    Nycol Doc 2, 1674
    Rcrd Nam 6, 1672
  Vinhagen
    Pearson, 1663
    Ship Lists, 1653, 1669
  Vinhogen
    Ship Lists, no date
  Vinhuygen
    Ship Lists, no date
  Vos
    Ship Lists, 1661
  Vries
    Rens Court, 1669
  Waterhout
    Rcrd Nam 1, 1655
  Woertman
    Berg Ref bp, 1691
    Bkln Ref bp, 1710
    King Co, 1678
    LI Source, 1695
Dominics
  VanLeeuwarden
    NY Ref mr, 1665
Douws
  Fonda
    Pearson, 1654
    Rens Court, 1670
  Smith
    Ship Lists, 1655
  Tallman
    Berg Ref mm, 1685
    NY Ref mr, 1686
    Tap Ref bp, 1709

Dries
  VanDriesbergen
    Ship Lists, 1642

E
Edsels
  VanRidding
    NY Ref mr, 1655
Edwards
  Banta
    Hack Ref mr, 1715
Egberts
  Banta
    Hack Ref bp, 1707, 1708,
    1709, 1712, 1713, 1718,
    1720
    Hack Ref mm, page xx
    Hack Ref mr, 1699, 1719
  Bratt
    Pearson, 1753
  VanNieuwenhuysen
    Rcrd Nam 7, 1659
  VanSchuttorp
    NY Ref mr, 1657
Elias
  Daas
    Fltb Ref bp, 1681
  DeKaarl
    Ship Lists, 1662
  DeKaerl
    Ship Lists, 1662
  VanBenschoten
    Ship Lists, 1662, no date
  Vreeland
    Berg Ref bp, 1701
    Hack Ref mr, 1700, 1703
    NY Ref mr, 1689
Emmens
  Zwollang
    Nycol Doc 1, 1655
Engelberts
  Loth
    NY Ref mr, 1662
  Lott
    King Co, 1684
  Mitspatskille
    NY Ref mr, 1680

VanEland
NY Ref mr, 1656
VanNamen
Ship Lists, no date
VanName
King Ref bp, 1682, 1683
Enochs
Vreeland
Hack Ref bp, 1696
Enoyse
Vreeland
Hack Ref mr, 1706
Ernests
Cock
Gen Entr 2, 1676
Etiel
Levy
NYC Court, 1712
Everts
Biscop
NY Ref bp, 1648
Bout
Brgr Frm, 1657
Fern Wlls, 1649
King Co, 1634
LI Source, 1668, 1695,
1698, 1700, 1703
NY Ref bp, 1641, 1644,
1645, 1647, 1649, 1650,
1653, 1654, 1656, 1669
NYC Wills, 1671
Nycol Doc 1, 1643
Orphan Mst, 1663
Rcrd Nam 1, 1654
Ship Lists, 1634, 1651,
1653, 1654
Cooper
Pearson, 1725
DeGoyer
Pearson, 1664
Duycking
NY Ref mr, 1666
Floid
Rcrd Nam 7, 1674
Hulft
Nycol Doc 1, 1617

Kerseboom
Berg Ref bp, 1667, 1669,
1673
Berg Ref dt, 1668
Berg Ref mm, 1665
NY Ref bp, 1678, 1681
Keteltas
NY Ref bp, 1669, 1670,
1671, 1673, 1674, 1680,
1683
NY Ref mr, 1687
Rcrd Nam 7, 1673
Kettelas
Ship Lists, no date
Maeter
King Pap, 1671
Molegh
Hack Ref bp, 1713, 1714,
1718
Moleg
Hack Ref mr, 1711
Molenaer
NY Ref bp, 1664
Rcrd Nam 6, 1667
Ship Lists, no date
Pells
King Ref bp, 1687
King Ref mr, 1676
NY Ref bp, 1671, 1673
NY Ref mr, 1670
Post
NYC Court, 1693
Schoonmaker
Pearson, 1661
VanBeukelaer
Berg Ref mr, 1707
VanDerGrift
Ship Lists, 1657
VanGelder
Hack Ref mr, 1706
VanKalcker
Nycol Doc 2, 1659
VanLansmeer
NY Ref mr, 1669
VanNorden
NY Ref mr, 1643
Vischer
Rcrd Nam 6, 1670

Wendel
Pearson, 1690
Wynkoop
Ship Lists, 1651, no date

F

Ferdinands
VanSicklen
King Co, 1694
Ferlyn
VanDerGouw
Ship Lists, 1631
Floris
Krum
Hack Ref mr, 1699
Fockens
Hermans
Ship Lists, no date
VanRhuyne
NY Ref mr, 1671
VanRomen
NY Ref mr, 1667, 1676
Frans
Bloodgood
Fltb Ref mr, 1677
Clow
Alb Ref bp, 1686, 1700,
1703, 1705
Alb Ref mm, 1683
Alb Ref mr, 1693
Atns Lth bp, 1705
NY Lth bp, 1705
Pearson, 1683
Croon
Nycol Doc 1, 1652
Hardick
King Ref bp, 1697
Pearson, 1737
Karreman
Orphan Mst, 1664, 1665
Langerth
King Ref bp, 1688
Langet
King Ref bp, 1683
Lange
King Ref bp, 1696

Frans (cont.)
Meerman
Nycol Doc 2, 1668
Oudewater
NY Ref mr, 1686
Outwater
Berg Ref mr, 1706
Pruyn
Alb Ref mm, 1683
Pearson, 1683
Reuth
NY Ref bp, 1707
VanAlstine
Pearson, 1700
VanBriston
NY Ref mr, 1656
VanDerBogart
Pearson, 1699
VanDerHoeven
Alb Ref bp, 1686
Vandermeulen
Brgr Frm, 1698
VanDerMulen
NY Ref bp, 1705
VanDyck
NY Ref bp, 1689, 1697, 1701, 1704
NY Ref mr, 1677, 1681, 1686
VanHarlem
NY Ref mr, 1664
VanHoesen
Fern Wlls, 1703
King Pap, 1666
NY Ref bp, 1640
Pearson, 1659
Ship Lists, 1646, no date
VanSale
Tap Ref bp, 1709
Fredericks
Blau
NY Ref bp, 1698
Bloom
NY Ref mr, 1697
Boogh
Alb Ref bp, 1689
Alb Ref mm, 1683
Alb Ref mr, 1686

Bosch
Pearson, 1689
Bout
Pearson, 1654
Rens Court, 1670, 1671
Rens Crsp 2, 1675
Ship Lists, 1642
Bouw
Pearson, 1689
Druger
Gen Entr 2, 1688
Lansing
Ship Lists, no date
Lent
LI Fam 2, 1638
Smith
Fern Wlls, 1689
Suydam
King Co, 1663
LI Fam 2, 1663
Ship Lists, 1663, no date
UytDenHage
NY Ref mr, 1660
VanBrasiel
NY Ref mr, 1671
VanDerGrist
Fltb Ref mr, 1682
VanDerKreeft
Bkln Ref mr, 1677
VanEveren
Pearson, 1663
VanEvery
Ship Lists, no date
VanFrank
Alb Ref bp, 1708, 1709
VanJevern
NY Ref mr, 1656
VanLeeuven
Fltb Ref bp, 1682
VanLeyden
Pearson, 1642
Ship Lists, 1642
VanLieuwen
King Co, 1652
VanPatten
Pearson, 1664
VanPetten
Ship Lists, no date

Wiltbank
Gen Entr 1, 1669

G
Gaasbeek
Chambers
Alb Ref bp, 1706
King Ref bp, 1697, 1707, 1710
NY Ref bp, 1708
Gaius
VanAelst
Brgr Frm, 1657
Gangeloffe
Villet
King Co, no date
Gangelofzen
Visscher
Orphan Mst, 1664
Gangolfs
Vischer
Nicl Lvl, 1664
NY Ref mr, 1659
Rcrd Nam 2, 1658
Ganitzee
Letelier
King Co, 1664
Gerberts
Cruiff
Pearson, 1654
Cruyff
Rens Court, 1668, 1669, 1670, 1671, 1672
Rens Crsp 1, 1659
Cruyf
Rens Crsp 1, 1668
Ship Lists, 1654
Gerbrants
Cruyf
Fern Wlls, 1663
VanGemoenepau
NY Ref mr, 1707
VanNorden
NY Ref mr, 1657
Gerrits
Backer
Pearson, 1670

Blauvelt
  Tap Ref bp, 1703
Brower
  NY Ref bp, 1656
  Pearson, 1676
  Rcrd Nam 1, 1655
Buitenhuis
  Brgr Frm, 1658
Buytenhuys
  Ship Lists, 1658
Cavalier
  NY Ref mr, 1693
Cock
  King Co, 1656
Compaen
  Rens Crsp 1, 1660
Constapel
  King Ref bp, 1707
Couwenhoven
  Bkln Ref bp, 1699
  Bkln Ref mr, 1695
  Fltb Ref bp, 1678, 1679,
  1680, 1681, 1682
  King Co, 1639
  Ship Lists, 1630
Croezen
  Fltb Ref mr, 1681
Decker
  King Ref bp, 1688, 1697,
  1701, 1710
  King Ref mr, 1704, 1709
DeHaas
  NY Ref bp, 1678
DeHonneur
  Pearson, 1679
DeVries
  Rcrd Nam 4, 1662
DeYoung
  NY Ref bp, 1681
Dorland
  Bkln Ref bp, 1674, 1692,
  1694
  Fltb Ref bp, 1680, 1684
  Fltb Ref mr, 1682, 1683
  King Co, 1656
  LI Source, 1689, 1690,
  1693, 1701
  Ship Lists, 1687

Dujon
  NY Ref bp, 1689
Greeff
  Pearson, 1661
Groll
  Rcrd Nam 3, 1661
Haas
  Fltb Ref bp, 1680
  King Co, 1680
Hagel
  Ship Lists, 1660
Klein
  Pearson, 1671
Lansing
  Pearson, 1694
Middagh
  King Co, 1693
Nordstrant
  LI Source, 1712
Papendorp
  Alb Ref bp, 1687
  Alb Ref mm, 1683
  Fern Wlls, 1689
  Fltb Ref bp, 1682
  Pearson, 1682
Paus
  Pearson, 1683
Ravenstine
  NY Ref bp, 1698, 1703
Roos
  Pearson, 1695
Schoonhoven
  Alb Ref bp, 1701
Sharp
  Rcrd Nam 4, 1663
Smith
  Rcrd Nam 1, 1653
Spoor
  Pearson, 1719
Stavast
  Gen Entr 2, 1677
Stoothoff
  King Co, 1698
Strycker
  Brgr Frm, 1657
  King Co, 1651
  Rcrd Nam 1, 1653
  Ship Lists, no date

Timmerman
  Ship Lists, 1644
Toffle
  Gen Entr 2, 1675
Torenburg
  Ship Lists, 1681
VanAllen
  Hack Ref bp, 1712, 1716,
  1721
VanAmersfort
  LI Fam 2, 1630
VanAmsterdam
  NY Ref mr, 1653
VanBenthuysen
  Rcrd Nam 3, 1659
VanBergen
  Alb Ref bp, 1687
  Alb Ref mr, 1686
  Fern Wlls, 1701
  Pearson, 1630
  Rens Crsp 2, 1683
  Ship Lists, 1630, no date
VanBocksel
  Rcrd Nam 1, 1655
VanBoxtel
  NY Ref bp, 1656, 1659
  NY Ref mr, 1655
VanBrakel
  Fern Wlls, 1709
  Pearson, 1699
VanBuytenhuys
  NY Ref bp, 1661, 1667
  Nycol Doc 2, 1664
VanCoetwyck
  NY Ref mr, 1662
VanCouwenhoven
  Bkln Ref bp, 1677, 1678
  Bkln Ref mm, 1664
  Gen Entr 1, 1664
  LI Fam 1, 1665
  LI Fam 2, 1630
  LI Source, 1676, 1687,
  1688, 1689, 1693, 1695,
  1697
  NY Ref bp, 1651
  Rcrd Nam 5, 1664
  Ship Lists, 1687

Patronymic/Surname Combinations

Gerrits (cont.)
  VanDenBerg
    Alb Ref bp, 1702, 1708
    Alb Ref mm, 1699
    Pearson, 1700
    Rens Crsp 1, 1658, 1659
  VanDerGrist
    NY Ref bp, 1660
  VanDerPoel
    Alb Ref bp, 1683
    Gen Entr 1, 1669
    Pearson, 1654
    Ship Lists, 1647, no date
  VanDerWerken
    Pearson, 1700
    Ship Lists, 1663
  VanDien
    Ship Lists, 1660
  VanDuyn
    Fltb Ref mr, 1691
    King Co, 1696
    LI Fam 2, 1664
    LI Source, 1699
    Ship Lists, 1687, no date
  VanFrank
    Alb Ref bp, 1705, 1708
    Schn Ref mr, 1701, 1704
  VanGesel
    Ship Lists, no date
  VanGezel
    Nycol Doc 2, 1659
  VanHalen
    Hack Ref bp, 1707, 1709,
      1710, 1714
  VanHarlem
    Hack Ref mr, 1706
    NY Ref mr, 1642
  VanHeerden
    King Pap, 1664
  VanHuysen
    Hack Ref bp, 1694
  VanLaer
    Fern Wlls, 1684
    NY Ref bp, 1662
    NY Ref mr, 1660
    Ship Lists, 1658, 1659
  VanLair
    Pearson, 1670

VanLeeuwen
  LI Source, 1652
VanLoockere
  NY Ref mr, 1675
VanLoon
  NY Ref mr, 1652
VanMarcken
  King Co, 1654
  Pearson, 1661
  Rens Court, 1668, 1669,
    1672
VanMarck
  Nicl Lvl, 1672
  Nycol Doc 2, 1673
  Rcrd Nam 5, 1665
VanMeulen
  Pearson, 1671
VanMydrecht
  NY Ref mr, 1667
VanNess
  NY Ref mr, 1654
  Pearson, 1736
  Ship Lists, 1645
VanNostrand
  King Co, 1687
VanOldenburg
  Pearson, 1662
VanPopersdorf
  NYC Wills, 1680
VanRavenstyn
  LI Fam 1, 1660
  NY Ref mr, 1681
VanRovenstein
  NYC Wills, 1692
VanSchaick
  Fern Wlls, 1668
  Pearson, 1637
  Rens Crsp 2, 1661
  Ship Lists, 1637, 1652,
    1658, no date
VanSchoenderwoert
  Pearson, 1642
VanSchoonderwoerdt
  Ship Lists, 1642
VanSchoonhoven
  Pearson, 1701
VanStuyvesant
  NY Ref mr, 1699

VanSutphin
  NY Ref mr, 1652, 1664,
    1668
VanSwoll
  Bkln Ref bp, 1661
  NY Ref mr, 1658, 1671
  Rcrd Nam 6, 1671
VanThuyl
  NY Ref mr, 1667
VanTricht
  NY Ref mr, 1660
  Rcrd Nam 3, 1660
VanVechten
  Alb Ref mm, 1683, 1692
  Pearson, 1683
VanVliet
  King Pap, 1663
VanVorst
  Alb Ref bp, 1689
  NY Ref bp, 1662
  NY Ref mr, 1662
  Pearson, 1671
  Rcrd Nam 4, 1662
VanVranken
  Pearson, 1705
VanVrieslant
  Brgr Frm, 1657
VanWagenen
  Berg Ref bp, 1710
  Berg Ref mr, 1710
  Hack Ref bp, 1718
VanWie
  Pearson, 1689
VanWorcum
  NY Ref mr, 1660
Vedder
  Schn Ref mr, 1715
Verwen
  Ship Lists, 1663
VerWey
  Alb Ref bp, 1689
  Alb Ref mr, 1692
  Alb Ref mr, 1698
Hendricks
  King Pap, 1665
  Pearson, 1689
  Rcrd Nam 6, 1670

Viele
  Alb Ref bp, 1684
Voorhees
  King Co, 1695
Vries
  Brgr Frm, 1657
Wyngart
  Alb Ref bp, 1703
  Pearson, 1670
  Rens Crsp 2, 1689
Geurts
  Cray
    NY Ref bp, 1653
  VanSchoonhoven
    Pearson, 1700
Gilberts
  Bogart
    Bkln Ref bp, 1662, 1663, 1678
    Bkln Ref mm, 1664
    Fltb Ref bp, 1678, 1680, 1681
    Fltb Ref mr, 1687
    King Co, 1711
    Nicl Lvl, 1671
    NY Ref bp, 1655, 1661, 1671, 1688, 1691
    Nycol Doc 2, 1665
    Pearson, 1658
    Rcrd Nam 4, 1662
    Ship Lists, 1687, no date
  Couwenhoven
    Ship Lists, no date
  Middagh
    Rcrd Nam 3, 1658
  UytenBogart
    NY Lth bp, 1704
  VanBarnevelt
    NY Ref mr, 1658
  VanBrakel
    Alb Ref mr, 1693
    Pearson, 1699
  VanDenBerg
    Alb Ref bp, 1701, 1706
    Alb Ref mm, 1683
    Nicl Lvl, 1672
    NY Ref mr, 1663
    Nycol Doc 3, 1664

Pearson, 1683
    Rcrd Nam 4, 1662
  VanMeteren
    King Co, 1663
    Nycol Doc 2, 1673
    Ship Lists, no date
  VanPelt
    King Co, 1685
  Verschier
    Ship Lists, 1687
  VerSchieur
    King Co, 1649
  VerSchuer
    Fltb Ref bp, 1682
Giles
  Cock
    NY Ref bp, 1658, 1660, 1661
    Nycol Doc 3, 1664
    Rcrd Nam 3, 1659
  Cook
    Orphan Mst, 1664, 1665
  DeMandeville
    King Co, 1680
    NY Ref mr, 1680
  DeYoung
    Rcrd Nam 3, 1660
  Fonda
    Pearson, 1674
  Kock
    Pearson, 1657
    Ship Lists, 1656
  Lanwaer
    Rcrd Nam 7, 1674
  Mandeville
    Fltb Ref bp, 1681
    Fltb Ref mr, 1680
    Hack Ref mm, 1686
    NY Ref mr, 1681
  Marshall
    Brgr Frm, 1659
    Ship Lists, 1658
  Metselaer
    Pearson, 1657
  Meyer
    NY Ref bp, 1704
    Pearson, 1676

VanBrugh
  Brgr Frm, 1657
  Nicl Lvl, 1667
  NY Ref bp, 1652, 1653
VerBrugh
  Rcrd Nam 1, 1653
Wageman
  Rcrd Nam 1, 1654
Goosens
  VanSchaick
    Pearson, 1681
  VanSchuildert
    Rcrd Nam 4, 1663
  VanTwiller
    Pearson, 1661
    Ship Lists, no date
Gothards
  VanHarlem
    NY Ref bp, 1661
    NY Ref mr, 1650
Gregors
  Hillebrant
    Pearson, 1658
    Ship Lists, 1658
    Hack Ref bp, 1717, 1718, 1720
  DeGroot
    Hack Ref mr, 1716
    King Co, 1677
    NY Ref bp, 1678, 1679, 1682, 1688
    NY Ref mr, 1677
    Rcrd Nam 7, 1674

H
Hans
  Barhyte
    Alb Ref bp, 1701
    Pearson, 1692
    Ship Lists, 1684
  Beergen
    Fltb Ref bp, 1681
  Bergen
    Bkln Ref bp, 1681, 1697, 1701, 1702, 1708
    Fltb Ref bp, 1678, 1679, 1680, 1681, 1682, 1684,

Hans (cont.)
  Bergen (cont.)
    1685, 1688
    Fltb Ref mr, 1678
    King Co, 1633
    LI Source, 1677
    NY Ref bp, 1704
    Ship Lists, 1687, no date
  Bruyenburgh
    King Co, 1639
  Bruynenburgh
    Ship Lists, 1687
  DeNoorman
    NY Ref bp, 1644
  Douw
    Ship Lists, no date
  Dreeper
    Pearson, 1694
  Graer
    Ship Lists, 1660
  Harding
    Hack Ref mm, page xx
  Harty
    Hack Ref mm, page xx
  Huyck
    Alb Ref bp, 1700
    Alb Ref mm, 1683
    Fern Wlls, 1705
  Huygh
    Pearson, 1679
  Jacobs
    Berg Ref bp, 1688, 1691
    Berg Ref mm, 1690
    Berg Ref mr, 1687
  Jeralemon
    Hack Ref mr, 1701
  Noorman
    NY Ref bp, 1642
  Scherp
    Pearson, 1674
  Spier
    Hack Ref mr, 1708
  Stevens
    Fltb Ref bp, 1685
  Toll
    Pearson, 1720
    Schn Ref bp, 1707, 1708

VanBergen
  Nicl Lvl, 1671
  Ship Lists, 1633
VanNostrand
  Hack Ref mm, page xx
  King Co, 1685
  Ship Lists, 1639
VanSweden
  Pearson, 1663
VanToll
  Pearson, 1697
Woertman
  LI Source, 1685
Hartmans
  Vreeland
    Berg Ref bp, 1710
    Berg Ref dt, 1692, 1697
    Berg Ref mr, 1697, 1699,
      1701, 1708
    Hack Ref bp, 1711
Hassens
  VanBreuckelen
    NY Ref mr, 1669
Hendricks
  Aaten
    Ship Lists, 1687
  Aten
    King Co, 1680
    LI Source, 1696
  Banta
    Hack Ref bp, 1699, 1706,
      1708, 1709, 1710, 1712,
      1714, 1715, 1716, 1718
    Hack Ref mm, 1709
    Hack Ref mr, 1703, 1705,
      1708
    NY Lth mr, 1705
  Bas
    King Co, 1682
    NY Ref mr, 1681
  Beekman
    Pearson, 1661
    Ship Lists, 1638, no date
  Blauvelt
    Ship Lists, no date
    Tap Ref bp, 1708
  Blau
    Rcrd Nam 7, 1674

Boeg
  NY Ref mr, 1678
Bommel
  King Co, 1662
Bond
  King Ref bp, 1696
  Schn Ref bp, 1704
Boogh
  NY Ref bp, 1677, 1681
  NY Ref mr, 1663
  Rcrd Nam 5, 1665
Bout
  Alb Ref bp, 1704, 1706
  Pearson, 1706
Brasser
  Fltb Ref mr, 1689
  King Ref bp, 1690
  NY Ref mr, 1689
Bresse
  King Co, 1689
  Ship Lists, 1687
Brevoort
  King Co, 1644
  LI Source, 1695
  NY Ref bp, 1695, 1701,
    1703, 1706
Bries
  Alb Ref mr, 1686
  Bkln Ref bp, 1698
  King Co, 1680
Briez
  LI Source, 1695
Brimes
  King Co, 1692
Brinckerhoff
  Berg Ref bp, 1709
  Berg Ref mm, 1707, 1709
  Berg Ref mr, 1682, 1708
  Hack Ref bp, 1703, 1705,
    1709, 1710, 1716
  Hack Ref mm, 1699
  Hack Ref mr, 1702, 1708
  NY Ref mr, 1708
Brisse
  LI Source, 1692
Bronckhorst
  Berg Ref mr, 1682

Patronymic/Surname Combinations

Brower
  Pearson, 1660
Browne
  Gen Entr 2, 1684
Bruyns
  Gen Entr 1, 1664
  King Co, 1685
  NY Ref bp, 1697
  Nycol Doc 2, 1673
  Pearson, 1662
  Rens Court, 1671, 1672
  Rens Crsp 1, 1667
Bruyn
  NY Ref bp, 1678
  Rens Court, 1668, 1670
  Ship Lists, 1677
Burger
  Alb Ref bp, 1706
  Pearson, 1700, 1706
Buys
  King Pap, 1665
Bye
  Pearson, 1675
  Christians
  NY Ref mr, 1659
Coopal
  Rcrd Nam 1, 1654
  Rens Crsp 1, 1661
Cooper
  Evjen, 1659
  NY Ref mr, 1659
  Rcrd Nam 5, 1664
  Ship Lists, 1659
DeBoogh
  NYC Wills, 1687
DeBoog
  Nicl Lvl, 1672
  NY Ref bp, 1658
DeBruyn
  Fern Wlls, 1702
  NY Ref bp, 1688
DeCromp
  Rcrd Nam 3, 1661
DeGojer
  Ship Lists, 1644
DeHaas
  Alb Ref mm, 1683
  Pearson, 1683

DeSweedt
  Pearson, 1675
DeWees
  Ship Lists, 1690
Douw
  Rens Crsp 2, 1684
Graef
  Pearson, 1684
Graff
  King Pap, 1661
Grootvelt
  NY Ref mr, 1706
Haan
  Brgr Frm, 1659
Haen
  Ship Lists, 1657
Hafte
  King Co, 1664
Hamelward
  Pearson, 1638
Harderwyck
  Orphan Mst, 1664
Harung
  NY Lth bp, 1709
Helling
  Berg Ref mr, 1695
Hoppe
  Hack Ref bp, 1710, 1716,
  1718, 1719, 1720
  Hack Ref mm, 1710
  Hack Ref mr, 1706, 1707
Kip
  Brgr Frm, 1657
  NY Ref bp, 1647, 1662,
  1668
  NY Ref mr, 1654
  Nycol Doc 1, 1644
  Rcrd Nam 5, 1664
  Ship Lists, 1637, no date
Kortright
  King Ref bp, 1702
Lery
  Pearson, 1663
Lock
  NY Ref bp, 1671, 1672
  NY Ref mr, 1671
  Rens Crsp 1, 1668

Lott
  King Co, 1692
Maet
  Pearson, 1654
Mandeville
  Hack Ref mr, 1708
Maul
  Rcrd Nam 3, 1661
Obee
  NY Ref bp, 1658, 1659
  Rcrd Nam 3, 1658
Obe
  Orphan Mst, 1663, 1664
Ostrom
  Berg Ref bp, 1684
  Berg Ref mr, 1672, 1678
  Fltb Ref mr, 1683
Ploeg
  King Ref mr, 1699
Pruyn
  Hack Ref mr, 1710
Pulman
  King Co, 1664
Riddenhaas
  Ship Lists, 1646
Rochen
  Nycol Doc 2, 1661
Roseboom
  Pearson, 1704
Rosekrans
  Evjen, 1657
  NY Ref bp, 1659
Rouse
  NY Ref bp, 1641
Salsbergen
  Rens Court, 1672
Schoonhoven
  Fern Wlls, 1692
  Pearson, 1654
Schoonmaker
  King Ref bp, 1698, 1699,
  1700, 1702
  King Ref mr, 1689
Schumacher
  King Ref mr, 1688
Sibinck
  Pearson, 1655

Hendricks (cont.)
Slecht
Fltb Ref mr, 1692
King Co, 1687
Smack
Fltb Ref bp, 1687
Fltb Ref mr, 1685
King Co, 1693
Snyder
NY Ref mr, 1653
Spier
Berg Ref bp, 1687, 1692
Berg Ref mr, 1698
NY Ref bp, 1703
NY Ref mr, 1683
Splinter
Nycol Doc 2, 1673
Steelman
Orphan Mst, 1664
Rcrd Nam 1, 1653
Stelman
King Co, 1651
Stilman
Rens Crsp 1, 1661
Suydam
King Co, 1684
LI Source, 1698
Sybinck
Rcrd Nam 5, 1664
TenBroeck
NY Ref bp, 1689
TenEyck
Pearson, 1733
Tery
Rens Court, 1670
UytVrieslandt
NY Ref mr, 1698
VanAlcmaer
NY Ref mr, 1662
VanAmersfort
NY Ref mr, 1668
VanBaal
Gen Entr 1, 1670
Nicl Lvl, 1670
NY Ref mr, 1683
Nycol Doc 2, 1677
Rcrd Nam 4, 1663

VanBaelen
Ship Lists, 1657
VanBael
Pearson, 1659
Rens Court, 1669, 1670,
1672
Rens Crsp 2, 1682
Ship Lists, 1653, 1657
VanBergen
NY Ref mr, 1650, 1657,
1683
VanBommel
Crt Assz, 1676
Nicl Lvl, 1672
NY Ref bp, 1658, 1660,
1662, 1677
NY Ref mr, 1662, 1682
NYC Wills, 1693
Nycol Doc 2, 1674
Rcrd Nam 5, 1664
VanBoswyck
NY Ref mr, 1692
VanBrevoort
NY Ref mr, 1670, 1673
VanBriel
Rcrd Nam 1, 1655
VanBuren
Alb Ref bp, 1702
Alb Ref mr, 1699
Pearson, 1701
Ship Lists, no date
VanCampen
NY Ref bp, 1661
Nycol Doc 3, 1664
Rcrd Nam 5, 1665
VanCortlandt
Rens Crsp 2, 1681
VanDenBerg
Alb Ref bp, 1688
Pearson, 1683
VanDenBriel
NY Ref bp, 1658, 1662
Vanderbilt
Rcrd Nam 1, 1653
VanDerBreets
King Co, 1687

VanDeventer
Brgr Frm, 1657
NY Ref mr, 1646
VanDoesburg
King Co, 1654
NY Ref mr, 1655
Pearson, 1698
Rcrd Nam 7, 1658
VanDort
NY Ref mr, 1652
VanDuisberg
NY Ref bp, 1656
VanEens
King Co, 1661
VanErlanger
Gen Entr 1, 1664
VanEs
Ship Lists, 1642
VanFeurden
NY Ref mr, 1693
VanGottenburgh
Pearson, 1663
VanGrist
NY Ref bp, 1681
VanGroeningen
NY Ref mr, 1659
VanGunst
Brgr Frm, 1657
Gen Entr 1, 1668
King Co, 1655
Nicl Lvl, 1669
NY Ref bp, 1665, 1668,
1672, 1679, 1683
NY Ref mr, 1685
Rcrd Nam 3, 1659
VanHamelwaard
Ship Lists, 1638
VanHarderwyck
Orphan Mst, 1663, 1664,
1665
Rcrd Nam 3, 1659
VanHarlem
NY Ref mr, 1655
VanHarstenhorst
Pearson, 1662
VanKeulen
Brgr Frm, 1657

Patronymic/Surname Combinations

VanLauven
   Rens Crsp 2, 1681
VanLeeuven
   Fltb Ref bp, 1681
   Fltb Ref mr, 1681
VanLeeuwen
   LI Source, 1670
   Ship Lists, no date
VanLoosereght
   Pearson, 1654
VanMeppel
   King Ref bp, 1663
   NY Ref mr, 1663, 1681
VanMiddelburg
   NY Ref mr, 1683
VanMispadtkill
   NY Ref mr, 1693
VanNess
   Fern Wlls, 1725
   Fltb Ref bp, 1679, 1680
   Pearson, 1643
   Ship Lists, 1641, no date
VanNorden
   Evjen, 1656
   NY Ref mr, 1656
VanOstrom
   Berg Ref bp, 1706
VanPutten
   NY Ref mr, 1655
VanReis
   Pearson, 1663
VanRodenkirk
   NY Ref mr, 1656
VanRys
   Rcrd Nam 5, 1664
VanSalsbergen
   Alb Ref mr, 1693
   Pearson, 1673
   Rens Court, 1672
VanSalsbury
   Nicl Lvl, 1671
VanSant
   King Ref mr, 1701
VanSchoonhoven
   Pearson, 1681
   Ship Lists, 1658, no date
VanSoest
   Pearson, 1630

VanSutphin
   NY Ref mr, 1657, 1664
VanUtrecht
   Pearson, 1654
VanWaerdenbroeck
   NY Ref mr, 1654
VanWagenen
   Hack Ref mr, 1721
VanWayen
   King Ref mr, 1684
VanWey
   King Pap, 1665
   Pearson, 1700, 1704
Varrevanger
   Pearson, 1661
   Rens Court, 1670
Varvanger
   Brgr Frm, 1657
   Nycol Doc 2, 1664
   Rcrd Nam 1, 1653
Verbraeck
   Pearson, 1668
Vogelsang
   Rcrd Nam 1, 1655
Volck
   Berg Ref bp, 1692
Vrooman
   Alb Ref mr, 1686
   Fltb Ref bp, 1683
   King Co, 1677
   Pearson, 1683
VVanBael
   Rens Court, 1671
Westercamp
   King Pap, 1662, 1665
   King Ref bp, 1662
   King Ref mr, 1664
Wils
   Bkln Ref bp, 1693
Wiltse
   Fltb Ref mr, 1690
Wynhard
   Fltb Ref bp, 1684
Yansz
   Rens Crsp 1, 1658
Yolcx
   King Co, 1692
   NY Ref mr, 1692

Zip
   NY Ref mr, 1656
Herberts
   Constapel
     Pearson, 1640
     Rens Crsp 1, 1661
     Ship Lists, 1642
   Cruyf
     Rcrd Nam 1, 1655
   VanCamp
     NY Ref bp, 1647
   VanDerBlass
     Pearson, 1640
   VanDeusen
     Pearson, 1736
Hermans
   Backer
     Fern Wlls, 1683
     Pearson, 1658
   Barkelo
     King Co, 1662
   Benthem
     NY Ref mr, 1673
   Boertgens
     Ship Lists, no date
   Brower
     King Pap, 1668
     Ship Lists, 1662, no date
   Bussing
     Ship Lists, 1673
   Coerten
     LI Fam 1, 1665
   Coort
     Brgr Frm, 1658
     Rcrd Nam 3, 1658
   Cort
     King Pap, 1665
   DeRaedt
     NY Ref bp, 1663
   Fesselet
     King Pap, 1664
   Gansevoort
     Rcrd Nam 1, 1655
     Rens Crsp 2, 1684
     Ship Lists, no date
   Hoffman
     Bkln Ref mr, 1663
     King Co, 1663

Hermans (cont.)
 Hun
  Alb Ref bp, 1702, 1704,
  1705, 1707, 1709
  Pearson, 1662
 Knickerbacker
  Alb Ref bp, 1701
  Pearson, 1708
 Lievens
  Alb Ref mm, 1683
 Lieversen
  Pearson, 1683
 Schutt
  NY Ref bp, 1651
  Ship Lists, 1649
 Tallman
  Berg Ref dt, 1674, 1687
  Tap Ref bp, 1706, 1710
 UytBohemen
  NY Ref mr, 1651
 Van Lemmet
  NY Ref mr, 1641
 VanAlcmaer
  NY Ref mr, 1664
 VanAmersfort
  Pearson, 1662
  Ship Lists, 1687
 VanBorkelo
  Berg Ref mr, 1697
  Fltb Ref bp, 1681
 VanDerBogart
  Alb Ref bp, 1684, 1685,
  1686, 1688
  Pearson, 1683
  Rens Crsp 2, 1683
 VanGansevoort
  Pearson, 1664
 VanHoesen
  NY Ref mr, 1641
 VanHun
  Pearson, 1681
 VanOetmarsen
  NY Ref mr, 1663
 VanThuyl
  Nycol Doc 2, 1661
 VanTurick
  Pearson, 1664

 VanVoorsthuysen
  NY Ref mr, 1660
 VanWitmont
  NY Ref mr, 1652
 Vischer
  Alb Ref bp, 1689, 1696,
  1699, 1700, 1701, 1702,
  1703, 1704, 1705, 1706,
  1708
  Alb Ref mm, 1683
  Alb Ref mr, 1686, 1692
  King Ref mr, 1695
  Pearson, 1701
 Vreeland
  Berg Ref bp, 1698, 1709
 Weaver
  Pearson, 1678
 Weendorp
  Pearson, 1663

Herricks
 Kranckheyt
  Tary Ref bp, 1697, 1699,
  1702, 1703, 1706, 1708
  Tary Ref mm, 1700?
  Tary Ref mr, 1708

Hertgers
 VanVee
  Ship Lists, 1645

Hertgerts
 VanVee
  Pearson, 1645

Hessels
 VanNewkirk
  NY Ref mr, 1667

Heymans
 Roosa
  Gen Entr 1, 1669
  King Pap, 1661, 1664
  King Ref bp, 1664, 1679,
  1705
  Nicl Lvl, 1667
  Ship Lists, no date

Hieronymus
 Volck
  Nycol Doc 5, 1708

Hillebrants
 VanDuyckhuysen
  Gen Entr 1, 1669

 VanDyckhuys
  King Co, 1661
Holgers
 Noorman
  Evjen, 1632
Horns
 Zeewis
  King Co, 1661
Huberts
 Blauvelt
  Hack Ref bp, 1719
  Hack Ref mr, 1709
  Tap Ref bp, 1706, 1708
 Brink
  Ship Lists, no date
 Egberts
  King Co, 1675
 Maul
  Brgr Frm, 1657
  King Co, 1641
  LI Source, 1693
  NY Ref bp, 1648, 1658
  Nycol Doc 1, 1650
  Rcrd Nam 1, 1653
 Sterrenvelt
  NY Ref bp, 1662
  Orphan Mst, 1665
  Rcrd Nam 3, 1661
  Ship Lists, 1660
 VanHarlem
  NY Ref mr, 1652
 VanVlissingen
  NY Ref mr, 1690
Huygens
 DeCley
  NY Ref mr, 1683
 DeKlein
  Bkln Ref bp, 1698
  King Co, 1683
  LI Source, 1693
  NY Ref bp, 1684, 1688,
  1698, 1702, 1704, 1706
  NY Ref mr, 1670, 1680,
  1704
  NYC Wills, 1695
  Rcrd Nam 6, 1670
  West Wills, 1735

Patronymic/Surname Combinations

Klein
  NY Ref bp, 1671
Rapalye
  Nycol Doc 1, 1652

I

Ides
  VanDerVorst
    Berg Ref mm, 1672, 1682
    Gen Entr 1, 1671
    NY Ref mr, 1671
  VanVorst
    NY Ref bp, 1687, 1689
    Tap Ref bp, 1705
  Waert
    NY Ref bp, 1657
Isaacs
  Fonda
    Pearson, 1732
  Lansing
    Pearson, 1747
  Planck
    NY Ref bp, 1639, 1640,
    1641, 1642, 1643, 1644,
    1646, 1648
  Van Hartevelt
    NY Ref bp, 1662
    Rcrd Nam 5, 1664
  VanBeeck
    NY Ref bp, 1655
  VanDeusen
    Brgr Frm, 1698
    NY Ref bp, 1700
    Pearson, 1740
  VanHoeck
    NY Ref bp, 1690, 1692
    NY Ref mr, 1695
    Pearson, 1658
  VanSartervelt
    LI Source, 1667
  VanVredenburgh
    NY Ref bp, 1667
    Ship Lists, no date
  VerPlanck
    Pearson, 1667
    Ship Lists, 1633
  Vredenburg
    NY Ref mr, 1664

J

Jacobs
  Backer
    Rcrd Nam 1, 1655
  Bamboes
    Rcrd Nam 2, 1658
    Rens Court, 1669
    Rens Crsp 1, 1658
  Bambus
    Pearson, 1657
  Banta
    Ship Lists, no date
  Beekman
    Pearson, 1746
  Bergen
    King Co, 1681
  Bierdrager
    Pearson, 1661
  Boerum
    King Co, 1617
  Borsboom
    NYC Wills, 1686
    Pearson, 1662
    Rens Court, 1668, 1670,
    1671
  Broersen
    King Pap, 1663
  Brower
    King Co, 1689
  Burhans
    Nicl Lvl, 1667
  Buys
    Brgr Frm, 1657
    King Co, 1653
    Rcrd Nam 1, 1655
  Bye
    Pearson, 1659
  Calebuys
    Rcrd Nam 1, 1654
  Carpenel
    Brgr Frm, 1657
    NY Ref bp, 1642
    NY Ref mr, 1641
    Rcrd Nam 7, 1657
  Clockluyer
    Pearson, 1661

Cole
  Brgr Frm, 1657
  King Ref bp, 1681
  King Ref mr, 1683
  Nycol Doc 2, 1663
  Rcrd Nam 1, 1654
Couwenhoven
  King Co, 1641
DeBruyn
  Ship Lists, 1649
Decker
  King Ref mr, 1704
DeGroot
  NY Ref bp, 1688, 1690
DeHart
  NY Ref bp, 1683
Delmont
  Alb Ref bp, 1702
DeVries
  King Co, 1667
  King Pap, 1664
  Nycol Doc 2, 1662
  Orphan Mst, 1666
  Rens Crsp 1, 1663
Elbins
  Nycol Doc 1, 1633
Elkens
  Pearson, 1618
Everson
  Pearson, 1744
Flodder
  Pearson, 1685
Freelinghuysen
  Ship Lists, no date
Frelinghuysen
  Ship Lists, 1720
Gardenier
  Pearson, 1683
  Rens Court, 1672
Gardner
  Alb Ref bp, 1685, 1689
  Alb Ref mr, 1692, 1695
  Fern Wlls, 1689, 1710
Glenn
  Pearson, 1699
Goewey
  NY Ref bp, 1706

Jacobs (cont.)
  Groesbeek
    Alb Ref bp, 1700, 1701
    Alb Ref mm, 1683
    Fern Wlls, 1707
    Pearson, 1661
    Ship Lists, no date
  Van Rotterdam
  Hallenbeck
    NY Lth bp, 1708
    Pearson, no date
    Rens Crsp 1, 1674
    Rens Crsp 2, 1687
    Ship Lists, no date
  Harberding
    NY Ref bp, 1671
  Harty
    NY Ref mr, 1668
    Ship Lists, 1663, 1685
  Hovenier
    King Ref bp, 1683
  Jansen
    King Pap, 1663
  Kieste
    King Co, 1691
  Lansing
    Pearson, 1734
  Larzelere
    King Co, 1677
  Loockermans
    Rcrd Nam 3, 1661
  Marcelis
    Rcrd Nam 6, 1668
  Marius
    Brgr Frm, 1657, 1683
    Crt Assz, 1668
    Gen Entr 2, 1677
    King Ref bp, 1681
    NY Ref bp, 1650, 1651,
    1657, 1659, 1661, 1664,
    1665, 1666, 1667, 1668,
    1674, 1676, 1677, 1678,
    1679, 1680, 1681, 1682,
    1684, 1686, 1687, 1688,
    1689, 1690, 1691, 1693,
    1695, 1696, 1702
    NY Ref mr, 1655
    NYC Court, 1693

NYC Wills, 1701, 1706
Nycol Doc 2, 1674
Pearson, 1663
Rcrd Nam 1, 1654
Mey
  Nycol Doc 1, 1620
Mooy
  Nycol Doc 2, 1677
Moy
  Rens Crsp 2, 1684
Noorthbrook
  King Co, 1667
Onnosel
  Rcrd Nam 3, 1661
Otterspoor
  King Pap, 1663
Outwater
  Ship Lists, no date
OuyVriesland
  NY Ref mr, 1666
Patervaer
  Rcrd Nam 1, 1654
Pott
  Rcrd Nam 3, 1660
Quick
  NY Ref bp, 1682, 1687
  NY Ref mr, 1682, 1683,
  1685
Roos
  Hack Ref mr, 1718
Roy
  Fern Wlls, 1643
Sardingh
  Ship Lists, 1663
Schermerhorn
  Alb Ref bp, 1684, 1685
  Fern Wlls, 1678
  Pearson, 1678
Schipper
  NY Ref bp, 1680
  NY Ref mr, 1678
Schnett
  NY Lth bp, 1710
Schooff
  NY Ref mr, 1658
Schout
  Pearson, 1697

Slicoten
  King Pap, 1667
Somerindink
  NY Ref bp, 1709
Sprong
  NY Ref mr, 1670
Steenwyck
  Rcrd Nam 1, 1653
Stille
  King Co, 1639
  NY Ref bp, 1646, 1660,
  1672
  NY Ref mr, 1659
  Nycol Doc 1, 1644
  Rcrd Nam 1, 1653
Stoll
  King Pap, 1670
  King Ref bp, 1685, 1689,
  1695
  King Ref mr, 1684
Strycker
  Bkln Ref bp, 1687
  King Co, 1673
Sutphin
  Fltb Ref bp, 1684
Suydam
  King Co, 1696
Swanevelt
  Ship Lists, 1652
Tolier
  Bogamr, 1677
  King Co, 1677
Turck
  Ship Lists, 1661
VanAmsterdam
  NY Ref mr, 1655
VanBeest
  NY Ref mr, 1662
VanBoerum
  LI Source, 1670, 1671,
  1675, 1687, no date
  Nycol Doc 2, 1664, 1665
  Ship Lists, 1687
VanBrugh
  NY Ref mr, 1670
VanCouwenhoven
  LI Fam 2, 1639

Patronymic/Surname Combinations

VanDeGrift
  King Co, 1667
VanDenNiyen
  Fltb Ref bp, 1680
VanDerGrift
  Bkln Ref bp, 1681
VanDerGrist
  Fltb Ref bp, 1680, 1681
  NY Ref mr, 1666
VanDerMeyen
  Fltb Ref bp, 1680
  Fltb Ref mr, 1678
VanDerMeyer
  King Co, 1678
VanDeusen
  Alb Ref bp, 1700, 1701,
  1702, 1703, 1706, 1709
  Alb Ref mm, 1683
  Pearson, 1683
VanDeventer
  King Co, 1719
VanDeWater
  King Co, 1669
VanDuyn
  NY Ref bp, 1687
VanEmbden
  NY Ref mr, 1660
VanEmmenes
  NY Ref mr, 1643
VanEtten
  King Ref mr, 1685
VanHarlem
  NY Ref mr, 1641
VanHertogenbosch
  NY Ref mr, 1650
VanHoesen
  Atns Lth bp, 1708, 1710
  NY Lth bp, 1708, 1710
VanHolstein
  King Pap, 1664
VanHoogharsteen
  NY Ref mr, 1658
VanHorn
  NY Ref mr, 1663
VanKuykenthal
  King Ref bp, 1706
VanLangendyck
  NY Ref mr, 1649

VanLeeuwen
  Ship Lists, 1660
VanMiddelburg
  NY Ref mr, 1657
VanNoortstrant
  Pearson, 1677
VanNoort
  King Co, 1667
VanNorden
  NY Ref bp, 1644
VanNortwyck
  King Co, 1662
VanNostrand
  King Ref bp, 1702
VanNuyse
  King Co, 1695
VanOostsanem
  Pearson, 1661
VanOstrand
  Alb Ref bp, 1687, 1688
  Alb Ref mm, 1683
  Alb Ref mr, 1688
  King Ref bp, 1689, 1699
VanRhenen
  Bkln Ref mr, 1661
VanRinsburgh
  Pearson, 1663
VanRotterdam
  NY Ref mr, 1699
  Pearson, 1661
VanSchermer
  Rcrd Nam 3, 1661
VanSchoenderwoert
  Pearson, 1636
  Ship Lists, 1640
VanSchooderwoert
  NY Ref mr, 1650
  Ship Lists, 1636
VanSchoonderwoerdt
  Rens Crsp 1, 1661
VanSteenwyck
  NY Ref mr, 1642
VanUtrecht
  NY Ref mr, 1662
VanUytdam
  NY Ref mr, 1689
VanVleckenstine
  NY Ref bp, 1673

VanVreeland
  NY Ref mr, 1642
VanWagenen
  King Ref bp, 1710
  Ship Lists, no date
VanWinckel
  Berg Ref bp, 1686, 1688,
  1689, 1690, 1692, 1696
  Berg Ref dt, 1692, 1708
  Berg Ref mm, 1676, 1677,
  1704
  Berg Ref mr, 1671, 1675,
  1676, 1695, 1699, 1703,
  1710
  Hack Ref bp, 1702, 1705,
  1718
  Hack Ref mm, 1696
  Hack Ref mr, 1703, 1712
  NY Ref bp, 1686
  NY Ref mr, 1676, 1707
VanWoert
  Pearson, 1636
  Ship Lists, no date
Verdon
  King Co, 1682
VerDuyn
  NY Ref bp, 1689, 1691,
  1694
Vis
  King Co, 1689
Vosburgh
  Pearson, 1657
Vreeland
  Ship Lists, 1633
Vries
  Rcrd Nam 4, 1662
Vroom
  Bkln Ref bp, 1681
Weesp
  Rcrd Nam 2, 1658
Wendel
  Pearson, 1749
Witzen
  Nycol Doc 1, 1614
Woertendyke
  NY Ref mr, 1709, 1710
Wolfe
  King Co, 1666

Jacobs (cont.)
Wolf
Bkln Ref bp, 1678
Fltb Ref bp, 1678
Wyngaerden
NY Ref mr, 1665
Zabriskie
Hack Ref bp, 1718
Jacques
Cortelyou
King Co, 1662
James
Fouchard
Brgr Frm, 1704
Minville
Brgr Frm, 1702
Jan Teunis
Tappan
Ship Lists, 1652
Jans
Abeel
Fern Wlls, 1678
King Co, 1664
NYC Wills, 1678
Pearson, 1659
Ship Lists, no date
Aemilius
Rens Crsp 1, 1656
Alcmaer
Nycol Doc 1, 1625
Amack
King Co, 1673
Ameland
King Co, 1699
Amerman
Fltb Ref bp, 1685
Amersfort
King Pap, 1663
Amerstede
King Pap, 1662
Amertman
LI Source, 1694, 1695
Ammerman
Ship Lists, 1687

Appel
Pearson, 1656
Rens Crsp 1, 1664
Ship Lists, 1649
Asdalen
Rcrd Nam 4, 1663
Backer
NY Ref bp, 1652, 1675,
1676
Nycol Doc 2, 1664
Rcrd Nam 6, 1668
Baker
Rcrd Nam 1, 1654
Bakker
Pearson, 1665
Ball
King Co, 1652
Bal
Pearson, 1660
Ship Lists, 1652
Bant
Berg Ref mr, 1697
NY Ref mr, 1697
Barkelo
King Co, 1672
Bastians
King Ref bp, 1694
Rcrd Nam 5, 1664
Been
Bkln Ref bp, 1662
Rcrd Nam 6, 1666
Bennet
King Co, 1696
Benson
Hack Ref bp, 1720
Berckelson
Rcrd Nam 7, 1673
Bergen
Fltb Ref bp, 1681
Berrien
Bkln Ref bp, 1681
Fltb Ref bp, 1678, 1681,
1683, 1685
King Co, 1670
LI Source, 1684
Berry
LI Source, 1683

Besems
NY Ref bp, 1660
Bestevaer
Gen Entr 1, 1669
Nycol Doc 2, 1658
Rcrd Nam 1, 1655
Rens Crsp 1, 1655, 1656,
1657, 1658, 1660, 1662,
1664
Rens Crsp 1, 1668
Ship Lists, 1657
Blaeck
NY Ref bp, 1668
Blauw
King Co, no date
Bleecker
Alb Ref bp, 1692, 1696,
1699, 1703
Alb Ref mm, 1683
Gen Entr 2, 1684
King Pap, 1665
King Ref bp, 1678
Nycol Doc 2, 1674
Pearson, 1666
Rens Court, 1668, 1669,
1671
Rens Crsp 2, 1683
Ship Lists, 1658, no date
Bloodgood
NY Ref bp, 1662
Ship Lists, no date
Bloom
Evjen, 1641
King Co, 1665
NY Ref mr, 1705
Ship Lists, 1637
Blycker
Rens Court, 1669
Boeckhout
NY Ref bp, 1679, 1683,
1688
NY Ref mr, 1699
Boerhol
Fltb Ref mr, 1690
King Co, 1690
Bogardus
Fern Wlls, 1663

Bogart
  Berg Ref mm, 1676
  Brgr Frm, 1702
  Gen Entr 1, 1670
  Hack Ref bp, 1719
  Hack Ref mm, 1687
  Hack Ref mr, 1718
  LI Source, 1687
  NY Ref bp, 1687, 1688,
    1689, 1705
  NY Ref mr, 1686, 1695
  Pearson, 1699
  Ship Lists, no date
Boomgart
  King Co, 1684
  LI Source, 1690, 1700
Bootsen
  Brgr Frm, 1659
Bosch
  Alb Ref bp, 1689, 1691
  Alb Ref mr, 1688
  NY Ref bp, 1664, 1689,
    1690, 1691, 1693, 1697
  NY Ref mr, 1690, 1694,
    1697
  Pearson, 1689
  Rcrd Nam 5, 1664
Bos
  Pearson, 1666
Brabander
  King Pap, 1662
  Nicl Lvl, 1667
Brandt
  Nycol Doc 2, 1630
Bratt
  Pearson, 1681
  Breested
  NY Ref bp, 1654, 1667,
    1674
Brevoort
  King Co, 1630
  Ship Lists, no date
Broer
  Ship Lists, 1655
Bronck
  Pearson, 1738

Brower
  Fltb Ref bp, 1678
  King Co, 1683
Bruynen
  Rcrd Nam 3, 1660
Bruyn
  Nycol Doc 2, 1661
Buys
  Berg Ref bp, 1685, 1699
  Berg Ref mr, 1684
  Bkln Ref bp, 1683, 1691,
    1694
  Bkln Ref mr, 1690
  Brgr Frm, 1698
  Fltb Ref bp, 1682
  King Co, 1684
  LI Fam 1, 1652
Calff
  Ship Lists, 1647
Cammega
  Fltb Ref bp, 1686, 1688
  King Co, 1679
CanCommel
  Rcrd Nam 1, 1665
Capteyn
  Hack Ref bp, 1698
Cap
  Hack Ref bp, 1704
Caspars
  Alb Ref bp, 1705
Claarbout
  Rcrd Nam 3, 1660
Clapper
  Brgr Frm, 1657
  Nicl Lvl, 1672
  NY Ref bp, 1658, 1659,
    1660, 1663, 1669
  NY Ref mr, 1657
  Nycol Doc 3, 1664
  Orphan Mst, 1664
  Rcrd Nam 1, 1655
  Ship Lists, 1655
Cleermaecker
  Ship Lists, 1648
Cloef
  Fltb Ref bp, 1687

Cloppenburg
  NY Ref mr, 1659
  Rcrd Nam 1, 1655
Cock
  NY Ref bp, 1688, 1689
Cocquyt
  NY Ref mr, 1662
Coevers
  Bkln Ref bp, 1663, 1680
  Fltb Ref bp, 1683
  NY Ref bp, 1680, 1684
Cole
  Nycol Doc 1, 1656
  Rcrd Nam 1, 1653
Coninck
  Rens Court, 1670
Conninck
  Pearson, 1654
Cooper
  Berg Ref dt, 1688, 1692
  Hack Ref bp, 1718
  Hack Ref mr, 1718
  King Co, 1655, 1675
  Nicl Lvl, 1667
  NY Ref bp, 1649
  Pearson, 1634
  Rcrd Nam 1, 1653
  Rcrd Nam 5, 1665
  Ship Lists, 1634, 1640,
    1652
Corbyn
  Rcrd Nam 4, 1662
Couwenhoven
  Bkln Ref mr, 1695
  Fltb Ref mr, 1691
  King Co, 1693
Covert
  Fltb Ref bp, 1680
  LI Source, 1694, 1698,
    1700
  NY Ref bp, 1691
  Ship Lists, 1687, no date
Cristman
  Rcrd Nam 1, 1653
Crol
  Pearson, 1630
Croom
  Pearson, 1660

Patronymic/Surname Combinations

Jans (cont.)
Croon
  Fern Wlls, 1694
  Nicl Lvl, 1667
  Nycol Doc 1, 1652
  Ship Lists, 1649, 1654
Damen
  Berg Ref mr, 1697
  Bkln Ref bp, 1680, 1681
  Bkln Ref mr, 1695
  Fern Wlls, 1649
  Fltb Ref bp, 1680, 1681
  Fltb Ref mr, 1679, 1681
  King Co, 1677
  NY Ref bp, 1649
  NY Ref mr, 1679
  Nycol Doc 1, 1644
  Pearson, 1634
  Ship Lists, 1634, 1651
Dam
  NY Ref bp, 1642, 1646, 1660
DeBoer
  Gen Entr 2, 1675
  Pearson, 1661
  Ship Lists, 1648
DeBrabander
  King Pap, 1662
  Ship Lists, 1651
DeCamp
  King Co, 1664
  Ship Lists, 1664, 1687
Decker
  King Ref bp, 1679, 1681, 1684, 1687, 1688, 1695, 1700, 1702
  King Ref mr, 1678, 1684, 1685
DeCuyper
  Rcrd Nam 1, 1653
DeDrayer
  NY Ref bp, 1659
Deenmarken
  NY Ref mr, 1659
DeGarmo
  Pearson, 1753
DeGroot
  Evjen, 1661

DeGuyt
  Rens Crsp 1, 1663
DeJones
  Gen Entr 1, 1670
DeJonge
  Rens Crsp 1, 1661, 1664
DeLange
  King Ref bp, 1663
DeLeeuw
  LI Fam 2, no date
DeMandeville
  Ship Lists, 1649
DeMare
  LI Source, 1694
DenHagenaer
  NY Ref bp, 1659
DeRuyter
  Ship Lists, 1636
DeSeeuw
  LI Fam 2, no date
DeSee
  King Co, 1660
DeVisscher
  Nicl Lvl, 1672
DeVos
  NY Ref mr, 1675
DeVries
  Pearson, 1656
DeWitt
  King Co, 1652
  Rens Crsp 1, 1660
  Ship Lists, 1687
DeYoung
  NY Ref bp, 1660, 1662, 1664
  NY Ref mr, 1659
  Rcrd Nam 1, 1653
  Ship Lists, 1652
Dey
  NYC Wills, 1693
DeZeeuw
  Bkln Ref bp, 1682
  Fltb Ref bp, 1682
Diffoer
  Alb Ref bp, 1705

Ditmars
  Evjen, 1643
  King Co, 1647
  Ship Lists, no date
Dominicus
  LI Fam 2, no date
Dommelaer
  Pearson, 1657
Dorland
  Bkln Ref bp, 1696
  Bkln Ref mr, 1695
  Bogart, 1672
  Fltb Ref bp, 1681
  Fltb Ref mr, 1692
  Gen Entr 2, 1676
  King Co, 1675
  Nicl Lvl, 1672
  Ship Lists, 1663
Douw
  Evjen, 1638
  Pearson, 1681
  Rens Crsp 1, 1658, 1659, 1661, 1662
  Rens Crsp 2, 1683
  Ship Lists, 1638, no date
Drats
  Fltb Ref bp, 1682
  Fltb Ref mr, 1682
  King Co, 1661
  NY Ref mr, 1682
  Rcrd Nam 2, 1658
Druyn
  LI Source, 1689
Dufoert
  NY Ref mr, 1698
Dye
  NY Ref bp, 1677
Eeckelen
  Rens Crsp 1, 1659
Eencluys
  Rens Court, 1670
  Ship Lists, 1641
Eggert
  NYC Wills, 1678
Emilius
  Nycol Doc 2, 1661
Engel
  Nycol Doc 1, 1618

Engsinck
  Ship Lists, 1660, no date
Fenn
  Gen Entr 2, 1684
Flansburgh
  Brgr Frm, 1683
  Gen Entr 2, 1684
  NY Ref bp, 1691
Flodder
  Nicl Lvl, 1665
  Pearson, 1638
  Rcrd Nam 1, 1654
  Rens Court, 1668, 1669,
  1670, 1671, 1672
  Rens Crsp 1, 1661, 1664
  Ship Lists, 1638, 1642
Fyn
  King Co, 1666
Galma
  Brgr Frm, 1657
  Nycol Doc 3, 1664
  Rcrd Nam 1, 1653
Gardenier
  Pearson, 1702
  Rens Court, 1672
  Ship Lists, 1638
Gardinier
  Ship Lists, no date
Gardner
  Alb Ref bp, 1701
Goes
  Alb Ref bp, 1687, 1700,
  1702
  Pearson, 1697
Goewey
  * Alb Ref bp, 1701, 1702,
  1704
  Pearson, 1702
Gravenhage
  NY Ref mr, 1671
Grever
  Rcrd Nam 2, 1658
Groenewout
  Rens Court, 1669, 1670,
  1671
Groenwoet
  Pearson, 1662

Gruis
  NY Ref bp, 1668
Hagenaar
  Orphan Mst, 1663, 1665
Hagener
  Brgr Frm, 1657
  Nycol Doc 3, 1664
  Rcrd Nam 4, 1663
Hallenbeck
  Alb Ref bp, 1707, 1709
  Atns Lth mr, 1709
  NY Lth bp, 1709
  NY Lth mr, 1709
  Pearson, 1707
Hap
  King Pap, 1661
  NY Ref bp, 1657
  Pearson, 1630
  Rens Crsp 2, 1685
  Ship Lists, 1645
Hardenbergh
  Ship Lists, no date
Hardenbrugh
  LI Fam 1, 1670
Hardenburgh
  Ship Lists, 1667
Haring
  NY Ref bp, 1688
  NY Ref mr, 1687
  Tap Ref bp, 1704
Hartmann
  Ship Lists, no date
Haughwout
  LI Fam 1, 1660
Heerings
  Hack Ref bp, 1694, 1711
Helmer
  Alb Ref mr, 1686
Henypot
  Ship Lists, 1639
Herttenbergh
  Pearson, 1664
Hesse
  Nycol Doc 1, 1633
Heyman
  NY Ref bp, 1652
Heyning
  NY Ref mr, 1667

Hoochsaet
  Nycol Doc 2, 1657
Hoogland
  Bkln Ref mr, 1662
  Crt Assz, 1679
  Fltb Ref bp, 1681, 1686
  King Co, 1657
  LI Source, 1689, 1694,
  1695, 1697, 1698
  Ship Lists, 1662, no date
Hoogstraten
  NY Ref bp, 1680
Hoog
  LI Source, 1701
Hoorn
  NY Ref bp, 1671
  Nycol Doc 2, 1659
  Pearson, 1659
  Rcrd Nam 3, 1659
Hotaling
  King Ref bp, 1679
Houten
  Nycol Doc 1, 1621
Houtsager
  King Pap, 1662
Huys
  Nycol Doc 1, 1656
  Rcrd Nam 1, 1654
  Rens Crsp 1, 1664
JanDenHans
  NY Ref bp, 1660
Jeralemon
  Alb Ref bp, 1702
Jeroloman
  Pearson, 1702
Jochems
  King Pap, 1662
Jonker
  Alb Ref mr, 1699
Jurianse
  King Co, 1688
Kamminga
  Ship Lists, 1687
Kapt
  Hack Ref bp, 1702
Kap
  Hack Ref bp, 1703

Patronymic/Surname Combinations

Jans (cont.)
Kitser
    Rcrd Nam 6, 1666
Kleermaker
    Pearson, 1683
Kleumpje
    Berg Ref dt, 1688
Klinckhamer
    Rcrd Nam 1, 1654
Klinckhammer
    Ship Lists, no date
Knickerbacker
    Alb Ref bmm, 1683
    Fern Wlls, 1708
    Pearson, 1682
    Rens Crsp 2, 1683
    Ship Lists, 1700, no date
Koninck
    NY Ref bp, 1665
    Ship Lists, 1663
Koningh
    Rens Court, 1671
Koorenbeurs
    Alb Ref bp, 1683
Krol
    Ship Lists, 13630
Kromenborch
    Pearson, 1657
Kunst
    King Ref bp, 1683, 1689
    King Ref mr, 1684
Laenen
    LI Source, 1687
Lamaker
    Pearson, 1659
Langedyck
    Brgr Frm, 1657
    King Ref bp, 1668
    NY Ref bp, 1698
    NY Ref mr, 1691
Langendike
    NYC Wills, 1698
Langestraat
    NY Ref bp, 1664, 1668,
    1670, 1679
    Orphan Mst, 1665

Langhaar
    NY Ref bp, 1705
    NY Ref mr, 1704
Lansing
    Pearson, 1695, 1748
Lay
    King Co, 1683
Leick
    King Co, 1696
Loisen
    Fltb Ref bp, 1681
    Fltb Ref mr, 1680
Loockermans
    Pearson, 1659
Looman
    Anjou Prb, 1663
    King Pap, 1665
    Pearson, 1661
Losericht
    Berg Ref bp, 1677
    Nicl Lvl, 1672
Loysen
    LI Source, 1690
Loy
    King Co, 1683
Lozier
    King Co, 1680
Lyndrayer
    Pearson, 1681
Marinus
    Ship Lists, no date
Marris
    Hack Ref mm, page xx
Maul
    NY Ref bp, 1677, 1680,
    1682, 1686, 1690, 1692
    NY Ref mr, 1675
    Ship Lists, no date
Mayer
    Ship Lists, 1662
Meet
    King Co, 1667
Merie
    Pearson, 1716
Mesier
    Nicl Lvl, 1672
    NY Ref bp, 1661, 1686,
    1687, 1689, 1698

Nycol Doc 2, 1673
    Rcrd Nam 6, 1673
Metselaer
    Pearson, 1718
Meyer
    Crt Assz, 1675
    Fern Wlls, 1693
    Gen Entr 2, 1685
    NY Ref bp, 1663, 1668,
    1678, 1689
    NY Ref mr, 1662
    NYC Court, 1697
    Nycol Doc 2, 1673
    Rcrd Nam 4, 1663
Middagh
    King Co, 1681
Mingaal
    Alb Ref mm, 1683
    Pearson, 1656
    Rcrd Nam 4, 1662
Minnelia
    Fltb Ref mr, 1689
Moesman
    Nicl Lvl, 1667
    NY Ref bp, 1661, 1664
    Nycol Doc 2, 1662
    Rcrd Nam 2, 1658
    Rens Crsp 1, 1655, 1663,
    1664
Molenaer
    Pearson, 1695
Mousman
    Gen Entr 1, 1664
Mynderts
    Pearson, 1629
Naerden
    Ship Lists, 1636
Nagel
    King Co, 1683
Nes
    Rcrd Nam 1, 1654
Nienghs
    Rcrd Nam 3, 1659
Noll
    NY Ref mr, 1692
Noorman
    Evjen, 1641, 1644, 1673
    Fern Wlls, 1673

Patronymic/Surname Combinations

NY Lth bp, 1710
NY Ref bp, 1646, 1647
NY Ref mr, 1662
Pearson, 1673
Rcrd Nam 2, 1658
Ship Lists, 1648
Noortstrant
Rens Court, 1668
Norman
LI Source, 1695
Nostrand
Ship Lists, 1638
Nykerk
Pearson, 1634
Oortstraet
King Pap, 1687
Oost
Rcrd Nam 6, 1671
OpBergen
NY Ref bp, 1688
Osterhout
King Pap, 1664
King Ref bp, 1683
Ship Lists, no date
Ostrom
Berg Ref bp, 1684
Berg Ref mr, 1666
King Co, 1660
LI Source, 1666
Ouderkerk
Pearson, 1681
Oudtlandt
Rcrd Nam 3, 1658
Outhout
Alb Ref bp, 1685
Gen Entr 1, 1664
Pearson, 1683
Rcrd Nam 2, 1656
Pier
King Ref bp, 1683, 1696
NY Ref bp, 1701
Pluvier
King Co, 1626
Pluyvier
Rcrd Nam 3, 1659
Poppen
NY Ref mr, 1669
Postma
King Pap, 1684

Post
Alb Ref mm, 1683
Alb Ref mr, 1692
Pearson, 1683
Poy
Rcrd Nam 2, 1658
Prall
King Ref bp, 1674
Ship Lists, no date
Prast
King Pap, 1671
Pratt
King Pap, 1671
Provoost
Nycol Doc 3, 1690
Pruyn
Alb Ref bp, 1683
Pearson, 1661
Rens Court, 1671
Ship Lists, no date
Purmerendt
NY Ref bp, 1672
Pyer
King Ref bp, 1681
Quisthout
Alb Ref mr, 1684
Rademacker
King Pap, 1670
Raeff
Nycol Doc 2, 1656
Ralemon
Berg Ref mr, 1696
Ralewyn
Berg Ref dt, 1694, 1696
Rapalye
King Co, 1623
NY Ref bp, 1653, 1658
Rcrd Nam 3, 16659
Ship Lists, 1623
Reur
Pearson, 1658
Rens Crsp 1, 1659, 1662
Ship Lists, 1651
Ribbide
Pearson, 1664
Ringo
Brgr Frm, 1657
Fern Wlls, 1646
NY Ref bp, 1648

Rcrd Nam 4, 1662
Rochel
Ship Lists, 1634
Roebel
Brgr Frm, 1657
Roll
NY Ref bp, 1697, 1700,
1702, 1706, 1709, 1710
Romer
NY Ref bp, 1665
NY Ref bp, 1699
Nycol Doc 4, 1698
Willems
Romeyn
Bkln Ref bp, 1686
Crt Assz, 1680
Fltb Ref bp, 1678, 1680,
1681, 1682, 1683, 1684
Fltb Ref mr, 1678
Gen Entr 2, 1676
Hack Ref bp, 1695, 1700
King Co, 1653
King Pap, 1662
Nicl Lvl, 1672
NY Ref bp, 1676
NY Ref mr, 1671, 1676
NYC Wills, 1702
Nycol Doc 2, 1664
Pearson, 1658
Rcrd Nam 3, 1659
Rens Court, 1672
Ship Lists, 1687
Rome
NY Ref bp, 1690, 1702
Romme
NY Ref mr, 1705
Romp
Nicl Lvl, 1667
Roosa
Brgr Frm, 1657, 1698
King Ref bp, 1699
King Ref mr, 1701
NY Ref bp, 1656, 1660,
1661, 1662, 1663, 1664,
1665, 1667, 1673, 1679,
1681, 1686, 1689
Nycol Doc 2, 1673
Rcrd Nam 1, 1654

Patronymic/Surname Combinations

Jans (cont.)
Roos
NYC Wills, 1697, 1698
Pearson, 1695
Roseboom
Pearson, 1662
Rens Court, 1672
Ship Lists, 1657, no date
Roy
Rcrd Nam 2, 1658
Ruyn
Rcrd Nam 7, 1658
Ruyter
Brgr Frm, 1657
King Co, 1639
LI Source, 1642, 1660
NY Ref bp, 1644, 1662
Nycol Doc 1, 1644
Pearson, 1638
Rcrd Nam 1, 1653
Ship Lists, 1638
Ruyting
Alb Ref bp, 1690
Pearson, 1690
Ryckman
Pearson, 1671
Rens Court, 1672
Rykskocht
NY Ref bp, 1704
Salsbergen
Pearson, 1706
Salsburg
Atns Lth bp, 1710
NY Lth bp, 1710
Sam
Rcrd Nam 3, 1660
Schaers
King Co, 1687
LI Source, 1695
Schagen
Nycol Doc 1, 1626
Schars
Bkln Ref bp, 1690
Fltb Ref mr, 1686
Scheel
Pearson, 1658
Schenck
King Co, 1675

Schepmoes
Anjou Prb, 1682
King Pap, 1667
King Ref bp, 1678, 1680,
1690, 1695, 1701, 1702
King Ref mr, 1703
NY Ref bp, 1643, 1645,
1647, 1648, 1654
NY Ref mr, 1656
NYC Wills, 1691
Rcrd Nam 1, 1648
Schermerhorn
Fern Wlls, 1688
Pearson, 1636
Ship Lists, 1636, 1645,
1650, no date
Schipper
Pearson, 1660
Scholl
LI Source, 1667
NY Ref bp, 1662, 1664,
1666, 1671
Ship Lists, 1659
Scholt
NY Ref mr, 1661
School
King Co, 1668
Schoonmaker
NY Ref bp, 1644
Schutt
Anjou Prb, 1706
King Pap, 1663, 1672
King Ref bp, 1664, 1682,
1683, 1684
Pearson, 1657
Rens Court, 1670
Rens Crsp 1, 1659, 1668
Seba
Anjou Prb, 1663
King Pap, 1665
Sebring
Bkln Ref bp1682, 1663
Seen
King Co, 1663
Seeuw
Bkln Ref bp, 1679, 1691
Fltb Ref bp, 1679

Seeu
Ship Lists, 1687
Slicoten
King Pap, 1666
Slot
Berg Ref bp, 1666, 1669
King Ref bp, 1681
NY Ref bp, 1660, 1687
NY Ref mr, 1672
Nycol Doc 2, 1673
Rcrd Nam 6, 1669
Rcrd Nam 7, 1674
Sluys
Rcrd Nam 4, 1662
Sluyter
NY Ref bp, 1657
Rcrd Nam 1, 1655
Slyckotem
Pearson, 1661
Smithing
Fltb Ref bp, 1685
King Co, 1660
Smith
Gen Entr 1, 1665
LI Source, 1694
NY Ref bp, 1642, 1662,
1667
Pearson, 1660
Rcrd Nam 2, 1658
Sneeding
NY Ref bp, 1668
Snyder
NY Ref bp, 1644, 1647,
16802
Solomons
Alb Ref mm, 1683
Spiering
NY Ref bp, 1663, 1667
Spiers
Rcrd Nam 3, 1659
Spier
Berg Ref bp, 1686, 1688
Berg Ref mr, 1684
Hack Ref mr, 1704, 1705,
1709, 1710
Nycol Doc 2, 1674
Ship Lists, 1660

Sprong
King Co, 1694
Staats
Bkln Ref bp, 1691, 1696
Bkln Ref mr, 1695
King Co, 1682
LI Source, 1689, 1693,
16943
NY Ref bp, 1706
Nycol Doc 2, 1661
Rcrd Nam 3, 1659
Rens Crsp 1, 1657, 1661
Ship Lists, 1687
Stavast
Crt Assz, 1668
Gen Entr 1, 1668
Nicl Lvl, 1673
NY Ref bp, 1687
Pearson, 1672, 1673
Rcrd Nam 6, 1666
Rens Court, 1670, 1671,
1672
Steenhalder
Berg Ref bp, 1667
Rcrd Nam 3, 1659
Steenwyck
King Ref bp, 1681, 1683
Stock
King Co, 1657
Stoerck
Rcrd Nam 2, 1656
Stoll
King Pap, 1661, 1665
King Ref mr, 1661, 1664
Nycol Doc 3, 1664
Pearson, 1630
Rcrd Nam 3, 1660
Rens Crsp 1, 1659, 1660
Rens Crsp 2, 1685
Ship Lists, 1645, 1650
Stol
Ship Lists, 1630
Stoutenburgh
King Pap, 1663, 1665
Pearson, 1646
Ship Lists, no date
Straatenmacker
NY Ref bp, 1705

Strycker
King Co, 1677
Ship Lists, 1687
Sutphin
Fltb Ref bp, 1681
Suyder
NY Ref bp, 1643
Swart
NY Ref bp, 1647
Tappan
Ship Lists, 1652
Terbush
Rens Court, 1669
Terhune
King Co, 1684
Tiebout
Ship Lists, no date
Timmerman
King Pap, 1674
Pearson, 1654
Ship Lists, 1649
Traphagen
King Co, 1658
NY Ref mr, 1658
Ship Lists, no date
Trimbel
King Co, 1662
Trynenburgh
Evjen, 1660
Rcrd Nam 3, 1660
Tubbing
NY Ref bp, 1650
Turkyen
Pearson, 1681
Turk
Pearson, 1659
Tuynier
NY Ref bp, 1666, 1684
UytDenemarken
NY Ref mr, 1677
UytDenHage
NY Ref mr, 1660
UytHessen
NY Ref mr, 1650
UytHolstein
NY Ref mr, 1653
Valentine
Berg Ref bp, 1701

Van Harlingen
NY Ref bp, 1682
Van Meteren
Ship Lists, 1687
VanAelokman
King Co, 1668
VanAeltemaer
King Co, 1668
VanAlstede
Alb Ref bp, 1705
VanAlstine
Alb Ref mr, 1689, 1694,
1698
Pearson, 1700
VanAmach
Ship Lists, 1687
VanAmersfort
King Pap, 1662, 1664
King Ref bp, 1663, 1665
NY Ref mr, 1681
VanAmsterdam
Pearson, 1642
Ship Lists, 1636
VanAntwerp
Alb Ref bp, 1692
Pearson, 1660
Ship Lists, no date
VanArnhem
Alb Ref bp, 1700, 1702,
1704, 1706, 1708
Alb Ref mr, 1696
NY Ref bp, 1701
Rcrd Nam 4, 1662
VanArnum
Alb Ref mm, 1699
Pearson, 1699
VanArsdalen
Fltb Ref bp, 1678, 1681,
1683
King Co, 1656
LI Source, 1688
Ship Lists, 1653, 1687
VanAschwoert
NY Ref mr, 1652
VanAurick
Brgr Frm, 1658
NY Ref mr, 1658
Rcrd Nam 3, 1660

Jans (cont.)
VanBaren
  Pearson, 1663
VanBatavia
  NY Ref mr, 1663
VanBerckels
  Rcrd Nam 3, 1660
VanBerkome
  NY Ref mr, 1703
VanBlercom
  Berg Ref mr, 1693, 1706
  Fltb Ref mr, 1693
  Hack Ref bp, 1707, 1708,
  1711, 1712, 1715, 1716,
  1717, 1719, 1720, 1721
  Hack Ref mr, 1710
  King Co, 1693
  NY Ref bp, 1704
VanBockhoven
  Fern Wlls, 1689
VanBoekhoven
  Pearson, 1662
VanBoertang
  NY Ref bp, 1654
VanBommel
  Alb Ref bp, 1686
  Pearson, 1685
VanBorkelo
  Ship Lists, 1662
VanBreda
  Pearson, 1639
  Ship Lists, 1639
VanBreestede
  Brgr Frm, 1657
  NY Ref bp, 1648, 1650,
  1652, 1656, 1658, 1659,
  1660, 1663, 1668
  NY Ref mr, 1643, 1646,
  1650, 16467
  Nycol Doc 3, 1664
  Rcrd Nam 2, 1656
  Ship Lists, 1636
VanBrefoort
  NY Ref mr, 1693
VanBremen
  Gen Entr 2, 1676
  NY Ref mr, 1643

Pearson, 1646
Ship Lists, 1646
VanBrestede
  Pearson, 1636
VanBreste
  Orphan Mst, 1665
VanBrest
  NY Ref mr, 1665
VanBreuckelen
  King Co, 1656
VanBrevoort
  Brgr Frm, 1695
  LI Source, 1695
  NY Ref bp, 1693
VanBroeckhuysen
  Ship Lists, 1637
VanBroekhuysen
  Pearson, 1636
  Ship Lists, 1636
VanBroutangie
  Rcrd Nam 1, 1654
VanBunick
  Ship Lists, 1636
VanBuytenhuys
  NY Ref bp, 1686
VanCampen
  King Co, 1668
  NY Ref mr, 1659
  Pearson, 1649
  Ship Lists, 1640
VanChristianstadt
  NY Ref mr, 1661
VanCleef
  King Co, 1683
  NY Ref bp, 1664, 1666,
  1669
VanCovert
  King Co, 1676
VanDam
  Nycol Doc 2, 1661
VanDanswyck
  King Ref bp, 1696, 1697
VanDeLangestraat
  NY Ref mr, 1657
  Rcrd Nam 3, 1659
VanDenBerg
  Alb Ref bp, 1702
  King Ref bp, 1703

NY Ref bp, 1647
NY Ref mr, 1688, 1694
Pearson, 1702
VanDenBosch
  Berg Ref mr, 1685
  King Ref bp, 1688, 1702
  Ship Lists, 1657
VanDenEnden
  NY Ref bp, 1647
VanDenHam
  Ship Lists, 1650
VanDerArck
  NY Ref bp, 1655
VanDerBeek
  Fltb Ref bp, 1678
  King Co, 1642
  Ship Lists, 1642
  Ship Lists, no date
Vanderbilt
  Berg Ref bp, 1678, 1681,
  1682, 1686, 1693
  Fltb Ref bp, 1677, 1678,
  1681
  Fltb Ref mr, 1687
  Jam Ref bp, 1707
  King Co, 1677
VanDerCleef
  NY Ref bp, 1668
  NY Ref mr, 1667
VanDerHam
  NY Ref bp, 1653, 1655,
  1657
  NY Ref mr, 1650
  Rcrd Nam 2, 1657
VanDerHeul
  NY Ref bp, 1689
VanDerHeyden
  Pearson, 1755
Vanderick
  King Co, 1676
VanDerKell
  Nycol Doc 3, 1666
VanDerKley
  Nycol Doc 2, 1657
VanDerLaen
  Pearson, 1661
VanDerMeer
  NY Ref mr, 1701

Patronymic/Surname Combinations

VanDerVeen
  King Co, 1661
  NY Ref bp, 1658, 1662,
  1679
  Nycol Doc 2, 1657
  Pearson, 1654
  Rcrd Nam 1, 1665
VanDerVeer
  Fltb Ref bp, 1679, 1682,
  1684
  King Co, 1659
  LI Fam 2, no date
  Ship Lists, 1659, no date
VanDerVenter
  Fltb Ref bp, 1687, 1688
VanDerVin
  Orphan Mst, 1663
VanDerVliet
  Bkln Ref bp, 1678, 1696
  King Co, 1660
  LI Source, 1660, 1680
VanDerVoort
  King Co, 1680
VanDerWerf
  Hack Ref mm, 1686
VanDeventer
  Fltb Ref mr, 1686
  King Co, 1695
  King Pap, 1670
  NY Ref mr, 1660
  NYC Wills, 1686
  Nycol Doc 2, 1674
  Rcrd Nam 4, 1662
  Ship Lists, 1687
VanDinter
  Nycol Doc 1, 1651
VanDitmars
  Evjen, 1664
  Fltb Ref bp, 1679, 1680
  LI Source, no date
  NY Ref mr, 1650, 1652
  Pearson, 1685
VanDockum
  NY Ref mr, 1647
VanDost
  King Pap, 1662
VanDuynkerken
  Pearson, 1660

VanDyck
  Bkln Ref bp, 1681, 1682,
  1684, 1688
  Fltb Ref bp, 1677, 1679,
  1680, 1681, 1682, 1683,
  1684
  Fltb Ref mr, 1680, 1694
  King Co, 1651
  NY Ref bp, 1674, 1675,
  1685, 1686, 1688
  NY Ref mr, 1673, 1674
  Ship Lists, 1687, no date
VanEbel
  Rcrd Nam 1, 1653
VanEdam
  Pearson, 1636
  Ship Lists, 1636
VanEeckelen
  Pearson, 1661
  Rens Crsp 1, 1659
VanEkel
  Rcrd Nam 1, 1653
VanElpendam
  NY Ref bp, 1649, 1659,
  16467
VanElsland
  Ship Lists, no date
VanEmbden
  NY Ref mr, 1644, 1662
VanEsselstine
  NY Ref mr, 1676
VanEtten
  King Pap, 1664
  King Ref bp, 1670, 1679,
  1681, 1683, 1684, 1688
  Nicl Lvl, 1667
  Ship Lists, 1652, no date
VanEveren
  NY Ref mr, 1642
VanEyckelen
  King Pap, 1661
VanFeurden
  NY Ref bp, 1685, 1690
  Nycol Doc 3, 1690
VanFewide
  Pearson, 1685

VanFlansburg
  NY Ref bp, 1680, 1682,
  1683, 1684, 1688, 1689
  NY Ref mr, 1680, 1687
VanFrederickstadt
  NY Ref mr, 1650
VanFrederikfort
  Pearson, 1662
VanFrurde
  King Co, 1664
VanGarder
  Ship Lists, 1658
VanGertruydenburgh
  Pearson, 1642
  Ship Lists, 1642
VanGerwen
  NY Ref bp, 1656
VanGesscher
  LI Source, 1696
VanGouda
  Fltb Ref mr, 1679
VanGroeningen
  NY Ref bp, 1647
  NY Ref mr, 1652
VanGroetenbaecken
  Rcrd Nam 1, 1654
VanGutsenhoven
  Rens Court, 1669
  Rens Crsp 1, 1659, 1662
VanHaert
  NY Ref mr, 1677
VanHalen
  NY Ref bp, 1667
VanHam
  Brgr Frm, 1657
  Rcrd Nam 1, 1655
VanHarlem
  Alb Ref bp, 1697
  NY Ref bp, 1646
  NY Ref mr, 1651, 1660
  Pearson, 1697
VanHartenburgh
  Rens Crsp 2, 1675
VanHasymes
  Bkln Ref bp, 1687
VanHeemstwaart
  Rcrd Nam 4, 1662, 1663

Jans (cont.)
VanHeemst
  King Co, 1661
VanHeerden
  NY Ref mr, 1677
VanHeerd
  NY Ref mr, 1654
VanHeyningen
  King Co, 1672
  NY Ref bp, 1686, 1688,
  1691
  NY Ref mr, 1672
  Rcrd Nam 6, 1671
  Ship Lists, 1662
VanHoesen
  Atns Lth bp, 1708
  King Ref bp, 1698
  NY Lth bp, 1705, 1708
  Pearson, 1694
  Rens Court, 1671, 1672
VanHolte
  Gen Entr 1, 1669
VanHoochsten
  Rcrd Nam 1, 1655
VanHoochten
  King Co, 1662
VanHoorstrant
  LI Source, no date
VanHorn
  King Pap, 1665
  NY Ref bp, 1659, 1663,
  1673, 1679, 1681, 1687
  NY Ref mr, 1659, 1666
  NYC Wills, 1689
  Pearson, 1661
  Rcrd Nam 3, 1660
VanHouten
  NY Ref bp, 1669
  Nycol Doc 3, 1664
VanIlpendam
  NY Ref bp, 1647
  Pearson, 1656
  Rens Court, 1669, 1672
VanKeuren
  Ship Lists, no date
VanKulenbergh
  Pearson, 1681

VanKuyk
  Ship Lists, 1662
VanLangendyck
  NY Ref bp, 1680, 1689,
  1691
  NY Ref mr, 1688
  Rcrd Nam 5, 1665
VanLangestraat
  NY Ref bp, 1661, 1666
  NY Ref mr, 1659, 1672
VanLenneps
  NY Ref bp, 1658
VanLeyden
  NY Ref bp, 1659, 1660
  NY Ref mr, 1659, 1675
  Pearson, 1656
  Rcrd Nam 1, 1655
  Ship Lists, 1649
VanLuane
  Fltb Ref mr, 1685
  King Co, 1654
VanLuisthout
  NY Ref bp, 1689
VanMaerden
  King Pap, 1670
VanMaesterlandt
  Ship Lists, 1630
VanMeckelen
  King Co, 1690
VanMekelen
  Fltb Ref mr, 1690
VanMeppel
  NY Ref bp, 1667
  NY Ref mr, 1682
  Rcrd Nam 3, 1659
VanMeteren
  Fltb Ref bp, 1683, 1687
  Fltb Ref mr, 1683
  King Co, 1663
  LI Source, 1695
VanMetren
  LI Source, 1683
VanMidwout
  NY Ref mr, 1686
VanMispadtkill
  NY Ref mr, 1695
VanNarden
  King Co, 1645

VanNess
  NY Ref bp, 1682
VanNeuerstrait
  NYC Wills, 1679
VanNewkirk
  Ship Lists, 1636
VanNimmegen
  NY Ref mr, 1657
VanNoordstrant
  LI Source, 1679
VanNoorstrant
  LI Source, 1679
VanNoortstrant
  Pearson, 1638
  Rens Court, 1672
VanNoort
  Ship Lists, 1661, no date
VanNooststrant
  Rens Court, 1668
VanNorden
  Hack Ref bp, 1712
  Hack Ref mr, 1717
  King NYGB, 1770
  King Pap, 1670
  NY Lth bp, 1704
  NY Lth mr, 1707
  NY Ref bp, 1648
  NY Ref mr, 1647
VanNordstrant
  Ship Lists, no date
VanNostrand
  King Co, 1685
  NY Ref bp, 1641
  Ship Lists, no date
VanNostrant
  NY Ref mr, 1652
VanNuxon
  NY Ref bp, 1660
VanNuyse
  King Co, 1651
VanNuys
  Fltb Ref bp, 1684, 1685,
  1687
  Ship Lists, 1687
VanObyn
  NY Ref bp, 1657

VanOldenburg
  Brgr Frm, 1659
  NY Ref bp, 1639, 1642,
    1643, 1646
  NY Ref mr, 1652
VanOogsten
  Berg Ref mr, 1672
VanOort
  King Pap, 1671
VanOosten
  King Pap, 1666
  NY Ref mr, 1666, 1672
VanOost
  NY Ref bp, 1659
VanOsterhout
  King Pap, 1663, 1665
  King Ref bp, 1663, 1665,
    1666, 1667, 1674, 1679,
    1681
  King Ref mr, 1682
  Nicl Lvl, 1667
  NY Ref bp, 1654, 1656
  NY Ref mr, 1653
VanOstrom
  Rcrd Nam 4, 1662
  Ship Lists, 1651
VanOtten
  Pearson, 1657
VanOtterspoor
  Pearson, 1658
VanPatten
  Fltb Ref bp, 1678
  King Ref bp, 1678
VanPelt
  Fltb Ref bp, 1681
  King Co, 1700
  LI Source, 1687
  NY Ref bp, 1700
  Ship Lists, 1687, no date
VanPurmarent
  King Co, 1656
VanPurmesendt
  NY Ref mr, 1656
VanRomen
  NY Ref bp, 1658, 1700
  NY Ref mr, 1691, 1699
VanRosenthal
  NY Ref bp, 1662

VanRotterdam
  Alb Ref bp, 1690
  Pearson, 1654
  Ship Lists, 1639, 1640
VanRuth
  Ship Lists, 1641
VanRuynderwolt
  NY Ref mr, 1674
VanSalee
  Ship Lists, 1652
VanSale
  Nicl Lvl, 1672
  Rcrd Nam 2, 166
VanSalsbergen
  Pearson, 1699
VanSalsbury
  Alb Ref bp, 1693, 1705,
    1707
  Alb Ref mr, 1689, 1698
VanSchalckwyck
  Brgr Frm, 1657
  NY Ref bp, 1652, 1657
  NY Ref mr, 1652
VanSchorel
  Rcrd Nam 1, 1655
VanSechten
  King Co, 1660
VanSpecherhorn
  Rcrd Nam 1, 1655
VanStAubin
  Rens Crsp 1, 1659
VanStavast
  Rens Court, 1672
VanSteenberg
  King Ref bp, 1699, 1700,
    1701, 1702, 1703, 1704
  King Ref mr, 1683
  Ship Lists, no date
VanSteenwyck
  King Pap, 1664
  King Ref bp, 1689
  Nicl Lvl, 1667
  NY Ref mr, 1654
VanStMarten
  NY Ref mr, 1672
VanStObin
  Pearson, 1657

VanStObyn
  Brgr Frm, 1657
  NY Ref bp, 1658, 1659
  Rcrd Nam 1, 1654
VanStockholm
  Pearson, 1658
VanStoutenburgh
  Anjou Prb, 1671
  King Pap, 1668
  Ship Lists, 1646
VanStraetkirk
  Brgr Frm, 1657
VanStrapelholm
  Gen Entr 1, 1667
VanStTobin
  Rens Crsp 1, 1659
VanSuermarter
  Brgr Frm, 1657
VanSutphin
  Ship Lists, 1687
VanSwoll
  NY Ref mr, 1652
VanTerGoes
  Rcrd Nam 3, 1660
VanTerIeverlant
  Brgr Frm, 1657
VanThuyl
  Fltb Ref bp, 1687, 1688
  LI Source, 1686
  NY Ref mr, 1686
  NYC Wills, 1696
VanTilburg
  Berg Ref bp, 1691, 1694
  NY Ref bp, 1690, 1692
VanTserooskerck
  NY Ref mr, 1660
VanTyne
  NYC Court, 1685
VanUtrecht
  Brgr Frm, 1657
  NY Ref bp, 1651, 1656,
    1658
  NY Ref mr, 1650
VaNuyse
  NYC Wills, 1694
VanUytrecht
  NY Ref mr, 1653

Patronymic/Surname Combinations

Jans (cont.)
VanVees
    Rcrd Nam 1, 1654
VanVliet
    Fltb Ref bp, 1678
    Ship Lists, 1687
VanVlissingen
    NY Ref bp, 1644
    NY Ref mr, 1640, 1664,
    1674, 1679, 1684, 1696
VanVogsten
    Berg Ref bp, 1673
VanVollenhoo
    King Pap, 1667
VanVollenhoven
    NY Ref bp, 1668
VanVoorden
    NY Ref mr, 1654
VanVoren
    NY Ref bp, 1671
VanWaalwyck
    Ship Lists, 1642
VanWarlwyck
    Pearson, 16462
VanWeeckendam
    Rcrd Nam 3, 1659
VanWerckendam
    NY Ref bp, 1666
    NY Ref mr, 1653
VanWesterhout
    King Co, 1664
    NY Ref mr, 1664
VanWey
    Pearson, 1682
VanWickelen
    Ship Lists, 1687
VanWicklen
    King Co, 1664
VanWien
    Rcrd Nam 6, 1671
VanWitmont
    NY Ref mr, 1674
VanWorden
    Hack Ref bp, 1712
VanWormer
    NY Ref mr, 1666
VanWytert
    Pearson, 1657

VanYsendyck
    NY Ref mr, 1654
VanZandt
    Pearson, 1753
VanZeeland
    Gen Entr 1, 1670
VanZuydtlandt
    NY Ref mr, 1659
Veerman
    Fltb Ref bp, 1681, 1682,
    1687
    NY Ref bp, 1677
Verbeeck
    Ship Lists, 1663
VerBrugh
    NY Ref bp, 1691
VerKerck
    Bkln Ref bp, 1682
    Fltb Ref bp, 1682
    Fltb Ref mr, 1681
Verkerken
    King Co, 1655
Verkerk
    LI Source, 1663
Verryn
    Gen Entr 1, 1664
    King Co, 1659
    Nicl Lvl, 1672
Verwen
    Ship Lists, 1663
Veryne
    Crt Assz, 1665
    Rcrd Nam 3, 1659
Vin
    NY Ref bp, 1679
Vischer
    Rcrd Nam 3, 1660
Volckert
    NY Ref mr, 1682
Vonck
    Rcrd Nam 1, 1653
Voorhees
    King Co, 1679
Voss
    NY Ref mr, 1671
Vredenburg
    NY Ref bp, 1665

Vreeland
    Berg Ref dt, 1697
    Ship Lists, no date
Vrooman
    Pearson, 1706
    Schn Ref mr, 1716
Wanshaer
    NY Ref bp, 1659
Weaver
    Rcrd Nam 6, 1667
Welckinghoff
    Ship Lists, 1650
Wemp
    Fern Wlls, 1664
Mynderts
    Pearson, 1663
    Pearson, 1699
Wendell
    Ship Lists, no date
Wendel
    Pearson, 1658, 1691
    Ship Lists, 1642, 1644
Westbroeck
    Rens Court, 1668
Westerbrook
    King Co, 1661
Westercamp
    Pearson, 1667
    Ship Lists, 1648
Westerhout
    Nycol Doc 2, 1673
West Wills, 1723
Whitbeck
    Alb Ref bp, 1700, 1702,
    1703, 1707
    Alb Ref mm, 1692
    Pearson, 1683
Wimp
    Alb Ref bp, 1684
Winckelhoek
    Rcrd Nam 2, 1656
Witt
    NY Ref bp, 1652
    Nycol Doc 2, 1665
    Rcrd Nam 2, 1656
Witzen
    Nycol Doc 2, 1657

Patronymic/Surname Combinations

Woertman
  Bkln Ref bp, 1684, 1686,
  1693, 1696
  Bkln Ref mr, 1691
  Fltb Ref bp, 1684
  King Co, 1647
  LI Source, 1671, 1679,
  1684, 1687, 1689, 1691,
  1692, 1694, 1695
  Nicl Lvl, 1672
  Ship Lists, 1687
Wolwesen
  King Co, 1680
Wyngart
  Pearson, 1726
WytStraat
  Rcrd Nam 4, 1662
Yoncker
  Pearson, 1703
Jeremiahs
  Prys
  NY Ref bp, 1697
  Spiering
  Brgr Frm, 1659
  Rcrd Nam 3, 1659
Jeromes
  Barhyte
  Pearson, 1713
  Bockqui
  Bkln Ref bp, 1678
  Rapalye
  Bkln Ref bp, 1678
  Bkln Ref mr, 1695
  King Co, 1690
Jochems
  Collier
  Rens Court, 1671
  Ketelhuyn
  Pearson, 1690
  Roelofsen
  NY Lth bp, 1708
  Schoonmaker
  Ship Lists, 1654, no date
  VanMiddelwout
  NY Ref mr, 1683
  VanMidwout
  NY Ref mr, 1693

VanValkenburgh
  Alb Ref bp, 1693, 1708
  Alb Ref mr, 1693, 1698
  Pearson, 1693
  Ship Lists, no date
Jonasse
  Douw
  Pearson, 1709
Jonas
  Douw
  Alb Ref bp, 1709
Joost
  Bruyn
  NY Ref bp, 1663
  DeMoulinars
  Ship Lists, 1683
  Duryee
  King Co, 1685
  LI Fam 1, 1686
  Hegeman
  King Co, 1687
  Ridder
  Ship Lists, 1687
  VanAelst
  NY Ref mr, 1647
  VanBrunt
  Ship Lists, 1653, 1687, no
  date
  VanCovelens
  Pearson, 1662
  VanElslant
  Tap Ref bp, 1700
  VanEyckelen
  King Pap, 1661
  VanHarlem
  NY Ref mr, 1660
  VanLinden
  Berg Ref mm, 1681
  VanMeerbeek
  NY Ref mr, 1649
  VanMeteren
  King Pap, 1664
  Ship Lists, no date
  VanRollegom
  LI Fam 1, 1640
  NY Ref bp, 1685, 1688,
  1689
  NYC Wills, 1692

Rens Crsp 2, 1675
VanWitmont
  NY Ref mr, 1658
Joris
  Alst
  NY Ref mr, 1689
  Bergen
  King Co, 1684
  Bowman
  King Co, 1693
  Brinckerhoff
  Fltb Ref bp, 1684, 1685
  Hack Ref bp, 1705, 1706
  King Co, 1632
  DeRapalye
  Bkln Ref bp, 1662
  Houten
  Nycol Doc 1, 1621
  Pearson, 1633
  Joerissen
  Bkln Ref mr, 1695
  Rapalye
  Fltb Ref bp, 1678, 1679,
  1680, 1681, 1682
  King Co, 1650
  NY Ref bp, 1655
  Remsen
  King Co, 1685
  Smith
  NY Ref bp, 1639
  Tienpoint
  Nycol Doc 1, 1644
  TonsonVanRitfort
  Brgr Frm, 1659
  Toonson
  Ship Lists, 1658
  VanAelst
  NY Ref mr, 1678, 1685
  VanDerVeer
  NY Ref mr, 1650
  VanElslant
  Hack Ref bp, 1695
  VanHersberg
  NY Ref mr, 1639
  VanHorn
  NY Ref bp, 1705, 1710

Joshua
  Kocherthal
    Nycol Doc 5, 1708
Josiahs
  Menevert
    Gen Entr 2, 1685
  VanRoen
    Berg Ref bp, 1686
Jurians
  Bakker
    Ship Lists, 1637
  Becker
    Gen Entr 1, 1669
    NY Ref bp, 1660
    Pearson, 1669
    Rcrd Nam 3, 1660
    Rens Court, 1668, 1669
  Haff
    King Co, 1679
  Hoff
    Fltb Ref bp, 1681
  Hogan
    Pearson, 1730
  Hortman
    NY Ref bp, 1710
  Klug
    NY Lth bp, 1710
  Lantsman
    Crt Assz, 1667
    NY Ref bp, 1661, 1666
    NY Ref mr, 1685
    Rcrd Nam 3, 1659
  Nagel
    King Co, 1697
  Paulus
    Hack Ref mm, page xx
  Post
    Pearson, 1667
  Probasco
    King Co, 1654
    LI Source, 1654
  Rinckhout
    Pearson, 1704
  Stoff
    Fltb Ref bp, 1681
  VanBergen
    NY Ref mr, 1672, 1695

VanCopenhagen
    NY Ref mr, 1657
VanDanzig
    NY Ref mr, 1699
VanDenBosch
    NY Ref mr, 1667
VanDyck
    King Co, 1701
VanHoesen
    Atns Lth bp, 1708, 1710
    NY Lth bp, 1708, 1710
    Pearson, 1699
VanOldenzeel
    NY Ref mr, 1660
Westervelt
    Hack Ref bp, 1719, 1720
    Hack Ref mr, 1718
Westfall
    King Pap, 1673, 1674
    King Ref mr, 1683
Justin
  VanBrunt
    King Co, 1653

K
Kapts
  VanBlercom
    Hack Ref mm, page xx
Kettelhuys
  VanCremyn
    Ship Lists, 1642
    King Co, 1651
  Sutphin
    Ship Lists, no date
Krynes
  Boelhont
    Ship Lists, 1663
  Cooper
    Ship Lists, 1657, no date
  VanHouten
    Ship Lists, 1640, 1642

L
Laanen
  VanPelt
    Bkln Ref bp, 1688

Labaties
  Fransman
    Ship Lists, 1637
Lamberts
  Bont
    Pearson, no date
  Cock
    Rens Crsp 1, 1654, 1656
  Cole
    King Co, 1639
    LI Source, 1642
    NY Ref bp, 1639
    Nycol Doc 1, 1644
  DeHeer
    Rcrd Nam 4, 1662
  DeHeest
    Bkln Ref mr, 1663
    King Co, 1663
  Dumont
    Gen Entr 2, 1686
  Loockermans
    Pearson, 1682
  Maul
    Gen Entr 2, 1682
    King Co, 1646
    NY Ref bp, 1677, 1678
    NY Ref mr, 1660, 1662,
    1668, 1686
    Rcrd Nam 3, 1661
    Ship Lists, no date
  Sassian
    Pearson, no date
  Smith
    Hack Ref bp, 1716, 1719,
    1720
    Tap Ref bp, 1706, 1710
  VanBremen
    Pearson, 1661
  VanDoorn
    Pearson, 1642
    Ship Lists, 1642
  VanDorland
    Ship Lists, 1644
  VanNorden
    NY Ref mr, 1654
  VanTeelickhuysen
    NY Ref mr, 1661

VanUtrecht
 NY Ref mr, 1651
VanValkenburgh
 Alb Ref bp, 1702
 Pearson, 1683
Latyns
 VanVerduym
 Ship Lists, 1636
 Verduyn
 Pearson, 1636
Lawrence
 Ackerman
 Bkln Ref bp, 1709
 Hack Ref bp, 1711, 1719,
 1721
 Hack Ref mr, 1707, 1710
 Appel
 Rcrd Nam 2, 1656
 Ship Lists, 1648
 Bogart
 Bkln Ref bp, 1663
 NY Ref bp, 1679
 Ship Lists, no date
 Tap Ref bp, 1696
 Cock
 NY Ref mr, 1657
 DeNoorman
 NY Ref bp, 1646
 Duyts
 King Co, 1642
 NY Ref bp, 1671
 NY Ref mr, 1667, 1673
 Ship Lists, 1668
 Kuykendaal
 Ship Lists, no date
 Noorman
 Evjen, 1631, 1639
 Ship Lists, 1631, 1658
 Popega
 NY Ref bp, 1702
 Poppinga
 NY Ref mr, 1689, 1691,
 1692
 Sluys
 NY Ref mr, 1686

Toers
 Berg Ref dt, 1674, 1682
 Berg Ref mm, 1672
 Hack Ref mr, 1703, 1704,
 1710
VanAllen
 Alb Ref bp, 1707, 1709
 Pearson, 1706
VanBoskirk
 Hack Ref bp, 1696, 1697,
 1699, 1712, 1716
 Hack Ref mr, 1711
VanBremen
 NY Ref mr, 1669
VanCleef
 Fltb Ref bp, 1687
VanDerVolgen
 Pearson, no date
 Ship Lists, no date
VanEsselstine
 NY Ref mr, 1646, 1649
VanGroeningen
 NY Ref mr, 1663
VanMispadt
 NY Ref mr, 1667
VanPurmerent
 Pearson, no date
VanRootsisil
 NY Ref mr, 1656
VanSchooderwoert
 NY Ref bp, 1675
VanSchoonderwoerdt
 LI Source, 1689
VanVlecheren
 Rcrd Nam 4, 1663
VanWurmdrink
 Pearson, 1709
Lazarus
 Stuyvesant
 NY Ref bp, 1672
Lefferts
 Haughwout
 LI Fam 1, no date
Lennerts
 Conine
 Alb Ref bp, 1687, 1689,
 1703, 1705
 Pearson, 1683

DeGrauw
 King Co, 1672
DeGraw
 NY Ref bp, 1684
 NY Ref mr, 1679
Geelgieter
 Ship Lists, 1647
Glenn
 Crt Assz, 1675
 Nicl Lvl, 1669
 Nycol Doc 1, 1656
 Pearson, 1639
 Rens Court, 1670, 1672
 Rens Crsp 1, 1656
 Ship Lists, 1639
Grauw
 NY Ref bp, 1690
Reinerse
 Fltb Ref mr, 1691
VanBrugh
 NY Ref bp, 1653
VanDeGrift
 King Co, 1648
VanDerGriff
 NYC Wills, 1670
VanDerGrift
 Orphan Mst, 1664, 1665
 Rcrd Nam 1, 1657
 Rens Crsp 1, 1659
 Ship Lists, 1657
VanDerGrist
 Brgr Frm, 1659
 Gen Entr 1, 1664
 LI Source, 1648
 NY Ref bp, 1648, 1655,
 1657, 1658, 1661, 1683,
 1685, 1687, 1691
 Nycol Doc 1, 1650
 Orphan Mst, 1664, 1665
 Pearson, 1658
Vandiegrist
 Brgr Frm, 1657
VanStavoren
 NY Ref mr, 1648
Louis
 Dubois
 King Ref bp, 1664

Louis (cont.)
Voe
Fltb Ref mr, 1689
Louwens
VanSchoondervooert
King Co, 1670
Lubberts
UytDeBeemster
NY Ref mr, 1655
VanDerGrist
Fltb Ref mr, 1682
VanDeRip
NY Ref mr, 1655
VanEdam
NY Ref mr, 1659
VanHarlem
NY Ref mr, 1651
VanRyp
LI Source, 1693
VanWessel
Orphan Mst, 1664, 1665
Westervelt
Berg Ref mr, 1688
Hack Ref bp, 1709, 1712,
1718, 1720
Hack Ref mm, 1687
Hack Ref mr, 1704, 1707,
1709
NY Ref mr, 1688
Ship Lists, no date
Lucas
Backer
Pearson, 1677
Coeyman
Alb Ref mm, 1683, 1692
Pearson, 1683
Hoogkerk
Alb Ref bp, 1701, 1709
Jans
NY Ref bp, 1703
Schouten
Ship Lists, 1657
VanHoogkerk
Alb Ref bp, 1704, 1705
Alb Ref mr, 1686
Pearson, 1686
VanVoorhees
Fltb Ref bp, 1680

Voorhees
King Co, 1698
Wyngart
Alb Ref bp, 1695, 1700,
1701, 1703, 1704, 1705,
1706, 1708, 1710
Alb Ref mr, 1694, 1695
Fern Wlls, 1690
Pearson, 1700
Ludwichs
Baech
Rcrd Nam 1, 1654

M

Marius
Groen
Alb Ref bp, 1709
King Ref bp, 1703
NY Ref bp, 1701, 1702,
1703, 1704, 1706, 1709
NY Ref mr, 1701
NYC Court, 1706
Pearson, 1709
Martins
Beekman
Pearson, 1673
Cregier
Pearson, 1734
Damen
Bkln Ref bp, 1680
Fltb Ref bp, 1680
DeWeaver
Pearson, 1689
Doorn
Anjou Prb, 1671
King Pap, 1664
King Ref bp, 1678
King Ref mr, 1661, 1684
Nicl Lvl, 1667
Pearson, 1686
Rcrd Nam 4, 1663
Dorn
King Pap, 1664
Esselstine
King Ref mr, 1702
Factor
Rcrd Nam 1, 1655

Hues
Rens Court, 1670
Huis
Pearson, 1658
Moer
Pearson, 1665
Rens Court, 1669, 1670
Roosevelt
Ship Lists, 1649, no date
Schenck
Bkln Ref bp, 1682
Fltb Ref bp, 1678, 1679,
1680, 1682, 1683, 1684,
1685, 1688
Fltb Ref mr, 1690
King Co, 1689
LI Fam 1, no date
LI Source, 1687, 1693,
1694, 1696
NYC Wills, 1688
Ship Lists, 1650, 1687, no
date
Smith
Pearson, 1683
UytDeWalebocht
NY Ref mr, 1696
VanAken
NY Ref mr, 1658
VanAlstine
Alb Ref bp, 1703
Pearson, 1703
Ship Lists, no date
VanBaston
NY Ref mr, 1678
VanBenthuysen
Alb Ref mm, 1683
Pearson, 1666
Ship Lists, no date
VanBergen
Alb Ref mm, 1683
Pearson, 1683
VanBuren
Alb Ref bp, 1701
Alb Ref mr, 1693
Pearson, 1742
VanCampen
NY Ref bp, 1660

VanCopenhagen
  NY Ref mr, 1660
  Pearson, 1659
VanDenBosch
  Nycol Doc 2, 1666
  Rcrd Nam 5, 1664
VanDeWalebocht
  NY Ref mr, 1691, 1692,
  1696
VanDoorn
  King Ref mr, 1682
VanEsselstine
  Alb Ref bp, 1707
  King Ref bp, 1687
  Pearson, 1705
VanLoonen
  NY Ref mr, 1659
VanRoosevelt
  NY Ref bp, 1652, 1654
VanRynsburgh
  Pearson, 1662
VanWolphen
  Rens Crsp 1, 1663, 1664,
  1668
Weaver
  Pearson, 1689
Wiltse
  Evjen, 1660
  NY Ref bp, 1701
Mathys
Banckert
  Tary Ref mm, 1699?
Brower
  Ship Lists, 1663
Buys
  NY Ref bp, 1684, 1693
Cooper
  NY Ref bp, 1661
  Tap Ref bp, 1706
DeReus
  Ship Lists, 1633
Goes
  Alb Ref mm, 1683
  Fern Wlls, 1697, 1705
  Gen Entr 1, 1669
  Pearson, 1683
Hols
  Ship Lists, no date

Hoppe
  Hack Ref bp, 1711, 1714
  Hack Ref mm, 1708
Hotaling
  Alb Ref mr, 1688
  Anjou Prb, 1671, 1702
  Gen Entr 1, 1668
  King Pap, 1664
  King Ref bp, 1664, 1665,
  1679, 1697, 1699
  Pearson, 1688
Willems
Laenen
  Ship Lists, 1687
Lanen
  Fltb Ref mr, 1679, 1690
Lane
  King Co, 1657
  LI Source, 1693
  NYC Wills, 1694
Luyster
  King Co, 1719
Muller
  Alb Ref bp, 1703, 1704,
  1706, 1709
Smack
  Fltb Ref bp, 1681, 1685
  King Co, 1654
  LI Source, 1687, no date
  Nycol Doc 2, 1674
  Ship Lists, 1687
VanAmsterdam
  Brgr Frm, 1657
  Pearson, 1654
VanBergen
  NY Ref mr, 1695
VanBuren
  NY Ref mr, 1673
VanDeCaep
  NY Ref bp, 1651
VanDerEyck
  Rcrd Nam 4, 1663
VanDerHeyden
  Pearson, 1700
  Rens Court, 1670
  Ship Lists, no date

VanDeusen
  Alb Ref bp, 1700, 1702,
  1708
  Alb Ref mm, 1694
  Alb Ref mr, 1695
  NY Ref bp, 1699
  Pearson, 1696
VanFraniker
  Pearson, 1635
VanLaeren
  Ship Lists, 1660
VanPelt
  Fltb Ref bp, 1679, 1681,
  1683, 1684, 1685, 1689,
  1690
  Fltb Ref mr, 1679
  King Co, 1646
VanStockholm
  NY Ref mr, 1661
Vlierboom
  Tap Ref bp, 1706
Maurits
Bout
  Rcrd Nam 4, 1663
Mauritz
Sluyswachter
  NY Ref bp, 1672, 1673,
  1678
Melchiors
Keet
  King Ref bp, 1701, 1725
VanBaes
  King Co, 1680
VanDerPoel
  Pearson, 1710
VanDeusen
  Alb Ref bp, 1702, 1707
  Pearson, 1691
Melyn
Antwerp
  Nycol Doc 1, 1650
Michels
Bergen
  King Co, 1689
DePaul
  Gen Entr 2, 1683
Goemonepa
  NY Ref mr, 1665

Michels (cont.)
  Messcher
    King Co, 1647
    Ship Lists, 1687
  Palmatier
    King Co, 1680
  Schuts
    NY Lth bp, 1706, 1708,
    1709, 1710
    NY Ref mr, 1703
  Sperling
    Hack Ref mr, 1709
  VanAmsterdam
    NY Ref mr, 1657
  VanCollumer Zyll
    NY Ref mr, 1654
  VanDelf
    NY Ref mr, 1665
  VanDerSchuere
    NY Ref bp, 1669
  VanDerVoort
    King Co, 1655
  VanEdam
    Pearson, 1637
  VanSchooderwoert
    NY Ref mr, 1673, 1686,
    1689
  Vreeland
    Berg Ref bp, 1685, 1686,
    1687, 1690, 1691, 1692,
    1693, 1694, 1698, 1705,
    1707, 1708, 1710
    Berg Ref dt, 1668, 1675,
    1682, 1683, 1688, 1690,
    1692, 1697, 1707, 1708,
    1710
    Berg Ref mr, 1670, 1681,
    1682, 1691
    Hack Ref bp, 1702, 1710
    NY Ref bp, 1677, 1678
    NY Ref mr, 1691
Monjeur
  DeLaMontagne
    King Ref bp, 1674, 1678,
    1682
Mynderts
  Bogart
    Pearson, 1647

Roseboom
  Pearson, 1728
Smith
  Pearson, 1703
VanDerBogart
  Fern Wlls, 1638
  Pearson, 1647
  Ship Lists, 1646
VanDoorn
  NY Ref mr, 1654
VanEveren
  Alb Ref bp, 1707, 1708
  Pearson, 1707
VanJevern
  Gen Entr 1, 1664
  NY Ref mr, 1660
VanVoorhees
  Fltb Ref bp, 1690

O

Odwaels
  Noorman
    Nycol Doc 2, 1661
Olivers
  Couwenhoven
    King Ref bp, 1663
  Rosebloom
    King Pap, 1661
Ottos
  VanThuyl
    Rcrd Nam 6, 1672
  VanTuyl
    Ship Lists, 1663

P

Pauls
  DuRues
    Ship Lists, 1663
  Jacquet
    Gen Entr 2, 1676
    NY Ref bp, 1655
    Nycol Doc 2, 1657
    Rcrd Nam 1, 1655
    Ship Lists, 1685
  Jongen
    Ship Lists, 1642

Noorman
  King Pap, 1662
VanBenthuysen
  Pearson, 1697
VanDerBeek
  Fltb Ref bp, 1681, 1683,
  1686
  King Co, 1647
VanDermonde
  NY Ref mr, 1640
VanDerVoort
  King Co, 1640
  Ship Lists, no date
VanDerWoert
  NY Ref bp, 1650, 1653
Pedro
  Alberto
    NY Ref bp, 1643
Peelens
  VanNewkirk
    Ship Lists, 1630
Pels
  VanSteltyn
    Ship Lists, 1642
Peter d'Italian
  Alberto
    NY Ref bp, 1645
Peters
  Bant
    NY Ref bp, 1679, 1690,
    1697
  Barroquier
    Pearson, 1654
  Beek
    NY Ref bp, 1687
  Bielefeld
    Ship Lists, 1626
  Bock
    Nycol Doc 1, 1652
  Bogart
    Hack Ref mr, 1713
  Borsboom
    Alb Ref mr, 1692
    Pearson, 1693
  Boschieter
    Nycol Doc 2, 1660

Bosch
  NY Ref bp, 1671, 1676,
  1678, 1685, 1687, 1695,
  1697
Bos
  Berg Ref bp, 1688
  NY Ref bp, 1691, 1699,
  1700, 1703
Bout
  Rens Court, 1671
Bronck
  Pearson, 1669
Brower
  Hack Ref bp, 1714
  Hack Ref mr, 1708
Buys
  Berg Ref bp, 1678, 1679,
  1682, 1684, 1686, 1689,
  1691
  Berg Ref mr, 1672
  Rcrd Nam 5, 1665
  Ship Lists, 1661, 1663
Cant
  LI Source, 1687
Carpyn
  Rcrd Nam 3, 1661
Claerhout
  Pearson, 1659
Clow
  Alb Ref mm, 1683
  Pearson, 1662
Coeyman
  Alb Ref bp, 1686
  Gen Entr 1, no date
  Pearson, 1636
  Rens Court, 1673
  Rens Crsp 1, 1660
  Rens Crsp 2, 1675, 1683
  Ship Lists, 1636, 1639,
  1640, 1650
Cooper
  Rcrd Nam 1, 1653
Coos
  Berg Ref dt, 1704
  Brgr Frm, 1657
  NY Ref mr, 1656
  Rcrd Nam 2, 1656, 1658

Corbyn
  Rcrd Nam 3, 1661
Couwenhoven
  King Co, no date
Cuyter
  LI Source, 1693
  NY Ref bp, 1642
  Nycol Doc 1, 1643
  Rcrd Nam 1, 1654
  Rcrd Nam 7, 1658
DeGroot
  Brgr Frm, 1657
  Hack Ref bp, 1716, 1718,
  1719, 1720, 1721
  Hack Ref mr, 1716
  NY Ref bp, 1650, 1688
  Orphan Mst, 1665
  Rcrd Nam 7, 1674
  Ship Lists, 1662, no date
DeHaas
  NY Ref bp, 1652, 1655
DeLascher
  Rcrd Nam 1, 1655
DeNoorman
  NY Ref bp, 1646
DeRoode
  Rens Court, 1669
DeVries
  Nycol Doc 1, 1642
Engelbert
  Hack Ref mr, 1718
Englebert
  Hack Ref bp, 1712
Groenvelt
  NY Ref bp, 1685
Haeswout
  Berg Ref mr, 1683
Harder
  Rcrd Nam 4, 1663
Haring
  NY Ref bp, 1669, 1679
  NY Ref mr, 1685
  Rcrd Nam 7, 1674
Haughwout
  LI Fam 1, 1675
Heerings
  Hack Ref bp, 1715, 1717,
  1719

Heyn
  Rens Crsp 1, 1656
Hogeboom
  King Pap, 1665
  Pearson, 1661
  Rens Court, 1669
  Rens Crsp 2, 1683
Houtsager
  Pearson, 1660
Jongen
  Ship Lists, 1637
Kenne
  King Co, 1660
Keteltas
  NY Ref bp, 1667, 1669,
  1670, 1671, 1672, 1673,
  1674, 1676, 1677
Kinne
  Fltb Ref bp, 1678, 1680,
  1683
Kleermaker
  Pearson, 1660
Kroock
  Nycol Doc 2, 1662
Kume
  Bkln Ref bp, 1686
  Ship Lists, 1663
Kuyter
  Ship Lists, 1637
Lansing
  Pearson, 1736
Lassen
  King Ref bp, 1684
  NY Lth bp, 1709
  Pearson, 1659
Lasse
  Ship Lists, 1659
Lock
  King Co, 1643
Loockermans
  Pearson, 1677
Lott
  King Co, 1654
Luyster
  King Co, 1697
  LI Source, 1693, 1695
  Ship Lists, 1687

Peters (cont.)

Mackelyck
King Co, 1664
LI Source, 1685, 1687

Makelik
Fltb Ref bp, 1681
LI Source, 1693

Marius
NY Ref bp, 1671

Mauritz
King Pap, 1669, 1670
Rcrd Nam 6, 1669

Mebie
Alb Ref bp, 1693
Pearson, 1683
Schn Ref bp, 1695

Meed
NY Ref bp, 1700
NY Ref mr, 1676

Mellott
NYC Wills, 1707

Melott
Brgr Frm, 1691, 1694
NYC Court, 1697

Menist
NY Ref bp, 1660, 1665
Rcrd Nam 3, 1659

Mevi
NY Ref bp, 1689

Meyer
Pearson, 1660

Meyn
Nycol Doc 2, 1661

Molenaer
NY Ref bp, 1644

Monfort
Fltb Ref bp, 1678, 1679,
1683
King Co, 1648
LI Fam 1, 1646

Mulder
Pearson, 1660

Muller
King Pap, 1664

Neby
NY Ref mr, 1687

Noorman
Evjen, 1639, 1660
King Pap, 1665
NY Ref bp, 1642, 1647

Norden
NY Ref bp, 1699

Nostrand
King Ref bp, 1699

Nucella
King Ref bp, 1696, 1700,
1701, 1703

Ostrander
Ship Lists, no date

Palmatier
Fltb Ref bp, 1680
King Co, 1654

Paulus
Hack Ref bp, 1720

Quackenbush
Alb Ref bp, 1685, 1688,
1689, 1690
Alb Ref mm, 1683
Alb Ref mr, 1683
Pearson, 1685
Rens Court, 1669

Roelofsen
NY Ref bp, 1653

Roode
Pearson, 1661
Rens Court, 1669

Roosa
NY Ref bp, 1642

Root
Pearson, 1661
Pearson, 1662

Sardam
Alb Ref bp, 1705

Schepmoes
King Pap, 1661

Schipper
King Pap, 1663

Scholl
Fltb Ref mr, 1680
NY Ref mr, 1680

Schuyler
Crt Assz, 1674
Gen Entr 1, 1667
King Ref bp, 1663
Nicl Lvl, 1665
NY Ref bp, 1674
NY Ref mr, 1657
Nycol Doc 3, 1664
Pearson, 1660
Rcrd Nam 4, 1663
Rens Court, 1669, 1670,
1671
Rens Crsp 1, 1657, 1659,
1660, 1661, 1664, 1668,
1672
Rens Crsp 2, 1681, 1683,
1687
Ship Lists, 1650, no date

Selenave
Brgr Frm, 1702

Sharp
Nycol Doc 1, 1650

Sloth
Hack Ref bp, 1699

Slot
Berg Ref bp, 1690
King Co, 1662
NY Ref bp, 1688, 1694
Rcrd Nam 1665, 1681
Ship Lists, 1650

Slyck
Pearson, 1685
Rens Court, 1669, 1671,
1672

Smith
NY Ref bp, 1656
Rcrd Nam 3, 1661

Staats
Bkln Ref bp, 1697
King Co, 1689
LI Source, 1694

Staeck
Evjen, 1660

Strycker
Fltb Ref bp, 1684
King Co, 1688

Patronymic/Surname Combinations

Suidam
  Pearson, 1705
Swart
  NY Ref bp, 1654
  Rcrd Nam 5, 1665
Tack
  King Pap, 1662, 1664
  King Ref bp, 1663
  King Ref mr, 1665
  Pearson, 1661
  Ship Lists, 1652, no date
Tempel
  Rcrd Nam 1, 1654
  Rens Crsp 1, 1655
Temper
  Pearson, 1657
  Rens Crsp 1, 1655, 1659
Timmerman
  Pearson, 1660
Tull
  Ship Lists, 1687
Tul
  King Co, 1657
UytHolstein
  NY Ref mr, 1652
Van Nort
  King Co, 1647
VanAlcmaer
  NY Ref bp, 1641, 1643
  NY Ref mr, 1643
  Pearson, 1653
VanAllen
  Alb Ref bp, 1707
  Pearson, 1689
VanAmsterdam
  Brgr Frm, 1657
  King Co, 1647
VanArbon
  NY Ref mr, 1663
VanBergen
  NY Ref bp, 1645
VanBlercom
  Hack Ref bp, 1719
VanBlydenstein
  Fltb Ref mr, 1682, 1684
  King Co, 1684

VanBolsart
  Brgr Frm, 1657
  Rcrd Nam 3, 1660
VanBolsuart
  Orphan Mst, 1664, 1665
VanBreda
  NY Ref mr, 1656
VanBremen
  NY Ref bp, 1663
VanBrugh
  Brgr Frm, 1657
  Nicl Lvl, 1667
  NY Ref bp, 1653, 1654,
  1660
  Nycol Doc 2, 1662
  Rcrd Nam 1, 1665
  Ship Lists, no date
VanBrutsteen
  NY Ref mr, 1641
VanCatalyn
  NY Ref bp, 1672
VanCopenhagen
  NY Ref mr, 1641, 1657
VanDeGujanes
  NY Ref mr, 1695
VanDerGoes
  Rcrd Nam 4, 1662
VanDerGrift
  NY Ref bp, 1679
VanDerGrist
  NY Ref bp, 1657
VanDerMeer
  NY Ref bp, 1697
VanDeusen
  Ship Lists, 1632, no date
VanDeventer
  King Co, 1662
  Ship Lists, no date
VanDeWater
  Fltb Ref bp, 1682
VanDockum
  Nycol Doc 2, 1665
VanEck
  King Co, 1632
VanEtten
  Pearson, 1658
VanGoestorp
  NY Ref mr, 1663

VanHamburg
  NY Ref mr, 1641, 1701
VanHarlem
  NY Ref mr, 1695
VanHasselt
  Brgr Frm, 1657
  Rcrd Nam 3, 1660
VanHaughwout
  Ship Lists, no date
VanHoesen
  NY Ref bp, 1640, 1643,
  1646
  NY Ref mr, 1652, 1657
VanHolstein
  Rcrd Nam 3, 1659
VanHorn
  NY Ref mr, 1672
VanLeeuven
  King Pap, 1664
  King Ref bp, 1688
  Nicl Lvl, 1667
VanLeyden
  NY Ref mr, 1652, 1664
  Pearson, 1661
VanLubeck
  NY Ref mr, 1676
VanMerven
  NY Ref mr, 1658
VanNess
  Fltb Ref bp, 1681, 1683
  King Co, 1677
  Rcrd Nam 7, 1672, 1673
VanNewkirk
  King Co, no date
VanOlinda
  Pearson, 1693
VanOstrander
  King Ref bp, 1706
VanQuackenbush
  NY Ref mr, 1674
VanRochel
  NY Ref mr, 1680
VanSeventer
  Pearson, 1659
VanSluyck
  Alb Ref mm, 1683
VanSluys
  NY Ref mr, 1665

Peters (cont.)
  VanSlyck
    Ship Lists, no date
  VanStruckhausen
    Brgr Frm, 1657
  VanTerGoude
    NY Ref mr, 16462
  VanTonsbergen
    NY Ref mr, 1641
  VanVaerden
    Brgr Frm, 1702
  VanVoorn
    NY Ref mr, 1706
  VanWoggelom
    Fern Wlls, 1682
    Pearson, 1671, 1682
  Veeltje
    Ship Lists, 1637
  VerBrugh
    NY Ref mr, 1658
    Rcrd Nam 1, 1653
    Rens Crsp 1, 1657, 1658
  Verhulst
    King Co, 1676
  Vosburgh
    Alb Ref mm, 1683
    King Pap, 1665
    Pearson, 1653
    Rens Crsp 1, 1659
    Ship Lists, 1649
  Vrooman
    Fern Wlls, 1684
    Pearson, 1684
  Vroom
    King Co, 1645
    LI Source, no date
    Ship Lists, 1645
  VVanDerGouw
    King Co, 1639
  VVanHaughwout
    Ship Lists, 1660
  Want
    NY Ref bp, 1688
  Weltman
    Gen Entr 2, 1676
  Wiltkock
    Rcrd Nam 2, 1658

Winnen
  Pearson, 1684
Winne
  Rens Court, 1671, 1672
Wyckoff
  Fltb Ref bp, 1679, 1680,
    1681, 1682, 1683, 1684,
    1685, 1688
  Fltb Ref mr, 1678, 1683
  King Co, 1677
  LI Fam 1, 1679
  LI Source, 1678
  NYC Wills, 1697
  Ship Lists, 1687
Philips
  Conine
    Alb Ref bp, 1687, 1706,
      1707, 1708
    Berg Ref mr, 1707
    NY Ref mr, 1707
    Pearson, 1708
  Demoer
    Pearson, 1693
  Gradus
    NY Ref bp, 1642
  Langelaan
    Fltb Ref bp, 1679
  Muller
    Pearson, 1663
  Ringo
    Rcrd Nam 7, 1674
  VanBolsart
    NY Ref mr, 1662
  VanMuyden
    NY Ref mr, 1662
  VanVelsen
    Rens Crsp 1, 1659
  VanVelthuysen
    Rens Crsp 1, 1654
  Velthuysen
    King Co, 1655
    Pearson, 1654
    Rens Crsp 1, 1654
  Waltman
    NY Ref mr, 1674
  Zerbe
    NY Lth mr, 1710

Piere
  Richards
    NYC Court, 1686
Pauls
  Richard
    King Ref bp, 1693
Potter
  Pottebacker
  Martins
    Pearson, 1659

R

Rees
  VanLipstadt
    NY Ref bp, 1656
Reinerse
  Myndert
    Pearson, 1706
  Smith
    Pearson, 1645
  VanBolsart
    Nycol Doc 3, 1664
  Wisselpenny
    Hack Ref mm, 1686
Rembrants
  VanAmsterdam
    NY Ref mr, 1655
Renatus
  DeLaSalle
    Rens Court, 1671
Reyers
  Lansing
    Pearson, 1693
  VanBlumenthal
    NY Ref mr, 1688
  VanBreuckelen
    NY Ref mr, 1665
  VanDeBeets
    Rcrd Nam 6, 1669
  VanDerBeer
    Nycol Doc 2, 1661
  VanDerBeets
    Rens Crsp 1, 1658, 1659,
      1663
Reyners
  Dirks
    Berg Ref mm, 1678

Spits
  Nycol Doc 2, 1664
VanGiesen
  Berg Ref mm, 1677
VanSicklen
  King Co, 1695
Wisselpenny
  Fltb Ref bp, 1679, 1681
  Fltb Ref mr, 1678, 1680,
  1681
  LI Source, 1680
Richards
  VanVranken
    Pearson, no date
Richard
  VanRochel
    NY Ref mr, 1664
Rips
  VanDam
    Alb Ref bp, 1684, 1700
    Nycol Doc 3, 1690
    Pearson, 1658
    Ship Lists, no date
Roelofs
  Bogart
    Hack Ref bp, 1718, 1720,
    1721
    Hack Ref mr, 1717
  DeGoyer
    Pearson, no date
    Rens Court, 1669
  Elting
    Berg Ref mr, 1672
  Jongerman
    Ship Lists, 1658
  Kidney
    Alb Ref mm, 1698
  Pottebacker
    NY Ref mr, 1663
  Schenck
    Fltb Ref bp, 1681, 1682,
    1683, 1684, 1685
    Fltb Ref mr, 1683, 1684,
    1687
    King Co, 1661
    Ship Lists, 1687

Sebring
  Berg Ref mm, 1682
  Bkln Ref bp, 1687
  Crt Assz, 1672
  Fltb Ref bp, 1682
  King Co, 1631
  Nicl Lvl, 1671
  Rcrd Nam 6, 1671
  Ship Lists, no date
Tysen
  Fltb Ref bp, 1682
VanDerWerken
  Alb Ref bp, 1702, 1704,
  1705, 1706, 1708
  Pearson, 1700
VanHamelwaard
  Ship Lists, 1639
VanHouten
  Ship Lists, no date
  Tary Ref bp, 1703
VanMalmuyden
  NY Ref mr, 1673
VanTappan
  Gen Entr 1, 1670
VanUytrecht
  NY Ref mr, 1653
VanVlecher
  NY Ref mr, 1665
Verkerken
  King Co, 1680
Westervelt
  Hack Ref bp, 1715, 1718,
  1719, 1720
  Hack Ref mr, 1710
Rogers
  Bleecker
    Pearson, 1749
  Moreau
    Rcrd Nam 4, 1663
  VanAmersfort
    NY Ref mr, 1666
  VanBrent
    Ship Lists, 1687
  VanBrunt
    Fltb Ref bp, 1683, 1684,
    1689
    Fltb Ref mr, 1683, 1685,
    1687

King Co, 1685
  LI Fam 2, 1653
  Ship Lists, 1687
VanWesop
  NY Ref mr, 1672, 1673
Rolants
  Van Hammelwart
  Pearson, 1638
Rombouts
  Petronellitie
    NY Ref bp, 1673
Romeyns
  Langestraat
    NY Ref bp, 1697
Roos
  VanDerlipstradt
    NY Ref bp, 1654
Rose
  Alberson
    King Ref bp, 1687
Rudolphs
  DeVries
    NY Ref mr, 1659
  Schenck
    Fltb Ref bp, 1682

S

Sam
  DeMaree
    Hack Ref mr, 1717
Samuels
  DeMaree
    Hack Ref bp, 1708, 1710,
    1715, 1717, 1718, 1719,
    1720
    Hack Ref mr, 1718
  Levy
    NYC Court, 1691
  Pruyn
    Pearson, 1752
Sanders
  Glenn
    Alb Ref bp, 1683, 1685
    Alb Ref mm, 1683
    Alb Ref mr, 1696, 1699
    Fern Wlls, 1685
    Gen Entr 2, 1685

Sanders (cont.)
 Glenn (cont.)
  Nicl Lvl, 1669
  NYC Wills, 1686
  Nycol Doc 3, 1688
  Pearson, 1695
  Rens Court, 1668, 1669,
   1670, 1671, 1672
  Rens Crsp 1, 1658, 1659,
   1662, 1670, 1672
  Rens Crsp 2, 1682, 1683,
   1687
  Schn Ref bp, 1694, 1700,
   1701, 1702, 1703, 1704,
   1706
 VanThuyl
  Gen Entr 1, 1664
 Vantiel
  Nycol Doc 3, 1664
Schermerhorn
 Winnen
  Alb Ref mm, 1683
Segers
 VanVoorhout
  Fern Wlls, 1663
  Pearson, 1642
  Rens Court, 1670
  Rens Crsp 1, 1656
  Rens Crsp 2, 1683
  Ship Lists, 1642, 1644, no
   date
Selyns
 Hendricksen
  NY Ref bp, 1663
Serix
 DeVries
  Nicl Lvl, 1672
Sheltons
 Broughton
  NYC Wills, 1705
  Ship Lists, 1637
 VanEdam
  Ship Lists, 1636
Siberse
 Banta
  Hack Ref bp, 1703, 1705,
   1706, 1708, 1709, 1711,
   1712, 1714, 1715, 1716,

  1717, 1718, 1719, 1720,
   1721
  Hack Ref mm, 1698
  Hack Ref mr, 1699, 1703,
   1705
Sickels
 VanWeenen
  Pearson, 1659
Siebolds
 VanLangendyck
  NY Ref mr, 1642
Simons
 Barroquier
  Pearson, 1653
 Bet
  Pearson, 1661
 Block
  NY Ref mr, 1674, 1697
 Boer
  Pearson, 1661
 Clum
  Pearson, 1653
  Rcrd Nam 1, 1654
  Rens Crsp 1, 1657
  Ship Lists, 1651
 Fradell
  Ship Lists, 1652
 Groot
  Pearson, 1654
 Michels
  Pearson, 1661
 Michiels
  Rens Crsp 1, 1663
 Mythousen
  LI Source, 1695
 Outhousen
  LI Source, 1695
 Uythuysen
  King Co, 1695
  LI Source, 1695
 VanAngola
  NY Ref bp, 1642
 VanArsdalen
  Fltb Ref bp, 1680, 1681,
   1683, 1684
  Fltb Ref mr, 1678, 1687
  King Co, 1687
  Ship Lists, 1687

 VanNordthorn
  NY Ref mr, 1646
 VanNostrand
  King Co, 1687
 VanOoscen
  Gen Entr 1, 1664
 VanOostsanen
  Pearson, 1661
 VanUythuysen
  Bkln Ref mr, 1685
 VanWinckel
  Berg Ref mr, 1701
  Hack Ref bp, 1702, 1709,
   1711, 1712, 1714
  Hack Ref mr, 1697, 1700,
   1704, 1705, 1706, 1708,
   1721
 Vedder
  Alb Ref bp, 1709
  Pearson, 1699
  Schn Ref bp, 1704, 1706
  Schn Ref mr, 1704
 Smith
  VanIckemsburgh
   Ship Lists, 1642
 Smit
  VanLochem
   NY Ref bp, 1655
 Solomons
  Goewey
   Alb Ref bp, 1701, 1702,
    1707, 1708
   NY Ref mr, 1707
   Pearson, 1683
  Metselaer
   King Ref mr, 1683
   NY Ref bp, 1708
 Staats
  DeGroot
   Hack Ref bp, 1715
 Stavast
  Yanzen
   Nycol Doc 3, 1664
 Stephens
  Cooper
   Ship Lists, 1654
  Cortlandt
   Rens Crsp 1, 1668

Patronymic/Surname Combinations

Croaet
  Ship Lists, 1638
Croat
  Pearson, 1637
Jongen
  Ship Lists, 1638
Mulder
  Pearson, 1682
  Ship Lists, 1660
Muller
  Alb Ref bp, 1683
  Rens Court, 1670
Van Cortlandt
  Rens Crsp 2, 1684
VanCortlandt
  Brgr Frm, 1659
  Evjen, 1637
  Gen Entr 1, 1664
  Nicl Lvl, 1667
  NY Ref bp, 1641, 1642,
  1643, 1644, 1645, 1646,
  1648, 1649, 1650, 1651,
  1653, 1655, 1656, 1657,
  1658, 1660, 1661, 1662,
  1666, 1672, 1675, 1677,
  1679, 1683, 16460
  Nycol Doc 1, 1649
  Orphan Mst, 1664
  Rcrd Nam 1, 1653
  Rens Crsp 1, 1655, 1657,
  1658, 1659, 1661, 1662,
  1663, 1664, 1665, 1666,
  1667, 1668, 1670, 1671,
  1673, 1674, no date
  Rens Crsp 2, 1669, 1678,
  1680, 1682, 1683
  Ship Lists, 1638, no date
VanDanzig
  NY Ref mr, 1699
VanDouveren
  NY Ref mr, 1692
VanSeyl
  Hack Ref bp, 1695

VanVoorhees
  Fltb Ref bp, 1678, 1680,
  1681, 1682, 1683, 1684,
  1685, 1687
  Fltb Ref mr, 1678, 1680,
  1681
  LI Source, no date
  Ship Lists, 1687
VanWyck
  NY Ref mr, 1642
VanZyl
  NY Ref bp, 1692
Voorhees
  Hack Ref mm, 1686
  King Co, 1660
Storms
  Bratt
    Pearson, 1699
  VanDerZee
    Pearson, 1699
Swagers
  VanAngola
    NY Ref bp, 1642, 1644
Sybrants
  Roelofsen
    King Pap, 1663
  VanDerHout
    King Pap, 1662
  VanSchaick
    Pearson, 1686
Syrachs
  DeVries
    King Co, 1660

T

Takels
  Heemstraat
    Alb Ref bp, 1701, 1702
    Pearson, 1701
  VanHeemstraat
    Alb Ref bp, 1704, 1706
Terss
  VanFraniker
    Ship Lists, 1635
Teunis
  Backer
    NY Ref bp, 1648

Baker
  LI Source, 1691
Beeregat
  Nycol Doc 1, 1649
Bogart
  Berg Ref bp, 1689, 1700
  Berg Ref mm, 1682
  Bkln Ref bp, 1693
  Fltb Ref bp, 1679, 1680,
  1682, 1684, 1685
  Fltb Ref mr, 1677, 1679,
  1681, 1689
  King Co, 1685
  NY Ref bp, 1691
Bosch
  Pearson, 1631
Bos
  Pearson, 1631
  Rens Court, 1668
  Ship Lists, 1631, 1637
Bratt
  Pearson, 1701
Burgtem
  NY Ref bp, 1657
Cleer
  LI Source, 1695
Clere
  LI Source, 1692, 1694,
  1696
Coevers
  Bkln Ref bp, 1690
  Fltb Ref bp, 1683
  Fltb Ref mr, 1682
  NY Ref bp, 1687
  NY Ref mr, 1680
Cole
  King Ref bp, 1683
Covert
  Fltb Ref mr, 1679, 1682
  King Co, 1677
Cray
  NY Ref bp, 1664
  NY Ref mr, 1658
  Rcrd Nam 1, 1655
Dam
  LI Source, 1695
DeHubert
  NY Ref mr, 1674

Patronymic/Surname Combinations

Teunis (cont.)
DeKey
Crt Assz, 1676
Fern Wlls, 1668
NY Ref bp, 1659, 1663,
1664, 1665, 1672, 1674,
1675, 1677, 1678, 1679,
1681
DeLooper
Pearson, 1656
Rcrd Nam 6, 1667
DeMetzelaer
Ship Lists, 1642
DeNys
Fltb Ref bp, 1681, 1682,
1685, 1687
King Co, 1667
DePaep
Pearson, 1660
DeReus
Pearson, 1631
Ship Lists, 1631
Dykehuys
LI Source, 1693
Glazemaecker
Pearson, 1658
Hellinck
Ship Lists, 1659
Helling
Berg Ref dt, 1685, 1697
Berg Ref mr, 1700
Hack Ref mr, 1700
Hoen
NY Ref bp, 1662
Hogeboom
Pearson, 1661
Huysman
Gen Entr 1, 1670
Kay
NYC Wills, 1671
Pearson, 1676
Key
Gen Entr 2, 1676
King Co, 1664
Nycol Doc 2, 1674
Rcrd Nam 1, 1661

Lanen
Fltb Ref mr, 1686
LI Source, 1687
NY Ref mr, 1686
Looper
Rcrd Nam 1, 1655
Metselaer
Fern Wlls, 1685
Pearson, 1685
Rens Crsp 2, 1681
Ship Lists, 1641
Middagh
Bkln Ref bp, 1662
Bkln Ref mm, 1664
King Co, 1657
NY Ref bp, 1660, 1661
Ship Lists, 1661, no date
Mingaal
Pearson, 1685
Mulder
Pearson, 1703
Noorman
Evjen, 1650
King Co, 1657
Nyssen
Fltb Ref bp, 1678
Fltb Ref mr, 1682, 1685
Oylensplegel
Pearson, 1645
Pelt
Nycol Doc 4, 1701
Pier
Hack Ref mr, 1708
King Ref bp, 1683, 1700
Quick
King NYGB, 1672
King Pap, 1665
King Ref bp, 1679, 1683,
1688
NY Ref bp, 1659, 1680
Pearson, 1661
Rcrd Nam 6, 1667
Rapalye
King Co, 1699
Robert
Berg Ref mr, 1686
Schay
NY Ref bp, 1647

Slackboom
NYC Wills, 1677
Slingerland
Pearson, 1705
Slyck
Rens Court, 1671, 1672
Swart
Alb Ref bp, 1691
Pearson, 1680, 1690
Tappan
Pearson, 1671
Rens Court, 1671
Rens Crsp 1, 1661
Rens Crsp 2, 1683
Ship Lists, 1652, 1662
TenEyck
NY Ref mr, 1689
Uylenspiegel
Ship Lists, 1642
VanAngola
NY Ref bp, 1641, 1643,
1645
VanBreuckelen
Pearson, 1631
Rens Court, 1670
Ship Lists, 1631
VanBronswyck
Pearson, 1684
VanCouverden
NY Ref mr, 1679
VanCovert
King Co, 1679
VanDenBos
Ship Lists, 1637
VanDerBeek
Alb Ref bp, 1683
Vanderbilt
Pearson, 1640
Ship Lists, 1640
VanDerHeyden
Nicl Lvl, 1669
VanDerVechte
Alb Ref bp, 1701
VanDeusen
Pearson, 1700
VanDuyckhuysen
Bkln Ref bp, 1677
Fltb Ref bp, 1681, 1684

Patronymic/Surname Combinations

VanDyckhuysen
  LI Source, 1687
VanDyckhuys
  King Co, 1643
  Ship Lists, 1687
VanDyck
  LI Source, 1687
VanEsselstine
  NY Ref mr, 1661
VanHouten
  Hack Ref bp, 1719
VanIselstein
  Ship Lists, 1658
VanLeyden
  NY Ref mr, 1649
  Pearson, 1642
VanLoenen
  Rens Crsp 1, 1659
VanLuyten
  Ship Lists, 1642
VanMerkerk
  Pearson, 1637
  Ship Lists, 1637
VanNieuwenhuysen
  NY Ref mr, 1707
VanNorden
  NY Ref mr, 1642, 1655
  Rcrd Nam 1, 1654
  Ship Lists, 1650
VanPelt
  Bkln Ref bp, 1687
  Fltb Ref bp, 1681, 1685,
  1689, 1690
  King Co, 1686
  LI Source, 1687, 1697
  Ship Lists, 1687
VanRotterdam
  NY Ref mr, 1664
VanSchlick
  Rens Crsp 2, 1683
  Ship Lists, 1634
VanSchoenderwoert
  Pearson, 1709
VanSchooderwoert
  Alb Ref bp, 1709
  Alb Ref mm, 1683

VanSlyck
  Pearson, 1641, 1661
  Rens Crsp 2, 1683
  Ship Lists, 1641, no date
VanThuyl
  NY Ref bp, 1661
  NY Ref mr, 1658
VanTilburg
  Brgr Frm, 1695
  NY Ref bp, 1689, 1694
  NY Ref mr, 1655, 1691
VanVechten
  Alb Ref bp, 1690, 1692,
  1701
  Alb Ref mm, 1683
  Alb Ref mr, 1689
  Fern Wlls, 1687, 1701
  Pearson, 1669
  Rens Court, 1668, 1670
  Rens Crsp 1, 1668
  Rens Crsp 2, 1680, 1683,
  1687, 1688
VanVelde
  Ship Lists, 1645
VanVelsen
  Pearson, 1664
VanVessen
  King Pap, 1664, 1665
VanVoorsthuysen
  NY Ref mr, 1659
VanWesop
  NY Ref mr, 1661
VanWestbroeck
  Pearson, 1663
  Rens Court, 1668
  Ship Lists, 1631
VanWoert
  Alb Ref bp, 1704
VanZell
  NY Ref mr, 1654
Vermeulen
  Ship Lists, 1659
VerWey
  Alb Ref bp, 1694
  Pearson, 1694

Theodurus
  Polhemus
    King Co, 1662
    LI Source, 1685, 1702
Thomas
  Baddie
    LI Source, 1670
  Berrow
    Brgr Frm, 1688
  Bloomenthal
    Alb Ref bp, 1709
  Hun
    Rens Crsp 1, 1660
    Ship Lists, no date
  Metselaer
    NY Ref bp, 1644, 1645
  Mingaal
    Alb Ref bp, 1701
    Alb Ref mm, 1683
    Alb Ref mr, 1685
    Rens Court, 1669, 1670
  Poppinga
    NY Ref mr, 1695
  Quick
    Nycol Doc 3, 1664
    Rcrd Nam 1, 1654
  Stridler
    Alb Ref bp, 1686
  VanBarnevelt
    NY Ref mr, 1659
  VanDyck
    Bkln Ref bp, 1690, 1695
    Fltb Ref mr, 1678, 1679,
    1689, 1692
    King Co, 1689
    Ship Lists, 1652, 1687
  VanRipen
    Ship Lists, no date
  VanStrabroeck
    Alb Ref mr, 1658
  VanUtrecht
    NY Ref mr, 1669
  VanWeely
    Rens Crsp 1, 1657
  VanWely
    Rens Crsp 1, 1654
  Vos
    Evjen, 1711

Thomas (cont.)
Whitbeck
Rens Court, 1669
Rens Crsp 1, 1658
Ship Lists, no date
Thompsons
Striddles
Rens Crsp 2, 1681
Struddles
NYC Wills, 1702
Westerhout
NYC Wills, 1694
Tiepkesz
Schellinger
Rens Crsp 1, 1657, 1658, 1659
Timothys
Vedam
Pearson, 1636
Titus
DeVries
Fltb Ref bp, 1682

U

Ulrichs
VanNewkirk
NY Ref mr, 1664

V

Volkerts
Bries
Ship Lists, 1655
DeBakker
Pearson, 1654
Douw
Alb Ref mm, 1683
Alb Ref mr, 1683, 1684
Pearson, 1690
Ship Lists, 1642
Hermans
NY Ref bp, 1694
Oly
Rcrd Nam 5, 1664

VanHoesen
Alb Ref bp, 1700
Atns Lth bp, 1707
Atns Lth mr, 1705, 1708
NY Lth bp, 1709
NY Lth mr, 1705, 1707
VanHusum
Evjen, 1705
VanNostrand
King Co, 1687
VanVechten
Pearson, 1747
Vedder
Fern Wlls, 1697
Pearson, 1654
Vos
VanBaden
Ship Lists, 1642

W

Walings
Vanderbilt
Ship Lists, 1636
VanWinckel
Berg Ref mr, 1710
Hack Ref bp, 1699
Hack Ref mr, 1710
Ship Lists, no date
Walters
NY Ref bp, 1688
Bkln Ref bp, 1688
Schotzina
NY Ref mr, 1663
VanBosch
King Co, 1659
Ship Lists, 1687
VanDenBosch
Fltb Ref bp, 1678, 1680, 1682, 1683, 1684
VanDerBosch
King Co, 1677
VanEsselstine
NY Ref bp, 1655
NY Ref mr, 1641
VanPelt
King Co, 1687

VanSchyven
Hack Ref bp, 1715
VanSterrevelt
King Pap, 1666
Wanshaer
VanStBenen
NY Ref bp, 1662
Wariverts
Bruman
King Co, 1677
Warners
Stoltin
Ship Lists, 1659
VanSchonevelt
NY Ref mr, 1656
Wartons
Marshall
Rcrd Nam 5, 1665
Wemp
Meinderts
Schn Ref bp, 1701
Wenzels
VanZant
Ship Lists, no date
Wessels
Backer
Pearson, 1633
Becker
Fern Wlls, 1681
DeYoung
NY Ref bp, 1670
Smith
Nycol Doc 2, 1674
Ten Broeck
Pearson, 1663
TenBroeck
Alb Ref bp, 1700, 1704
Alb Ref mm, 1683
King Pap, 1673
King Ref bp, 1678, 1682
Nicl Lvl, 1672
NY Ref bp, 1671, 1674, 1678, 1679, 1680, 1682, 1684, 1686, 1688, 1690
Rens Crsp 2, 1678
Ship Lists, no date

Patronymic/Surname Combinations

UytOostVrieslant
  NY Ref mr, 1658
VanArnhem
  NY Ref mr, 1655, 1667,
  1668
VanColen
  NY Ref mr, 1654
VanDortrecht
  NY Ref mr, 1675
VanNorden
  NY Ref mr, 1669
VanTolhuys
  NY Ref mr, 1679
VanUtrecht
  NY Ref mr, 1656, 1664
VanWessen
  NY Ref mr, 1670

Wiertse

Banta
  Hack Ref bp, 1715, 1716,
  1717, 1718, 1719, 1720

Willems

Backer
  Nycol Doc 2, 1674
  Pearson, 1657
Bakker
  Rcrd Nam 1, 1654
Barkelo
  King Co, 1680
Beekman
  King Co, 1647
Beer
  Rcrd Nam 2, 1658
Bennet
  Bkln Ref bp, 1682, 1687
  Bkln Ref mm, 1677
  Fltb Ref bp, 1680, 1681,
  1682, 1683, 1685
  King Co, 1662
  LI Fam 1, 1636
  LI Source, 1686, 1689,
  1698
  NY Ref bp, 1685, 1686,
  1705
  NY Ref mr, 1686, 1690
  Ship Lists, 1687

Boerum
  King Co, 1642
  Ship Lists, no date
Bootsen
  Pearson, 1684
Boreklo
  Ship Lists, 1687
Brandt
  King Ref bp, 1681
Brower
  Alb Ref mr, 1692
Cooperslaeger
  King Pap, 1671
Cornell
  King Co, 1681
  LI Fam 1, 1688
  LI Source, 1679
Couwenhoven
  King Co, 1676
Cram
  LI Source, 1679
Croon
  NYC Court, 1693
DeBeer
  Rens Crsp 1, 1658
  Ship Lists, 1657
Dubois
  King Ref bp, 1664
Esselstine
  King Co, 1661
  NY Ref bp, 1650, 1669
  Rcrd Nam 1, 1654
Ester
  Rcrd Nam 2, 1658
Gesscher
  Berg Ref dt, 1696
Groesbeek
  Pearson, 1746
Heyvelt
  Rens Crsp 1, 1660
Kettelas
  Ship Lists, no date
Krum
  Fern Wlls, 1699
  King Co, 1677
  King Pap, 1668
  King Ref bp, 1678, 1681
  King Ref mr, 1668

LI Fam 2, no date
  NY Ref bp, 1685
  NYC Wills, 1699
Loosdrecht
  Berg Ref mm, 1667
Megapolensis
  Nycol Doc 2, 1674
Munnick
  King Pap, 1663
  Nycol Doc 2, 1663
Neering
  NY Ref bp, 1681, 1687,
  1691
  NY Ref mr, 1680
Neringh
  LI Source, 1694
Noortryck
  King Pap, 1671
Oosterum
  Pearson, 1631
Ostrom
  Ship Lists, 1631
Otten
  Pearson, 1703
Romeyn
  NY Ref bp, 1694, 1695,
  1697, 1699, 1700, 1701,
  1702, 1704, 1708, 1709
  NY Ref mr, 1684
Rome
  Brgr Frm, 1698
  NY Ref bp, 1687, 1689,
  1692, 1702, 1703, 1707
  NY Ref mr, 1684
Rom
  NY Ref bp, 1687
Roome
  NYC Court, 1702
  NYC Wills, 1706
Schagen
  Nycol Doc 2, 1657
Schoon
  King Pap, 1664
  Pearson, 1661
Schryver
  King Ref bp, 1682

Patronymic/Surname Combinations

Willems (cont.)
Schutt
  King Ref bp, 1696
  Ship Lists, 1646
Schyven
  King Ref bp, 1682
Scuth
  Pearson, 1646
  Ship Lists, 1646
Staats
  LI Source, 1700
Stuyvesant
  Gen Entr 1, 1665
  King Pap, 1673
  King Ref mr, 1681
  NY Ref bp, 1678, 1679,
  1683, 1685, 1687, 1691
  NY Ref mr, 1672, 1681
  Rcrd Nam 7, 1674
UytOldenburger
  NY Ref mr, 1660
VanAmsterdam
  NY Ref mr, 1660
VanAmsterd
  NY Ref bp, 1648
  NY Ref mr, 1685
VanBaasle
  Pearson, 1642
  Ship Lists, 1642
VanBoerum
  Fltb Ref mr, 1684
  LI Source, 1649, 1687,
  1689
VanBorcklo
  Ship Lists, 1687
VanBorkelo
  Fltb Ref bp, 1680, 1681
  Fltb Ref mr, 1679
VanBuren
  King Ref bp, 1698
VanCoppernol
  Pearson, 1676
VanCouwenhoven
  LI Fam 2, 1662
  Ship Lists, 1687
VanDenBerg
  Alb Ref bp, 1700, 1708
  Fern Wlls, 1706

Pearson, 1670
VanDenBosch
  Brgr Frm, 1657
  NY Ref mr, 1665
  Rcrd Nam 1, 1655
VanDerSchuere
  NY Ref bp, 1689
VanDeSchuyven
  King Ref bp, 1703, 1704
VanDeventer
  Berg Ref bp, 1693
VanEngen
  King Co, 1657
VanEsselstine
  NY Ref bp, 1658, 1661
  Rcrd Nam 2, 1658
VanGeescher
  King Co, 1696
VanGesscher
  LI Source, 1696
VanHeerden
  Pearson, 1662
VanHouten
  Hack Ref mm, page xx
  Hack Ref mr, 1712
VanLeyden
  NY Ref bp, 1664
VanMeeuwis
  NY Ref mr, 1693
VanMeppel
  NY Ref mr, 1662
VanNewkirk
  NY Ref mr, 1663
VanNuys
  Fltb Ref bp, 1685
VanSluyck
  Alb Ref bp, 1688, 1689
  Alb Ref mr, 1688, 1690,
  1696
VanSlyck
  Pearson, 1687
VanWestervelt
  LI Source, 1697
VanWesterv
  King Co, 1697
VanWicklen
  Fltb Ref bp, 1709
VanWoutbergh

Pearson, 1677
Vertein
  King Co, 1661
Wee
  NYC Wills, 1667
Witt
Romeyn
  NY Ref bp, 1696
Wolferts
Couwenhoven
  King Co, 1631
  NY Ref bp, 1655
  NYC Wills, 1670
  Nycol Doc 1, 1643
Krast
  Fltb Ref bp, 1680
VanAmersfort
  NY Ref mr, 1640
VanCouwenhoven
  Gen Entr 1, 1664
  LI Fam 2, 1630
  NY Ref bp, 1655
  NY Ref mr, 1655
  Rcrd Nam 1, 1653
Wollewevers
Schaats
  Alb Ref mm, 1683
Wooderts
Ruyter
  NY Ref bp, 1678
Wybrechts
Spoor
  Pearson, 1685
VanHarlingen
  Pearson, 1662
Wygands
VanColen
  NY Ref mr, 1662
Wynants
VanBreuckelen
  NY Ref mr, 1690
VanDenBerg
  Pearson, 1749

VanDerPoel
>Alb Ref bp, 1683, 1685,
>1689, 1691, 1703
>Alb Ref mm, 1683
>NY Ref bp, 1690
>Pearson, 1683

VanEck
>King Co, 1663

VanGroeningen
>NY Ref mr, 1683

Y

Ysbrants
Timmer
>Pearson, 1662

Z

Zacharias
DeVries
>Fltb Ref bp, 1682

Sluys
>NYC Wills, 1686
>Nycol Doc 2, 1674
>Rcrd Nam 6, 1671

VanGroeningen
>NY Ref mr, 1655

Names, Names and More Names

HELPFUL HINTS REGARDING SURNAMES

Place Identifiers as Surnames:

New settlers in America were often identified not only by a patronymic signifying the father but also by a phrase telling something about the place of origin. The Dutch term "van" or the German term "von" were used at the beginning of the phrase. Sometimes in Dutch phraseology, "de", "der" or "ter" was inserted meaning "of" or "of the", Van der Water meaning of the water. In the French language prefixes "de" "des" "du" or "le" meant of. (The word to which the prefix is attached should show whether the name could be Dutch or French.). Not only do we have Van and Van Der but we also come across Van Den and then what seems like a contraction of Van Der, namely, Ver as in Verplanck. Less often we come across Uyt Den and Uyt Der for out of. These also become contracted to become Ten and Ter as in Ten Broeck and Terbush (at/near the brook or bush).

In a short article titled "Surnames" appearing in the NEHG Register, July 1849, we are told by B. H. Dixon that "A common prefix to Dutch family names is the word 'de', which is here generally supposed to mean 'of', and to denote a French extraction. This is, however, incorrect, it being in the former language the article 'the', as, for example, de Wit, the White; de Bruyn, the Brown; de Kock, the Cook; de Jong, the Young; de Koster, the Sexton; de Vries, the Friesian; de Waal, the Walloon, etc, synonymous with our English names White, Brown, Cook, Young, etc.

"It is also prefixed in its different genders and cases as `t Hooft (het Hoofd), the Head; in't Veld (in het Veld), in the Field; der Kinderen, of the Children; van der Hegge, of the Hedge; van den Berg, of the Hill; uit den Boogaard, out or from the Orchard; equivalent to our Head, Field, etc.

"'Te', 'ten', and 'ter' meaning 'at' or 'to', are also often used as, te Water, at the Water; ten Heugel, at the Hill; ter Winkel, at the Shop.

"The Dutch preposition 'van' before family names answers to the French "de", "of" and was in early times seldom borne but by nobles, being placed before the names of their castles or estates.

"In later days, however, when family names came more generally into use, many added to their Christian names their places of birth or residence, which were retained as family names; as van Gent, of Ghent; van Bern, of Bern; van den Haag, of the Hague; van Cleef, of Cleves; van Buren, of Buren. This latter is derived from the village of Buren, in Gelderland. It was formerly a domain of the Princess of Orange-Nassau, and many of them bore the title of Counts of Buren. Our Ex-President's family is, however, in no wise related to them; his name probably originated from his ancestor having hailed from that town."

A further discussion of Van and Von used as predicates is found in an article written by Susanna Matthes for the NYGandB *Record* in Oct 1893. The following is extracted from that article:

"It is a common mistake of Americans to think that the 'van' before a Dutch name signifies nobility. In the Low Countries, that is, in the kingdoms of the Netherlands and of Belgium, 'van' has no particular meaning. Names with 'van' are to be read on shops as well as on the doors of the most aristocratic mansions. The humblest persons have it as well as the most refined. On the other hand, a great number of the oldest families are without it. In Germany, 'von' means noble, and all persons belonging to the nobility have 'von' before their family names, without any exception. Persons who do not belong to the nobility cannot put 'von' before their names, as they have no right to do so, and would be found out directly if they assumed it, and make themselves ridiculous. But in case of a man being knighted for some reason or other, he has the right to put 'von' before his family name.

"Among the family names in America, the bearers of which came over from the Netherlands in the 16th and 17th centuries, many terminate in 'us'. At that time the only means of correspondence between scientific persons from different countries was in Latin, which became so much the fashion that many people Latinized their names. Families with names such as Stratenus, Mollerus, and Cramerus inform us that the ancestors of these families must have been prominent, educated men.

These would be called people of good family or old family. We may find a person as Hugo DeGroot becoming Hugo Grotius only to revert back again to the DeGroot surname.

"The provinces of the Netherlands are extremely small but each continues to keep its own distinct character. The Province of Friesland has a different language so that other Dutchman have a difficult time in understanding them. Family names in Friesland generally terminate in 'a' as in Van Cysingha, Kingma, Camminga, Van Heemstra, and Postma. Their Christian names are also peculiar and don't lend themselves to easy translation. Men named Sjoust, Jouwert, and Skato and women named Wietkske, Vrouwke, and Tcota are not unusual.

Names, Names and More Names

"There are many family names in the Netherlands that belong to individuals far apart in the social scale of life. Van Buren is a very common name in Holland, but there was a family van Buren, now extinct, who were of such high and ancient blood that the late Queen Sophia, when travelling incognito, did so under the name of Countess van Buren. No one is allowed to make any alteration in the family name by adding, deleting, or changing a single letter, or assuming or dropping the predicate 'van'. A special license must be obtained to do so. There can scarcely be a mistake about a name in Holland, whereas the descendants of the Dutch in America may have taken 'van' or dropped it, and may have changed several letters in their names so as to make them unrecognizable to the Dutch ear."

A surname using a place name of origin might refer to a province, a city, a small area or a natural feature. Examples:

Province:	Van Brabant	
City:	Van Arnhem	
Area:	Van Winkle	
Feature:	Van Tassel or Texel	Isle of Texel
	Van Buskirk	woods + church
	Ter Broogh	bridge
	Townsend	end of the town

Sometimes the place identifier continued in use as the family surname; other times it may only appear in one or two entries while the patronymic persisted for some time before a permanent surname was adopted, such as the case of Hendrick Jansen Ostrom who was initially identified as Hendrick Jansen Van Schalckwyck. (New York Reformed Church baptisms Nov 1652 and Jun 1657) then adopted a van Oosteroom designation before becoming simply Ostrom or Ostrum (The Record, New York GandB Society, "The Dutcher Family" 1909 p. 191).

In the Osterhout family of Ulster County, New York, we find that at one time there were at least two families in the community being fathered by someone named Jan. A means of identifying one from the other was the place of origin. Thus the family of Jan van Oosterhout assumed the surname Van Oosterhout in the first generation. While many families retained the Van designation, the Oosterhout family dropped it in the next generation so that they may be found in the index under Van Osterhout for one generation and under Osterhout in another generation.

In actual practice, modern German indexes ignore the von designation and simply index all surnames by the main word in the surname. In searching American records it is important to look for the names with and without the prefix word.

Names, Names and More Names

Further development and examples of patronymics changing to placename identifier surnames may be found by referring to *Searching for Colonial Dutch Ancestors* by David M. Riker in vol 63 No. 3 pages 1-4 of "De Halve Maen" published Sep 1990.

Characteristic Names:

Many times an individual was identified by a characteristic and this became the surname adopted by the family. De Groote is an example of a surname which first identified a large man. DeWitt would have been the white one or a man who had either light skin or hair. Swartz or Schwartz was someone with dark complexion or with black hair. The following lists some examples:

English	German
Old	Alt
Long	Lange
Short	Kleine
Large	Grosse
Young	Jung

Occupation Names:

An obvious choice for surnames identifying an individual would be the occupational name. This was especially appropriate since sons often assumed their fathers occupation and hence the surname would continue to be appropriate to the one using it. Naturally over time the surname continued while the occupation may have changed.

This practice appears in many nationalities such as English, German, and Dutch names. A few examples include:

English,	German,	Dutch	meaning
Smith	Schmidt, -	Gow	blacksmith
Butcher	Metselaer		
Cooper	Kuyper,	Cooper	(barrel maker)
Weaver	Weber.	Wever	weaver
Carpenter	Zimmerman		carpenter
Miller	Mueller		
Roofer		Decker	roofer
Streetmaker		Straetmaker	roadmaker

The occupational name might be further changed by the use of the form which meant son of such as McGowan which would be son of a Gow or smith. Slight spelling variations might help to differentiate different branches of a family so that Zimmerman and Zimmermann or Schmidt and Schmitt could provide those slight differences

Anglicized Names:

In searching for some surnames, especially those of German origin, it is important to be aware of the English version of that name. Frequently the English or Americanized version of a surname occurred during the nineteenth century. For example, the German name Weber became Weaver in common usage. In this regard it may be helpful to look in a German English dictionary for the German equivalent of an English name and consider tracing further back, looking for the German form. We may be easily fooled into thinking that a surname is of the origin of the language in which it presently appears but it was common, especially for occupational surnames, to assume the translated form of common usage and so Schmidt became Smith, Mueller became Miller, and Weber became Weaver. While a French name was likely to undergo spelling changes, a name like DuBois usually continues with some variation of the French form while many German and some Dutch names lost all resemblance to their origin and took on the English form of the name.

During the twentieth century, there was a stigma against German sounding names, since Germany was the enemy during the world wars. Just as sauerkraut became victory cabbage, many families changed their names to an Americanized form. The changes concerning most genealogists, however, occurred a century or more earlier when the impetus must have been simply to function more efficiently in the new country and to adopt American ways.

Feminine Form of Surname:

Early German ministers often added the suffix "-in" or "n" to a surname. This can cause confusion when the researcher is confronted with a name such as Anna Landin. Should we assume her surname to be Landon/Landen or is it Land/Lant/Lent? A John Landin wouldn't have presented such a problem but because Anna is a female, we can't be certain if her family name received the feminine ending or not. Fortunately, this custom did not exist for an extended period of time in this country. Obviously, the feminine form did not mean that the surname was usually spelled with the "in" ending. Therefore when a surname first occurs with a woman sponsor for a baptism or as the mother's maiden name and has the "in" ending, it may generally be assumed that this is only given as the feminine form of the name and that the name is usually found without the "in" ending unless there is other evidence to the contrary.

Many beginning genealogists frequently identify a family with a particular religion and neglect to search records of other nearby churches. Actually, when the religious service could not be performed in the church preferred by the family, perhaps because the minister was unavailable, another nearby minister was often chosen for the baptism, marriage or death and the activity recorded in his church's record. Novices also assume that travel was difficult in colonial times and consequently do not search records far from the place of known residence. However, a study of church histories will help to identify the minister who served a particular area and it is his home church that contains the record of his ministry. Usually an event recorded far from home indicates that the minister had traveled and not the participants. But with the availability of travel by boat it was not uncommon for marriages and baptisms of the same family to take place in widely separated communities.

New York Dutch Reformed Church and the Old Dutch Church of Kingston, New York are two early reformed churches which contain records of baptisms of children from a wide geographic area. The Kingston church acted as the mother church for a great many congregations in the mid-Hudson area and the records were kept in Kingston before record books were established in the later congregations.

New York Lutheran Church ministers traveled up and down the Hudson to minister to congregations meeting in churches, barns and private homes throughout the settled areas of New York and parts of New Jersey. A less obvious wide ranging set of records is that at Athens (Loonenburg), south of Albany. The Rev. Berkenmeyer, the minister who resided there, had formerly served from a base in New York City and then resigned the southern portion of his congregation and assumed the duties for the northern part, establishing his base at a place he considered to be centrally located.

In most cases, the Lutheran church records provide birth dates in contrast to many of the Reformed records which only give the baptism dates. Fortunately babies were baptized soon after birth so that baptismal dates can give an approximation of the birth date. The Lutherans were likely to record both dates. In contrast, the Reformed church records offer the greater likelihood that a mother's maiden name would be recorded at the time of the baptism. This practice continued through the nineteenth century, aiding many genealogies by adding women's maiden names even if a baptism of only one of her children appears in a Reformed church record.

Early Dutch and German marriage records provide a wealth of information which serve to identify an individual and recite his history. The marriages of the New York Dutch Reformed Church, the Old Dutch Church of Kingston, New York and the Athens Lutheran church are famous in this respect. The groom's place of origin, his father's name, his marital status (i.e. single or widowed) and perhaps his place of residence may be listed as well as similar information for the wife. In cases where the marriage of an individual gives the father's name, a patronymic clue may have been provided allowing the researcher to find more information about the family. If we are provided with the father's given name only, then the search is more involved. If, for example, Jacob Ostrom is said to be the son of Jan, one could subtract 21 years from the date of the marriage and use that as an approximate date for a search for the birth of a child of that given name, born to an appropriate father named Jan.

Section II

GIVEN NAMES

In the given name section of this book, we will consider just given names and their use in helping us to solve research problems. Through the years, many changes have occurred in forms of the names as well as the choice of names which were bestowed upon the children. The 17th and 18th centuries found the members of the Society of Friends selecting many obscure and Biblical names such as Zophar, Eliphalet, and Zebulon and names that implied temperament such as Beloved, Resolved, and Preserved.

When only educated or professional people could read and write, it was customary for the clergy to Latinize given names providing us with variations such as Wilhelmus for Willem, Gregorus for Gregory, Everhardus for Evert, etc. This in turn was the forerunner of the equivalent nicknames for these given names of Helmus, Goris, and Hardus.

The 19th century produced an abundance of surnames appearing as children's given names. A popular fad was to bestow the mother's family name as the given name on the child so that there was a proliferation of names such as Whitney, Ford, Montgomery, etc. The 20th century continued this trend of seeking the unique by using names such as Rock, Stone, Forest, and Storm (although the latter can be found in the New York-New Jersey church records as early as the 17th century in Storm Van Der Zee).

The tables in this section are provided so that the family historian can easily determine alternate and
equivalent names in use during the 17th century and early part of the 18th in the New York-New Jersey, Dutch-English period of that region.

Consider the following:

Diminutive Dutch name forms:
Various suffix forms were used for a female name. -tje or -tie made the name feminine as in Maritje-Maria, or Paultje-Paula and -tjen or -tien can occur as a diminutive form of the name such as in Jannetjen. It was also considered a term of endearment. This system is not at all archaic. Consider present day terms of endearment such as Rosie, Nelly, and Barbie. Our sons are not exempt either when we become aware that Eddie, Willie, Teddy, Bobby, Johnnie, and Franky are very common and they suggest familiarity. As can be imagined this diminutive form may not have been preserved through the lifetime of the individual and the name could appear in other forms at more formal occasions.

Interchangeable letters:

Note that the letters "i" and "j"; and "ij" and "y" appear interchangeably in the Dutch language as written in the early church records. The initial letters "K" and "C" are also found used interchangeably. Other pairs that are also confused or substituted for each other can be

g-h,
b-p,
f-v,
g-k,
s-z,
k-q,
d-t

If the spelling of the name in which you have an interest contains any of the above letters, make sure that you pursue that name with the alternate letter.

Use of Patronymic Middle Initial:

Long after the use of a Patronymic for a middle name had disappeared, many families, especially the descendants of the German Palatines, continued the practice of using a patronymic middle initial. Thus John A. Weaver was the son of Adam, clearly a different individual from John J. Weaver who was the son of John. (The manuscripts of the period of about 1800-1860, commonly wrote the capital letter I and J almost identically. When used as a middle initial, therefore, the researcher is faced with the problem of determining whether the scribe meant an "I" or a "J". Since there are far more given names beginning with J such as Jacob and John than given names beginning with I such as Isaac, we would tend to assume the middle initial was a J unless there was reason to believe otherwise.) The patronymic middle initial seems always to have been used as just the initial and the full middle name never appeared. The child probably was not baptized with the initial but when the need arose later on in life to identify him from others in the community with the same name, the patronymic initial was utilized.

In a Dutch family, the patronymic middle initial may be found in the family of Simon H. Van Ness born in 1729, the son of Hendrick Van Ness. Simon had three sons, Henry, Giles, and Jacob who each had a son who was named Simon. The logical means of identifying these individuals who were of similar age and lived in proximity of each other was the use of a middle initial of their father's name resulting in men named Simon H., Simon G. and Simon J. It may be pointed out that this is not as crystal clear as could be desired. (A puzzle should not be too easy or you would become bored.) It turns out that Giles was sometimes spelled Yellis, a Dutch form of the word. Therefore Simon G. could at times be called Simon Y. Also since J. and I. were interchangeable, Simon J. might be called Simon I. (see David M. Riker, "The Ancestors and Descendants of Simon Van Ness and Hester DeLamater" Manuscript dated 1984 or refer to "de Halve Maen" Vol LXIII No. 3 p. 2, "Searching for Colonial Dutch Ancestors" by the same author)

German Multiple Given Names:

In Germany and in the first generations of the 1710 Palatines we find that families may favor a form of a saint's name as the first name given to each of their children while the second name is the significant name and the name of common usage. Thus we might find a family naming sons John Jacob, John Peter, and John Paul with the children actually being called Jacob, Peter, and Paul. Of course in the early German records the name might be written "Johan Jacob" or "Joh: Jacob" or any number of various forms. In addition there is likely to be a child named simply Johannes or John and known by that name.

This same honoring of saints may be found with female children, most commonly with Anna as the first name given as Anna Maria, Anna Margaret, Anna Gertrude, etc. When the family migrated sometimes the first name would be ignored, other times the second name might be omitted. It is important to consider this possibility in the struggle to correctly identify individuals.

The researcher should be aware that German families from Catholic backgrounds may prefer to use the baptismal date rather than a child's actual birth date. In fact, some churches and families did not keep a record of the birth date, only the baptism date. This may account for the slight difference in age at death recorded on tombstones which don't seem to match with the actual birth date of the individual.

If a child died young, it was common to name a second child with that same name so that the name would be carried on. Usually when we find a second child of the same name we can assume that the first child has died. However, in a few cases, as pointed out by Henry Z Jones of Palatine Emigration fame, there is evidence that a family had two children of the same name ("The Palatine Families of New York" page xxv and 363). Perhaps they were differentiated by nicknames, we can only speculate on the reasons why the two children received the same name. Was the first individual sickly and not expected to survive? Were there multiple relatives of the same name which the family wished to honor?

The practice of naming a successive child, using the name of one deceased, was common in Dutch and their early families. It is useful to remember that families were large but infant mortality was high. The family struggled to maintain its traditions and preserve its identity through the use of the names given to the children.

Dutch relatives/mothers:

In the Dutch church records the mother's name may appear with the patronymic or with the surname which her family had assumed. It is useful to assemble the entire family group showing the children of the couple as each baptism is recorded, augmented with known information from a will or a bible record. An analysis of the family naming system, use of sponsors and mother's name as recorded in the various baptismal records will greatly aid in identifying the previous generation. Be aware that the mother's name may be written differently in different baptisms as in the case of Jan Middagh's wife who was Geertje Teunisse in the baptism of her first child in 1696 and Geertje Claerwater at the baptism of another child in 1699. This was not two different people but she is being described first as the daughter of Teunisse and second as a member of the Claerwater family. These variations may be further complicated by the use of nicknames, equivalents such as Gertrude vs Geesje and by the use of multiple given names such as an Anna Maria who later appears as Maria. The information in TABLES 2A and 2B will be useful in resolving some of these problems.

As we will discover, since daughters were often named for the grandmothers , aunts and other female relatives, it is always important to analyze the persons who were chosen as sponsors at the baptism. Many times their names were the same as the child's and they were either the grandparents or some family member with the same given name as the honoree.

Considering the difficulties provided by language, variations in name forms and lack of vital records, the best approach for the genealogist is to record all references to members of the family during the period in question. Analyze the information by studying the selection of sponsors, the naming patterns and references to the parents. Even instances in which the parents stood as sponsors for possible brothers and sisters families can provide useful information. Often this will give a much clearer picture of the family in question and provide the lineage with more surety than would otherwise be possible. Remember that it is not a certainty that all children will be found within one church record. Be sure to search a wide area for references to the family. In this regard the published records available through Kinship, 60 Cedar Heights Road, Rhinebeck, NY 12572 or found listed on the internet at http://www.kinshipny.com will be helpful. The Kinship baptism records have also been published on CD-ROM by Ancestry in a form which is very easy to search. Marriage records of the area are available on CD-ROM from Broderbund, "Marriage Index: Selected Areas of New York, 1639-1916", prepared by Kinship, CD 401.

Names, Names and More Names

Using the Tables:

The primary value of the tables which follow is that other forms of a given name are provided for the family historian. These alternate forms should be used in assembling family groups. A further value is to alert the researcher to the possibilities that exist for any given name. For example, if it is known that a certain male ancestor went by the name "Bert", then, by using these tables, the searcher will be advised to also look for Adelbert, Albert, Engelbert, Gilbert, and Robert. Similarly for a female named "Dina", equivalents such as Albertina, Bernadine, Blandina, Christina, and Gerardina should be considered.

The given name equivalents tables can be used to combine entries for persons whose first name appears in many variations. The list of names, nicknames and variants given in these tables should be helpful in identifying given names which may have been used by the same individual. Since phonetic spelling provides many additional variations of the name used by an individual, the researcher must face the challenge by sorting through the many possibilities and identifying the facts. Novice genealogists who are accustomed to several generations of consistent spelling of a name can easily be identified by their unwillingness to accept variations in the spelling of their ancestor's names. The experienced genealogist accepts the possibility, if not the probability, that names come in a variety of forms.

Tables of Name Equivalents and Dutch/English conversions as found in early records of New York and New Jersey.

Table 2A
Given Name Equivalents: Dutch to English

Aadriannus...... Adrian	Ada......... Adelheid	Aechtje........ Agatha
Aadrianus....... Adrian	Ada............ Adolf	Aeffie .... Eva
Aaentle.......... Anna	Adaleentje...... Adeline	Aefje............. Eva
Aafje............. Eva	Adda......... Adeline	Aefjee............ Eva
Aafjee............ Eva	Ade............ Adam	Aegidius .... Aegeus
Aafyee........... Eva	Ade .... Adolf	Aegt........... Agatha
Aaghie......... Agatha	Adel........... Adolf	Aeltie .... Alida
Aaghje......... Agatha	Adela .... Adelia	Aeltje .... Alida
Aagie.......... Agatha	Adela.......... Adolf	Aender .... Andrew
Aagje .... Agatha	Adele .... Adelheid	Aenenietje....... Agnes
Aagjen .... Agatha	Adelheid......... Alida	Aengenietye...... Agnes
Aagt........... Agatha	Adelheyd..... Adelaide	Aentie.......... Anna
Aal............. Alida	Adeli .... Adam	Aerriel .... Ariel
Aalt .... Arthur	Aderianus....... Adrian	Aert........... Arthur
Aalte........... Alida	Aderjanus....... Adrian	Aertje .... Artelia?
Aaltje .... Alida	Adi............ Adolf	Aertje......... Artina?
Aanken.......... Anna	Adje........... Adolf	Aetje............ Eva
Aant............ Anna	Ado .... Adolf	Aevje .... Eva
Aantie.......... Anna	Adolff.......... Adolf	After........... Arthur
Aantje.......... Anna	Adolfus........ Adolf	Agatha.......... Agnes
Aantonny ...... Anthony	Adolphus .... Adolf	Agestinus ...... August
Aarend .... Aaron	Adreaen .... Adrian	Aget........... Agatha
Aarie........... Aaron	Adreannis....... Adrian	Agetli .... Agatha
Aaron.......... Adrian	Adreyanes ..... Adrian	Aggenetye .... Agnes
Aart .... Arthur	Adriaantje ..... Adrian	Aggie .... Agatha
Aartje .... Artelia?	Adriaantje...... Adriana	Agi............ Agatha
Aartje......... Artina?	Adriaen .... Adriana	Agidius .... Aegeus
Aary .... Aaron	Adrian......... Aaron	Agie........... Agatha
Abedy .... Obadiah	Adrian........ Harriet	Agilhart .... Eilardus
Abegail .... Abigail	Adriance...... Adrienne	Agite .... Agatha
Abelke .... Albertina	Adrianis........ Adrian	Agje........... Agatha
Aberaam...... Abraham	Adriann ...... Adriana	Agneiteta .... Agnes
Aberam ...... Abraham	Adrians .... Adrian	Agnes.......... Agatha
Abertus......... Albert	Adrianus .... Adrian	Agniet .... Agnes
Abia .... Obadiah	Adrieannus..... Adrian	Agnietie......... Agnes
Abiegeil .... Abigail	Adriieyaanis .... Adrian	Agnietje......... Agnes
Abiegel .... Abigail	Adriyanis .... Adrian	Agnita .... Agnes
Abiegiel .... Abigail	Adriyannis ...... Adrian	Agnitje.......... Agnes
Abigel .... Abigail	Adryianis .... Adrian	Agt............ Agatha
Abijah .... Obadiah	Adur .... Arthur	Agti .... Agatha
Abraam ...... Abraham	Adurli.......... Arthur	Agustes .... August
Abram .... Abraham	Aebi .... Abraham	Agustus .... August
Absulom ...... Absalom	Aebi .... Adelbert	Agye........... Agatha
Achijas .... Aegeus	Aebi .... Evert	Ahasuerus...... Azariah
Achye.......... Agatha	Aeche.......... Agatha	Aile........... Adelheid

Given Name Equivalents: Dutch to English

Ailff . . . . Adolf	Ander . . . . Andrew	Appel . . . . Albert
Ailke . . . . Adelheid	Andres . . . . Andrew	Arabella . . . . Isabella
Ainers . . . . Andrew	Andries . . . . Andrew	Arend . . . . Aaron
Aitje . . . . Ida	Andris . . . . Andrew	Arendt . . . . Aaron
Akbutje . . . . Egberta	Anenietje . . . . Agnes	Arent . . . . Aaron
Al . . . . Albert	Anesli . . . . Agnes	Ariaan . . . . Aaron
Al . . . . Alfred	Angenitie . . . . Agnes	Ariaan . . . . Adrian
Alabartus . . . . Albert	Anghe . . . . Agnes	Ariaantie . . . . Adriana
Alana . . . . Helena	Angie . . . . Angelica	Ariaen . . . . Adrian
Albardt . . . . Albert	Anglica . . . . Angelica	Arianntje . . . . . . Adriana
Albart . . . . Albert	Angonietje . . . . . . Agnes	Ariannus . . . . Adrian
Albartus . . . . Albert	Anke . . . . Anna	Arians . . . . Adrian
Alberic . . . . Albert	Anken . . . . Anna	Ariantje . . . . Adrian
Albertina . . . . . . Christina	Ankje . . . . Annesen	Ariantje . . . . Adriana
Albrecht . . . . Albert	Ann . . . . Nancy	Ariantje . . . . Harriet
Aldert . . . . Albert?	Anna . . . . Hannah	Arianus . . . . Adrian
Alebartus . . . . Albert	Annaatje . . . . Anna	Arie . . . . Aaron
Alef . . . . Adolf	Annaka . . . . Anna	Arien . . . . Adrian
Aleke . . . . Adelheid	Annake . . . . Anna	Aris . . . . Aaron
Alena . . . . . . Magdalena	Annatie . . . . Anna	Arnaud . . . . Arnold
Alethea . . . . Althea	Annatje . . . . Anna	Arnke . . . . Arnold
Aletta . . . . Letitia	Annatye . . . . Anna	Arnout . . . . Arnold
Alewijn . . . . Alvin	Annechet . . . . Anna	Arnt . . . . Arnold
Alexzander . . . Alexander	Anneckie . . . . . . Anna	Arnulfus . . . . Arnold
Alf . . . . Adolf	Anneke . . . . Anna	Aron . . . . Aaron
Alf . . . . Alfred	Annesen . . . . Anna	Arriaantje . . . . . . Adriana
Alida . . . . Adelaide	Anni . . . . Anna	Art . . . . Arthur
Alida . . . . Adelheid	Annie . . . . Anna	Ary . . . . Aaron
Alida . . . . Alice	Anning . . . . Anna	Aryaennis . . . . Adrian
Allert . . . . Aldert	Annitje . . . . Anna	Aryannis . . . . Adrian
Alof . . . . Adolf	Annitye . . . . Anna	Aryje . . . . Aaron
Alta . . . . Alida	Anno . . . . Arnold	Asa . . . . Asenath
Altgen . . . . Adelheid	Anstadt . . . . . Anastasius	Asael . . . . Asel
Altie . . . . Alida	Anthoni . . . . Anthony	Asam . . . . Erasmus
Altje . . . . Alida	Antie . . . . Anna	Aser . . . . Erasmus
Alva . . . . Alvin	Antine . . . . Anthony	Asia . . . . Gesia
Alyd . . . . Adelaide	Antje . . . . Anna	Asmus . . . . Erasmus
Alyf . . . . Adolf	Antoine . . . . . . Anthony	Asseltje . . . . Ursula
Alzander . . . . . Alexander	Antoni . . . . Anthony	Assepoester . . . Cinderella
Amas . . . . Amos	Antonius . . . . . Anthony	Asseurus . . . . Azariah
Ami . . . . Amy	Antony . . . . Anthony	Assmann . . . . . Erasmus
Ammel . . . . . . Emmerich	Antusch . . . . . . Anthony	Assuerus . . . . . . Azariah
Ammon . . . . Aman	Antys . . . . Anthony	Ate . . . . Adrian
Amy . . . . Amelia	Aosseltje . . . . Ursula	Augst . . . . August
Anatie . . . . Anna	Apel . . . . Albert	Augustus . . . . . . August
Anatye . . . . Anna	Apitz . . . . Adelbert	Aujke . . . . Octavius
Anczel . . . . Hans	Apke . . . . Egbert	Auke . . . . Octavius
Andel . . . . Joanna	Apolonia . . . . Apollonia	Aukes . . . . August

Auleide . . . . Adelheid	Barrend . . . . Barent	Bele . . . . Sybil
Aurie . . . . Aaron	Barrinicke . . . . Veronica	Beleke . . . . Sybil
Aust . . . . August	Bart . . . . . . Bartholomew	Beletje . . . . Isabella
Austen . . . . August	Barte . . . . Bertha	Belettie . . . . Isabella
Aute . . . . Adrian	Bartelmus . Bartholomew	Beletye . . . . Isabella
Ayl . . . . Adelheid	Barthel . . . . Bartel	Belia . . . . Sybil
Baachie . . . . Bertha	Bartje . . . . Barbara	Belietie . . . . Isabella
Baaltje . . . . Polly	Bartje . . . . Bertha	Belige . . . . Sybil
Baartje . . . . Barbara	Bartol . . . Bartholomew	Belitie . . . . Isabella
Baata . . . . Bertha	Bas . . . . Bastian	Belitje . . . . Isabella
Bab . . . . Barbara	Basche . . . . Bastian	Bell . . . . Arabella
Babe . . . . Barbara	Baschele . . . . . . Bastian	Bell . . . . Isabella
Bacca . . . . Rebecca	Bastaan . . . . Bastian	Bella . . . . Isabella
Badeloch . . . . . . Beatrice	Baste . . . . Bastian	Bella . . . . Sybil
Badje . . . . Barbara	Bastel . . . . Bastian	Belye . . . . Sybil
Baldus . . . . Baltus	Bastiaan . . . . Bastian	Belyntrie . . . . Patricia
Baleke . . . . Baldwin	Bastiaen . . . . . . Bastian	Belytie . . . . Isabella
Balko . . . . Baldwin	Bastle . . . . Bastian	Ben . . . . Benjamin
Balles . . . . Baltus	Bat . . . . . . Bartholomew	Bendix . . . . Benedict
Ballie . . . . Isabella	Bata . . . . Bertha	Bene . . . . Benedict
Ballie . . . . Polly	Batha . . . . Bertha	Benedict . . . . . Bernard
Bally . . . . Polly	Batie . . . . Bathilda	Beneke . . . . . . Benedict
Balster . . . . Baltus	Batje . . . . Bathilda	Benieman . . . Benjamin
Balt . . . . Baltus	Batt . . . . . Bartholomew	Beniemen . . . Benjamin
Balthazar . . . . . . Baltus	Battist . . . . Baptist	Benjaman . . . Benjamin
Balthus . . . . Baltus	Beata . . . . Bertha	Benjamen . . . Benjamin
Baltus . . . . . . Archibald	Beatrix . . . . Beatrice	Benje . . . . Benjamin
Baltus . . . . . . Theobald	Becca . . . . Rebecca	Benjemen . . . Benjamin
Balz . . . . Baltus	Becht . . . . Berthold	Benny . . . . . . Benjamin
Balzer . . . . Baltus	Bechte . . . . Bertha	Bentz . . . . Benedict
Bapp . . . . Barbara	Bechtgin . . . . . Berthold	Benyamen . . . Benjamin
Bapper . . . . Baptist	Becki . . . . Rebecca	Benz . . . . Bernard
Baranicke . . . . Veronica	Beda . . . . Elizabeth	Beppo . . . . Joseph
Barbara . . . . Bertha	Beele . . . . Elizabeth	Berbe . . . . Barbara
Barbartie . . . . . Barbara	Beele . . . . Sybil	Beretje . . . . . Bernadine
Barber . . . . Barbara	Beelgen . . . . Sybil	Berlt . . . . Berthold
Barbera . . . . . . Barbara	Beelitie . . . . Isabella	Bernhard . . . . Benedict
Bardolph . . . . . Barthol	Beelitje . . . . Isabella	Berno . . . . Bernard
Barendt . . . . Barent	Beeltgen . . . . Sybil	Bernt . . . . Bernard
Barenicke . . . . Veronica	Beeltje . . . . . Isabella	Berranecke . . . . Veronica
Barent . . . . Bernard	Beertje . . . Bernadine	Berrent . . . . Barent
Barentje . . . . Bernadine	Behne . . . . Bernard	Bersheba . . . . Bathsheba
Baretje . . . . Barbara	Behrda . . . . Bertha	Bert . . . . Adelbert
Baretl . . . . . Bartholomew	Beilgen . . . . Sybil	Bert . . . . Albert
Barint . . . . Barent	Bekyntrie . . . . . Patience	Bert . . . . Berthold
Barnardus . . . . Bernard	Bel . . . . Isabella	Bert . . . . Engelbert
Barnicke . . . . . Veronica	Bela . . . . Elizabeth	Bert . . . . Gilbert
Barranicke . . . . Veronica	Bele . . . . Elizabeth	Bert . . . . Robert

Given Name Equivalents: Dutch to English

Berteli . . . . Bertha	Bolte . . . . Baldwin	Burger . . . . . . Burkhard?
Bertes . . . . Adelbert	Bonifaas . . . . . . Boniface	Burgun . . . . Burger
Bertha . . . . Elizabeth	Bool . . . . Boele	Burki . . . . . . Burkhard
Berthe . . . . Bartholomew	Bopp . . . . Baptist	Burtis . . . . Albert
Berthel . . . . Bartholomew	Borger . . . . Burger	Bury . . . . Burkhard
Bertho . . . . Berthold	Bork . . . . Burkhard	Busse . . . . Burkhard
Bertke . . . . Bertha	Boso . . . . Burkhard	Butz . . . . Burkhard
Bertolf . . . . Bartholf	Bosse . . . . Burkhard	Caatje . . . . Catherine
Bertsch . . . . . . Berthold	Boudewyn . . . . Baldwin	Cades . . . . Thaddius
Bertus . . . . Albert	Boudje . . . . Baldwin	Caes . . . . Cornelius
Berzo . . . . Berthold	Bourgoon . . . . . . Burger	Caetrina . . . . . . Catherine
Bestgen . . . . Bastian	Brachie . . . . Bridget	Caharina . . . . Catherine
Bestian . . . . Bastian	Bram . . . . Abraham	Cairekje . . . . . . Gertrude
Beterse . . . . Patricia	Brandt . . . . . . Rembrant	Calep . . . . Caleb
Beth . . . . Elizabeth	Brant . . . . Rembrant	Calip . . . . Caleb
Betje . . . . Bathilda	Brasch . . . . Ambrose	Calvijn . . . . Calvin
Betsch . . . . Berthold	Brechie . . . . Bridget	Carel . . . . Carl
Betterdin . . . . . Elizabeth	Brechtel . . . . . Adelbert	Carius . . . . Eucharius
Betterse . . . . Patricia	Brecthje . . . . Bridget	Carl . . . . Charles
Betti . . . . Elizabeth	Bregge . . . . Bridget	Carly . . . . Caroline
Betto . . . . Berthold	Breggie . . . . Bridget	Carolus . . . . Carl
Betty . . . . Elizabeth	Breghie . . . . Bridget	Caroly . . . . Caroline
Betz . . . . Bernard	Breghje . . . . Bridget	Carroline . . . . . . Caroline
Betza . . . . Elizabeth	Breghye . . . . . . Bridget	Carsten . . . . Christian
Bevelia . . . . Beverly	Bregije . . . . Bridget	Carstiena . . . . . Christina
Bias . . . . Tobias	Bregje . . . . Bridget	Carye . . . . Caroline
Bielgen . . . . Sybil	Bregtie . . . . Bridget	Case . . . . Cornelius
Bietje . . . . Elizabeth	Bregye . . . . Bridget	Caspar . . . . Jasper
Bilgin . . . . Sybil	Breidte . . . . Bridget	Caspares . . . . Caspar
Bill . . . . William	Breltje . . . . Cornelia	Casparis . . . . Caspar
Billa . . . . Sybil	Bridlin . . . . Bridget	Casparus . . . . Caspar
Bille . . . . Sybil	Briell . . . . Bridget	Casper . . . . Caspar
Billy . . . . William	Briette . . . . Bridget	Cassia . . . . Keziah
Bina . . . . Sabina	Brigael . . . . Bridget	Catalintje . . . . . . Caroline
Bine . . . . Sabina	Brigitta . . . . Bridget	Catalyntje . . . . . Caroline
Bingel . . . . Sabina	Brom . . . . Abraham	Catarina . . . . . . Catherine
Birdie . . . . Birdella	Brose . . . . Ambrose	Cateryne . . . . Catherine
Birdie . . . . Bridget	Broseck . . . . . . Ambrose	Cathalyna . . . . . Caroline
Birkle . . . . Burkhard	Brosius . . . . . . Ambrose	Catharena . . . Catherine
Birthe . . . . Bertha	Brossken . . . . . Ambrose	Catharia . . . . . Catherine
Bischle . . . . Baptist	Bruna . . . . . . Brunhilda	Cathariena . . . Catherine
Blanca . . . . Blanche	Brus . . . . Ambrose	Catharina . . . . Catherine
Blass . . . . Blasius	Bryn . . . . Bryan?	Catharyn . . . . Catherine
Blesse . . . . Blasius	Brynse . . . . Bryan?	Cathlyntje . . . . . Caroline
Boele . . . . Baldwin?	Bucko . . . . Burkhard	Cathrina . . . . . . Catherine
Boldwijn . . . . . . Baldwin	Burga . . . . Walburg	Catiena . . . . . . Catherine
Boldwyn . . . . . . Baldwin	Burge . . . . Burkhard	Catlintie . . . . Caroline
Bolo . . . . Boele	Burgei . . . . Walburg	Catlyntje . . . . . . Caroline

Given Name Equivalents: Dutch to English

Catreina...... Catherine	Christopher.... Christian	Constantia.... Constance
Catriena...... Catherine	Christyntje..... Christina	Constantine... Constance
Catrina....... Catherine	Cibilla.......... Sybil	Constantyn ... Constance
Catrine....... Catherine	Cillia .... Cecilia	Conze .... Conrad
Catrinna...... Catherine	Cina........ Kunigunda	Coonraat....... Conrad
Catrintje...... Catherine	Cinda .... Cinderella	Coosje.......... James
Catrintye .... Catherine	Cindy ...... Cinderella	Corndt .... Conrad
Catryntje .... Catherine	Cine........ Kunigunda	Cornelea ...... Cornelia
Caty......... Catherine	Claas........ Nicholas	Corneleia...... Cornelia
Ceelitie .... Cecelia	Clabis .... Nicholas	Corneles .... Cornelius
Ceerles .... Carl	Cladious .... Claude	Corneleya ..... Cornelia
Ceerlez .... Carl	Claeck........ Nicholas	Cornelisen .... Cornelius
Celetje .... Cecilia	Claertje .... Clara	Cornelize.... Cornelius
Celitjen .... Cecelia	Claes......... Nicholas	Cornelya ...... Cornelia
Celia .... Cecilia	Claesje .... Nicole	Cors .... Cornelius
Celie .... Cecilia	Clais .... Nicholas	Corstiaan ..... Christian
Cellep .... Caleb	Clasje......... Clarissa	Cort .... Conrad
Cerstena ...... Christina	Clasje......... Nicole	Cosyne....... Christina?
Cervaes .... Servis	Classje .... Nicole	Cousyn .... Cosyne
Charel .... Carl	Claudia......... Nicole	Covert .... Godfrey
Charels .... Carl	Claus......... Nicholas	Cozina........ Cosyne
Charich .... George	Clausie .... Clarissa	Cozinus .... Cosyne
Charil .... Carl	Clean.......... Kilian	Creisteaen..... Christian
Charitas....... Charity	Clese......... Nicholas	Creisteaer... Christopher
Charitea....... Charity	Clesschen ..... Nicholas	Cresce .... Christian
Charity .... Gertrude	Clobes........ Nicholas	Cresten....... Christina
Charles .... Carl	Clos .... Nicholas	Crestena ...... Christina
Charlina ..... Caroline	Cloudy .... Claudia	Crestiena ..... Christina
Charlotta ..... Charlotte	Clowes ...... Nicholas	Crestina ...... Christina
Chatarina..... Catherine	Cniertje ..... Kunigunda	Crestoffel ... Christopher
Chawchee ...... Charity	Cob............ Jacob	Crissen .... Christina
Cheerelz.......... Carl	Coba......... Jacobina	Cristina....... Christina
Cheiltje .... Cornelia	Cobe .... Jacob	Cristofel .... Christopher
Chieltje .... Cornelia	Cobes .... Jacob	Cristoffel.... Christopher
Chime.......... James	Cobus .... Jacob	Critje .... Margaret
Chresta....... Christian	Coen.......... Conrad	Cryenus....... Quirinus
Chrestina ..... Christina	Coenraat....... Conrad	Cryn .... Quirinus
Chris .... Christian	Coenradt....... Conrad	Cryne .... Quirinus
Chris .... Christina	Coenraet....... Conrad	Cryntje....... Catherine
Christ .... Christian	Cole .... Nicholas	Cuiertie ...... Kunigunda
Christe .... Christina	Comman .... Conrad	Cumczele.... Kunigunda
Christeaen..... Christian	Commetje ... Commertje	Cunckil ..... Kunigunda
Christiaen ..... Christian	Comnertje ... Commertje	Cunera..... Kunigunda
Christian.... Christopher	Conclo .... Conrad	Cuniertie .... Kunigunda
Christiena ..... Christina	Conczemann .... Conrad	Cunigunde ... Kunigunda
Christina...... Albertina	Cone........ Conrad	Cunira ..... Kunigunda
Christing...... Christina	Conkil........ Conrad	Cunkele .... Conrad
Christoffel... Christopher	Conkulo ...... Conrad	Cuntze ...... Kunigunda

Given Name Equivalents: Dutch to English

Cy . . . . Cyrus	Delefferins . . Deliverance	Diedlof . . . . Didlove
Cytie . . . . Sophia	Delefverins . . Deliverance	Diehm . . . . Ditmar
Czyliox . . . . Cyriacus	Deleverence . Deliverance	Diele . . . . Ottilia
Daaf . . . . David	Deleverens . . Deliverance	Dielman . . . . . . Dietrich
Daam . . . . Adam	Deleverins . . Deliverance	Dielo . . . . Dietrich
Daan . . . . Daniel	Delfverins . . . Deliverance	Diemo . . . . Ditmar
Daatje . . . . Alida	Delia . . . . Adelia	Diena . . . . Blandina
Daatje . . . . Charity	Deliefferins . . Deliverance	Diena . . . . Dinah
Daem . . . . Adam	Delifferins . . Deliverance	Dientje . . . . . Bernadine
Dahm . . . . Adam	Dell . . . . Adelbert	Diepes . . . . Matthew
Dammas . . . . . . Thomas	Delverins . . . Deliverance	Diepil . . . . Dietrich
Dammo . . . . . Dankmar	Denel . . . . Daniel	Dierckje . . . . . Theodora
Daneil . . . . Daniel	Dennel . . . . Daniel	Dierderick . . . . . Dietrich
Danel . . . . Daniel	Dennert . . . . . Degenhard	Dietel . . . . Dietrich
Dange . . . . Anthony	Dentin . . . . Denton	Dietleip . . . . Didlove
Dankmar . . . . . . Ditmar	Denys . . . . Dennis	Dietleyous . . . . . . Didlove
Dannel . . . . Daniel	Denys . . . . . . Dionysius	Dietloip . . . . Didlove
Danyel . . . . Daniel	Dercjee . . . . . Theodora	Dieto . . . . Dietrich
Darckis . . . . . Theodora	Derck . . . . Dirk	Dietrich . . . . . . Theodore
Darkus . . . . . Theodora	Dercketie . . . . Theodora	Dietsch . . . . . . Dietrich
Dauvie . . . . David	Dercktie . . . . Theodora	Dietzel . . . . Dietrich
Davet . . . . David	Dercktje . . . . Theodora	Dieuwer . . . . . Deborah
Davida . . . . Tabitha	Derckye . . . . . Theodora	Dievertje . . . . . Deborah
Davidt . . . . David	Dereck . . . . Dirk	Diewertje . . . . Deborah
Davit . . . . David	Derick . . . . Dirk	Dik . . . . Richard
DeLifferins . . Deliverance	Derick . . . . . . Theodore	Dikman . . . . . . Dyckman
Debbora . . . . . . Deborah	Derjck . . . . Dirk	Diktus . . . . Benedict
Debes . . . . Matthew	Derk . . . . Dirk	Dileman . . . . . . Dietrich
Debiss . . . . Matthew	Derreck . . . . Dirk	Dilge . . . . Ottilia
Debora . . . . Deborah	Derrick . . . . Dirk	Dilich . . . . Dietrich
Debra . . . . Deborah	Derrick . . . . . Theodore	Diliga . . . . Ottilia
Debus . . . . Matthew	Deryck . . . . Dirk	Dilo . . . . Dietrich
Deczel . . . . Dietrich	Deryee . . . . . . Theodora	Dimphinia . . . . Delphine
Deddo . . . . Dietrich	Dese . . . . Andrew	Dina . . . . Bernadine
Dedi . . . . Theodore	Desin . . . . . . Gerardina	Dina . . . . Blandina
Dee . . . . Deborah	Deter . . . . Dietrich	Dina . . . . Dinah
Deel . . . . Adelheid	Detlef . . . . Didlove	Dina . . . . Gerardina
Deerick . . . . Dirk	Devertjen . . . . Deborah	Dinah . . . . Albertina
Degen . . . . . . Degenhard	Dewer . . . . Deborah	Dinah . . . . . . Gerardina
Dehmel . . . . Thomas	Dewes . . . . Matthew	Dine . . . . Christina
Dehn . . . . Degenhard	Dewetje . . . . . . Deborah	Dinnies . . . . Dennis
Deiderick . . . . Theodore	Dibbora . . . . . Deborah	Dins . . . . Dennis
Deinart . . . . . Degenhard	Dibra . . . . Deborah	Dion . . . . Dionysius
Deis . . . . Matthew	Diclof . . . . Didlove	Dionesius . . . . Dionysius
Deise . . . . Matthew	Diebel . . . . Theobald	Dionys . . . . . . Dionysius
Dela . . . . Adelheid	Diebold . . . . . . Theobald	Diple . . . . Dietrich
Dele . . . . Adelheid	Diede . . . . Dietrich	Dippel . . . . Dietrich
Deleferins . . . Deliverance	Diederick . . . . Theodore	Dirck . . . . Dirk

Given Name Equivalents: Dutch to English

Dirck . . . . Theodore	Dorle . . . . Theodore	Dysskin . . . . Matthew
Dirckie . . . . . . Theodora	Dorli . . . . Theodore	Dytlouff . . . . Didlove
Dirckje . . . . . . Theodora	Dorothea . . . . . . Dorothy	Dyze . . . . Dietrich
Dircktie . . . . . . Theodora	Dort . . . . Dorothy	Eagie . . . . Agatha
Dirckye . . . . . Theodora	Dortchen . . . . . Dorothy	Eamon . . . . Amon
Dirick . . . . Theodore	Dorte . . . . Dorothy	Ebbe . . . . Abigail
Dirk . . . . Dietrich	Dortel . . . . Dorothy	Ebbegal . . . . Abigail
Dirk . . . . Richard	Dortje . . . . Dorothy	Ebbegel . . . . Abigail
Dirk . . . . Theodore	Dorus . . . . Theodore	Ebbegil . . . . Abigail
Dirkje . . . . Theodora	Douwe . . . . Douw	Ebbertje . . . . Abigail
Dirrickje . . . . . Theodora	Dow . . . . Douw	Ebbi . . . . Ebenezer
Disse . . . . Matthew	Dowie . . . . Douw	Ebbie . . . . Ebenezer
Diteleve . . . . Detlef	Drebes . . . . Andrew	Ebbo . . . . Evert
Ditlo . . . . Didlove	Drees . . . . Andrew	Ebegel . . . . Abigail
Ditmar . . . . . . Dankmar	Dreis . . . . Andrew	Ebel . . . . Abel
Ditmas . . . . . . Dankmar	Dresel . . . . Andrew	Eberwin . . . . Erwin
Ditmis . . . . . . Dankmar	Dreus . . . . Andrew	Ebiegel . . . . Abigail
Dittel . . . . Ottilia	Drew . . . . Andrew	Echelo . . . . Eckhard
Ditters . . . . Diethard	Drickes . . . . Henry	Echtje . . . . Agatha
Ditzel . . . . Dietrich	Dries . . . . Andrew	Eckel . . . . Eckhard
Divertje . . . . Deborah	Driess . . . . Andrew	Eckerle . . . . Eckhard
Dix . . . . Benedict	Drucke . . . . . . Gertrude	Ecklo . . . . Eckhard
Dixie . . . . Benedicta	Druda . . . . Gertrude	Ed . . . . Edmond
Dodo . . . . Dorothy	Druda . . . . . . Irmtraud	Ed . . . . Edward
Dolde . . . . Berthold	Drudeke . . . . . Gertrude	Ede . . . . Ide
Dolf . . . . Adolf	Drudel . . . . . . Gertrude	Edman . . . . . . Edmond
Dolfi . . . . Rudolf	Drudischen . . . . Gertrude	Edo . . . . Ide
Dolfus . . . . Adolf	Druide . . . . . . Gertrude	Edsart . . . . Eckhard
Doll . . . . Berthold	Drut . . . . Gertrude	Eduaart . . . . Edward
Dolly . . . . Dorothy	Drutchen . . . . . Gertrude	Eduard . . . . Edward
Domincus . . . . Dominick	Drutke . . . . . . Gertrude	Edwaerdt . . . . . . Edward
Domingo . . . . . Dominick	Drutte . . . . Gertrude	Eechtje . . . . Agatha
Donge . . . . Anthony	Duggie . . . . Douglas	Eef . . . . Eva
Dongis . . . . Anthony	Dulde . . . . Berthold	Eefje . . . . Eva
Dongus . . . . Anthony	Dulf . . . . Rudolf	Eefrem . . . . Ephraim
Donich . . . . . . Anthony	Dumes . . . . Thomas	Eegelo . . . . Eckhard
Donigiss . . . . . . Anthony	Durcktie . . . . . Theodora	Eegfe . . . . Agatha
Donisi . . . . Dionysius	Duredel . . . . . . Dorothy	Eelet . . . . Helena
Donjes . . . . Anthony	Dures . . . . Theodore	Eemet . . . . Emma
Door . . . . Dorothy	Durle . . . . Dorothy	Eemetie . . . . Emma
Doortje . . . . . . Dorothy	Durli . . . . Arthur	Eemie . . . . Emma
Doostie . . . . . . Theodosia	Durli . . . . Dorothy	Eemus . . . . Amos
Dorcas . . . . . . Theodora	Dutti . . . . Dorothy	Eester . . . . Esther
Dorcken . . . . . Dorothy	Dyanzo . . . . Dinah	Eestther . . . . Esther
Dorel . . . . Dorothy	Dyna . . . . Dinah	Eetie . . . . Ida
Dores . . . . Theodore	Dyntje . . . . Dinah	Eeverdt . . . . Evert
Dorken . . . . . . Dorothy	Dypil . . . . Dietrich	Eevert . . . . Evert
Dorle . . . . Dorothy	Dyrck . . . . Dirk	Efa . . . . Eva

Given Name Equivalents: Dutch to English

Effe. . . . . Eva	Elheid. . . . . . . Adelheid	Emmen. . . . . Amon
Effee. . . . . Euphemia	Elia. . . . . Adelheid	Emmenentje. . . . . Emma
Effie . . . . Eva	Elida . . . . Alida	Emmerens . . . . . . Emma
Efie. . . . . Eva	Eliesabeth. . . . . Elizabeth	Emmetie. . . . . Emma
Efrom . . . . Ephraim	Eliezabet. . . . . . Elizabeth	Emmetje. . . . . Emma
Efte. . . . . Eva	Eliezabeth. . . . . Elizabeth	Emogene. . . . . . Imogene
Egberth . . . . Abigail	Elisabeth . . . . . Elizabeth	Emus. . . . . Amos
Egbertje. . . . . Abigail	Elisbeth . . . . . . Elizabeth	Emyche . . . . . Emmerich
Egeno . . . . Eckhard	Elisha . . . . Elijah	En . . . . Anna
Eget. . . . . Agatha	Elishah . . . . Elijah	Ena . . . . Anna
Egge . . . . Eckhard	Eliza. . . . . Elizabeth	Enderle . . . . Andrew
Eghertje. . . . . Abigail	Elizabet . . . . . . Elizabeth	Enders . . . . Andrew
Egid . . . . Agidius	Elizabeth . . . . Bertha	Endres . . . . Andrew
Egino . . . . Eckhard	Eljias . . . . Elias	Endris . . . . Andrew
Egiz . . . . Agidius	Elke . . . . Adelheid	Endro. . . . . Andrew
Egje. . . . . Agatha	Ella . . . . Helena	Endru. . . . . Andrew
Egle. . . . . Agatha	Elle. . . . . Adelheid	Engel. . . . . Angel
Eheimbricho. . Emmerich	Elle. . . . . Alexander	Engelbart. . . . . Engelbert
Ehl . . . . Adelheid	Elli . . . . Helena	Engelt . . . . Angelica
Ehrle. . . . . Erhard	Eloise. . . . . Louise	Engeltie. . . . . . . Angelica
Eibart. . . . . Albert	Eloy. . . . . Eligius	Engeltje. . . . . . . Angelica
Eibel. . . . . Albert	Els . . . . Alsie	Engentie . . . . . . Angelica
Eida . . . . Ida	Elsebit . . . . . . Elizabeth	Engiel . . . . Engel
Eike . . . . Agnes	Elsee. . . . . Elsie	Engletie. . . . . . . Angelica
Eike . . . . Eckhard	Elsewed . . . . . Elizabeth	Enni. . . . . Anna
Eile. . . . . Adelheid	Elsje. . . . . Elsie	Enny. . . . . Anna
Eilert. . . . . Eilardus	Elslin . . . . Elizabeth	Enretta. . . . . . . Henrietta
Eilika . . . . Adelheid	Eltie . . . . Alida	Enrik . . . . Henry
Eilsa. . . . . Elizabeth	Eltje. . . . . Alida	Ensel . . . . Hans
Eilse. . . . . Elsie	Eltje . . . . Elsie	Entenie . . . . Anthony
Eilsee . . . . Elsie	Elwert. . . . . Albert	Epje. . . . . Egbert
Eilsjen . . . . Elsie	Elyane. . . . . Julia	Epke . . . . Egbert
Eilsyen . . . . Elsie	Elyas. . . . . Elias	Eppo . . . . Evert
Eisther . . . . Esther	Elyzabet . . . . . . Elizabeth	Ermedrudis . . . Irmtraud
Eitje . . . . Ida	Elyzabeth . . . . Elizabeth	Ermel . . . . Irmgard
Ela . . . . Adelheid	Elze . . . . Elizabeth	Erne . . . . Arnold
Elbardt . . . . Albert	Elzee. . . . . Elsie	Ernie . . . . Ernest
Elbert . . . . Albert	Embercho. . . . Emmerich	Ernst . . . . Ernest
Elbrat . . . . Albert	Embricho . . . . Emmerich	Erny . . . . Arnold
Elbrecht . . . . Albert	Emche . . . . . . Emmerich	Ersula . . . . Ursula
Elchgen. . . . . . Adelheid	Emecho . . . . . Emmerich	Esaias . . . . Isaiah
Eldert . . . . Aldert	Emeda . . . . Emma	Esopus . . . . Aesop
Eldred. . . . . Aldert	Emee . . . . Emma	Esse . . . . Elsie
Elena. . . . . Helena	Emerensje . . . . . Emma	Ester . . . . Esther
Elesebath . . . . Elizabeth	Emie . . . . Emma	Esther . . . . Hester
Eleyde. . . . . . . Adelheid	Emilia . . . . Emeline	Esthers. . . . . Esther
Elgen . . . . Elizabeth	Emma . . . . Emeline	Ethelred . . . . Audrey
Elgin. . . . . Adelheid	Emma . . . . Emily	Ethelyn. . . . . Ethel

Given Name Equivalents: Dutch to English

Ethilrede . . . . . . Audrey
Etje. . . . . Eva
Eubel . . . . Albert
Evardt . . . . Evert
Evatje . . . . Eva
Eve . . . . Eva
Evelyn . . . . Evaline
Everard . . . . Evert
Everdt . . . . Evert
Everhardus . . . . Evert
Ewart . . . . Evert
Ewe . . . . Eva
Ewout. . . . . Evert
Exgye. . . . . Agatha
Eyke . . . . Eycke
Eylheit . . . . Adelheid
Eyntie. . . . . Anna
Eyntje. . . . . Anna
Eytic . . . . Ida
Eytie . . . . Ida
Ezechias . . . . . . Hezekiah
Ezegeel . . . . Ezechiel
Faas . . . . Gervas
Fannetje . . . . Fanny
Fanny . . . . Frances
Febe . . . . Phebe
Febi . . . . Phebe
Febie . . . . Phebe
Feebi . . . . Phebe
Fei . . . . Sophia
Feige . . . . Sophia
Feigin . . . . Sophia
Feilleph . . . . Philip
Feit . . . . Vitus
Feitie . . . . Sophia
Felcke. . . . . Sybil
Felipe . . . . Philip
Fell . . . . Valentine
Felt . . . . Valentine
Felte. . . . . Valentine
Feltes . . . . Valentine
Feltine . . . . Valentine
Femetien . . . . . . Sophia
Femmete . . . . . . Sophia
Femmetie. . . . . . Sophia
Femmetje. . . . . . Sophia
Femmettie . . . . . Sophia
Femmetye . . . . . Sophia

Femmitje . . . . . . Sophia
Fendel . . . . . Ferdinand
Ferdel. . . . . . Ferdinand
Ferges. . . . . . Ferdinand
Fertel . . . . . . Ferdinand
Feupe . . . . Volpert
Fey . . . . Sophia
Feytie. . . . . Sophia
Feytje. . . . . Sophia
Fia. . . . . Sophia
Fiche . . . . Sophia
Fick. . . . . Sophia
Ficke . . . . Sophia
Fie. . . . . Sophia
Fiebie . . . . Phebe
Fiekchen . . . . . . Sophia
Fieken . . . . Sophia
Fiene. . . . . . . Josephine
Fietje . . . . Sophia
Fige . . . . Sophia
Fijnsan . . . . Vincent
Fike . . . . Victoria
File . . . . Philomena
Filep . . . . Philip
Filgin . . . . Sophia
Filip . . . . Philip
Filips. . . . . Philip
Filo . . . . Philomena
Fina . . . . Josephine
Fincent . . . . Vincent
Finchen . . . . . Josephine
Finna . . . . Josephine
Fletje . . . . Sophia
Fliep . . . . Philip
Fliepse . . . . Philip
Flip . . . . Philip
Floortje . . . . Flora
Floortje. . . . . Florentina
Flora . . . . Florentina
Florence. . . . . Flora
Floris . . . . Flora
Floris . . . . Florian
Flourtje . . . . Flora
Flyp. . . . . Philip
Focken . . . . . . Volkert
Fockilo . . . . . . Volpert
Foilep . . . . Volpert
Fokke . . . . Volkert

Folbert . . . . Volkert
Folkert . . . . Volkert
Fons. . . . . Alphonse
Fonse. . . . . . . Alphonse
Foupel. . . . . Volpert
Francijntje . . . . . Frances
Francina. . . . . . . Frances
Franck . . . . Francis
Francois . . . . . . Francis
Francoy. . . . . . . Francis
Francoys . . . . . . Francis
Francyntie . . . . . Frances
Frank . . . . Francis
Frans . . . . Francis
Franscyntje. . . . . Frances
Fransus. . . . . . . Francis
Fransytie. . . . . . Frances
Fred . . . . Alfred
Fred . . . . Ferdinand
Fred . . . . Frederick
Fred. . . . . Godfrey
Freddie . . . . . . Frederick
Frederik . . . . . Frederick
Frederika. . . . . Frederica
Fredo . . . . Frederick
Fredrick . . . . . Frederick
Freek . . . . Frederick
Freena . . . . Veronica
Frein. . . . . Ephraim
Freins . . . . Severin
Frek . . . . Frederick
Frem. . . . . Ephraim
Freme . . . . Ephraim
Frena . . . . Veronica
Frenck . . . . Francis
Frenckel . . . . Frank
Frengs. . . . . Severin
Frenky . . . . Frances
Frenne . . . . Veronica
Frenz . . . . Francis
Frerich . . . . . Frederick
Frerick . . . . . Frederick
Frerk. . . . . . . Frederick
Freyntje . . . . . . Frances
Fricke . . . . . . Frederick
Fried . . . . Frederick
Friedel . . . . Godfrey
Frieder . . . . . . Frederick

Frieder . . . . Godfrey	Gaspard . . . . Caspar	Gerarda . . . . Charity
Friedes . . . . Godfrey	Gat . . . . Garret	Gerarda . . . . . . Geraldine
Friedlon . . . . . Frederick	Gate . . . . Agatha	Gerarda . . . . Grace
Friele . . . . Frederick	Gebel . . . . Godfrey	Gerardus . . . . Garret
Frielo . . . . Frederick	Gebelo . . . . Godfrey	Gerbrand . . . . Gerbrant
Frielove . . . . Freelove	Gebeno . . . . Godfrey	Gerbrechta . . Gerbrantina
Frigge . . . . Frederica	Gebert . . . . Godfrey	Geresolveert . . . Resolved
Frika . . . . Frederica	Gebes . . . . Gebhard	Geresolvert . . . . Resolved
Friko . . . . Frederick	Gebje . . . . Rachel	Geretie . . . . Gerarda
Frilo . . . . Frederick	Gebke . . . . Gebhard	Geridt . . . . Garret
Frily . . . . Frederick	Geerd . . . . Gertrude	Gering . . . . Gerhard
Frina . . . . Veronica	Geert . . . . Gerhard	Geritie . . . . Gerarda
Frinckye . . . . . . Frances	Geert . . . . Gertrude	Geritje . . . . Gerarda
Frings . . . . Severin	Geertje . . . . . . Gertrude	Gerjet . . . . Gerhard
Frit . . . . Godfrey	Geertruyd . . . . Gertrude	Gerke . . . . Gerhard
Frits . . . . Frederick	Geertruyt . . . . Gertrude	Gerlin . . . . Gerhard
Fritschi . . . . . Frederick	Geese . . . . Gerarda	Gero . . . . Gerhard
Fritsje . . . . . . Frederica	Geesje . . . . Augusta	Gerrebrecht . Gerbrantina
Fritzi . . . . Frederica	Geesje . . . . Gerarda	Gerret . . . . Garret
Fritzo . . . . Frederick	Geesje . . . . Grace	Gerretie . . . . . . Gerarda
Fron . . . . Veronica	Geeske . . . . Gerarda	Gerrid . . . . Garret
Fronn . . . . Veronica	Geesknana . . . . Gerarda	Gerridt . . . . Garret
Froutje . . . . Sophia	Gehardus . . . . . . Garret	Gerrit . . . . Garret
Fryntgen . . . . . Catherine	Gehrt . . . . Gerhard	Gerritje . . . . . . Gerarda
Fulbert . . . . Volkert	Gehse . . . . Gerarda	Gerson . . . . Gershom
Fulkard . . . . Volkert	Geil . . . . Kilian	Gert . . . . Garret
Fulpracht . . . . . . Volpert	Geila . . . . Gertrude	Gert . . . . Gertrude
Fyhe . . . . Sophia	Geiljongh . . . . . William	Gerta . . . . Gertrude
Fyllia . . . . Sybil	Geisbert . . . . Gilbert	Gertchen . . . . . Gertrude
Fyte . . . . Vitus	Geisel . . . . Giselle	Gerti . . . . Gertrude
Fytie . . . . Ida	Geitze . . . . Giselle	Gertie . . . . Gertrude
Fytie . . . . Sophia	Gela . . . . Gertrude	Gertjen . . . . . . Gertrude
Fytje . . . . Sophia	Gelante . . . . Anna	Gertke . . . . Gertrude
Fytle . . . . Sophia	Gele . . . . Gertrude	Gertrude . . . . . . Charity
Fytyje . . . . Sophia	Geleyn . . . . Giles	Gertrude . . . . . Gerarda
Gabergel . . . . . . Gabriel	Gelina . . . . Julia	Gerung . . . . . . Gerhard
Gabert . . . . Godfrey	Gellis . . . . Giles	Gesa . . . . Gerarda
Gabl . . . . Gabriel	Gelud . . . . Gertrude	Gesa . . . . Giselle
Gail . . . . Abigail	Gelyn . . . . Giles	Gescha . . . . . . Gertrude
Gajus . . . . Gaius	Gemes . . . . James	Gesche . . . . . . Gertrude
Garabrach . . Gerbrantina	Gene . . . . Juliane	Geseke . . . . . . Gertrude
Garabrand . . . . Gerbrant	Georg . . . . George	Gesine . . . . . . Gertrude
Gard . . . . Garret	George . . . . Uriah	Getze . . . . Giselle
Garrabrant . . . . Gerbrant	Gepie . . . . Gerarda	Geuert . . . . Godfrey
Garret . . . . Gerard	Gepje . . . . Rachel	Gibel . . . . Godfrey
Garret . . . . Gerhard	Geppert . . . . . . Gebhard	Gide . . . . Agidius
Garrit . . . . Garret	Gerard . . . . Garret	Gidi . . . . Agidius
Gashia . . . . Gerarda	Gerard . . . . Gerhard	Gidion . . . . Gideon

Given Name Equivalents: Dutch to English

Giel . . . . Michael	Godeke . . . . Godfrey	Gottert . . . . Gothard
Gielam . . . . William	Godel . . . . Godfrey	Gotti . . . . Godfrey
Giele . . . . Kilian	Godert . . . . Gothard	Gotz . . . . Godfrey
Gieles . . . . Agidius	Godet . . . . Goodeth	Gotze . . . . Godfrey
Gieljam . . . . William	Godevaart . . . . . Geoffrey	Gotzi . . . . Godfrey
Gierd . . . . Gerhard	Godevaart . . . . . . Godfrey	Gotzmann . . . . . . Godfrey
Giertje . . . . Gertrude	Godevart . . . . . . Godfrey	Goverd . . . . Godfrey
Giesel . . . . Giselle	Godfried . . . . . . Godfrey	Goze . . . . Godwin
Gija . . . . Gilbert	Godith . . . . Goodeth	Gozen . . . . Godwin
Gijs . . . . Gilbert	Godje . . . . Goodeth	Gozewijn . . . . Godwin
Gijsbertus . . . . . . Gilbert	Godlief . . . . Gotlieb	Gozewin . . . . Godwin
Gile . . . . Gilbert	Godlief . . . . . Theophilus	Gozzo . . . . Godfrey
Gilgen . . . . Gilbert	Godo . . . . Godfrey	Grades . . . . Gerhard
Giliam . . . . William	Goedyth . . . . . . Goodeth	Grarda . . . . Gertrude
Gilies . . . . Giles	Goeffrey . . . . Godfrey	Gratiosa . . . . Gracius
Giljon . . . . William	Goerd . . . . Godfrey	Grees . . . . Grace
Gilles . . . . Agidius	Goes . . . . Godwin	Greesje . . . . Grace
Gilles . . . . Giles	Goeze . . . . Godfrey	Greesje . . . . Lucretia
Gillis . . . . Giles	Goffert . . . . Godfrey	Greet . . . . Margaret
Gilljon . . . . William	Goline . . . . Julian	Greetie . . . . . . Margaret
Gillmann . . . . . . Agidius	Golyn . . . . Julian	Gregoris . . . . . . Gregory
Gillo . . . . Agidius	Gonda . . . . . . Hillegond	Gregorius . . . . . . Gregory
Gilly . . . . Agidius	Goose . . . . Godwin	Gregorus . . . . . Gregory
Gils . . . . Agidius	Goosen . . . . . . Augusta?	Grein . . . . Quirinus
Gils . . . . Gilbert	Goosen . . . . . . Godwina	Gretchen . . . . Margaret
Gine . . . . Regina	Goossen . . . . . . Godwin	Gretli . . . . Margaret
Gipelo . . . . Giselle	Gooze . . . . Godwin	Gretzen . . . . . . Margaret
Girge . . . . George	Gorch . . . . George	Grickel . . . . . . Agricola
Gisa . . . . Giselle	Gores . . . . Gregory	Griesse . . . . Grace
Gisbert . . . . Gilbert	Goris . . . . Gregory	Grieta . . . . Margaret
Gisch . . . . Gerarda	Gorjes . . . . Gregory	Grietie . . . . . . Margaret
Gisela . . . . Giselle	Gorris . . . . Gregory	Grietje . . . . . . Margaret
Giselbert . . . . . . Giselle	Gorrius . . . . . . Gregory	Griettie . . . . . . Margaret
Gishum . . . . . . Gershom	Gort . . . . Gothard	Gritli . . . . Margaret
Gisle . . . . Giselle	Gorus . . . . Gregory	Gritschi . . . . . Margaret
Giso . . . . Giselle	Gose . . . . August?	Gritta . . . . Margaret
Giszil . . . . Giselle	Gose . . . . Godwin	Grogel . . . . Gregory
Gita . . . . Bridget	Gose . . . . Gustave?	Grolmes . . . Hieronymus
Gitty . . . . Gertrude	Gosen . . . . August	Grommes . . . Hieronymus
Gitty . . . . Kitty	Gosen . . . . Godwina	Gronlein . . . Hieronymus
Gleen . . . . Julian	Gosewyntie . . . . Godwina	Grutschi . . . . . Margaret
Gobbert . . . . . . Godfrey	Gosta . . . . August	Gualterus . . . . . . Walter
Gobelius . . . . . . Godfrey	Gosyntje . . . . . Godwina	Gualtier . . . . Walter
Godaard . . . . . . Gothard	Gotfried . . . . . . Godfrey	Gubil . . . . Godfrey
Godard . . . . . . Gothard	Gotje . . . . Godfrey	Gudeste . . . . Judah
Godardina . . . . Geraldine	Gotsch . . . . Godfrey	Guert . . . . Godfrey
Goddard . . . . . . Gothard	Gotsche . . . . . . Godfrey	Guido . . . . Guy
Goddert . . . . . . Gothard	Gottel . . . . Godfrey	Guilem . . . . William

Given Name Equivalents: Dutch to English

Guiliam . . . . William	Hanne . . . . Joanna	Hauser . . . . Baltus
Guiljam . . . . William	Hanne . . . . John	Hazecha . . . . . . Hedwich
Guilliam . . . . William	Hannes . . . . John	Hazecha . . . . . . Hezekiah
Guisbert . . . . Gilbert	Hans . . . . John	Hebbele . . . . . . Hedwich
Guleyn . . . . Julian	Hansje . . . . Joanna	Hebel . . . . Hedwich
Gumpel . . . . . . Gumpert	Happel . . . . Albert	Heberardus . . . . . . Evert
Gunkelo . . . . . Gumpert	Haramanis . . . . Herman	Heccehardus . . . Eckhard
Gunner . . . . Gunther	Haramanus . . . . Herman	Hechardus . . . . . Eckhard
Gunpilo . . . . . . Gumpert	Harbart . . . . Herbert	Heckter . . . . Hector
Guntzel . . . . Gunther	Harck . . . . Hercules	Hedda . . . . Hedwich
Gurgel . . . . George	Harcke . . . . Hercules	Hede . . . . Hedwich
Gussein . . . . . Gershom	Harckse . . . . . Hercules	Hedel . . . . Hedwich
Gust . . . . August	Hard . . . . Bernard	Hedi . . . . Hedwich
Gustaaf . . . . August	Hard . . . . Gerhard	Hedken . . . . Hedwich
Gustaaf . . . . Gustave	Haremanis . . . . . Herman	Heebilo . . . . Hedwich
Gustetl . . . . August	Hark . . . . Hercules	Heide . . . . Helwich
Gutechin . . . . Judah	Harke . . . . Hercules	Heike . . . . Henry
Gutste . . . . Judah	Harklis . . . . Hercules	Heiko . . . . Henry
Guyten . . . . Gooden	Harkueles . . . . . Hercules	Heilecke . . . . . . Adelheid
Gylo . . . . Gilbert	Harkules . . . . . . Hercules	Heilo . . . . Henry
Gyppel . . . . Giselle	Harkulis . . . . . Hercules	Heiltje . . . . Hilda
Gysbert . . . . Gilbert	Harkulius . . . . Hercules	Hein . . . . Henry
Gysbertje . . . . . . Gilberta	Harm . . . . Herman	Heinclo . . . . Henry
Gyslben . . . . Gilbert	Harman . . . . . . Herman	Heineke . . . . Henry
Gyslbert . . . . Gilbert	Harmanas . . . . Herman	Heinel . . . . Henry
Hades . . . . Bernard	Harmanis . . . . . Herman	Heinemann . . . . . . Henry
Hadken . . . . . . Hedwich	Harme . . . . Herman	Heinkel . . . . Henry
Haggans . . . . . . Aegeus	Harmel . . . . . . Herman	Heinko . . . . Henry
Haggaus . . . . . . Aegeus	Harmen . . . . . . Herman	Heino . . . . Henry
Haggeus . . . . . . Aegeus	Harmena . . . . . Hermina	Heinsel . . . . Henry
Hagha . . . . Agatha	Harmenas . . . . Herman	Heintje . . . . Henrietta
Haiquiez . . . . . . Agatha	Harmke . . . . . Hermina	Heintje . . . . Henry
Haiseli . . . . John	Harmpje . . . . . Hermina	Heintze . . . . Henry
Halheyde . . . . . Adelheid	Harmpji . . . . . . Herman	Heintze . . . . John
Halmagh . . . . . . William	Harmsie . . . . . Hermina	Heinzo . . . . Henry
Hamman . . . . John	Haro . . . . Herman	Heiri . . . . Henry
Hanatie . . . . Hannah	Harpert . . . . . . Herbert	Heis . . . . Matthew
Hanatje . . . . Hannah	Harreck . . . . . Hercules	Heise . . . . Henry
Hanatys . . . . Hannah	Harriet . . . . . . Henrietta	Heitchen . . . . . Hedwich
Hanemann . . . . . . John	Harry . . . . Henry	Hel . . . . Adelheid
Hank . . . . Henry	Hart . . . . Bernard	Hela . . . . Helena
Hanke . . . . John	Hartman . . . . . Herman	Helche . . . . Hilda
Hankey . . . . . . Henrietta	Hasa . . . . Hedwich	Helchin . . . . . . Adelheid
Hanman . . . . John	Haseke . . . . . . Hedwich	Heleche . . . . . Adelheid
Hanna . . . . Hannah	Hassel . . . . Hessel	Helecke . . . . . Adelheid
Hannah . . . . Anna	Hasueras . . . . . Azariah	Helena . . . . . Magdalena
Hannatje . . . . . . Hannah	Hattie . . . . Harriet	Heling . . . . Helena
Hannatye . . . . . Hannah	Hausel . . . . Baltus	Hella . . . . Helena

Given Name Equivalents: Dutch to English

Hellegonda. . . . . . . Hilda
Helletjen . . . . Helena
Helletpe. . . . . Hilda
Helletye . . . . Hilda
Helltje . . . . Hilda
Helm . . . . William
Helma. . . . . . Wilhelmina
Helmer. . . . . . . William
Helmes. . . . . . . William
Helmet . . . . William
Helmi. . . . . William
Helmig. . . . . William
Helmke . . . . William
Helmus . . . . Helmich
Heltjen. . . . . Hilda
Helyas. . . . . Elias
Helytje. . . . . Helena
Heman. . . . . Herman
Hemmo . . . . Herman
Hendereckus. . . . . Henry
Henderick. . . . . . . Henry
Henderickas . . . . . Henry
Henderickes . . . . . Henry
Henderickis . . . . . Henry
Hendericus . . . . . Henry
Henderikus . . . . . Henry
Hendreck . . . . Henry
Hendrekus . . . . . . Henry
Hendrica . . . . . Henrietta
Hendrick . . . . Henry
Hendrickes . . . . . Henry
Hendrickje. . . . Henrietta
Hendrickye. . . . Henrietta
Hendricus. . . . . . . Henry
Hendriekje. . . . Henrietta
Hendrik . . . . Henry
Hengin . . . . Henry
Henkel . . . . Henry
Henkyn. . . . . Henry
Henlyn . . . . Henry
Henne. . . . . Henry
Hennekin . . . . Henry
Hennemann . . . . . Henry
Henner . . . . Henry
Hennes . . . . John
Henning . . . . Henry
Henock . . . . Enoch
Henrick . . . . Henry

Henrietta. . . . . . Harriet
Henrikus. . . . . . . Henry
Henry. . . . . Hercules
Henschel. . . . . . . Henry
Henschel. . . . . John
Henselm . . . . Ansel
Hentgin. . . . . Henry
Hentje . . . . . . Henrietta
Hentze . . . . Henry
Henzo . . . . Henry
Heppy . . . . Abigail
Hercilius. . . . . Hercules
Herck. . . . . . . Hercules
Hercules . . . . Henry
Hermanus . . . . Herman
Hermeli . . . . . . Herman
Hermje . . . . . . Harmina
Hernestus . . . . . . Ernest
Herreck . . . . . Hercules
Herrick. . . . . . Hercules
Herrick. . . . . . Hercules
Herrickse . . . . Hercules
Herrik . . . . . . Hercules
Herrikz. . . . . . Hercules
Herrikze . . . . . Hercules
Hervey. . . . . Harvey
Herwin . . . . Erwin
Heseke . . . . . . Hedwich
Hesje . . . . Hester
Hess . . . . Matthew
Hesse. . . . . Herman
Hesselius . . . . . . Hessel
Hesther . . . . Hester
Heta . . . . Hedwich
Hete . . . . Hedwich
Hetgin. . . . . . . Hedwich
Hetichin . . . . . Hedwich
Hetje . . . . Albertina
Hetta. . . . . Hedwich
Hettichin . . . . . Hedwich
Hettie . . . . Harriet
Hetty . . . . Hester
Hetzel . . . . Herman
Hevlyn . . . . Evaline
Heyliche . . . . . Adelheid
Heyltje . . . . Hilda
Heyltjen . . . . Hilda
Hias . . . . Matthew

Hickel . . . . Helena
Hiellegontie . . . . . Hilda
Hielletie. . . . . Hilda
Hielletje. . . . . Hilda
Hieronimus . Hieronymus
Hieronymus. . . . . Jerome
Hiesl . . . . Matthew
Hilchen . . . . Helena
Hild . . . . Hilda
Hildegard . . . . Hillegond
Hilgen . . . . Helena
Hilla . . . . Hilda
Hille . . . . Hilda
Hillegond. . . . . . . Hilda
Hillegonda . . . . . . Hilda
Hilletje. . . . . Hilda
Hillitje . . . . Hilda
Hillund . . . . Hilda
Hinke . . . . Henry
Hinnerk . . . . Henry
Hinrich . . . . Henry
Hinrik. . . . . Henry
Hintzel . . . . Henry
Hipp . . . . Hippoletus
Hiscock . . . . Isaac
Hiskca . . . . . . Hezekiah
Hiskia . . . . . . Hezekiah
Hittebel . . . . . Mehitabel
Hold. . . . . Reinhold
Holda . . . . Hilda
Holder . . . . . . Reinhold
Holger. . . . . . . Volkert
Hubert . . . . Herbert
Hubrecht . . . . . Herbert
Hugo . . . . Hugh
Hugue . . . . Hugh
Huib . . . . Hubert
Huig . . . . Hugh
Huigen. . . . . Hugh
Hulda . . . . Hilda
Hulda . . . . . . Hillegond
Humfridus . . . Humphrey
Humfried . . . . Humphrey
Humfry. . . . . . Humphrey
Hupraid. . . . . . . Hubert
Huybert . . . . Hubert
Huygen . . . . Hugh
Hydde. . . . . Hedwich

Given Name Equivalents: Dutch to English

Ilyer	Hieronymus	Jacobus	James	Japil	Jacob
Hylie	Hilda	Jacomina	Jemima	Japje	Jacobina
Ibel	Isabella	Jacomyntie	Jemima	Jappje	Jacobina
Iddo	Ide	Jacomyntje	Jemima	Jaquemne	Jemima
Iden	Ide	Jacop	Jacob	Jaquemyntie	Jemima
Ielmer	Ethelmar	Jacquemina	Jemima	Jaques	Jacob
Ifje	Eva	Jacques	Jack	Jarvis	George
Ijbitje	Abigail	Jacques	Jacob	Jasper	Caspar
Ikee	Agatha	Jaepie	Jacob	Jassawa	Joshua
Ikee	Eycke	Jaepje	Jacob	Jassewa	Joshua
Iliane	Juliane	Jaggi	Jacob	Jassewil	Joshua
Illetie	Alida	Jahn	John	Jassuel	Joshua
Ilsa	Elizabeth	Jakob	Jacob	Jaszewil	Joshua
Immel	Emmerich	Jakobus	Jacob	Jeams	James
Immetje	Emma	Jakomina	Jemima	Jeanne	Janet
Immicha	Emma	James	Jacob	Jeannetie	Janet
Ina	Regina	James	Jacob	Jeartie	Gertrude
Ingber	Inga	Jamesina	Jacobina	Jeckel	Jacob
Inkrees	Increase	Janche	Janet	Jeems	James
Iost	Joseph	Jane	Janet	Jeffers	Godfrey
Ipke	Eva?	Janetie	Janet	Jeffery	Godfrey
Isaack	Isaac	Janetje	Janet	Jefta	Jeptha
Isaak	Isaac	Janeton	Jonathan	Jeggeli	Jacob
Isabel	Elizabeth	Janietie	Janet	Jelette	Julia
Isabella	Arabella	Janietje	Janet	Jelitje	Julia
Isac	Isaac	Janije	Janet	Jelmer	Ethelmar
Isack	Isaac	Janitie	Janet	Jeltje	Gallia
Iseck	Isaac	Janne	John	Jemeima	Jemima
Isick	Isaac	Janneke	Janet	Jemema	Jemima
Ita	Judith	Janneken	Joanna	Jemina	Jemima
Ite	Judith	Jannetan	Jonathan	Jemmea	Jemima
Izaak	Isaac	Jannetie	Janet	Jems	James
Jaan	Janet	Jannetje	Janet	Jemyma	Jemima
Jaantje	Janet	Jannettye	Janet	Jemyna	Jemima
Jaap	Jacob	Janni	John	Jeneke	Janet
Jaapie	Jacob	Jannieke	Janet	Jenfrit	Godfrey
Jaapje	Jacobina	Jannitie	Janet	Jengen	Janet
Jaapje	Janet	Jannitje	Janet	Jenike	Janet
Jabbo	Jacob	Jannitye	Janet	Jenne	Janet
Jack	John	Janny	John	Jenne	John
Jackel	Jacob	Jansje	Janet	Jennecke	Janet
Jacket	Jacob	Jantia	Janet	Jenneke	Janet
Jacob	James	Jantina	Janet	Jenni	John
Jacoba	Jacobina	Jantje	Janet	Jennica	Janet
Jacobes	Jacob	Janus	Adrian	Jennie	Janet
Jacobia	Jacobina	Jany	John	Jennike	Janet
Jacobje	Jacobina	Japic	Jacob	Jenny	Janet
Jacobus	Jacob	Japik	Jacob	Jeramius	Jeremiah

Jeramyas . . . . . Jeremiah	Jockel . . . . Jacob	Josie. . . . . Josina
Jeremeies . . . . . Jeremiah	Jocki . . . . Jacob	Josina . . . . Justina
Jeremia . . . . . . Jeremiah	Joe . . . . Joseph	Josop. . . . . Joseph
Jeremias . . . . . . Jeremiah	Jofrid . . . . Godfrey	Josoph . . . . Joseph
Jeremies . . . . . . Jeremiah	Joggeli. . . . . Jacob	Josua . . . . Joshua
Jeremy . . . . Jeremiah	Joghem. . . . . Jochem	Josyna. . . . . Josina
Jeremyas . . . . Jeremiah	Johan . . . . John	Josyntje. . . . . Josina
Jerg. . . . . George	Johanis . . . . John	Jottichin . . . . Judah
Jerig . . . . George	Johanneke . . . . . . Janet	Jous . . . . Joris
Jerimyas . . . . . Jeremiah	Johannes. . . . . John	Jozef . . . . Joseph
Jero . . . . . . Hieronymus	Johannis . . . . John	Jozefina. . . . . . Josephine
Jerome. . . . Hieronymus	Johnatan . . . . . . Jonathan	Jozie . . . . Joseph
Jeronimus . . Hieronymus	Johnaton. . . . . . Jonathan	Jozua. . . . . Joshua
Jesaias . . . . Josiah	Joide. . . . . Judah	Ju . . . . Hugh
Jesays . . . . Josiah	Jonah . . . . Jonas	Judah . . . . Judas
Jesia . . . . Josiah	Jonatan. . . . . . . Jonathan	Judah . . . . Judith
Jesyntje. . . . . Josina	Jones. . . . . Jonas	Jude . . . . Judah
Jesynze . . . . Josina	Joneton. . . . . . . Jonathan	Judick. . . . . Judith
Jetje . . . . Henrietta	Jonis . . . . Jonas	Judinta . . . . Judith
Jetze. . . . . Godfrey	Jonitia . . . . Janet	Juerry . . . . George
Jeuriaen . . . . George	Jonus. . . . . Jonas	Juliaantje. . . . . . . Juliane
Jeurian . . . . George	Joonje . . . . Janet	Jupp . . . . Joseph
Jeurie . . . . George	Jooris . . . . George	Jurge. . . . . George
Jezaus. . . . . Isaiah	Jooryder . . . . . . George	Jurgen. . . . . George
Jezia. . . . . Josiah	Joosdt . . . . Joseph	Jurian . . . . George
Jezyna. . . . . Josina	Joosje. . . . . Josina	Jurn . . . . George
Jezyntie. . . . . Josina	Joost . . . . Joseph	Jurrian . . . . George
Jezyntje. . . . . Josina	Jopje. . . . . Jacob	Jurrie . . . . George
Jid . . . . Agidius	Joppes. . . . . Jacob	Jurrien . . . . George
Jilles. . . . . Giles	Jores. . . . . George	Jurry . . . . George
Jillis . . . . Giles	Jorge. . . . . George	Jury. . . . . George
Jira . . . . Ira	Jorgel . . . . George	Jusken . . . . August
Jittje . . . . Ida	Joris . . . . George	Justje. . . . . Justina
Joachim . . . . Jochem	Jorius . . . . George	Jutge. . . . . Judith
Joakemis . . . . . . Jochem	Jorn . . . . George	Jutta . . . . Judith
Joan . . . . Janet	Jorus. . . . . George	Jutte . . . . Judith
Joana . . . . Janet	Joryeer . . . . George	Kaat. . . . . Catherine
Joanis. . . . . John	Joryer . . . . George	Kaatje . . . . Catherine
Joanna . . . . Janet	Joryjer. . . . . George	Kaderl . . . . Catherine
Joannis . . . . John	Josef . . . . Joseph	Kanieltje. . . . . Kunigunda
Joaptie. . . . . Jacob	Josep. . . . . Joseph	Karel . . . . Carl
Jobbi. . . . . Jacob	Josepha. . . . . . Josephine	Kareltje . . . . . . Caroline
Jobje. . . . . Jacob	Josephat . . . . . . Joseph	Karolina . . . . . Caroline
Jocamyna . . . . . Jemima	Josephine . . . . . . Josina	Karsten . . . . . . Christian
Jocamyntie . . . . Jemima	Josey. . . . . . . Josephine	Karyuss . . . . . Eucharius
Jocheemus . . . . Jochem	Josi. . . . . Josina	Kas . . . . Caspar
Jochim . . . . Jochem	Josia . . . . Josephine	Kasper . . . . Caspar
Jochum . . . . . . Jochem	Josie . . . . Josephine	Kassen . . . . Christian

Given Name Equivalents: Dutch to English

Kasten . . . . Christian	Ko . . . . Jacob	Kunike . . . . Conrad
Kate . . . . Catherine	Koba . . . . Jacob	Kunisa . . . . . Kunigunda
Katel . . . . Catherine	Kobel . . . . Jacob	Kunkelo . . . . Conrad
Kathe . . . . Catherine	Kobes . . . . Jacob	Kunna . . . . . Kunigunda
Kathl . . . . Catherine	Kobi . . . . Jacob	Kuno . . . . Conrad
Kathy . . . . Catherine	Kobus . . . . Jacob	Kunz . . . . Conrad
Katili . . . . Catherine	Koen . . . . Conrad	Kunzela . . . . Kunigunda
Katri . . . . Catherine	Koenraet . . . . . . Conrad	Kunzelin . . . . Conrad
Katrijn . . . . . . Catherine	Koert . . . . Conrad	Kure . . . . Conrad
Katryntje . . . . Catherine	Koert . . . . Curtis	Kurri . . . . Conrad
Katter . . . . . . Catherine	Koes . . . . Christian	Kutsch . . . . Conrad
Katterl . . . . . . Catherine	Kohn . . . . Conrad	Kyrn . . . . Quirinus
Katti . . . . Catherine	Koneiung . . . . Kunigunda	Lackje . . . . Rachel
Kederin . . . . . Catherine	Konert . . . . Conrad	Laenette . . . . Lena
Kee . . . . Cornelia	Konne . . . . Conrad	Lakas . . . . Lucas
Kees . . . . Cornelius	Konne . . . . . Kunigunda	Lambrecht . . . . . Lambert
Keesje . . . . Cornelius	Kontzele . . . . . Kunigunda	Lammert . . . . . . Lambert
Keetje . . . . Cornelia	Koob . . . . Jacob	Lammertje . . . Lambertina
Keltie . . . . Alida	Koos . . . . Jacob	Lammetje . . . Lambertina
Kerdel . . . . Carl	Koosje . . . . Jacobina	Lana . . . . Lena
Kerstan . . . . Christian	Kord . . . . Conrad	Landolph . . . . . Randolph
Kerstanus . . . . . Christian	Kordel . . . . Carl	Laney . . . . Eleanor
Kersten . . . . . . Christian	Koris . . . . Cornelius	Lare . . . . Hillary
Kerstyne . . . . . Christina	Kornelia . . . . . Cornelia	Laure . . . . Lawrence
Kesia . . . . Keziah	Kors . . . . Cornelius	Laurenis . . . . . Lawrence
Ketterle . . . . . Catherine	Korsjaan . . . . . Christian	Laurens . . . . . . Lawrence
Ketterlin . . . . . Catherine	Krees . . . . Cornelius	Laurentz . . . . . Lawrence
Kiersten . . . . . Christian	Krein . . . . Quirinus	Laurenz . . . . . . Lawrence
Killeaen . . . . Kilian	Kreingen . . . . . Catherine	Laurus . . . . Lourus
Kit . . . . Christopher	Krelis . . . . Cornelius	Lavyntje . . . . Lavina
Kitt . . . . Christopher	Krelius . . . . . . Cornelius	Layah . . . . Lea
Kitty . . . . Catherine	Kress . . . . Christian	Leaya . . . . Lea
Klaar . . . . Clara	Krienes . . . . . . Quirinus	Ledina . . . . Lydia
Klaartje . . . . Clara	Krin . . . . Catherine	Leeiaa . . . . Lea
Klaas . . . . Nicholas	Kris . . . . Christian	Leeja . . . . Lea
Klaasje . . . . Clarissa	Krischan . . . . . Christian	Leen . . . . Leonard
Klaatje . . . . Claudia	Krisje . . . . Christina	Leena . . . . Lena
Klaes . . . . Nicholas	Kristel . . . . Christina	Leendert . . . . . . Leonard
Klass . . . . Nicholas	Kristiaan . . . . . Christian	Leendredt . . . . . Leonard
Klasyne . . . . Clarissa	Kristijntje . . . . Christina	Leenna . . . . Lena
Klaywitz . . . . . . Nicholas	Kruschen . . . . Christian	Leent . . . . Leonard
Klazina . . . . Clarissa	Kryn . . . . Quirinus	Leentje . . . . Lena
Klement . . . . . . Clement	Krynchgin . . . . Catherine	Leeya . . . . Lea
Klobes . . . . Nicholas	Kueni . . . . Conrad	Leffers . . . . Leffert
Klosel . . . . Nicholas	Kuenrat . . . . . . Conrad	Lehene . . . . . . Magdalena
Knelles . . . . . . Cornelius	Kuhn . . . . Conrad	Lehrd . . . . Leonard
Kniertee . . . . Kunigunda	Kun . . . . Conrad	Lei . . . . Eligius
Kniertje . . . . Kunigunda	Kunemann . . . . . Conrad	Leia . . . . Lea

Given Name Equivalents: Dutch to English

Leick . . . . Lucas	Liedea . . . . Lydia	Lola . . . . Dolores
Leintgen . . . . . . Helena	Liedia . . . . Lydia	Lon . . . . Lawrence
Leli . . . . Lena	Liedya . . . . Lydia	Lons . . . . Lawrence
Lemmert . . . . . Lambert	Liena . . . . Lena	Loodewyck . . . . Ludwich
Lena . . . . Helena	Lienchgen . . . Magdalena	Lore . . . . Lawrence
Lena . . . . . . Magdalena	Lienert . . . . Leonard	Lorenchen . . . . Laurentia
Lenah . . . . Lena	Liengen . . . . Helena	Lori . . . . Lawrence
Lenchen . . . . Lena	Lienhard . . . . . Leonard	Lortz . . . . Lawrence
Leneke . . . . Lena	Lientje . . . . Caroline	Lotje . . . . Charlotte
Leneli . . . . Lena	Liert . . . . Leonard	Lotze . . . . Ludwich
Lenert . . . . Leonard	Liesabet . . . . . Elizabeth	Lotzeya . . . . . . Luitgard
Lenhard . . . . . . Leonard	Liesabeth . . . . Elizabeth	Louckil . . . . Luitgard
Leni . . . . Lena	Liesebeth . . . . Elizabeth	Lourens . . . . . Lawrence
Lennert . . . . . . Leonard	Lieve . . . . Leo	Lourus . . . . Louis?
Lenoor . . . . Eleanor	Liewe . . . . Leo	Louw . . . . Lawrence
Lenz . . . . Lancelot	Lijsbert . . . . Elizabeth	Louwerins . . . . Lawrence
Lenz . . . . Leonard	Lijsje . . . . Eliza	Louwrens . . . . . Lawrence
Leo . . . . Leopold	Lindis . . . . Edellind	Lovis . . . . Ludwich
Leon . . . . Leonard	Line . . . . Magdalena	Lowerens . . . . . Lawrence
Leonoor . . . . . . Eleanor	Linje . . . . Lena	Lowies . . . . Eloise
Leonora . . . . . . Eleanor	Linnart . . . . . . Leonard	Lowies . . . . Louis
Leret . . . . Leonard	Lipmann . . . . . . Philip	Lowisa . . . . Louisa
Lerrence . . . . Lawrence	Lippe . . . . Philip	Lowrus . . . . Lourus
Let . . . . Adeline	Lipperl . . . . Philip	Loy . . . . Eligius
Letje . . . . Adeline	Lipps . . . . Philip	Loyse . . . . Louis
Letje . . . . Letitia	Lippus . . . . Philip	Luas . . . . Lucas
Leuckel . . . . . . Luitgard	Lisabeth . . . . . Elizabeth	Lubbers . . . . . . Lubbert
Leuntje . . . . . Apollonia	Lisichin . . . . . Elizabeth	Luca . . . . Luitgard
Leuntje . . . . Lubbert	Litt . . . . Hippoletus	Lucco . . . . Ludwich
Leur . . . . Louis	Liubert . . . . Lubbert	Lucia . . . . Lucy
Leverens . . . . Lawrence	Liudike . . . . . . Ludwich	Luckas . . . . Lucas
Leverins . . . . . Lawrence	Livinus . . . . Levi	Lucke . . . . Ludwich
Levinus . . . . Leo	Livyntje . . . . Lena	Luckel . . . . Ludwich
Levyntje . . . . Lena	Liza . . . . Elizabeth	Luckeley . . . . . Ludwich
Levyntje . . . . Lena	Lizzie . . . . Elizabeth	Luckhard . . . . . Ludwich
Lewis . . . . Louis	Ljesbeth . . . . . Elizabeth	Luczchen . . . . . Ludwich
Lewts . . . . Ludwich	Locza . . . . Luitgard	Lucze . . . . Luitgard
Lexel . . . . Alexander	Lodewyck . . . . Ludwich	Ludbrecht . . . . . Lubbert
Ley . . . . Eligius	Lodewyk . . . . Ludwich	Lude . . . . Ludwich
Leya . . . . Lea	Lodowyck . . . . Ludwich	Ludeke . . . . Lothar
Leyn . . . . . . Magdalena	Loew . . . . Louis	Ludeke . . . . . . Ludwich
Leynje . . . . Lena	Lof . . . . Adolf	Ludel . . . . Ludwich
Lezart . . . . Eliza	Logkele . . . . . . Luitgard	Luder . . . . Ludwich
Libby . . . . Elizabeth	Lohr . . . . Lawrence	Ludmilla . . . . Lulu
Licharde . . . . . Luitgard	Loi . . . . Eligius	Ludovicus . . . . . . Louis
Lidda . . . . Adelheid	Loisl . . . . Eloise	Ludovicus . . . . Ludwich
Liddy . . . . Adelheid	Lokil . . . . Luitgard	Luer . . . . Louis
Lidia . . . . Lydia	Lola . . . . Delores	Lues . . . . Eligius

Given Name Equivalents: Dutch to English

Luewes. . . . . Louis	Maatje. . . . . Martha	Manuel . . . . Emanuel
Luhr. . . . . Lothar	Mable . . . . Mehitable	Manus . . . . Herman
Luir . . . . Louis	Machiel . . . . Michael	Manz . . . . Mangold
Lukarde. . . . . . . Luitgard	Machtel . . . . . Magdalena	Mappus . . . Bartholomew
Luke . . . . Lucas	Machteld . . . . Magdalena	Mara. . . . . Maria
Luklei . . . . Ludwich	Mack . . . . Marcus	Maraatje . . . . Maria
Lur . . . . Louis	Madalena. . . . Magdalena	Maragriet . . . . . Margaret
Lurtz . . . . Lawrence	Madalentie. . . Magdalena	Maragrietie. . . . Margaret
Luthe. . . . . Ludwich	Madel . . . . . . Magdalena	Maragriettie . . . Margaret
Lutter . . . . Ludwich	Madele . . . . . Magdalena	Maragrietye . . . Margaret
Lutygo . . . . Ludwich	Madelein . . . . Magdalena	Maragritie. . . . . Margaret
Lutyke . . . . Ludwich	Madeli . . . . . . Magdalena	Maragryettie . . . Margaret
Lutz. . . . . Ludwich	Maden . . . . . . Magdalena	Maratie . . . . Maria
Lutza. . . . . Lucy	Mades . . . . Matthew	Marceles . . . . . . Marshal
Lutzel . . . . Lucy	Madge . . . . Margaret	Mardalena . . . Magdalena
Lutzo. . . . . Ludwich	Madi . . . . Magdalena	Marei . . . . Maria
Luuerins . . . . . Lawrence	Madla . . . . . . Magdalena	Mareiia . . . . Maria
Luwert . . . . Lubbert	Maeritje . . . . Maria	Mareile . . . . Maria
Luwje. . . . . Louis	Maerte. . . . . Martin	Mareitie . . . . Maria
Luykas. . . . . Lucas	Maertie . . . . Maria	Mareitje . . . . Maria
Luyr. . . . . Louis	Maertje . . . . Maria	Marelia . . . . Maria
Luytje . . . . Lucas	Maes . . . . Bartholomew	Mareten . . . . Martin
Luza . . . . Lucy	Maes . . . . Thomas	Marethe . . . . Maria
Luzeile . . . . Lucy	Maeyke . . . . Maria	Marethen . . . . . . Maria
Luzel. . . . . Lucy	Magda . . . . . Magdalena	Maretie . . . . Maria
Luzi . . . . Lucy	Magdaleentje . Magdalena	Maretje . . . . Maria
Luzscha. . . . . Lucy	Magdaleetje . . Magdalena	Mareytie . . . . Maria
Luzze. . . . . Ludwich	Magdalena. . . . . . Helena	Margarita . . . . . Margaret
Lydea . . . . Lydia	Magdaletie. . . Magdalena	Margaritta. . . . . Margaret
Lyenchgin. . . . Magdalena	Mageel. . . . . Michael	Marget . . . . Margaret
Lyes . . . . Elias	Magel . . . . . . Magdalena	Margitta . . . . . . Margaret
Lymon . . . . Simon	Maghdaleena . Magdalena	Margriet . . . . . . Margaret
Lyntje . . . . Lena	Maghiel . . . . Michael	Margrieta . . . . . Margaret
Lys . . . . Elizabeth	Magiel . . . . Michael	Margriete . . . . . Margaret
Lysbert . . . . Elizabeth	Magle . . . . . . Magdalena	Margrietie. . . . . Margaret
Lysbet. . . . . Elizabeth	Magrytie . . . . . . Margaret	Margrietje. . . . . Margaret
Lysbeth . . . . Elizabeth	Magtelt . . . . . Magdalena	Margrietze . . . . Margaret
Lysje . . . . Eliza	Maigel . . . . . . Margaret	Margritje . . . . . Margaret
Maacke . . . . Maria	Maike . . . . Maria	Mari . . . . Maria
Maaicke . . . . Maria	Mais . . . . Bartholomew	Maria . . . . Martha
Maaike . . . . Maria	Makeel. . . . . Michael	Maria. . . . . Mary
Maaritje . . . . Maria	Maleschi . . . . . Malachi	Mariah . . . . Maria
Maarten . . . . Martin	Malle. . . . . Molly	Marian . . . . Maria
Maartie . . . . Maria	Mally. . . . . Molly	Maricka . . . . Maria
Maartje . . . . Maria	Maneke. . . . . . . Mangold	Marie . . . . Maria
Maartje . . . . Martha	Manes . . . . Herman	Mariea . . . . Maria
Maas . . . . . Bartholomew	Mangel . . . . Mangold	Mariedel . . . . Maria
Maas . . . . Thomas	Mann . . . . Mangold	Marieiia . . . . Maria

Given Name Equivalents: Dutch to English

Marietie . . . . Maria	Martynnus . . . . . Martin	Maykje . . . . Maria
Marietje . . . . Maria	Martyntie . . . . . Martina	Mayna. . . . . . . Imogene
Marietta . . . . Maria	Martyntje . . . . . . Martina	Mazeries . . . . . . Marjorie
Marigiettie . . . . Margaret	Martynus . . . . . . Martin	Mazre . . . . Marjorie
Mariken . . . . Maria	Marx. . . . . Marcus	Mebess . . . Bartholomew
Marin . . . . Marinus	Mary. . . . . Maria	Mebs . . . . . Bartholomew
Maris. . . . . Maurice	Mary. . . . . Polly	Meccla . . . . . . Mathilda
Marite. . . . . Maria	Marya . . . . Maria	Mechel . . . . . . Mathilda
Marites . . . . Maria	Maryette . . . . Maria	Mechteld. . . . . . Mathilda
Maritje . . . . Maria	Marygriethe . . . Margaret	Mechthild . . . . . Mathilda
Maritjen . . . . Maria	Marytie . . . . Maria	Meckel . . . . . . Mathilda
Mark . . . . Marcus	Marytje . . . . Maria	Meckele . . . . . Mathilda
Marka. . . . . Maria	Marytyntie . . . . . Martina	Meckelia. . . . . . Mathilda
Marlene. . . . . Magdalena	Masere . . . . Marjorie	Meckla . . . . . . Mathilda
Marragriet . . . . Margaret	Mass . . . . . Bartholomew	Meckle . . . . . . Mathilda
Marragrieta . . . Margaret	Massey. . . . . . . Thomas	Mecklie. . . . . . Mathilda
Marragrietie . . . Margaret	Mateis . . . . Matthew	Meeno. . . . . Minnie
Marregante . . Magdalena	Mateues. . . . . . . Matthew	Meensje. . . . . . . Minnie
Marregieta . . . . Margaret	Mateves. . . . . . . Matthew	Meenske . . . . Minnie
Marregrietie . . . Margaret	Matewes . . . . . Matthew	Mees . . . . Bartholomew
Marregrietta . . . Margaret	Matewis. . . . . . . Matthew	Meewes . . . Bartholomew
Marreten . . . . . . Martin	Matheus . . . . . Matthew	Meg . . . . Margaret
Marrethen . . . . . . Martin	Mathias . . . . . . Matthew	Meigel . . . . Michael
Marretie . . . . Maria	Mathys . . . . . . Matthew	Meindert. . . . . . Maynard
Marretje . . . . Maria	Matie. . . . . Martha	Meinhard . . . . . Maynard
Marretye . . . . Maria	Matje. . . . . Martha	Meino . . . . Minnie
Marrietta. . . . . . . Maria	Matje . . . . Mathilda	Meinsje . . . . Minnie
Marritius . . . . . Maurice	Matle. . . . . . . Magdalena	Meintje. . . . . . . Jemima
Marritje. . . . . Maria	Mattes . . . . Matthew	Meitza. . . . . . . Mathilda
Marryetie . . . . . . Maria	Mattheus . . . . . Matthew	Meiza . . . . Mathilda
Marrytie . . . . Maria	Matthias . . . . . Matthew	Mekkels . . . . . Mathilda
Marselis. . . . . . Marshal	Matthis . . . . . . Matthew	Melbert . . . . . Melchior
Mart . . . . Maria	Matthys . . . . . . Matthew	Melchar . . . . . Melchior
Marta . . . . Martha	Matthysse . . . . Matthew	Melchert. . . . . Melchior
Marta. . . . . Martin	Matthyus . . . . . Matthew	Mele. . . . . Melchior
Martaleentje. . Magdalena	Mattius . . . . . . Matthew	Melgert. . . . . . Melchior
Marte. . . . . Martin	Matyas. . . . . . . Matthew	Melke. . . . . . . Melchior
Marteines. . . . . . Martin	Matys . . . . Matthew	Mella. . . . . Amelia
Martha . . . . Maria	Matz . . . . Matthew	Melle . . . . Melchior
Marthen. . . . . . . Martin	Maue . . . . . Bartholomew	Menassus . . . . . Maynard
Marthinnus . . . . Martin	Maurus . . . . . . Maurice	Mene . . . . Imogene
Marthynnus . . . . Martin	Maus . . . . Bartholomew	Mengel . . . . . . Mangold
Martie. . . . . Maria	Mavous. . . . . . . Marcus	Menikes . . . . . . Dominic
Martie . . . . Martin	Mawe. . . . . Bartholomew	Menno. . . . . Minnie
Martines . . . . . . Martin	Max . . . . . . Maximilian	Mensie . . . . . . Mensje
Martinis . . . . Martin	Mayke. . . . . Maria	Menzel. . . . . . . Herman
Martinus . . . . . . Martin	Mayke . . . . Marjory	Merbel . . . . Mabel
Martje. . . . . Maria	Mayken . . . . Maria	Merci . . . . Martha

Given Name Equivalents: Dutch to English

Merck . . . . Markoff	Mies . . . . Maria	Myndert . . . . . . Maynard
Merga . . . . Maria	Mieteke . . . . Maria	Mynett . . . . Minnie
Merityen . . . . Maria	Mietje . . . . Maria	Mynni . . . . Minnie
Merkel . . . . Marcus	Mietzerl . . . . Maria	Mynno . . . . Minnie
Merkellin . . . . Markward	Miezel . . . . Maria	Mynnotie . . . . . . Minnie
Merkelo . . . . . Markward	Miggi . . . . . Wilhelmina	Myno . . . . Minnie
Merkle . . . . Marcus	Mijntje . . . . . Wilhelmina	Mynotie . . . . Minnie
Mermel . . . . Mabel	Milly . . . . Millicent	Myntie . . . . Minnie
Merreytje . . . . Maria	Mimmeli . . . . Maria	Na . . . . Nancy
Merriam . . . . . . Miriam	Mimmi . . . . Maria	Naatje . . . . Anna
Merritje . . . . Maria	Mina . . . . . . Wilhelmina	Naeltie . . . . Nelly
Merselies . . . . . . Marshal	Minchen . . . . Wilhelmina	Nafje . . . . Agnes
Merten . . . . Martin	Mincke . . . . Minnie	Nan . . . . Anna
Mertin . . . . Martin	Minckes . . . . . . Dominic	Nancy . . . . Anna
Merytyen . . . . Maria	Mingo . . . . Dominic	Nandel . . . . Anna
Mes . . . . . Bartholomew	Minicus . . . . . . Dominic	Nandel . . . . . Ferdinand
Meta . . . . Mathilda	Minikes . . . . . . Dominic	Nanne . . . . Anna
Metje . . . . . . Magdalena	Minne . . . . Dominic	Nanni . . . . Anna
Metje . . . . Martha	Minnie . . . . Wilhelmina	Nante . . . . . . Ferdinand
Metje . . . . Mathilda	Mino . . . . Minnie	Nantje . . . . Anna
Metke . . . . Mathilda	Minochy . . . . Wilhelmina	Nardes . . . . Bernard
Metta . . . . Mathilda	Minske . . . . Mensje	Nat . . . . Nathaniel
Mettelde . . . . . Mathilda	Mintgen . . . . . Wilhelmina	Necklaes . . . . . Nicholas
Mettild . . . . . . Mathilda	Miri . . . . Maria	Neeklas . . . . . . Nicholas
Mettje . . . . Martha	Mirl . . . . Maria	Neel . . . . Cornelius
Mettus . . . . Matthew	Mirtel . . . . Martin	Neeltje . . . . Nelly
Mettys . . . . Matthew	Mirzel . . . . Maria	Neely . . . . Nelly
Metys . . . . Matthew	Mitzi . . . . Maria	Neesie . . . . Agnes
Metze . . . . Mathilda	Mizzi . . . . Maria	Neesken . . . . Agnes
Meus . . . . Bartholomew	Mobius . . . Bartholomew	Neisa . . . . Agnes
Mewes . . . Bartholomew	Molly . . . . Mary	Nella . . . . Helena
Mewis . . . Bartholomew	Mone . . . . Monica	Nellchen . . . . Helena
Mews . . . . Bartholomew	Morica . . . . Marjory	Nelle . . . . Petronella
Mewus . . . Bartholomew	Morice . . . . . . Maurice	Nelles . . . . Cornelius
Meyne . . . . Imogene	Morinus . . . . . . Marinus	Nelletie . . . . Nelly
Meyne . . . . Minnie	Mort . . . . Mortimer	Nelletje . . . . Nelly
Meynno . . . . Minnie	Mosis . . . . Moses	Nelli . . . . Helena
Meyno . . . . Minnie	Mosus . . . . Moses	Nellies . . . . . . Cornelius
Meynou . . . . Minnie	Mouris . . . . . . Maurice	Nellitie . . . . Nelly
Mezza . . . . Mathilda	Mouwies . . . . . Maurice	Nelly . . . . Cornelia
Mia . . . . Maria	Moyse . . . . Thomas	Neltie . . . . Nelly
Mias . . . . Jeremiah	Moyses . . . . Moses	Nemeyjar . . . . . Nehemiah
Michel . . . . Michael	Mundel . . . . . Siegmond	Nencie . . . . Nancy
Michiel . . . . Michael	Mundi . . . . . . Siegmond	Nesa . . . . Agnes
Mie . . . . Maria	Muno . . . . Minnie	Nese . . . . Agnes
Miekchen . . . . Maria	Mutz . . . . Hartmut	Neselin . . . . Agnes
Mieke . . . . Maria	Myn . . . . Dominic	Nesi . . . . Agnes
Miel . . . . Maria	Myna . . . . Minnie	Net . . . . Nathaniel

Given Name Equivalents: Dutch to English

Nete . . . . Agnes	Obed. . . . . Obadiah	Pauel. . . . . Paul
Nethaniel . . . . . Nathaniel	Odde. . . . . Otto	Paulius . . . . Paul
Netta. . . . . Agnes	Ode. . . . . Otto	Paullus . . . . Paul
Netta . . . . Joanna	Odel . . . . Adam	Paultje . . . . Paulina
Nettchen . . . . . . Joanna	Odeli. . . . . Adam	Paulus. . . . . Paul
Netteneel . . . . Nathaniel	Odo. . . . . Otto	Paulyntje. . . . . . Paulina
Neysa . . . . Agnes	Oelfert . . . . Oliver	Pauwelis . . . . Paul
Nicholaas . . . . Nicholas	Oetje. . . . . Agnes	Pawel . . . . Paul
Nicholaes . . . . Nicholas	Oetje. . . . . Agnes	Paylyntie . . . . . . Paulina
Nickel. . . . . . . Nicholas	Oeycke . . . . Agnes	Pecens . . . . Patience
Nicklaes . . . . . Nicholas	Okenus . . . . . . Octavius	Peczgin. . . . . . . Patricia
Nicklas . . . . . . Nicholas	Okie . . . . Octavius	Peeck. . . . . Peek
Niclaas . . . . . . Nicholas	Oktee . . . . Octavius	Peesjiens . . . . . Patience
Nicolaas . . . . . Nicholas	Oledo. . . . . Alida	Peg. . . . . Margaret
Nicolass . . . . . Nicholas	Oletgen . . . . . . Adelheid	Peggie . . . . . . Margaret
Nicole. . . . . Claudia	Olfert . . . . Oliver	Peggy . . . . Margaret
Niefje . . . . Agnes	Olmes . . . . Hieronymus	Pelcke . . . . Sybil
Niels . . . . Cornelius	Olof . . . . Oliver	Penny. . . . . . . Penelope
Nies . . . . Agnes	Olphert. . . . . Oliver	Pepil. . . . . Patricia
Niese. . . . . Agnes	Omfrey. . . . . Humphrey	Peppe. . . . . Patricia
Niesen. . . . . Agnes	Onimus . . . . Hieronymus	Peppi. . . . . Joseph
Niesje . . . . Agnes	Onno. . . . . Arnold	Percy . . . . Persis
Niesse. . . . . Agnes	Ootie . . . . Otilia	Peres . . . . Peter
Niessje . . . . Agnes	Opitz. . . . . Adelbert	Perter . . . . Peter
Niesye. . . . . Agnes	Ordewin . . . . . . Ortwin	Pesens. . . . . . . Patience
Nijs . . . . Dionysius	Orety . . . . Dorothy	Pesensie . . . . . Patience
Niklas . . . . Nicholas	Orschel . . . . Ursula	Petertje. . . . . . . Patricia
Nilies. . . . . . . Cornelius	Orseli. . . . . Ursula	Peterus. . . . . Peter
Nilletie . . . . Nelly	Orselina . . . . Ursula	Petiens . . . . . . Patience
Nillie . . . . Nelly	Orseltie . . . . Ursula	Petirsche . . . . . Patricia
Nisje. . . . . Agnes	Orthea . . . . Dorothy	Petres . . . . Peter
Nisse. . . . . Agnes	Orthia . . . . Dorothy	Petris. . . . . Peter
Nisse. . . . . Nicholas	Osschil. . . . . Ursula	Petronela . . . . Petronella
Nissi . . . . Agnes	Osseltje . . . . Ursula	Petrus . . . . Peter
Nitsche . . . . . . Nicholas	Otho . . . . Otto	Petschke . . . . Peter
Nitzel . . . . Agnes	Otte. . . . . Otto	Petz. . . . . Bernard
Noach . . . . Noah	Ottel . . . . Otto	Peubie . . . . Phebe
Nol . . . . Arnold	Otti . . . . Otto	Pfie . . . . Sophia
Nolde. . . . . Arnold	Ouke. . . . . Octavius	Pheben. . . . . Phebe
Noldeke. . . . . . . Arnold	Outie. . . . . Agnes	Phebie . . . . Phebe
Noll. . . . . Arnold	Outie . . . . Otilia	Pheebie . . . . Phebe
Nolte . . . . Arnold	Pabel. . . . . Paul	Phelitjah. . . . . . Philetus
Nulde. . . . . Arnold	Pagel. . . . . Paul	Phema . . . . . Euphemia
Nuschi . . . . Ursula	Pakke. . . . . . . Margaret	Phige. . . . . Sophia
Nyngel . . . . Benigna	Parvel . . . . Paul	Philamon . . . . . . Philip
Nys . . . . Dionysius	Paryntie. . . . . . Patience	Phile . . . . . . Philomena
Obadja . . . . . . Obadiah	Patty. . . . . Patricia	Philiph . . . . Philip
Obaje . . . . Obadiah	Patze . . . . Patricia	Philipus. . . . . Philip

Given Name Equivalents: Dutch to English

Phlip . . . . Philip	Ragel . . . . Rachel	Renz . . . . Reinhard
Phoebe . . . . Phebe	Raghel . . . . Rachel	Resel . . . . Rosella
Phya . . . . Sophia	Rahel . . . . Rachel	Resolveert . . . . . Resolved
Pierre . . . . Peter	Ralph . . . . Roelof	Ressardt . . . . Richard
Piet . . . . Peter	Ram . . . . Rembrant	Ressart . . . . Richard
Pieter . . . . Peter	Ranche . . . . Rosina	Ressel . . . . Rosella
Pieternelle . . . Petronella	Randolph . . . . . . Randal	Resserdt . . . . Richard
Pietertje . . . . . . Patricia	Rasana . . . . Rosina	Resula . . . . Rosella
Pietje . . . . . . Petronella	Rase . . . . Erasmus	Resull . . . . Resolved
Pietronella . . . Petronella	Rasi . . . . Erasmus	Resull . . . . Rosella
Pietsch . . . . Peter	Rasmus . . . . Erasmus	Resulla . . . . . . Resolved
Pilten . . . . Hippoletus	Rassmann . . . . . Erasmus	Resulla . . . . Rosella
Pip . . . . Philip	Rebakah . . . . . . Rebecca	Resyntje . . . . Rosina
Pironella . . . . . Petronella	Rebbecca . . . . . Rebecca	Retchen . . . . . . Margaret
Pironelle . . . . . Petronella	Rebecke . . . . . . Rebecca	Reyckje . . . . . . Frederica
Piter . . . . Peter	Rebeckke . . . . . Rebecca	Reyess . . . . Reyer
Pitter . . . . Peter	Reda . . . . Margaret	Reyk . . . . Ulrich
Pleuntje . . . . . . Apollonia	Redel . . . . Margaret	Reynchin . . . . . Reinhard
Ploentje . . . . . . Apollonia	Rees . . . . Andrew	Reynold . . . . . Reinhard
Plone . . . . Apollonia	Rega . . . . Regina	Reysard . . . . Richard
Plonia . . . . Apollonia	Regel . . . . Regina	Reyyer . . . . Reyer
Polly . . . . Mary	Reghel . . . . Rachel	Rhyntje . . . . Rachel
Polte . . . . Hippoletus	Regi . . . . Regina	Ria . . . . Maria
Poltel . . . . . . Hippoletus	Reich . . . . Richard	Rias . . . . Zachariah
Poltus . . . . . . Hippoletus	Reigerl . . . . Regina	Richel . . . . Henry
Poulus . . . . Paul	Reimerick . . . . Rymerick	Richeli . . . . Richard
Pouw . . . . Paul	Reimond . . . . Raymond	Rick . . . . Richard
Pouweles . . . . Paul	Reindel . . . . . . Reinhard	Ricka . . . . Frederica
Pouwelis . . . . Paul	Reindert . . . . . Reinhard	Rickel . . . . Frederica
Powel . . . . Paul	Reineke . . . . . Reinhard	Rickel . . . . Ulrich
Powles . . . . Paul	Reiner . . . . Reinhard	Rickert . . . . Richard
Prada . . . . Prudence	Reinert . . . . . . Reinhard	Rickli . . . . . . Frederica
Prechtl . . . . Rupert	Reinhard . . . . . Reynold	Riecke . . . . Frederica
Preciens . . . . . . Patience	Reini . . . . Reinhard	Riehl . . . . Rudolf
Preyntie . . . . . . Penelope	Reinnaert . . . . Reinhard	Riehle . . . . Rudolf
Preyntje . . . . . . Patience	Reinoud . . . . . Reinhard	Rietje . . . . Maria
Prientje . . . . . . Penelope	Reinsch . . . . . Reinhard	Rietschel . . . . . . Rudolf
Prudy . . . . Prudence	Reintje . . . . . . Reinhard	Rijkaard . . . . Richard
Pryne . . . . Penelope	Reitzle . . . . Henry	Rijkerd . . . . Richard
Pult . . . . Hippoletus	Rem . . . . Rembrant	Rijn . . . . Reyner
Quiryn . . . . Quirinus	Rem . . . . Rems	Rijpert . . . . Rupert
Raagel . . . . Rachel	Renard . . . . . . Reinhard	Rik . . . . Henry
Rabecca . . . . . . Rebecca	Rendel . . . . . . Reinhard	Rika . . . . Frederica
Rabecka . . . . . . Rebecca	Rene . . . . Veronica	Rike . . . . Frederica
Rabeecka . . . . Rebecca	Renke . . . . . Reinhold	Rilke . . . . Rudolf
Radel . . . . Meinrad	Rensie . . . . Rosina	Rining . . . . . . Catherine
Radser . . . . Roger	Rentje . . . . Rosina	Rip . . . . Rupert
Raedjert . . . . Roger	Renz . . . . Lawrence	Risherd . . . . Richard

Given Name Equivalents: Dutch to English

Rissard .... Richard	Rosena .... Rosina	Ruttiger .... Rudiger
Rissardt .... Richard	Rosert .... Richard	Rychard .... Richard
Rissart .... Richard	Rosul .... Rosella	Ryck .... Richard
Risserd .... Richard	Rotger.......... Roger	Ryckje .... Frederica
Risserdt .... Richard	Roudle........ Rudolf	Ryer .... Reyer
Rissert .... Richard	Rozamond ... Rosamond	Ryerse.......... Reyer
Rita .... Margaret	Ruben .... Reuben	Ryerson......... Reyer
Rithsardt ...... Richard	Rubi .... Rupert	Ryetze.......... Henry
Rithzart .... Richard	Ruckel........ Rudiger	Ryjardt........ Richard
Ritsch .... Richard	Rucker .... Roger	Ryk .... Richard
Ritsert .... Richard	Ruclo......... Rudiger	Rykaard .... Richard
Ritsier .... Richard	Rudel.......... Rudolf	Rynberg...... Rymerick
Ritze........... Henry	Rudelft........ Rudolf	Ryndert ...... Reinhard
Rob........... Robert	Rudelo........ Rudolf	Ryntje .... Catherine
Robbardt .... Robert	Rudengerus .... Rudiger	Saal .... Solomon
Robbart........ Robert	Rudi .... Rudolf	Saam.......... Samuel
Robbedt........ Robert	Rudiger......... Roger	Saar .... Sarah
Robben......... Robin	Rudolph....... Rudolf	Saara.......... Sarah
Robberdt .... Robert	Ruef........... Rudolf	Saartie.......... Sarah
Robbert........ Robert	Ruetsch .... Rudolf	Saartje.......... Sarah
Robberthus ..... Robert	Ruf .... Rudolf	Saatje .... Sarah
Robbet......... Robert	Rugger .... Roger	Sabel .... Isabella
Robbin .... Robin	Rugkil .... Rudiger	Sachariah .... Zachariah
Robert......... Rupert	Ruhle.......... Rudolf	Saddie.......... Sarah
Rockel........ Rudiger	Rule........... Rudolf	Saertje.......... Sarah
Roedolf .... Rudolf	Rulef.......... Ralph	Safeiia .... Sophia
Roeland ...... Rowland	Ruliph.......... Ralph	Safeija .... Sophia
Roelof.......... Ralph	Rulke.......... Rudolf	Safya .... Sophia
Roger......... Rudiger	Rulle .... Rudolf	Safytie .... Sophia
Rogier.......... Roger	Rulmann ...... Rudolf	Salemen ...... Solomon
Rogkens....... Rudiger	Rulo .... Rudolf	Sali .... Rosina
Rohle......... Rudiger	Ruodi......... Rudolf	Sali............ Sally
Rohle.......... Rudolf	Ruoff .... Rudolf	Sally .... Sarah
Roille.......... Roelof	Rupel.......... Rupert	Salomon...... Solomon
Rolef .... Roelof	Rupli .... Rupert	Sam .... Samuel
Roleke .... Roelof	Ruplo .... Rupert	Samel .... Samuel
Rolf .... Roelof	Ruppel......... Rupert	Samewel ...... Samuel
Rolfe .... Roelof	Ruppes .... Rupert	Sammel........ Samuel
Rolke.......... Rudolf	Ruprecht ...... Rupert	Sammiel ...... Samuel
Rollekin .... Roelof	Rusje .... Ruth	Sammul ...... Samuel
Rollmann ...... Roelof	Rut .... Roger	Samson ..... Sampson
Rollo .... Roelof	Rutger.......... Roger	Sander ..... Alexander
Rolof .... Roelof	Rutgert .... Roger	Sanna .... Susan
Rolph.......... Roelof	Rutje........... Ruth	Sanne .... Susan
Rombout ..... Rumbold	Rutsen .... Roger	Sanneke .... Susan
Roosje .... Rose	Rutsert........ Richard	Sannertje....... Susan
Roosje .... Rosetta	Rutsjert .... Richard	Sannertje....... Susan
Roppel......... Rupert	Rutt .... Rudolf	Sannetan...... Jonathan

Given Name Equivalents: Dutch to English

Sanni . . . . Susan	Selle . . . . Salome	Sinche. . . . . Cynthia
Santje . . . . Susan	Sem . . . . Samuel	Sippel . . . . Siegbert
Sapheya . . . . Sophia	Seman . . . . Simon	Sitske . . . . Cynthia
Saphia . . . . Sophia	Semion. . . . . Simon	Sitt. . . . . Siegbert
Saphya. . . . . Sophia	Semmuel. . . . . . . Samuel	Sizo . . . . Siegfried
Sara . . . . Sarah	Sens. . . . . Vincentia	Sizzo . . . . Siegbert
Sarah . . . . Sally	Senzel . . . . Vincentia	Sjaeck . . . . Jacques
Sarahette . . . . Sarah	Seppeli . . . . . . Josephine	Sjarel . . . . Charles
Sare . . . . Sarah	Sepperli. . . . . Joseph	Sjoert. . . . . Siegbert
Sarel . . . . Carl	Seppi. . . . . Joseph	Smiaa. . . . . Hezekiah
Sartye . . . . Sarah	Servas . . . . Servis	Soers. . . . . Siegbert
Sasze. . . . . Sarah	Seu . . . . Sarah	Soert . . . . Siegbert
Sate . . . . Sally	Seufert . . . . Siegfried	Soetje . . . . Susan
Saul . . . . Solomon	Sevfya . . . . Sophia	Soff . . . . Sophia
Sautie . . . . Sarah	Sevold. . . . . Siebold	Sofya . . . . Sophia
Schack . . . . Jacob	Seybout . . . . Sybout	Sophya. . . . . Sophia
Schaffried. . . . . . Godfrey	Seytie . . . . Cynthia	Sosar . . . . Susan
Schani . . . . John	Seytie. . . . . Sophia	Sourt . . . . Siegbert
Scheifahrt . . . . . Siegfried	Seytje. . . . . Sophia	Staas . . . . Staats
Schonette . . . . Janet	Shaan . . . . Christian	Staats . . . . Eustace
Schorschel . . . . . George	Shark. . . . . Richard	Stacius . . . . Eustis
Seba . . . . Siegbert	Sherrard . . . . Gerard	Staes . . . . Staats
Sebastian. . . . . . . Bastian	Shuart . . . . Siegbert	Staets . . . . Staats
Sebel . . . . Joseph	Siaque. . . . . Jacob	Stafanus . . . . . . Stephen
Sebert . . . . Siegbert	Siaques . . . . Jacob	Stans . . . . . . Constance
Sebi. . . . . Joseph	Siba . . . . Siebold	Stavanus. . . . . . Stephen
Sebring. . . . . . . Sybrant	Sibe . . . . Siebold	Stebe . . . . Stephen
Seel . . . . Marshal	Sibi. . . . . Siebold	Stebin . . . . Stephen
Seertie. . . . . Sarah	Siebel . . . . Siegbert	Steentje. . . . . . Christina
Seeuw . . . . Sarah	Siefert . . . . Siegbert	Steeven . . . . . . Stephen
Sefa. . . . . Josephine	Siegbert . . . . . . Siebold	Stefanis . . . . . . Stephen
Sefe. . . . . Josephine	Siegbert . . . . . Siegfried	Steffanus . . . . . Stephen
Sefeytie . . . . Sophia	Siegel. . . . . Siegbert	Steffel. . . . . Stephen
Seffi . . . . Josephine	Siegel . . . . Siegmond	Steffen . . . . Stephen
Sefia . . . . Sophia	Sierick. . . . . . . Siegbert	Stefferl . . . . Stephen
Sefie . . . . Sophia	Sierride . . . . Charity	Steffi . . . . Stephen
Sefried . . . . . . Siegfried	Sierrity . . . . Charity	Stella . . . . Estella
Sefytie . . . . Sophia	Sievert. . . . . . Siegmond	Stennes . . . . August
Seibel . . . . Siegbert	Sieze. . . . . Siegfried	Stephanis . . . . . Stephen
Seichen. . . . . . Josephine	Sigelo . . . . . . Siegmond	Stephchin. . . . . Stephen
Seidel . . . . Siegbert	Sigimund. . . . . Siegmond	Stevants . . . . . . Stephen
Seiffert. . . . . . . Siegbert	Sijmen . . . . Simon	Stevanus. . . . . . Stephen
Seintie . . . . Josina	Silja. . . . . Cecilia	Steve . . . . Stephen
Seizz . . . . Siegbert	Silly. . . . . Sylvia	Steven . . . . Stephen
Seletje . . . . Cecilia	Simeon. . . . . Simon	Stevens. . . . . . . Stephen
Selie . . . . Cecilia	Simson . . . . Sampson	Stevin. . . . . Stephen
Selie . . . . Sally	Sina . . . . Josina	Steyne. . . . . . . Christina
Selitje . . . . Cecelia	Sina. . . . . Rosina	Steyntje. . . . . . Christina

Given Name Equivalents: Dutch to English

Sthebe . . . . Stephen	Tammo . . . . . Dankmar	Thieme . . . . Ditmar
Stina. . . . . Christina	Tammus. . . . . . Thomas	Thies. . . . . Matthew
Stine. . . . . Christina	Tamus . . . . Thomas	Thiess . . . . Matthew
Stini . . . . Christina	Tanna. . . . . Anna	Thijsie . . . . Mattina
Stinnes. . . . . August	Tanneken . . . . Anna	Thilde. . . . . Mathilda
Stoffel. . . . . Christopher	Tatie . . . . Charity	Thiloman . . . . . . Dietrich
Stoffer . . . . Christopher	Tatje . . . . Charity	Tholde . . . . Berthold
Stynichen . . . . Christina	Tebes . . . . Matthew	Thom. . . . . Thomas
Styntie . . . . . . Christina	Tebout . . . . Theobald	Thoman . . . . Thomas
Subolt. . . . . Siebold	Tedi. . . . . Theodore	Thomel . . . . Thomas
Suff . . . . Sophia	Teemer . . . . Timothy	Thommes. . . . . . Thomas
Suffia. . . . . Sophia	Teeuw . . . . Matthew	Thoms . . . . Thomas
Suffie. . . . . Sophia	Teeuwis . . . . Matthew	Thomus . . . . Thomas
Suffridus . . . . . Siegfried	Teiwes. . . . . Matthew	Thone . . . . Anthony
Sukey . . . . Susan	Tepelo . . . . Dietrich	Thonges. . . . . . . Anthony
Susana . . . . Susan	Terrothe. . . . . . . Dorothy	Thonis . . . . Anthony
Susane . . . . Susan	Teryntje . . . . . . Catherine	Thons . . . . Anthony
Susanna . . . . Susan	Teunis . . . . Anthony	Thres. . . . . Theresa
Suse . . . . Susan	Teuntje . . . . . . Antoinette	Thuennius . . . . Anthony
Suzana . . . . Susan	Teuntje . . . . Eunice	Thuinnas . . . . . . Anthony
Suze . . . . Susan	Teus . . . . Matthew	Thuintie . . . . . Antoinette
Swaan . . . . Swan	Teves. . . . . Matthew	Thuinus . . . . . . Anthony
Swaen . . . . Swan	Tewis. . . . . Matthew	Thum. . . . . Thomas
Swantie. . . . . . . Swantje	Tews . . . . Matthew	Thune . . . . Anthony
Sweer . . . . Azariah	Thabyita . . . . . . Tabitha	Thungis . . . . . . Anthony
Sybe. . . . . Siegbert	Thabytha . . . . . . Tabitha	Thunies . . . . . . Anthony
Syboud. . . . . Sybout	Thamar . . . . . . Timothy	Thunis . . . . Anthony
Syboudt . . . . Sybout	Thamer . . . . . . Timothy	Thunnas. . . . . . Anthony
Sybouwt . . . . Sybout	Thaniel . . . . . Nathaniel	Thunnis . . . . . . Anthony
Sybrichse . . . . . Siegbert	Thebs . . . . Matthew	Thunnius . . . . . Anthony
Sybuldus . . . . . . Siebold	Thederl . . . . . Theodore	Thunus . . . . . . Anthony
Syczel . . . . Siegfried	Theibs. . . . . . . Matthew	Thuunnis . . . . . Anthony
Syer . . . . Josiah	Theinhart. . . . Degenhard	Thymen . . . . . . Timothy
Sylas . . . . Silas	Theis. . . . . Matthew	Thymon . . . . . . Timothy
Syles . . . . Silas	Theiss . . . . Matthew	Thys . . . . Matthew
Symon . . . . Simon	Thele. . . . . Dietrich	Thysje . . . . Mattina?
Syntje . . . . Cynthia	Theodo . . . . Dietrich	Tiebald. . . . . . . Theobald
Sytje . . . . Sophia	Theodorus. . . . Theodore	Tiebes . . . . Matthew
Taatje . . . . Charity	Theresa . . . . Tracy	Tiebout . . . . . . Theobald
Tacy. . . . . Anastasia	Thetje . . . . Theodore	Tieleman . . . . . . Dietrich
Tades . . . . Thaddius	Theums . . . . . . Anthony	Tienes . . . . Martin
Taisso. . . . . Christian	Theunis . . . . . . Anthony	Tientje . . . . . . Albertina
Taitje. . . . . Charity	Theuntje . . . . . . Eunice	Tietje . . . . Letitia
Taleke. . . . . . . Adelheid	Thewes . . . . . . Matthew	Tietye . . . . Letitia
Tam . . . . Thomas	Theynert . . . . Degenhard	Tigenhardus. . Degenhard
Tamacha. . . . . . . Phebe	Thiede. . . . . . . Dietrich	Tiges . . . . Matthew
Tammaes . . . . . Thomas	Thiele . . . . Dietrich	Tigges . . . . Matthew
Tammes . . . . . . Thomas	Thielmann . . . . Dietrich	Tijmen . . . . Timothy

Given Name Equivalents: Dutch to English

Tijs	Matthew	Tracy	Theresa	Uhlig	Ulrich
Tijte	Titus	Tradchen	Gertrude	Ule	Ulrich
Tildchen	Mathilda	Traudel	Gertrude	Ulin	Ulrich
Tileman	Dietrich	Treasje	Theresa	Ulli	Ulrich
Tiletje	Albertina	Treinel	Catherine	Ulritz	Ulrich
Tiletje	Letitia	Treintie	Catherine	Ultschi	Ulrich
Till	Mathilda	Tressje	Theresa	Umphrey	Humphrey
Tilla	Mathilda	Trienchen	Catherine	Urech	Ulrich
Tillmann	Dietrich	Trientie	Catherine	Uriah	George
Tilly	Letitia	Trijn	Catherine	Urle	Ulrich
Tilly	Ottilia	Trina	Catherine	Ursel	Ursula
Timme	Ditmar	Trineli	Catherine	Urseltje	Ursula
Timotius	Timothy	Trudel	Gertrude	Ursi	Ursula
Tina	Albertina	Trudi	Gertrude	Ury	George
Tina	Martina	Trudy	Gertrude	Ury	Uriah
Tine	Albertina	Trui	Gertrude	Urzili	Ursula
Tiney	Martina	Truitje	Gertrude	Utz	Ulrich
Tippel	Dietrich	Truytje	Gertrude	Uz	Ulrich
Tisje	Letitia	Tryntie	Catherine	Vaaz	Servatius
Tit	Letitia	Tryntje	Catherine	Vacius	Servatius
Titje	Letitia	Tsassen	Christian	Vaes	Servatius
Titzel	Dietrich	Tuenes	Anthony	Valentijn	Valentine
Tjaatie	Charity	Tunes	Anthony	Valentyn	Valentine
Tjaatje	Charity	Tunie	Antoinette	Valtin	Valentine
Tjadtje	Charity	Tunis	Anthony	Vaupel	Volpert
Tjerck	George	Tunis	Dennis	Vefe	Geneva
Tjerck	Theodore	Tunnes	Antoinette	Velten	Valentine
Tobeas	Tobias	Turet	Dorothy	Veltin	Valentine
Tobyas	Tobias	Turi	Arthur	Veltje	Valentine
Toff	Christopher	Tyatje	Charity	Veupe	Volpert
Toffels	Christopher	Tyle	Ottilia	Veva	Geneva
Tolde	Berthold	Tymen	Timothy	Vevele	Geneva
Tomas	Thomas	Tymon	Timothy	Vevi	Geneva
Tomatius	Timothy	Tyne	Martina	Vibbardt	Vibbard
Tomes	Thomas	Tys	Matthew	Vige	Victoria
Tommes	Thomas	Tysje	Mattina	Vike	Victoria
Toms	Thomas	Tytje	Letitia	Viki	Victoria
Tomus	Thomas	Tytzil	Dietrich	Vikli	Victoria
Tone	Anthony	Tzyna	Kunigunda	Viny	Lavina
Tonges	Anthony	Uarritie	Maria	Vits	Vitus
Tonies	Anthony	Uda	Ute	Vlypse	Philip
Tonis	Anthony	Udo	Otto	Vockel	Volpert
Tonjes	Anthony	Udo	Ulrich	Volkers	Volkert
Tonke	Anthony	Ueli	Ulrich	Volzo	Volpert
Tonnes	Anthony	Uelk	Ulrich	Vopel	Volpert
Tonnies	Anthony	Uerich	Ulrich	Voypel	Volpert
Toon	Anthony	Uetz	Ulrich	Vredrick	Frederick
Toontje	Antoinette	Uhl	Ulrich	Vrein	Veronica

Given Name Equivalents: Dutch to English

Vrenele....... Veronica	Wenzel .... Werner	Wilma...... Wilhelmina
Vroa......... Veronica	Wenzo......... Werner	Wilt .... William
Vrona .... Veronica	Wernz......... Werner	Wiltz.......... William
Vroutie .... Sophia	Wessel .... Werner	Wilyum........ William
Vroutjie .... Sophia	Wetti .... Barbara	Wim........... William
Vrouwete ...... Sophia	Wetzel......... Werner	Wimpje..... Wilhelmina
Vyntje.......... Lavina	Wetzile .... Werner	Wina .... Sabina
Wabe......... Barbara	Weybrug...... Wybrecht	Winand....... Wynant
Wali............ Wally	Weynt .... Lavinia	Winans .... Wynant
Walich .... Wallace	Weyntje .... Lavinia	Winant .... Wynant
Walig .... Wallace	Wiart.......... Wygert	Winlin......... Wynant
Walleran .... Walran	Wiberich ..... Wybrecht	Winne .... Lavinia
Wally......... Walburg	Wibrant........ Wynant	Winsan .... Vincent
Walpel.......... Wally	Wibregh...... Wybrecht	Wintie .... Lavinia
Walpert........ Volpert	Wickel........ Ludwich	Wintye .... Lavinia
Walpodo....... Volpert	Wickes ...... Ludwich	Wipo .... Wipert
Walpracht ..... Volpert	Wiczel .... Wygand	Witzel .... Werner
Walra .... Walran	Widsel .... Werner	Wobbe........ Walburg
Walrandt ...... Walran	Wier .... Edward?	Wold .... Walter
Walraven ...... Walran	Wiert......... Edward?	Wolefert ...... Wolfert
Walt .... Oswald	Wiert.......... Wygert	Wolfard........ Wolfert
Walti .... Walter	Wigel .... Hedwich	Wolfardt .... Wolfert
Wander........ Wendel	Wigelo .... Wygand	Wolfart .... Wolfert
Warnaerts ..... Werner	Wiggel........ Ludwich	Wolffert........ Wolfert
Warner........ Werner	Wilemeintie.. Wilhelmina	Wolgmarus .... Volkmar
Wassel......... Wessel	Wilhelmentie. Wilhelmina	Wollefard ..... Wolfert
Wastel......... Bastian	Wilhelmina .... Minnie	Wollefart...... Wolfert
Wat .... Walter	Wilhelmius .... William	Wolpertus ..... Volpert
Watschel .... Bastian	Wilhelmus .... William	Wolprath....... Volpert
Watzold....... Werner	Wilielmus ..... William	Wolt .... Oswald
Weart.......... Wygert	Wilke .... William	Wolter .... Walter
Wecelinus ..... Werner	Wilko .... William	Woltje .... Walter
Weczelo .... Werner	Wille.......... William	Wolvert........ Wolfert
Weillem ...... William	Willekin .... William	Wout .... Walter
Weillemeintie Wilhelmina	Willem .... William	Wouter......... Walter
Weintie .... Lavinia	Willemfye ... Wilhelmina	Wouters .... Walter
Weintie....... Winafred	Willemintie .. Wilhelmina	Wubgen....... Walburg
Weiske .... Agnes	Willemintje .. Wilhelmina	Wulprat........ Volpert
Weldechen ..... Oswald	Willempie ... Wilhelmina	Wybracht ..... Wybrecht
Welemeintie . Wilhelmina	Willempje ... Wilhelmina	Wybrant ...... Wynant
Wellem........ William	Willemtje.... Wilhelmina	Wybren .... Wynant
Wellimyntie.. Wilhelmina	Willemyn.... Wilhelmina	Wybrug ...... Wybrecht
Welter .... Walter	Willemyntie.. Wilhelmina	Wydt........... Wyatt?
Welti .... Walter	Williem........ William	Wyentie .... Lavinia
Wenckel ...... Werner	Willim .... William	Wygbrant....... Wynant
Wencz......... Werner	Willium .... William	Wygel .... Wygand
Wenkelo ...... Werner	Willum .... William	Wyllem........ William
Wensan........ Vincent	Wilm .... William	Wynand....... Wynant

Given Name Equivalents: Dutch to English

Wynefrid...... Winafred	Zanneke .... Susan	Zybout .... Sybout
Wyntie......... Lavinia	Zannetan ..... Jonathan	Zyfie .... Sophia
Wyntje......... Lavinia	Zara .... Sarah	Zyfitie .... Sophia
Wyntje .... Winafred	Zarel .... Carl	Zyne .... Kunigunda
Wyntye........ Lavinia	Zarels .... Carl	Zytie .... Sophia
Wyt........... Wyatt?	Zefeytie .... Sophia	Zytken .... Sophia
Xander ...... Alexander	Zefya .... Sophia	
Xandi .... Alexander	Zeger.......... Seger	
Yacob .... Jacob	Zeia .... Lucy	
Yacus .... Jacob	Zeieli .... Lucy	
Yan............. John	Zeigen.......... Lucy	
Yannetan...... Jonathan	Zeims .... James	
Yannittie........ Janet	Zeje .... Lucy	
Yawn .... Adrian	Zena .... Rosina	
Ydje .... Ida	Zenta .... Vincentia	
Ydtje............. Ida	Zenzel ...... Vincentia	
Yellis .... Giles	Zenzi .... Vincentia	
Yke............ Agnes	Zephronia ...... Sophia	
Ymecha .... Emma	Zerves .... Servatius	
Yoidin.......... Judah	Zetze.......... Cecelia	
Yokum .... Jochem	Zeytie.......... Sophia	
Yoost.......... Joseph	Zharel .... Carl	
Yope .... Joseph	Ziele .... Cecelia	
Yoris .... George	Zielietie .... Cecilia	
Yoseph........ Joseph	Zigi............. Lucy	
Yost........... Joseph	Zilge .... Cecelia	
Yrasmuz .... Erastus	Zilie .... Lucy	
Yria.............. Ira	Zilla .... Cecelia	
Yria........... Uriah	Zillchen........ Cecelia	
Yrietje .... Margaret	Zilli........... Cecelia	
Ysaak.......... Isaac	Zirves .... Servatius	
Ysac........... Isaac	Ziska.......... Francis	
Ysack.......... Isaac	Ziskus......... Francis	
Ysaeck .... Isaac	Ziss........... Francis	
Ysaque.......... Isaac	Zissi .... Francis	
Ythel............. Ida	Zita .... Theresa	
Ytie.............. Ida	Zjarritjen....... Charity	
Ytje.............. Ida	Zoch........ Zachariah	
Yurie.......... George	Zophya .... Sophia	
Yurie.......... Uriah	Zosel.......... Susan	
Zaarel .... Carl	Zuff........... Sophia	
Zacariah ..... Zachariah	Zus............ Susan	
Zach........ Zachariah	Zusana .... Susan	
Zacharias .... Zachariah	Zusanna .... Susan	
Zachary..... Zachariah	Zusel.......... Susan	
Zacherl..... Zachariah	Zusi .... Susan	
Zandaer ..... Alexander	Zutz .... Susan	
Zander ...... Alexander	Zwantje .... Swantje	

Table 2B
Given Name Equivalents: English to Dutch

Aaron . . . . Aarend	Adam . . . . Dahm	Adelheid . . . . . . Oletgen
Aaron. . . . . Aarie	Adam . . . . Odel	Adelheid. . . . . . . Taleke
Aaron . . . . Aary	Adam. . . . . Odeli	Adelia . . . . Adela
Aaron. . . . . Adrian	Adelaide. . . . . Adelheyd	Adelia . . . . Delia
Aaron . . . . Arend	Adelaide. . . . . Alida	Adeline. . . . . Adaleentje
Aaron. . . . . . : . . . Arendt	Adelaide . . . . Alyd	Adeline. . . . . Adda
Aaron . . . . Arent	Adelbert . . . . Aebi	Adeline . . . . Let
Aaron. . . . . Ariaan	Adelbert . . . . Apitz	Adeline . . . . Letje
Aaron . . . . Arie	Adelbert. . . . . Bert	Adolf . . . . Ada
Aaron. . . . . Aris	Adelbert . . . . Bertes	Adolf . . . . Ade
Aaron . . . . Aron	Adelbert . . . . . Brechtel	Adolf. . . . . Adel
Aaron . . . . Ary	Adelbert. . . . . Dell	Adolf . . . . Adela
Aaron. . . . . Aryje	Adelbert . . . . Opitz	Adolf. . . . . Adi
Aaron . . . . Aurie	Adelheid. . . . . Ada	Adolf. . . . . Adje
Abel . . . . Ebel	Adelheid . . . . Adele	Adolf . . . . Ado
Abigail . . . . Abegail	Adelheid. . . . . Aile	Adolf. . . . . Adolff
Abigail . . . . Abiegeil	Adelheid. . . . . Ailke	Adolf. . . . . Adolfus
Abigail . . . . Abiegel	Adelheid . . . . Aleke	Adolf . . . . Adolphus
Abigail . . . . Abiegiel	Adelheid. . . . . Alida	Adolf . . . . Ailff
Abigail . . . . Abigel	Adelheid . . . . Altgen	Adolf . . . . Alef
Abigail . . . . Ebbe	Adelheid . . . . . . Auleide	Adolf . . . . Alf
Abigail . . . . Ebbegal	Adelheid . . . . Ayl	Adolf . . . . Alof
Abigail . . . . Ebbegel	Adelheid . . . . Deel	Adolf . . . . Alyf
Abigail . . . . Ebbegil	Adelheid . . . . Dela	Adolf . . . . Dolf
Abigail. . . . . Ebbertje	Adelheid . . . . Dele	Adolf . . . . Dolfus
Abigail . . . . Ebegel	Adelheid . . . . Ehl	Adolf. . . . . Lof
Abigail . . . . Ebiegel	Adelheid. . . . . Eile	Adrian. . . . . . Aadriannus
Abigail . . . . Egberth	Adelheid . . . . Eilika	Adrian. . . . . . . Aadrianus
Abigail. . . . . . . Egbertje	Adelheid . . . . Ela	Adrian. . . . . . . Aderjanus
Abigail. . . . . . . Eghertje	Adelheid. . . . . . Elchgen	Adrian . . . . Adreaen
Abigail . . . . Gail	Adelheid. . . . . . . Eleyde	Adrian. . . . . . . Adreannis
Abigail . . . . Heppy	Adelheid. . . . . Elgin	Adrian . . . . . . Adreyanes
Abigail. . . . . Ijbitje	Adelheid. . . . . . . Elheid	Adrian . . . . . . Adriaantje
Abraham. . . . . . Aberaam	Adelheid. . . . . Elia	Adrian . . . . Adrianis
Abraham . . . . . . Aberam	Adelheid . . . . Elke	Adrian . . . . Adrians
Abraham . . . . . . Abraam	Adelheid . . . . Elle	Adrian . . . . Adrianus
Abraham . . . . Abram	Adelheid . . . . . . Eylheit	Adrian. . . . . . Adrieannus
Abraham . . . . Aebi	Adelheid. . . . . Halheyde	Adrian . . . . Adriieyaanis
Abraham . . . . Bram	Adelheid . . . . Hel	Adrian . . . . Adriyanis
Abraham . . . . Brom	Adelheid. . . . . . Helchin	Adrian . . . . . . Adriyannis
Absalom . . . . . . Absulom	Adelheid . . . . . Heleche	Adrian . . . . Adryianis
Adam . . . . Ade	Adelheid . . . . . Helecke	Adrian . . . . Ariaan
Adam . . . . Adeli	Adelheid . . . . . Heyliche	Adrian . . . . Ariaen
Adam . . . . Daam	Adelheid . . . . Lidda	Adrian . . . . Ariannus
Adam . . . . Daem	Adelheid . . . . Liddy	Adrian . . . . Arians

Given Name Equivalents: English to Dutch

Adrian . . . . Ariantje	Agatha . . . . Eegfe	Agnes . . . . Nies
Adrian . . . . Arianus	Agatha . . . . Eget	Agnes . . . . Niese
Adrian . . . . Arien	Agatha . . . . Egje	Agnes . . . . Niesen
Adrian . . . . . . Aryaennis	Agatha . . . . Egle	Agnes . . . . Niesje
Adrian . . . . Aryannis	Agatha . . . . Exgye	Agnes . . . . Niesse
Adrian . . . . Ate	Agatha . . . . Gate	Agnes . . . . Niessje
Adrian . . . . Aute	Agatha . . . . Hagha	Agnes . . . . Niesye
Adrian . . . . Janus	Agatha . . . . Haiquiez	Agnes . . . . Nisje
Adrian . . . . Yawn	Agatha . . . . Ikee	Agnes . . . . Nisse
Adriana . . . . . . Adriaantje	Agidius . . . . Egid	Agnes . . . . Nissi
Adriana . . . . Adriaen	Agidius . . . . Egiz	Agnes . . . . Nitzel
Adriana . . . . Adriann	Agidius . . . . Gide	Agnes . . . . Oetie
Adriana . . . . Ariaantie	Agidius . . . . Gidi	Agnes . . . . Oetje
Adriana . . . . . . Arianntje	Agidius . . . . Gieles	Agnes . . . . Oeycke
Adriana . . . . Ariantje	Agidius . . . . Gils	Agnes . . . . Outie
Adriana . . . . . . Arriaantje	Agidius . . . . Gilles	Agnes . . . . Weiske
Adrienne . . . . . . Adriance	Agidius . . . . . . Gillmann	Agnes . . . . Yke
Aegeus . . . . Achijas	Agidius . . . . Gilly	Agricola . . . . Grickel
Aegeus . . . . . . Aegidius	Agidius . . . . Gillo	Albert . . . . Abertus
Aegeus . . . . Agidius	Agidius . . . . Jid	Albert . . . . Al
Aegeus . . . . . . Haggans	Agnes . . . . . . Aenenietje	Albert . . . . Alabartus
Aegeus . . . . . . Haggaus	Agnes . . . . . Aengenietye	Albert . . . . Albardt
Aegeus . . . . . . Haggeus	Agnes . . . . Agatha	Albert . . . . Albart
Aesop . . . . Esopus	Agnes . . . . . . Aggenetye	Albert . . . . Albartus
Agatha . . . . Aaghie	Agnes . . . . Agneiteta	Albert . . . . Alberic
Agatha . . . . Aaghje	Agnes . . . . Agniet	Albert . . . . Albrecht
Agatha . . . . Aagie	Agnes . . . . Agnietie	Albert . . . . . . Alebartus
Agatha . . . . Aagje	Agnes . . . . Agnietje	Albert . . . . Apel
Agatha . . . . Aagjen	Agnes . . . . Agnita	Albert . . . . Appel
Agatha . . . . Aagt	Agnes . . . . Agnitje	Albert . . . . Bert
Agatha . . . . Achye	Agnes . . . . . . Anenietje	Albert . . . . Bertus
Agatha . . . . Aeche	Agnes . . . . Anesli	Albert . . . . Burtis
Agatha . . . . Aechtje	Agnes . . . . . . Angenitie	Albert . . . . Eibart
Agatha . . . . Aegt	Agnes . . . . Anghe	Albert . . . . Eibel
Agatha . . . . Aget	Agnes . . . . . Angonietje	Albert . . . . Elbardt
Agatha . . . . Agetli	Agnes . . . . Eike	Albert . . . . Elbert
Agatha . . . . Aggie	Agnes . . . . Nafje	Albert . . . . Elbrat
Agatha . . . . Agi	Agnes . . . . Neesie	Albert . . . . . . Elbrecht
Agatha . . . . Agie	Agnes . . . . . . Neesken	Albert . . . . Elwert
Agatha . . . . Agite	Agnes . . . . Neisa	Albert . . . . Eubel
Agatha . . . . Agje	Agnes . . . . Nesa	Albert . . . . Happel
Agatha . . . . Agnes	Agnes . . . . Nesi	Albert? . . . . Aldert
Agatha . . . . Agt	Agnes . . . . Nese	Albertina . . . . . . Abelke
Agatha . . . . Agti	Agnes . . . . Neselin	Albertina . . . . . Christina
Agatha . . . . Agye	Agnes . . . . Nete	Albertina . . . . . . Dinah
Agatha . . . . Eagie	Agnes . . . . Netta	Albertina . . . . Hetje
Agatha . . . . Echtje	Agnes . . . . Neysa	Albertina . . . . . Tientje
Agatha . . . . . . Eechtje	Agnes . . . . Niefje	Albertina . . . . . Tiletje

Given Name Equivalents: English to Dutch

Albertina	Tina
Albertina	Tine
Aldert	Allert
Aldert	Eldert
Aldert	Eldred
Alexander	Alexzander
Alexander	Alzander
Alexander	Elle
Alexander	Lexel
Alexander	Sander
Alexander	Xander
Alexander	Xandi
Alexander	Zandaer
Alexander	Zander
Alfred	Al
Alfred	Alf
Alfred	Fred
Alice	Alida
Alida	Aal
Alida	Aalte
Alida	Aaltje
Alida	Adelheid
Alida	Aeltie
Alida	Aeltje
Alida	Alta
Alida	Altie
Alida	Altje
Alida	Daatje
Alida	Elida
Alida	Eltie
Alida	Eltje
Alida	Illetie
Alida	Keltie
Alida	Oledo
Alphonse	Fons
Alphonse	Fonse
Alsie	Els
Althea	Alethea
Alvin	Alewijn
Alvin	Alva
Aman	Ammon
Ambrose	Brasch
Ambrose	Brose
Ambrose	Broseck
Ambrose	Brosius
Ambrose	Brossken
Ambrose	Brus
Amelia	Amy
Amelia	Mella
Amon	Eamon
Amon	Emmen
Amos	Amas
Amos	Eemus
Amos	Emus
Amy	Ami
Anastasia	Tacy
Anastasius	Anstadt
Andrew	Aender
Andrew	Ainers
Andrew	Ander
Andrew	Andres
Andrew	Andries
Andrew	Andris
Andrew	Dese
Andrew	Drebes
Andrew	Drees
Andrew	Dreis
Andrew	Dresel
Andrew	Dreus
Andrew	Drew
Andrew	Dries
Andrew	Driess
Andrew	Enderle
Andrew	Enders
Andrew	Endres
Andrew	Endris
Andrew	Endro
Andrew	Endru
Andrew	Rees
Angel	Engel
Angelica	Angie
Angelica	Anglica
Angelica	Engelt
Angelica	Engeltie
Angelica	Engeltje
Angelica	Engentie
Angelica	Engletie
Anna	Aaentle
Anna	Aanken
Anna	Aant
Anna	Aantie
Anna	Aantje
Anna	Aentie
Anna	Anatie
Anna	Anatye
Anna	Anke
Anna	Anken
Anna	Annaatje
Anna	Annaka
Anna	Annake
Anna	Annatie
Anna	Annatje
Anna	Annatye
Anna	Annechet
Anna	Anneckie
Anna	Anneke
Anna	Annesen
Anna	Anni
Anna	Annie
Anna	Anning
Anna	Annitje
Anna	Annitye
Anna	Antie
Anna	Antje
Anna	En
Anna	Ena
Anna	Enni
Anna	Enny
Anna	Eyntie
Anna	Eyntje
Anna	Gelante
Anna	Hannah
Anna	Naatje
Anna	Nan
Anna	Nancy
Anna	Nandel
Anna	Nanne
Anna	Nanni
Anna	Nantje
Anna	Tanna
Anna	Tanneken
Annesen	Ankje
Ansel	Henselm
Anthony	Aantonny
Anthony	Anthoni
Anthony	Antine
Anthony	Antoine
Anthony	Antoni
Anthony	Antonius
Anthony	Antony
Anthony	Antusch
Anthony	Antys
Anthony	Dange
Anthony	Donge

Anthony . . . . Dongis	Arabella . . . . Bell	August . . . . Gustetl
Anthony . . . . Dongus	Arabella . . . . Isabella	August . . . . Jusken
Anthony . . . . . . Donich	Archibald . . . . . . Baltus	August . . . . Stennes
Anthony . . . . . . Donigiss	Ariel . . . . Aerriel	August . . . . Stinnes
Anthony . . . . Donjes	Arnold . . . . Anno	August? . . . . Gose
Anthony . . . . . . Entenie	Arnold . . . . Arnaud	Augusta . . . . Geesje
Anthony . . . . . . Teunis	Arnold . . . . Arnke	Augusta? . . . . . . Goosen
Anthony . . . . . . Theums	Arnold . . . . Arnout	Azariah . . . . . Ahasuerus
Anthony . . . . . . Theunis	Arnold . . . . Arnt	Azariah . . . . . . Asseurus
Anthony . . . . Thone	Arnold . . . . . . Arnulfus	Azariah . . . . . . Assuerus
Anthony . . . . . . Thonges	Arnold . . . . Erne	Azariah . . . . . . Hasueras
Anthony . . . . . . Thonis	Arnold . . . . Erny	Azariah . . . . Sweer
Anthony . . . . . . Thons	Arnold . . . . Nol	Baldwin . . . . Baleke
Anthony . . . . Thuennius	Arnold . . . . Nolde	Baldwin . . . . Balko
Anthony . . . . . Thuinnas	Arnold . . . . . . Noldeke	Baldwin . . . . . Boldwijn
Anthony . . . . . . Thuinus	Arnold . . . . Noll	Baldwin . . . . . . Boldwyn
Anthony . . . . Thune	Arnold . . . . Nolte	Baldwin . . . . Bolte
Anthony . . . . . . Thungis	Arnold . . . . Nulde	Baldwin . . . . Boudewyn
Anthony . . . . . . Thunies	Arnold . . . . Onno	Baldwin . . . . Boudje
Anthony . . . . . . Thunis	Artelia? . . . . Aartje	Baldwin? . . . . Boele
Anthony . . . . . Thunnas	Artelia? . . . . Aertje	Baltus . . . . Baldus
Anthony . . . . . . Thunnis	Arthur . . . . Aalt	Baltus . . . . Balzer
Anthony . . . . Thunnius	Arthur . . . . Aart	Baltus . . . . Balles
Anthony . . . . . . Thunus	Arthur . . . . Adur	Baltus . . . . Balster
Anthony . . . . Thuunnis	Arthur . . . . Adurli	Baltus . . . . Balt
Anthony . . . . Tone	Arthur . . . . Aert	Baltus . . . . . . Balthazar
Anthony . . . . Tonges	Arthur . . . . After	Baltus . . . . Balthus
Anthony . . . . Tonies	Arthur . . . . Art	Baltus . . . . Balz
Anthony . . . . Tonis	Arthur . . . . Durli	Baltus . . . . Hausel
Anthony . . . . Tonjes	Arthur . . . . Turi	Baltus . . . . Hauser
Anthony . . . . Tonke	Artina? . . . . Aartje	Baptist . . . . Bapper
Anthony . . . . . . Tonnes	Artina? . . . . Aertje	Baptist . . . . Battist
Anthony . . . . . . Tonnies	Asel . . . . Asael	Baptist . . . . Bischle
Anthony . . . . Toon	Asenath . . . . Asa	Baptist . . . . Bopp
Anthony . . . . Tuenes	Audrey . . . . Ethelred	Barbara . . . . Baartje
Anthony . . . . Tunes	Audrey . . . . . . Ethilrede	Barbara . . . . Bab
Anthony . . . . Tunis	August . . . . . . Agestinus	Barbara . . . . Babe
Antoinette . . . . . Teuntje	August . . . . Agustes	Barbara . . . . Badje
Antoinette . . . . Thuintie	August . . . . Agustus	Barbara . . . . Bapp
Antoinette . . . . . Toontje	August . . . . . . Augustus	Barbara . . . . . Barbartie
Antoinette . . . . . . Tunie	August . . . . Augst	Barbara . . . . Barber
Antoinette . . . . . Tunnes	August . . . . Aukes	Barbara . . . . . . Barbera
Apollonia . . . . Apolonia	August . . . . Aust	Barbara . . . . Baretje
Apollonia . . . . . Leuntje	August . . . . Austen	Barbara . . . . Bartje
Apollonia . . . . . Pleuntje	August . . . . Gosen	Barbara . . . . Berbe
Apollonia . . . . . Ploentje	August . . . . Gosta	Barbara . . . . Wabe
Apollonia . . . . . . Plone	August . . . . Gust	Barbara . . . . Wetti
Apollonia . . . . . . Plonia	August . . . . Gustaaf	Barent . . . . Barendt

Given Name Equivalents: English to Dutch

Barent . . . . Barint	Bathilda . . . . Batje	Bertha . . . . Beata
Barent . . . . Barrend	Bathilda . . . . Betje	Bertha . . . . Bechte
Bartel . . . . Barthel	Bathsheba . . . . Bersheba	Bertha . . . . Behrda
Barent . . . . Berrent	Beatrice . . . . . Badeloch	Bertha . . . . Berteli
Bartholf . . . . . . Bardolph	Beatrice . . . . Beatrix	Bertha . . . . Bertke
Bartholf . . . . Bertolf	Benedict . . . . Bendix	Bertha . . . . Birthe
Bartholomew . . . . . Bart	Benedict . . . . Bene	Bertha . . . . . . Elizabeth
Bartholomew . Bartelmus	Benedict . . . . Beneke	Berthold . . . . Becht
Bartholomew . . . . . Baretl	Benedict . . . . Bentz	Berthold . . . . . Bechtgin
Bartholomew . . . Bartol	Benedict . . . . Bernhard	Berthold . . . . Berlt
Bartholomew . . . . . . Bat	Benedict . . . . Diktus	Berthold . . . . Bert
Bartholomew . . . . . . Batt	Benedict . . . . Dix	Berthold . . . . Bertho
Bartholomew . . . Berthe	Benedicta . . . . Dixie	Berthold . . . . Bertsch
Bartholomew . . . . Berthel	Benigna . . . . Nyngel	Berthold . . . . Berzo
Bartholomew . . . . . Maas	Benjamin . . . . Ben	Berthold . . . . Betsch
Bartholomew . . . . . Maes	Benjamin . . . Benieman	Berthold . . . . Betto
Bartholomew . . . . . Mais	Benjamin . . . Beniemen	Berthold . . . . Dolde
Bartholomew . . . Mappus	Benjamin . . . Benjaman	Berthold . . . . Doll
Bartholomew· . . . . . Mass	Benjamin . . . Benjamen	Berthold . . . . Dulde
Bartholomew . . . . . Maue	Benjamin . . . . Benje	Berthold . . . . Tholde
Bartholomew . . . . . Maus	Benjamin . . . Benjemen	Berthold . . . . Tolde
Bartholomew . . . . . Mawe	Benjamin . . . . . . Benny	Beverly . . . . Bevelia
Bartholomew . . . . . Mebs	Benjamin . . . Benyamen	Birdella . . . . Birdie
Bartholomew . . . Mebess	Bernadine . . . . . Barentje	Blanche . . . . Blanca
Bartholomew . . . . . Mees	Bernadine . . . . . . Beertje	Blandina . . . . Diena
Bartholomew . . . Meewes	Bernadine . . . . . Beretje	Blandina . . . . Dina
Bartholomew . . . . . . Mes	Bernadine . . . . . Dientje	Blasius . . . . Blass
Bartholomew . . . . Meus	Bernadine . . . . Dina	Blasius . . . . Blesse
Bartholomew . . . Mewes	Bernard . . . . Barent	Boele . . . . Bolo
Bartholomew . . . Mewis	Bernard . . . . Barnardus	Boele . . . . Bool
Bartholomew . . . . . Mews	Bernard . . . . Behne	Boniface . . . . . . Bonifaas
Bartholomew . . . Mewus	Bernard . . . . . Benedict	Bridget . . . . Birdie
Bartholomew . . . Mobius	Bernard . . . . Benz	Bridget . . . . Brachie
Bastian . . . . Bas	Bernard . . . . Berno	Bridget . . . . Brechie
Bastian . . . . Basche	Bernard . . . . Bernt	Bridget . . . . Brecthje
Bastian . . . . Baschele	Bernard . . . . Betz	Bridget . . . . Bregge
Bastian . . . . Bastaan	Bernard . . . . Hades	Bridget . . . . Breggie
Bastian . . . . Baste	Bernard . . . . . .· . . Hard	Bridget . . . . Breghie
Bastian . . . . Bastel	Bernard . . . . Hart	Bridget . . . . Breghje
Bastian . . . . Bastiaan	Bernard . . . . Nardes	Bridget . . . . Breghye
Bastian . . . . Bastiaen	Bernard . . . . Petz	Bridget . . . . Bregije
Bastian . . . . Bastle	Bertha . . . . . . Baachie	Bridget . . . . Bregje
Bastian . . . . Bestgen	Bertha . . . . Baata	Bridget . . . . Bregtie
Bastian . . . . Bestian	Bertha . . . . Barbara	Bridget . . . . Bregye
Bastian . . . . . . Sebastian	Bertha . . . . Barte	Bridget . . . . Breidte
Bastian . . . . Wastel	Bertha . . . . Bartje	Bridget . . . . Bridlin
Bastian . . . . . . Watschel	Bertha . . . . Bata	Bridget . . . . Briell
Bathilda . . . . Batie	Bertha . . . . Batha	Bridget . . . . Briette

Given Name Equivalents: English to Dutch

Bridget . . . . Brigael	Caroline . . . . . Cathlyntje	Catherine . . . . Katri
Bridget . . . . Brigitta	Caroline. . . . . . . Catlintie	Catherine . . . . Katterl
Bridget. . . . . Gita	Caroline . . . . . . Catlyntje	Catherine . . . . Katter
Brunhilda . . . . Bruna	Caroline . . . . . . Charlina	Catherine. . . . . Katti
Bryan? . . . . Bryn	Caroline . . . . Kareltje	Catherine . . . . Katrijn
Bryan? . . . . Brynse	Caroline . . . . . . Karolina	Catherine . . . . . Katryntje
Burger. . . . . Borger	Caroline. . . . . Lientje	Catherine . . . . . . Kederin
Burger . . . . . . Bourgoon	Caspar . . . . Caspares	Catherine . . . . . . Ketterle
Burger . . . . Burgun	Caspar. . . . . Casparis	Catherine. . . . . . Ketterlin
Burkhard . . . . Birkle	Caspar . . . . Casparus	Catherine. . . . . Kitty
Burkhard . . . . Bork	Caspar. . . . . Casper	Catherine . . . . . Kreingen
Burkhard . . . . Boso	Caspar. . . . . Gaspard	Catherine. . . . . Krin
Burkhard . . . . Bosse	Caspar . . . . Jasper	Catherine . . . . Krynchgin
Burkhard . . . . . . Bucko	Caspar . . . . Kas	Catherine . . . . Rining
Burkhard . . . . . . Burge	Caspar . . . . Kasper	Catherine . . . . Ryntje
Burkhard . . . . Burki	Catherine . . . . Caatje	Catherine . . . . . . Teryntje
Burkhard . . . . Bury	Catherine. . . . . . Caetrina	Catherine. . . . . . . Treinel
Burkhard . . . . . . Busse	Catherine . . . . . Caharina	Catherine . . . . . . Treintie
Burkhard . . . . Butz	Catherine . . . . . Catarina	Catherine . . . . Trienchen
Burkhard? . . . . . . Burger	Catherine . . . . . Cateryne	Catherine . . . . . . Trientie
Caleb. . . . . Calep	Catherine . . . . Catharena	Catherine . . . . Trijn
Caleb . . . . Calip	Catherine. . . . . . Catharia	Catherine . . . . Trina
Caleb . . . . Cellep	Catherine . . . . Cathariena	Catherine . . . . Trineli
Calvin. . . . . Calvijn	Catherine. . . . . Catharina	Catherine . . . . . . Tryntie
Carl . . . . Carel	Catherine . . . . . Catharyn	Catherine . . . . . . Tryntje
Carl . . . . Carolus	Catherine. . . . . . Cathrina	Cecelia . . . . Ceelitie
Carl . . . . Ceerles	Catherine . . . . . . Catiena	Cecilia . . . . Celetje
Carl . . . . Ceerlez	Catherine. . . . . . Catreina	Cecilia . . . . Celia
Carl . . . . Charel	Catherine. . . . . . Catriena	Cecilia . . . . Celie
Carl . . . . Charels	Catherine. . . . . . . Catrina	Cecelia . . . . Celitjen
Carl . . . . Charil	Catherine. . . . . . . Catrine	Cecilia . . . . Cillia
Carl . . . . Charles	Catherine. . . . . . Catrinna	Cecilia . . . . Seletje
Carl. . . . . Cheerelz	Catherine. . . . . . Catrintje	Cecilia . . . . Selie
Carl . . . . Karel	Catherine . . . . . Catrintye	Cecilia . . . . Selitje
Carl . . . . Kerdel	Catherine . . . . . Catryntje	Cecilia. . . . . Silja
Carl . . . . Kordel	Catherine. . . . . Caty	Cecilia. . . . . Zetze
Carl . . . . Sarel	Catherine. . . . Chatarina	Cecilia . . . . Ziele
Carl . . . . Zaarel	Catherine. . . . . . Cryntje	Cecilia . . . . Zielietie
Carl . . . . Zarel	Catherine . . . . . Fryntgen	Cecilia . . . . Zilge
Carl . . . . Zarels	Catherine. . . . . Kaat	Cecilia . . . . Zilla
Carl . . . . Zharel	Catherine . . . . . . Kaatje	Cecilia. . . . . . . Zillchen
Caroline . . . . Carly	Catherine . . . . . . Kaderl	Cecilia. . . . . Zilli
Caroline . . . . Caroly	Catherine. . . . . Kate	Charity. . . . . . . Charitas
Caroline. . . . . Carroline	Catherine . . . . Katel	Charity. . . . . . . Charitea
Caroline. . . . . Carye	Catherine . . . . . . Kathe	Charity . . . . . Chawchee
Caroline. . . . . Catalintje	Catherine . . . . Kathl	Charity . . . . Daatje
Caroline. . . . . Catalyntje	Catherine . . . . . . Kathy	Charity. . . . . . . Gerarda
Caroline. . . . . Cathalyna	Catherine . . . . Katili	Charity . . . . . . Gertrude

Given Name Equivalents: English to Dutch

Charity . . . . Sierride	Christina . . . . . Christiena	Claudia . . . . Klaatje
Charity . . . . Sierrity	Christina . . . . . . Christing	Claudia . . . . Nicole
Charity . . . . Tatie	Christina . . . . . Christyntje	Clement . . . . Klement
Charity . . . . Taatje	Christina . . . . Cresten	Commertje . . . Commetje
Charity . . . . Taitje	Christina . . . . . . Crestena	Commertje . . . Comnertje
Charity . . . . Tatje	Christina . . . . . Crestiena	Conrad . . . . Coen
Charity . . . . Tjaatie	Christina . . . . . . Crestina	Conrad . . . . . . Coenraat
Charity . . . . Tjaatje	Christina . . . . Crissen	Conrad . . . . . . Coenradt
Charity . . . . Tjadtje	Christina . . . . Cristina	Conrad . . . . . . Coenraet
Charity . . . . Tyatje	Christina . . . . Dine	Conrad . . . . Comman
Charity . . . . . . Zjarritjen	Christina . . . . . Kerstyne	Conrad . . . . Cone
Charles . . . . Carl	Christina . . . . Krisje	Conrad . . . . Conclo
Charles . . . . Sjarel	Christina . . . . Kristel	Conrad . . . . Conczemann
Charlotte . . . . . Charlotta	Christina . . . . Kristijntje	Conrad . . . . Conkil
Charlotte . . . . Lotje	Christina . . . . . . Steentje	Conrad . . . . Conkulo
Christian . . . . . . Carsten	Christina . . . . Steyne	Conrad . . . . Conze
Christian . . . . . . Chresta	Christina . . . . . . Steyntje	Conrad . . . . . . Coonraat
Christian . . . . Chris	Christina . . . . Stina	Conrad . . . . Corndt
Christian . . . . Christ	Christina . . . . Stine	Conrad . . . . Cort
Christian . . . . Christeaen	Christina . . . . Stini	Conrad . . . . Cunkele
Christian . . . . Christiaen	Christina . . . . Stynichen	Conrad . . . . Koen
Christian . . . Christopher	Christina . . . . . . Styntie	Conrad . . . . . . Koenraet
Christian . . . Corstiaan	Christina? . . . . . . Cosyne	Conrad . . . . Koert
Christian . . . . Creisteaen	Christopher . . . Christian	Conrad . . . . Kohn
Christian . . . . . . Cresce	Christopher . . Christoffel	Conrad . . . . Konert
Christian . . . . . . Karsten	Christopher . . Creisteaer	Conrad . . . . Konne
Christian . . . . . . Kassen	Christopher . . Crestoffel	Conrad . . . . Kord
Christian . . . . . . Kasten	Christopher . . . Cristofel	Conrad . . . . Kueni
Christian . . . . . . Kerstan	Christopher . . . Cristoffel	Conrad . . . . . . Kuenrat
Christian . . . . Kerstanus	Christopher . . . . Kit	Conrad . . . . Kuhn
Christian . . . . . . Kersten	Christopher . . . . Kitt	Conrad . . . . Kun
Christian . . . . . Kiersten	Christopher . . . . . Stoffel	Conrad . . . . . Kunemann
Christian . . . . Koes	Christopher . . . . . Stoffer	Conrad . . . . Kunike
Christian . . . . . Korsjaan	Christopher . . . . . . Toff	Conrad . . . . . . Kunkelo
Christian . . . . Kress	Christopher . . . . . Toffels	Conrad . . . . Kuno
Christian . . . . Kris	Cinderella . . . Assepoester	Conrad . . . . Kunz
Christian . . . . . Krischan	Cinderella . . . . Cinda	Conrad . . . . . . Kunzelin
Christian . . . . . Kristiaan	Cinderella . . . . Cindy	Conrad . . . . Kure
Christian . . . . Kruschen	Clara . . . . Claertje	Conrad . . . . Kurri
Christian . . . . Shaan	Clara . . . . Klaar	Conrad . . . . Kutsch
Christian . . . . Taisso	Clara . . . . Klaartje	Constance . . . . Constantia
Christian . . . . Tsassen	Clarissa . . . . Clasje	Constance . . . Constantine
Christina . . . . . Albertina	Clarissa . . . . Clausie	Constance . . . Constantyn
Christina . . . . Carstiena	Clarissa . . . . Klaasje	Constance . . . . Stans
Christina . . . . . . Cerstena	Clarissa . . . . Klasyne	Cornelia . . . . Breltje
Christina . . . . Chrestina	Clarissa . . . . . Klazina	Cornelia . . . . Cheiltje
Christina . . . . Chris	Claude . . . . Cladious	Cornelia . . . . Chieltje
Christina . . . . . . Christe	Claudia . . . . Cloudy	Cornelia . . . . . Cornelea

Cornelia . . . . . . Corneleia	David . . . . Daaf	Didlove. . . . . . Dietleyous
Cornelia . . . . . Corneleya	David. . . . . Dauvie	Didlove . . . . Dietloip
Cornelia . . . . . . Cornelya	David. . . . . Davet	Didlove. . . . . Ditlo
Cornelia . . . . Kee	David . . . . Davidt	Didlove . . . . Dytlouff
Cornelia . . . . Keetje	David . . . . Davit	Diethard . . . . Ditters
Cornelia . . . . . . Kornelia	Deborah . . . . . . Debbora	Dietrich . . . . Deczel
Cornelia . . . . Nelly	Deborah . . . . Debora	Dietrich . . . . Deddo
Cornelius . . . . Caes	Deborah . . . . Debra	Dietrich. . . . . Deter
Cornelius . . . . Case	Deborah. . . . . Dee	Dietrich. . . . . Diede
Cornelius . . . . Corneles	Deborah . . . . Devertjen	Dietrich. . . . . . Dielman
Cornelius . . . . Cornelisen	Deborah. . . . . . . Dewer	Dietrich . . . . Dielo
Cornelius . . . . . Cornelize	Deborah. . . . . . Dewetje	Dietrich . . . . Diepil
Cornelius . . . . Cors	Deborah . . . . . . Dibbora	Dietrich . . . . . Dierderick .
Cornelius . . . . Kees	Deborah . . . . Dibra	Dietrich. . . . . Dietel
Cornelius . . . . Keesje	Deborah . . . . . . Dieuwer	Dietrich . . . . Dieto
Cornelius. . . . . . . Knelles	Deborah . . . . . . Dievertje	Dietrich . . . . Dietsch
Cornelius . . . . Koris	Deborah . . . . Diewertje	Dietrich . . . . Dietzel
Cornelius . . . . Kors	Deborah. . . . . . . Divertje	Dietrich. . . . . . Dileman
Cornelius. . . . . Krees	Degenhard . . . . . . Degen	Dietrich . . . . Dilich
Cornelius. . . . . . . Krelis	Degenhard. . . . . . . Dehn	Dietrich. . . . . Dilo
Cornelius. . . . . . Krelius	Degenhard . . . . Deinart	Dietrich . . . . Diple
Cornelius. . . . . Neel	Degenhard. . . . Dennert	Dietrich . . . . Dippel
Cornelius . . . . Nelles	Degenhard. . . Theinhart	Dietrich. . . . . Dirk
Cornelius . . . . Nellies	Degenhard . . . . Theynert	Dietrich . . . . Ditzel
Cornelius . . . . Niels	Degenhard. . Tigenhardus	Dietrich . . . . Dypil
Cornelius. . . . . Nilies	Deliverance. . . Deleferins	Dietrich . . . . Dyze
Cosyne . . . . Cousyn	Deliverance . . Delefferins	Dietrich . . . . Tepelo
Cosyne. . . . . Cozina	Deliverance . . Delefverins	Dietrich . . . . Thele
Cosyne . . . . Cozinus	Deliverance . Deleverence	Dietrich . . . . Theodo
Curtis. . . . . Koert	Deliverance. . Deleverens	Dietrich . . . . Thiede
Cynthia . . . . Seytie	Deliverance . . Deleverins	Dietrich . . . . Thiele
Cynthia. . . . . Sinche	Deliverance. . . Delfverins	Dietrich . . . . Thielmann
Cynthia . . . . Sitske	Deliverance. . Deliefferins	Dietrich . . . . . Thiloman
Cynthia . . . . Syntje	Deliverance . . Delifferins	Dietrich . . . . . Tieleman
Cyriacus . . . . Czyliox	Deliverance. . DeLifferins	Dietrich . . . . Tileman
Cyrus . . . . Cy	Deliverance . . . Delverins	Dietrich . . . . . . Tillmann
Daniel . . . . Daan	Delores . . . . Lola	Dietrich . . . . Tippel
Daniel . . . . Daneil	Delphine . . . . Dimphinia	Dietrich . . . . Titzel
Daniel. . . . . Danel	Dennis . . . . Denys	Dietrich . . . . Tytzil
Daniel. . . . . Dannel	Dennis . . . . Dinnies	Dinah . . . . Diena
Daniel . . . . Danyel	Dennis . . . . Dins	Dinah . . . . Dina
Daniel. . . . . Denel	Dennis. . . . . Tunis	Dinah . . . . Dyanzo
Daniel. . . . . Dennel	Denton. . . . . Dentin	Dinah. . . . . Dyna
Dankmar . . . . . . Dammo	Detlef. . . . . Diteleve	Dinah. . . . . Dyntje
Dankmar. . . . . . . Ditmar	Didlove. . . . . Detlef	Dionysius . . . . Denys
Dankmar. . . . . . . Ditmas	Didlove. . . . . Diclof	Dionysius . . . . Dion
Dankmar . . . . Ditmis	Didlove. . . . . . . Diedlof	Dionysius . . . . Dionesius
Dankmar . . . . . . Tammo	Didlove . . . . Dietleip	Dionysius. . . . . . . Dionys

Dionysius . . . . Donisi	Dorothy . . . . Orthea	Eligius. . . . . Ley
Dionysius . . . . Nijs	Dorothy . . . . Orthia	Eligius. . . . . Loi
Dionysius . . . . Nys	Dorothy. . . . . . . Terrothe	Eligius . . . . Loy
Dirk. . . . . Deerick	Dorothy . . . . Turet	Eligius. . . . . Lues
Dirk . . . . Dereck	Douglas . . . . Duggie	Elijah . . . . Elisha
Dirk . . . . Derck	Douw . . . . Douwe	Elijah . . . . Elishah
Dirk . . . . Derick	Douw . . . . Dow	Eliza . . . . Lezart
Dirk . . . . Derjck	Douw . . . . Dowie	Eliza. . . . . Lijsje
Dirk. . . . . Derk	Dyckman . . . . . Dikman	Eliza . . . . Lysje
Dirk . . . . Derreck	Ebenezer. . . . . Ebbi	Elizabeth . . . . Beda
Dirk. . . . . Derrick	Ebenezer . . . . Ebbie	Elizabeth . . . . Beele
Dirk . . . . Deryck	Eckhard. . . . . . . Echelo	Elizabeth . . . . Bela
Dirk . . . . Dirck	Eckhard. . . . . Eckel	Elizabeth . . . . Bertha
Dirk . . . . Dyrck	Eckhard . . . . . . Eckerle	Elizabeth . . . . Beth
Ditmar . . . . Dankmar	Eckhard . . . . Ecklo	Elizabeth . . . . Betterdin
Ditmar. . . . . Diehm	Eckhard . . . . Edsart	Elizabeth . . . . Betti
Ditmar. . . . . Diemo	Eckhard . . . . Eegelo	Elizabeth . . . . Betty
Ditmar . . . . Thieme	Eckhard . . . . Egeno	Elizabeth . . . . Betza
Ditmar. . . . . Timme	Eckhard . . . . Egge	Elizabeth . . . . Bietje
Dolores . . . . Lola	Eckhard . . . . Egino	Elizabeth . . . . Eilsa
Dominic . . . . . . Menikes	Eckhard . . . . Eike	Elizabeth . . . . Elesebath
Dominic . . . . . . Minckes	Eckhard . . . Heccehardus	Elizabeth . . . . Elgen
Dominic . . . . Mingo	Eckhard. . . . . Hechardus	Elizabeth. . . . . Eliesabeth
Dominic. . . . . . . Minicus	Edellind . . . . Lindis	Elizabeth. . . . . Eliezabet
Dominic. . . . . . . Minikes	Edmond. . . . . Ed	Elizabeth. . . . Eliezabeth
Dominic . . . . Minne	Edmond . . . . Edman	Elizabeth . . . . Elisabeth
Dominic . . . . Myn	Edward . . . . Ed	Elizabeth . . . . . . Elisbeth
Dominick . . . . Domincus	Edward . . . . . . Eduaart	Elizabeth . . . . Eliza
Dominick . . . . . Domingo	Edward . . . . Eduard	Elizabeth . . . . . . Elizabet
Dorothy . . . . Dodo	Edward . . . . . Edwaerdt	Elizabeth . . . . Elsebit
Dorothy . . . . Dolly	Edward? . . . . Wier	Elizabeth . . . . . . Elsewed
Dorothy . . . . Door	Edward?. . . . . Wiert	Elizabeth . . . . Elslin
Dorothy . . . . . . Doortje	Egbert . . . . Apke	Elizabeth . . . . . . Elyzabet
Dorothy . . . . . Dorcken	Egbert . . . . Epje	Elizabeth . . . . . Elyzabeth
Dorothy. . . . . Dorel	Egbert . . . . Epke	Elizabeth . . . . Elze
Dorothy . . . . . . Dorken	Egberta. . . . . Akbutje	Elizabeth. . . . . Ilsa
Dorothy. . . . . Dorle	Eilardus . . . . Agilhart	Elizabeth . . . . Isabel
Dorothy . . . . . Dorothea	Eilardus . . . . Eilert	Elizabeth . . . . Libby
Dorothy. . . . . Dort	Eleanor . . . . Laney	Elizabeth . . . . . Liesabet
Dorothy . . . . . Dortchen	Eleanor . . . . Lenoor	Elizabeth . . . . Liesabeth
Dorothy. . . . . Dorte	Eleanor . . . . . . Leonoor	Elizabeth . . . . Liesebeth
Dorothy . . . . Dortel	Eleanor . . . . . . Leonora	Elizabeth. . . . . . Lijsbert
Dorothy . . . . Dortje	Elias . . . . Eljias	Elizabeth . . . . . Lisabeth
Dorothy . . . . . . Duredel	Elias. . . . . Elyas	Elizabeth . . . . . Lisichin
Dorothy. . . . . Durle	Elias. . . . . Helyas	Elizabeth . . . . Liza
Dorothy . . . . Durli	Elias . . . . Lyes	Elizabeth . . . . Lizzie
Dorothy . . . . Dutti	Eligius. . . . . Eloy	Elizabeth . . . . . . Ljesbeth
Dorothy. . . . . Orety	Eligius. . . . . Lei	Elizabeth . . . . Lysbet

Given Name Equivalents: English to Dutch

Elizabeth . . . . Lys	Ephraim . . . . Freme	Eva. . . . . Etje
Elizabeth . . . . Lysbert	Erasmus. . . . . Asam	Eva . . . . Evatje
Elizabeth . . . . . . Lysbeth	Erasmus . . . . Aser	Eva. . . . . Eve
Eloise . . . . Loisl	Erasmus. . . . . . . Asmus	Eva . . . . Ewe
Eloise . . . . Lowies	Erasmus . . . . . . Assmann	Eva. . . . . Ifje
Elsie . . . . Eilse	Erasmus . . . . Rase	Eva? . . . . Ipke
Elsie . . . . Eilsee	Erasmus . . . . Rasi	Evaline. . . . . Evelyn
Elsie . . . . Eilsjen	Erasmus. . . . . . Rasmus	Evaline. . . . . Hevlyn
Elsie . . . . Eilsyen	Erasmus . . . . Rassmann	Evert. . . . . Aebi
Elsie. . . . . Elsee	Erastus . . . . Yrasmuz	Evert . . . . Ebbo
Elsie. . . . . Elsje	Erhard. . . . . Ehrle	Evert. . . . . Eeverdt
Elsie . . . . Eltje	Ernest . . . . Ernie	Evert. . . . . Eevert
Elsie. . . . . Elzee	Ernest . . . . Ernst	Evert . . . . Eppo
Elsie . . . . Esse	Ernest. . . . . . . Hernestus	Evert . . . . Evardt
Emanuel . . . . Manuel	Erwin . . . . Eberwin	Evert . . . . Everard
Emeline . . . . Emilia	Erwin . . . . Herwin	Evert . . . . Everdt
Emeline . . . . Emma	Estella . . . . Stella	Evert . . . . . . Everhardus
Emily . . . . Emma	Esther. . . . . Eester	Evert . . . . Ewart
Emma. . . . . Eemet	Esther . . . . Eestther	Evert. . . . . Ewout
Emma . . . . Eemetie	Esther . . . . Eisther	Evert . . . . . Heberardus
Emma. . . . . Eemie	Esther . . . . Ester	Eycke . . . . Ikee
Emma . . . . Emeda	Esther. . . . . Esthers	Eycke . . . . Eyke
Emma . . . . Emee	Ethel. . . . . Ethelyn	Ezechiel . . . . Ezegeel
Emma . . . . . Emerensje	Ethelmar . . . . Ielmer	Fanny . . . . Fannetje
Emma . . . . Emie	Ethelmar . . . . Jelmer	Ferdinand . . . . . . Fendel
Emma . . . . Emmenentje	Eucharius. . . . . . . Carius	Ferdinand. . . . . . . Ferdel
Emma . . . . . Emmerens	Eucharius . . . . . Karyuss	Ferdinand. . . . . . . Ferges
Emma. . . . . Emmetie	Eunice . . . . Teuntje	Ferdinand . . . . . . Fertel
Emma. . . . . Emmetje	Eunice . . . . . . Theuntje	Ferdinand . . . . Fred
Emma . . . . Immetje	Euphemia . . . . Effee	Ferdinand . . . . . Nandel
Emma. . . . . . . Immicha	Euphemia . . . . . Phema	Ferdinand . . . . . . Nante
Emma . . . . Ymecha	Eustace . . . . Staats	Flora . . . . Floortje
Emmerich . . . . . Ammel	Eustis . . . . Stacius	Flora. . . . . Florence
Emmerich. . Eheimbricho	Eva. . . . . Aafje	Flora. . . . . Floris
Emmerich. . . . Embercho	Eva. . . . . Aafjee	Flora . . . . Flourtje
Emmerich . . . . Embricho	Eva. . . . . Aafyee	Florentina. . . . . . Floortje
Emmerich . . . . . Emche	Eva . . . . Aeffie	Florentina . . . . . . Flora
Emmerich . . . . Emecho	Eva. . . . . Aefje	Florian . . . . Floris
Emmerich . . . . Emyche	Eva. . . . . Aefjee	Frances. . . . . Fanny
Emmerich . . . . . Immel	Eva . . . . Aetje	Frances . . . . . Francijntje
Engel . . . . Engiel	Eva . . . . Aevje	Frances. . . . . . . Francina
Engelbert. . . . . Bert	Eva . . . . Eef	Frances . . . . . Francyntie
Engelbert. . . . Engelbart	Eva. . . . . Eefje	Frances. . . . . Franscyntje
Enoch . . . . Henock	Eva. . . . . Efa	Frances. . . . . . . Fransytie
Ephraim . . . . Eefrem	Eva. . . . . Effe	Frances . . . . Frenky
Ephraim . . . . Efrom	Eva. . . . . Effie	Frances . . . . . . Freyntje
Ephraim. . . . . Frein	Eva. . . . . Efie	Frances . . . . . . Frinckye
Ephraim. . . . . Frem	Eva. . . . . Efte	Francis . . . . Franck

Given Name Equivalents: English to Dutch

Francis . . . . Francois
Francis. . . . . . . Francoy
Francis . . . . Francoys
Francis . . . . Frank
Francis . . . . Frans
Francis. . . . . . . Fransus
Francis . . . . Frenck
Francis . . . . Frenz
Francis. . . . . Ziska
Francis. . . . . . . Ziskus
Francis. . . . . Ziss
Francis . . . . Zissi
Frank . . . . Frenckel
Frederica. . . . Frederika
Frederica . . . . . . Frigge
Frederica . . . . Frika
Frederica . . . . . . Fritsje
Frederica . . . . . . Fritzi
Frederica . . . . . Reyckje
Frederica. . . . . . . Ricka
Frederica . . . . . . Rickel
Frederica . . . . . . Rickli
Frederica . . . . . . Riecke
Frederica . . . . Rika
Frederica . . . . Rike
Frederica . . . . . . Ryckje
Frederick . . . . Fred
Frederick . . . . . Freddie
Frederick . . . . Frederik
Frederick . . . . . . Fredo
Frederick . . . . Fredrick
Frederick . . . . . . Freek
Frederick . . . . Frek
Frederick . . . . Frerich
Frederick . . . . . Frerick
Frederick. . . . . . . Frerk
Frederick . . . . . . Fricke
Frederick. . . . . . . Fried
Frederick . . . . . Frieder
Frederick . . . . Friedlon
Frederick . . . . . . Friele
Frederick . . . . . . Frielo
Frederick. . . . . . . Friko
Frederick . . . . . . Frilo
Frederick . . . . . . Frily
Frederick . . . . . . Frits
Frederick . . . . . Fritschi
Frederick . . . . . . Fritzo

Frederick . . . . Vredrick
Freelove . . . . . . Frielove
Gabriel . . . . . . Gabergel
Gabriel . . . . Gabl
Gaius. . . . . Gajus
Gallia . . . . Jeltje
Garret. . . . . Gard
Garret . . . . Garrit
Garret . . . . Gat
Garret . . . . . . Gehardus
Garret . . . . Gerard
Garret . . . . . . Gerardus
Garret. . . . . Geridt
Garret. . . . . Gerret
Garret . . . . Gerrid
Garret. . . . . . . Gerridt
Garret . . . . Gerrit
Garret . . . . Gert
Gebhard . . . . Gebes
Gebhard . . . . . . Gebke
Gebhard. . . . . . Geppert
Geneva. . . . . Vefe
Geneva . . . . Veva
Geneva . . . . Vevele
Geneva. . . . . Vevi
Geoffrey . . . . Godevaart
George . . . . Charich
George . . . . Georg
George. . . . . Girge
George . . . . Gorch
George. . . . . . . Gurgel
George. . . . . Jarvis
George. . . . . Jerg
George . . . . Jerig
George . . . . . . Jeuriaen
George . . . . Jeurian
George . . . . Jeurie
George . . . . Jooris
George . . . . . . Jooryder
George. . . . . Jorge
George . . . . Jorgel
George . . . . Jores
George . . . . Joris
George . . . . Jorius
George . . . . Jorn
George. . . . . Jorus
George . . . . . . Joryeer
George . . . . Joryer

George. . . . . Joryjer
George . . . . Juerry
George. . . . . Jurge
George. . . . . Jurgen
George . . . . Jurian
George . . . . Jurn
George . . . . Jurrian
George . . . . Jurrie
George . . . . Jurrien
George . . . . Jurry
George. . . . . Jury
George . . . . Schorschel
George. . . . . Tjerck
George. . . . . Uriah
George . . . . Ury
George . . . . Yoris
George . . . . Yurie
Geraldine. . . . . . Gerarda
Geraldine . . . . Godardina
Gerard . . . . Garret
Gerard . . . . . . Sherrard
Gerarda . . . . Gashia
Gerarda. . . . . Geese
Gerarda . . . . Geesje
Gerarda. . . . . . . Geeske
Gerarda. . . . . Geesknana
Gerarda . . . . Gehse
Gerarda. . . . . Gepie
Gerarda. . . . . . . Geretie
Gerarda . . . . Geritie
Gerarda . . . . Geritje
Gerarda . . . . . . Gerretie
Gerarda . . . . . . Gerritje
Gerarda . . . . . Gertrude
Gerarda . . . . Gesa
Gerarda. . . . . Gisch
Gerardina . . . . . . Desin
Gerardina . . . . Dina
Gerardina . . . . . . Dinah
Gerbrant . . . Garabrand
Gerbrant . . . Garrabrant
Gerbrant . . . . Gerbrand
Gerbrantina . . Garabrach
Gerbrantina. . Gerbrechta
Gerbrantina . Gerrebrecht
Gerhard . . . . Garret
Gerhard. . . . . Gehrt
Gerhard. . . . . . . Gerard

Given Name Equivalents: English to Dutch

Gerhard . . . . Gering	Gertrude . . . . . . Jeartie	Giselle . . . . Gyppel
Gerhard . . . . Geert	Gertrude . . . . . Tradchen	Godfrey . . . . Covert
Gerhard . . . . Gerjet	Gertrude . . . . . . Traudel	Godfrey . . . . Fred
Gerhard . . . . Gerke	Gertrude . . . . . . Trudel	Godfrey . . . . Friedel
Gerhard . . . . Gerlin	Gertrude . . . . Trudi	Godfrey . . . . Frieder
Gerhard . . . . Gero	Gertrude . . . . Trudy	Godfrey . . . . Friedes
Gerhard . . . . . . Gerung	Gertrude . . . . Trui	Godfrey . . . . Frit
Gerhard . . . . Gierd	Gertrude . . . . . . Truitje	Godfrey . . . . Gabert
Gerhard . . . . Grades	Gertrude . . . . . . Truytje	Godfrey . . . . Gebel
Gerhard . . . . Hard	Gervas . . . . Faas	Godfrey . . . . Gebelo
Gershom . . . . . . Gerson	Gesia . . . . Asia	Godfrey . . . . . . Gebeno
Gershom . . . . . . Gishum	Gideon . . . . Gidion	Godfrey . . . . Gebert
Gershom . . . . . Gussein	Gilbert . . . . Bert	Godfrey . . . . Geuert
Gertrude . . . . . Cairekje	Gilbert . . . . Geisbert	Godfrey . . . . Gibel
Gertrude . . . . . . Charity	Gilbert . . . . Gija	Godfrey . . . . Gobbert
Gertrude . . . . . . Drucke	Gilbert . . . . Gijs	Godfrey . . . . . . Gobelius
Gertrude . . . . Druda	Gilbert . . . . . Gijsbertus	Godfrey . . . . . . Godeke
Gertrude . . . . . Drudeke	Gilbert . . . . Gile	Godfrey . . . . Godel
Gertrude . . . . . . Drudel	Gilbert . . . . Gilgen	Godfrey . . . . . Godevaart
Gertrude . . . . Drudischen	Gilbert . . . . Gils	Godfrey . . . . . . Godevart
Gertrude . . . . . . Druide	Gilbert . . . . Gisbert	Godfrey . . . . . . Godfried
Gertrude . . . . Drut	Gilbert . . . . Guisbert	Godfrey . . . . Godo
Gertrude . . . . . Drutchen	Gilbert . . . . Gylo	Godfrey . . . . . Goeffrey
Gertrude . . . . . . Drutke	Gilbert . . . . Gysbert	Godfrey . . . . Goerd
Gertrude . . . . Drutte	Gilbert . . . . Gyslben	Godfrey . . . . Goeze
Gertrude . . . . Geerd	Gilbert . . . . Gyslbert	Godfrey . . . . Goffert
Gertrude . . . . Geert	Gilberta . . . . . . Gysbertje	Godwin . . . . Goose
Gertrude . . . . . . Geertje	Giles . . . . Geleyn	Godwin . . . . Gose
Gertrude . . . . Geertruyd	Giles . . . . Gellis	Godfrey . . . . Gotfried
Gertrude . . . . Geertruyt	Giles . . . . Gelyn	Godfrey . . . . Gotje
Gertrude . . . . Geila	Giles . . . . Gilies	Godfrey . . . . Gotsch
Gertrude . . . . Gela	Giles . . . . Gilles	Godfrey . . . . . . Gotsche
Gertrude . . . . Gele	Giles . . . . Gillis	Godfrey . . . . Gottel
Gertrude . . . . . . Gelud	Giles . . . . Jilles	Godfrey . . . . Gotti
Gertrude . . . . Gert	Giles . . . . Jillis	Godfrey . . . . Gotz
Gertrude . . . . . Gertchen	Giles . . . . Yellis	Godfrey . . . . Gotze
Gertrude . . . . . . Gerta	Giselle . . . . Gesa	Godfrey . . . . Gotzi
Gertrude . . . . Gerti	Giselle . . . . Geisel	Godfrey . . . . . . Gotzmann
Gertrude . . . . . . Gertie	Giselle . . . . Geitze	Godfrey . . . . . . Goverd
Gertrude . . . . . . Gertjen	Giselle . . . . Getze	Godfrey . . . . Gozzo
Gertrude . . . . . . Gertke	Giselle . . . . Giesel	Godfrey . . . . Gubil
Gertrude . . . . . . Gescha	Giselle . . . . Gipelo	Godfrey . . . . Guert
Gertrude . . . . . . Gesche	Giselle . . . . Gisa	Godfrey . . . . Jeffers
Gertrude . . . . . . Geseke	Giselle . . . . Gisela	Godfrey . . . . Jeffery
Gertrude . . . . . . Gesine	Giselle . . . . . Giselbert	Godfrey . . . . Jenfrit
Gertrude . . . . . . Giertje	Giselle . . . . Gisle	Godfrey . . . . Jetze
Gertrude . . . . Gitty	Giselle . . . . Giso	Godfrey . . . . Jofrid
Gertrude . . . . . . Grarda	Giselle . . . . Giszil	Godfrey . . . . . . Schaffried

200

Given Name Equivalents: English to Dutch

Godwin . . . . Goes	Hannah . . . . Anna	Helena . . . . Hella
Godwin . . . . Goossen	Hannah . . . . Hanatie	Helena . . . . Helletjen
Godwin . . . . Gooze	Hannah . . . . Hanatje	Helena . . . . Hilchen
Godwin . . . . Goze	Hannah . . . . . . Hanatys	Helena . . . . Hickel
Godwin . . . . Gozen	Hannah . . . . Hanna	Helena . . . . Hilgen
Godwin . . . . . . Gozewijn	Hannah . . . . Hannatje	Helena . . . . Leintgen
Godwin . . . . Gozewin	Hannah . . . . . Hannatye	Helena . . . . Lena
Godwina . . . . . . Goosen	Hans . . . . Anczel	Helena . . . . Liengen
Godwina . . . . Gosen	Hans . . . . Ensel	Helena . . . . . Magdalena
Godwina . . . . . Gosyntje	Harmina . . . . . . Hermje	Helena . . . . Nella
Godwina . . . Gosewyntie	Harriet . . . . Adrian	Helena . . . . Nellchen
Gooden . . . . Guyten	Harriet . . . . Ariantje	Helena . . . . Nelli
Goodeth . . . . Godet	Harriet . . . . Hattie	Helmich . . . . Helmus
Goodeth . . . . Godith	Harriet . . . . . . Henrietta	Helwich . . . . Heide
Goodeth . . . . Godje	Harriet . . . . . . Hettie	Henrietta . . . . Enretta
Goodeth . . . . . . Goedyth	Hartmut . . . . Mutz	Henrietta . . . . . . Harriet
Gothard . . . . . . Godaard	Harvey . . . . Hervey	Henrietta . . . . . . Hankey
Gothard . . . . Godard	Hector . . . . Heckter	Henrietta . . . . . . Heintje
Gothard . . . . . Goddard	Hedwich . . . . . . Hadken	Henrietta . . . . Hendrica
Gothard . . . . . . Goddert	Hedwich . . . . Hasa	Henrietta . . . Hendrickje
Gothard . . . . Godert	Hedwich . . . . . . Haseke	Henrietta . . . Hendriekje
Gothard . . . . Gort	Hedwich . . . . . Hazecha	Henrietta . . . Hendrickye
Gothard . . . . . . Gottert	Hedwich . . . . Hebbele	Henrietta . . . . . . Hentje
Gotlieb . . . . Godlief	Hedwich . . . . Hebel	Henrietta . . . . Jetje
Grace . . . . Geesje	Hedwich . . . . Hedda	Henry . . . . Drickes
Grace . . . . Gerarda	Hedwich . . . . Hede	Henry . . . . Enrik
Grace . . . . Grees	Hedwich . . . . Hedel	Henry . . . . Hank
Grace . . . . Greesje	Hedwich . . . . Hedi	Henry . . . . Harry
Grace . . . . Griesse	Hedwich . . . . . . Hedken	Henry . . . . Heike
Gracius . . . . Gratiosa	Hedwich . . . . . . Heebilo	Henry . . . . Heiko
Gregory . . . . Gores	Hedwich . . . . . Heitchen	Henry . . . . Heilo
Gregory . . . . Goris	Hedwich . . . . Heseke	Henry . . . . Hein
Gregory . . . . Gorjes	Hedwich . . . . Heta	Henry . . . . Heinclo
Gregory . . . . Gorris	Hedwich . . . . Hete	Henry . . . . Heineke
Gregory . . . . Gorrius	Hedwich . . . . Hetgin	Henry . . . . Heinel
Gregory . . . . Gorus	Hedwich . . . . . Hettichin	Henry . . . . . Heinemann
Gregory . . . . . . Gregoris	Hedwich . . . . . Hetichin	Henry . . . . Heinkel
Gregory . . . . . Gregorius	Hedwich . . . . Hetta	Henry . . . . Heinko
Gregory . . . . . Gregorus	Hedwich . . . . Hydde	Henry . . . . Heino
Gregory . . . . Grogel	Hedwich . . . . Wigel	Henry . . . . Heinsel
Gumpert . . . . . . Gumpel	Helena . . . . Alana	Henry . . . . Heinzo
Gumpert . . . . . . Gunkelo	Helena . . . . Eelet	Henry . . . . Heintje
Gumpert . . . . . . Gunpilo	Helena . . . . Elena	Henry . . . . Heintze
Gunther . . . . Gunner	Helena . . . . Ella	Henry . . . . Heiri
Gunther . . . . Guntzel	Helena . . . . Elli	Henry . . . . Heise
Gustave . . . . Gose	Helena . . . . Hela	Henry . . . . Henderick
Gustave . . . . Gustaaf	Helena . . . . Heling	Henry . . . . Henderickas
Guy . . . . Guido	Helena . . . . Helytje	Henry . . . . . Hendereckus

Given Name Equivalents: English to Dutch

Henry . . . . . Henderickes	Hercules . . . . . Harkulis	Hezekiah . . . . Hiskca
Henry . . . . . Henderickis	Hercules . . . . . Harkulius	Hezekiah . . . . Hiskia
Henry . . . . . . Hendericus	Hercules . . . . . . Harreck	Hezekiah . . . . Smiaa
Henry . . . . . . Henderikus	Hercules . . . . Henry	Hieronymus. . . . Grolmes
Henry . . . . Hendreck	Hercules. . . . . . Hercilius	Hieronymus. . . Grommes
Henry . . . . . . Hendrekus	Hercules. . . . . Herck	Hieronymus . . . Gronlein
Henry. . . . . . . Hendricus	Hercules . . . . . . Herreck	Hieronymus . Hieronimus
Henry . . . . Hendrick	Hercules. . . . . . . Herrick	Hieronymus . . . . . . Hyer
Henry . . . . . Hendrickes	Hercules. . . . . . . Herrick	Hieronymus. . . . . . . Jero
Henry . . . . Hendrik	Hercules . . . . Herrickse	Hieronymus. . . . . Jerome
Henry . . . . Hengin	Hercules . . . . Herrik	Hieronymus . . Jeronimus
Henry . . . . Henkel	Hercules. . . . . . . Herrikz	Hieronymus . . . . . Olmes
Henry. . . . . Henkyn	Hercules . . . . . . Herrikze	Hieronymus . . . . Onimus
Henry . . . . Henlyn	Herman . . . . . Haramanis	Hilda . . . . Heiltje
Henry. . . . . Henne	Herman . . . . Haramanus	Hilda. . . . . Helche
Henry . . . . . . Hennekin	Herman . . . . . Haremanis	Hilda. . . . . . . Hellegonda
Henry . . . . Hennemann	Herman. . . . . Harm	Hilda. . . . . Helletpe
Henry. . . . . Henner	Herman . . . . Harman	Hilda . . . . Helletye
Henry . . . . Henning	Herman . . . . Harmanas	Hilda . . . . Helltje
Henry . . . . Henrick	Herman . . . . . Harmanis	Hilda . . . . Heltjen
Henry. . . . . . . Henrikus	Herman . . . . Hermanus	Hilda . . . . Heyltje
Henry. . . . . . . Henschel	Herman . . . . Harme	Hilda . . . . Heyltjen
Henry. . . . . Hentgin	Herman . . . . Harmel	Hilda . . . . . . Hiellegontie
Henry . . . . Hentze	Herman . . . . Hermeli	Hilda. . . . . Hielletie
Henry. . . . . Henzo	Herman . . . . Harmen	Hilda. . . . . Hielletje
Henry. . . . . . . Hercules	Herman . . . . Harmenas	Hilda . . . . Hild
Henry . . . . Hinke	Herman . . . . Harmpji	Hilda . . . . Hilla
Henry . . . . Hinnerk	Herman . . . . Haro	Hilda . . . . Hille
Henry. . . . . Hinrich	Herman . . . . . Hartman	Hilda. . . . . Hillegond
Henry. . . . . Hinrik	Herman. . . . . Heman	Hilda. . . . . . . Hillegonda
Henry . . . . Hintzel	Herman . . . . Hemmo	Hilda. . . . . Hilletje
Henry. . . . . Reitzle	Herman. . . . . Hesse	Hilda . . . . Hillitje
Henry. . . . . Richel	Herman . . . . Hetzel	Hilda . . . . Hillund
Henry. . . . . Rik	Herman . . . . Manes	Hilda . . . . Holda
Henry. . . . . Ritze	Herman. . . . . Manus	Hilda . . . . Hulda
Henry. . . . . Ryetze	Herman. . . . . . . Menzel	Hilda . . . . Hylie
Herbert . . . . Harbart	Hermina. . . . . Harmena	Hillary. . . . . Lare
Herbert . . . . Harpert	Hermina . . . . . . Harmke	Hillegond . . . . Gonda
Herbert . . . . Hubert	Hermina . . . . . . Harmpje	Hillegond . . . . Hildegard
Herbert . . . . . . Hubrecht	Hermina . . . . . . Harmsie	Hillegond . . . . Hulda
Hercules. . . . . Harck	Hessel . . . . Hassel	Hippoletus . . . . Hipp
Hercules . . . . Harcke	Hessel . . . . Hesselius	Hippoletus. . . . . Litt
Hercules . . . . . Harckse	Hester . . . . Esther	Hippoletus. . . . . . . Pilten
Hercules. . . . . Hark	Hester . . . . Hesje	Hippoletus . . . . Polte
Hercules. . . . . . . Harke	Hester . . . . Hesther	Hippoletus . . . . . . Poltel
Hercules . . . . Harklis	Hester . . . . Hetty	Hippoletus . . . . . . Poltus
Hercules. . . . . Harkueles	Hezekiah. . . . . . Ezechias	Hippoletus . . . . Pult
Hercules . . . . . . Harkules	Hezekiah . . . . . . Hazecha	Hubert . . . . Huib

Given Name Equivalents: English to Dutch

Hubert . . . . Hupraid	Isaac . . . . Izaak	Jacob . . . . Jaques
Hubert . . . . Huybert	Isaac . . . . Ysaak	Jacob . . . . Jeckel
Hugh . . . . Hugo	Isaac . . . . Ysac	Jacob . . . . Jeggeli
Hugh . . . . Hugue	Isaac . . . . Ysack	Jacob . . . . Joaptie
Hugh . . . . Huig	Isaac . . . . Ysaeck	Jacob . . . . Jobbi
Hugh . . . . Huigen	Isaac . . . . Ysaque	Jacob . . . . Jobje
Hugh . . . . Huygen	Isabella . . . . Arabella	Jacob . . . . Jockel
Hugh . . . . Ju	Isabella . . . . Ballie	Jacob . . . . Jocki
Humphrey . . . Humfridus	Isabella . . . . Beelitie	Jacob . . . . Joggeli
Humphrey . . . Humfried	Isabella . . . . Beelitje	Jacob . . . . Jopje
Humphrey . . . . . Humfry	Isabella . . . . Beeltje	Jacob . . . . Joppes
Humphrey . . . . . Omfrey	Isabella . . . . Bel	Jacob . . . . Ko
Humphrey . . . . Umphrey	Isabella . . . . Beletje	Jacob . . . . Koba
Ida . . . . Aitje	Isabella . . . . Belettie	Jacob . . . . Kobel
Ide . . . . Ede	Isabella . . . . Beletye	Jacob . . . . Kobes
Ide . . . . Edo	Isabella . . . . Belietie	Jacob . . . . Kobi
Ida . . . . Eetie	Isabella . . . . Belitie	Jacob . . . . Kobus
Ida . . . . Eida	Isabella . . . . Belitje	Jacob . . . . Koob
Ida . . . . Eitje	Isabella . . . . Belytie	Jacob . . . . Koos
Ida . . . . Eytic	Isabella . . . . Bell	Jacob . . . . Schack
Ida . . . . Eytie	Isabella . . . . Bella	Jacob . . . . Siaque
Ida . . . . Fytie	Isabella . . . . Ibel	Jacob . . . . Siaques
Ide . . . . Iddo	Isabella . . . . Sabel	Jacob . . . . Yacob
Ide . . . . Iden	Isaiah . . . . Esaias	Jacob . . . . Yacus
Ida . . . . Jittje	Isaiah . . . . Jezaus	Jacobina . . . . Coba
Ida . . . . Ydje	Jack . . . . Jacques	Jacobina . . . . Jaapje
Ida . . . . Ydtje	Jacob . . . . Cob	Jacobina . . . . Jacoba
Ida . . . . Ythel	Jacob . . . . Cobe	Jacobina . . . . . . Jacobia
Ida . . . . Ytie	Jacob . . . . Cobes	Jacobina . . . . . . Jacobje
Ida . . . . Ytje	Jacob . . . . Cobus	Jacobina . . . . . Jamesina
Imogene . . . . . . Emogene	Jacob . . . . Jaap	Jacobina . . . . Japje
Imogene . . . . Mayna	Jacob . . . . Jaapie	Jacobina . . . . Jappje
Imogene . . . . Mene	Jacob . . . . Jabbo	Jacobina . . . . . . Koosje
Imogene . . . . Meyne	Jacob . . . . Jackel	Jacques . . . . Sjaeck
Increase . . . . Inkrees	Jacob . . . . Jacket	James . . . . Chime
Inga . . . . Ingber	Jacob . . . . Jacobes	James . . . . Coosje
Ira . . . . Jira	Jacob . . . . Jacobus	James . . . . Gemes
Ira . . . . Yria	Jacob . . . . Jacop	James . . . . Jacob
Irmgard . . . . Ermel	Jacob . . . . Jacques	James . . . . Jacobus
Irmtraud . . . . Druda	Jacob . . . . Jaepie	James . . . . Jeams
Irmtraud . . . Ermedrudis	Jacob . . . . Jaepje	James . . . . Jeems
Isaac . . . . Hiscock	Jacob . . . . Jaggi	James . . . . Jems
Isaac . . . . Isaack	Jacob . . . . Jakob	James . . . . Zeims
Isaac . . . . Isaak	Jacob . . . . Jakobus	Janet . . . . Jaan
Isaac . . . . Isac	Jacob . . . . James	Janet . . . . Jaantje
Isaac . . . . Isack	Jacob . . . . Japic	Janet . . . . Jaapje
Isaac . . . . Iseck	Jacob . . . . Japik	Janet . . . . Janche
Isaac . . . . Isick	Jacob . . . . Japil	Janet . . . . Jane

Janet	Janetie	Jemima	Jemema	John	Jany
Janet	Janetje	Jemima	Jemmea	John	Jenne
Janet	Janietie	Jemima	Jemyma	John	Jenni
Janet	Janietje	Jemima	Jemyna	John	Joanis
Janet	Janije	Jemima	Jocamyna	John	Joannis
Janet	Janitie	Jemima	Jocamyntie	John	Johan
Janet	Janneke	Jemima	Meintje	John	Johanis
Janet	Jannetie	Jeptha	Jefta	John	Johannis
Janet	Jannetje	Jeremiah	Jeramius	John	Johannes
Janet	Jannettye	Jeremiah	Jeremy	John	Schani
Janet	Jannieke	Jeremiah	Jeramyas	John	Yan
Janet	Jannitie	Jeremiah	Jeremeies	Jonas	Jonah
Janet	Jannitje	Jeremiah	Jeremia	Jonas	Jones
Janet	Jannitye	Jeremiah	Jeremias	Jonas	Jonis
Janet	Jansje	Jeremiah	Jeremies	Jonas	Jonus
Janet	Jantia	Jeremiah	Jeremyas	Jonathan	Janeton
Janet	Jantina	Jeremiah	Jerimyas	Jonathan	Jannetan
Janet	Jantje	Jeremiah	Mias	Jonathan	Johnatan
Janet	Jeanne	Jerome	Hieronymus	Jonathan	Johnaton
Janet	Jeannetie	Joanna	Andel	Jonathan	Jonatan
Janet	Jeneke	Joanna	Janneken	Jonathan	Joneton
Janet	Jengen	Joanna	Hanne	Jonathan	Sannetan
Janet	Jenike	Joanna	Hansje	Jonathan	Yannetan
Janet	Jenne	Joanna	Netta	Jonathan	Zannetan
Janet	Jennecke	Joanna	Nettchen	Joris	Jous
Janet	Jenneke	Jochem	Joachim	Joseph	Beppo
Janet	Jennica	Jochem	Joakemis	Joseph	Iost
Janet	Jennie	Jochem	Jocheemus	Joseph	Joe
Janet	Jennike	Jochem	Jochim	Joseph	Joosdt
Janet	Jenny	Jochem	Jochum	Joseph	Joost
Janet	Joan	Jochem	Joghem	Joseph	Josef
Janet	Joana	Jochem	Yokum	Joseph	Josep
Janet	Joanna	John	Haiseli	Joseph	Josephat
Janet	Johanneke	John	Hamman	Joseph	Josop
Janet	Jonitia	John	Hanemann	Joseph	Josoph
Janet	Joonje	John	Hanke	Joseph	Jozef
Janet	Schonette	John	Hanman	Joseph	Jozie
Janet	Yannittie	John	Hanne	Joseph	Jupp
Jasper	Caspar	John	Hannes	Joseph	Peppi
Jemima	Jacomina	John	Hans	JJoseph	Sebel
Jemima	Jacomyntie	John	Heintze	oseph	Sebi
Jemima	Jacomyntje	John	Hennes	Joseph	Sepperli
Jemima	Jacquemina	John	Henschel	Joseph	Seppi
Jemima	Jakomina	John	Jack	Joseph	Yope
Jemima	Jaquemne	John	Jahn	Joseph	Yoseph
Jemima	Jaquemyntie	John	Janne	Joseph	Yoost
Jemima	Jemina	John	Janni	Joseph	Yost
Jemima	Jemeima	John	Janny	Josephine	Fiene

Given Name Equivalents: English to Dutch

Josephine . . . . Fina	Judith . . . . Judah	Lambert . . . . . Lambrecht
Josephine. . . . . . Finchen	Judith. . . . . Judick	Lambert . . . . . . Lammert
Josephine . . . . Finna	Judith . . . . Judinta	Lambert . . . . . . Lemmert
Josephine. . . . . . Josepha	Judith. . . . . Jutge	Lambertina. . . Lammertje
Josephine. . . . . Josey	Judith . . . . Jutta	Lambertina . . . Lammetje
Josephine . . . . Josia	Judith . . . . Jutte	Lancelot . . . . Lenz
Josephine . . . . Josie	Julia. . . . . Elyane	Laurentia . . . . Lorenchen
Josephine. . . . . Jozefina	Julia. . . . . Gelina	Lavina . . . . Lavyntje
Josephine. . . . . Sefa	Julia . . . . Jelette	Lavina . . . . Viny
Josephine. . . . . Sefe	Julia . . . . Jelitje	Lavina. . . . . Vyntje
Josephine . . . . Seffi	Julian . . . . Gleen	Lavinia . . . . Weintie
Josephine. . . . . Seichen	Julian. . . . . Goline	Lavinia . . . . Weynt
Josephine . . . . . Seppeli	Julian. . . . . Golyn	Lavinia . . . . Weyntje
Joshua . . . . Jassawa	Julian. . . . . Guleyn	Lavinia . . . . Winne
Joshua . . . . Jassewa	Juliane . . . . Gene	Lavinia . . . . Wintie
Joshua . . . . Jassewil	Juliane. . . . . Iliane	Lavinia . . . . Wintye
Joshua. . . . . Jassuel	Juliane. . . . . . Juliaantje	Lavinia . . . . . . Wyentie
Joshua . . . . Jaszewil	Justina . . . . Josina	Lavinia . . . . Wyntje
Joshua. . . . . Josua	Justina. . . . . Justje	Lavinia . . . . Wyntie
Joshua. . . . . Jozua	Keziah. . . . . Cassia	Lavinia. . . . . Wyntye
Josiah . . . . Jesaias	Keziah . . . . Kesia	Lawrence. . . . . Laure
Josiah . . . . Jesays	Kilian. . . . . Clean	Lawrence . . . . . Laurenis
Josiah . . . . Jesia	Kilian. . . . . Geil	Lawrence . . . . . . Laurens
Josiah . . . . Jezia	Kilian . . . . Giele	Lawrence . . . . . Laurentz
Josiah . . . . Syer	Kilian . . . . Killeaen	Lawrence . . . . . . Laurenz
Josina. . . . . Jesyntje	Kitty. . . . . Gitty	Lawrence . . . . . Lerrence
Josina . . . . Jesynze	Kunigunda. . . . . Cina	Lawrence . . . . . Leverens
Josina. . . . . Jezyna	Kunigunda. . . . . Cine	Lawrence. . . . . . Leverins
Josina. . . . . Jezyntie	Kunigunda . . . . Cniertje	Lawrence . . . . Lohr
Josina. . . . . Jezyntje	Kunigunda . . . . Cuiertie	Lawrence . . . . Lon
Josina. . . . . Joosje	Kunigunda . . . Cumczele	Lawrence . . . . Lons
Josina . . . . . . Josephine	Kunigunda . . . . Cunckil	Lawrence . . . . Lore
Josina. . . . . Josi	Kunigunda. . . . . Cunera	Lawrence. . . . . Lori
Josina. . . . . Josie	Kunigunda . . . Cuniertie	Lawrence . . . . Lortz
Josina. . . . . Josyna	Kunigunda . . . Cunigunde	Lawrence . . . . . Lourens
Josina. . . . . Josyntje	Kunigunda . . . . . Cunira	Lawrence. . . . . Louw
Josina . . . . Seintie	Kunigunda . . . . . Cuntze	Lawrence . . . . Louwerins
Josina . . . . Sina	Kunigunda. . . . Kanieltje	Lawrence. . . . . Louwrens
Judah. . . . . Gudeste	Kunigunda . . . . Kniertee	Lawrence . . . . Lowerens
Judah . . . . Gutechin	Kunigunda . . . . Kniertje	Lawrence . . . . Lurtz
Judah . . . . Gutste	Kunigunda . . . Koneiung	Lawrence . . . . . Luuerins
Judah. . . . . Joide	Kunigunda . . . . . Konne	Lawrence . . . . Renz
Judah . . . . Jottichin	Kunigunda. . . . Kontzele	Lea . . . . Layah
Judah . . . . Jude	Kunigunda. . . . . Kunisa	Lea . . . . Leaya
Judah. . . . . Yoidin	Kunigunda . . . . . Kunna	Lea. . . . . Leeiaa
Judas . . . . Judah	Kunigunda . . . . Kunzela	Lea . . . . Leeja
Judith . . . . Ita	Kunigunda. . . . . . Tzyna	Lea . . . . Leeya
Judith . . . . Ite	Kunigunda . . . . . . Zyne	Lea . . . . Leia

Given Name Equivalents: English to Dutch

Lea	Leya	Letitia	Tytje	Ludwich	Lewts
Leffert	Leffers	Levi	Livinus	Ludwich	Liudike
Lena	Laenette	Lothar	Ludeke	Ludwich	Lodewyck
Lena	Lana	Lothar	Luhr	Ludwich	Lodewyk
Lena	Leena	Louis	Leur	Ludwich	Loodewyck
Lena	Leenna	Louis	Lewis	Ludwich	Lovis
Lena	Leentje	Louis	Loew	Ludwich	Lucco
Lena	Leli	Louis	Loyse	Ludwich	Lucke
Lena	Lenah	Louis	Lowies	Ludwich	Luckel
Lena	Lenchen	Louis	Ludovicus	Ludwich	Luckeley
Lena	Leneke	Louis	Luer	Ludwich	Luckhard
Lena	Leneli	Louis	Luewes	Ludwich	Luczchen
Lena	Leni	Louis	Luir	Ludwich	Lude
Lena	Levyntje	Louis	Lur	Ludwich	Ludeke
Lena	Levyntje	Louis	Luwje	Ludwich	Ludel
Lena	Leynje	Louis	Luyr	Ludwich	Luder
Lena	Liena	Louis?	Lourus	Ludwich	Ludovicus
Lena	Linje	Louise	Eloise	Ludwich	Lodowyck
Lena	Livyntje	Louisa	Lowisa	Ludwich	Lotze
Lena	Lyntje	Lourus	Laurus	Ludwich	Luklei
Leo	Levinus	Lourus	Lowrus	Ludwich	Luthe
Leo	Lieve	Lubbert	Leuntje	Ludwich	Lutter
Leo	Liewe	Lubbert	Liubert	Ludwich	Lutyke
Leonard	Leen	Lubbert	Lubbers	Ludwich	Lutz
Leonard	Leendert	Lubbert	Ludbrecht	Ludwich	Lutzo
Leonard	Leendredt	Lubbert	Luwert	Ludwich	Lutygo
Leonard	Leent	Lucas	Lakas	Ludwich	Luzze
Leonard	Lehrd	Lucas	Leick	Ludwich	Wickel
Leonard	Lenert	Lucas	Luas	Ludwich	Wickes
Leonard	Lenhard	Lucas	Luckas	Ludwich	Wiggel
Leonard	Lennert	Lucas	Luke	Luitgard	Leuckel
Leonard	Lenz	Lucas	Luykas	Luitgard	Licharde
Leonard	Leon	Lucas	Luytje	Luitgard	Locza
Leonard	Leret	Lucretia	Greesje	Luitgard	Logkele
Leonard	Lienert	Lucy	Lucia	Luitgard	Lokil
Leonard	Lienhard	Lucy	Luzscha	Luitgard	Lotzeya
Leonard	Liert	Lucy	Lutza	Luitgard	Louckil
Leonard	Linnart	Lucy	Lutzel	Luitgard	Luca
Leopold	Leo	Lucy	Luza	Luitgard	Lucze
Letitia	Aletta	Lucy	Luzeile	Luitgard	Lukarde
Letitia	Letje	Lucy?	Luzel	Lulu	Ludmilla
Letitia	Tietje	Lucy	Luzi	lydia	Ledina
Letitia	Tietye	Lucy	Zeieli	lydia	Lidia
Letitia	Tiletje	Lucy	Zeigen	lydia	Liedea
Letitia	Tilly	Lucy	Zeia	lydia	Liedia
Letitia	Tisje	Lucy	Zeje	lydia	Liedya
Letitia	Tit	Lucy	Zigi	lydia	Lydea
Letitia	Titje	Lucy	Zilie	Mabel	Merbel

Given Name Equivalents: English to Dutch

Mabel. . . . . Mermel	Margaret . . . . . Gretchen	Margaret . . . . Rita
Magdalena. . . . . . Helena	Margaret. . . . . . . Greetie	Margaret . . . . Yrietje
Magdalena. . . . . . . Alena	Margaret . . . . Gretli	Maria. . . . . Maacke
Magdalena. . . . . . Lehene	Margaret. . . . . . . Gretzen	Maria . . . . Maaicke
Magdalena . . . . Lena	Margaret. . . . . Grieta	Maria . . . . Maaike
Magdalena . . . . Leyn	Margaret . . . . Grietie	Maria . . . . Maaritje
Magdalena . . . Lienchgen	Margaret . . . . Grietje	Maria . . . . Maartie
Magdalena. . . . . Line	Margaret. . . . . . . Griettie	Maria . . . . Maartje
Magdalena. . . . Lyenchgin	Margaret . . . . Gritli	Maria . . . . Maeritje
Magdalena . . . . . Machtel	Margaret . . . . . . Gritschi	Maria . . . . Maertie
Magdalena . . . . Machteld	Margaret . . . . Gritta	Maria . . . . Maertje
Magdalena. . . . Madalena	Margaret . . . . . Grutschi	Maria . . . . Maeyke
Magdalena. . . Madalentie	Margaret . . . . Madge	Maria . . . . Maike
Magdalena . . . . . . Madel	Margaret. . . . . Magrytie	Maria. . . . . Mara
Magdalena . . . . . Madele	Margaret . . . . Maigel	Maria . . . . Maraatje
Magdalena . . . Madelein	Margaret . . . . Maragriet	Maria . . . . Maratie
Magdalena. . . . . Madeli	Margaret. . . Maragrietie	Maria . . . . Marei
Magdalena. . . . . Maden	Margaret . . Maragriettie	Maria . . . . Mareiia
Magdalena . . . . . . Madi	Margaret . . . Maragrietye	Maria . . . . Mareile
Magdalena . . . . . . Madla	Margaret. . . . Maragritie	Maria . . . . Mareitie
Magdalena . . . . . Magda	Margaret . . Maragryettie	Maria . . . . Mareitje
Magdalena . Magdaleentje	Margaret . . . . . Margarita	Maria . . . . Marelia
Magdalena . . Magdaleetje	Margaret. . . . Margaritta	Maria . . . . Marethen
Magdalena . . . Magdaletie	Margaret . . . . Marget	Maria . . . . Maretie
Magdalena . . . . . . Magel	Margaret . . . . . Margitta	Maria . . . . Maretje
Magdalena . Maghdaleena	Margaret. . . . . Margriet	Maria . . . . Mareytie
Magdalena . . . . . . Magle	Margaret . . . . Margrieta	Maria . . . . Mari
Magdalena . . . . . Magtelt	Margaret . . . . Margriete	Maria . . . . Mariah
Magdalena . . . Mardalena	Margaret. . . . Margrietie	Maria . . . . Marian
Magdalena. . . . . Marlene	Margaret. . . . Margrietje	Maria . . . . Maricka
Magdalena . . Marregante	Margaret . . . Margrietze	Maria . . . . Marie
Magdalena. . Martaleentje	Margaret . . . . Margritje	Maria . . . . Mariea
Magdalena. . . . . . Matle	Margaret . . . Marigiettie	Maria . . . . . . Mariedel
Magdalena. . . . . . Metje	Margaret . . . Marragriet	Maria . . . . Marieiia
Malachi . . . . . Maleschi	Margaret . . Marragrieta	Maria . . . . Marietie
Mangold. . . . . . Maneke	Margaret. . Marragrietie	Maria . . . . Marietje
Mangold . . . . . . Mangel	Margaret . . . . Marregieta	Maria . . . . Marietta
Mangold . . . . Mann	Margaret . . Marregrietie	Maria . . . . Mariken
Mangold . . . . Manz	Margaret . . Marregrietta	Maria. . . . . Marite
Mangold . . . . . . Mengel	Margaret . . . Marygriethe	Maria . . . . Marites
Marcus . . . . Mack	Margaret . . . . Meg	Maria . . . . Maritje
Marcus . . . . Mark	Margaret. . . . . . . Pakke	Maria . . . . Maritjen
Marcus. . . . . Marx	Margaret. . . . . Peg	Maria . . . . Marka
Marcus. . . . . . . Mavous	Margaret . . . . . . Peggie	Maria . . . . Marretie
Marcus . . . . Merkel	Margaret . . . . . . Peggy	Maria . . . . Marretje
Marcus . . . . Merkle	Margaret . . . . Reda	Maria . . . . . . Marretye
Margaret . . . . Critje	Margaret . . . . Redel	Maria. . . . . . . Marrietta
Margaret . . . . Greet	Margaret . . . . . Retchen	Maria. . . . . Marritje

Given Name Equivalents: English to Dutch

Maria . . . . Marryetie	Marshal . . . . Marselis	Mathilda . . . . . . Meckelia
Maria . . . . Marrytie	Marshal . . . . Seel	Mathilda . . . . Meckla
Maria . . . . Mart	Martha . . . . Maartje	Mathilda . . . . Meckle
Maria . . . . Martha	Martha . . . . Maatje	Mathilda . . . . Mecklie
Maria . . . . Martie	Martha . . . . Maria	Mathilda . . . . Meitza
Maria . . . . Martje	Martha . . . . Marta	Mathilda . . . . Meiza
Maria . . . . Mary	Martha . . . . Matie	Mathilda . . . . . Mekkels
Maria . . . . Marya	Martha . . . . Matje	Mathilda . . . . Meta
Maria . . . . Maryette	Martha . . . . Merci	Mathilda . . . . Metje
Maria . . . . Marytie	Martha . . . . Metje	Mathilda . . . . Metke
Maria . . . . Mayke	Martha . . . . Mettje	Mathilda . . . . Metta
Maria . . . . Mayken	Martin . . . . Maarten	Mathilda . . . . . Mettelde
Maria . . . . Maykje	Martin . . . . Maerte	Mathilda . . . . Mettild
Maria . . . . Merga	Martin . . . . Mareten	Mathilda . . . . . . Metze
Maria . . . . Merityen	Martin . . . . . . Marreten	Mathilda . . . . Mezza
Maria . . . . . . Merreytje	Martin . . . . . Marrethen	Mathilda . . . . Thilde
Maria . . . . Merytyen	Martin . . . . Marta	Mathilda . . . . . Tildchen
Maria . . . . Mia	Martin . . . . Marte	Mathilda . . . . Till
Maria . . . . Mie	Martin . . . . . . Marteines	Mathilda . . . . Tilla
Maria . . . . . . Miekchen	Martin . . . . Marthen	Matthew . . . . Debes
Maria . . . . Mieke	Martin . . . . Marthinnus	Matthew . . . . Debiss
Maria . . . . Miel	Martin . . . . Marthynnus	Matthew . . . . Debus
Maria . . . . Mieteke	Martin . . . . Martie	Matthew . . . . Dewes
Maria . . . . Mietje	Martin . . . . Martines	Matthew . . . . Diepes
Maria . . . . Mietzerl	Martin . . . . Martinis	Matthew . . . . Deis
Maria . . . . Miezel	Martin . . . . . . Martinus	Matthew . . . . Deise
Maria . . . . Mimmeli	Martin . . . . . Martynnus	Matthew . . . . Disse
Maria . . . . Mimmi	Martin . . . . . . Martynus	Matthew . . . . . . Dysskin
Maria . . . . Miri	Martin . . . . Merten	Matthew . . . . Hess
Maria . . . . Mirl	Martin . . . . Mertin	Matthew . . . . Heis
Maria . . . . Mirzel	Martin . . . . Mirtel	Matthew . . . . Hias
Maria . . . . Mitzi	Martin . . . . Tienes	Matthew . . . . Hiesl
Maria . . . . Mizzi	Martina . . . . . Martyntie	Matthew . . . . Mades
Maria . . . . Ria	Martina . . . . . Martyntje	Matthew . . . . Mateis
Maria . . . . Rietje	Martina . . . . Marytyntie	Matthew . . . . . . Mateues
Maria . . . . Uarritie	Martina . . . . Tina	Matthew . . . . . . Mateves
Marinus . . . . Marin	Martina . . . . Tiney	Matthew . . . . . Matewes
Marinus . . . . . . Morinus	Martina . . . . Tyne	Matthew . . . . . . Matewis
Marjorie . . . . . . Masere	Mary . . . . Maria	Matthew . . . . . Matheus
Marjorie . . . . . Mazeries	Mary . . . . Molly	Matthew . . . . . . Mathias
Marjorie . . . . Mazre	Mary . . . . Polly	Matthew . . . . Mathys
Marjory . . . . Mayke	Mathilda . . . . Matje	Matthew . . . . Mattes
Marjory . . . . Morica	Mathilda . . . . Meccla	Matthew . . . . . Mattheus
Markoff . . . . Merck	Mathilda . . . . . . Mechel	Matthew . . . . . Matthias
Markward . . . Merkellin	Mathilda . . . . . Mechteld	Matthew . . . . . . Matthis
Markward . . . . Merkelo	Mathilda . . . . Mechthild	Matthew . . . . . . Matthys
Marshal . . . . . Marceles	Mathilda . . . . . . Meckel	Matthew . . . . Matthysse
Marshal . . . . . Merselies	Mathilda . . . . . Meckele	Matthew . . . . . Matthyus

Matthew . . . . Mattius	Melchior . . . . Mele	Nancy . . . . Nencie
Matthew . . . . Matyas	Melchior . . . . . . Melgert	Nathaniel . . . . Nat
Matthew . . . . Matys	Melchior . . . . Melke	Nehemiah . . . . . Nemeyjar
Matthew . . . . Matz	Melchior . . . . Melle	Nathaniel . . . . Net
Matthew . . . . Mettus	Mensje . . . . Mensie	Nathaniel . . . . . Nethaniel
Matthew . . . . Mettys	Mensje . . . . Minske	Nathaniel . . . . . Netteneel
Matthew . . . . Metys	Michael . . . . Machiel	Nathaniel . . . . . . Thaniel
Matthew . . . . Teves	Michael . . . . Mageel	Nelly . . . . Naeltie
Matthew . . . . Thebs	Michael . . . . Maghiel	Nelly . . . . Neeltje
Matthew . . . . Tebes	Michael . . . . Magiel	Nelly . . . . Neely
Matthew . . . . Teeuw	Michael . . . . Makeel	Nelly . . . . Nelletie
Matthew . . . . . . Teeuwis	Michael . . . . Meigel	Nelly . . . . Nelletje
Matthew . . . . Teiwes	Michael . . . . Michel	Nelly . . . . Nellitie
Matthew . . . . Teus	Michael . . . . . . Michiel	Nelly . . . . Neltie
Matthew . . . . Tewis	Michael . . . . Giel	Nelly . . . . Nilletie
Matthew . . . . Tews	Millicent . . . . Milly	Nelly . . . . Nillie
Matthew . . . . Theibs	Minnie . . . . Meeno	Nicholas . . . . Claas
Matthew . . . . Theis	Minnie . . . . Meensje	Nicholas . . . . Clabis
Matthew . . . . Theiss	Minnie . . . . . . Meenske	Nicholas . . . . Claeck
Matthew . . . . Thewes	Minnie . . . . Meino	Nicholas . . . . Claes
Matthew . . . . Thies	Minnie . . . . Meinsje	Nicholas . . . . Clais
Matthew . . . . Thiess	Minnie . . . . Menno	Nicholas . . . . Claus
Matthew . . . . Thys	Minnie . . . . Meyne	Nicholas . . . . Clese
Matthew . . . . Tiebes	Minnie . . . . Meynno	Nicholas . . . . . Clesschen
Matthew . . . . Tiges	Minnie . . . . Meyno	Nicholas . . . . Clobes
Matthew . . . . Tigges	Minnie . . . . Meynou	Nicholas . . . . Clos
Matthew . . . . Tijs	Minnie . . . . Mincke	Nicholas . . . . Clowes
Matthew . . . . Tys	Minnie . . . . Mino	Nicholas . . . . Klaas
Mattina . . . . Thijsie	Minnie . . . . Muno	Nicholas . . . . Klaes
Mattina . . . . Tysje	Minnie . . . . Myna	Nicholas . . . . Klass
Mattina? . . . . Thysje	Minnie . . . . Mynett	Nicholas . . . . . . Klaywitz
Maurice . . . . Maris	Minnie . . . . Mynni	Nicholas . . . . Klobes
Maurice . . . . . . Mouwies	Minnie . . . . Mynno	Nicholas . . . . Klosel
Maurice . . . . Maurus	Minnie . . . . . . Mynnotie	Nicholas . . . . . Necklaes
Maurice . . . . . Marritius	Minnie . . . . Myno	Nicholas . . . . . . Neeklas
Maurice . . . . . . Morice	Minnie . . . . Mynotie	Nicholas . . . . Nicholaas
Maurice . . . . . . Mouris	Minnie . . . . Myntie	Nicholas . . . . Nicholaes
Maximilian . . . . Max	Minnie . . . . . Wilhelmina	Nicholas . . . . Nickel
Maynard . . . . . Meindert	Miriam . . . . . . Merriam	Nicholas . . . . . . Nicklaes
Maynard . . . . Meinhard	Molly . . . . Malle	Nicholas . . . . Nicklas
Maynard . . . . Menassus	Molly . . . . Mally	Nicholas . . . . . . Niclaas
Maynard . . . . . Myndert	Monica . . . . Mone	Nicholas . . . . . Nicolaas
Mehitabel . . . . . Hittebel	Mortimer . . . . Mort	Nicholas . . . . . Nicolass
Mehitable . . . . . . Mable	Moses . . . . Mosis	Nicholas . . . . . . Niklas
Meinrad . . . . Radel	Moses . . . . Mosus	Nicholas . . . . Nisse
Melchior . . . . . Melbert	Moses . . . . Moyses	Nicholas . . . . . . Nitsche
Melchior . . . . . Melchar	Nancy . . . . Ann	Nicole . . . . Claesje
Melchior . . . . . Melchert	Nancy . . . . Na	Nicole . . . . Clasje

Given Name Equivalents: English to Dutch

Nicole . . . . Classje	Patricia . . . . . . Belyntrie	Petronella . . . . Nelle
Nicole . . . . Claudia	Patricia . . . . Beterse	Petronella . . . . Petronela
Noah . . . . Noach	Patricia . . . . Betterse	Petronella . . . Pieternelle
Obadiah . . . . Abedy	Patricia . . . . Patty	Petronella . . . . Pietje
Obadiah . . . . Abia	Patricia . . . . Patze	Petronella . . . Pietronella
Obadiah . . . . Abijah	Patricia . . . . Peczgin	Petronella . . . . . Pironella
Obadiah . . . . Obadja	Patricia . . . . Pepil	Petronella . . . . . Pironelle
Obadiah . . . . Obaje	Patricia . . . . Peppe	Phebe . . . . Febe
Obadiah . . . . Obed	Patricia . . . . Petertje	Phebe . . . . Febi
Octavius . . . . Aujke	Patricia . . . . . Petirsche	Phebe . . . . Febie
Octavius . . . . Auke	Patricia . . . . Pietertje	Phebe . . . . Feebi
Octavius . . . . Okie	Paul . . . . Pabel	Phebe . . . . Fiebie
Octavius . . . . Oktee	Paul . . . . Pagel	Phebe . . . . Peubie
Octavius . . . . Ouke	Paul . . . . Parvel	Phebe . . . . Pheben
Octavius . . . . . . Okenus	Paul . . . . Pauel	Phebe . . . . Phebie
Oliver . . . . Oelfert	Paul . . . . Paulius	Phebe . . . . Pheebie
Oliver . . . . Olfert	Paul . . . . Paullus	Phebe . . . . Phoebe
Oliver . . . . Olof	Paul . . . . Paulus	Phebe . . . . . . Tamacha
Oliver . . . . Olphert	Paul . . . . Pauwelis	Philetus . . . . . . Phelitjah
Ortwin . . . . . . Ordewin	Paul . . . . Pawel	Philip . . . . Feilleph
Oswald . . . . Walt	Paul . . . . Powel	Philip . . . . Felipe
Oswald . . . . Weldechen	Paul . . . . Powles	Philip . . . . Filep
Oswald . . . . Wolt	Paul . . . . Poulus	Philip . . . . Filip
Otilia . . . . Ootie	Paul . . . . Pouw	Philip . . . . Filips
Otilia . . . . Outie	Paul . . . . Pouweles	Philip . . . . Fliep
Ottilia . . . . Diele	Paul . . . . Pouwelis	Philip . . . . Fliepse
Ottilia . . . . Dilge	Paulina . . . . . . Paylyntie	Philip . . . . Flip
Ottilia . . . . Diliga	Paulina . . . . Paultje	Philip . . . . Flyp
Ottilia . . . . Dittel	Paulina . . . . . . Paulyntje	Philip . . . . Lipmann
Ottilia . . . . Tilly	Peek . . . . Peeck	Philip . . . . Lippe
Ottilia . . . . Tyle	Penelope . . . . Penny	Philip . . . . Lipperl
Otto . . . . Odde	Penelope . . . . . Preyntie	Philip . . . . Lipps
Otto . . . . Ode	Penelope . . . . . . Prientje	Philip . . . . Lippus
Otto . . . . Odo	Penelope . . . . Pryne	Philip . . . . . . Philamon
Otto . . . . Otho	Persis . . . . Percy	Philip . . . . Philiph
Otto . . . . Otte	Peter . . . . Peres	Philip . . . . Philipus
Otto . . . . Ottel	Peter . . . . Perter	Philip . . . . Phlip
Otto . . . . Otti	Peter . . . . Peterus	Philip . . . . Pip
Otto . . . . Udo	Peter . . . . Petres	Philip . . . . Vlypse
Patience . . . . . Bekyntrie	Peter . . . . Petris	Philomena . . . . File
Patience . . . . . . Paryntie	Peter . . . . Petrus	Philomena . . . . Filo
Patience . . . . . . Pecens	Peter . . . . Petschke	Philomena . . . . . . Phile
Patience . . . . . . Peesjiens	Peter . . . . Pierre	Polly . . . . Baaltje
Patience . . . . Pesens	Peter . . . . Piet	Polly . . . . Ballie
Patience . . . . . . Pesensie	Peter . . . . Pieter	Polly . . . . Bally
Patience . . . . . . Petiens	Peter . . . . Pietsch	Polly . . . . Mary
Patience . . . . . . Preciens	Peter . . . . Piter	Prudence . . . . Prada
Patience . . . . . . Preyntje	Peter . . . . Pitter	Prudence . . . . Prudy

Given Name Equivalents: English to Dutch

Quirinus....... Cryenus	Reinhard ..... Reinsch	Richard ..... Rithsardt
Quirinus .... Cryn	Reinhard ...... Reintje	Richard .... Ritsch
Quirinus .... Cryne	Reinhard ...... Renard	Richard .... Ritsert
Quirinus .... Grein	Reinhard ...... Rendel	Richard .... Ritsier
Quirinus .... Krein	Reinhard .... Renz	Richard ...... Rithzart
Quirinus .... Krienes	Reinhard ..... Reynchin	Richard .... Rosert
Quirinus .... Kryn	Reinhard ..... Reynold	Richard........ Rutsert
Quirinus .... Kyrn	Reinhard ..... Ryndert	Richard .... Rutsjert
Quirinus .... Quiryn	Reinhold........ Hold	Richard ...... Rychard
Rachel.......... Gebje	Reinhold ...... Holder	Richard .... Ryck
Rachel.......... Gepje	Reinhold .... Renke	Richard........ Ryjardt
Rachel .... Lackje	Rembrant....... Brandt	Richard .... Ryk
Rachel......... Raagel	Rembrant .... Brant	Richard...... Rykaard
Rachel.......... Ragel	Rembrant .... Ram	Richard......... Shark
Rachel......... Raghel	Rembrant .... Rem	Robert........... Bert
Rachel.......... Rahel	Rems .... Rem	Robert........... Rob
Rachel......... Reghel	Resolved ... Geresolveert	Robert...... Robbardt
Rachel .... Rhyntje	Resolved .... Geresolvert	Robert........ Robbart
Ralph.......... Roelof	Resolved.... Resolveert	Robert........ Robbedt
Ralph.......... Rulef	Resolved ...... Resull	Robert....... Robberdt
Ralph.......... Ruliph	Resolved ...... Resulla	Robert........ Robbert
Randal....... Randolph	Reuben .... Ruben	Robert .... Robberthus
Randolph..... Landolph	Reyer......... Reyess	Robert......... Robbet
Raymond ..... Reimond	Reyer......... Reyyer	Robin......... Robben
Rebecca .... Bacca	Reyer .... Ryer	Robin .... Robbin
Rebecca .... Becca	Reyer......... Ryerse	Roelof.......... Ralph
Rebecca .... Becki	Reyer........ Ryerson	Roelof.......... Roille
Rebecca ...... Rabecca	Reyner.......... Rijn	Roelof .... Rolef
Rebecca ...... Rabecka	Reynold ..... Reinhard	Roelof .... Roleke
Rebecca .... Rabeecka	Richard .... Dik	Roelof .... Rolf
Rebecca ...... Rebakah	Richard.......... Dirk	Roelof .... Rolfe
Rebecca .... Rebbecca	Richard......... Reich	Roelof........ Rollekin
Rebecca ...... Rebecke	Richard...... Ressardt	Roelof....... Rollmann
Rebecca .... Rebeckke	Richard........ Ressart	Roelof .... Rollo
Regina .... Gine	Richard...... Resserdt	Roelof .... Rolof
Regina .... Ina	Richard .... Reysard	Roelof.......... Rolph
Regina .... Rega	Richard....... Richeli	Roger .... Radser
Regina.......... Regel	Richard.......... Rick	Roger .... Raedjert
Regina........... Regi	Richard........ Rickert	Roger.......... Rogier
Regina........ Reigerl	Richard...... Rijkaard	Roger.......... Rotger
Reinhard ..... Reindel	Richard ...... Rijkerd	Roger .... Rucker
Reinhard...... Reindert	Richard ...... Risherd	Roger......... Rudiger
Reinhard ..... Reineke	Richard ...... Rissard	Roger......... Rugger
Reinhard .... Reiner	Richard....... Rissardt	Roger............. Rut
Reinhard....... Reinert	Richard........ Rissart	Roger .... Rutgert
Reinhard .... Reini	Richard........ Risserd	Roger .... Rutsen
Reinhard.... Reinnaert	Richard...... Risserdt	Roger.......... Rutger
Reinhard...... Reinoud	Richard .... Rissert	Rosamond ... Rozamond

Rose . . . . Roosje	Rudolf . . . . Rulle	Sarah . . . . Saddie
Rosella . . . . Resel	Rudolf . . . . Rulmann	Sarah . . . . Saertje
Rosella . . . . Ressel	Rudolf . . . . Rulo	Sarah . . . . Sally
Rosella . . . . Resula	Rudolf . . . . Ruodi	Sarah . . . . Sara
Rosella . . . . Resull	Rudolf . . . . Ruoff	Sarah . . . . Sarahette
Rosella . . . . Resulla	Rudolf . . . . Rutt	Sarah . . . . Sare
Rosella . . . . Rosul	Rumbold . . . . . Rombout	Sarah . . . . Sartye
Rosina . . . . Ranche	Rupert . . . . Prechtl	Sarah . . . . Sasze
Rosina . . . . Rasana	Rupert . . . . Rijpert	Sarah . . . . Sautie
Rosina . . . . Rensie	Rupert . . . . Rip	Sarah . . . . Seertie
Rosina . . . . Rentje	Rupert . . . . Robert	Sarah . . . . Seeuw
Rosina . . . . Resyntje	Rupert . . . . Roppel	Sarah . . . . Seu
Rosetta . . . . Roosje	Rupert . . . . Rubi	Sarah . . . . Zara
Rosina . . . . Rosena	Rupert . . . . Rupel	Seger . . . . Zeger
Rosina . . . . Sali	Rupert . . . . Rupli	Servatius . . . . Vaaz
Rosina . . . . Sina	Rupert . . . . Ruplo	Servatius . . . . Vacius
Rosina . . . . Zena	Rupert . . . . Ruppel	Servatius . . . . Vaes
Rowland . . . . . . Roeland	Rupert . . . . Ruppes	Servatius . . . . . . Zerves
Rudiger . . . . Rockel	Rupert . . . . Ruprecht	Servatius . . . . Zirves
Rudiger . . . . Roger	Ruth . . . . Rusje	Servis . . . . Cervaes
Rudiger . . . . Rogkens	Ruth . . . . Rutje	Servis . . . . Servas
Rudiger . . . . Rohle	Rymerick . . . . Reimerick	Severin . . . . Freins
Rudiger . . . . Ruckel	Rymerick . . . . . . Rynberg	Severin . . . . Frengs
Rudiger . . . . Ruclo	Sabina . . . . Bina	Severin . . . . Frings
Rudiger . . . . Rudengerus	Sabina . . . . Bine	Siebold . . . . Sevold
Rudiger . . . . Rugkil	Sabina . . . . Bingel	Siebold . . . . Siba
Rudiger . . . . Ruttiger	Sabina . . . . Wina	Siebold . . . . Sibe
Rudolf . . . . Dolfi	Sally . . . . Sali	Siebold . . . . Sibi
Rudolf . . . . Dulf	Sally . . . . Sarah	Siebold . . . . Siegbert
Rudolf . . . . Riehl	Sally . . . . Sate	Siebold . . . . Subolt
Rudolf . . . . Riehle	Sally . . . . Selie	Siebold . . . . Sybuldus
Rudolf . . . . . . Rietschel	Salome . . . . Selle	Siegbert . . . . Seba
Rudolf . . . . Rilke	Sampson . . . . . . Samson	Siegbert . . . . Sebert
Rudolf . . . . Roedolf	Sampson . . . . . . Simson	Siegbert . . . . Seibel
Rudolf . . . . Rohle	Samuel . . . . Saam	Siegbert . . . . Seidel
Rudolf . . . . Rolke	Samuel . . . . Sam	Siegbert . . . . Seiffert
Rudolf . . . . Roudle	Samuel . . . . Samel	Siegbert . . . . Seizz
Rudolf . . . . Rudel	Samuel . . . . . . Samewel	Siegbert . . . . Shuart
Rudolf . . . . Rudelft	Samuel . . . . Sammel	Siegbert . . . . Siebel
Rudolf . . . . Rudelo	Samuel . . . . Sammiel	Siegbert . . . . Siefert
Rudolf . . . . Rudi	Samuel . . . . Sammul	Siegbert . . . . Siegel
Rudolf . . . . Rudolph	Samuel . . . . Sem	Siegbert . . . . Sierick
Rudolf . . . . Ruef	Samuel . . . . . . Semmuel	Siegbert . . . . Sippel
Rudolf . . . . Ruetsch	Sarah . . . . Saar	Siegbert . . . . Sitt
Rudolf . . . . Ruf	Sarah . . . . Saara	Siegbert . . . . Sizzo
Rudolf . . . . Ruhle	Sarah . . . . Saartie	Siegbert . . . . Sjoert
Rudolf . . . . Rule	Sarah . . . . Saartje	Siegbert . . . . Soers
Rudolf . . . . Rulke	Sarah . . . . Saatje	Siegbert . . . . Soert

Siegbert . . . . Sourt	Sophia . . . . Fie	Sophia . . . . Zytken
Siegbert. . . . . Sybe	Sophia . . . . . . Fiekchen	Sophia . . . . Zytie
Siegbert . . . . . . Sybrichse	Sophia . . . . Fieken	Staats . . . . Staas
Siegfried . . . . . Scheifahrt	Sophia . . . . Fietje	Staats . . . . Staes
Siegfried . . . . Sefried	Sophia . . . . Fige	Staats . . . . Staets
Siegfried . . . . Seufert	Sophia . . . . Filgin	Stephen . . . . Stafanus
Siegfried . . . . . . Siegbert	Sophia . . . . Fletje	Stephen. . . . . . . Stavanus
Siegfried. . . . . Sieze	Sophia. . . . . Froutje	Stephen . . . . Stebe
Siegfried . . . . Sizo	Sophia . . . . Fyhe	Stephen . . . . Stebin
Siegfried . . . . . Suffridus	Sophia . . . . Fytie	Stephen . . . . Steeven
Siegfried . . . . Syczel	Sophia . . . . Fytje	Stephen . . . . Stefanis
Siegmond . . . . . Mundel	Sophia . . . . Fytle	Stephen . . . . . . Steffanus
Siegmond. . . . . . . Mundi	Sophia. . . . . Fytyje	Stephen. . . . . Steffel
Siegmond . . . . . . Siegel	Sophia . . . . Pfie	Stephen . . . . Steffen
Siegmond. . . . . . Sievert	Sophia . . . . Phige	Stephen . . . . Stefferl
Siegmond . . . . . . Sigelo	Sophia . . . . Phya	Stephen . . . . Steffi
Siegmond. . . . . Sigimund	Sophia . . . . . Safeiia	Stephen . . . . . Stephanis
Silas . . . . Sylas	Sophia . . . . Safeija	Stephen. . . . . Stephchin
Silas . . . . Syles	Sophia . . . . Safya	Stephen . . . . Stevants
Simon . . . . Lymon	Sophia . . . . Safytie	Stephen. . . . . . Stevanus
Simon . . . . Seman	Sophia . . . . Sapheya	Stephen . . . . Steve
Simon. . . . . Semion	Sophia . . . . Saphia	Stephen . . . . Steven
Simon . . . . Sijmen	Sophia. . . . . Saphya	Stephen. . . . . . . Stevens
Simon. . . . . Simeon	Sophia . . . . Sefeytie	Stephen. . . . . Stevin
Simon . . . . Symon	Sophia . . . . Sefia	Stephen . . . . Sthebe
Solomon . . . . Saal	Sophia . . . . Sefie	Susan . . . . Sanna
Solomon . . . . . Salemen	Sophia . . . . Sefytie	Susan . . . . Sanne
Solomon . . . . . Salomon	Sophia . . . . Sevfya	Susan . . . . . . Sanneke
Solomon . . . . Saul	Sophia. . . . . Seytie	Susan. . . . . . . Sannertje
Sophia . . . . Cytie	Sophia. . . . . Seytje	Susan. . . . . . . Sannertje
Sophia. . . . . Fei	Sophia . . . . Soff	Susan . . . . Sanni
Sophia . . . . Feige	Sophia . . . . Sofya	Susan . . . . Santje
Sophia . . . . Feigin	Sophia. . . . . . . Sophya	Susan . . . . Soetje
Sophia . . . . Feitie	Sophia . . . . Suff	Susan . . . . Sosar
Sophia . . . . . . Femetien	Sophia. . . . . Suffia	Susan . . . . Sukey
Sophia . . . . . . Femmete	Sophia. . . . . Suffie	Susan . . . . Suse
Sophia. . . . . . Femmetie	Sophia . . . . Sytje	Susan . . . . Susana
Sophia. . . . . . Femmetje	Sophia . . . . Vroutie	Susan . . . . Susane
Sophia . . . . . Femmettie	Sophia . . . . Vroutjie	Susan . . . . Susanna
Sophia . . . . . Femmetye	Sophia . . . . . . Vrouwete	Susan . . . . Suzana
Sophia . . . . . . Femmitje	Sophia . . . . Zefeytie	Susan . . . . Suze
Sophia . . . . Fey	Sophia . . . . Zefya	Susan . . . . . . Zanneke
Sophia. . . . . Feytie	Sophia . . . . . Zephronia	Susan. . . . . Zosel
Sophia. . . . . Feytje	Sophia. . . . . Zeytie	Susan . . . . Zusi
Sophia. . . . . Fia	Sophia . . . . Zophya	Susan . . . . Zus
Sophia . . . . Fiche	Sophia . . . . Zuff	Susan . . . . Zusana
Sophia . . . . Fick	Sophia . . . . Zyfie	Susan . . . . Zusanna
Sophia. . . . . Ficke	Sophia . . . . Zyfitie	Susan. . . . . Zusel

Given Name Equivalents: English to Dutch

Susan . . . . Zutz	Theodora. . . . . . Deryee	Thomas. . . . . Thom
Swan . . . . Swaen	Theodora . . . . . Dierckje	Thomas . . . . Thoman
Swan . . . . Swaan	Theodora. . . . . . Dircktie	Thomas . . . . Thomel
Swantje. . . . . . . Swantie	Theodora . . . . . . Dirckje	Thomas. . . . . Thommes
Swantje . . . . Zwantje	Theodora . . . . . Dirckye	Thomas . . . . Thoms
Sybil . . . . Beele	Theodora . . . . Dirkje	Thomas . . . . Thomus
Sybil. . . . . Beelgen	Theodora . . . . Dirrickje	Thomas. . . . . Thum
Sybil . . . . Beeltgen	Theodora . . . . . . Dirckie	Thomas . . . . Tomas
Sybil . . . . Beilgen	Theodora . . . . . . Dorcas	Thomas . . . . Tomes
Sybil . . . . Bele	Theodora . . . . . Durcktie	Thomas. . . . . . . Tommes
Sybil . . . . Beleke	Theodore . . . . Dedi	Thomas . . . . Toms
Sybil. . . . . Belia	Theodore . . . . Deiderick	Thomas . . . . Tomus
Sybil. . . . . Belige	Theodore. . . . . . . Derick	Timothy . . . . Teemer
Sybil. . . . . Bella	Theodore . . . . . . Derrick	Timothy . . . . Thamar
Sybil . . . . Belye	Theodore . . . . Diederick	Timothy . . . . Thamer
Sybil . . . . Bielgen	Theodore. . . . . . Dietrich	Timothy . . . . Thymen
Sybil . . . . Bilgin	Theodore . . . . Dirck	Timothy . . . . Thymon
Sybil . . . . Billa	Theodore . . . . . . Dirick	Timothy . . . . Tijmen
Sybil . . . . Bille	Theodore . . . . . . Dores	Timothy. . . . . . . Timotius
Sybil. . . . . Cibilla	Theodore . . . . Dirk	Timothy . . . . . Tomatius
Sybil. . . . . Felcke	Theodore . . . . . . Dorle	Timothy . . . . Tymen
Sybil. . . . . Fyllia	Theodore . . . . Dorli	Timothy . . . . Tymon
Sybil . . . . Pelcke	Theodore . . . . . . Dorus	Titus . . . . Tijte
Sybout . . . . Seybout	Theodore . . . . . . Dures	Tobias . . . . Bias
Sybout. . . . . Syboud	Theodore. . . . . Tedi	Tobias . . . . Tobeas
Sybout . . . . Syboudt	Theodore . . . . . Thederl	Tobias . . . . Tobyas
Sybout. . . . . . . Sybouwt	Theodore. . . Theodorus	Tracy . . . . Theresa
Sybout. . . . . Zybout	Theodore . . . . . . Thetje	Ulrich . . . . Reyk
Sybrant. . . . . . . Sebring	Theodore . . . . . . Tjerck	Ulrich. . . . . Rickel
Sylvia . . . . Silly	Theodosia. . . . . Doostie	Ulrich . . . . Udo
Tabitha . . . . Davida	Theophilus . . . . Godlief	Ulrich . . . . Ueli
Tabitha . . . . . . Thabyita	Theresa . . . . Thres	Ulrich . . . . Uelk
Tabitha . . . . . . Thabytha	Theresa . . . . Tracy	Ulrich . . . . Uerich
Thaddius. . . . . . . Cades	Theresa . . . . Treasje	Ulrich . . . . Uetz
Thaddius . . . . Tades	Theresa . . . . Tressje	Ulrich . . . . Uhl
Theobald . . . . . . Baltus	Theresa . . . . Zita	Ulrich . . . . Uhlig
Theobald . . . . . . Diebel	Thomas. . . . . . Dammas	Ulrich . . . . Ule
Theobald . . . . . Diebold	Thomas . . . . . . Dehmel	Ulrich . . . . Ulin
Theobald . . . . . . Tebout	Thomas. . . . . . . Dumes	Ulrich . . . . Ulli
Theobald. . . . . . Tiebald	Thomas . . . . Maas	Ulrich . . . . Ulritz
Theobald . . . . . Tiebout	Thomas . . . . Maes	Ulrich . . . . Ultschi
Theodora . . . . . Darckis	Thomas. . . . . . Massey	Ulrich . . . . Urech
Theodora . . . . . Darkus	Thomas . . . . Moyse	Ulrich . . . . Urle
Theodora . . . . . Dercjee	Thomas. . . . . Tam	Ulrich . . . . Utz
Theodora. . . . Dercketie	Thomas . . . . . Tammaes	Ulrich . . . . Uz
Theodora . . . . Dercktie	Thomas . . . . . . Tammes	Uriah. . . . . George
Theodora . . . . Dercktje	Thomas . . . . . . Tammus	Uriah . . . . Yria
Theodora . . . . . Derckye	Thomas . . . . Tamus	Uriah . . . . Yurie

Given Name Equivalents: English to Dutch

Uriah . . . . Ury	Victoria . . . . Viki	Wally . . . . Walpel
Ursula. . . . . Aosseltje	Victoria. . . . . Vikli	Walran . . . . Walleran
Ursula. . . . . Asseltje	Vincent . . . . Fijnsan	Walran . . . . Walra
Ursula . . . . Ersula	Vincent . . . . Fincent	Walran . . . . . . Walrandt
Ursula . . . . Nuschi	Vincent. . . . . Wensan	Walran . . . . . . Walraven
Ursula . . . . Orschel	Vincent . . . . Winsan	Walter . . . . Gualterus
Ursula. . . . . Orseli	Vincentia . . . . Sens	Walter . . . . Gualtier
Ursula. . . . . . . Orselina	Vincentia . . . . Senzel	Walter . . . . Walti
Ursula . . . . Orseltie	Vincentia . . . . Zenta	Walter . . . . Wat
Ursula. . . . . Osschil	Vincentia . . . . Zenzel	Walter . . . . Welter
Ursula . . . . Osseltje	Vincentia . . . . Zenzi	Walter . . . . Welti
Ursula . . . . Urzili	Vitus. . . . . Feit	Walter . . . . Wold
Ursula . . . . Ursi	Vitus . . . . Fyte	Walter . . . . Wolter
Ursula . . . . Ursel	Vitus. . . . . Vits	Walter . . . . Woltje
Ursula . . . . Urseltje	Volkert . . . . Focken	Walter . . . . Wout
Ute. . . . . Uda	Volkert . . . . Fokke	Walter. . . . . Wouter
Valentine . . . . Fell	Volkert . . . . Folbert	Walter . . . . Wouters
Valentine . . . . Felt	Volkert . . . . Fulbert	Wendel. . . . . . . Wander
Valentine. . . . . . . Felte	Volkert. . . . . . . Fulkard	Werner . . . . . Warnaerts
Valentine. . . . . . . Feltes	Volkert. . . . . Holger	Werner . . . . Warner
Valentine . . . . . . Feltine	Volkert. . . . . . . Volkers	Werner. . . . . . . Watzold
Valentine. . . . . Valentijn	Volkert . . . . Folkert	Werner . . . . . . Wenckel
Valentine . . . . . Valentyn	Volkmar . . . . Wolgmarus	Werner . . . . . Wecelinus
Valentine . . . . Valtin	Volpert . . . . Feupe	Werner. . . . . Wencz
Valentine. . . . . . Velten	Volpert . . . . Fockilo	Werner . . . . . . Weczelo
Valentine. . . . . . Veltin	Volpert . . . . Foilep	Werner . . . . . . Wenkelo
Valentine . . . . Veltje	Volpert. . . . . . . Foupel	Werner . . . . . . Wenzel
Veronica. . . . Baranicke	Volpert. . . . . Fulpracht	Werner. . . . . . . Wenzo
Veronica. . . . Barenicke	Volpert. . . . . . . Vaupel	Werner. . . . . . . Wernz
Veronica. . . . . Barnicke	Volpert . . . . Veupe	Werner . . . . Wessel
Veronica . . . Barranicke	Volpert. . . . . . . Vockel	Werner. . . . . . . Wetzel
Veronica . . . Barrinicke	Volpert. . . . . Volzo	Werner . . . . . . Wetzile
Veronica. . . Berranecke	Volpert . . . . Vopel	Werner . . . . Widsel
Veronica . . . . . . Freena	Volpert. . . . . . . Voypel	Werner . . . . Witzel
Veronica . . . . Frena	Volpert . . . . . . Walpert	Wessel . . . . Wassel
Veronica . . . . . . Frenne	Volpert . . . . . Walpodo	Wilhelmina. . . . . Helma
Veronica. . . . . . . Frina	Volpert . . . . Walpracht	Wilhelmina . . . . . Miggi
Veronica. . . . . . . Fron	Volpert . . . . Wolpertus	Wilhelmina . . . Mijntje
Veronica. . . . . . . Fronn	Volpert. . . . . Wolprath	Wilhelmina. . . . . . Mina
Veronica. . . . . . . Rene	Volpert. . . . . . Wulprat	Wilhelmina . . . Minchen
Veronica. . . . . Vrenele	Walburg . . . . Burga	Wilhelmina . . . Minochy
Veronica . . . . Vroa	Walburg. . . . . . . Burgei	Wilhelmina . . . . Minnie
Veronica. . . . . . . Vrona	Walburg. . . . . Wally	Wilhelmina. . . . Mintgen
Veronica . . . . Vrein	Walburg. . . . . . Wobbe	Wilhelmina Weillemeintie
Vibbard. . . . . . Vibbardt	Walburg. . . . . . Wubgen	Wilhelmina . Welemeintie
Victoria . . . . Fike	Wallace . . . . Walich	Wilhelmina . . Wellimyntie
Victoria . . . . Vige	Wallace . . . . Walig	Wilhelmina. . Wilemeintie
Victoria . . . . Vike	Wally. . . . . Wali	Wilhelmina . Wilhelmentie

Given Name Equivalents: English to Dutch

Wilhelmina . . . Willemfye	William . . . . Wim
Wilhelmina . . Willemintie	William . . . . Wyllem
Wilhelmina . . Willemintje	Winafred . . . . . . Weintie
Wilhelmina . . . . Willemtje	Winafred . . . . . . Wynefrid
Wilhelmina . . . Willempie	Winafred . . . . Wyntje
Wilhelmina . . . Willempje	Wipert . . . . Wipo
Wilhelmina . . . . Willemyn	Wolfert . . . . Wolefert
Wilhelmina . . Willemyntie	Wolfert . . . . Wolfard
Wilhelmina . . . . . . Wilma	Wolfert . . . . Wolfardt
Wilhelmina . . . . . Wimpje	Wolfert . . . . Wolfart
William . . . . Bill	Wolfert . . . . Wolffert
William . . . . Billy	Wolfert . . . . . Wollefard
William . . . . . Geiljongh	Wolfert . . . . Wollefart
William . . . . Gielam	Wolfert . . . . Wolvert
William . . . . Gieljam	Wyatt? . . . . Wydt
William . . . . Giliam	Wyatt? . . . . Wyt
William . . . . Giljon	Wybrecht . . . . . . Weybrug
William . . . . Guilem	Wybrecht . . . . . Wiberich
William . . . . Guiliam	Wybrecht . . . . . . Wibregh
William . . . . Guiljam	Wybrecht . . . . Wybracht
William . . . . Guilliam	Wybrecht . . . . . . Wybrug
William . . . . Gilljon	Wygand . . . . Wiczel
William . . . . Halmagh	Wygand . . . . Wigelo
William . . . . Helm	Wygand . . . . Wygel
William . . . . Helmer	Wygert . . . . Weart
William . . . . Helmes	Wygert . . . . Wiart
William . . . . Helmet	Wygert . . . . Wiert
William . . . . Helmi	Wynant . . . . Wibrant
William . . . . Helmig	Wynant . . . . Winand
William . . . . Helmke	Wynant . . . . Winans
William . . . . Weillem	Wynant . . . . Winant
William . . . . Wellem	Wynant . . . . Winlin
William . . . . . Wilhelmius	Wynant . . . . Wybrant
William . . . . . Wilhelmus	Wynant . . . . Wybren
William . . . . . . Wilielmus	Wynant . . . . Wygbrant
William . . . . Wilke	Wynant . . . . Wynand
William . . . . Wilko	Zachariah . . . . Rias
William . . . . Wille	Zachariah . . . . Sachariah
William . . . . Willekin	Zachariah . . . . . Zacariah
William . . . . Willem	Zachariah . . . . Zach
William . . . . Williem	Zachariah . . . . Zacharias
William . . . . Willim	Zachariah . . . . . . Zachary
William . . . . Willium	Zachariah . . . . . . Zacherl
William . . . . Willum	Zachariah . . . . Zoch
William . . . . Wilm	
William . . . . Wilt	
William . . . . Wiltz	
William . . . . Wilyum	

Section III

FATHER AND MOTHER PAIRS - 17th Century

This final section might be called "The section of last resort" and can become useful to the researcher if both previous sections of this book have not yielded positive results. This section might provide the research breakthrough but it's value is limited by the commonness of the names being searched, whether or not the time period is early enough, and the geographic location being searched.

Dutch and German Naming Conventions:

Before beginning to discuss naming conventions, it is important to point out that the conventions were not followed by every family and in all periods of time but were used with enough frequency that we may expect to see evidence of the convention in families from New York and New Jersey through the 18th century. Many times being aware of the system can provide the researcher with the tools that are needed to bring a genealogy closer to successful completion.

The typical family, both of Dutch and also of German origin who settled in New York-New Jersey seemed to prefer a system of naming the first two children of each sex in honor of the grandparents of the same sex. Usually the father's father was the name chosen for the first male child. If that grandparent was still living, he would usually stand as the male sponsor for that child's baptism. The second male child would then be named for the mother's father and the succeeding male children were likely to be named for uncles and others whom the family wished to honor. Daughters names were also selected based upon grandparents names when this system was used.

Perhaps a hypothetical example would be the best way to illustrate this concept: If patronymics were also being used, all children of Jacob (_____) would be (_____) Jacobs. Suppose, therefore, that children of Jacob Leonards and Maria Jans were:

> Leonard Jacobs
> Jans Jacobs
> Elizabeth Jacobs
> Sophia Jacobs
> Jacob Jacobs
> Maria Jacobs

After having gathered this family grouping, we could readily presume that:
1. The patronymic system of naming is in use.
2. The paternal grandparents were Leonard and Elizabeth.
3. The maternal grandparents were Jans and Sophia.

Names, Names and More Names

Sponsors at the baptisms of the above children would be a great help in ascertaining whether or not we were on the right track. Of course, the main assumptions here are that:

1. The family was using patronymics, and
2. We have located all of the early children in this family.

A word of caution – obviously some patronymics are very common so that all those with the patronymic "Jans" are not likely to be brothers. Just as it is true that all those whose father's given name is John, that does not make them siblings. However, conversely, if one male has the patronymic of Jans and another the patronymic of Jacobs, it is not very likely that they are siblings – they could be cousins or even half-brothers by sharing the same mother, but probably not brothers.

Another factor to consider is that if, when a family grouping has been gathered, there is a seeming discrepancy in the naming system, an earlier child may have died and the name reused for a newborn child. At other times children are named out of sequence to honor some different recently deceased family member.

The name of the wife should be considered an important clue in determining the identity of her husband's family even if her surname is unknown. Her first name, especially if an unusual name such as Petronella or Kunigonda, will help to show the identity of her husband by comparing baptism and marriage entries for couples with the same first names. Occasionally the wife will be identified with a surname or a patronymic which will appear in index entries and this, in turn, could lead to the surname of her husband.

This third section will be of particular value to you if you are working in the 17th century or very early in the 18th century and:

1. You've established the grandparents given names from the sequence of grandchildren names already discovered, or
2. You already know the parents given names and are searching for additional children of that couple suspecting that they may occasionally be found with their patronymic.

The value of TABLE 3 is dependent upon the uniqueness of the given names involved. The research will be more certain of a valid match with male given names, for example, of Clement or Ide rather than Hendrick or a mother's given name of Jemima or Ursula rather than Anna. Since a father's name of Jan, John, Johannes, etc was just too common to be of any great value, it was decided to omit that name from the listing.

The following tables were derived from church baptism and marriage records prior to 1700 in the New York/New Jersey area and were selected if:

Names, Names and More Names

1. A father's and a mother's name were both recorded and
2. the father's given name was not Jan, John, Johannes., etc

List of church records used together with the abbreviations found in the table:

Alb Ref - Albany, Reformed Church baptisms + marriages
Berg Ref - Bergen, NJ Reformed Church baptisms + marriages
Bkln Ref - Brooklyn, NY Reformed Church baptisms + marriages
Fltb Ref - Flatbush, NY Reformed Church baptisms + marriages
Hack Ref - Hackensack, NJ Reformed Church baptisms + marriages
King Ref - Kingston, NY Reformed Church baptisms + marriages
King NYGB - Kingston, NY Reformed Church (pub in *The Record*) baptisms + marriages
NPal Ref - New Platz, NY Reformed church baptisms
NY Ref - New York City Reformed Church baptisms + marriages
Schn Ref - Schenectady, NY Reformed Church baptisms + marriages
Tap Ref - Tappan, NY Reformed Church baptisms + marriages
Tary Ref - Tarrytown, NY Reformed Church baptisms + marriages

Table 3A
Father/Mother Pairs Directory

A

Abel

Anna
NY Ref bp, 1662, 1664, 1667, 1669, 1671

Catherine
Berg Ref bp, 1698, 1699
Hack Ref bp, 1699

Abraham

Agatha
King Ref bp, 1697
NPal Ref bp, 1696, 1698
NY Ref bp, 1650

Alida
Berg Ref bp, 1695
Fltb Ref bp, 1681
Hack Ref bp, 1696, 1697
NY Ref bp, 1684, 1685, 1689, 1690, 1691, 1693

Anna
Alb Ref bp, 1692, 1694, 1695
Berg Ref bp, 1688, 1690
Hack Ref bp, 1699
King Ref bp, 1695, 1697
NY Ref bp, 1665, 1683, 1685, 1693, 1694, 1696, 1697
Tary Ref bp, 1698

Catherine
Alb Ref bp, 1692, 1695, 1698
NY Ref bp, 1656, 1660, 1662, 1664, 1668, 1671, 1673, 1676, 1685, 1686, 1688, 1690, 1692, 1694, 1695, 1696, 1698

Catlintje
NY Ref bp, 1697, 1699

Cecilia
King Ref bp, 1683, 1685, 1688, 1689

Christina
Fltb Ref bp, 1680

Cornelia
Bkln Ref bp, 1697, 1699
NY Ref bp, 1682, 1684, 1686, 1689, 1691, 1694, 1695

Elizabeth
Berg Ref bp, 1691, 1692
NY Ref bp, 1692, 1694, 1696, 1698

Elsie
Alb Ref bp, 1697, 1698
King Ref bp, 1694, 1697
NY Ref bp, 1661, 1668

Frances
NY Ref bp, 1659, 1661, 1663, 1667, 1669, 1671

Geesje
Alb Ref bp, 1691, 1694, 1697

Gertrude
Alb Ref bp, 1692, 1695
Bkln Ref bp, 1699
NY Ref bp, 1693, 1695

Harmina
NY Ref bp, 1697, 1699

Helena
NY Ref bp, 1688

Hester
NY Ref bp, 1698

Janet
Berg Ref bp, 1686, 1688
Bkln Ref bp, 1678, 1695
Fltb Ref bp, 1678, 1680

Jemima
King Ref bp, 1699
NY Ref bp, 1664, 1666, 1668, 1673, 1676, 1685, 1692, 1694, 1698

Lavinia
NY Ref bp, 1696

Magdalena
King Ref bp, 1688

Margaret
King Ref bp, 1682, 1694, 1696
NPal Ref bp, 1684, 1687, 1689, 1693
NY Ref bp, 1643, 1655, 1662, 1666, 1682, 1685, 1686, 1691, 1699
Tap Ref bp, 1694, 1697
Tary Ref bp, 1699

Maria
Alb Ref bp, 1694, 1696, 1698
King Ref bp, 1682, 1694
NPal Ref bp, 1683, 1686, 1690, 1691, 1696
NY Ref bp, 1655, 1657, 1660, 1662, 1664, 1680, 1687, 1692, 1698

Mathilda
NY Ref bp, 1658, 1659, 1661, 1664, 1667, 1671, 1674

Rebecca
NY Ref bp, 1693, 1695

Sarah
NY Ref bp, 1696, 1697, 1699

Sophia
Berg Ref bp, 1692, 1694, 1696
NY Ref bp, 1689, 1691, 1692, 1693, 1695, 1697

Adam

Alida
NY Ref bp, 1678

Anna
NY Ref bp, 1690

Magdalena
Bkln Ref bp, 1660, 1662
NY Ref bp, 1662, 1672

Margaret
Alb Ref bp, 1697
Schn Ref bp, 1699

Adam (cont.)
  Maria
    Bkln Ref bp, 1692, 1695,
    1696, 1699
  Mathilda
    King Ref bp, 1693, 1695,
    1698
  Nelly
    NY Ref bp, 1663, 1665,
    1666, 1667, 1670
Adolf
  Agatha
    NY Ref bp, 1666
  Eva
    NY Ref bp, 1657, 1669
  Maria
    NY Ref bp, 1671, 1673,
    1677, 1679, 1682, 1684,
    1686, 1692, 1698
Adrian
  Abigail
    Berg Ref bp, 1667
    NY Ref bp, 1669
  Agnes
    Bkln Ref bp, 1682
    Fltb Ref bp, 1680, 1682
    NY Ref bp, 1685
  Anna
    Bkln Ref bp, 1686
    Fltb Ref bp, 1678, 1683
    NY Ref bp, 1691, 1693,
    1695, 1697, 1698, 1699
  Catherine
    Berg Ref bp, 1678, 1679,
    1680, 1681, 1682, 1684,
    1686, 1688, 1689, 1690,
    1691
    NY Ref bp, 1673, 1675,
    1678, 1679, 1680, 1681,
    1682, 1685
  Clara
    NY Ref bp, 1663
  Elizabeth
    Fltb Ref bp, 1678, 1680
    NY Ref bp, 1665, 1668,
    1671, 1674
  Isabel
    NY Ref bp, 1665

Janet
  Bkln Ref bp, 1685, 1689
  Fltb Ref bp, 1685
  NY Ref bp, 1666
Margaret
  NY Ref bp, 1662
Maria
  Berg Ref bp, 1688
  NY Ref bp, 1678
Martina
  NY Ref bp, 1664
Rachel
  King Ref bp, 1693
Rebecca
  NY Ref bp, 1665, 1667,
  1670, 1674, 1676, 1678
Wilhelmina
  Bkln Ref bp, 1686
  Fltb Ref bp, 1678, 1680,
  1683
Aegeus
  Janet
    Bkln Ref bp, 1682, 1687
    Fltb Ref bp, 1677, 1679,
    1680
  Judith
    NY Ref bp, 1664, 1671,
    1673
Aert
  Alida
    King Ref bp, 1697
  Anna
    King Ref bp, 1661
  Bridget
    Bkln Ref bp, 1662
    NY Ref bp, 1661
  Catherine
    NY Ref bp, 1692, 1693,
    1695, 1698
  Elizabeth
    Bkln Ref bp, 1699
  Gertrude
    Berg Ref bp, 1696
  Gracius
    Fltb Ref bp, 1682
  Margaret
    King Ref bp, 1663

Maria
  NY Ref bp, 1699
Nelly
  Fltb Ref bp, 1688
Susan
  NY Ref bp, 1641
Albert
  Adriana
    NY Ref bp, 1658
  Catherine
    NY Ref bp, 1659, 1686,
    1688, 1690, 1693, 1696,
    1698
  Catlintje
    Bkln Ref bp, 1695
  Elsie
    NY Ref bp, 1653, 1656,
    1658, 1669, 1670, 1672,
    1674, 1677, 1679, 1681,
    1683
  Helena
    Hack Ref bp, 1694, 1699
  Henrietta
    Berg Ref bp, 1690
    Fltb Ref bp, 1680, 1682,
    1684, 1685
  Hester
    Alb Ref bp, 1696, 1698
  Hilda
    Bkln Ref bp, 1698
    Fltb Ref bp, 1664, 1666,
    1681, 1683, 1685
  Janet
    NY Ref bp, 1680, 1682,
    1685, 1687, 1689, 1694,
    1695
  Julia
    Berg Ref bp, 1690
  Lavinia
    Hack Ref bp, 1694, 1695
    King Ref bp, 1664
  Magdalena
    Hack Ref bp, 1694, 1696
  Margaret
    Bkln Ref bp, 1685
    Fltb Ref bp, 1685
    NY Ref bp, 1663, 1666,
    1667, 1669

Father/Mother Pairs Directory

Maria
    Alb Ref bp, 1659, 1693,
    1694, 1696, 1698
    Tary Ref bp, 1698
Nelly
    Alb Ref bp, 1692
Patricia
    King Ref bp, 1680, 1683,
    1685
Petronella
    NY Ref bp, 1689, 1691,
    1694, 1696
Wilhelmina
    Bkln Ref bp, 1692
    Tap Ref bp, 1695, 1697

Aldert
Christina
    Fltb Ref bp, 1677, 1680,
    1681, 1684
    NY Ref bp, 1691
Henrietta
    NY Ref bp, 1657
Margaret
    NY Ref bp, 1661

Alexander
Christina
    King Ref bp, 1687
Elizabeth
    NY Ref bp, 1689, 1691,
    1694, 1696
Elsie
    Berg Ref bp, 1693
    Fltb Ref bp, 1683
Emma
    NY Ref bp, 1673
Janet
    NY Ref bp, 1669
Judith
    NY Ref bp, 1667
Margaret
    NY Ref bp, 1656
Maria
    King Ref bp, 1698
    NY Ref bp, 1668

Ambrose
Adriana
    NY Ref bp, 1661, 1665,
    1671

Andrew
Adriana
    Alb Ref bp, 1697, 1699
Agnes
    NY Ref bp, 1651, 1656,
    1659, 1662, 1667, 1669
Anna
    Fltb Ref bp, 1679, 1680
    Hack Ref bp, 1699
    NY Ref bp, 1675, 1677,
    1679, 1681, 1683, 1684,
    1685, 1687, 1689, 1691,
    1692, 1694, 1695, 1696,
    1697, 1698, 1699
Catherine
    Alb Ref bp, 1693, 1696
    NY Ref bp, 1655, 1657,
    1660, 1669, 1671, 1673,
    1687
Cecilia
    NY Ref bp, 1656
Cornelia
    Alb Ref bp, 1694, 1697
    NY Ref bp, 1696, 1698,
    1699
Elizabeth
    NY Ref bp, 1691, 1692,
    1694, 1696, 1698
Engel
    Alb Ref bp, 1692, 1694,
    1698
Frances
    NY Ref bp, 1673
Gertrude
    Bkln Ref bp, 1695
    NY Ref bp, 1656, 1658,
    1661, 1673, 1676
Gooden
    NY Ref bp, 1664
Hilda
    King Ref bp, 1661, 1662
Ida
    Alb Ref bp, 1693, 1695,
    1698
Isabel
    NY Ref bp, 1662

Janet
    King Ref bp, 1683, 1684,
    1686, 1688, 1692, 1694,
    1695, 1697, 1699
    NY Ref bp, 1673, 1676,
    1677, 1694
Joanna
    Berg Ref bp, 1694, 1696,
    1699
Margaret
    Alb Ref bp, 1693
Maria
    Fltb Ref bp, 1684, 1686
    King Ref bp, 1678, 1680,
    1684, 1685, 1688, 1691
    NY Ref bp, 1657, 1660,
    1689, 1691, 1692, 1694,
    1696, 1698, 1699
Patience
    Berg Ref bp, 1691
    NY Ref bp, 1678, 1684
Sophia
    NY Ref bp, 1672, 1677,
    1679, 1681, 1684, 1686,
    1689

Anthony
Anna
    Bkln Ref bp, 1683, 1686
    Fltb Ref bp, 1679, 1681,
    1684
Catherine
    Alb Ref bp, 1693, 1695,
    1697
    Berg Ref bp, 1679, 1680,
    1682, 1686, 1688, 1689,
    1690
Christina
    Berg Ref bp, 1686, 1688
    NY Ref bp, 1682, 1684
Dorothy
    NY Ref bp, 1657
Elizabeth
    Alb Ref bp, 1699
    Bkln Ref bp, 1688, 1690,
    1692
    NY Ref bp, 1659, 1661,
    1663, 1666, 1685, 1697

Anthony (cont.)

Gertrude
Berg Ref bp, 1676

Henrietta
NY Ref bp, 1699

Hester
NY Ref bp, 1667

Isabel
NY Ref bp, 1698

Janet
King Ref bp, 1678, 1695,
1696, 1697, 1699
NY Ref bp, 1671

Josina
NY Ref bp, 1678, 1685,
1687, 1691

Madeline
Bkln Ref bp, 1690

Magdalena
Fltb Ref bp, 1679, 1681,
1684, 1685

Margaret
NY Ref bp, 1655, 1660

Maria
Alb Ref bp, 1694, 1696
Fltb Ref bp, 1682, 1684
King Ref bp, 1662, 1664,
1666, 1668, 1671, 1674
NY Ref bp, 1690, 1696,
1699

Nelly
NY Ref bp, 1682

Petronella
King Ref bp, 1682, 1684,
1686

Susan
NY Ref bp, 1682, 1688,
1690, 1692, 1694, 1696

Wilhelmina
Alb Ref bp, 1692, 1695,
1698

Arent

Abigail
King Ref bp, 1666

Alida
King Ref bp, 1689
NY Ref bp, 1692, 1696

Anna
Fltb Ref bp, 1680
NY Ref bp, 1657

Catherine
King Ref bp, 1695, 1698

Christina
Bkln Ref bp, 1677
Fltb Ref bp, 1677
NY Ref bp, 1666, 1672

Elizabeth
King Ref bp, 1688, 1692,
1697, 1699

Eva
NY Ref bp, 1680, 1681,
1684, 1686, 1692, 1694

Geesje
King Ref bp, 1664, 1668
NY Ref bp, 1661

Gertrude
Alb Ref bp, 1691, 1694,
1697

Gilberta
NY Ref bp, 1664, 1667,
1669, 1673

Hester
NY Ref bp, 1691, 1693,
1695, 1699

Hilda
Bkln Ref bp, 1681, 1686,
1693, 1695
Fltb Ref bp, 1678, 1681,
1682, 1684

Isabel
NY Ref bp, 1661, 1664,
1669, 1671

Janet
Alb Ref bp, 1692
NY Ref bp, 1695

Madeline
Bkln Ref bp, 1696

Margaret
NY Ref bp, 1659

Maria
Alb Ref bp, 1698
Fltb Ref bp, 1680
King Ref bp, 1674, 1679,
1685, 1687, 1694, 1696,
1698

NY Ref bp, 1663, 1672,
1684

Rachel
King Ref bp, 1680, 1683,
1684, 1686, 1688, 1696

Rebecca
NY Ref bp, 1663, 1671

Sarah
Alb Ref bp, 1691, 1694
NY Ref bp, 1681, 1682,
1684, 1687, 1689
Schn Ref bp, 1696, 1699

Susan
NY Ref bp, 1661, 1664,
1669, 1670, 1674, 1675,
1677

Wyntje
King Ref bp, 1682

Arnold

Adriana
NY Ref bp, 1670, 1672,
1674

Cornelia
NY Ref bp, 1679, 1681

Janet
NY Ref bp, 1676, 1678,
1680, 1683, 1685, 1688,
1693

August

Anna
NY Ref bp, 1668, 1669,
1670, 1681, 1683, 1698

Janet
NY Ref bp, 1652, 1656,
1658, 1660, 1662

Maria
Alb Ref bp, 1692

Azariah

Nelly
NY Ref bp, 1679

Sarah
Alb Ref bp, 1698

B

Ballerand

Margaret
King Ref bp, 1664

Father/Mother Pairs Directory

Baltus
  Catherine
    Berg Ref bp, 1688
    King Ref bp, 1697
    NY Ref bp, 1687, 1690
  Engel
    NY Ref bp, 1662, 1663
  Frances
    Berg Ref bp, 1685
  Margaret
    NY Ref bp, 1671
  Maria
    NY Ref bp, 1667, 1670,
    1672, 1677, 1679, 1682,
    1685

Barent
  Agatha
    NY Ref bp, 1658
  Alida
    Fltb Ref bp, 1680
  Anna
    NY Ref bp, 1666, 1670
  Catherine
    Bkln Ref bp, 1696
    Fltb Ref bp, 1685
  Catlintje
    NY Ref bp, 1663
  Christina
    NY Ref bp, 1644, 1652,
    1675
  Deborah
    NY Ref bp, 1691, 1692,
    1694, 1697
  Gertrude
    Alb Ref bp, 1691, 1694,
    1695, 1696, 1699
    Berg Ref bp, 1697
    NY Ref bp, 1658, 1691
  Hilda
    Bkln Ref bp, 1693, 1696,
    1698
  Ida
    Bkln Ref bp, 1663
    Fltb Ref bp, 1685
  Janet
    NY Ref bp, 1690, 1692,
    1695, 1698

  Joanna
    NY Ref bp, 1687, 1690,
    1692
  Magdalena
    Fltb Ref bp, 1680
    King Ref bp, 1678, 1683
    NY Ref bp, 1676
  Margaret
    Bkln Ref bp, 1664
    NY Ref bp, 1660, 1697,
    1699
  Maria
    NY Ref bp, 1655, 1657,
    1677, 1680
  Nicole
    King Ref bp, 1663
    NY Ref bp, 1665
  Rachel
    NY Ref bp, 1695
  Sarah
    NY Ref bp, 1686, 1689,
    1691, 1694, 1697, 1698,
    1699
    Tary Ref bp, 1697, 1699
  Sophia
    Bkln Ref bp, 1659, 1661,
    1664
  Volkje
    Alb Ref bp, 1691, 1693
    Schn Ref bp, 1695, 1697

Bartel
  Eleanor
    Berg Ref bp, 1695, 1697
  Harmina
    NY Ref bp, 1663, 1668
  Helena
    Bkln Ref bp, 1695

Bartholomew
  Gertrude
    NY Ref bp, 1689, 1691,
    1693, 1695, 1697, 1699

Bastian
  Alida
    Berg Ref bp, 1690, 1693
  Anna
    NY Ref bp, 1697
  Maria
    NY Ref bp, 1660

  Theodora
    Alb Ref bp, 1693, 1696

Bay
  Anna
    NY Ref bp, 1667

Benjamin
  Alida
    King Ref bp, 1687, 1689
  Bernadine
    NY Ref bp, 1696
  Cornelia
    NY Ref bp, 1694, 1696,
    1699
  Ellen
    King Ref bp, 1680
  Elsie
    King Ref bp, 1678, 1679,
    1682, 1684, 1686
    NY Ref bp, 1672, 1673,
    1691, 1692, 1694, 1696,
    1699
  Gerarda
    NY Ref bp, 1695
  Judith
    NY Ref bp, 1680, 1683,
    1686, 1689, 1694
  Magdalena
    King Ref bp, 1696, 1699
  Sarah
    NY Ref bp, 1671
  Sophia
    NY Ref bp, 1699

Benoni
  Elizabeth
    Alb Ref bp, 1693, 1696
    NY Ref bp, 1690

Bernard
  Alida
    Fltb Ref bp, 1682
    NY Ref bp, 1670, 1672,
    1674, 1677, 1678, 1679,
    1685
  Elizabeth
    NY Ref bp, 1689, 1691,
    1693, 1695, 1698, 1699
  Elsie
    NY Ref bp, 1699

Father/Mother Pairs Directory

Boele
  Bayken
    NY Ref bp, 1661, 1662
Borgenson
  Catlintje
    Bkln Ref bp, 1676
Boschman
  Sarah
    NY Ref bp, 1690
Bouwen
  Maria
    NY Ref bp, 1674
Broer
  Cornelia
    King Ref bp, 1688, 1693,
    1696, 1698
Bruyn
  Elizabeth
    King Ref bp, 1683, 1684,
    1686, 1687, 1694, 1697,
    1699
  Gerarda
    King Ref bp, 1683
Burger
  Catherine
    Fltb Ref bp, 1680
    NY Ref bp, 1686
  Elsie
    King Ref bp, 1685, 1688
  Engel
    NY Ref bp, 1640, 1642,
    1647, 1650, 1652, 1653,
    1657, 1659, 1661, 1664

C

Caesar
  Judith
    NY Ref bp, 1652
Carl
  Anna
    NY Ref bp, 1695, 1697
  Catherine
    Berg Ref bp, 1696
    Bkln Ref bp, 1662, 1664
    NY Ref bp, 1659, 1679,
    1684

Catlintje
  NY Ref bp, 1657
Elizabeth
  Alb Ref bp, 1691, 1695,
  1698
  Bkln Ref bp, 1688
  Fltb Ref bp, 1681, 1684
  NY Ref bp, 1686
Helena
  NY Ref bp, 1650
Lena
  Bkln Ref bp, 1696, 1699
Margaret
  NY Ref bp, 1689, 1691,
  1692, 1695, 1697, 1698
Maria
  King Ref bp, 1694, 1696,
  1699
  NY Ref bp, 1676, 1693
Sophia
  NY Ref bp, 1659
Caspar
  Agnes
    NY Ref bp, 1699
  Alida
    Alb Ref bp, 1691, 1693,
    1696, 1697
  Catherine
    NY Ref bp, 1697, 1699
  Elizabeth
    NY Ref bp, 1689, 1695,
    1699
  Janet
    Berg Ref bp, 1667
    NY Ref bp, 1653, 1656,
    1658, 1660, 1663, 1665,
    1670, 1697, 1699
  Lavinia
    NY Ref bp, 1694
  Louisa
    Fltb Ref bp, 1678, 1679,
    1681, 1683
  Magdalena
    NY Ref bp, 1686, 1688,
    1689

Maria
  NY Ref bp, 1687, 1695,
  1697
  Tap Ref bp, 1697
  Tary Ref bp, 1697
Nelly
  Berg Ref bp, 1686
  NY Ref bp, 1667, 1681
Charles
  Adriana
    Berg Ref bp, 1680, 1682
  Catherine
    Berg Ref bp, 1682, 1692,
    1694
Christian
  Anna
    NY Ref bp, 1663, 1665,
    1666, 1668
  Catherine
    Berg Ref bp, 1666
    NY Ref bp, 1658, 1660,
    1662, 1664, 1668
  Engel
    NY Ref bp, 1659, 1662
  Gertrude
    NY Ref bp, 1670, 1672,
    1674, 1676, 1678, 1681,
    1683, 1684, 1685, 1687,
    1691
  Janet
    NY Ref bp, 1657
  Maria
    Alb Ref bp, 1693, 1697
  Nelly
    NY Ref bp, 1669, 1683,
    1687
  Patricia
    NY Ref bp, 1691
  Petronella
    NY Ref bp, 1693, 1695,
    1698
Christopher
  Anna
    Bkln Ref bp, 1693, 1695
    NY Ref bp, 1657, 1659,
    1662, 1664, 1670

Father/Mother Pairs Directory

Catherine
  NY Ref bp, 1662, 1664,
  1666, 1667, 1669, 1672,
  1675, 1676, 1678, 1680,
  1681, 1682
Catlintje
  NY Ref bp, 1699
Christina
  Alb Ref bp, 1691, 1694
  NY Ref bp, 1670
Gertrude
  Bkln Ref bp, 1682
  Fltb Ref bp, 1679, 1680,
  1682, 1684
Helena
  NY Ref bp, 1699
Ida
  Bkln Ref bp, 1682, 1687
  Fltb Ref bp, 1682, 1685
Janet
  Berg Ref bp, 1686, 1688,
  1692, 1693
Maria
  King Ref bp, 1665
  NY Ref bp, 1681
Clement
Anna
  NY Ref bp, 1681, 1683,
  1685, 1686, 1689, 1694,
  1696
Janet
  NY Ref bp, 1681
Joanna
  Bkln Ref bp, 1679
  Fltb Ref bp, 1679
Conrad
Adriana
  King Ref bp, 1694, 1696,
  1697
Catherine
  Alb Ref bp, 1692, 1694,
  1696, 1698
Elsie
  NY Ref bp, 1679, 1682,
  1685, 1688, 1690, 1693
Gerarda
  Alb Ref bp, 1698

Isabel
  NY Ref bp, 1675, 1678,
  1680, 1684, 1687, 1690
Maria
  NY Ref bp, 1656, 1658,
  1659, 1662, 1664
Cornelius
Abigail
  NY Ref bp, 1682, 1684
Adriana
  NY Ref bp, 1642, 1651,
  1655
Agatha
  Bkln Ref bp, 1684
Agnes
  NY Ref bp, 1685, 1687,
  1688, 1690
Alida
  Berg Ref bp, 1689
  Bkln Ref bp, 1693, 1695,
  1697, 1699
  Fltb Ref bp, 1683
  NY Ref bp, 1682, 1684,
  1685, 1691
  Tap Ref bp, 1695, 1696
Anna
  Bkln Ref bp, 1682, 1696,
  1698
  Fltb Ref bp, 1679, 1682,
  1685, 1688
  King Ref bp, 1665, 1667,
  1679, 1680, 1684, 1687,
  1698
  NY Ref bp, 1660, 1663,
  1664, 1666, 1669, 1671,
  1672, 1673, 1674, 1676,
  1677, 1678, 1681, 1689,
  1691, 1695, 1696, 1697
  Tary Ref bp, 1698, 1699
Artelia
  Bkln Ref bp, 1687
Barbara
  King Ref bp, 1692, 1693,
  1696, 1699
  NY Ref bp, 1691
Bernadine
  NY Ref bp, 1665, 1669,
  1676

Catherine
  Bkln Ref bp, 1686
  Fltb Ref bp, 1679, 1682,
  1684, 1689
  Hack Ref bp, 1694
  NY Ref bp, 1653, 1661,
  1694, 1696, 1697, 1698,
  1699
Catlintje
  Tap Ref bp, 1697
Christina
  NY Ref bp, 1656, 1657,
  1658, 1659, 1661, 1662,
  1666, 1668, 1680
Clara
  Alb Ref bp, 1696, 1697
  Schn Ref bp, 1698
Cornelia
  Alb Ref bp, 1691, 1694
  Berg Ref bp, 1677
  Bkln Ref bp, 1680
  Fltb Ref bp, 1680
  King Ref bp, 1687, 1696,
  1698
  NY Ref bp, 1690, 1696
Elizabeth
  Bkln Ref bp, 1698
  Fltb Ref bp, 1682
  King Ref bp, 1678, 1682,
  1684, 1687
  NY Ref bp, 1655, 1660,
  1665
Elsie
  King Ref bp, 1696, 1698
Eunice
  NY Ref bp, 1660, 1672
Eva
  King Ref bp, 1697
  NY Ref bp, 1662, 1697
Gertrude
  Alb Ref bp, 1693, 1695,
  1698
  Bkln Ref bp, 1679, 1681,
  1682, 1690, 1691
  Fltb Ref bp, 1679, 1681,
  1682, 1683
  NY Ref bp, 1658, 1661,
  1669, 1677, 1694

Cornelius (cont.)
  Henrietta
    Berg Ref bp, 1685, 1688
    Bkln Ref bp, 1678
    Fltb Ref bp, 1678
    NY Ref bp, 1683
  Hester
    NY Ref bp, 1676
  Hilda
    Alb Ref bp, 1691, 1693,
    1696
    NY Ref bp, 1658, 1660,
    1663, 1665, 1667, 1669,
    1672, 1675, 1677
  Janet
    Berg Ref bp, 1687, 1691
    Bkln Ref bp, 1697, 1699
    Fltb Ref bp, 1678, 1681,
    1683
    Hack Ref bp, 1695, 1696,
    1697
    King Ref bp, 1683, 1684,
    1685, 1687, 1689, 1692,
    1694, 1696, 1699
    NY Ref bp, 1676, 1680,
    1681, 1685, 1692, 1694
  Jemima
    King Ref bp, 1693
  Joanna
    Bkln Ref bp, 1699
  Lena
    NY Ref bp, 1675
  Leonora
    King Ref bp, 1693
  Madeline
    Berg Ref bp, 1678, 1679,
    1681, 1683, 1684, 1686
  Magdalena
    Berg Ref bp, 1687, 1690
    Bkln Ref bp, 1679, 1696
    Fltb Ref bp, 1681
    NY Ref bp, 1678, 1680,
    1681, 1687
  Margaret
    Hack Ref bp, 1697, 1699
    NY Ref bp, 1659, 1661,
    1664, 1666, 1669, 1671,
    1674, 1676, 1696, 1697

Maria
  Alb Ref bp, 1691, 1692,
  1696, 1697, 1698
  Fltb Ref bp, 1681
  King Ref bp, 1668, 1671,
  1686, 1687, 1689, 1692,
  1694, 1696, 1698, 1699
  NY Ref bp, 1658, 1663,
  1679, 1681, 1682, 1684,
  1685, 1686, 1687, 1688,
  1689, 1690, 1691, 1692,
  1693, 1695, 1696, 1697,
  1698, 1699
Mathilda
  Berg Ref bp, 1682, 1694,
  1698
  NY Ref bp, 1666, 1671,
  1673, 1679, 1681, 1688,
  1694
Merritje
  Bkln Ref bp, 1681
Nelly
  Fltb Ref bp, 1688
  King Ref bp, 1679, 1682
  NY Ref bp, 1664, 1666,
  1667, 1670, 1672, 1673,
  1676, 1678, 1679, 1680,
  1684, 1688
Nicole
  NY Ref bp, 1656
Rachel
  King Ref bp, 1692, 1695,
  1699
  NY Ref bp, 1657, 1694
Sarah
  NY Ref bp, 1685, 1687,
  1689, 1691, 1694, 1695,
  1699
Sophia
  Berg Ref bp, 1687, 1692,
  1694, 1695, 1696, 1697,
  1699
  NY Ref bp, 1687, 1689,
  1694
Susan
  Alb Ref bp, 1694
  NY Ref bp, 1696, 1697

Theodora
  Fltb Ref bp, 1689
Wilhelmina
  NY Ref bp, 1695, 1699
Cosine
  Catherine
    NY Ref bp, 1699
  Margaret
    Tap Ref bp, 1496
  Maria
    Tap Ref bp, 1498
  Sophia
    NY Ref bp, 1640
Court
  Maria
    Fltb Ref bp, 1678, 1680,
    1683
    NY Ref bp, 1676

D

Daniel
  Alida
    Fltb Ref bp, 1680
    NY Ref bp, 1663, 1666
  Anna
    King Ref bp, 1666
    NY Ref bp, 1668, 1673,
    1675, 1681, 1684, 1685,
    1687, 1688
  Catherine
    Bkln Ref bp, 1699
  Christina
    NY Ref bp, 1683, 1685,
    1687, 1690, 1692, 1694
  Deborah
    Alb Ref bp, 1696, 1698
  Elizabeth
    Alb Ref bp, 1696, 1697,
    1699
    NY Ref bp, 1678
  Engel
    NY Ref bp, 1696, 1698
  Helena
    NY Ref bp, 1698
  Jemima
    NY Ref bp, 1661

Father/Mother Pairs Directory

Judith
  NY Ref bp, 1686
Maria
  Alb Ref bp, 1692
  Fltb Ref bp, 1680
  NY Ref bp, 1674, 1677,
  1679, 1681
  Schn Ref bp, 1695
Nelly
  Bkln Ref bp, 1698
Sarah
  Bkln Ref bp, 1691
  Fltb Ref bp, 1679, 1681,
  1687
  NY Ref bp, 1674, 1675,
  1677, 1679, 1680, 1681,
  1683, 1685, 1686, 1688,
  1689
Theodora
  Alb Ref bp, 1699

David
Alida
  NY Ref bp, 1687
Anna
  Berg Ref bp, 1696
  Hack Ref bp, 1697, 1699
  NY Ref bp, 1671, 1673,
  1675, 1678, 1680, 1683,
  1686, 1690, 1693, 1694,
  1698
Catherine
  NY Ref bp, 1670, 1671,
  1672, 1673, 1676, 1677,
  1679, 1682, 1685, 1687,
  1688
Christina
  NY Ref bp, 1697, 1699
Cornelia
  King Ref bp, 1692, 1696
Elizabeth
  NY Ref bp, 1690, 1695,
  1697
Elsie
  Alb Ref bp, 1694, 1697
Esther
  Tary Ref bp, 1698

Helena
  NY Ref bp, 1684, 1686,
  1692, 1694, 1695, 1698
Hilda
  NY Ref bp, 1681, 1683,
  1684, 1686, 1688
Isabel
  King Ref bp, 1688
Janet
  NY Ref bp, 1658, 1659,
  1662, 1665
Joanna
  Alb Ref bp, 1695, 1697
Letitia
  NY Ref bp, 1660
Maria
  NY Ref bp, 1662, 1666
Rachel
  Alb Ref bp, 1692
  Berg Ref bp, 1679, 1680
  Bkln Ref bp, 1696
  Fltb Ref bp, 1681
  NY Ref bp, 1676, 1677
  Schn Ref bp, 1696
Sarah
  Hack Ref bp, 1699

Deliverance
Engel
  NY Ref bp, 1696

Dennis
see also Tunis
Elizabeth
  NY Ref bp, 1662, 1665,
  1667
Joanna
  King Ref bp, 1699
Judith
  NY Ref bp, 1682
Maria
  Bkln Ref bp, 1695

Denton
Abigail
  Bkln Ref bp, 1679
  Fltb Ref bp, 1679

Didlove
Elsie
  NY Ref bp, 1681, 1683,
  1684, 1687

Dinckrick
Elizabeth
  Fltb Ref bp, 1685

Dionysius
Helena
  Bkln Ref bp, 1692
  Fltb Ref bp, 1689
Lena
  Fltb Ref bp, 1687

Dirk
Adriana
  NY Ref bp, 1694, 1696,
  1698
Agatha
  Bkln Ref bp, 1680
  Fltb Ref bp, 1680
  NY Ref bp, 1657, 1659
Agnes
  King Ref bp, 1671, 1679,
  1680, 1684, 1689
  NY Ref bp, 1673, 1676
Alida
  Fltb Ref bp, 1681, 1683,
  1685
Anna
  Alb Ref bp, 1692, 1696
  Bkln Ref bp, 1699
  Fltb Ref bp, 1681, 1684,
  1686
  King Ref bp, 1686, 1688,
  1695, 1697, 1699
  NY Ref bp, 1656, 1661,
  1666, 1673, 1695
Catherine
  Fltb Ref bp, 1677
  King Ref bp, 1697, 1698,
  1699
  NY Ref bp, 1694
  Tap Ref bp, 1698
Catlintje
  Bkln Ref bp, 1698
  NY Ref bp, 1696
Elizabeth
  Berg Ref bp, 1673
  Bkln Ref bp, 1670, 1684,
  1689, 1692
  Fltb Ref bp, 1681, 1684,
  1687, 1689

Dirk (cont.)
Elizabeth (cont.)
NY Ref bp, 1666, 1668,
1672, 1673, 1674, 1676,
1678, 1680, 1681, 1682,
1687, 1692, 1699
Esther
Hack Ref bp, 1695
Eva
NY Ref bp, 1676, 1681,
1684, 1686, 1687, 1689,
1691, 1694
Gerarda
NY Ref bp, 1659, 1668,
1669, 1671, 1674, 1677,
1678, 1681, 1684, 1687
Gertrude
NY Ref bp, 1659, 1661
Henrietta
NY Ref bp, 1693, 1696,
1698
Hester
Hack Ref bp, 1699
Janet
NY Ref bp, 1654, 1656,
1673, 1678
Joanna
NY Ref bp, 1680
Lavinia
NY Ref bp, 1656, 1659
Margaret
King Ref bp, 1665
Maria
Alb Ref bp, 1693
Bkln Ref bp, 1661, 1664,
1673, 1678, 1680, 1684,
1686
Fltb Ref bp, 1678, 1680,
1681, 1684
King Ref bp, 1678, 1680,
1684, 1687
NY Ref bp, 1662, 1666,
1667, 1669, 1672, 1695,
1698
Schn Ref bp, 1695, 1698
Mattina
NY Ref bp, 1693, 1696,
1699

Nelly
NY Ref bp, 1670
Patricia
NY Ref bp, 1662
Rachel
Alb Ref bp, 1692, 1694,
1695, 1697, 1699
NY Ref bp, 1678, 1682
Rosella
NY Ref bp, 1679
Sarah
Bkln Ref bp, 1685, 1686,
1688, 1690, 1692
Fltb Ref bp, 1685
Sophia
Alb Ref bp, 1694, 1696,
1698
King Ref bp, 1692
NY Ref bp, 1663, 1667,
16646
Ursula
NY Ref bp, 1675, 1677,
1679, 1682, 1684, 1687,
1689
Dominic
Dorothy
NY Ref bp, 1695, 1697,
1699
Douw
Theodora
NY Ref bp, 1662, 1665,
1669

E
Edward
Anna
King Ref bp, 1675
Elsie
Berg Ref bp, 1690, 1693,
1695, 1696, 1698
Hack Ref bp, 1696
Gertrude
King Ref bp, 1689
NY Ref bp, 1682, 1685,
1687, 1690
Josina
Alb Ref bp, 1698

Egbert
Anna
Hack Ref bp, 1695
King Ref bp, 1684, 1686,
1688, 1692, 1694, 1696,
1698
NY Ref bp, 1656, 1692,
1693
Elsie
NY Ref bp, 1679, 1682,
1685, 1687, 1689, 1697
Eva
NY Ref bp, 1694
Gertrude
NY Ref bp, 1662
Harmina
NY Ref bp, 1662
Jacobina
NY Ref bp, 1661, 1664,
1667
Maria
Alb Ref bp, 1691
King Ref bp, 1692, 1695,
1698
Elias
Anna
King Ref bp, 1694, 1698
NY Ref bp, 1681, 1682,
1684
Bernadine
Fltb Ref bp, 1685
Catherine
Alb Ref bp, 1691
Catlintje
NY Ref bp, 1672
Cornelia
NY Ref bp, 1673, 1675,
1676, 1679, 1681, 1683
Elizabeth
King Ref bp, 1697
NY Ref bp, 1679, 1682
Margaret
Berg Ref bp, 1676, 1678
NY Ref bp, 1666, 1668,
1669, 1672, 1674, 1676,
1678

Father/Mother Pairs Directory

Maria
NY Ref bp, 1675, 1677,
1679, 1680, 1683, 1686,
1689, 1696
Ellebrandt
Alida
King Ref bp, 1689
Emanuel
Maria
King Ref bp, 1694, 1697
Engelbert
Cornelia
Fltb Ref bp, 1684
NY Ref bp, 1682, 1696
Enoch
Catherine
NY Ref bp, 1693, 1696,
1698
Theodora
NY Ref bp, 1671, 1673,
1675, 1677, 1678, 1680,
1683, 1687
Ephraim
Elizabeth
NY Ref bp, 1680, 1684,
1687, 1688
Eustace
Barbara
Berg Ref bp, 1678
NY Ref bp, 1680, 1688
Evert
Alida
NY Ref bp, 1682
Anna
Alb Ref bp, 1691, 1692,
1695, 1697, 1699
Bridget
NY Ref bp, 1673, 1676
Catherine
NY Ref bp, 1691
Charity
King Ref bp, 1698, 1699
Elizabeth
Alb Ref bp, 1691, 1693,
1695, 1697
Bkln Ref bp, 1672
NY Ref bp, 1690, 1697

Gertrude
King Ref bp, 1693, 1695,
1697, 1699
Henrietta
NY Ref bp, 1652, 1656,
1657, 1659, 1660
Janet
King Ref bp, 1661, 1665
NY Ref bp, 1673, 1675,
1677, 1680, 1682, 1684,
1685, 1688
Joanna
NY Ref bp, 1687, 1689,
1690, 1692, 1695, 11698
Josina
Alb Ref bp, 1692, 1694,
1696
Judith
NY Ref bp, 1671
Margaret
Alb Ref bp, 1696
NY Ref bp, 1697
Maria
NY Ref bp, 1674, 1675,
1676, 1678, 1680, 1683,
1684, 1686, 1688, 1690,
1692
Mathilda
NY Ref bp, 1686, 1687,
1688, 1690, 1694, 1696,
1698
Patience
NY Ref bp, 1694, 1696,
1699
Patricia
NY Ref bp, 1692
Sophia
Bkln Ref bp, 1678, 1684,
1690
Fltb Ref bp, 1680, 1684, 1687
NY Ref bp, 1677, 1682

F
Ferdinand
Eva
Fltb Ref bp, 1681

Florian
Catlintje
NY Ref bp, 1685
Helena
NY Ref bp, 1681, 1694
Francis
Adriana
King Ref bp, 1693
Alida
NY Ref bp, 1666
Anna
NY Ref bp, 1673, 1675,
1677, 1689
Barbara
NY Ref bp, 1667, 1669,
1671, 1673, 1675, 1676,
1677, 1680, 1682, 1684
Catherine
Alb Ref bp, 1692
King Ref bp, 1694
NY Ref bp, 1661, 1680,
1681, 1683, 1684, 1686,
1689, 1690, 1693, 1695,
1697, 1699
Catlintje
Berg Ref bp, 1686
Delia
NY Ref bp, 1663
Dorothy
NY Ref bp, 1692
Elizabeth
NY Ref bp, 1660, 1665,
1666, 1667, 1669, 1672,
1675, 1697, 1699
Elsie
Alb Ref bp, 1692, 1694,
1696
Emma
NY Ref bp, 1657
Gertrude
Fltb Ref bp, 1679, 1681
NY Ref bp, 1664, 1671,
1674, 1677, 1686
Helena
NY Ref bp, 1684, 1687,
1689
Hester
NY Ref bp, 1674

231

Francis (cont.)
Isabel
NY Ref bp, 1672, 1673, 1675
Janet
Hack Ref bp, 1696, 1699
King Ref bp, 1663, 1665
NY Ref bp, 1656, 1660, 1668, 1687, 1691
Lena
NY Ref bp, 1687, 1689
Lucretia
Fltb Ref bp, 1681
NY Ref bp, 1683, 1686
Margaret
King Ref bp, 1697
Maria
Berg Ref bp, 1692
King Ref bp, 1695, 1697, 1699
NY Ref bp, 1659, 1663, 1665, 1669
Rebecca
King Ref bp, 1684, 1685
NY Ref bp, 1687, 1689, 1691, 1693, 1695, 1696
Rosella
Tary Ref bp, 1697, 1698
Sophia
Alb Ref bp, 1691, 1692
NY Ref bp, 1656
Walburg
NY Ref bp, 1662
Fred
Catherine
Berg Ref bp, 1679, 1681, 1684, 1692, 1693
NY Ref bp, 1658, 1660, 1673, 1675, 1679, 1684, 1687, 1694
Christina
NY Ref bp, 1659, 1662, 1665, 1674, 1675
Dina
Bkln Ref bp, 1663, 1694
Fltb Ref bp, 1681, 1683
Elizabeth
Alb Ref bp, 1691

King Ref bp, 1682, 1685, 1694
NY Ref bp, 1658, 1660, 1667, 1669, 1672, 1673, 1677, 1679, 1681, 1683, 1692
Engel
King Ref bp, 1667, 1671, 1675, 1679, 1684, 1686
Frances
King Ref bp, 1693, 1695, 1697, 1698
Hester
King Ref bp, 1684
NY Ref bp, 1678, 1680, 1682
Lea
NY Ref bp, 1688
Lydia
Bkln Ref bp, 1699
Margaret
Alb Ref bp, 1693, 1695, 1696, 1699
King Ref bp, 1665, 1667, 1679
NY Ref bp, 1657, 1659, 1661, 1663, 1664, 1665, 1667, 1669, 1670, 1671, 1673, 1676

G

Gabriel
Catherine
NY Ref bp, 1659
Christina
NY Ref bp, 1660
Gertrude
Bkln Ref bp, 1695, 1696, 1698
Janet
NY Ref bp, 1658, 1693, 1694, 1696
Garret
Abigail
NY Ref bp, 1660
Agatha
Berg Ref bp, 1678, 1683

Agnes
Berg Ref bp, 1682, 1684, 1695, 1697, 1699
NY Ref bp, 1693, 1695, 1697, 1699
Alida
NY Ref bp, 1653, 1656
Anna
Berg Ref bp, 1667, 1675, 1678
Bkln Ref bp, 1662, 1689, 1692, 1694, 1698
Fltb Ref bp, 1686
King Ref bp, 1694, 1697
NY Ref bp, 1662, 1663, 1665, 1672, 1678
Barbara
Alb Ref bp, 1697, 1699
Catherine
Alb Ref bp, 1691, 1693, 1695
Berg Ref bp, 1695, 1696, 1698
NY Ref bp, 1660, 1663, 1665, 1667, 1686, 1687, 1689, 1690, 1691, 1692, 1694, 1695, 1697, 1698, 1699
Schn Ref bp, 1696, 1698
Catlintje
Tary Ref bp, 1697
Christina
Fltb Ref bp, 1684
Clara
King Ref bp, 1682, 1684, 1686, 1689, 1692, 1694
Cornelia
Bkln Ref bp, 1692, 1693, 1696, 1697
Fltb Ref bp, 1685
NY Ref bp, 1666
Dorothy
NY Ref bp, 1697, 1699
Elizabeth
Alb Ref bp, 1695, 1696, 1699
Bkln Ref bp, 1699
Fltb Ref bp, 1681, 1685,

1687, 1690
NY Ref bp, 1674, 1676,
1686, 1691, 1693, 1695,
1697, 1698
Elsie
Fltb Ref bp, 1677, 1681,
1683
NY Ref bp, 1694, 1695,
1696
Eva
NY Ref bp, 1675, 1681,
1685
Gertrude
Fltb Ref bp, 1681, 1683,
1685
King Ref bp, 1699
Harmina
Berg Ref bp, 1667
NY Ref bp, 1656, 1665,
1669
Hester
NY Ref bp, 1665, 1682
Hilda
King Ref bp, 1694, 1696,
1698
NY Ref bp, 1664
Isabel
Berg Ref bp, 1694, 1697,
1699
NY Ref bp, 1677, 1682,

1684, 1687, 1689, 1696,
1698, 1699
Janet
Bkln Ref bp, 1687, 1694
King Ref bp, 1686
NY Ref bp, 1695, 1697,
1699
Josina
NY Ref bp, 1680, 1682
Lavinia
Fltb Ref bp, 1677, 1679,
1682, 1685
NY Ref bp, 1681, 1683
Lena
King Ref bp, 1694
Letitia
NY Ref bp, 1672

Madeline
Bkln Ref bp, 1694
Magdalena
Bkln Ref bp, 1684
Fltb Ref bp, 1681, 1682,
1684, 1689
King Ref bp, 1661, 1684,
1686, 1687, 1691
NY Ref bp, 1693, 1694,
1696, 1698
Margaret
King Ref bp, 1688, 1695,
1698
NY Ref bp, 1657, 1671
Maria
Alb Ref bp, 1693, 1695,
1697
Bkln Ref bp, 1695
NY Ref bp, 1648, 1657,
1659, 1661, 1666, 1668,
1670, 1677, 1680, 1683,
1684, 1685, 1687, 1688,
1689, 1690, 1691, 1693,
1695, 1698
Nelly
Bkln Ref bp, 1662, 1677
Fltb Ref bp, 1677
Hack Ref bp, 1696
NY Ref bp, 1683, 1684,
1687, 1689, 1691

Petronella
King Ref bp, 1680, 1685,
1687, 1694, 1697, 1699
Sarah
Alb Ref bp, 1695, 1697,
1699
NY Ref bp, 1694, 1695,
1697, 1699
Sophia
Berg Ref bp, 1684, 1686,
1688
Hack Ref bp, 1699
NY Ref bp, 1664, 1666,
1673, 1674, 1675, 1677,
1680, 1682, 1684

Susan
NY Ref bp, 1682, 1684,
1689, 1690, 1694, 1696,
1697, 1699
Wilhelmina
Fltb Ref bp, 1685, 1687
George see also Joris, Jurian
Adriana
NY Ref bp, 1695, 1697
Agnes
Alb Ref bp, 1693, 1697
Bkln Ref bp, 1687, 1689
NY Ref bp, 1694
Alida
King Ref bp, 1688
Anna
King Ref bp, 1686, 1689,
1691, 1695, 1697, 1699
Barbara
King Ref bp, 1662, 1664,
1666, 1668, 1684
Catherine
NY Ref bp, 1658, 1662
Elizabeth
King Ref bp, 1675
Emma
Alb Ref bp, 1695
Eva
NY Ref bp, 1699
Frederica
Berg Ref bp, 1684, 1691
NY Ref bp, 1668, 1670,
1672, 1677, 1680, 1686
Gerarda
Hack Ref bp, 1696
NY Ref bp, 1696, 1697,
1699
Harmina
NY Ref bp, 1659, 1661,
1663, 1665, 1667, 1669,
1671, 1673, 1674, 1677
Hester
Bkln Ref bp, 1679, 1683,
1694
Fltb Ref bp, 1679, 1681,
1683
NY Ref bp, 1674, 1675,
1677, 1681, 1685, 1687

George (cont.)
Janet
NY Ref bp, 1679, 1682,
1684, 1687, 1690, 1695
Magdalena
NY Ref bp, 1688
Margaret
NY Ref bp, 1675, 1682
Maria
King Ref bp, 1661, 1663,
1666
NY Ref bp, 1698
Sophia
Alb Ref bp, 1691, 1698
Veronica
Tap Ref bp, 1695, 1697
Wilhelmina
NY Ref bp, 1699
Gerbrant
Maria
Berg Ref bp, 1679, 1691,
1696
Bkln Ref bp, 1682, 1691
Fltb Ref bp, 1682
NY Ref bp, 1675, 1677,
1679, 1684, 1687, 1689,
1693, 1696
Gerdin
Susan
NY Ref bp, 1665
Gideon
Catherine
Alb Ref bp, 1696
Theodora
Alb Ref bp, 1696
Gilbert
Barbara
Alb Ref bp, 1692, 1695,
1698
Catherine
NY Ref bp, 1658, 1672
Elizabeth
NY Ref bp, 1659
Schn Ref bp, 1695
Gertrude
King Ref bp, 1679, 1683,
1686, 1688
NY Ref bp, 1677

Henrietta
NY Ref bp, 1667
Janet
Bkln Ref bp, 1690, 1693,
1699
Fltb Ref bp, 1677, 1679,
1681, 1683, 1685, 1689
NY Ref bp, 1689, 1692,
1694, 1697, 1699
Margaret
King Ref bp, 1696
Rachel
King Ref bp, 1664, 1682,
1684, 1686, 1688, 1692,
1696, 1698
Sophia
Fltb Ref bp, 1678, 1680,
1683
Wilhelmina
NY Ref bp, 1661, 1662,
1664, 1666, 1667, 1668,
1670, 1672, 1674, 1675,
1678
Giles
Christina
NY Ref bp, 1661, 1664
Henrietta
NY Ref bp, 1669, 1674,
1680, 1684
Janet
Alb Ref bp, 1693, 1695
Rachel
Alb Ref bp, 1696, 1698
Godfrey
Adriana
NY Ref bp, 1641
Gregory
Engel
Bkln Ref bp, 1695
Gustave
Anna
NY Ref bp, 1658

H
Haeck
Abigail
NY Ref bp, 1662

Hartman
Elizabeth
NY Ref bp, 1677
Maria
Berg Ref bp, 1675, 1677,
1678, 1680, 1683, 1685,
1693, 1695, 1698
NY Ref bp, 1681, 1683,
1685, 1687, 1691
Helle (Kelm)
Janet
NY Ref bp, 1695
Hendrick
Abigail
NY Ref bp, 1656, 1657,
1672, 1674, 1677, 1678
Adriana
King Ref bp, 1694, 1695,
1698
NY Ref bp, 1686
Agnes
Hack Ref bp, 1696
NY Ref bp, 1691, 1692
Alida
King Ref bp, 1664, 1666,
1699
NY Ref bp, 1657, 1658,
1659, 1661, 1669
Anna
Alb Ref bp, 1692, 1695,
1696, 1697
Bkln Ref bp, 1683
Fltb Ref bp, 1681, 1683,
1684, 1685, 1687, 1688
King Ref bp, 1678, 1684,
1686, 1688, 1689, 1697,
1699, 16979
NY Ref bp, 1661, 1662,
1664, 1678, 1680, 1681,
1682, 1685, 1686, 1688,
1689, 1690, 1691, 1692,
1694
Catherine
Alb Ref bp, 1692, 1693,
1694, 1695, 1696, 1697,
1698, 1699
King Ref bp, 1675, 1679,
1680, 1682, 1684, 1686,

1688, 1689, 1692, 1694,
1696, 1697, 1699
NY Ref bp, 1656, 1657,
1658, 1662, 1666, 1674,
1680, 1681, 1684, 1685,
1686, 1687, 1689, 1692,
1694
Tary Ref bp, 1697, 1699
Catlintje
Alb Ref bp, 1691, 1693,
1695, 1697, 1699
Cecilia
NY Ref bp, 1662
Clara
NY Ref bp, 1699
Cornelia
Alb Ref bp, 1693, 1696,
1698
King Ref bp, 1689, 1691,
1694, 1696, 1699
Deborah
Alb Ref bp, 1693, 1695,
1697, 1698
King Ref bp, 1685
Elizabeth
NY Ref bp, 1657, 1699
Elsie
King Ref bp, 1663, 1665,
1669
NY Ref bp, 1672, 1674,
1677, 1679, 1684, 1685,
1686, 1688, 1692, 1697
Frances
NY Ref bp, 1686
Gerarda
King Ref bp, 1692
Gertrude
Bkln Ref bp, 1660, 1661,
1677, 1687, 1693, 1696
Fltb Ref bp, 1681, 1684
King Ref bp, 1689, 1692,
1694, 1695, 1697, 1699
NY Ref bp, 1651, 1655,
1658, 1662, 1665, 1674,
1677, 1691
Godwina
NY Ref bp, 1674

Harmina
NY Ref bp, 1654
Helena
NY Ref bp, 1657, 1663
Hester
Bkln Ref bp, 1693
Fltb Ref bp, 1688
Ida
Berg Ref bp, 1668
Bkln Ref bp, 1666, 1683
Fltb Ref bp, 1680, 1683,
1685
NY Ref bp, 1675, 1678
Isabel
NY Ref bp, 1680, 1696,
1699
Janet
Fltb Ref bp, 1681
King Ref bp, 1682, 1684,
1688, 1692, 1695, 1697
NY Ref bp, 1671, 1672,
1673, 1674, 1675, 1676,
1678, 1679, 1681, 1682,
1683, 1684, 1686, 1688,
1690, 1693, 1695, 1697,
1698, 1699
Joanna
King Ref bp, 1682, 1683,
1688, 1693
Josina
Bkln Ref bp, 1683, 1690
Fltb Ref bp, 1681, 1683
NY Ref bp, 1677
Kunigunda
Fltb Ref bp, 1679
Lavinia
King Ref bp, 1695, 1696
NY Ref bp, 1655, 1664,
1668, 1676, 1679, 1699
Magdalena
NY Ref bp, 1655, 1663,
1665, 1667
Margaret
Berg Ref bp, 1667
King Ref bp, 1660, 1663,
1665, 1667
NY Ref bp, 1660, 1662,
1663, 1665, 1669, 1670,

1672, 1673, 1674, 1675,
1678, 1682
Maria
Alb Ref bp, 1692, 1693,
1695, 1697
Berg Ref bp, 1680, 1682,
1683, 1684, 1685
Bkln Ref bp, 1682, 1685,
1688, 1690, 1693, 1698
Fltb Ref bp, 1680, 1682,
1683, 1685
Hack Ref bp, 1696, 1699
King Ref bp, 1688, 1691
NY Ref bp, 1656, 1658, 1661,
1663, 1666, 1671, 1673,
1674, 1675, 1676, 1677,
1678, 1679, 1680, 1681,
1682, 1683, 1685, 1686,
1687, 1689, 1690, 1692, 1699
Schn Ref bp, 1695, 1697
Martha
NY Ref bp, 1674, 1676,
1679, 1680, 1682, 1687,
1693, 1696, 1697, 1699
Nelly
Alb Ref bp, 1694, 1698,
1699
King Ref bp, 1679, 1680,
1683, 1685, 1687
NY Ref bp, 1670, 1672,
1675, 1676, 1678, 1680,
1681, 1684, 1686
Nicole
Berg Ref bp, 1679, 1681
Bkln Ref bp, 1661, 1685
Fltb Ref bp, 1685
NY Ref bp, 1677, 1679
Patience
NY Ref bp, 1675
Petronella
King Ref bp, 1683
NY Ref bp, 1676, 1678,
1680, 1686, 1689, 1693,
1697
Rachel
King Ref bp, 1688
NY Ref bp, 1660, 1662,
1666, 1668, 1672, 1675

Hendrick (cont.)
Rosella
NY Ref bp, 1657, 1671
Sarah
King Ref bp, 1698
NY Ref bp, 1644, 1661,
1663, 1666, 1669, 1675,
1678, 1690, 1692, 1694,
1697, 1699
Sophia
NY Ref bp, 1683, 1684,
1686, 1689, 1694, 1695,
1697
Susan
NY Ref bp, 1655, 1657,
1659, 1663, 1666, 1668
Herbert
Maria
Alb Ref bp, 1696, 1697
Hercules
Lavinia
NY Ref bp, 1644, 1657,
1659, 1662, 1666, 1668,
1670, 1675, 1681
Herman
Abigail
Bkln Ref bp, 1697
Anna
NY Ref bp, 1682
Bridget
NY Ref bp, 1683, 1685,
1687
Catherine
Fltb Ref bp, 1679
NY Ref bp, 1659, 1660,
1691
Christina
King Ref bp, 1684
NY Ref bp, 1686, 1688,
1690
Clara
NY Ref bp, 1656
Elizabeth
Alb Ref bp, 1692, 1695,
1699
NY Ref bp, 1699

Eunice
NY Ref bp, 1689, 1693,
1696, 1698
Gerarda
NY Ref bp, 1689
Gertrude
Hack Ref bp, 1696, 1699
NY Ref bp, 1691
Janet
NY Ref bp, 1677, 1678
Lavinia
NY Ref bp, 1660
Madeline
King Ref bp, 1662, 1663,
1666, 1667
Magdalena
NY Ref bp, 1659, 1674,
1687
Margaret
Alb Ref bp, 1692, 1698
Bkln Ref bp, 1679
Fltb Ref bp, 1679, 1681
NY Ref bp, 1658, 1685,
1687, 1688, 1690, 1693,
1694
Schn Ref bp, 1696
Maria
Alb Ref bp, 1692, 1693,
1696
NY Ref bp, 1664, 1677,
1679
Nelly
NY Ref bp, 1695
Rachel
King Ref bp, 1696, 1698,
1699
Sarah
NY Ref bp, 1667
Susan
NY Ref bp, 1669
Wybrecht
Fltb Ref bp, 1681
NY Ref bp, 1686
Hessel
Elizabeth
Berg Ref bp, 1691

Heyman
Anna
King Ref bp, 1689, 1696,
1698
Margaret
King Ref bp, 1679, 1684,
1686
Maria
NY Ref bp, 1684, 1687,
1689, 1692, 1694, 1696,
1699
Hieronymus
Anna
Bkln Ref bp, 1685, 1687
Fltb Ref bp, 1682, 1685
NY Ref bp, 1671, 1673,
1676, 1690
Joanna
NY Ref bp, 1661, 1663,
1666
Nelly
NY Ref bp, 1696
Rebecca
Alb Ref bp, 1691
Susan
NY Ref bp, 1684, 1686,
1688, 1690, 1693, 1696
Hubert
Henrietta
King Ref bp, 1680, 1684,
1685, 1687, 1694, 1697,
1699
Janet
NY Ref bp, 1663
Maria
Alb Ref bp, 1694
NY Ref bp, 1656, 1657,
1659, 1660, 1663, 1667,
1695, 1697, 1699
Sarah
King Ref bp, 1696, 1698
Wilhelmina
NY Ref bp, 1680, 1682,
1684, 1687
Hugh
Janet
King Ref bp, 1679, 1682

Louisa
   NY Ref bp, 1687
Maria
   King Ref bp, 1695, 1698
   NPal Ref bp, 1690, 1691,
   1693, 1696, 1699
Humphrey
Anna
   King Ref bp, 1684, 1686,
   1689, 1694, 1697

I

Ide
Hilda
   Berg Ref bp, 1666
   NY Ref bp, 1657, 1659,
   1662
Isabel
   NY Ref bp, 1686, 1687,
   1689, 1691, 1692
Isaac
Abigail
   Alb Ref bp, 1693, 1695,
   1698
Alida
   NY Ref bp, 1690, 1691,
   1693, 1695, 1698
Anna
   Alb Ref bp, 1692, 1694,
   1696, 1697, 1699
   NY Ref bp, 1687, 1690
Catherine
   NY Ref bp, 1656
Catlintje
   NY Ref bp, 1662, 1664,
   1666, 1669, 1681, 1682,
   1685, 1687, 1689, 1692,
   1694
Christina
   King Ref bp, 1697
   NY Ref bp, 1681
Cornelia
   Berg Ref bp, 1692, 1694,
   1696, 1699
   Hack Ref bp, 1699
   NY Ref bp, 1675, 1679,
   1683, 1685, 1687, 1691,

1693, 1696, 1699
Dorothy
   Alb Ref bp, 1692, 1695,
   16998
   NY Ref bp, 1679
Elizabeth
   NY Ref bp, 1657, 1659,
   1662, 1664, 1667, 1669,
   1672, 1682, 1684, 1686,
   1688, 1689, 1692, 1694,
   1696, 1697, 1699
Eunice
   Alb Ref bp, 1693
Gertrude
   Fltb Ref bp, 1688, 1690
Harmina
   NY Ref bp, 1686, 1687,
   1689, 1692
Hester
   NY Ref bp, 1696, 1698
Janet
   Alb Ref bp, 1699
   King Ref bp, 1692, 1694,
   1697, 1699
   NY Ref bp, 1659, 1662,
   1665, 1666, 1670, 1687,
   1694, 1696, 1697, 1699
Judith
   Alb Ref bp, 1698
Lavinia
   Fltb Ref bp, 1690
Lena
   Bkln Ref bp, 1698
Louisa
   NY Ref bp, 1685

Margaret
   NY Ref bp, 1684, 1685,
   1687, 1690
Maria
   Alb Ref bp, 1692, 1695,
   1696, 1697, 1699
   Fltb Ref bp, 1688
   NPal Ref bp, 1684, 1687,
   1690
   NY Ref bp, 1664, 1665,
   1666, 1667, 1669, 1670,
   1675, 1678, 1689, 1690,

1693, 1695, 1697, 1699
   Schn Ref bp, 1694
Mathilda
   NY Ref bp, 1698
Nelly
   NY Ref bp, 1691, 1692,
   1694, 1696, 1697, 1698,
   1699
Petronella
   NY Ref bp, 1670, 1672
Prudence
   NY Ref bp, 1695, 1697,
   1699
Sarah
   Bkln Ref bp, 1699
   NY Ref bp, 1645, 1655,
   1657, 1660, 1662, 1663,
   1666, 1669, 1685, 1686,
   1687, 1688, 1690, 1691,
   1692, 1693, 1694, 1695,
   1696, 1697, 1698, 1699
Susan
   Alb Ref bp, 1691, 1693
   NY Ref bp, 1686, 1688,
   1690, 1693, 1696
   Schn Ref bp, 1695, 1697
Temperance
   NY Ref bp, 1682, 1684
Isaiah
Cornelia
   Hack Ref bp, 1699
Eva
   Alb Ref bp, 1691
   Schn Ref bp, 1694, 1696
Janet
   NY Ref bp, 1688

J

Jacob
see also Jacques
Adriana
   King Ref bp, 1663
Alida
   Berg Ref bp, 1676, 1678,
   1681, 1686, 1689, 1692
   NY Ref bp, 1672, 1674,
   1676, 1677, 1678, 1680,

Jacob (cont.)

Alida (cont.)
1682, 1686, 1687, 1689,
1690, 1692, 1695, 1696,
1697, 1698, 1699
Tary Ref bp, 1699

Anna
Alb Ref bp, 1692, 1693,
1695, 1696, 1697, 1698
Bkln Ref bp, 1684, 1686,
1687, 1689, 1696, 1699
Fltb Ref bp, 1684, 1685
King Ref bp, 1666, 1668,
1670, 1679, 1680, 1684,
1686, 1688, 1696, 1698
NY Ref bp, 1664, 1674,
1675, 1677, 1680, 1682,
1685, 1687, 1690, 1691,
1693, 1694, 1695, 1696,
1697, 1698, 1699

Barbara
King Ref bp, 1680
NY Ref bp, 1695
Tap Ref bp, 1697

Bernadine
King Ref bp, 1687

Catherine
Alb Ref bp, 1692, 1695,
1697
Fltb Ref bp, 1685
Hack Ref bp, 1686
NY Ref bp, 1655, 1656,
1657, 1660, 1663, 1664,
1665, 1680, 1682, 1684,
1685, 1688, 1690, 1691,
1692, 1694, 1697, 1698

Catlintje
NY Ref bp, 1665

Christina
Fltb Ref bp, 1680
NY Ref bp, 1678, 1689,
1694

Cornelia
Hack Ref bp, 1698
NY Ref bp, 1656, 1662,
1665, 1673, 1674, 1677,
1680, 1684, 1694

Dorothy
Alb Ref bp, 1693, 1697
King Ref bp, 1699

Elizabeth
Alb Ref bp, 1692
Bkln Ref bp, 1683
Fltb Ref bp, 1678, 1680,
1682, 1683
NY Ref bp, 1675, 1679,
1683, 1689, 1692, 1696,
1698, 1699
Schn Ref bp, 1695, 1698

Elsie
Bkln Ref bp, 1684
Fltb Ref bp, 1678, 1681,
1684, 1688
NY Ref bp, 1664, 1665,
1667, 1669, 1671, 1673,
1676

Engel
Bkln Ref bp, 1684, 1687
Fltb Ref bp, 1684
NY Ref bp, 1667, 1669,
1673, 1676, 1678

Eva
NY Ref bp, 1694, 1697,
1698, 1699

Gerarda
Fltb Ref bp, 1679, 1683
NY Ref bp, 1664

Gertrude
Alb Ref bp, 1692, 1693,
1694, 1698
King Ref bp, 1678, 1683,
1692, 1694, 1695, 1696,
1697, 1699
NY Ref bp, 1671, 1689,
1691

Henrietta
Alb Ref bp, 1691, 1694,
1697

Hilda
NY Ref bp, 1659, 1660,
1662, 1665, 1668, 1670,
1672, 1675, 1677, 1679,
1680, 1682, 1686, 16664

Isabel
King Ref bp, 1679, 1680,
1694, 1697

Janet
Alb Ref bp, 1692, 1695,
1698
Fltb Ref bp, 1684
King Ref bp, 1685, 1699
NY Ref bp, 1680, 1681,
1684, 1686, 1689, 1691,
1694, 1696, 1699

Jemima
Alb Ref bp, 1698
Schn Ref bp, 1697

Judith
Alb Ref bp, 1693, 1696
King Ref bp, 1698

Lydia
NY Ref bp, 1673

Magdalena
King Ref bp, 1685
NY Ref bp, 1658, 1660,
1678, 1681, 1683, 1686,
1689, 1692, 1694, 1697

Margaret
Berg Ref bp, 1696, 1697,
1698, 1699
King Ref bp, 1671, 1678,
1684, 1696, 1698, 1699
NY Ref bp, 1655, 1656,
1657, 1658, 1659, 1660,
1664, 1678, 1679, 1681,
1683, 1685, 1688, 1690,
1692, 1695, 1696, 1698

Maria
Alb Ref bp, 1698
Bkln Ref bp, 1681, 1690,
1691, 1693, 1694, 1697,
1698, 1699
Fltb Ref bp, 1679, 1680,
1681
Hack Ref bp, 1696, 1698,
1699
King Ref bp, 1661, 1663,
1665, 1666, 1678, 1683,
1686, 1687, 1688, 1693
NPal Ref bp, 1689, 1699
NY Ref bp, 1655, 1656,

1660, 1664, 1666, 1668,
1669, 1671, 1672, 1673,
1676, 1678, 1680, 1681,
1682, 1683, 1684, 1685,
1686, 1687, 1689, 1690,
1692, 1698

Nelly
  NY Ref bp, 1693, 1695,
  1698
Patricia
  Berg Ref bp, 1697, 1699
  NY Ref bp, 1699
Rachel
  King Ref bp, 1696, 1697,
  1699
Rebecca
  NY Ref bp, 1655, 1658,
  1661, 1664, 1667
Ruth
  NY Ref bp, 1694, 1696,
  1698
Sarah
  Alb Ref bp, 1695
  King Ref bp, 1679, 1680,
  1682, 1685, 1686, 1688,
  1689, 1693, 1699, 16979
  NY Ref bp, 1657, 1666,
  1668, 1695, 1696, 1698,
  1699
Sophia
  Bkln Ref bp, 1682, 1683,
  1696
  Fltb Ref bp, 1680, 1682,
  1683, 1685, 1688
  NY Ref bp, 1667, 1668,
  1670, 1671, 1672, 1674,
  1676
Theodora
  King Ref bp, 1699
Wybrecht
  Berg Ref bp, 1682
  Hack Ref bp, 1698, 1699

Jacques
see also Jacob
Adriana
  Fltb Ref bp, 1679

Anna
  NY Ref bp, 1691, 1692,
  1694, 1696, 1699
Catherine
  NY Ref bp, 1674
Eva
  NY Ref bp, 1686, 1691,
  1695, 1698
Lydia
  NY Ref bp, 1665, 1668,
  1671
Maria
  Fltb Ref bp, 1679, 1681,
  1687, 1688
  NY Ref bp, 1665, 1670,
  1671, 1674, 1676, 1678,
  1679, 1682
Sarah
  Fltb Ref bp, 1681
Wybrecht
  Hack Ref bp, 1696

Jafort
Catherine
  NY Ref bp, 1677, 1683

James
Elizabeth
  King Ref bp, 1697, 1698
  NY Ref bp, 1685, 1686,
  1688, 1693, 1697
Janet
  NY Ref bp, 1668, 1670,
  1672, 1674, 1676, 1678,
  1680, 1683, 1686
Margaret
  Bkln Ref bp, 1699
  King Ref bp, 1689
Maria
  NY Ref bp, 1681, 1695
Sarah
  King Ref bp, 1689, 1694,
  1698

Jeffers
Maria
  NY Ref bp, 1699

Jeremiah
Anna
  NY Ref bp, 1689, 1692,
  1695

Catherine
  King Ref bp, 1675
Elizabeth
  King Ref bp, 1697
  NY Ref bp, 1678
Janet
  NY Ref bp, 1688, 1690,
  1692, 1694, 1695, 1697,
  1699
Rachel
  Schn Ref bp, 1698

Jesse
Maria
  NY Ref bp, 1696, 1698

Jochem
Anna
  Alb Ref bp, 1691
  King Ref bp, 1692, 1694,
  1695, 1698
  NY Ref bp, 1696, 1698
Christina
  NY Ref bp, 1679, 1682,
  1686
Elizabeth
  King Ref bp, 1682, 1683,
  1686, 1687, 1693, 1695,
  1697
Emma
  NY Ref bp, 1665, 1672,
  1674
Engel
  Hack Ref bp, 1686
Eva
  Alb Ref bp, 1692, 1695
Jemima
  Fltb Ref bp, 1687
Magdalena
  Fltb Ref bp, 1681, 1685,
  1689
  NY Ref bp, 1658
Maria
  Bkln Ref bp, 1696
  NY Ref bp, 1699
Petronella
  King Ref bp, 1682, 1683,
  1684, 1685, 1687
Sarah
  King Ref bp, 1678

Jonas
  Catherine
    NY Ref bp, 1661
  Magdalena
    Alb Ref bp, 1692
Jonathan
  Catherine
    Alb Ref bp, 1697
    NY Ref bp, 1680, 1682,
      1683, 1687, 1689, 1692,
      1694, 1697
  Frances
    NY Ref bp, 1682, 1685
  Judith
    Bkln Ref bp, 1697
  Lavinia
    NY Ref bp, 1694, 1695,
      1699
  Lea
    Schn Ref bp, 1695, 1697
  Maria
    Schn Ref bp, 1696, 1698
  Sarah
    NY Ref bp, 1694
Joris
  see also George, Jurian
  Adriana
    NY Ref bp, 1683, 1686,
      1692, 1695, 1698
  Anna
    Bkln Ref bp, 1693, 1695, 1697,
      1699
    NY Ref bp, 1691, 1692,
      1694, 1696, 1698
  Catherine
    Bkln Ref bp, 1661, 1664
    NY Ref bp, 1666, 1678,
      1692
  Elizabeth
    NY Ref bp, 1689, 1692,
      1694
  Gerarda
    NY Ref bp, 1655, 1657,
      1659, 1661, 1669, 1672,
      1675, 1677
  Janet
    King Ref bp, 1
    NY Ref bp, 1

Joanna
  King Ref bp, 1680
Magdalena
  NY Ref bp, 1678, 1680,
    1683
Maria
  Bkln Ref bp, 1695, 1699
  King Ref bp, 1696, 1697,
    1699
  NY Ref bp, 1667, 1669,
    1672, 1674, 1677, 1680,
    1683
Nelly
  Bkln Ref bp, 1696
Rebecca
  Bkln Ref bp, 1678
  NY Ref bp, 1652, 1664
Sarah
  Bkln Ref bp, 1688, 1690,
    1694
  Fltb Ref bp, 1679, 1681,
    1682, 1684
  NY Ref bp, 1681, 1696
Wilhelmina
  NY Ref bp, 1696
Joseph
  Anna
    NY Ref bp, 1657, 1659,
      1661, 1689, 1696, 1698
  Catherine
    NY Ref bp, 1689, 1692,
      1695, 1697, 1699
  Christina
    NY Ref bp, 1658, 1660,
      1663, 1664, 1666, 1669
  Constance
    Alb Ref bp, 1696
  Elizabeth
    Bkln Ref bp, 1695
    Fltb Ref bp, 1687, 1690
    King Ref bp, 1672, 1678,
      1680
    NY Ref bp, 1682, 1684,
      1694, 1696, 1698
  Frances
    NY Ref bp, 1693

Huberta
  Alb Ref bp, 1693, 1695,
    1698
Jemima
  Alb Ref bp, 1693, 1696
  NY Ref bp, 1656, 1658,
    1661
Josephine
  NY Ref bp, 1663
Madeline
  Bkln Ref bp, 1681, 1686,
    1693
Magdalena
  Bkln Ref bp, 1681, 1684
  Fltb Ref bp, 1679, 1681,
    1684
  NY Ref bp, 1687
Margaret
  NY Ref bp, 1696, 1698
Maria
  King Ref bp, 1682
  NY Ref bp, 1655, 1669,
    1672, 1675, 1678, 1684,
    1685, 1691, 1695
Nelly
  Fltb Ref bp, 1682, 1684
Rachel
  Alb Ref bp, 1691, 1694
Sarah
  King Ref bp, 1683, 1686,
    1689, 1695
Sophia
  Alb Ref bp, 1693, 1695, 1698
  Bkln Ref bp, 1680, 1687
  Fltb Ref bp, 1678, 1680,
    1682, 1685
  King Ref bp, 1664
  NY Ref bp, 1661, 1667,
    1692, 1696
Joshua
  Engel
    NY Ref bp, 1696
Josiah
  Alida
    Bkln Ref bp, 1684, 1687,
      1699
    Fltb Ref bp, 1682, 1684
    NY Ref bp, 1691, 1696

Nelly
    Fltb Ref bp, 1680
Jurian
see also George, Joris
    Catherine
        NY Ref bp, 1655
    Veronica
        Hack Ref bp, 1699
Justus
    Anna
        NY Ref bp, 1698, 1699
    Catherine
        NY Ref bp, 1676, 1679,
        1682, 1687, 1690

K

Kilian
    Janet
        Tary Ref bp, 1697

L

Lambert
    Barbara
        NY Ref bp, 1661
    Harmina
        Bkln Ref bp, 1672
        Fltb Ref bp, 1678, 1681
    Henrietta
        King Ref bp, 1663, 1666,
        1670
        NY Ref bp, 1661
    Janet
        Alb Ref bp, 1691, 1693,
        1695, 1696, 1698, 1699
    Letitia
        Fltb Ref bp, 1679, 1683
        NY Ref bp, 1697
    Margaret
        NY Ref bp, 1683, 1685,
        1689, 1691
        Tap Ref bp, 1695, 1698
    Maria
        NY Ref bp, 1667, 1692
    Sophia
        Fltb Ref bp, 1682, 1685,
        1687, 1689

Lawrence
    Alberta
        Alb Ref bp, 1691
    Alida
        Fltb Ref bp, 1679, 1681,
        1683, 1687
        NY Ref bp, 1681, 1685,
        1688, 1690, 1693, 1695,
        1699
    Anna
        NY Ref bp, 1663, 1667,
        1698
    Catherine
        NY Ref bp, 1689, 1691,
        1692, 1694, 1696, 1698,
        1699
    Frances
        NY Ref bp, 1673, 1675,
        1677, 1679, 1681, 1683,
        1691
    Gertrude
        Hack Ref bp, 1686
        NY Ref bp, 1680, 1685
    Henrietta
        Hack Ref bp, 1696, 1699
    Hilda
        NY Ref bp, 1670, 1674,
        1677, 1679, 1681, 1682,
        1684, 1686
    Janet
        Berg Ref bp, 1666
        NY Ref bp, 1659, 1686,
        1688, 1691, 1696, 1698
    Joanna
        NY Ref bp, 1693, 1695,
        1696
    Kunigunda
        Bkln Ref bp, 1689
        Fltb Ref bp, 1679, 1681,
        1683, 1685
    Laurentia
        King Ref bp, 1680
    Margaret
        Bkln Ref bp, 1693
        Fltb Ref bp, 1680, 1682,
        1684
        NY Ref bp, 1677, 1678,
        1687, 1691

Maria
    Alb Ref bp, 1691
    NY Ref bp, 1674, 1676,
    1679, 1682, 1685, 1686,
    1687, 1693
Sarah
    Bkln Ref bp, 1667
    NY Ref bp, 1659, 1661,
    1662, 1663, 1666, 1668,
    1670, 1671, 1672, 1673,
    1674, 1677, 1678, 1680,
    1681, 1683
Leffert
    Abigail
        Bkln Ref bp, 1684, 1692
        Fltb Ref bp, 1682, 1684
        NY Ref bp, 1686
Leonard
    Christina
        Bkln Ref bp, 1691
        NY Ref bp, 1679, 1681,
        1683, 1686, 1689, 1695
    Elizabeth
        NY Ref bp, 1690, 1691,
        1692, 1694, 1696, 1698,
        1699
    Gertrude
        NY Ref bp, 1685, 1687,
        1689, 1691, 1694, 1696,
        1699
    Janet
        NY Ref bp, 1676, 1690,
        1699
    Madeline
        Bkln Ref bp, 1698
    Magdalena
        NY Ref bp, 1684, 1686,
        1688, 1690, 1694, 1696
    Maria
        King Ref bp, 1679, 1680,
        1683, 1684, 1686, 1689
        NY Ref bp, 1669, 1673, 1694
Louis
    Anna
        Bkln Ref bp, 1661, 1664
        Hack Ref bp, 1698, 1699
        NY Ref bp, 1658

Louis (cont.)
Catherine
King Ref bp, 1661, 1664,
1667, 1671, 1675
NY Ref bp, 1669
Catlintje
NY Ref bp, 1680
Hillary
NY Ref bp, 1665
Margaret
King Ref bp, 1682, 1683,
1685, 1686, 1688, 1694,
1698
Maria
King Ref bp, 1678, 1682,
1698
NPal Ref bp, 1684, 1687
Lourus
Frances
Berg Ref bp, 1685, 1687,
1689, 1694, 1696
Gertrude
Berg Ref bp, 1682
Margaret
Berg Ref bp, 1667
Lubbert
Hilda
Berg Ref bp, 1682, 1685
Hack Ref bp, 1686, 1694
NY Ref bp, 1681
Lucas
Agatha
NY Ref bp, 1669
Alida
NY Ref bp, 1656
Anna
King Ref bp, 1697, 1699
NY Ref bp, 1655, 1656,
1657, 1658, 1661, 1662,
1663
Barbara
Bkln Ref bp, 1699
Fltb Ref bp, 1683
Catherine
Alb Ref bp, 1692, 1693
Fltb Ref bp, 1677
NY Ref bp, 1671, 1678,
1681, 1683, 1685, 1688,
1690, 1693

Catlintje
Bkln Ref bp, 1686
Fltb Ref bp, 1679, 1681,
1683
Clara
NY Ref bp, 1665
Eva
NY Ref bp, 1657, 1660,
1662, 1663, 1665, 1667,
1670, 1671, 1673, 1675,
1676, 1679, 1682
Judith
Alb Ref bp, 1693, 1695,
1698
Maria
Alb Ref bp, 1693
Rachel
NY Ref bp, 1684, 1686,
1689, 1692, 1695, 1698,
1699
Sarah
NY Ref bp, 1677
Ludwich
Agnes
NY Ref bp, 1655, 1657
Janet
Hack Ref bp, 1694, 1696
King Ref bp, 1684
Maria
King Ref bp, 1697

M

Mangold
Anna
NY Ref bp, 1694, 1697,
1699
Marcelis
Patricia
Berg Ref bp, 1682, 1684,
1694, 1699
NY Ref bp, 1687, 1690,
1696
Marcus
Elizabeth
Bkln Ref bp, 1662
NY Ref bp, 1658, 1659,
1665, 1669

Hester
NY Ref bp, 1693
Marinus
Petronella
King Ref bp, 1685, 1688,
1695, 1697, 1699
Martin
Anna
Bkln Ref bp, 1677, 1682
Fltb Ref bp, 1677, 1682,
1684, 1685, 1688, 1689
NY Ref bp, 1664, 1666,
1669, 1671, 1673, 1685
Catherine
NY Ref bp, 1696
Elizabeth
NY Ref bp, 1643
Emma
NY Ref bp, 1665, 1666
Henrietta
NY Ref bp, 1663, 1665,
1667, 1668, 1674
Janet
Alb Ref bp, 1692, 1693,
1695, 1698
NY Ref bp, 1660, 1662,
1665, 1669, 1690
Magdalena
NY Ref bp, 1676, 1678,
1681
Margaret
Hack Ref bp, 1696, 1699
NY Ref bp, 1657, 1699
Maria
Bkln Ref bp, 1693
NY Ref bp, 1661, 1673,
1695
Nelly
Alb Ref bp, 1692, 1694,
1695
NY Ref bp, 1693, 1694,
1696, 1698
Sarah
NY Ref bp, 1696
Sophia
Schn Ref bp, 1697
Susan
NY Ref bp, 1664

Father/Mother Pairs Directory

Matthew
Alida
King Ref bp, 1661, 1699
Anna
Berg Ref bp, 1673, 1678,
1680, 1682, 1684
Hack Ref bp, 1686, 1695
King Ref bp, 1696
NY Ref bp, 1660, 1671
Catherine
Alb Ref bp, 1699
Berg Ref bp, 1668, 1687,
1688, 1690, 1692, 1693,
1694, 1696, 1699
Hack Ref bp, 1696, 1699
King Ref bp, 1693
NY Ref bp, 1656, 1657,
1669, 1680, 1687, 1688,
1693, 1694, 1696, 1698,
1699
Charity
King Ref bp, 1678, 1679,
1680, 1682, 1684, 1685,
1687, 1689, 1692, 1694,
1696
Cornelia
Alb Ref bp, 1692, 1695,
1697
Bkln Ref bp, 1696
Deborah
Tary Ref bp, 1697
Elizabeth
NY Ref bp, 1676, 1678,
1679, 1681, 1685, 1688
Gertrude
NY Ref bp, 1690
Janet
King Ref bp, 1682, 1684,
1689, 1694, 1697, 1699
NY Ref bp, 1673, 1680,
1696, 1698, 1699
Magdalena
King Ref bp, 1686
Margaret
King Ref bp, 1679, 1682,
1683, 1686, 1688, 1692,
1694, 1699

Maria
Alb Ref bp, 1694
Bkln Ref bp, 1682, 1693
Fltb Ref bp, 1682, 1684
King Ref bp, 1680, 1684,
1688, 1694, 1697
NY Ref bp, 1669, 1670, 1672,
1674, 1676, 1677, 1679,
1681, 1686, 1689, 1699
Sarah
King Ref bp, 1698, 1797
Sophia
Bkln Ref bp, 1695, 1699
NY Ref bp, 1661
Susan
Alb Ref bp, 1696, 1698,
1699
Maurice
Anna
Bkln Ref bp, 1697
NY Ref bp, 1691, 1693,
1696
Maynard
Catherine
NY Ref bp, 1667
Elizabeth
NY Ref bp, 1674
Helena
Alb Ref bp, 1692
NY Ref bp, 1696
Janet
NY Ref bp, 1682, 1683,
1685, 1687, 1690, 1693
Maria
Fltb Ref bp, 1682
NY Ref bp, 1661, 1666,
1670, 1673, 1695
Rachel
Alb Ref bp, 1697
Sarah
King Ref bp, 1694, 1697,
1699
Melchior
Bridget
NY Ref bp, 1679
Catherine
Alb Ref bp, 1697, 1699

Elizabeth
Alb Ref bp, 1693, 1695
Engel
Alb Ref bp, 1691
Gertrude
Bkln Ref bp, 1681, 1683
Fltb Ref bp, 1681, 1683
NY Ref bp, 1672, 1687
Susan
King Ref bp, 1678, 1682
Michael
Alida
King Ref bp, 1662
Anna
King Ref bp, 1678, 1682,
1684, 1687
NY Ref bp, 1659, 1660,
1661
Christina
Bkln Ref bp, 1699
Frances
Hack Ref bp, 1696
Helena
NY Ref bp, 1696, 1698
Henrietta
Bkln Ref bp, 1674
Fltb Ref bp, 1679
NY Ref bp, 1671, 1676
Janet
NY Ref bp, 1691, 1694
Letitia
Alb Ref bp, 1692, 1695,
1699
Margaret
NY Ref bp, 1677
Maria
NY Ref bp, 1655, 1656
Nelly
Bkln Ref bp, 1680, 1694,
1699
Fltb Ref bp, 1680, 1682,
1684, 1690
Sophia
Bkln Ref bp, 1678
Fltb Ref bp, 1678, 1680
NY Ref bp, 1651, 1654,
1656, 1658

Michael (cont.)
  Susan
    NY Ref bp, 1688
Moses
  Hester
    King Ref bp, 1685, 1687,
    1688, 1695, 1697, 1699
    NY Ref bp, 1691
  Janet
    NY Ref bp, 1696, 1698
  Maria
    King Ref bp, 1680, 1682,
    1684, 1686, 1688, 1691,
    1695, 1698
    NY Ref bp, 1680

N

Nanning
  Alida
    Alb Ref bp, 1692, 1694,
    1696, 1698
Nathan
  Anna
    NY Ref bp, 1665, 1667,
    1670, 1679, 1683
  Hester
    Tap Ref bp, 1695
    Tary Ref bp, 1698
  Margaret
    NY Ref bp, 1679, 1681,
    1683, 1685, 1690
  Maria
    NY Ref bp, 1687
  Sarah
    NY Ref bp, 1664, 1676
Nicasius
  Anna
    Hack Ref bp, 1697
Nicholas
  Agnes
    NY Ref bp, 1657
  Alida
    NY Ref bp, 1662, 1664,
    1667, 1675, 1677, 1680
  Anna
    Berg Ref bp, 1667, 1676,
    1678, 1680, 1682, 1698
    NY Ref bp, 1651, 1657,

1659, 1663, 1664, 1669,
1671, 1673, 1676, 1678,
1682
  Barbara
    NY Ref bp, 1663, 1685
  Bernadine
    NY Ref bp, 1662, 1691,
    1695
  Catherine
    Bkln Ref bp, 1690
    Fltb Ref bp, 1678
    Hack Ref bp, 1697, 1699
    NY Ref bp, 1663, 1664,
    1667, 1670, 1675, 1695,
    1697
  Catlintje
    NY Ref bp, 1669, 1671,
    1674, 1680, 1691
  Christina
    Bkln Ref bp, 1686
    Fltb Ref bp, 1681, 1683
    King Ref bp, 1682
  Cornelia
    King Ref bp, 1682, 1684,
    1687, 1692, 1695, 1698
  Elizabeth
    Alb Ref bp, 1691, 1693
    Bkln Ref bp, 1694
    NY Ref bp, 1683, 1685,
    1687, 1689, 1691
    Schn Ref bp, 1696
  Engel
    King Ref bp, 1683, 1684,
    1687, 1692, 1693
    NY Ref bp, 1681
  Eva
    Alb Ref bp, 1692
    NY Ref bp, 1659
  Gerarda
    NY Ref bp, 1668
  Gertrude
    NY Ref bp, 1648, 1686,
    1687
  Helena
    Fltb Ref bp, 1684
  Hilda
    Bkln Ref bp, 1692
    King Ref bp, 1683, 1685,

1687, 1689
    NY Ref bp, 1691, 1692,
    1694, 1697, 1699
  Isabel
    NY Ref bp, 1697
  Janet
    Bkln Ref bp, 1693, 1699
    NY Ref bp, 1656, 1658,
    1674, 1676, 1678, 1681,
    1683, 1684, 1686, 1689,
    1691, 1693, 1695
  Jemima
    Berg Ref bp, 1685, 1687,
    1694, 1696, 1699
    NY Ref bp, 1669, 1685,
    1691, 1694
  Kunigunda
    NY Ref bp, 1672, 1675,
    1682, 1686, 1688
  Lambertina
    NY Ref bp, 1662
  Lea
    Alb Ref bp, 1691
  Lucretia
    NY Ref bp, 1680, 1681,
    1683, 1685, 1688
  Lydia
    NY Ref bp, 1656, 1657,
    1661, 1664, 1666, 1668
  Margaret
    NY Ref bp, 1668, 1681,
    1684, 1686, 1699
  Maria
    Alb Ref bp, 1693
    Berg Ref bp, 1680, 1689
    NY Ref bp, 1655, 1661,
    1663, 1664, 1666, 1667,
    1671, 1673, 1675, 1676,
    1678, 1680, 1681, 1682,
    1683, 1684, 1685, 1687,
    1689, 1691, 1693, 1694,
    1695, 1698
  Nelly
    NY Ref bp, 1653
  Rebecca
    NY Ref bp, 1685

Sarah
Fltb Ref bp, 1679, 1681, 1683
NY Ref bp, 1676, 1682, 1686, 1688, 1690, 1692, 1693

Susan
NY Ref bp, 1652, 1656, 1659, 1661, 1662, 1664, 1666, 1667, 1668, 1670, 1672, 1673, 1675, 1677, 1679, 1681

Wilhelmina
Berg Ref bp, 1688, 1692

O

Obadiah
Margaret
NY Ref bp, 1671

Octavius
Magdalena
Bkln Ref bp, 1662

Oliver
Anna
NY Ref bp, 1655, 1658
Margaret
NY Ref bp, 1683, 1686, 1688, 1691, 1695, 1698

Omie
Anna
Alb Ref bp, 1692
Louisa
King Ref bp, 1689

Otto
Engel
NY Ref bp, 1668, 1669, 1672, 1674, 1676, 1678, 1680, 1681, 1684, 1686
Janet
NY Ref bp, 1665
Margaret
NY Ref bp, 1694

Oufreen
Sophia
NY Ref bp, 1689

P

Palbel
Elsie
Fltb Ref bp, 1687

Patrick
Margaret
King Ref bp, 1687, 1693
Marjory
King Ref bp, 1689, 1691, 1695, 1697, 1699
Sophia
Alb Ref bp, 1697

Paul
Alida
NY Ref bp, 1664, 1666, 1669, 1671, 1673, 1677, 1678, 1679, 1682
Anna
NY Ref bp, 1694, 1695
Apollonia
NY Ref bp, 1675
Catherine
Berg Ref bp, 1667, 1679
NY Ref bp, 1661, 1663, 1670, 1675
Cecilia
NY Ref bp, 1664, 1667, 1670, 1673, 1675, 1678
Elizabeth
Fltb Ref bp, 1679, 1681
King Ref bp, 1665, 1667, 1673, 1678, 1682, 1684
Janet
NY Ref bp, 1655, 1696, 1699
Maria
NY Ref bp, 1656, 1663, 1689, 1691, 1692, 1695, 1697
Nicole
NY Ref bp, 1663
Sarah
Bkln Ref bp, 1678, 1681
Fltb Ref bp, 1678, 1679, 1680, 1681
NY Ref bp, 1683, 1687, 1688

Peek
Maria
NY Ref bp, 1698

Peter
Adriana
Alb Ref bp, 1693, 1695, 1696, 1697
Agatha
NPal Ref bp, 1683, 1687
NY Ref bp, 1656, 1658, 1660, 1668
Agnes
Bkln Ref bp, 1681
Fltb Ref bp, 1681
NY Ref bp, 1664, 1666, 1668, 1677
Alberta
NY Ref bp, 1658
Alet
King Ref bp, 1679
Alida
Alb Ref bp, 1693, 1694, 1696
NY Ref bp, 1656, 1660, 1669
Anna
Bkln Ref bp, 1661, 1663, 1684, 1688, 1694, 1695, 1696, 1697
Fltb Ref bp, 1680, 1682, 1684, 1685
NY Ref bp, 1659, 1667, 1673, 1676, 1677, 1678, 1680, 1696, 1698, 1699
Barbara
Bkln Ref bp, 1695
Bathilda
NY Ref bp, 1678, 1680, 1681, 1682, 1687, 1690, 1692, 1694
Blandina
NY Ref bp, 1675, 1679, 1681, 1683
Bridget
NY Ref bp, 1657
Catherine
Alb Ref bp, 1692, 1694, 1696, 1698

Peter (cont.)

Catherine (cont.)
Berg Ref bp, 1688, 1691
Bkln Ref bp, 1661, 1662,
1697
Fltb Ref bp, 1680, 1682,
1684
Hack Ref bp, 1696
King Ref bp, 1684, 1687
NY Ref bp, 1666, 1697,
1699, 16989

Christina
Bkln Ref bp, 1699

Constance
Alb Ref bp, 1697
King Ref bp, 1689

Cornelia
Bkln Ref bp, 1688, 1691,
1693, 1696
NY Ref bp, 1697, 1698,
1699

Deborah
Fltb Ref bp, 1685
King Ref bp, 1693, 1698
NY Ref bp, 1664, 1666,
1670, 1673, 1675

Elizabeth
Berg Ref bp, 1677, 1680,
1682, 1685, 1687
Fltb Ref bp, 1691
King Ref bp, 1680, 1683,
1686, 1688
NY Ref bp, 1663, 1667,
1668, 1670, 1672, 1673,
1675, 1678, 1683, 1686,
1687, 1689, 1692, 1694,
1697, 1699

Elsie
NY Ref bp, 1652, 1657,
1695

Emma
Alb Ref bp, 1691

Engel
NY Ref bp, 1678, 1679,
1681, 1684

Esther
King Ref bp, 1697

Eva
King Ref bp, 1698
NY Ref bp, 1658, 1660,
1662, 1666

Frances
NY Ref bp, 1661, 1668,
1669

Gerarda
NY Ref bp, 1669, 1671,
1673, 1675

Gertrude
King Ref bp, 1682, 1693,
1695, 1697, 1699
NY Ref bp, 1662, 1664,
1677, 1679, 1689, 1691,
1693, 1696, 1698

Godwina
NY Ref bp, 1676

Harmina
NY Ref bp, 1666

Helena
NY Ref bp, 1694, 1697

Henrietta
Alb Ref bp, 1697, 1698
Berg Ref bp, 1676, 1678,
1681, 1684
Hack Ref bp, 1686
King Ref bp, 1680, 1683,
1685
NY Ref bp, 1671, 1673,
1676

Hester
King Ref bp, 1694
NY Ref bp, 1667, 1669,
1672, 1675, 1678, 1682,
1684, 1685, 1687, 1689,
1692, 1694, 1696, 1699

Hilda
King Ref bp, 1697, 1699

Isabel
Hack Ref bp, 1696, 1698
NY Ref bp, 1685, 1687,
1688, 1690, 1692, 1693,
1695

Janet
Alb Ref bp, 1693, 1695,
1697, 1699
Bkln Ref bp, 1681, 1684,
1690
Fltb Ref bp, 1681, 1684
Hack Ref bp, 1696
King Ref bp, 1661, 1683,
1686, 1688, 1691, 1693,
1694, 1697, 1698, 1699
NY Ref bp, 1659, 1675,
1676, 1679, 1682, 1684,
1686, 1688, 1691, 1693,
1696

Jemima
Hack Ref bp, 1698
NY Ref bp, 1657

Joanna
Alb Ref bp, 1692, 1695,
1697

Josina
NY Ref bp, 1674, 1679

Judith
NY Ref bp, 1648, 1653,
1658, 1661, 1665, 1672,
1674, 1676, 1678

Lavinia
Alb Ref bp, 1691
King Ref bp, 1662
NY Ref bp, 1659

Lydia
NY Ref bp, 1697

Margaret
Bkln Ref bp, 1663, 1681,
1686
Fltb Ref bp, 1678, 1679,
1681, 1683
King Ref bp, 1662, 1693
NY Ref bp, 1660, 1662,
1664, 1666, 1671, 1675,
1685, 1688
Tap Ref bp, 1696, 1698
Tary Ref bp, 1699

Maria
Alb Ref bp, 1692, 1694,
1696, 1698
Berg Ref bp, 1666, 1669
Bkln Ref bp, 1688, 1698

Fltb Ref bp, 1679, 1680,
1681, 1687, 1688
King Ref bp, 1678, 1680
NY Ref bp, 1655, 1657,
1658, 1659, 1661, 1662,
1663, 1664, 1666, 1667,
1668, 1671, 1673, 1674,
1675, 1677, 1680, 1681,
1682, 1685, 1688, 1689,
1691, 1692, 1693, 1694,
1695, 1696, 1697, 1698
Martha
King Ref bp, 1697
Nelly
King Ref bp, 1692, 1694,
1695
Patience
Bkln Ref bp, 1695
Petronella
Bkln Ref bp, 1692
NY Ref bp, 1685
Rachel
NY Ref bp, 1659, 1662,
1699
Rebecca
King Ref bp, 1682, 1684,
1686, 1688, 1695, 1698
NY Ref bp, 1667, 1690,
1693, 1694, 1696, 1697,
1699
Sarah
Bkln Ref bp, 1687, 1696,
1698
Fltb Ref bp, 1681
NY Ref bp, 1656, 1685,
1688, 1689, 1691, 1695,
1697, 1699
Sophia
Bkln Ref bp, 1664
NY Ref bp, 1687, 1689,
1691, 1694, 1697
Susan
Fltb Ref bp, 1688, 1690
Hack Ref bp, 1697
NY Ref bp, 1666, 1686,
1693, 1697

Philip
Agatha
NY Ref bp, 1668
Anna
NY Ref bp, 1695, 1697
Catherine
Alb Ref bp, 1692, 1694,
1697
NY Ref bp, 1678
Elizabeth
Alb Ref bp, 1693
King Ref bp, 1689
NY Ref bp, 1692
Schn Ref bp, 1697
Eva
NY Ref bp, 1666
Gerarda
NY Ref bp, 1667
Gertrude
NY Ref bp, 1656
Hilda
NY Ref bp, 1696, 1698
Lavinia
Alb Ref bp, 1693, 1694,
1698
Margaret
NY Ref bp, 1673, 1682
Maria
Alb Ref bp, 1693, 1695,
1697
NY Ref bp, 1662
Sarah
King Ref bp, 1686, 1688
NY Ref bp, 1681

Q
Quirinus
Nelly
Fltb Ref bp, 1687

R
Randolph
Margaret
Bkln Ref bp, 1684
Fltb Ref bp, 1684
Martha
Fltb Ref bp, 1684

Rembrant
Cornelia
NY Ref bp, 1683, 1686,
1690
Janet
Bkln Ref bp, 1662
NY Ref bp, 1673
Margaret
Alb Ref bp, 1696, 1698
Maria
Fltb Ref bp, 1682, 1684,
1688
Resolved
Anna
NY Ref bp, 1657
Reyer
Adriana
Alb Ref bp, 1693
Jemima
NY Ref bp, 1689, 1693,
1695, 1698
Maria
NY Ref bp, 1682
Rebecca
NY Ref bp, 1697, 1698
Reyner
Catlintje
King Ref bp, 1670
NY Ref bp, 1665, 1666
Clara
NY Ref bp, 1699
Constance
Berg Ref bp, 1686
Elizabeth
Fltb Ref bp, 1681, 1683
Janet
Bkln Ref bp, 1696
Fltb Ref bp, 1679, 1682,
1684, 1689
NY Ref bp, 1657, 1660,
1685, 1695
Nicole
NY Ref bp, 1693, 1696
Susan
NY Ref bp, 1661, 1663,
1665, 1668, 1670, 1673,
1675, 1678, 1681, 1685

Father/Mother Pairs Directory

Reyner (cont.)
Theodora
Berg Ref bp, 1666
NY Ref bp, 1659, 1670, 1673
Richard
Anna
NY Ref bp, 1660, 1661,
1664, 1667, 1672
Catherine
NY Ref bp, 1673, 1675,
1678, 1681, 1684, 1687
Dorothy
NY Ref bp, 1689
Elizabeth
Berg Ref bp, 166
Goodeth
King Ref bp, 1684, 1687
Janet
NY Ref bp, 1673
Judith
King Ref bp, 1685
Lavinia
King Ref bp, 1699
Madeline
NPal Ref bp, 1698
Magdalena
King Ref bp, 1693, 1696
Maria
Fltb Ref bp, 1681
NY Ref bp, 1680, 1688,
1691, 1694, 1695, 1698
Sarah
NY Ref bp, 1667
Sophia
NY Ref bp, 1682, 1684
Susan
NY Ref bp, 1692
Robert
Alida
Alb Ref bp, 1692, 1694,
1698
Anna
NY Ref bp, 1697
Catherine
NY Ref bp, 1685, 1687,
1689

Christina
NY Ref bp, 1677, 1678,
1683, 1685, 1688, 1689,
1690, 1693, 1695
Cornelia
Alb Ref bp, 1691, 1694,
1696
Elizabeth
King Ref bp, 1679, 1680,
1684, 1687
Frances
NY Ref bp, 1695, 1697
Gerarda
Tary Ref bp, 1698
Gertrude
Berg Ref bp, 1692, 1694,
1697, 1699
NY Ref bp, 1692
Helena
NY Ref bp, 1695
Jemima
NY Ref bp, 1691
Lavinia
Alb Ref bp, 1692, 1694,
1696, 1699
NY Ref bp, 1694
Margaret
Alb Ref bp, 1698
King Ref bp, 1682, 1687
Maria
Alb Ref bp, 1693
King Ref bp, 1685
NY Ref bp, 1684, 1685,
1687, 1691, 1693, 1695
Roelof
Agnes
King Ref bp, 1679, 1682,
1684, 1685
Alida
Fltb Ref bp, 1685
King Ref bp, 1665, 1667,
1679, 1683, 1686
Anna
Fltb Ref bp, 1678, 1682,
1684

Catherine
Bkln Ref bp, 1682, 1684,
1695
Fltb Ref bp, 1682, 1684
Eva
King Ref bp, 1662, 1664,
1667, 1673
Gerarda
NY Ref bp, 1653, 1656,
1661, 1664, 1667
Gertrude
Alb Ref bp, 1692, 1693
NY Ref bp, 1648
Ida
NY Ref bp, 1671, 1673,
1677
Susan
Berg Ref bp, 1685
Hack Ref bp, 1695, 1698
Ursula
Hack Ref bp, 1686, 1694,
1696, 1699
NY Ref bp, 1691
Roger
Gertrude
Fltb Ref bp, 1685
Hester
Alb Ref bp, 1696
Lavinia
Alb Ref bp, 1693, 1696
Maria
NY Ref bp, 1696
Nelly
Hack Ref bp, 1698
Sophia
NY Ref bp, 1686, 1690
Romeyn
Nelly
NY Ref bp, 1661
Rupert
Sarah
NY Ref bp, 1685, 1686,
1688, 1690, 1692, 1694,
1695, 1699, 16979

Father/Mother Pairs Directory

S

Sampson
  Catherine
    Alb Ref bp, 1692, 1694,
    1696
    NY Ref bp, 1698
Samuel
  Adriana
    NY Ref bp, 1692, 1694,
    1696, 1698
  Agnes
    NY Ref bp, 1683, 1684,
    1685, 1694, 1695, 1697,
    1699
  Anna
    King Ref bp, 1689
    NY Ref bp, 1656, 1692
  Catherine
    NY Ref bp, 1699
  Catlintje
    Bkln Ref bp, 1691, 1698
    NY Ref bp, 1695
  Deborah
    NY Ref bp, 1660, 1661,
    1663, 1667, 1689
  Helena
    Alb Ref bp, 1693, 1696,
    1699
  Hester
    NY Ref bp, 1790
  Janet
    Berg Ref bp, 1667, 1673
    NY Ref bp, 1658, 1660
  Joanna
    NY Ref bp, 1689, 1690,
    1694, 1697
  Margaret
    NY Ref bp, `1698, 1695,
    1696
    Tary Ref bp, 1699
  Maria
    Berg Ref bp, 1681
    Hack Ref bp, 1694, 1697,
    1699
    NY Ref bp, 1665, 1679,
    1680, 1681, 1685, 1695,
    1698

Ruth
    Berg Ref bp, 1683
Susan
    Alb Ref bp, 1692
    Schn Ref bp, 1695, 1696,
    1699
Seger
  Sophia
    NY Ref bp, 1687, 1690
Servis
  Gertrude
    NY Ref bp, 1698
Siebold
  Maria
    Berg Ref bp, 1680, 1682,
    1684, 1685
    Hack Ref bp, 1694, 1696,
    1699
Siegbert
  Ida
    Berg Ref bp, 1666
    NY Ref bp, 1664
Simon
  Agnes
    King Ref bp, 1697
  Anna
    Alb Ref bp, 1696
    Berg Ref bp, 1676, 1678,
    1682, 1686, 1688, 1690
    Bkln Ref bp, 1660, 1661,
    1664, 1671, 1674
    King Ref bp, 1682, 1684,
    1686, 1688
    NY Ref bp, 1656, 1657,
    1658, 1660, 1662, 1666,
    1667, 1668, 1676, 1678,
    1680, 1684
  Catherine
    NY Ref bp, 1689, 1692,
    1695, 1698
  Elizabeth
    King Ref bp, 1679
    NPal Ref bp, 1683, 1684
  Eva
    King Ref bp, 1694

Gertrude
    Alb Ref bp, 1692, 1697
    Fltb Ref bp, 1680, 1682,
    1684, 1685
    NY Ref bp, 1677, 1687
    Schn Ref bp, 1695
  Hester
    NY Ref bp, 1694
  Isabel
    King Ref bp, 1693, 1694,
    1697, 1699
  Janet
    NY Ref bp, 1687, 1689,
    1691, 1693, 1696, 1699
  Lavinia
    NY Ref bp, 1663, 1665,
    1668, 1672, 1673, 1675,
    1679, 1682
  Magdalena
    NY Ref bp, 1659, 1662,
    1665
  Maria
    Bkln Ref bp, 1681
    Fltb Ref bp, 1681
    King Ref bp, 1684, 1686,
    1689
  Nelly
    King Ref bp, 1696, 1698
  Patricia
    Fltb Ref bp, 1678
  Petronella
    King Ref bp, 1694
  Rachel
    Alb Ref bp, 1693
    NY Ref bp, 1695, 1697
  Wilhelmina
    NY Ref bp, 1693, 1695
  Ypje
    NY Ref bp, 1699
Solomon
  Anna
    Fltb Ref bp, 1689
    NY Ref bp, 1656, 1691,
    1694, 1695
  Barbara
    NY Ref bp, 1653

Solomon (cont.)

Catherine
King Ref bp, 1691, 1693, 1697
Janet
King Ref bp, 1699
Maria
NY Ref bp, 1666, 1668, 1671, 1674, 1676
Susan
NY Ref bp, 1681

Stephen

Anna
NY Ref bp, 1697, 1799
Gertrude
NY Ref bp, 1672, 1674, 1677, 1678, 1680, 1682, 1683, 1685, 1687, 1688, 1694, 1696, 1698
Maria
NY Ref bp, 1697, 1699

Swan

Anna
NY Ref bp, 1669, 1672
Christina
Fltb Ref bp, 1681

Sybout

Maria
NY Ref bp, 1670, 1672, 1676, 1680, 1684, 1687, 1689, 1693

Sylvester

Elizabeth
NY Ref bp, 1676

T

Tades

Anna
NY Ref bp, 1684

Thaddius

Alida
NY Ref bp, 1686
Anna
Berg Ref bp, 1680, 1682, 1684, 1689

Theodore

Artelia
Bkln Ref bp, 1685, 1693, 1697
Fltb Ref bp, 1680, 1681
Margaret
Bkln Ref bp, 1694

Thomas

Agnes
Alb Ref bp, 1692, 1694, 1697, 1699
NY Ref bp, 1695
Alida
NY Ref bp, 1696, 1697, 1699
Anna
Alb Ref bp, 1696
Bkln Ref bp, 1694
King Ref bp, 1682, 1684
NY Ref bp, 1681, 1686, 1696
Barbara
NY Ref bp, 1656
Catherine
Berg Ref bp, 1691, 1694, 1696
NY Ref bp, 1686, 1688, 1689, 1691, 1693, 1694, 1696, 1697
Christina
NY Ref bp, 1676
Deborah
NY Ref bp, 1669, 1672, 1685, 1687, 1689
Elizabeth
Fltb Ref bp, 1680
King Ref bp, 1683, 1686, 1689, 1692, 1694, 1697, 1699
NPal Ref bp, 1693
NY Ref bp, 1650, 1682
Tary Ref bp, 1699
Elsie
NY Ref bp, 1659, 1661, 1664, 1674, 1678, 1681, 1683, 1695
Emma
Berg Ref bp, 1692

Engel
NY Ref bp, 1674, 1676, 1678, 1698
Eunice
Alb Ref bp, 1692
NY Ref bp, 1694, 1696
Frances
Bkln Ref bp, 1697
Hack Ref bp, 1696
NY Ref bp, 1699
Gerarda
NY Ref bp, 1664, 1666, 1667, 1669, 1672, 1674, 1676, 1678
Gertrude
Alb Ref bp, 1694
King Ref bp, 1696, 1698
NY Ref bp, 1692
Harmina
NY Ref bp, 1681, 1683, 1689, 1698
Hester
NY Ref bp, 1691, 1697
Hilda
Fltb Ref bp, 1681
Janet
Berg Ref bp, 1692, 1693
Fltb Ref bp, 1680
King Ref bp, 1695, 1698
NY Ref bp, 1656, 1658, 1697
Jemima
King Ref bp, 1679, 1680, 1682, 1684, 1687, 1688
Joanna
NY Ref bp, 1688
Letitia
NY Ref bp, 1671
Margaret
Berg Ref bp, 1674, 1680
Fltb Ref bp, 1680
Hack Ref bp, 1694
NY Ref bp, 1657, 1694, 1696

Maria
  Alb Ref bp, 1693, 1697
  Berg Ref bp, 1668
  Bkln Ref bp, 1681, 1697
  Fltb Ref bp, 1681
  King Ref bp, 1684, 1686,
    1688, 1689, 1692, 1695,
    1697, 1699
  NY Ref bp, 1653, 1658,
    1659, 1660, 1662, 1663,
    1664, 1666, 1667, 1668,
    1670, 1672, 1673, 1674,
    1675, 1677, 1679, 1681,
    1695, 1698
Nelly
  NY Ref bp, 1665, 1667,
    1669, 1671, 1673
Rymerick
  King Ref bp, 1679, 1683,
    1686, 1688, 1695
Susan
  Hack Ref bp, 1699
Timothy
  Elizabeth
    NY Ref bp, 1682
  Hester
    NY Ref bp, 1687, 1689,
      1696, 1698
  Margaret
    NY Ref bp, 1677, 1678,
      1679, 1682, 1685, 1686,
      1687
Titus
  Janet
    Bkln Ref bp, 1663
    Fltb Ref bp, 1679, 1682
Tobias
  Alida
    NY Ref bp, 1678, 1680,
      1682
  Anna
    NY Ref bp, 1685, 1686,
      1688, 1689, 1691, 1693,
      1695, 1696, 1698
  Elizabeth
    Bkln Ref bp, 1694, 1698
    NY Ref bp, 1685, 1687,
      1690, 1692, 1696

Janet
  NY Ref bp, 1655
Tunis
  see also Dennis
  Adriana
    King Ref bp, 1694, 1696,
      1698, 1699
  Anna
    NY Ref bp, 1675, 1682,
      1683, 1685, 1687, 1688,
      1690, 1692, 1694, 1697
  Barbara
    Bkln Ref bp, 1661, 1663
  Bridget
    Tap Ref bp, 1695, 1697
  Catherine
    Alb Ref bp, 1695
    Berg Ref bp, 1687
    Bkln Ref bp, 1696
    NY Ref bp, 1679, 1680,
      1685, 1688, 1691, 1692,
      1698
    Tap Ref bp, 1696, 1698
  Clara
    King Ref bp, 1697
  Elizabeth
    Bkln Ref bp, 1667
    Schn Ref bp, 1694, 1696
  Elsie
    NY Ref bp, 1691, 1692,
      1693
  Engel
    NY Ref bp, 1655
  Gerarda
    NY Ref bp, 1688
  Gertrude
    King Ref bp, 1679, 1682,
      1684, 1686, 1688, 1692,
      1695
  Helena
    NY Ref bp, 1681, 1682,
      1684, 1686, 1688, 1689,
      1691, 1693, 1695, 1697,
      1699
  Isabel
    NY Ref bp, 1640, 1644
  Janet
    Alb Ref bp, 1696, 1698

    Fltb Ref bp, 1678, 1681,
      1689
    NY Ref bp, 1674, 1676,
      1677, 1679, 1681, 1685,
      1686
  Margaret
    Alb Ref bp, 1694
    NY Ref bp, 1697
  Maria
    King Ref bp, 1678, 1679,
      1680, 1683, 1684, 1686,
      1688, 1694
    NY Ref bp, 1692, 1694,
      1696
  Sarah
    Bkln Ref bp, 1661
    King Ref bp, 1696, 1698,
      1699
    NY Ref bp, 1655, 1657,
      1660, 1665, 1668, 1699
  Sophia
    NY Ref bp, 1680, 1682,
      1684, 1685, 1687, 1689,
      1691, 1692, 1693, 1695,
      1697, 1699
  Wilhelmina
    King Ref bp, 1697, 1699

U

Ulrich
  Sarah
    NY Ref bp, 1656
Urban
  Maria
    NY Ref bp, 1690, 1691

V

Valentine
  Maria
    NY Ref bp, 1665, 1671,
      1674
Victor
  Nicole
    NY Ref bp, 1681, 1683,
      1688, 1690, 1692, 1695,
      1697

Father/Mother Pairs Directory

Vincent
Adriana
NY Ref bp, 1687, 1689,
1691, 1694, 1695, 1696
Volkert
Anna
Bkln Ref bp, 1680, 1682
Fltb Ref bp, 1682, 1683
NY Ref bp, 1686
Elizabeth
Bkln Ref bp, 1698, 16968
Janet
Schn Ref bp, 1698
Maria
Alb Ref bp, 1692
Sarah
Fltb Ref bp, 1681, 1685
Hack Ref bp, 1686

W

Waling
Catherine
Berg Ref bp, 1677, 1680,
1682, 1687, 1690
Wallace
Catherine
NY Ref bp, 1672, 1674,
1685
Charity
NY Ref bp, 1677
Walran
Catherine
King Ref bp, 1691, 1693,
1698, 1699
Margaret
King Ref bp, 1667, 1674,
1679
Walraven
Hester
NY Ref bp, 1668
Kunigunda
NY Ref bp, 1669
Walter
Anna
NY Ref bp, 1673, 1674,
1682, 1697, 1699

Catherine
Bkln Ref bp, 1692, 1695
NY Ref bp, 1671, 1673,
1675, 1678, 1685, 1687
Cornelia
Alb Ref bp, 1697, 1699
Dorothy
Fltb Ref bp, 1682
NY Ref bp, 1667, 1668,
1671, 1676, 1688
Janet
Alb Ref bp, 1696, 1698
Maria
Bkln Ref bp, 1687
Fltb Ref bp, 1690
NY Ref bp, 1671, 1673,
1675, 1678
Nelly
Alb Ref bp, 1691
Fltb Ref bp, 1684
NY Ref bp, 1690
Wendel
Alida
Berg Ref bp, 1694, 1695,
1697
Deborah
NY Ref bp, 1672, 1676
Elizabeth
NY Ref bp, 1679, 1682,
1690
Werner
Anna
Alb Ref bp, 1697
King Ref bp, 1671, 1680,
1683, 1685, 1688
NY Ref bp, 1656, 1657,
1659, 1660, 1662
Deborah
NY Ref bp, 1668, 1670
Margaret
King Ref bp, 1693, 1695,
1698
Wessel
Alida
NY Ref bp, 1679
Catherine
Alb Ref bp, 1692, 1694,
1696, 1698

Gertrude
NY Ref bp, 1653, 1656,
1659
Jemima
King Ref bp, 1695, 1697
NY Ref bp, 1694, 1696,
1699
Maria
King Ref bp, 1678, 1679,
1682, 1683, 1685, 1686,
1688
NY Ref bp, 1672
Patience
Berg Ref bp, 1696   *
Susan
NY Ref bp, 1692, 1694,
1696, 1698
William
Adriana
Fltb Ref bp, 1690
King Ref bp, 1679, 1680,
1683, 1686
NY Ref bp, 1678, 1689
Agnes
Bkln Ref bp, 1664
Alida
Bkln Ref bp, 1662, 1689
NY Ref bp, 1659, 1680,
1683, 1695, 1698
Anna
Alb Ref bp, 1693, 1695,
1696, 1698
Berg Ref bp, 1691, 1695,
1697, 1699
Bkln Ref bp, 1683, 1686,
1688
Fltb Ref bp, 1685
Hack Ref bp, 1699
King Ref bp, 1678, 1680,
1683
NY Ref bp, 1661, 1666,
1671, 1672, 1673, 1675,
1677, 1678, 1679, 1681,
1682, 1685, 1688, 1689,
1691, 1692, 1694, 1695,
1696, 1697, 1699

Father/Mother Pairs Directory

Apollonia
King Ref bp, 1682, 1684, 1687
NY Ref bp, 1665, 1667, 1669, 1671, 1673, 1675, 1677, 1682

Bathilda
Bkln Ref bp, 1679

Beatrice
NY Ref bp, 1696

Catherine
Alb Ref bp, 1692, 1694, 1696, 1698
Berg Ref bp, 1696
King Ref bp, 1664, 1665, 1668, 1680, 1683, 1688, 1689, 1693
NY Ref bp, 1656, 1661, 1671, 1672, 1674, 1677, 1678, 1679, 1681, 1682, 1683, 1685, 1687, 1689, 1691, 1694, 1696, 1697, 1699
Schn Ref bp, 1696, 1698

Catlintje
NY Ref bp, 1696

Christina
Bkln Ref bp, 1694
NY Ref bp, 1664, 1665, 1678, 1680, 1682, 1688, 1692

Cornelia
King Ref bp, 1694, 1696, 1698
NY Ref bp, 1659

Deborah
Bkln Ref bp, 1682, 1683
Fltb Ref bp, 1682, 1683

Eleanor
King Ref bp, 1678, 1682, 1688

Elizabeth
Alb Ref bp, 1691, 1692, 1693, 1695, 1697
Berg Ref bp, 1695
Bkln Ref bp, 1684, 1687
Fltb Ref bp, 1678, 1684
King Ref bp, 1685, 1686, 1688
NY Ref bp, 1662, 1670, 1676, 1678, 1681, 1683, 1684, 1688, 1690, 1691, 1694, 1695, 1696, 1697, 1698
Tary Ref bp, 1698

Elsie
Fltb Ref bp, 1682
NY Ref bp, 1668

Engel
NY Ref bp, 1672, 1675, 1677, 1680, 1682, 1694

Gertrude
Alb Ref bp, 1692, 1698, 1699
Bkln Ref bp, 1663
NY Ref bp, 1661

Goodeth
King Ref bp, 1694, 1696, 1699

Harmina
NY Ref bp, 1654

Helena
Fltb Ref bp, 1678, 1682
NY Ref bp, 1690, 1691, 1694, 1696, 1698

Henrietta
Bkln Ref bp, 1677, 1688, 1694
Fltb Ref bp, 1677, 1683

Hilda
King Ref bp, 1699
NY Ref bp, 1693, 1696, 1699

Isabel
Berg Ref bp, 1677
Fltb Ref bp, 1680

Janet
Berg Ref bp, 1677, 1680, 1682, 1685, 1687, 1693, 1696, 1699
Bkln Ref bp, 1695
Fltb Ref bp, 1679, 1681, 1687, 1688
King Ref bp, 1679, 1683, 1687, 1692
NY Ref bp, 1660, 1663, 1665, 1667, 1671, 1672, 1678, 1680, 1681, 1682, 1685, 1687, 1688, 1689, 1691, 1693, 1695, 1696, 1699

Josephine
Bkln Ref bp, 1662

Judith
King Ref bp, 1698
NY Ref bp, 1688

Lavinia
NY Ref bp, 1659, 1661, 1663

Leonora
King Ref bp, 1674, 1683, 1684, 1686

Magdalena
NY Ref bp, 1693, 1694, 1695, 1696, 1697, 1699
Tary Ref bp, 1698

Margaret
King Ref bp, 1671, 1682, 1683, 1686, 1688, 1692
NY Ref bp, 1664, 1666, 1667, 1669, 1673, 1674, 1680, 1681, 1683, 1685, 1686, 1688, 1690, 1692, 1694, 1696

Maria
Alb Ref bp, 1692, 1695, 1697
Fltb Ref bp, 1678, 1680, 1682, 1685
Hack Ref bp, 1696
NY Ref bp, 1667, 1669, 1673, 1683, 1686, 1690, 1693, 1694, 1695, 1696, 1698, 1699

William (cont.)
  Martha
    King Ref bp, 1682, 1684,
    1685
  Martina
    Alb Ref bp, 1693, 1695,
    1697
    Berg Ref bp, 1686, 1692
    Hack Ref bp, 1698
    NY Ref bp, 1688
  Mattina
    NY Ref bp, 1656, 1658,
    1660
  Nelly
    King Ref bp, 1695, 1699
  Petronella
    NY Ref bp, 1695, 1697,
    1699
  Priscilla
    NY Ref bp, 1674, 1676,
    1678
  Rachel
    NY Ref bp, 1687, 1689,
    1690, 1693, 1696, 1699
  Rebecca
    NY Ref bp, 1681
  Sarah
    NY Ref bp, 1658, 1673,
    1681, 1685, 1687, 1689
  Sophia
    Alb Ref bp, 1697, 1699
  Susan
    King Ref bp, 1678, 1682,
    1684, 1686, 1688
    NY Ref bp, 1678, 1684,
    1687, 1690, 1699
  Theodora
    NY Ref bp, 1665, 1667
  Walburg
    NY Ref bp, 1669, 1675,
    1678, 1680
  Wilhelmina
    Hack Ref bp, 1686
    NY Ref bp, 1684, 1699
Wolfert
  Gertrude
    NY Ref bp, 1671, 1674,
    1677, 1680

Margaret
  NY Ref bp, 1666, 1698
Maria
  NY Ref bp, 1693, 1696
  Tary Ref bp, 1698
Wyatt
  Janet
    NY Ref bp, 1680, 1684,
    1687, 1692
Wynant
  Anna
    Bkln Ref bp, 1663
    NY Ref bp, 1680, 1683,
    1686
  Elizabeth
    NY Ref bp, 1684

Z

Zachariah
  Alida
    NY Ref bp, 1687, 1689
  Maria
    NY Ref bp, 1694, 1695,
    1698

Table 3B
Mother/Father Pairs Directory

A

Abigail
  Adrian
    Berg Ref bp, 1667
    NY Ref bp, 1669
  Arent
    King Ref bp, 1666
  Cornelius
    NY Ref bp, 1682, 1684
  Denton
    Bkln Ref bp, 1679
    Fltb Ref bp, 1679
  Garret
    NY Ref bp, 1660
  Haeck
    NY Ref bp, 1662
  Hendrick
    NY Ref bp, 1656, 1657,
    1672, 1674, 1677, 1678
  Herman
    Bkln Ref bp, 1697
  Isaac
    Alb Ref bp, 1693, 1695,
    1698
  Leffert
    Bkln Ref bp, 1684, 1692
    Fltb Ref bp, 1682, 1684
    NY Ref bp, 1686

Adriana
  Albert
    NY Ref bp, 1658
  Ambrose
    NY Ref bp, 1661, 1665,
    1671
  Andrew
    Alb Ref bp, 1697, 1699
  Arnold
    NY Ref bp, 1670, 1672,
    1674
  Charles
    Berg Ref bp, 1680, 1682
  Conrad
    King Ref bp, 1694, 1696,
    1697

  Cornelius
    NY Ref bp, 1642, 1651,
    1655
  Dirk
    NY Ref bp, 1694, 1696,
    1698
  Francis
    King Ref bp, 1693
  George
    NY Ref bp, 1695, 1697
  Godfrey
    NY Ref bp, 1641
  Hendrick
    King Ref bp, 1694, 1695,
    1698
    NY Ref bp, 1686
  Jacob
    King Ref bp, 1663
  Jacques
    Fltb Ref bp, 1679
  Joris
    NY Ref bp, 1683, 1686,
    1692, 1695, 1698
  Peter
    Alb Ref bp, 1693, 1695,
    1696, 1697
  Reyer
    Alb Ref bp, 1693
  Samuel
    NY Ref bp, 1692, 1694,
    1696, 1698
  Tunis
    King Ref bp, 1694, 1696,
    1698, 1699
  Vincent
    NY Ref bp, 1687, 1689,
    1691, 1694, 1695, 1696
  William
    Fltb Ref bp, 1690
    King Ref bp, 1679, 1680,
    1683, 1686
    NY Ref bp, 1678, 1689

Agatha
  Abraham
    King Ref bp, 1697
    NPal Ref bp, 1696, 1698
    NY Ref bp, 1650
  Adolf
    NY Ref bp, 1666
  Barent
    NY Ref bp, 1658
  Cornelius
    Bkln Ref bp, 1684
  Dirk
    Bkln Ref bp, 1680
    Fltb Ref bp, 1680
    NY Ref bp, 1657, 1659
  Garret
    Berg Ref bp, 1678, 1683
  Lucas
    NY Ref bp, 1669
  Peter
    NPal Ref bp, 1683, 1687
    NY Ref bp, 1656, 1658,
    1660, 1668
  Philip
    NY Ref bp, 1668

Agnes
  Adrian
    Bkln Ref bp, 1682
    Fltb Ref bp, 1680, 1682
    NY Ref bp, 1685
  Andrew
    NY Ref bp, 1651, 1656,
    1659, 1662, 1667, 1669
  Caspar
    NY Ref bp, 1699
  Cornelius
    NY Ref bp, 1685, 1687,
    1688, 1690
  Dirk
    King Ref bp, 1671, 1679,
    1680, 1684, 1689
    NY Ref bp, 1673, 1676

Agatha (cont.)

Garret
Berg Ref bp, 1682, 1684,
1695, 1697, 1699
NY Ref bp, 1693, 1695,
1697, 1699
George
Alb Ref bp, 1693, 1697
Bkln Ref bp, 1687, 1689
NY Ref bp, 1694
Hendrick
Hack Ref bp, 1696
NY Ref bp, 1691, 1692
Ludwich
NY Ref bp, 1655, 1657
Nicholas
NY Ref bp, 1657
Peter
Bkln Ref bp, 1681
Fltb Ref bp, 1681
NY Ref bp, 1664, 1666,
1668, 1677
Roelof
King Ref bp, 1679, 1682,
1684, 1685
Samuel
NY Ref bp, 1683, 1684,
1685, 1694, 1695, 1697,
1699
Simon
King Ref bp, 1697
Thomas
Alb Ref bp, 1692, 1694,
1697, 1699
NY Ref bp, 1695
William
Bkln Ref bp, 1664

Alberta

Lawrence
Alb Ref bp, 1691
Peter
NY Ref bp, 1658

Alet

Peter
King Ref bp, 1679

Alida

Abraham
Berg Ref bp, 1695
Fltb Ref bp, 1681
Hack Ref bp, 1696, 1697
NY Ref bp, 1684, 1685,
1689, 1690, 1691, 1693
Adam
NY Ref bp, 1678
Aert
King Ref bp, 1697
Arent
King Ref bp, 1689
NY Ref bp, 1692, 1696
Barent
Fltb Ref bp, 1680
Bastian
Berg Ref bp, 1690, 1693
Benjamin
King Ref bp, 1687, 1689
Bernard
Fltb Ref bp, 1682
NY Ref bp, 1670, 1672,
1674, 1677, 1678, 1679,
1685
Caspar
Alb Ref bp, 1691, 1693,
1696, 1697
Cornelius
Berg Ref bp, 1689
Bkln Ref bp, 1693, 1695,
1697, 1699
Fltb Ref bp, 1683
NY Ref bp, 1682, 1684,
1685, 1691
Tap Ref bp, 1695, 1696
Daniel
Fltb Ref bp, 1680
NY Ref bp, 1663, 1666
David
NY Ref bp, 1687
Dirk
Fltb Ref bp, 1681, 1683,
1685
Ellebrandt
King Ref bp, 1689
Evert
NY Ref bp, 1682

Francis

NY Ref bp, 1666
Garret
NY Ref bp, 1653, 1656
George
King Ref bp, 1688
Hendrick
King Ref bp, 1664, 1666,
1699
NY Ref bp, 1657, 1658,
1659, 1661, 1669
Isaac
NY Ref bp, 1690, 1691,
1693, 1695, 1698
Jacob
Berg Ref bp, 1676, 1678,
1681, 1686, 1689, 1692
NY Ref bp, 1672, 1674,
1676, 1677, 1678, 1680,
1682, 1686, 1687, 1689,
1690, 1692, 1695, 1696,
1697, 1698, 1699
Tary Ref bp, 1699
Josiah
Bkln Ref bp, 1684, 1687,
1699
Fltb Ref bp, 1682, 1684
NY Ref bp, 1691, 1696
Lawrence
Fltb Ref bp, 1679, 1681,
1683, 1687
NY Ref bp, 1681, 1685,
1688, 1690, 1693, 1695,
1699
Lucas
NY Ref bp, 1656
Matthew
King Ref bp, 1661, 1699
Michael
King Ref bp, 1662
Nanning
Alb Ref bp, 1692, 1694,
1696, 1698
Nicholas
NY Ref bp, 1662, 1664,
1667, 1675, 1677, 1680
Paul
NY Ref bp, 1664, 1666,

1669, 1671, 1673, 1677,
1678, 1679, 1682
Peter
Alb Ref bp, 1693, 1694,
1696
NY Ref bp, 1656, 1660,
1669
Robert
Alb Ref bp, 1692, 1694,
1698
Roelof
Fltb Ref bp, 1685
King Ref bp, 1665, 1667,
1679, 1683, 1686
Thaddius
NY Ref bp, 1686
Thomas
NY Ref bp, 1696, 1697,
1699
Tobias
NY Ref bp, 1678, 1680,
1682
Wendel
Berg Ref bp, 1694, 1695,
1697
Wessel
NY Ref bp, 1679
William
Bkln Ref bp, 1662, 1689
NY Ref bp, 1659, 1680,
1683, 1695, 1698
Zachariah
NY Ref bp, 1687, 1689
Anna
Abel
NY Ref bp, 1662, 1664,
1667, 1669, 1671
Abraham
Alb Ref bp, 1692, 1694,
1695
Berg Ref bp, 1688, 1690
Hack Ref bp, 1699
King Ref bp, 1695, 1697
NY Ref bp, 1665, 1683,
1685, 1693, 1694, 1696,
1697
Tary Ref bp, 1698

Adam
NY Ref bp, 1690
Adrian
Bkln Ref bp, 1686
Fltb Ref bp, 1678, 1683
NY Ref bp, 1691, 1693,
1695, 1697, 1698, 1699
Aert
King Ref bp, 1661
Andrew
Fltb Ref bp, 1679, 1680
Hack Ref bp, 1699
NY Ref bp, 1675, 1677,
1679, 1681, 1683, 1684,
1685, 1687, 1689, 1691,
1692, 1694, 1695, 1696,
1697, 1698, 1699
Anthony
Bkln Ref bp, 1683, 1686
Fltb Ref bp, 1679, 1681,
1684
Arent
Fltb Ref bp, 1680
NY Ref bp, 1657
August
NY Ref bp, 1668, 1669,
1670, 1681, 1683, 1698
Barent
NY Ref bp, 1666, 1670
Bastian
NY Ref bp, 1697
Bay
NY Ref bp, 1667
Carl
NY Ref bp, 1695, 1697
Christian
NY Ref bp, 1663, 1665,
1666, 1668
Christopher
Bkln Ref bp, 1693, 1695
NY Ref bp, 1657, 1659,
1662, 1664, 1670
Clement
NY Ref bp, 1681, 1683,
1685, 1686, 1689, 1694,
1696

Cornelius
Bkln Ref bp, 1682, 1696,
1698
Fltb Ref bp, 1679, 1682,
1685, 1688
King Ref bp, 1665, 1667,
1679, 1680, 1684, 1687,
1698
NY Ref bp, 1660, 1663,
1664, 1666, 1669, 1671,
1672, 1673, 1674, 1676,
1677, 1678, 1681, 1689,
1691, 1695, 1696, 1697
Tary Ref bp, 1698, 1699
Daniel
King Ref bp, 1666
NY Ref bp, 1668, 1673,
1675, 1681, 1684, 1685,
1687, 1688
David
Berg Ref bp, 1696
Hack Ref bp, 1697, 1699
NY Ref bp, 1671, 1673,
1675, 1678, 1680, 1683,
1686, 1690, 1693, 1694,
1698
Dirk
Alb Ref bp, 1692, 1696
Bkln Ref bp, 1699
Fltb Ref bp, 1681, 1684,
1686
King Ref bp, 1686, 1688,
1695, 1697, 1699
NY Ref bp, 1656, 1661,
1666, 1673, 1695
Edward
King Ref bp, 1675
Egbert
Hack Ref bp, 1695
King Ref bp, 1684, 1686,
1688, 1692, 1694, 1696,
1698
NY Ref bp, 1656, 1692,
1693
Elias
King Ref bp, 1694, 1698
NY Ref bp, 1681, 1682,
1684

Anna (cont.)

Evert
Alb Ref bp, 1691, 1692, 1695, 1697, 1699

Francis
NY Ref bp, 1673, 1675, 1677, 1689

Garret
Berg Ref bp, 1667, 1675, 1678
Bkln Ref bp, 1662, 1689, 1692, 1694, 1698
Fltb Ref bp, 1686
King Ref bp, 1694, 1697
NY Ref bp, 1662, 1663, 1665, 1672, 1678

George
King Ref bp, 1686, 1689, 1691, 1695, 1697, 1699

Gustave
NY Ref bp, 1658

Hendrick
Alb Ref bp, 1692, 1695, 1696, 1697
Bkln Ref bp, 1683
Fltb Ref bp, 1681, 1683, 1684, 1685, 1687, 1688
King Ref bp, 1678, 1684, 1686, 1688, 1689, 1697, 1699, 16979
NY Ref bp, 1661, 1662, 1664, 1678, 1680, 1681, 1682, 1685, 1686, 1688, 1689, 1690, 1691, 1692, 1694

Herman
NY Ref bp, 1682

Heyman
King Ref bp, 1689, 1696, 1698

Hieronymus
Bkln Ref bp, 1685, 1687
Fltb Ref bp, 1682, 1685
NY Ref bp, 1671, 1673, 1676, 1690

Humphrey
King Ref bp, 1684, 1686, 1689, 1694, 1697

Isaac
Alb Ref bp, 1692, 1694, 1696, 1697, 1699
NY Ref bp, 1687, 1690

Jacob
Alb Ref bp, 1692, 1693, 1695, 1696, 1697, 1698
Bkln Ref bp, 1684, 1686, 1687, 1689, 1696, 1699
Fltb Ref bp, 1684, 1685
King Ref bp, 1666, 1668, 1670, 1679, 1680, 1684, 1686, 1688, 1696, 1698
NY Ref bp, 1664, 1674, 1675, 1677, 1680, 1682, 1685, 1687, 1690, 1691, 1693, 1694, 1695, 1696, 1697, 1698, 1699

Jacques
NY Ref bp, 1691, 1692, 1694, 1696, 1699

Jeremiah
NY Ref bp, 1689, 1692, 1695

Jochem
Alb Ref bp, 1691
King Ref bp, 1692, 1694, 1695, 1698
NY Ref bp, 1696, 1698

Joris
Bkln Ref bp, 1693, 1695, 1697, 1699
NY Ref bp, 1691, 1692, 1694, 1696, 1698

Joseph
NY Ref bp, 1657, 1659, 1661, 1689, 1696, 1698

Justus
NY Ref bp, 1698, 1699

Lawrence
NY Ref bp, 1663, 1667, 1698

Louis
Bkln Ref bp, 1661, 1664
Hack Ref bp, 1698, 1699
NY Ref bp, 1658

Lucas
King Ref bp, 1697, 1699
NY Ref bp, 1655, 1656, 1657, 1658, 1661, 1662, 1663

Mangold
NY Ref bp, 1694, 1697, 1699

Martin
Bkln Ref bp, 1677, 1682
Fltb Ref bp, 1677, 1682, 1684, 1685, 1688, 1689
NY Ref bp, 1664, 1666, 1669, 1671, 1673, 1685

Matthew
Berg Ref bp, 1673, 1678, 1680, 1682, 1684
Hack Ref bp, 1686, 1695
King Ref bp, 1696
NY Ref bp, 1660, 1671

Maurice
Bkln Ref bp, 1697
NY Ref bp, 1691, 1693, 1696

Michael
King Ref bp, 1678, 1682, 1684, 1687
NY Ref bp, 1659, 1660, 1661

Nathan
NY Ref bp, 1665, 1667, 1670, 1679, 1683

Nicasius
Hack Ref bp, 1697

Nicholas
Berg Ref bp, 1667, 1676, 1678, 1680, 1682, 1698
NY Ref bp, 1651, 1657, 1659, 1663, 1664, 1669, 1671, 1673, 1676, 1678, 1682

Oliver
NY Ref bp, 1655, 1658

Omie
Alb Ref bp, 1692

Paul
NY Ref bp, 1694, 1695

Peter
 Bkln Ref bp, 1661, 1663,
 1684, 1688, 1694, 1695,
 1696, 1697
 Fltb Ref bp, 1680, 1682,
 1684, 1685
 NY Ref bp, 1659, 1667,
 1673, 1676, 1677, 1678,
 1680, 1696, 1698, 1699
Philip
 NY Ref bp, 1695, 1697
Resolved
 NY Ref bp, 1657
Richard
 NY Ref bp, 1660, 1661,
 1664, 1667, 1672
Robert
 NY Ref bp, 1697
Roelof
 Fltb Ref bp, 1678, 1682,
 1684
Samuel
 King Ref bp, 1689
 NY Ref bp, 1656, 1692
Simon
 Alb Ref bp, 1696
 Berg Ref bp, 1676, 1678,
 1682, 1686, 1688, 1690
 Bkln Ref bp, 1660, 1661,
 1664, 1671, 1674
 King Ref bp, 1682, 1684,
 1686, 1688
 NY Ref bp, 1656, 1657,
 1658, 1660, 1662, 1666,
 1667, 1668, 1676, 1678,
 1680, 1684
Solomon
 Fltb Ref bp, 1689
 NY Ref bp, 1656, 1691,
 1694, 1695
Stephen
 NY Ref bp, 1697, 1799
Swan
 NY Ref bp, 1669, 1672
Tades
 NY Ref bp, 1684

Thaddius
 Berg Ref bp, 1680, 1682,
 1684, 1689
Thomas
 Alb Ref bp, 1696
 Bkln Ref bp, 1694
 King Ref bp, 1682, 1684
 NY Ref bp, 1681, 1686, 1696
Tobias
 NY Ref bp, 1685, 1686,
 1688, 1689, 1691, 1693,
 1695, 1696, 1698
Tunis
 NY Ref bp, 1675, 1682,
 1683, 1685, 1687, 1688,
 1690, 1692, 1694, 1697
Volkert
 Bkln Ref bp, 1680, 1682
 Fltb Ref bp, 1682, 1683
 NY Ref bp, 1686
Walter
 NY Ref bp, 1673, 1674,
 1682, 1697, 1699
Werner
 Alb Ref bp, 1697
 King Ref bp, 1671, 1680,
 1683, 1685, 1688
 NY Ref bp, 1656, 1657,
 1659, 1660, 1662
William
 Alb Ref bp, 1693, 1695,
 1696, 1698
 Berg Ref bp, 1691, 1695,
 1697, 1699
 Bkln Ref bp, 1683, 1686,
 1688
 Fltb Ref bp, 1685
 Hack Ref bp, 1699
 King Ref bp, 1678, 1680,
 1683
 NY Ref bp, 1661, 1666,
 1671, 1672, 1673, 1675,
 1677, 1678, 1679, 1681,
 1682, 1685, 1688, 1689,
 1691, 1692, 1694, 1695,
 1696, 1697, 1699

Wynant
 Bkln Ref bp, 1663
 NY Ref bp, 1680, 1683,
 1686
Apollonia
 Paul
 NY Ref bp, 1675
 William
 King Ref bp, 1682, 1684,
 1687
 NY Ref bp, 1665, 1667,
 1669, 1671, 1673, 1675,
 1677, 1682
Artelia
 Cornelius
 Bkln Ref bp, 1687
 Theodore
 Bkln Ref bp, 1685, 1693,
 1697
 Fltb Ref bp, 1680, 1681

B

Barbara
 Cornelius
 King Ref bp, 1692, 1693,
 1696, 1699
 NY Ref bp, 1691
 Eustace
 Berg Ref bp, 1678
 NY Ref bp, 1680, 1688
 Francis
 NY Ref bp, 1667, 1669,
 1671, 1673, 1675, 1676,
 1677, 1680, 1682, 1684
 Garret
 Alb Ref bp, 1697, 1699
 George
 King Ref bp, 1662, 1664,
 1666, 1668, 1684
 Gilbert
 Alb Ref bp, 1692, 1695,
 1698
 Jacob
 King Ref bp, 1680
 NY Ref bp, 1695
 Tap Ref bp, 1697

Mother/Father Pairs Directory

Barbara (cont.)
Lambert
NY Ref bp, 1661
Lucas
Bkln Ref bp, 1699
Fltb Ref bp, 1683
Nicholas
NY Ref bp, 1663, 1685
Peter
Bkln Ref bp, 1695
Solomon
NY Ref bp, 1653
Thomas
NY Ref bp, 1656
Tunis
Bkln Ref bp, 1661, 1663

Bathilda
Peter
NY Ref bp, 1678, 1680,
1681, 1682, 1687, 1690,
1692, 1694
William
Bkln Ref bp, 1679

Bayken
Boele
NY Ref bp, 1661, 1662

Beatrice
William
NY Ref bp, 1696

Bernadine
Benjamin
NY Ref bp, 1696
Cornelius
NY Ref bp, 1665, 1669,
1676
Elias
Fltb Ref bp, 1685
Jacob
King Ref bp, 1687
Nicholas
NY Ref bp, 1662, 1691,
1695

Blandina
Peter
NY Ref bp, 1675, 1679,
1681, 1683

Bridget
Aert
Bkln Ref bp, 1662
NY Ref bp, 1661
Evert
NY Ref bp, 1673, 1676
Herman
NY Ref bp, 1683, 1685,
1687
Melchior
NY Ref bp, 1679
Peter
NY Ref bp, 1657
Tunis
Tap Ref bp, 1695, 1697

C

Catherine
Abel
Berg Ref bp, 1698, 1699
Hack Ref bp, 1699
Abraham
Alb Ref bp, 1692, 1695,
1698
NY Ref bp, 1656, 1660,
1662, 1664, 1668, 1671,
1673, 1676, 1685, 1686,
1688, 1690, 1692, 1694,
1695, 1696, 1698
Adrian
Berg Ref bp, 1678, 1679,
1680, 1681, 1682, 1684,
1686, 1688, 1689, 1690,
1691
NY Ref bp, 1673, 1675,
1678, 1679, 1680, 1681,
1682, 1685
Aert
NY Ref bp, 1692, 1693,
1695, 1698
Albert
NY Ref bp, 1659, 1686,
1688, 1690, 1693, 1696,
1698

Andrew
Alb Ref bp, 1693, 1696
NY Ref bp, 1655, 1657,
1660, 1669, 1671, 1673,
1687
Anthony
Alb Ref bp, 1693, 1695,
1697
Berg Ref bp, 1679, 1680,
1682, 1686, 1688, 1689,
1690
Arent
King Ref bp, 1695, 1698
Baltus
Berg Ref bp, 1688
King Ref bp, 1697
NY Ref bp, 1687, 1690
Barent
Bkln Ref bp, 1696
Fltb Ref bp, 1685
Burger
Fltb Ref bp, 1680
NY Ref bp, 1686
Carl
Berg Ref bp, 1696
Bkln Ref bp, 1662, 1664
NY Ref bp, 1659, 1679,
1684
Caspar
NY Ref bp, 1697, 1699
Charles
Berg Ref bp, 1682, 1692,
1694
Christian
Berg Ref bp, 1666
NY Ref bp, 1658, 1660,
1662, 1664, 1668
Christopher
NY Ref bp, 1662, 1664,
1666, 1667, 1669, 1672,
1675, 1676, 1678, 1680,
1681, 1682
Conrad
Alb Ref bp, 1692, 1694,
1696, 1698

Mother/Father Pairs Directory

Cornelius
- Bkln Ref bp, 1686
- Fltb Ref bp, 1679, 1682, 1684, 1689
- Hack Ref bp, 1694
- NY Ref bp, 1653, 1661, 1694, 1696, 1697, 1698, 1699

Cosine
- NY Ref bp, 1699

Daniel
- Bkln Ref bp, 1699

David
- NY Ref bp, 1670, 1671, 1672, 1673, 1676, 1677, 1679, 1682, 1685, 1687, 1688

Dirk
- Fltb Ref bp, 1677
- King Ref bp, 1697, 1698, 1699
- NY Ref bp, 1694
- Tap Ref bp, 1698

Elias
- Alb Ref bp, 1691

Enoch
- NY Ref bp, 1693, 1696, 1698

Evert
- NY Ref bp, 1691

Francis
- Alb Ref bp, 1692
- King Ref bp, 1694
- NY Ref bp, 1661, 1680, 1681, 1683, 1684, 1686, 1689, 1690, 1693, 1695, 1697, 1699

Fred
- Berg Ref bp, 1679, 1681, 1684, 1692, 1693
- NY Ref bp, 1658, 1660, 1673, 1675, 1679, 1684, 1687, 1694

Gabriel
- NY Ref bp, 1659

Garret
- Alb Ref bp, 1691, 1693, 1695
- Berg Ref bp, 1695, 1696, 1698
- NY Ref bp, 1660, 1663, 1665, 1667, 1686, 1687, 1689, 1690, 1691, 1692, 1694, 1695, 1697, 1698, 1699
- Schn Ref bp, 1696, 1698

George
- NY Ref bp, 1658, 1662

Gideon
- Alb Ref bp, 1696

Gilbert
- NY Ref bp, 1658, 1672

Hendrick
- Alb Ref bp, 1692, 1693, 1694, 1695, 1696, 1697, 1698, 1699
- King Ref bp, 1675, 1679, 1680, 1682, 1684, 1686, 1688, 1689, 1692, 1694, 1696, 1697, 1699
- NY Ref bp, 1656, 1657, 1658, 1662, 1666, 1674, 1680, 1681, 1684, 1685, 1686, 1687, 1689, 1692, 1694
- Tary Ref bp, 1697, 1699

Herman
- Fltb Ref bp, 1679
- NY Ref bp, 1659, 1660, 1691

Isaac
- NY Ref bp, 1656

Jacob
- Alb Ref bp, 1692, 1695, 1697
- Fltb Ref bp, 1685
- Hack Ref bp, 1686
- NY Ref bp, 1655, 1656, 1657, 1660, 1663, 1664, 1665, 1680, 1682, 1684, 1685, 1688, 1690, 1691, 1692, 1694, 1697, 1698

Jacques
- NY Ref bp, 1674

Jafort
- NY Ref bp, 1677, 1683

Jeremiah
- King Ref bp, 1675

Jonas
- NY Ref bp, 1661

Jonathan
- Alb Ref bp, 1697
- NY Ref bp, 1680, 1682, 1683, 1687, 1689, 1692, 1694, 1697

Joris
- Bkln Ref bp, 1661, 1664
- NY Ref bp, 1666, 1678, 1692

Joseph
- NY Ref bp, 1689, 1692, 1695, 1697, 1699

Jurian
- NY Ref bp, 1655

Justus
- NY Ref bp, 1676, 1679, 1682, 1687, 1690

Lawrence
- NY Ref bp, 1689, 1691, 1692, 1694, 1696, 1698, 1699

Louis
- King Ref bp, 1661, 1664, 1667, 1671, 1675
- NY Ref bp, 1669

Lucas
- Alb Ref bp, 1692, 1693
- Fltb Ref bp, 1677
- NY Ref bp, 1671, 1678, 1681, 1683, 1685, 1688, 1690, 1693

Martin
- NY Ref bp, 1696

Matthew
- Alb Ref bp, 1699
- Berg Ref bp, 1668, 1687, 1688, 1690, 1692, 1693, 1694, 1696, 1699
- Hack Ref bp, 1696, 1699
- King Ref bp, 1693

Mother/Father Pairs Directory

Catherine (cont.)

Matthew (cont.)
NY Ref bp, 1656, 1657,
1669, 1680, 1687, 1688,
1693, 1694, 1696, 1698,
1699

Maynard
NY Ref bp, 1667

Melchior
Alb Ref bp, 1697, 1699

Nicholas
Bkln Ref bp, 1690
Fltb Ref bp, 1678
Hack Ref bp, 1697, 1699
NY Ref bp, 1663, 1664,
1667, 1670, 1675, 1695,
1697

Paul
Berg Ref bp, 1667, 1679
NY Ref bp, 1661, 1663,
1670, 1675

Peter
Alb Ref bp, 1692, 1694,
1696, 1698
Berg Ref bp, 1688, 1691
Bkln Ref bp, 1661, 1662,
1697
Fltb Ref bp, 1680, 1682,
1684
Hack Ref bp, 1696
King Ref bp, 1684, 1687
NY Ref bp, 1666, 1697,
1699, 16989

Philip
Alb Ref bp, 1692, 1694,
1697
NY Ref bp, 1678

Richard
NY Ref bp, 1673, 1675,
1678, 1681, 1684, 1687

Robert
NY Ref bp, 1685, 1687,
1689

Roelof
Bkln Ref bp, 1682, 1684,
1695
Fltb Ref bp, 1682, 1684

Sampson
Alb Ref bp, 1692, 1694,
1696
NY Ref bp, 1698

Samuel
NY Ref bp, 1699

Simon
NY Ref bp, 1689, 1692,
1695, 1698

Solomon
King Ref bp, 1691, 1693,
1697

Thomas
Berg Ref bp, 1691, 1694,
1696
NY Ref bp, 1686, 1688,
1689, 1691, 1693, 1694,
1696, 1697

Tunis
Alb Ref bp, 1695
Berg Ref bp, 1687
Bkln Ref bp, 1696
NY Ref bp, 1679, 1680,
1685, 1688, 1691, 1692,
1698
Tap Ref bp, 1696, 1698

Waling
Berg Ref bp, 1677, 1680,
1682, 1687, 1690

Wallace
NY Ref bp, 1672, 1674,
1685

Walran
King Ref bp, 1691, 1693,
1698, 1699

Walter
Bkln Ref bp, 1692, 1695
NY Ref bp, 1671, 1673,
1675, 1678, 1685, 1687

Wessel
Alb Ref bp, 1692, 1694,
1696, 1698

William
Alb Ref bp, 1692, 1694,
1696, 1698
Berg Ref bp, 1696
King Ref bp, 1664, 1665,
1668, 1680, 1683, 1688,

1689, 1693
NY Ref bp, 1656, 1661,
1671, 1672, 1674, 1677,
1678, 1679, 1681, 1682,
1683, 1685, 1687, 1689,
1691, 1694, 1696, 1697,
1699
Schn Ref bp, 1696, 1698

Catlintje

Abraham
NY Ref bp, 1697, 1699

Albert
Bkln Ref bp, 1695

Barent
NY Ref bp, 1663

Borgenson
Bkln Ref bp, 1676

Carl
NY Ref bp, 1657

Christopher
NY Ref bp, 1699

Cornelius
Tap Ref bp, 1697

Dirk
Bkln Ref bp, 1698
NY Ref bp, 1696

Elias
NY Ref bp, 1672

Florian
NY Ref bp, 1685

Francis
Berg Ref bp, 1686

Garret
Tary Ref bp, 1697

Hendrick
Alb Ref bp, 1691, 1693,
1695, 1697, 1699

Isaac
NY Ref bp, 1662, 1664,
1666, 1669, 1681, 1682,
1685, 1687, 1689, 1692,
1694

Jacob
NY Ref bp, 1665

Louis
NY Ref bp, 1680

Mother/Father Pairs Directory

Lucas
  Bkln Ref bp, 1686
  Fltb Ref bp, 1679, 1681,
    1683
  Nicholas
    NY Ref bp, 1669, 1671,
    1674, 1680, 1691
  Reyner
    King Ref bp, 1670
    NY Ref bp, 1665, 1666
  Samuel
    Bkln Ref bp, 1691, 1698
    NY Ref bp, 1695
  William
    NY Ref bp, 1696

Cecilia
  Abraham
    King Ref bp, 1683, 1685,
    1688, 1689
  Andrew
    NY Ref bp, 1656
  Hendrick
    NY Ref bp, 1662
  Paul
    NY Ref bp, 1664, 1667,
    1670, 1673, 1675, 1678

Charity
  Evert
    King Ref bp, 1698, 1699
  Matthew
    King Ref bp, 1678, 1679,
    1680, 1682, 1684, 1685,
    1687, 1689, 1692, 1694,
    1696
  Wallace
    NY Ref bp, 1677

Christina
  Abraham
    Fltb Ref bp, 1680
  Aldert
    Fltb Ref bp, 1677, 1680,
    1681, 1684
    NY Ref bp, 1691
  Alexander
    King Ref bp, 1687
  Anthony
    Berg Ref bp, 1686, 1688
    NY Ref bp, 1682, 1684

Arent
  Bkln Ref bp, 1677
  Fltb Ref bp, 1677
  NY Ref bp, 1666, 1672
Barent
  NY Ref bp, 1644, 1652,
  1675
Christopher
  Alb Ref bp, 1691, 1694
  NY Ref bp, 1670
Cornelius
  NY Ref bp, 1656, 1657,
  1658, 1659, 1661, 1662,
  1666, 1668, 1680
Daniel
  NY Ref bp, 1683, 1685,
  1687, 1690, 1692, 1694
David
  NY Ref bp, 1697, 1699
Fred
  NY Ref bp, 1659, 1662,
  1665, 1674, 1675
Gabriel
  NY Ref bp, 1660
Garret
  Fltb Ref bp, 1684
Giles
  NY Ref bp, 1661, 1664
Herman
  King Ref bp, 1684
  NY Ref bp, 1686, 1688,
  1690
Isaac
  King Ref bp, 1697
  NY Ref bp, 1681
Jacob
  Fltb Ref bp, 1680
  NY Ref bp, 1678, 1689,
  1694
Jochem
  NY Ref bp, 1679, 1682,
  1686
Joseph
  NY Ref bp, 1658, 1660,
  1663, 1664, 1666, 1669
Leonard
  Bkln Ref bp, 1691
  NY Ref bp, 1679, 1681,

  1683, 1686, 1689, 1695
Michael
  Bkln Ref bp, 1699
Nicholas
  Bkln Ref bp, 1686
  Fltb Ref bp, 1681, 1683
  King Ref bp, 1682
Peter
  Bkln Ref bp, 1699
Robert
  NY Ref bp, 1677, 1678,
  1683, 1685, 1688, 1689,
  1690, 1693, 1695
Swan
  Fltb Ref bp, 1681
Thomas
  NY Ref bp, 1676
William
  Bkln Ref bp, 1694
  NY Ref bp, 1664, 1665,
  1678, 1680, 1682, 1688,
  1692

Clara
  Adrian
    NY Ref bp, 1663
  Cornelius
    Alb Ref bp, 1696, 1697
    Schn Ref bp, 1698
  Garret
    King Ref bp, 1682, 1684,
    1686, 1689, 1692, 1694
  Hendrick
    NY Ref bp, 1699
  Herman
    NY Ref bp, 1656
  Lucas
    NY Ref bp, 1665
  Reyner
    NY Ref bp, 1699
  Tunis
    King Ref bp, 1697

Constance
  Joseph
    Alb Ref bp, 1696
  Peter
    Alb Ref bp, 1697
    King Ref bp, 1689

Constance (cont.)
Reyner
Berg Ref bp, 1686
Cornelia
Abraham
Bkln Ref bp, 1697, 1699
NY Ref bp, 1682, 1684,
1686, 1689, 1691, 1694,
1695
Andrew
Alb Ref bp, 1694, 1697
NY Ref bp, 1696, 1698,
1699
Arnold
NY Ref bp, 1679, 1681
Benjamin
NY Ref bp, 1694, 1696,
1699
Broer
King Ref bp, 1688, 1693,
1696, 1698
Cornelius
Alb Ref bp, 1691, 1694
Berg Ref bp, 1677
Bkln Ref bp, 1680
Fltb Ref bp, 1680
King Ref bp, 1687, 1696,
1698
NY Ref bp, 1690, 1696
David
King Ref bp, 1692, 1696
Elias
NY Ref bp, 1673, 1675,
1676, 1679, 1681, 1683
Engelbert
Fltb Ref bp, 1684
NY Ref bp, 1682, 1696
Garret
Bkln Ref bp, 1692, 1693,
1696, 1697
Fltb Ref bp, 1685
NY Ref bp, 1666
Hendrick
Alb Ref bp, 1693, 1696,
1698
King Ref bp, 1689, 1691,
1694, 1696, 1699

Isaac
Berg Ref bp, 1692, 1694,
1696, 1699
Hack Ref bp, 1699
NY Ref bp, 1675, 1679,
1683, 1685, 1687, 1691,
1693, 1696, 1699
Isaiah
Hack Ref bp, 1699
Jacob
Hack Ref bp, 1698
NY Ref bp, 1656, 1662,
1665, 1673, 1674, 1677,
1680, 1684, 1694
Matthew
Alb Ref bp, 1692, 1695,
1697
Bkln Ref bp, 1696
Nicholas
King Ref bp, 1682, 1684,
1687, 1692, 1695, 1698
Peter
Bkln Ref bp, 1688, 1691,
1693, 1696
NY Ref bp, 1697, 1698,
1699
Rembrant
NY Ref bp, 1683, 1686,
1690
Robert
Alb Ref bp, 1691, 1694,
1696
Walter
Alb Ref bp, 1697, 1699
William
King Ref bp, 1694, 1696,
1698
NY Ref bp, 1659

D

Deborah
Barent
NY Ref bp, 1691, 1692,
1694, 1697
Daniel
Alb Ref bp, 1696, 1698

Hendrick
Alb Ref bp, 1693, 1695,
1697, 1698
King Ref bp, 1685
Matthew
Tary Ref bp, 1697
Peter
Fltb Ref bp, 1685
King Ref bp, 1693, 1698
NY Ref bp, 1664, 1666,
1670, 1673, 1675
Samuel
NY Ref bp, 1660, 1661,
1663, 1667, 1689
Thomas
NY Ref bp, 1669, 1672,
1685, 1687, 1689
Wendel
NY Ref bp, 1672, 1676
Werner
NY Ref bp, 1668, 1670
William
Bkln Ref bp, 1682, 1683
Fltb Ref bp, 1682, 1683
Delia
Francis
NY Ref bp, 1663
Dina
Fred
Bkln Ref bp, 1663, 1694
Fltb Ref bp, 1681, 1683
Dorothy
Anthony
NY Ref bp, 1657
Dominic
NY Ref bp, 1695, 1697,
1699
Francis
NY Ref bp, 1692
Garret
NY Ref bp, 1697, 1699
Isaac
Alb Ref bp, 1692, 1695,
16998
NY Ref bp, 1679
Jacob
Alb Ref bp, 1693, 1697
King Ref bp, 1699

Richard
NY Ref bp, 1689
Walter
Fltb Ref bp, 1682
NY Ref bp, 1667, 1668,
1671, 1676, 1688

E

Eleanor
Bartel
Berg Ref bp, 1695, 1697
William
King Ref bp, 1678, 1682,
1688
Elizabeth
Abraham
Berg Ref bp, 1691, 1692
NY Ref bp, 1692, 1694,
1696, 1698
Adrian
Fltb Ref bp, 1678, 1680
NY Ref bp, 1665, 1668,
1671, 1674
Aert
Bkln Ref bp, 1699
Alexander
NY Ref bp, 1689, 1691,
1694, 1696
Andrew
NY Ref bp, 1691, 1692,
1694, 1696, 1698
Anthony
Alb Ref bp, 1699
Bkln Ref bp, 1688, 1690,
. 1692
NY Ref bp, 1659, 1661,
1663, 1666, 1685, 1697
Arent
King Ref bp, 1688, 1692,
1697, 1699
Benoni
Alb Ref bp, 1693, 1696
NY Ref bp, 1690
Bernard
NY Ref bp, 1689, 1691,
1693, 1695, 1698, 1699

Bruyn
King Ref bp, 1683, 1684,
1686, 1687, 1694, 1697,
1699
Carl
Alb Ref bp, 1691, 1695,
1698
Bkln Ref bp, 1688
Fltb Ref bp, 1681, 1684
NY Ref bp, 1686
Caspar
NY Ref bp, 1689, 1695,
1699
Cornelius
Bkln Ref bp, 1698
Fltb Ref bp, 1682
King Ref bp, 1678, 1682,
1684, 1687
NY Ref bp, 1655, 1660,
1665
Daniel
Alb Ref bp, 1696, 1697,
1699
NY Ref bp, 1678
David
NY Ref bp, 1690, 1695,
1697
Dennis
NY Ref bp, 1662, 1665,
1667
Dinckrick
Fltb Ref bp, 1685
Dirk
Berg Ref bp, 1673
Bkln Ref bp, 1670, 1684,
1689, 1692
Fltb Ref bp, 1681, 1684,
1687, 1689
NY Ref bp, 1666, 1668,
1672, 1673, 1674, 1676,
1678, 1680, 1681, 1682,
1687, 1692, 1699
Elias
King Ref bp, 1697
NY Ref bp, 1679, 1682
Ephraim
NY Ref bp, 1680, 1684,
1687, 1688

Evert
Alb Ref bp, 1691, 1693,
1695, 1697
Bkln Ref bp, 1672
NY Ref bp, 1690, 1697
Francis
NY Ref bp, 1660, 1665,
1666, 1667, 1669, 1672,
1675, 1697, 1699
Fred
Alb Ref bp, 1691
King Ref bp, 1682, 1685,
1694
NY Ref bp, 1658, 1660,
1667, 1669, 1672, 1673,
1677, 1679, 1681, 1683,
1692
Garret
Alb Ref bp, 1695, 1696,
1699
Bkln Ref bp, 1699
Fltb Ref bp, 1681, 1685,
1687, 1690
NY Ref bp, 1674, 1676,
1686, 1691, 1693, 1695,
1697, 1698
George
King Ref bp, 1675
Gilbert
NY Ref bp, 1659
Schn Ref bp, 1695
Hartman
NY Ref bp, 1677
Hendrick
NY Ref bp, 1657, 1699
Herman
Alb Ref bp, 1692, 1695,
1699
NY Ref bp, 1699
Hessel
Berg Ref bp, 1691
Isaac
NY Ref bp, 1657, 1659,
1662, 1664, 1667, 1669,
1672, 1682, 1684, 1686,
1688, 1689, 1692, 1694,
1696, 1697, 1699

Mother/Father Pairs Directory

Elizabeth (cont.)

Jacob
Alb Ref bp, 1692
Bkln Ref bp, 1683
Fltb Ref bp, 1678, 1680,
1682, 1683
NY Ref bp, 1675, 1679,
1683, 1689, 1692, 1696,
1698, 1699
Schn Ref bp, 1695, 1698
James
King Ref bp, 1697, 1698
NY Ref bp, 1685, 1686,
1688, 1693, 1697
Jeremiah
King Ref bp, 1697
NY Ref bp, 1678
Jochem
King Ref bp, 1682, 1683,
1686, 1687, 1693, 1695,
1697
Joris
NY Ref bp, 1689, 1692,
1694
Joseph
Bkln Ref bp, 1695
Fltb Ref bp, 1687, 1690
King Ref bp, 1672, 1678,
1680
NY Ref bp, 1682, 1684,
1694, 1696, 1698
Leonard
NY Ref bp, 1690, 1691,
1692, 1694, 1696, 1698,
1699
Marcus
Bkln Ref bp, 1662
NY Ref bp, 1658, 1659,
1665, 1669
Martin
NY Ref bp, 1643
Matthew
NY Ref bp, 1676, 1678,
1679, 1681, 1685, 1688
Maynard
NY Ref bp, 1674
Melchior
Alb Ref bp, 1693, 1695

Nicholas
Alb Ref bp, 1691, 1693
Bkln Ref bp, 1694
NY Ref bp, 1683, 1685,
1687, 1689, 1691
Schn Ref bp, 1696
Paul
Fltb Ref bp, 1679, 1681
King Ref bp, 1665, 1667,
1673, 1678, 1682, 1684
Peter
Berg Ref bp, 1677, 1680,
1682, 1685, 1687
Fltb Ref bp, 1691
King Ref bp, 1680, 1683,
1686, 1688
NY Ref bp, 1663, 1667,
1668, 1670, 1672, 1673,
1675, 1678, 1683, 1686,
1687, 1689, 1692, 1694,
1697, 1699
Philip
Alb Ref bp, 1693
King Ref bp, 1689
NY Ref bp, 1692
Schn Ref bp, 1697
Reyner
Fltb Ref bp, 1681, 1683
Richard
Berg Ref bp, 166
Robert
King Ref bp, 1679, 1680,
1684, 1687
Simon
King Ref bp, 1679
NPal Ref bp, 1683, 1684
Sylvester
NY Ref bp, 1676
Thomas
Fltb Ref bp, 1680
King Ref bp, 1683, 1686,
1689, 1692, 1694, 1697,
1699
NPal Ref bp, 1693
NY Ref bp, 1650, 1682
Tary Ref bp, 1699
Timothy
NY Ref bp, 1682

Tobias
Bkln Ref bp, 1694, 1698
NY Ref bp, 1685, 1687,
1690, 1692, 1696
Tunis
Bkln Ref bp, 1667
Schn Ref bp, 1694, 1696
Volkert
Bkln Ref bp, 1698, 16968
Wendel
NY Ref bp, 1679, 1682,
1690
William
Alb Ref bp, 1691, 1692,
1693, 1695, 1697
Berg Ref bp, 1695
Bkln Ref bp, 1684, 1687
Fltb Ref bp, 1678, 1684
King Ref bp, 1685, 1686,
1688
NY Ref bp, 1662, 1670,
1676, 1678, 1681, 1683,
1684, 1688, 1690, 1691,
1694, 1695, 1696, 1697,
1698
Tary Ref bp, 1698
Wynant
NY Ref bp, 1684
Ellen
Benjamin
King Ref bp, 1680
Elsie
Abraham
Alb Ref bp, 1697, 1698
King Ref bp, 1694, 1697
NY Ref bp, 1661, 1668
Albert
NY Ref bp, 1653, 1656,
1658, 1669, 1670, 1672,
1674, 1677, 1679, 1681,
1683
Alexander
Berg Ref bp, 1693
Fltb Ref bp, 1683
Benjamin
King Ref bp, 1678, 1679,
1682, 1684, 1686
NY Ref bp, 1672, 1673,

1691, 1692, 1694, 1696,
1699
Bernard
NY Ref bp, 1699
Burger
King Ref bp, 1685, 1688
Conrad
NY Ref bp, 1679, 1682,
1685, 1688, 1690, 1693
Cornelius
King Ref bp, 1696, 1698
David
Alb Ref bp, 1694, 1697
Didlove
NY Ref bp, 1681, 1683,
1684, 1687
Edward
Berg Ref bp, 1690, 1693,
1695, 1696, 1698
Hack Ref bp, 1696
Egbert
NY Ref bp, 1679, 1682,
1685, 1687, 1689, 1697
Francis
Alb Ref bp, 1692, 1694,
1696
Garret
Fltb Ref bp, 1677, 1681,
1683
NY Ref bp, 1694, 1695,
1696
Hendrick
King Ref bp, 1663, 1665,
1669
NY Ref bp, 1672, 1674,
1677, 1679, 1684, 1685,
1686, 1688, 1692, 1697
Jacob
Bkln Ref bp, 1684
Fltb Ref bp, 1678, 1681,
1684, 1688
NY Ref bp, 1664, 1665,
1667, 1669, 1671, 1673,
1676
Palbel
Fltb Ref bp, 1687

Peter
NY Ref bp, 1652, 1657,
1695
Thomas
NY Ref bp, 1659, 1661,
1664, 1674, 1678, 1681,
1683, 1695
Tunis
NY Ref bp, 1691, 1692,
1693
William
Fltb Ref bp, 1682
NY Ref bp, 1668
Emma
Alexander
NY Ref bp, 1673
Francis
NY Ref bp, 1657
George
Alb Ref bp, 1695
Jochem
NY Ref bp, 1665, 1672,
1674
Martin
NY Ref bp, 1665, 1666
Peter
Alb Ref bp, 1691
Thomas
Berg Ref bp, 1692
Engel
Andrew
Alb Ref bp, 1692, 1694,
1698
Baltus
NY Ref bp, 1662, 1663
Burger
NY Ref bp, 1640, 1642,
1647, 1650, 1652, 1653,
1657, 1659, 1661, 1664
Christian
NY Ref bp, 1659, 1662
Daniel
NY Ref bp, 1696, 1698
Deliverance
NY Ref bp, 1696
Fred
King Ref bp, 1667, 1671,
1675, 1679, 1684, 1686

Gregory
Bkln Ref bp, 1695
Jacob
Bkln Ref bp, 1684, 1687
Fltb Ref bp, 1684
NY Ref bp, 1667, 1669,
1673, 1676, 1678
Jochem
Hack Ref bp, 1686
Joshua
NY Ref bp, 1696
Melchior
Alb Ref bp, 1691
Nicholas
King Ref bp, 1683, 1684,
1687, 1692, 1693
NY Ref bp, 1681
Otto
NY Ref bp, 1668, 1669,
1672, 1674, 1676, 1678,
1680, 1681, 1684, 1686
Peter
NY Ref bp, 1678, 1679,
1681, 1684
Thomas
NY Ref bp, 1674, 1676,
1678, 1698
Tunis
NY Ref bp, 1655
William
NY Ref bp, 1672, 1675,
1677, 1680, 1682, 1694
Esther
David
Tary Ref bp, 1698
Dirk
Hack Ref bp, 1695
Peter
King Ref bp, 1697
Eunice
Cornelius
NY Ref bp, 1660, 1672
Herman
NY Ref bp, 1689, 1693,
1696, 1698
Isaac
Alb Ref bp, 1693

Mother/Father Pairs Directory

Eunice (cont.)
Thomas
Alb Ref bp, 1692
NY Ref bp, 1694, 1696
Eva
Adolf
NY Ref bp, 1657, 1669
Arent
NY Ref bp, 1680, 1681,
1684, 1686, 1692, 1694
Cornelius
King Ref bp, 1697
NY Ref bp, 1662, 1697
Dirk
NY Ref bp, 1676, 1681,
1684, 1686, 1687, 1689,
1691, 1694
Egbert
NY Ref bp, 1694
Ferdinand
Fltb Ref bp, 1681
Garret
NY Ref bp, 1675, 1681,
1685
George
NY Ref bp, 1699
Isaiah
Alb Ref bp, 1691
Schn Ref bp, 1694, 1696
Jacob
NY Ref bp, 1694, 1697,
1698, 1699
Jacques
NY Ref bp, 1686, 1691,
1695, 1698
Jochem
Alb Ref bp, 1692, 1695
Lucas
NY Ref bp, 1657, 1660,
1662, 1663, 1665, 1667,
1670, 1671, 1673, 1675,
1676, 1679, 1682
Nicholas
Alb Ref bp, 1692
NY Ref bp, 1659

Peter
King Ref bp, 1698
NY Ref bp, 1658, 1660,
1662, 1666
Philip
NY Ref bp, 1666
Roelof
King Ref bp, 1662, 1664,
1667, 1673
Simon
King Ref bp, 1694

F

Frances
Abraham
NY Ref bp, 1659, 1661,
1663, 1667, 1669, 1671
Andrew
NY Ref bp, 1673
Baltus
Berg Ref bp, 1685
Fred
King Ref bp, 1693, 1695,
1697, 1698
Hendrick
NY Ref bp, 1686
Jonathan
NY Ref bp, 1682, 1685
Joseph
NY Ref bp, 1693
Lawrence
NY Ref bp, 1673, 1675,
1677, 1679, 1681, 1683,
1691
Lourus
Berg Ref bp, 1685, 1687,
1689, 1694, 1696
Michael
Hack Ref bp, 1696
Peter
NY Ref bp, 1661, 1668,
1669
Robert
NY Ref bp, 1695, 1697
Thomas
Bkln Ref bp, 1697
Hack Ref bp, 1696
NY Ref bp, 1699

Frederica
George
Berg Ref bp, 1684, 1691
NY Ref bp, 1668, 1670,
1672, 1677, 1680, 1686

G

Geesje
Abraham
Alb Ref bp, 1691, 1694,
1697
Arent
King Ref bp, 1664, 1668
NY Ref bp, 1661
Gerarda
Benjamin
NY Ref bp, 1695
Bruyn
King Ref bp, 1683
Conrad
Alb Ref bp, 1698
Dirk
NY Ref bp, 1659, 1668,
1669, 1671, 1674, 1677,
1678, 1681, 1684, 1687
George
Hack Ref bp, 1696
NY Ref bp, 1696, 1697,
1699
Hendrick
King Ref bp, 1692
Herman
NY Ref bp, 1689
Jacob
Fltb Ref bp, 1679, 1683
NY Ref bp, 1664
Joris
NY Ref bp, 1655, 1657,
1659, 1661, 1669, 1672,
1675, 1677
Nicholas
NY Ref bp, 1668
Peter
NY Ref bp, 1669, 1671,
1673, 1675
Philip
NY Ref bp, 1667
Robert
Tary Ref bp, 1698

Roelof
NY Ref bp, 1653, 1656,
1661, 1664, 1667
Thomas
NY Ref bp, 1664, 1666,
1667, 1669, 1672, 1674,
1676, 1678
Tunis
NY Ref bp, 1688
Gertrude
Abraham
Alb Ref bp, 1692, 1695
Bkln Ref bp, 1699
NY Ref bp, 1693, 1695
Aert
Berg Ref bp, 1696
Andrew
Bkln Ref bp, 1695
NY Ref bp, 1656, 1658,
1661, 1673, 1676
Anthony
Berg Ref bp, 1676
Arent
Alb Ref bp, 1691, 1694,
1697
Barent
Alb Ref bp, 1691, 1694,
1695, 1696, 1699
Berg Ref bp, 1697
NY Ref bp, 1658, 1691
Bartholomew
NY Ref bp, 1689, 1691,
1693, 1695, 1697, 1699
Christian
NY Ref bp, 1670, 1672,
* 1674, 1676, 1678, 1681,
1683, 1684, 1685, 1687,
1691
Christopher
Bkln Ref bp, 1682
Fltb Ref bp, 1679, 1680,
1682, 1684

Cornelius
Alb Ref bp, 1693, 1695,
1698
Bkln Ref bp, 1679, 1681,
1682, 1690, 1691
Fltb Ref bp, 1679, 1681,
1682, 1683
NY Ref bp, 1658, 1661,
1669, 1677, 1694
Dirk
NY Ref bp, 1659, 1661
Edward
King Ref bp, 1689
NY Ref bp, 1682, 1685,
1687, 1690
Egbert
NY Ref bp, 1662
Evert
King Ref bp, 1693, 1695,
1697, 1699
Francis
Fltb Ref bp, 1679, 1681
NY Ref bp, 1664, 1671,
1674, 1677, 1686
Gabriel
Bkln Ref bp, 1695, 1696,
1698
Garret
Fltb Ref bp, 1681, 1683,
1685
King Ref bp, 1699
Gilbert
King Ref bp, 1679, 1683,
1686, 1688
NY Ref bp, 1677
Hendrick
Bkln Ref bp, 1660, 1661,
1677, 1687, 1693, 1696
Fltb Ref bp, 1681, 1684
King Ref bp, 1689, 1692,
1694, 1695, 1697, 1699
NY Ref bp, 1651, 1655,
1658, 1662, 1665, 1674,
1677, 1691
Herman
Hack Ref bp, 1696, 1699
NY Ref bp, 1691

Isaac
Fltb Ref bp, 1688, 1690
Jacob
Alb Ref bp, 1692, 1693,
1694, 1698
King Ref bp, 1678, 1683,
1692, 1694, 1695, 1696,
1697, 1699
NY Ref bp, 1671, 1689,
1691
Lawrence
Hack Ref bp, 1686
NY Ref bp, 1680, 1685
Leonard
NY Ref bp, 1685, 1687,
1689, 1691, 1694, 1696,
1699
Lourus
Berg Ref bp, 1682
Matthew
NY Ref bp, 1690
Melchior
Bkln Ref bp, 1681, 1683
Fltb Ref bp, 1681, 1683
NY Ref bp, 1672, 1687
Nicholas
NY Ref bp, 1648, 1686,
1687
Peter
King Ref bp, 1682, 1693,
1695, 1697, 1699
NY Ref bp, 1662, 1664,
1677, 1679, 1689, 1691,
1693, 1696, 1698
Philip
NY Ref bp, 1656
Robert
Berg Ref bp, 1692, 1694,
1697, 1699
NY Ref bp, 1692
Roelof
Alb Ref bp, 1692, 1693
NY Ref bp, 1648
Roger
Fltb Ref bp, 1685
Servis
NY Ref bp, 1698

Gertrude (cont.)

Simon
Alb Ref bp, 1692, 1697
Fltb Ref bp, 1680, 1682,
1684, 1685
NY Ref bp, 1677, 1687
Schn Ref bp, 1695

Stephen
NY Ref bp, 1672, 1674,
1677, 1678, 1680, 1682,
1683, 1685, 1687, 1688,
1694, 1696, 1698

Thomas
Alb Ref bp, 1694
King Ref bp, 1696, 1698
NY Ref bp, 1692

Tunis
King Ref bp, 1679, 1682,
1684, 1686, 1688, 1692,
1695

Wessel
NY Ref bp, 1653, 1656,
1659

William
Alb Ref bp, 1692, 1698,
1699
Bkln Ref bp, 1663
NY Ref bp, 1661

Wolfert
NY Ref bp, 1671, 1674,
1677, 1680

Gilberta

Arent
NY Ref bp, 1664, 1667,
1669, 1673

Godwina

Hendrick
NY Ref bp, 1674

Peter
NY Ref bp, 1676

Gooden

Andrew
NY Ref bp, 1664

Goodeth

Richard
King Ref bp, 1684, 1687

William
King Ref bp, 1694, 1696,
1699

Gracius

Aert
Fltb Ref bp, 1682

H

Harmina

Abraham
NY Ref bp, 1697, 1699

Bartel
NY Ref bp, 1663, 1668

Egbert
NY Ref bp, 1662

Garret
Berg Ref bp, 1667
NY Ref bp, 1656, 1665,
1669

George
NY Ref bp, 1659, 1661,
1663, 1665, 1667, 1669,
1671, 1673, 1674, 1677

Hendrick
NY Ref bp, 1654

Isaac
NY Ref bp, 1686, 1687,
1689, 1692

Lambert
Bkln Ref bp, 1672
Fltb Ref bp, 1678, 1681

Peter
NY Ref bp, 1666

Thomas
NY Ref bp, 1681, 1683,
1689, 1698

William
NY Ref bp, 1654

Helena

Abraham
NY Ref bp, 1688

Albert
Hack Ref bp, 1694, 1699

Bartel
Bkln Ref bp, 1695

Carl
NY Ref bp, 1650

Christopher
NY Ref bp, 1699

Daniel
NY Ref bp, 1698

David
NY Ref bp, 1684, 1686,
1692, 1694, 1695, 1698

Dionysius
Bkln Ref bp, 1692
Fltb Ref bp, 1689

Florian
NY Ref bp, 1681, 1694

Francis
NY Ref bp, 1684, 1687,
1689

Hendrick
NY Ref bp, 1657, 1663

Maynard
Alb Ref bp, 1692
NY Ref bp, 1696

Michael
NY Ref bp, 1696, 1698

Nicholas
Fltb Ref bp, 1684

Peter
NY Ref bp, 1694, 1697

Robert
NY Ref bp, 1695

Samuel
Alb Ref bp, 1693, 1696,
1699

Tunis
NY Ref bp, 1681, 1682,
1684, 1686, 1688, 1689,
1691, 1693, 1695, 1697,
1699

William
Fltb Ref bp, 1678, 1682
NY Ref bp, 1690, 1691,
1694, 1696, 1698

Henrietta

Albert
Berg Ref bp, 1690
Fltb Ref bp, 1680, 1682,
1684, 1685

Aldert
NY Ref bp, 1657

Mother/Father Pairs Directory

Anthony
  NY Ref bp, 1699
Cornelius
  Berg Ref bp, 1685, 1688
  Bkln Ref bp, 1678
  Fltb Ref bp, 1678
  NY Ref bp, 1683
Dirk
  NY Ref bp, 1693, 1696,
  1698
Evert
  NY Ref bp, 1652, 1656,
  1657, 1659, 1660
Gilbert
  NY Ref bp, 1667
Giles
  NY Ref bp, 1669, 1674,
  1680, 1684
Hubert
  King Ref bp, 1680, 1684,
  1685, 1687, 1694, 1697,
  1699
Jacob
  Alb Ref bp, 1691, 1694,
  1697
Lambert
  King Ref bp, 1663, 1666,
  1670
  NY Ref bp, 1661
Lawrence
  Hack Ref bp, 1696, 1699
Martin
  NY Ref bp, 1663, 1665,
  1667, 1668, 1674
Michael
  Bkln Ref bp, 1674
  Fltb Ref bp, 1679
  NY Ref bp, 1671, 1676
Peter
  Alb Ref bp, 1697, 1698
  Berg Ref bp, 1676, 1678,
  1681, 1684
  Hack Ref bp, 1686
  King Ref bp, 1680, 1683,
  1685
  NY Ref bp, 1671, 1673,
  1676

William
  Bkln Ref bp, 1677, 1688,
  1694
  Fltb Ref bp, 1677, 1683
Hester
  Abraham
  NY Ref bp, 1698
Albert
  Alb Ref bp, 1696, 1698
Anthony
  NY Ref bp, 1667
Arent
  NY Ref bp, 1691, 1693,
  1695, 1699
Cornelius
  NY Ref bp, 1676
Dirk
  Hack Ref bp, 1699
Francis
  NY Ref bp, 1674
Fred
  King Ref bp, 1684
  NY Ref bp, 1678, 1680,
  1682
Garret
  NY Ref bp, 1665, 1682
George
  Bkln Ref bp, 1679, 1683,
  1694
  Fltb Ref bp, 1679, 1681,
  1683
  NY Ref bp, 1674, 1675,
  1677, 1681, 1685, 1687
Hendrick
  Bkln Ref bp, 1693
  Fltb Ref bp, 1688
Isaac
  NY Ref bp, 1696, 1698
Marcus
  NY Ref bp, 1693
Moses
  King Ref bp, 1685, 1687,
  1688, 1695, 1697, 1699
  NY Ref bp, 1691
Nathan
  Tap Ref bp, 1695
  Tary Ref bp, 1698

Peter
  King Ref bp, 1694
  NY Ref bp, 1667, 1669,
  1672, 1675, 1678, 1682,
  1684, 1685, 1687, 1689,
  1692, 1694, 1696, 1699
Roger
  Alb Ref bp, 1696
Samuel
  NY Ref bp, 1790
Simon
  NY Ref bp, 1694
Thomas
  NY Ref bp, 1691, 1697
Timothy
  NY Ref bp, 1687, 1689,
  1696, 1698
Walraven
  NY Ref bp, 1668
Hilda
  Albert
  Bkln Ref bp, 1698
  Fltb Ref bp, 1664, 1666,
  1681, 1683, 1685
Andrew
  King Ref bp, 1661, 1662
Arent
  Bkln Ref bp, 1681, 1686,
  1693, 1695
  Fltb Ref bp, 1678, 1681,
  1682, 1684
Barent
  Bkln Ref bp, 1693, 1696,
  1698
Cornelius
  Alb Ref bp, 1691, 1693,
  1696
  NY Ref bp, 1658, 1660,
  1663, 1665, 1667, 1669,
  1672, 1675, 1677
David
  NY Ref bp, 1681, 1683,
  1684, 1686, 1688
Garret
  King Ref bp, 1694, 1696,
  1698
  NY Ref bp, 1664

Mother/Father Pairs Directory

Hilda (cont.)

Ide
Berg Ref bp, 1666
NY Ref bp, 1657, 1659, 1662

Jacob
NY Ref bp, 1659, 1660, 1662, 1665, 1668, 1670, 1672, 1675, 1677, 1679, 1680, 1682, 1686, 16664

Lawrence
NY Ref bp, 1670, 1674, 1677, 1679, 1681, 1682, 1684, 1686

Lubbert
Berg Ref bp, 1682, 1685
Hack Ref bp, 1686, 1694
NY Ref bp, 1681

Nicholas
Bkln Ref bp, 1692
King Ref bp, 1683, 1685, 1687, 1689
NY Ref bp, 1691, 1692, 1694, 1697, 1699

Peter
King Ref bp, 1697, 1699

Philip
NY Ref bp, 1696, 1698

Thomas
Fltb Ref bp, 1681

William
King Ref bp, 1699
NY Ref bp, 1693, 1696, 1699

Hillary

Louis
NY Ref bp, 1665

Huberta

Joseph
Alb Ref bp, 1693, 1695, 1698

Ida
Andrew
Alb Ref bp, 1693, 1695, 1698

Barent
Bkln Ref bp, 1663
Fltb Ref bp, 1685

Christopher
Bkln Ref bp, 1682, 1687
Fltb Ref bp, 1682, 1685

Hendrick
Berg Ref bp, 1668
Bkln Ref bp, 1666, 1683
Fltb Ref bp, 1680, 1683, 1685
NY Ref bp, 1675, 1678

Roelof
NY Ref bp, 1671, 1673, 1677

Siegbert
Berg Ref bp, 1666
NY Ref bp, 1664

I

Isabel

Adrian
NY Ref bp, 1665

Andrew
NY Ref bp, 1662

Anthony
NY Ref bp, 1698

Arent
NY Ref bp, 1661, 1664, 1669, 1671

Conrad
NY Ref bp, 1675, 1678, 1680, 1684, 1687, 1690

David
King Ref bp, 1688

Francis
NY Ref bp, 1672, 1673, 1675

Garret
Berg Ref bp, 1694, 1697, 1699
NY Ref bp, 1677, 1682, 1684, 1687, 1689, 1696, 1698, 1699

Hendrick
NY Ref bp, 1680, 1696, 1699

Ide
NY Ref bp, 1686, 1687, 1689, 1691, 1692

Jacob
King Ref bp, 1679, 1680, 1694, 1697

Nicholas
NY Ref bp, 1697

Peter
Hack Ref bp, 1696, 1698
NY Ref bp, 1685, 1687, 1688, 1690, 1692, 1693, 1695

Simon
King Ref bp, 1693, 1694, 1697, 1699

Tunis
NY Ref bp, 1640, 1644

William
Berg Ref bp, 1677
Fltb Ref bp, 1680

J

Jacobina

Egbert
NY Ref bp, 1661, 1664, 1667

Janet

Abraham
Berg Ref bp, 1686, 1688
Bkln Ref bp, 1678, 1695
Fltb Ref bp, 1678, 1680

Adrian
Bkln Ref bp, 1685, 1689
Fltb Ref bp, 1685
NY Ref bp, 1666

Aegeus
Bkln Ref bp, 1682, 1687
Fltb Ref bp, 1677, 1679, 1680

Albert
NY Ref bp, 1680, 1682, 1685, 1687, 1689, 1694, 1695

Alexander
NY Ref bp, 1669

Andrew
King Ref bp, 1683, 1684, 1686, 1688, 1692, 1694, 1695, 1697, 1699
NY Ref bp, 1673, 1676, 1677, 1694

Mother/Father Pairs Directory

Anthony
King Ref bp, 1678, 1695,
1696, 1697, 1699
NY Ref bp, 1671
Arent
Alb Ref bp, 1692
NY Ref bp, 1695
Arnold
NY Ref bp, 1676, 1678,
1680, 1683, 1685, 1688,
1693
August
NY Ref bp, 1652, 1656,
1658, 1660, 1662
Barent
NY Ref bp, 1690, 1692,
1695, 1698
Caspar
Berg Ref bp, 1667
NY Ref bp, 1653, 1656,
1658, 1660, 1663, 1665,
1670, 1697, 1699
Christian
NY Ref bp, 1657
Christopher
Berg Ref bp, 1686, 1688,
1692, 1693
Clement
NY Ref bp, 1681
Cornelius
Berg Ref bp, 1687, 1691
Bkln Ref bp, 1697, 1699
Fltb Ref bp, 1678, 1681,
1683
Hack Ref bp, 1695, 1696,
1697
King Ref bp, 1683, 1684,
1685, 1687, 1689, 1692,
1694, 1696, 1699
NY Ref bp, 1676, 1680,
1681, 1685, 1692, 1694
David
NY Ref bp, 1658, 1659,
1662, 1665
Dirk
NY Ref bp, 1654, 1656,
1673, 1678

Evert
King Ref bp, 1661, 1665
NY Ref bp, 1673, 1675,
1677, 1680, 1682, 1684,
1685, 1688
Francis
Hack Ref bp, 1696, 1699
King Ref bp, 1663, 1665
NY Ref bp, 1656, 1660,
1668, 1687, 1691
Gabriel
NY Ref bp, 1658, 1693,
1694, 1696
Garret
Bkln Ref bp, 1687, 1694
King Ref bp, 1686
NY Ref bp, 1695, 1697,
1699
George
NY Ref bp, 1679, 1682,
1684, 1687, 1690, 1695
Gilbert
Bkln Ref bp, 1690, 1693,
1699
Fltb Ref bp, 1677, 1679,
1681, 1683, 1685, 1689
NY Ref bp, 1689, 1692,
1694, 1697, 1699
Giles
Alb Ref bp, 1693, 1695
Helle (Kelm)
NY Ref bp, 1695
Hendrick
Fltb Ref bp, 1681
King Ref bp, 1682, 1684,
1688, 1692, 1695, 1697
NY Ref bp, 1671, 1672,
1673, 1674, 1675, 1676,
1678, 1679, 1681, 1682,
1683, 1684, 1686, 1688,
1690, 1693, 1695, 1697,
1698, 1699
Herman
NY Ref bp, 1677, 1678
Hubert
NY Ref bp, 1663
Hugh
King Ref bp, 1679, 1682

Isaac
Alb Ref bp, 1699
King Ref bp, 1692, 1694,
1697, 1699
NY Ref bp, 1659, 1662,
1665, 1666, 1670, 1687,
1694, 1696, 1697, 1699
Isaiah
NY Ref bp, 1688
Jacob
Alb Ref bp, 1692, 1695,
1698
Fltb Ref bp, 1684
King Ref bp, 1685, 1699
NY Ref bp, 1680, 1681,
1684, 1686, 1689, 1691,
1694, 1696, 1699
James
NY Ref bp, 1668, 1670,
1672, 1674, 1676, 1678,
1680, 1683, 1686
Jeremiah
NY Ref bp, 1688, 1690,
1692, 1694, 1695, 1697,
1699
Joris
King Ref bp, 1675
NY Ref bp, 1678
Kilian
Tary Ref bp, 1697
Lambert
Alb Ref bp, 1691, 1693,
1695, 1696, 1698, 1699
Lawrence
Berg Ref bp, 1666
NY Ref bp, 1659, 1686,
1688, 1691, 1696, 1698
Leonard
NY Ref bp, 1676, 1690,
1699
Ludwich
Hack Ref bp, 1694, 1696
King Ref bp, 1684
Martin
Alb Ref bp, 1692, 1693,
1695, 1698
NY Ref bp, 1660, 1662,
1665, 1669, 1690

Mother/Father Pairs Directory

Janet (cont.)
  Matthew
    King Ref bp, 1682, 1684,
    1689, 1694, 1697, 1699
    NY Ref bp, 1673, 1680,
    1696, 1698, 1699
  Maynard
    NY Ref bp, 1682, 1683,
    1685, 1687, 1690, 1693
  Michael
    NY Ref bp, 1691, 1694
  Moses
    NY Ref bp, 1696, 1698
  Nicholas
    Bkln Ref bp, 1693, 1699
    NY Ref bp, 1656, 1658,
    1674, 1676, 1678, 1681,
    1683, 1684, 1686, 1689,
    1691, 1693, 1695
  Otto
    NY Ref bp, 1665
  Paul
    NY Ref bp, 1655, 1696,
    1699
  Peter
    Alb Ref bp, 1693, 1695,
    1697, 1699
    Bkln Ref bp, 1681, 1684,
    1690
    Fltb Ref bp, 1681, 1684
    Hack Ref bp, 1696
    King Ref bp, 1661, 1683,
    1686, 1688, 1691, 1693,
    1694, 1697, 1698, 1699
    NY Ref bp, 1659, 1675,
    1676, 1679, 1682, 1684,
    1686, 1688, 1691, 1693,
    1696
  Rembrant
    Bkln Ref bp, 1662
    NY Ref bp, 1673
  Reyner
    Bkln Ref bp, 1696
    Fltb Ref bp, 1679, 1682,
    1684, 1689
    NY Ref bp, 1657, 1660,
    1685, 1695
  Richard
    NY Ref bp, 1673

Samuel
    Berg Ref bp, 1667, 1673
    NY Ref bp, 1658, 1660
  Simon
    NY Ref bp, 1687, 1689,
    1691, 1693, 1696, 1699
  Solomon
    King Ref bp, 1699
  Thomas
    Berg Ref bp, 1692, 1693
    Fltb Ref bp, 1680
    King Ref bp, 1695, 1698
    NY Ref bp, 1656, 1658,
    1697
  Titus
    Bkln Ref bp, 1663
    Fltb Ref bp, 1679, 1682
  Tobias
    NY Ref bp, 1655
  Tunis
    Alb Ref bp, 1696, 1698
    Fltb Ref bp, 1678, 1681,
    1689
    NY Ref bp, 1674, 1676,
    1677, 1679, 1681, 1685,
    1686
  Volkert
    Schn Ref bp, 1698
  Walter
    Alb Ref bp, 1696, 1698
  William
    Berg Ref bp, 1677, 1680,
    1682, 1685, 1687, 1693,
    1696, 1699
    Bkln Ref bp, 1695
    Fltb Ref bp, 1679, 1681,
    1687, 1688
    King Ref bp, 1679, 1683,
    1687, 1692
    NY Ref bp, 1660, 1663,
    1665, 1667, 1671, 1672,
    1678, 1680, 1681, 1682,
    1685, 1687, 1688, 1689,
    1691, 1693, 1695, 1696,
    1699
  Wyatt
    NY Ref bp, 1680, 1684,
    1687, 1692

Jemima
  Abraham
    King Ref bp, 1699
    NY Ref bp, 1664, 1666,
    1668, 1673, 1676, 1685,
    1692, 1694, 1698
  Cornelius
    King Ref bp, 1693
  Daniel
    NY Ref bp, 1661
  Jacob
    Alb Ref bp, 1698
    Schn Ref bp, 1697
  Jochem
    Fltb Ref bp, 1687
  Joseph
    Alb Ref bp, 1693, 1696
    NY Ref bp, 1656, 1658,
    1661
  Nicholas
    Berg Ref bp, 1685, 1687,
    1694, 1696, 1699
    NY Ref bp, 1669, 1685,
    1691, 1694
  Peter
    Hack Ref bp, 1698
    NY Ref bp, 1657
  Reyer
    NY Ref bp, 1689, 1693,
    1695, 1698
  Robert
    NY Ref bp, 1691
  Thomas
    King Ref bp, 1679, 1680,
    1682, 1684, 1687, 1688
  Wessel
    King Ref bp, 1695, 1697
    NY Ref bp, 1694, 1696,
    1699
Joanna
  Andrew
    Berg Ref bp, 1694, 1696,
    1699
  Barent
    NY Ref bp, 1687, 1690,
    1692
  Clement
    Bkln Ref bp, 1679
    Fltb Ref bp, 1679

Cornelius
 Bkln Ref bp, 1699
David
 Alb Ref bp, 1695, 1697
Dennis
 King Ref bp, 1699
Dirk
 NY Ref bp, 1680
Evert
 NY Ref bp, 1687, 1689,
 1690, 1692, 1695, 11698
Hendrick
 King Ref bp, 1682, 1683,
 1688, 1693
Hieronymus
 NY Ref bp, 1661, 1663,
 1666
Joris
 King Ref bp, 1680
Lawrence
 NY Ref bp, 1693, 1695,
 1696
Peter
 Alb Ref bp, 1692, 1695,
 1697
Samuel
 NY Ref bp, 1689, 1690,
 1694, 1697
Thomas
 NY Ref bp, 1688
Josephine
Joseph
 NY Ref bp, 1663
William
 Bkln Ref bp, 1662
Josina
Anthony
 NY Ref bp, 1678, 1685,
 1687, 1691
Edward
 Alb Ref bp, 1698
Evert
 Alb Ref bp, 1692, 1694,
 1696
Garret
 NY Ref bp, 1680, 1682

Hendrick
 Bkln Ref bp, 1683, 1690
 Fltb Ref bp, 1681, 1683
 NY Ref bp, 1677
Peter
 NY Ref bp, 1674, 1679
Judith
Aegeus
 NY Ref bp, 1664, 1671,
 1673
Alexander
 NY Ref bp, 1667
Benjamin
 NY Ref bp, 1680, 1683,
 1686, 1689, 1694
Caesar
 NY Ref bp, 1652
Daniel
 NY Ref bp, 1686
Dennis
 NY Ref bp, 1682
Evert
 NY Ref bp, 1671
Isaac
 Alb Ref bp, 1698
Jacob
 Alb Ref bp, 1693, 1696
 King Ref bp, 1698
Jonathan
 Bkln Ref bp, 1697
Lucas
 Alb Ref bp, 1693, 1695,
 1698
Peter
 NY Ref bp, 1648, 1653,
 1658, 1661, 1665, 1672,
 1674, 1676, 1678
Richard
 King Ref bp, 1685
William
 King Ref bp, 1698
 NY Ref bp, 1688
Julia
Albert
 Berg Ref bp, 1690

K

Kunigunda
Hendrick
 Fltb Ref bp, 1679
Lawrence
 Bkln Ref bp, 1689
 Fltb Ref bp, 1679, 1681,
 1683, 1685
Nicholas
 NY Ref bp, 1672, 1675,
 1682, 1686, 1688
Walraven
 NY Ref bp, 1669

L

Lambertina
Nicholas
 NY Ref bp, 1662
Laurentia
Lawrence
 King Ref bp, 1680
Lavinia
Abraham
 NY Ref bp, 1696
Albert
 Hack Ref bp, 1694, 1695
 King Ref bp, 1664
Caspar
 NY Ref bp, 1694
Dirk
 NY Ref bp, 1656, 1659
Garret
 Fltb Ref bp, 1677, 1679,
 1682, 1685
 NY Ref bp, 1681, 1683
Hendrick
 King Ref bp, 1695, 1696
 NY Ref bp, 1655, 1664,
 1668, 1676, 1679, 1699
Hercules
 NY Ref bp, 1644, 1657,
 1659, 1662, 1666, 1668,
 1670, 1675, 1681
Herman
 NY Ref bp, 1660
Isaac
 Fltb Ref bp, 1690

Lavinia (cont.)
Jonathan
NY Ref bp, 1694, 1695, 1699
Peter
Alb Ref bp, 1691
King Ref bp, 1662
NY Ref bp, 1659
Philip
Alb Ref bp, 1693, 1694, 1698
Richard
King Ref bp, 1699
Robert
Alb Ref bp, 1692, 1694, 1696, 1699
NY Ref bp, 1694
Roger
Alb Ref bp, 1693, 1696
Simon
NY Ref bp, 1663, 1665, 1668, 1672, 1673, 1675, 1679, 1682
William
NY Ref bp, 1659, 1661, 1663
Lea
Fred
NY Ref bp, 1688
Jonathan
Schn Ref bp, 1695, 1697
Nicholas
Alb Ref bp, 1691
Lena
Carl
Bkln Ref bp, 1696, 1699
Cornelius
NY Ref bp, 1675
Dionysius
Fltb Ref bp, 1687
Francis
NY Ref bp, 1687, 1689
Garret
King Ref bp, 1694
Isaac
Bkln Ref bp, 1698

Leonora
Cornelius
King Ref bp, 1693
William
King Ref bp, 1674, 1683, 1684, 1686
Letitia
David
NY Ref bp, 1660
Garret
NY Ref bp, 1672
Lambert
Fltb Ref bp, 1679, 1683
NY Ref bp, 1697
Michael
Alb Ref bp, 1692, 1695, 1699
Thomas
NY Ref bp, 1671
Louisa
Caspar
Fltb Ref bp, 1678, 1679, 1681, 1683
Hugh
NY Ref bp, 1687
Isaac
NY Ref bp, 1685
Omie
King Ref bp, 1689
Lucretia
Francis
Fltb Ref bp, 1681
NY Ref bp, 1683, 1686
Nicholas
NY Ref bp, 1680, 1681, 1683, 1685, 1688
Lydia
Fred
Bkln Ref bp, 1699
Jacob
NY Ref bp, 1673
Jacques
NY Ref bp, 1665, 1668, 1671
Nicholas
NY Ref bp, 1656, 1657, 1661, 1664, 1666, 1668

Peter
NY Ref bp, 1697

M
Madeline
Anthony
Bkln Ref bp, 1690
Arent
Bkln Ref bp, 1696
Cornelius
Berg Ref bp, 1678, 1679, 1681, 1683, 1684, 1686
Garret
Bkln Ref bp, 1694
Herman
King Ref bp, 1662, 1663, 1666, 1667
Joseph
Bkln Ref bp, 1681, 1686, 1693
Leonard
Bkln Ref bp, 1698
Richard
NPal Ref bp, 1698
Magdalena
Abraham
King Ref bp, 1688
Adam
Bkln Ref bp, 1660, 1662
NY Ref bp, 1662, 1672
Albert
Hack Ref bp, 1694, 1696
Anthony
Fltb Ref bp, 1679, 1681, 1684, 1685
Barent
Fltb Ref bp, 1680
King Ref bp, 1678, 1683
NY Ref bp, 1676
Benjamin
King Ref bp, 1696, 1699
Caspar
NY Ref bp, 1686, 1688, 1689

Cornelius
  Berg Ref bp, 1687, 1690
  Bkln Ref bp, 1679, 1696
  Fltb Ref bp, 1681
  NY Ref bp, 1678, 1680,
  1681, 1687
Garret
  Bkln Ref bp, 1684
  Fltb Ref bp, 1681, 1682,
  1684, 1689
  King Ref bp, 1661, 1684,
  1686, 1687, 1691
  NY Ref bp, 1693, 1694,
  1696, 1698
George
  NY Ref bp, 1688
Hendrick
  NY Ref bp, 1655, 1663,
  1665, 1667
Herman
  NY Ref bp, 1659, 1674,
  1687
Jacob
  King Ref bp, 1685
  NY Ref bp, 1658, 1660,
  1678, 1681, 1683, 1686,
  1689, 1692, 1694, 1697
Jochem
  Fltb Ref bp, 1681, 1685,
  1689
  NY Ref bp, 1658
Jonas
  Alb Ref bp, 1692
Joris
  NY Ref bp, 1678, 1680,
  1683
Joseph
  Bkln Ref bp, 1681, 1684
  Fltb Ref bp, 1679, 1681,
  1684
  NY Ref bp, 1687
Leonard
  NY Ref bp, 1684, 1686,
  1688, 1690, 1694, 1696
Martin
  NY Ref bp, 1676, 1678,
  1681

Matthew
  King Ref bp, 1686
Octavius
  Bkln Ref bp, 1662
Richard
  King Ref bp, 1693, 1696
Simon
  NY Ref bp, 1659, 1662,
  1665
William
  NY Ref bp, 1693, 1694,
  1695, 1696, 1697, 1699
  Tary Ref bp, 1698
Margaret
Abraham
  King Ref bp, 1682, 1694,
  1696
  NPal Ref bp, 1684, 1687,
  1689, 1693
  NY Ref bp, 1643, 1655,
  1662, 1666, 1682, 1685,
  1686, 1691, 1699
  Tap Ref bp, 1694, 1697
  Tary Ref bp, 1699
Adam
  Alb Ref bp, 1697
  Schn Ref bp, 1699
Adrian
  NY Ref bp, 1662
Aert
  King Ref bp, 1663
Albert
  Bkln Ref bp, 1685
  Fltb Ref bp, 1685
  NY Ref bp, 1663, 1666,
  1667, 1669
Aldert
  NY Ref bp, 1661
Alexander
  NY Ref bp, 1656
Andrew
  Alb Ref bp, 1693
Anthony
  NY Ref bp, 1655, 1660
Arent
  NY Ref bp, 1659
Ballerand
  King Ref bp, 1664

Baltus
  NY Ref bp, 1671
Barent
  Bkln Ref bp, 1664
  NY Ref bp, 1660, 1697,
  1699
Carl
  NY Ref bp, 1689, 1691,
  1692, 1695, 1697, 1698
Cornelius
  Hack Ref bp, 1697, 1699
  NY Ref bp, 1659, 1661,
  1664, 1666, 1669, 1671,
  1674, 1676, 1696, 1697
Cosine
  Tap Ref bp, 1496
Dirk
  King Ref bp, 1665
Elias
  Berg Ref bp, 1676, 1678
  NY Ref bp, 1666, 1668,
  1669, 1672, 1674, 1676,
  1678
Evert
  Alb Ref bp, 1696
  NY Ref bp, 1697
Francis
  King Ref bp, 1697
Fred
  Alb Ref bp, 1693, 1695,
  1696, 1699
  King Ref bp, 1665, 1667,
  1679
  NY Ref bp, 1657, 1659,
  1661, 1663, 1664, 1665,
  1667, 1669, 1670, 1671,
  1673, 1676
Garret
  King Ref bp, 1688, 1695,
  1698
  NY Ref bp, 1657, 1671
George
  NY Ref bp, 1675, 1682
Gilbert
  King Ref bp, 1696
Hendrick
  Berg Ref bp, 1667
  King Ref bp, 1660, 1663,

Mother/Father Pairs Directory

Margaret (cont.)

Hendrick (cont.)
1665, 1667
NY Ref bp, 1660, 1662,
1663, 1665, 1669, 1670,
1672, 1673, 1674, 1675,
1678, 1682

Herman
Alb Ref bp, 1692, 1698
Bkln Ref bp, 1679
Fltb Ref bp, 1679, 1681
NY Ref bp, 1658, 1685,
1687, 1688, 1690, 1693,
1694
Schn Ref bp, 1696

Heyman
King Ref bp, 1679, 1684,
1686

Isaac
NY Ref bp, 1684, 1685,
1687, 1690

Jacob
Berg Ref bp, 1696, 1697,
1698, 1699
King Ref bp, 1671, 1678,
1684, 1696, 1698, 1699
NY Ref bp, 1655, 1656,
1657, 1658, 1659, 1660,
1664, 1678, 1679, 1681,
1683, 1685, 1688, 1690,
1692, 1695, 1696, 1698

James
Bkln Ref bp, 1699
King Ref bp, 1689

Joseph
NY Ref bp, 1696, 1698

Lambert
NY Ref bp, 1683, 1685,
1689, 1691
Tap Ref bp, 1695, 1698

Lawrence
Bkln Ref bp, 1693
Fltb Ref bp, 1680, 1682,
1684
NY Ref bp, 1677, 1678,
1687, 1691

Louis
King Ref bp, 1682, 1683,
1685, 1686, 1688, 1694,
1698

Lourus
Berg Ref bp, 1667

Martin
Hack Ref bp, 1696, 1699
NY Ref bp, 1657, 1699

Matthew
King Ref bp, 1679, 1682,
1683, 1686, 1688, 1692,
1694, 1699

Michael
NY Ref bp, 1677

Nathan
NY Ref bp, 1679, 1681,
1683, 1685, 1690

Nicholas
NY Ref bp, 1668, 1681,
1684, 1686, 1699

Obadiah
NY Ref bp, 1671

Oliver
NY Ref bp, 1683, 1686,
1688, 1691, 1695, 1698

Otto
NY Ref bp, 1694

Patrick
King Ref bp, 1687, 1693

Peter
Bkln Ref bp, 1663, 1681,
1686
Fltb Ref bp, 1678, 1679,
1681, 1683
King Ref bp, 1662, 1693
NY Ref bp, 1660, 1662,
1664, 1666, 1671, 1675,
1685, 1688
Tap Ref bp, 1696, 1698
Tary Ref bp, 1699

Philip
NY Ref bp, 1673, 1682

Randolph
Bkln Ref bp, 1684
Fltb Ref bp, 1684

Rembrant
Alb Ref bp, 1696, 1698

Robert
Alb Ref bp, 1698
King Ref bp, 1682, 1687

Samuel
NY Ref bp, `1698, 1695,
1696
Tary Ref bp, 1699

Theodore
Bkln Ref bp, 1694

Thomas
Berg Ref bp, 1674, 1680
Fltb Ref bp, 1680
Hack Ref bp, 1694
NY Ref bp, 1657, 1694,
1696

Timothy
NY Ref bp, 1677, 1678,
1679, 1682, 1685, 1686,
1687

Tunis
Alb Ref bp, 1694
NY Ref bp, 1697

Walran
King Ref bp, 1667, 1674,
1679

Werner
King Ref bp, 1693, 1695,
1698

William
King Ref bp, 1671, 1682,
1683, 1686, 1688, 1692
NY Ref bp, 1664, 1666,
1667, 1669, 1673, 1674,
1680, 1681, 1683, 1685,
1686, 1688, 1690, 1692,
1694, 1696

Wolfert
NY Ref bp, 1666, 1698

Maria

Abraham
Alb Ref bp, 1694, 1696,
1698
King Ref bp, 1682, 1694
NPal Ref bp, 1683, 1686,
1690, 1691, 1696
NY Ref bp, 1655, 1657,
1660, 1662, 1664, 1680,
1687, 1692, 1698

Adam
  Bkln Ref bp, 1692, 1695,
  1696, 1699
Adolf
  NY Ref bp, 1671, 1673,
  1677, 1679, 1682, 1684,
  1686, 1692, 1698
Adrian
  Berg Ref bp, 1688
  NY Ref bp, 1678
Aert
  NY Ref bp, 1699
Albert
  Alb Ref bp, 1659, 1693,
  1694, 1696, 1698
  Tary Ref bp, 1698
Alexander
  King Ref bp, 1698
  NY Ref bp, 1668
Andrew
  Fltb Ref bp, 1684, 1686
  King Ref bp, 1678, 1680,
  1684, 1685, 1688, 1691
  NY Ref bp, 1657, 1660,
  1689, 1691, 1692, 1694,
  1696, 1698, 1699
Anthony
  Alb Ref bp, 1694, 1696
  Fltb Ref bp, 1682, 1684
  King Ref bp, 1662, 1664,
  1666, 1668, 1671, 1674
  NY Ref bp, 1690, 1696,
  1699
Arent
  Alb Ref bp, 1698
* Fltb Ref bp, 1680
  King Ref bp, 1674, 1679,
  1685, 1687, 1694, 1696,
  1698
  NY Ref bp, 1663, 1672,
  1684
August
  Alb Ref bp, 1692
Baltus
  NY Ref bp, 1667, 1670,
  1672, 1677, 1679, 1682,
  1685

Barent
  NY Ref bp, 1655, 1657,
  1677, 1680
Bastian
  NY Ref bp, 1660
Bouwen
  NY Ref bp, 1674
Carl
  King Ref bp, 1694, 1696,
  1699
  NY Ref bp, 1676, 1693
Caspar
  NY Ref bp, 1687, 1695,
  1697
  Tap Ref bp, 1697
  Tary Ref bp, 1697
Christian
  Alb Ref bp, 1693, 1697
Christopher
  King Ref bp, 1665
  NY Ref bp, 1681
Conrad
  NY Ref bp, 1656, 1658,
  1659, 1662, 1664
Cornelius
  Alb Ref bp, 1691, 1692,
  1696, 1697, 1698
  Fltb Ref bp, 1681
  King Ref bp, 1668, 1671,
  1686, 1687, 1689, 1692,
  1694, 1696, 1698, 1699
  NY Ref bp, 1658, 1663, 1679,
  1681, 1682, 1684, 1685,
  1686, 1687, 1688, 1689,
  1690, 1691, 1692, 1693,
  1695, 1696, 1697, 1698, 1699
Cosine
  Tap Ref bp, 1498
Court
  Fltb Ref bp, 1678, 1680,
  1683
  NY Ref bp, 1676
Daniel
  Alb Ref bp, 1692
  Fltb Ref bp, 1680
  NY Ref bp, 1674, 1677,
  1679, 1681
  Schn Ref bp, 1695

David
  NY Ref bp, 1662, 1666
Dennis
  Bkln Ref bp, 1695
Dirk
  Alb Ref bp, 1693
  Bkln Ref bp, 1661, 1664,
  1673, 1678, 1680, 1684,
  1686
  Fltb Ref bp, 1678, 1680,
  1681, 1684
  King Ref bp, 1678, 1680,
  1684, 1687
  NY Ref bp, 1662, 1666,
  1667, 1669, 1672, 1695,
  1698
  Schn Ref bp, 1695, 1698
Egbert
  Alb Ref bp, 1691
  King Ref bp, 1692, 1695,
  1698
Elias
  NY Ref bp, 1675, 1677,
  1679, 1680, 1683, 1686,
  1689, 1696
Emanuel
  King Ref bp, 1694, 1697
Evert
  NY Ref bp, 1674, 1675,
  1676, 1678, 1680, 1683,
  1684, 1686, 1688, 1690,
  1692
Francis
  Berg Ref bp, 1692
  King Ref bp, 1695, 1697,
  1699
  NY Ref bp, 1659, 1663,
  1665, 1669
Garret
  Alb Ref bp, 1693, 1695,
  1697
  Bkln Ref bp, 1695
  NY Ref bp, 1648, 1657,
  1659, 1661, 1666, 1668,
  1670, 1677, 1680, 1683,
  1684, 1685, 1687, 1688,
  1689, 1690, 1691, 1693,
  1695, 1698

Mother/Father Pairs Directory

Maria (cont.)
George
King Ref bp, 1661, 1663,
1666
NY Ref bp, 1698
Gerbrant
Berg Ref bp, 1679, 1691,
1696
Bkln Ref bp, 1682, 1691
Fltb Ref bp, 1682
NY Ref bp, 1675, 1677,
1679, 1684, 1687, 1689,
1693, 1696
Hartman
Berg Ref bp, 1675, 1677,
1678, 1680, 1683, 1685,
1693, 1695, 1698
NY Ref bp, 1681, 1683,
1685, 1687, 1691
Hendrick
Alb Ref bp, 1692, 1693,
1695, 1697
Berg Ref bp, 1680, 1682,
1683, 1684, 1685
Bkln Ref bp, 1682, 1685,
1688, 1690, 1693, 1698
Fltb Ref bp, 1680, 1682,
1683, 1685
Hack Ref bp, 1696, 1699
King Ref bp, 1688, 1691
NY Ref bp, 1656, 1658, 1661,
1663, 1666, 1671, 1673,
1674, 1675, 1676, 1677,
1678, 1679, 1680, 1681,
1682, 1683, 1685, 1686,
1687, 1689, 1690, 1692, 1699
Schn Ref bp, 1695, 1697
Herbert
Alb Ref bp, 1696, 1697
Herman
Alb Ref bp, 1692, 1693,
1696
NY Ref bp, 1664, 1677,
1679
Heyman
NY Ref bp, 1684, 1687,
1689, 1692, 1694, 1696,
1699

Hubert
Alb Ref bp, 1694
NY Ref bp, 1656, 1657,
1659, 1660, 1663, 1667,
1695, 1697, 1699
Hugh
King Ref bp, 1695, 1698
NPal Ref bp, 1690, 1691,
1693, 1696, 1699
Isaac
Alb Ref bp, 1692, 1695,
1696, 1697, 1699
Fltb Ref bp, 1688
NPal Ref bp, 1684, 1687,
1690
NY Ref bp, 1664, 1665,
1666, 1667, 1669, 1670,
1675, 1678, 1689, 1690,
1693, 1695, 1697, 1699
Schn Ref bp, 1694
Jacob
Alb Ref bp, 1698
Bkln Ref bp, 1681, 1690,
1691, 1693, 1694, 1697,
1698, 1699
Fltb Ref bp, 1679, 1680,
1681
Hack Ref bp, 1696, 1698,
1699
King Ref bp, 1661, 1663,
1665, 1666, 1678, 1683,
1686, 1687, 1688, 1693
NPal Ref bp, 1689, 1699
NY Ref bp, 1655, 1656,
1660, 1664, 1666, 1668,
1669, 1671, 1672, 1673,
1676, 1678, 1680, 1681,
1682, 1683, 1684, 1685,
1686, 1687, 1689, 1690,
1692, 1698
Jacques
Fltb Ref bp, 1679, 1681,
1687, 1688
NY Ref bp, 1665, 1670,
1671, 1674, 1676, 1678,
1679, 1682
James
NY Ref bp, 1681, 1695

Jeffers
NY Ref bp, 1699
Jesse
NY Ref bp, 1696, 1698
Jochem
Bkln Ref bp, 1696
NY Ref bp, 1699
Jonathan
Schn Ref bp, 1696, 1698
Joris
Bkln Ref bp, 1695, 1699
King Ref bp, 1696, 1697,
1699
NY Ref bp, 1667, 1669,
1672, 1674, 1677, 1680,
1683
Joseph
King Ref bp, 1682
NY Ref bp, 1655, 1669,
1672, 1675, 1678, 1684,
1685, 1691, 1695
Lambert
NY Ref bp, 1667, 1692
Lawrence
Alb Ref bp, 1691
NY Ref bp, 1674, 1676,
1679, 1682, 1685, 1686,
1687, 1693
Leonard
King Ref bp, 1679, 1680,
1683, 1684, 1686, 1689
NY Ref bp, 1669, 1673,
1694
Louis
King Ref bp, 1678, 1682,
1698
NPal Ref bp, 1684, 1687
Lucas
Alb Ref bp, 1693
Ludwich
King Ref bp, 1697
Martin
Bkln Ref bp, 1693
NY Ref bp, 1661, 1673,
1695
Matthew
Alb Ref bp, 1694
Bkln Ref bp, 1682, 1693

Mother/Father Pairs Directory

Fltb Ref bp, 1682, 1684
King Ref bp, 1680, 1684,
1688, 1694, 1697
NY Ref bp, 1669, 1670,
1672, 1674, 1676, 1677,
1679, 1681, 1686, 1689,
1699

Maynard
Fltb Ref bp, 1682
NY Ref bp, 1661, 1666,
1670, 1673, 1695

Michael
NY Ref bp, 1655, 1656

Moses
King Ref bp, 1680, 1682,
1684, 1686, 1688, 1691,
1695, 1698
NY Ref bp, 1680

Nathan
NY Ref bp, 1687

Nicholas
Alb Ref bp, 1693
Berg Ref bp, 1680, 1689
NY Ref bp, 1655, 1661,
1663, 1664, 1666, 1667,
1671, 1673, 1675, 1676,
1678, 1680, 1681, 1682,
1683, 1684, 1685, 1687,
1689, 1691, 1693, 1694,
1695, 1698

Paul
NY Ref bp, 1656, 1663,
1689, 1691, 1692, 1695,
1697

Peek
NY Ref bp, 1698

Peter
Alb Ref bp, 1692, 1694,
1696, 1698
Berg Ref bp, 1666, 1669
Bkln Ref bp, 1688, 1698
Fltb Ref bp, 1679, 1680,
1681, 1687, 1688
King Ref bp, 1678, 1680
NY Ref bp, 1655, 1657,
1658, 1659, 1661, 1662,
1663, 1664, 1666, 1667,
1668, 1671, 1673, 1674,

1675, 1677, 1680, 1681,
1682, 1685, 1688, 1689,
1691, 1692, 1693, 1694,
1695, 1696, 1697, 1698

Philip
Alb Ref bp, 1693, 1695,
1697
NY Ref bp, 1662

Rembrant
Fltb Ref bp, 1682, 1684,
1688

Reyer
NY Ref bp, 1682

Richard
Fltb Ref bp, 1681
NY Ref bp, 1680, 1688,
1691, 1694, 1695, 1698

Robert
Alb Ref bp, 1693
King Ref bp, 1685
NY Ref bp, 1684, 1685,
1687, 1691, 1693, 1695

Roger
NY Ref bp, 1696

Samuel
Berg Ref bp, 1681
Hack Ref bp, 1694, 1697,
1699
NY Ref bp, 1665, 1679,
1680, 1681, 1685, 1695,
1698

Siebold
Berg Ref bp, 1680, 1682,
1684, 1685
Hack Ref bp, 1694, 1696,
1699

Simon
Bkln Ref bp, 1681
Fltb Ref bp, 1681
King Ref bp, 1684, 1686,
1689

Solomon
NY Ref bp, 1666, 1668,
1671, 1674, 1676

Stephen
NY Ref bp, 1697, 1699

Sybout
NY Ref bp, 1670, 1672,
1676, 1680, 1684, 1687,
1689, 1693

Thomas
Alb Ref bp, 1693, 1697
Berg Ref bp, 1668
Bkln Ref bp, 1681, 1697
Fltb Ref bp, 1681
King Ref bp, 1684, 1686,
1688, 1689, 1692, 1695,
1697, 1699
NY Ref bp, 1653, 1658,
1659, 1660, 1662, 1663,
1664, 1666, 1667, 1668,
1670, 1672, 1673, 1674,
1675, 1677, 1679, 1681,
1695, 1698

Tunis
King Ref bp, 1678, 1679,
1680, 1683, 1684, 1686,
1688, 1694
NY Ref bp, 1692, 1694,
1696

Urban
NY Ref bp, 1690, 1691

Valentine
NY Ref bp, 1665, 1671,
1674

Volkert
Alb Ref bp, 1692

Walter
Bkln Ref bp, 1687
Fltb Ref bp, 1690
NY Ref bp, 1671, 1673,
1675, 1678

Wessel
King Ref bp, 1678, 1679,
1682, 1683, 1685, 1686,
1688
NY Ref bp, 1672

William
Alb Ref bp, 1692, 1695,
1697
Fltb Ref bp, 1678, 1680,
1682, 1685
Hack Ref bp, 1696
NY Ref bp, 1667, 1669,

Maria (cont.)
William (cont.)
1673, 1683, 1686, 1690,
1693, 1694, 1695, 1696,
1698, 1699
Wolfert
NY Ref bp, 1693, 1696
Tary Ref bp, 1698
Zachariah
NY Ref bp, 1694, 1695,
1698

Marjory
Patrick
King Ref bp, 1689, 1691,
1695, 1697, 1699

Martha
Hendrick
NY Ref bp, 1674, 1676,
1679, 1680, 1682, 1687,
1693, 1696, 1697, 1699
Peter
King Ref bp, 1697
Randolph
Fltb Ref bp, 1684
William
King Ref bp, 1682, 1684,
1685

Martina
Adrian
NY Ref bp, 1664
William
Alb Ref bp, 1693, 1695,
1697
Berg Ref bp, 1686, 1692
Hack Ref bp, 1698
NY Ref bp, 1688

Mathilda
Abraham
NY Ref bp, 1658, 1659,
1661, 1664, 1667, 1671,
1674
Adam
King Ref bp, 1693, 1695,
1698

Cornelius
Berg Ref bp, 1682, 1694,
1698
NY Ref bp, 1666, 1671,
1673, 1679, 1681, 1688,
1694
Evert
NY Ref bp, 1686, 1687,
1688, 1690, 1694, 1696,
1698
Isaac
NY Ref bp, 1698

Mattina
Dirk
NY Ref bp, 1693, 1696,
1699
William
NY Ref bp, 1656, 1658,
1660

Merritje
Cornelius
Bkln Ref bp, 1681

N

Nelly
Adam
NY Ref bp, 1663, 1665,
1666, 1667, 1670
Aert
Fltb Ref bp, 1688
Albert
Alb Ref bp, 1692
Anthony
NY Ref bp, 1682
Azariah
NY Ref bp, 1679
Caspar
Berg Ref bp, 1686
NY Ref bp, 1667, 1681
Christian
NY Ref bp, 1669, 1683,
1687
Cornelius
Fltb Ref bp, 1688
King Ref bp, 1679, 1682
NY Ref bp, 1664, 1666,
1667, 1670, 1672, 1673,

1676, 1678, 1679, 1680,
1684, 1688
Daniel
Bkln Ref bp, 1698
Dirk
NY Ref bp, 1670
Garret
Bkln Ref bp, 1662, 1677
Fltb Ref bp, 1677
Hack Ref bp, 1696
NY Ref bp, 1683, 1684,
1687, 1689, 1691
Hendrick
Alb Ref bp, 1694, 1698,
1699
King Ref bp, 1679, 1680,
1683, 1685, 1687
NY Ref bp, 1670, 1672,
1675, 1676, 1678, 1680,
1681, 1684, 1686
Herman
NY Ref bp, 1695
Hieronymus
NY Ref bp, 1696
Isaac
NY Ref bp, 1691, 1692,
1694, 1696, 1697, 1698,
1699
Jacob
NY Ref bp, 1693, 1695,
1698
Joris
Bkln Ref bp, 1696
Joseph
Fltb Ref bp, 1682, 1684
Josiah
Fltb Ref bp, 1680
Martin
Alb Ref bp, 1692, 1694,
1695
NY Ref bp, 1693, 1694,
1696, 1698
Michael
Bkln Ref bp, 1680, 1694,
1699
Fltb Ref bp, 1680, 1682,
1684, 1690

Nicholas
NY Ref bp, 1653
Peter
King Ref bp, 1692, 1694, 1695
Quirinus
Fltb Ref bp, 1687
Roger
Hack Ref bp, 1698
Romeyn
NY Ref bp, 1661
Simon
King Ref bp, 1696, 1698
Thomas
NY Ref bp, 1665, 1667, 1669, 1671, 1673
Walter
Alb Ref bp, 1691
Fltb Ref bp, 1684
NY Ref bp, 1690
William
King Ref bp, 1695, 1699

Nicole
Barent
King Ref bp, 1663
NY Ref bp, 1665
Cornelius
NY Ref bp, 1656
Hendrick
Berg Ref bp, 1679, 1681
Bkln Ref bp, 1661, 1685
Fltb Ref bp, 1685
NY Ref bp, 1677, 1679
Paul
NY Ref bp, 1663
Reyner
NY Ref bp, 1693, 1696
Victor
NY Ref bp, 1681, 1683, 1688, 1690, 1692, 1695, 1697

P

Patience
Andrew
Berg Ref bp, 1691
NY Ref bp, 1678, 1684

Evert
NY Ref bp, 1694, 1696, 1699
Hendrick
NY Ref bp, 1675
Peter
Bkln Ref bp, 1695
Wessel
Berg Ref bp, 1696

Patricia
Albert
King Ref bp, 1680, 1683, 1685
Christian
NY Ref bp, 1691
Dirk
NY Ref bp, 1662
Evert
NY Ref bp, 1692
Jacob
Berg Ref bp, 1697, 1699
NY Ref bp, 1699
Marcelis
Berg Ref bp, 1682, 1684, 1694, 1699
NY Ref bp, 1687, 1690, 1696
Simon
Fltb Ref bp, 1678

Petronella
Albert
NY Ref bp, 1689, 1691, 1694, 1696
Anthony
King Ref bp, 1682, 1684, 1686
Christian
NY Ref bp, 1693, 1695, 1698
Garret
King Ref bp, 1680, 1685, 1687, 1694, 1697, 1699
Hendrick
King Ref bp, 1683
NY Ref bp, 1676, 1678, 1680, 1686, 1689, 1693, 1697

Isaac
NY Ref bp, 1670, 1672
Jochem
King Ref bp, 1682, 1683, 1684, 1685, 1687
Marinus
King Ref bp, 1685, 1688, 1695, 1697, 1699
Peter
Bkln Ref bp, 1692
NY Ref bp, 1685
Simon
King Ref bp, 1694

William
NY Ref bp, 1695, 1697, 1699

Priscilla
William
NY Ref bp, 1674, 1676, 1678

Prudence
Isaac
NY Ref bp, 1695, 1697, 1699

R

Rachel
Adrian
King Ref bp, 1693
Arent
King Ref bp, 1680, 1683, 1684, 1686, 1688, 1696
Barent
NY Ref bp, 1695
Cornelius
King Ref bp, 1692, 1695, 1699
NY Ref bp, 1657, 1694
David
Alb Ref bp, 1692
Berg Ref bp, 1679, 1680
Bkln Ref bp, 1696
Fltb Ref bp, 1681
NY Ref bp, 1676, 1677
Schn Ref bp, 1696

Rachel (cont.)
Dirk
Alb Ref bp, 1692, 1694,
1695, 1697, 1699
NY Ref bp, 1678, 1682
Gilbert
King Ref bp, 1664, 1682,
1684, 1686, 1688, 1692,
1696, 1698
Giles
Alb Ref bp, 1696, 1698
Hendrick
King Ref bp, 1688
NY Ref bp, 1660, 1662,
1666, 1668, 1672, 1675
Herman
King Ref bp, 1696, 1698,
1699
Jacob
King Ref bp, 1696, 1697,
1699
Jeremiah
Schn Ref bp, 1698
Joseph
Alb Ref bp, 1691, 1694
Lucas
NY Ref bp, 1684, 1686,
1689, 1692, 1695, 1698,
1699
Maynard
Alb Ref bp, 1697
Peter
NY Ref bp, 1659, 1662,
1699
Simon
Alb Ref bp, 1693
NY Ref bp, 1695, 1697
William
NY Ref bp, 1687, 1689,
1690, 1693, 1696, 1699
Rebecca
Abraham
NY Ref bp, 1693, 1695
Adrian
NY Ref bp, 1665, 1667,
1670, 1674, 1676, 1678
Arent
NY Ref bp, 1663, 1671

Francis
King Ref bp, 1684, 1685
NY Ref bp, 1687, 1689,
1691, 1693, 1695, 1696
Hieronymus
Alb Ref bp, 1691
Jacob
NY Ref bp, 1655, 1658,
1661, 1664, 1667
Joris
Bkln Ref bp, 1678
NY Ref bp, 1652, 1664
Nicholas
NY Ref bp, 1685

Peter
King Ref bp, 1682, 1684,
1686, 1688, 1695, 1698
NY Ref bp, 1667, 1690,
1693, 1694, 1696, 1697,
1699
Reyer
NY Ref bp, 1697, 1698
William
NY Ref bp, 1681
Rosella
Dirk
NY Ref bp, 1679
Francis
Tary Ref bp, 1697, 1698
Hendrick
NY Ref bp, 1657, 1671
Ruth
Jacob
NY Ref bp, 1694, 1696,
1698
Samuel
Berg Ref bp, 1683
Rymerick
Thomas
King Ref bp, 1679, 1683,
1686, 1688, 1695

S
Sarah
Abraham
Ref bp, 1696, 1697,

Arent
Alb Ref bp, 1691, 1694
NY Ref bp, 1681, 1682,
1684, 1687, 1689
Schn Ref bp, 1696, 1699
Azariah
Alb Ref bp, 1698
Barent
NY Ref bp, 1686, 1689,
1691, 1694, 1697, 1698,
1699
Tary Ref bp, 1697, 1699
Benjamin
NY Ref bp, 1671
Boschman
NY Ref bp, 1690
Cornelius
NY Ref bp, 1685, 1687,
1689, 1691, 1694, 1695,
1699
Daniel
Bkln Ref bp, 1691
Fltb Ref bp, 1679, 1681,
1687
NY Ref bp, 1674, 1675,
1677, 1679, 1680, 1681,
1683, 1685, 1686, 1688,
1689
David
Hack Ref bp, 1699
Dirk
Bkln Ref bp, 1685, 1686,
1688, 1690, 1692
Fltb Ref bp, 1685
Garret
Alb Ref bp, 1695, 1697,
1699
NY Ref bp, 1694, 1695,
1697, 1699
Hendrick
King Ref bp, 1698
NY Ref bp, 1644, 1661,
1663, 1666, 1669, 1675,
1678, 1690, 1692, 1694,
1697, 1699
Herman
NY Ref bp, 1667

Hubert
King Ref bp, 1696, 1698
Isaac
Bkln Ref bp, 1699
NY Ref bp, 1645, 1655,
1657, 1660, 1662, 1663,
1666, 1669, 1685, 1686,
1687, 1688, 1690, 1691,
1692, 1693, 1694, 1695,
1696, 1697, 1698, 1699
Jacob
Alb Ref bp, 1695
King Ref bp, 1679, 1680,
1682, 1685, 1686, 1688,
1689, 1693, 1699, 16979
NY Ref bp, 1657, 1666,
1668, 1695, 1696, 1698,
1699
Jacques
Fltb Ref bp, 1681
James
King Ref bp, 1689, 1694,
1698
Jochem
King Ref bp, 1678
Jonathan
NY Ref bp, 1694
Joris
Bkln Ref bp, 1688, 1690,
1694
Fltb Ref bp, 1679, 1681,
1682, 1684
NY Ref bp, 1681, 1696
Joseph
King Ref bp, 1683, 1686,
1689, 1695
Lawrence
Bkln Ref bp, 1667
NY Ref bp, 1659, 1661,
1662, 1663, 1666, 1668,
1670, 1671, 1672, 1673,
1674, 1677, 1678, 1680,
1681, 1683
Lucas
NY Ref bp, 1677
Martin
NY Ref bp, 1696

Matthew
King Ref bp, 1698, 1797
Maynard
King Ref bp, 1694, 1697,
1699
Nathan
NY Ref bp, 1664, 1676
Nicholas
Fltb Ref bp, 1679, 1681,
1683
NY Ref bp, 1676, 1682,
1686, 1688, 1690, 1692,
1693
Paul
Bkln Ref bp, 1678, 1681
Fltb Ref bp, 1678, 1679,
1680, 1681
NY Ref bp, 1683, 1687,
1688
Peter
Bkln Ref bp, 1687, 1696,
1698
Fltb Ref bp, 1681
NY Ref bp, 1656, 1685,
1688, 1689, 1691, 1695,
1697, 1699
Philip
King Ref bp, 1686, 1688
NY Ref bp, 1681
Richard
NY Ref bp, 1667
Rupert
NY Ref bp, 1685, 1686,
1688, 1690, 1692, 1694,
1695, 1699, 16979
Tunis
Bkln Ref bp, 1661
King Ref bp, 1696, 1698,
1699
NY Ref bp, 1655, 1657,
1660, 1665, 1668, 1699
Ulrich
NY Ref bp, 1656
Volkert
Fltb Ref bp, 1681, 1685
Hack Ref bp, 1686

William
NY Ref bp, 1658, 1673,
1681, 1685, 1687, 1689
Sophia
Abraham
Berg Ref bp, 1692, 1694,
1696
NY Ref bp, 1689, 1691,
1692, 1693, 1695, 1697
Andrew
NY Ref bp, 1672, 1677,
1679, 1681, 1684, 1686,
1689
Barent
Bkln Ref bp, 1659, 1661,
1664
Benjamin
NY Ref bp, 1699
Carl
NY Ref bp, 1659
Cornelius
Berg Ref bp, 1687, 1692,
1694, 1695, 1696, 1697,
1699
NY Ref bp, 1687, 1689,
1694
Cosine
NY Ref bp, 1640
Dirk
Alb Ref bp, 1694, 1696,
1698
King Ref bp, 1692
NY Ref bp, 1663, 1667,
16646
Evert
Bkln Ref bp, 1678, 1684,
1690
Fltb Ref bp, 1680, 1684,
1687
NY Ref bp, 1677, 1682
Francis
Alb Ref bp, 1691, 1692
NY Ref bp, 1656
Garret
Berg Ref bp, 1684, 1686,
1688
Hack Ref bp, 1699
NY Ref bp, 1664, 1666,

Mother/Father Pairs Directory

Sophia (cont.)
Garret (cont.)
1673, 1674, 1675, 1677,
1680, 1682, 1684
George
Alb Ref bp, 1691, 1698
Gilbert
Fltb Ref bp, 1678, 1680,
1683
Hendrick
NY Ref bp, 1683, 1684,
1686, 1689, 1694, 1695,
1697
Jacob
Bkln Ref bp, 1682, 1683,
1696
Fltb Ref bp, 1680, 1682,
1683, 1685, 1688
NY Ref bp, 1667, 1668,
1670, 1671, 1672, 1674,
1676
Joseph
Alb Ref bp, 1693, 1695,
1698
Bkln Ref bp, 1680, 1687
Fltb Ref bp, 1678, 1680,
1682, 1685
King Ref bp, 1664
NY Ref bp, 1661, 1667,
1692, 1696
Lambert
Fltb Ref bp, 1682, 1685,
1687, 1689
Martin
Schn Ref bp, 1697
Matthew
Bkln Ref bp, 1695, 1699
NY Ref bp, 1661
Michael
Bkln Ref bp, 1678
Fltb Ref bp, 1678, 1680
NY Ref bp, 1651, 1654,
1656, 1658
Oufreen
NY Ref bp, 1689
Patrick
Alb Ref bp, 1697

Peter
Bkln Ref bp, 1664
NY Ref bp, 1687, 1689,
1691, 1694, 1697
Richard
NY Ref bp, 1682, 1684
Roger
NY Ref bp, 1686, 1690
Seger
NY Ref bp, 1687, 1690
Tunis
NY Ref bp, 1680, 1682,
1684, 1685, 1687, 1689,
1691, 1692, 1693, 1695,
1697, 1699
William
Alb Ref bp, 1697, 1699
Susan
Aert
NY Ref bp, 1641
Anthony
NY Ref bp, 1682, 1688,
1690, 1692, 1694, 1696
Arent
NY Ref bp, 1661, 1664,
1669, 1670, 1674, 1675,
1677
Cornelius
Alb Ref bp, 1694
NY Ref bp, 1696, 1697
Garret
NY Ref bp, 1682, 1684,
1689, 1690, 1694, 1696,
1697, 1699
Gerdin
NY Ref bp, 1665
Hendrick
NY Ref bp, 1655, 1657,
1659, 1663, 1666, 1668
Herman
NY Ref bp, 1669
Hieronymus
NY Ref bp, 1684, 1686,
1688, 1690, 1693, 1696
Isaac
Alb Ref bp, 1691, 1693
NY Ref bp, 1686, 1688,
1690, 1693, 1696

Schn Ref bp, 1695, 1697
Martin
NY Ref bp, 1664
Matthew
Alb Ref bp, 1696, 1698,
1699
Melchior
King Ref bp, 1678, 1682
Michael
NY Ref bp, 1688
Nicholas
NY Ref bp, 1652, 1656,
1659, 1661, 1662, 1664,
1666, 1667, 1668, 1670,
1672, 1673, 1675, 1677,
1679, 1681
Peter
Fltb Ref bp, 1688, 1690
Hack Ref bp, 1697
NY Ref bp, 1666, 1686,
1693, 1697
Reyner
NY Ref bp, 1661, 1663,
1665, 1668, 1670, 1673,
1675, 1678, 1681, 1685
Richard
NY Ref bp, 1692
Roelof
Berg Ref bp, 1685
Hack Ref bp, 1695, 1698
Samuel
Alb Ref bp, 1692
Schn Ref bp, 1695, 1696,
1699
Solomon
NY Ref bp, 1681
Thomas
Hack Ref bp, 1699
Wessel
NY Ref bp, 1692, 1694,
1696, 1698
William
King Ref bp, 1678, 1682,
1684, 1686, 1688
NY Ref bp, 1678, 1684,
1687, 1690, 1699

T

Temperance
Isaac
  NY Ref bp, 1682, 1684
Theodora
Bastian
  Alb Ref bp, 1693, 1696
Cornelius
  Fltb Ref bp, 1689
Daniel
  Alb Ref bp, 1699
Douw
  NY Ref bp, 1662, 1665,
  1669
Enoch
  NY Ref bp, 1671, 1673,
  1675, 1677, 1678, 1680,
  1683, 1687
Gideon
  Alb Ref bp, 1696
Jacob
  King Ref bp, 1699
Reyner
  Berg Ref bp, 1666
  NY Ref bp, 1659, 1670,
  1673
William
  NY Ref bp, 1665, 1667

U

Ursula
Dirk
  NY Ref bp, 1675, 1677,
  1679, 1682, 1684, 1687,
  1689
Roelof
  Hack Ref bp, 1686, 1694,
  1696, 1699
  NY Ref bp, 1691

V

Veronica
George
  Tap Ref bp, 1695, 1697
Jurian
  Hack Ref bp, 1699

Volkje
Barent
  Alb Ref bp, 1691, 1693
  Schn Ref bp, 1695, 1697

W

Walburg
Francis
  NY Ref bp, 1662
William
  NY Ref bp, 1669, 1675,
  1678, 1680
Wilhelmina
Adrian
  Bkln Ref bp, 1686
  Fltb Ref bp, 1678, 1680,
  1683
Albert
  Bkln Ref bp, 1692
  Tap Ref bp, 1695, 1697
Anthony
  Alb Ref bp, 1692, 1695,
  1698
Cornelius
  NY Ref bp, 1695, 1699
Garret
  Fltb Ref bp, 1685, 1687
George
  NY Ref bp, 1699
Gilbert
  NY Ref bp, 1661, 1662,
  1664, 1666, 1667, 1668,
  1670, 1672, 1674, 1675,
  1678
Hubert
  NY Ref bp, 1680, 1682,
  1684, 1687 .
Joris
  NY Ref bp, 1696
Nicholas
  Berg Ref bp, 1688, 1692
Simon
  NY Ref bp, 1693, 1695
Tunis
  King Ref bp, 1697, 1699

William
  Hack Ref bp, 1686
  NY Ref bp, 1684, 1699
Wybrecht
Herman
  Fltb Ref bp, 1681
  NY Ref bp, 1686
Jacob
  Berg Ref bp, 1682
  Hack Ref bp, 1698, 1699
Jacques
  Hack Ref bp, 1696
Wyntje
Arent
  King Ref bp, 1682

Y

Ypje
Simon
  NY Ref bp, 1699

Table 3C
Groom/Bride Pairs Directory

A

Abel
  Catherine
    Berg Ref mr, 1696

Abel (d)
  Anna
    NY Ref Ch mr, 1685
  Gertrude
    NY Ref Ch mr, 1647

Abraham
  Agatha
    NPal Ref mr, 1694
    NY Ref Ch mr, 1647
  Alida
    Berg Ref mr, 1683
    Fltb Ref mr, 1683
    NY Ref Ch mr, 1683
  Anna
    Alb Ref mr, 1696
    NY Ref Ch mr, 1692, 1695, 1698
    Schn Ref mr, 1696
  Catherine
    Alb Ref mr, 1689
    NY Ref Ch mr, 1659
  Catlintje
    NY Ref Ch mr, 1694, 1697
  Cecilia
    King Ref mr, 1682
  Cornelia
    Fltb Ref mr, 1692
    NY Ref Ch mr, 1681
  Elizabeth
    NY Ref Ch mr, 1690
  Elsie
    Alb Ref mr, 1696
  Frances
    NY Ref Ch mr, 1656
  Frances (d)
    NY Ref Ch mr, 1691
  Geesje
    Alb Ref mr, 1687
  Gertrude
    Alb Ref mr, 1691
    Bkln Ref mr, 1695

    Fltb Ref mr, 1690
    NY Ref Ch mr, 1642, 1693, 1696
  Harmina
    NY Ref Ch mr, 1694
  Helena
    NY Ref Ch mr, 1685
  Hester
    Alb Ref mr, 1699
    NY Ref Ch mr, 1697
    Schn Ref mr, 1699
  Jemima
    Alb Ref mr, 1697
    NY Ref Ch mr, 1662, 1691
  Margaret
    Berg Ref mr, 1698
    NY Ref Ch mr, 1681, 1691, 1698
  Maria
    Alb Ref mr, 1694, 1698
    King Ref mr, 1676
    NY Ref Ch mr, 1684
  Maria (d)
    NY Ref Ch mr, 1663
  Mathilda
    NY Ref Ch mr, 1656
  Rachel
    Tary Ref mr, 1698
  Rebecca
    NY Ref Ch mr, 1689
  Sarah
    NY Ref Ch mr, 1695
  Sophia
    Berg Ref mr, 1691
  Vroutje
    NY Ref Ch mr, 1689

Abraham (d)
  Elizabeth
    Alb Ref mr, 1692
    NY Ref Ch mr, 1685
  Frances
    Berg Ref mr, 1691

Adam
  Janet
    NY Ref Ch mr, 1647

  Magdalena
    NY Ref Ch mr, 1645, 1661
  Margaret
    Alb Ref mr, 1697
  Margaret (d)
    Alb Ref mr, 1697
  Maria
    Fltb Ref mr, 1690
  Mathilda
    Alb Ref mr, 1690
  Nelly
    NY Ref Ch mr, 1660

Adam (d)
  Anna
    Alb Ref mr, 1691
  Elsie
    NY Ref Ch mr, 1670
  Janet
    NY Ref Ch mr, 1659
  Magdalena
    NY Ref Ch mr, 1663
  Nelly
    NY Ref Ch mr, 1676

Adolf
  Maria
    NY Ref Ch mr, 1671

Adrian
  Abigail (d)
    NY Ref Ch mr, 1672
  Agnes
    NY Ref Ch mr, 1660
  Anna
    NY Ref Ch mr, 1690
  Catherine
    Alb Ref mr, 1699
    Berg Ref mr, 1672, 1677
    NY Ref Ch mr, 1673
  Elizabeth
    NY Ref Ch mr, 1679
  Elsie
    NY Ref Ch mr, 1643
  Isabel
    NY Ref Ch mr, 1685
  Judith (d)
    NY Ref Ch mr, 1663

(d) = deceased at time the spouse remarried

Adrian (cont.)
Luytje
NY Ref Ch mr, 1672
Margaret
NY Ref Ch mr, 1656
Margaret (d)
NY Ref Ch mr, 1643
Maria
Berg Ref mr, 1686
NY Ref Ch mr, 1645
Maria (d)
Alb Ref mr, 1685
NY Ref Ch mr, 1679
Mattina
NY Ref Ch mr, 1663
Nelly
Fltb Ref mr, 1686
Susan (d)
NY Ref Ch mr, 1685
Volkje
Alb Ref mr, 1685
Adrian (d)
Agnes
NY Ref Ch mr, 1663
Catherine
Berg Ref mr, 1691
Margaret
NY Ref Ch mr, 1664
Aegeus
Judith
NY Ref Ch mr, 1663
Aelst
Gertrude
NY Ref Ch mr, 1695
Aert
Alida
King Ref mr, 1684, 1695
Catherine
Berg Ref mr, 1692
NY Ref Ch mr, 1692
Gertrude
Berg Ref mr, 1695
King Ref mr, 1661
Gertrude (d)
King Ref mr, 1682, 1684
Janet
King Ref mr, 1682

Nelly
Fltb Ref mr, 1686
NY Ref Ch mr, 1686
Aert (d)
Alida
King Ref mr, 1698
Anna
King Ref mr, 1665
Lavinia
NY Ref Ch mr, 1662
Susan
NY Ref Ch mr, 1645
Albert
Adriana
NY Ref Ch mr, 1656
Alida
NY Ref Ch mr, 1645
Alida (d)
NY Ref Ch mr, 1683
Catherine
NY Ref Ch mr, 1648, 1685
Catlintje
Fltb Ref mr, 1689
Elpkin
NY Ref Ch mr, 1652
Elsie
NY Ref Ch mr, 1668
Hester
Hack Ref mr, 1695
Hilda
King Ref mr, 1664
Hilda (d)
NY Ref Ch mr, 1652
Isabel
NY Ref Ch mr, 1699
Janet
NY Ref Ch mr, 1679
Julia
Fltb Ref mr, 1681
Magdalena
Berg Ref mr, 1676
Margaret
Fltb Ref mr, 1683
NY Ref Ch mr, 1666
Maria
Alb Ref mr, 1693
NY Ref Ch mr, 1641
Schn Ref mr, 1699

Minnie
Fltb Ref mr, 1684
Nelly
King Ref mr, 1664
Petronella
NY Ref Ch mr, 1688
Sarah
Fltb Ref mr, 1683
NY Ref Ch mr, 1683
Albert (d)
Alida
King Ref mr, 1665
Elizabeth
NY Ref Ch mr, 1659
Elsie
NY Ref Ch mr, 1664
Margaret
NY Ref Ch mr, 1672
Wilhelmina
King Ref mr, 1668
Aldert
Henrietta
NY Ref Ch mr, 1656
Petronella
King Ref mr, 1696
Rachel
King Ref mr, 1698
Sarah
NY Ref Ch mr, 1656
Alexander
see also Sander
Elizabeth
NY Ref Ch mr, 1688
Janet
Fltb Ref mr, 1690
Maria
NY Ref Ch mr, 1663
Ambrose
Maria
NY Ref Ch mr, 1644
Ambrose (d)
Adriana
NY Ref Ch mr, 1691
Amos (d)
Lydia
NY Ref Ch mr, 1687

Groom/Bride Pairs Directory

Andrew
  Adriana
    Alb Ref mr, 1697
  Agnes (d)
    NY Ref Ch mr, 1656
  Anna
    NY Ref Ch mr, 1642, 1660,
    1674, 1684
  Cornelia
    NY Ref Ch mr, 1695
  Elizabeth
    NY Ref Ch mr, 1690
  Elsie
    Alb Ref mr, 1697
  Gertrude
    NY Ref Ch mr, 1672
  Henrietta
    Fltb Ref mr, 1690
  Ida
    Alb Ref mr, 1692
  Janet
    Fltb Ref mr, 1692
    King Ref mr, 1682
  Jemima
    NY Ref Ch mr, 1698
  Joanna
    Berg Ref mr, 1688
  Lambertina
    NY Ref Ch mr, 1652
  Margaret
    NY Ref Ch mr, 1666
  Maria
    Fltb Ref mr, 1683
    NY Ref Ch mr, 1655, 1656,
    1688, 1689
  Patience
    Berg Ref mr, 1668
  Sophia
    NY Ref Ch mr, 1671
  Vroutje
    Berg Ref mr, 1671
  Wits
    NY Ref Ch mr, 1655
Andrew (d)
  Agnes
    NY Ref Ch mr, 1682
  Anna
    NY Ref Ch mr, 1664

  Gertrude
    NY Ref Ch mr, 1660
  Hilda
    King Ref mr, 1664
  Maria
    Fltb Ref mr, 1687
    NY Ref Ch mr, 1662
Anke
  Abigail
    NY Ref Ch mr, 1661
  Anna (d)
    NY Ref Ch mr, 1661
Anthony
  Anna
    NY Ref Ch mr, 1653
  Catherine
    Alb Ref mr, 1692
  Catlintje (d)
    NY Ref Ch mr, 1641
  Dina
    NY Ref Ch mr, 1695
  Elizabeth
    Alb Ref mr, 1698
    Fltb Ref mr, 1684
    King Ref mr, 1696
    NY Ref Ch mr, 1696
  Engel (d)
    Alb Ref mr, 1684
  Frances
    NY Ref Ch mr, 1644
  Gertrude
    Alb Ref mr, 1684
  Henrietta
    NY Ref Ch mr, 1698
  Isabel
    NY Ref Ch mr, 1697
  Janet
    Berg Ref mr, 1692
    King Ref mr, 1667
  Josina
    NY Ref Ch mr, 1685
  Lucy
    NY Ref Ch mr, 1641
  Maria
    Fltb Ref mr, 1682
    NY Ref Ch mr, 1654, 1672
  Maria (d)
    NY Ref Ch mr, 1685

  Ruth
    King Ref mr, 1683
  Wilhelmina
    Alb Ref mr, 1685
Anthony (d)
  Anna
    Alb Ref mr, 1689
  Catherine
    NY Ref Ch mr, 1659
  Elizabeth
    Bkln Ref mr, 1695
  Magdalena
    NY Ref Ch mr, 1659
Arent
  Alida
    King Ref mr, 1687
  Anna
    Bkln Ref mr, 1662
    NY Ref Ch mr, 1694
  Christina
    NY Ref Ch mr, 1665
  Christina (d)
    NY Ref Ch mr, 1685
  Deborah
    NY Ref Ch mr, 1678
  Elizabeth
    King Ref mr, 1686
    NY Ref Ch mr, 1685
  Elizabeth (d)
    NY Ref Ch mr, 1695
  Gertrude
    Alb Ref mr, 1688
  Gertrude (d)
    NY Ref Ch mr, 1665
  Gilberta
    NY Ref Ch mr, 1660
  Gilberta (d)
    NY Ref Ch mr, 1679
  Helena
    NY Ref Ch mr, 1695
  Hester
    NY Ref Ch mr, 1690
  Hilda
    Fltb Ref mr, 1677
  Isabel
    NY Ref Ch mr, 1660

(d) = deceased at time the
spouse remarried

Arent (cont.)
  Janet
    Alb Ref mr, 1684
    NY Ref Ch mr, 1665
  Maria
    Alb Ref mr, 1686, 1698
    King NYGB, 1670
    NY Ref Ch mr, 1679, 1695
  Mattina
    Bkln Ref mr, 1663
  Rebecca
    Bkln Ref mr, 1662
  Sarah
    King Ref mr, 1698
    NY Ref Ch mr, 1680
  Sarah (d)
    NY Ref Ch mr, 1690
  Susan
    NY Ref Ch mr, 1673
  Susan (d)
    NY Ref Ch mr, 1678

Arent (d)
  Agnes
    NY Ref Ch mr, 1647
  Catherine
    NY Ref Ch mr, 1656
  Isabel
    NY Ref Ch mr, 1685
  Lena
    NY Ref Ch mr, 1661
  Rachel
    King Ref mr, 1698

Arnold
  Adriana
    NY Ref Ch mr, 1669
  Adriana (d)
    NY Ref Ch mr, 1675
  Janet
    NY Ref Ch mr, 1675

August
  Anna
    NY Ref Ch mr, 1666, 1697
  Catherine
    Alb Ref mr, 1699
  Janet
    NY Ref Ch mr, 1651

August (d)
  Anna
    NY Ref Ch mr, 1691

Azariah
  Anna
    NY Ref Ch mr, 1690
  Nelly
    NY Ref Ch mr, 1676
  Sarah
    Alb Ref mr, 1697

B

Baltus
  Maria
    NY Ref Ch mr, 1664

Barent
  Agatha
    NY Ref Ch mr, 1657
  Alida
    King Ref mr, 1698
  Anna
    NY Ref Ch mr, 1652, 1664
  Catherine
    Alb Ref mr, 1699
    Fltb Ref mr, 1684
    NY Ref Ch mr, 1662
    Schn Ref mr, 1699
  Catlintje
    Berg Ref mr, 1698
  Christina
    NY Ref Ch mr, 1641, 1675
  Deborah
    NY Ref Ch mr, 1690
  Elsie
    NY Ref Ch mr, 1654
  Gertrude
    Alb Ref mr, 1687
  Gertrude (d)
    NY Ref Ch mr, 1671
  Hilda
    Fltb Ref mr, 1692
  Janet
    NY Ref Ch mr, 1687
  Joanna
    NY Ref Ch mr, 1686
  Margaret
    NY Ref Ch mr, 1658, 1660
  Maria
    NY Ref Ch mr, 1671, 1686
  Sarah
    NY Ref Ch mr, 1685
  Sophia
    NY Ref Ch mr, 1658
  Ursula (d)
    NY Ref Ch mr, 1660

Barent (d)
  Elsie
    NY Ref Ch mr, 1656
  Joanna
    NY Ref Ch mr, 1694

Barne (d)
  Elizabeth
    NY Ref Ch mr, 1645

Bartel
  Eleanor
    Berg Ref mr, 1695
  Harmina
    NY Ref Ch mr, 1662

Bartel (d)
  Gertrude
    NY Ref Ch mr, 1666

Bartholomew
  Adriana
    Alb Ref mr, 1699
  Agatha
    Alb Ref mr, 1698
  Cornelia
    Alb Ref mr, 1686
  Gertrude
    NY Ref Ch mr, 1688

Bartholomew (d)
  Wilhelmina
    NY Ref Ch mr, 1680

Bastian
  Alida
    Berg Ref mr, 1688
  Anna
    NY Ref Ch mr, 1689
  Isabel
    NY Ref Ch mr, 1646
  Maria
    NY Ref Ch mr, 1659, 1680

Benjamin
Anna
Alb Ref mr, 1693
NY Ref Ch mr, 1699
Bernadine
Alb Ref mr, 1688
Cornelia
NY Ref Ch mr, 1693
Elsie
NY Ref Ch mr, 1671
Engel
Alb Ref mr, 1692
Lavinia
Fltb Ref mr, 1688
Maria
NY Ref Ch mr, 1693
Sarah
NY Ref Ch mr, 1670
Sophia
Alb Ref mr, 1699
NY Ref Ch mr, 1697

Benoni
Elizabeth
Alb Ref mr, 1686

Bernard
Alida
NY Ref Ch mr, 1669
Elizabeth
NY Ref Ch mr, 1688
Elsie
NY Ref Ch mr, 1698
Maria
NY Ref Ch mr, 1687

Bouwen
Maria
* NY Ref Ch mr, 1674

Brayer (d)
Elizabeth
NY Ref Ch mr, 1697

Bruno
Elizabeth
Fltb Ref mr, 1682
King Ref mr, 1682

Bruyn
Geesje
NY Ref Ch mr, 1681

Bruyn (d)
Geesje
NY Ref Ch mr, 1688

Burger
Engel
NY Ref Ch mr, 1639

C

Carl
Anna
Alb Ref mr, 1688
Elizabeth
Fltb Ref mr, 1680
Helena
NY Ref Ch mr, 1648
Maria
Fltb Ref mr, 1691
NY Ref Ch mr, 1675
Sarah
NY Ref Ch mr, 1647

Caspar
Agnes
NY Ref Ch mr, 1699
Anna
NY Ref Ch mr, 1682
Catherine
Berg Ref mr, 1671
NY Ref Ch mr, 1696
Dorothy (d)
NY Ref Ch mr, 1652
Elizabeth
NY Ref Ch mr, 1687
Gertrude
NY Ref Ch mr, 1664
Janet
NY Ref Ch mr, 1652, 1695
Janet (d)
NY Ref Ch mr, 1685
Lavinia
NY Ref Ch mr, 1693
Magdalena
NY Ref Ch mr, 1685
Susan (d)
NY Ref Ch mr, 1682

Caspar (d)
Geesje
NY Ref Ch mr, 1652

Charles
Catherine
Berg Ref mr, 1678
Catlintje
NY Ref Ch mr, 1652
Margaret
Fltb Ref mr, 1687
Maria
King Ref mr, 1693

Christian
Agnes
NY Ref Ch mr, 1693
Anna
NY Ref Ch mr, 1665
Catherine
NY Ref Ch mr, 1657
Christina
NY Ref Ch mr, 1657
Engel
NY Ref Ch mr, 1658
Gertrude
NY Ref Ch mr, 1668
Patricia
Fltb Ref mr, 1689
Petronella
NY Ref Ch mr, 1692

Christopher
Catherine
NY Ref Ch mr, 1660, 1661
Catlintje
NY Ref Ch mr, 1697
Gertrude
Fltb Ref mr, 1678
Janet
Berg Ref mr, 1684
Janet (d)
Berg Ref mr, 1698
Maria
NY Ref Ch mr, 1656
Sarah
Berg Ref mr, 1698

Christopher (d)
Catherine
Fltb Ref mr, 1688
NY Ref Ch mr, 1688
Maria
NY Ref Ch mr, 1671

(d) = deceased at time the
spouse remarried

Claude (d)
  Hester
    NY Ref Ch mr, 1687
Clement
  Anna
    NY Ref Ch mr, 1680
Conrad
  Adriana
    Alb Ref mr, 1693
  Anna
    NY Ref Ch mr, 1682
  Apollonia
    Hack Ref mr, 1698
  Catherine
    Alb Ref mr, 1688
  Geesje
    Alb Ref mr, 1697
  Isabel
    NY Ref Ch mr, 1675
  Janet
    NY Ref Ch mr, 1678
  Maria (d)
    NY Ref Ch mr, 1682
Cornelius
  Abigail
    NY Ref Ch mr, 1682
  Abigail (d)
    NY Ref Ch mr, 1685
  Adriana
    Alb Ref mr, 1689
    Fltb Ref mr, 1683
    NY Ref Ch mr, 1683
  Agatha
    Fltb Ref mr, 1683
    Schn Ref mr, 1699
  Agnes (d)
    NY Ref Ch mr, 1692
  Alida
    Berg Ref mr, 1681
    Fltb Ref mr, 1681, 1682,
    1687
    NY Ref Ch mr, 1645
  Anna
    Bkln Ref mr, 1695
    NY Ref Ch mr, 1659, 1675,
    1680, 1689
  Anna (d)
    Alb Ref mr, 1689

Barbara
  King Ref mr, 1688
Bernadine
  NY Ref Ch mr, 1661
Catherine
  Bkln Ref mr, 1685
  Fltb Ref mr, 1685
  NY Ref Ch mr, 1659, 1693
Catherine (d)
  King Ref mr, 1684
  NY Ref Ch mr, 1683
Christina
  NY Ref Ch mr, 1646, 1655,
  1678
Clara
  Alb Ref mr, 1696
Cornelia
  King Ref mr, 1685
  NY Ref Ch mr, 1688
Elizabeth
  NY Ref Ch mr, 1692
Elizabeth (d)
  NY Ref Ch mr, 1659
Elsie
  King Ref mr, 1684, 1695
Eva
  King Ref mr, 1696
  NY Ref Ch mr, 1661, 1696
Gertrude
  Fltb Ref mr, 1678
  NY Ref Ch mr, 1665
Henrietta (d)
  Hack Ref mr, 1699
Hilda
  NY Ref Ch mr, 1654, 1657
Isabel (d)
  NY Ref Ch mr, 1662
Janet
  King Ref mr, 1684, no date
  NY Ref Ch mr, 1696
Joanna
  Bkln Ref mr, 1696
Josina
  NY Ref Ch mr, 1659
Lavinia
  NY Ref Ch mr, 1662
Lievyntie
  NY Ref Ch mr, 1673

Magdalena
  Berg Ref mr, 1677
  Bkln Ref mr, 1691
  Hack Ref mr, 1699
  NY Ref Ch mr, 1652
Margaret
  King Ref mr, 1698
  NY Ref Ch mr, 1658, 1672,
  1695
Maria
  Alb Ref mr, 1689, 1695
  Fltb Ref mr, 1691
  Hack Ref mr, 1696
  King Ref mr, 1685
  NY Ref Ch mr, 1658, 1665,
  1666, 1677, 1680, 1685,
  1688, 1694
Maria (d)
  NY Ref Ch mr, 1693
Mathilda
  Berg Ref mr, 1681
  NY Ref Ch mr, 1665
Nelly
  Fltb Ref mr, 1687
  King Ref mr, 1667
  NY Ref Ch mr, 1662
Nelly (d)
  NY Ref Ch mr, 1678
Nicole
  NY Ref Ch mr, 1642
Nicole (d)
  NY Ref Ch mr, 1659
Sarah
  Bkln Ref mr, 1686
  NY Ref Ch mr, 1669, 1684
Sophia
  Berg Ref mr, 1685
Susan
  Alb Ref mr, 1693
Wilhelmina
  NY Ref Ch mr, 1658, 1693
Cornelius (d)
  Adriana
    Alb Ref mr, 1693
    NY Ref Ch mr, 1656
  Alida
    NY Ref Ch mr, 1644

Groom/Bride Pairs Directory

Anna
 NY Ref Ch mr, 1661, 1686
Apollonia
 NY Ref Ch mr, 1659
Catherine
 Alb Ref mr, 1692
 NY Ref Ch mr, 1657
Christina
 NY Ref Ch mr, 1681
Elizabeth
 Alb Ref mr, 1691
Eunice
 NY Ref Ch mr, 1686
Gertrude
 NY Ref Ch mr, 1671
Henrietta
 Berg Ref mr, 1698
Magdalena
 NY Ref Ch mr, 1657, 1683
Margaret
 NY Ref Ch mr, 1686
Maria
 NY Ref Ch mr, 1663
Nicole
 King Ref mr, 1662
Sarah
 NY Ref Ch mr, 1683
Cosine
Catlintje
 NY Ref Ch mr, 1699

D

Daniel
Anna
 Alb Ref mr, 1696
 NY Ref Ch mr, 1686
Catherine
 NY Ref Ch mr, 1661
Christina
 Fltb Ref mr, 1681
 NY Ref Ch mr, 1681
Deborah
 Alb Ref mr, 1695
Elizabeth
 Alb Ref mr, 1696, 1697
Engel
 Berg Ref mr, 1692

Geesje
 Hack Ref mr, 1696
Helena
 NY Ref Ch mr, 1696
Margaret
 NY Ref Ch mr, 1685
Maria
 Schn Ref mr, 1696
Maria (d)
 NY Ref Ch mr, 1685
Nelly
 Fltb Ref mr, 1685
Sarah
 NY Ref Ch mr, 1673, 1674
Theodora
 Alb Ref mr, 1698
Daniel (d)
Catherine
 Fltb Ref mr, 1679
David
Anna
 Berg Ref mr, 1692
Catherine
 NY Ref Ch mr, 1668
Catlintje
 NY Ref Ch mr, 1657
Christina
 NY Ref Ch mr, 1659, 1696
Cornelia
 King Ref mr, 1689
Elizabeth
 NY Ref Ch mr, 1689
Elsie
 Alb Ref mr, 1694
Helena
 Fltb Ref mr, 1681
 NY Ref Ch mr, 1681, 1691
Helena (d)
 NY Ref Ch mr, 1699
Joanna
 Alb Ref mr, 1695
Letitia
 NY Ref Ch mr, 1658
Maria
 NY Ref Ch mr, 1692, 1699
Rachel
 NY Ref Ch mr, 1675, 1694

Sarah
 Hack Ref mr, 1697
David (d)
Elpkin
 NY Ref Ch mr, 1652
Deliverance
Engel
 NY Ref Ch mr, 1695
Dennis
Rachel
 NY Ref Ch mr, 1696
Didlove
Elsie
 NY Ref Ch mr, 1680
Didlove (d)
Elsie
 NY Ref Ch mr, 1689
Dietrich
Catherine
 Fltb Ref mr, 1678
Dietrich (d)
Eunice
 NY Ref Ch mr, 1657
Dionysius
Elizabeth
 Fltb Ref mr, 1682
Helena
 Fltb Ref mr, 1685
Maria
 Fltb Ref mr, 1691
Dirk
Adriana
 NY Ref Ch mr, 1650, 1693
Agatha
 NY Ref Ch mr, 1650
Anna
 Alb Ref mr, 1686
 Bkln Ref mr, 1662
 King Ref mr, 1685
 NY Ref Ch mr, 1654, 1663,
 1664
Anna (d)
 NY Ref Ch mr, 1691
Catherine
 Berg Ref mr, 1698
 King Ref mr, 1662, 1695
Catlintje
 NY Ref Ch mr, 1669

(d) = deceased at time the
spouse remarried

Groom/Bride Pairs Directory

Dirk (cont.)
Elizabeth
 Berg Ref mr, 1672
 Fltb Ref mr, 1684
 NY Ref Ch mr, 1657, 1672,
  1684, 1698
Elizabeth (d)
 NY Ref Ch mr, 1672
Emma
 NY Ref Ch mr, 1672
Eva
 NY Ref Ch mr, 1675
Geesje
 NY Ref Ch mr, 1658, 1667
Gertrude
 NY Ref Ch mr, 1659, 1660
Henrietta
 NY Ref Ch mr, 1691
Hester
 Berg Ref mr, 1681
Janet
 King Ref mr, 1698
 NY Ref Ch mr, 1641, 1670
Janet (d)
 NY Ref Ch mr, 1659
Lavinia (d)
 NY Ref Ch mr, 1663
Magdalena
 King Ref mr, 1692
Maria
 Fltb Ref mr, 1691
 NY Ref Ch mr, 1646, 1660,
  1687
Rachel
 Alb Ref mr, 1687
 NY Ref Ch mr, 1677, 1679
Sophia
 Alb Ref mr, 1687
 Berg Ref mr, 1698
 NY Ref Ch mr, 1695
Theodora (d)
 NY Ref Ch mr, 1670
Ursula
 NY Ref Ch mr, 1674
Wybrecht (d)
 NY Ref Ch mr, 1677

Dirk (d)
Anna
 Fltb Ref mr, 1679
Catherine
 NY Ref Ch mr, 1657
Elizabeth
 NY Ref Ch mr, 1688
Gertrude
 NY Ref Ch mr, 1687
Ida
 Alb Ref mr, 1693
Maria
 NY Ref Ch mr, 1695
Ditmar
Gerarda
 Bkln Ref mr, 1664
 NY Ref Ch mr, 1664
Dominic
Dorothy
 NY Ref Ch mr, 1694
Frances
 NY Ref Ch mr, 1652
Magdalena
 Fltb Ref mr, 1689
Rebecca
 Alb Ref mr, 1699
Dominic (d)
Maria
 NY Ref Ch mr, 1689
Douw
Catherine
 Fltb Ref mr, 1688
Maria
 Alb Ref mr, 1685

E

Edward
Elizabeth
 Berg Ref mr, 1684
Elsie
 Berg Ref mr, 1688
 NY Ref Ch mr, 1688
Gertrude
 Berg Ref mr, 1681
 NY Ref Ch mr, 1681
Helena
 NY Ref Ch mr, 1692

Maria
 Alb Ref mr, 1699
Sarah
 NY Ref Ch mr, 1674
Edward (d)
Janet
 NY Ref Ch mr, 1645
Sarah
 NY Ref Ch mr, 1689
Egbert
Anna
 King Ref mr, 1684
 NY Ref Ch mr, 1639
Elsie
 NY Ref Ch mr, 1678
Engel
 NY Ref Ch mr, 1641
Gertrude
 NY Ref Ch mr, 1662
Egbert (d)
Harmina
 NY Ref Ch mr, 1664
Egmont
Anna
 NY Ref Ch mr, 1642
Elias
Catlintje
 NY Ref Ch mr, 1671
Cornelia
 Hack Ref mr, 1697
 NY Ref Ch mr, 1672
Elizabeth
 NY Ref Ch mr, 1678
Margaret
 NY Ref Ch mr, 1665
Maria
 NY Ref Ch mr, 1674
Elias (d)
Anna
 NY Ref Ch mr, 1686
Catherine
 Alb Ref mr, 1695
Cornelia
 NY Ref Ch mr, 1692
Elken
Janet
 NY Ref Ch mr, 1647

Elsy
  Elizabeth
    NY Ref Ch mr, 1697
Emanuel
  Christina
    NY Ref Ch mr, 1644
  Dorothy
    NY Ref Ch mr, 1653
  Dorothy (d)
    NY Ref Ch mr, 1689
  Maria
    NY Ref Ch mr, 1671, 1689
  Phizithiaen
    NY Ref Ch mr, 1642
Engelbert
  Cornelia
    NY Ref Ch mr, 1678
Enoch
  Elizabeth (d)
    NY Ref Ch mr, 1699
  Margaret
    Berg Ref mr, 1691
    NY Ref Ch mr, 1691
  Maria
    NY Ref Ch mr, 1699
  Theodora
    Berg Ref mr, 1670
    NY Ref Ch mr, 1670
  Theodora (d)
    Berg Ref mr, 1691
    NY Ref Ch mr, 1691
Ephraim
  Elizabeth
    NY Ref Ch mr, 1679
Ephraim (d)
  Elizabeth
    NY Ref Ch mr, 1692
Evert
  Anna
    Alb Ref mr, 1688
  Bridget
    NY Ref Ch mr, 1670
  Catherine
    NY Ref Ch mr, 1690
  Charity
    King Ref mr, 1697
  Elizabeth
    Alb Ref mr, 1686

Elsie
    NY Ref Ch mr, 1657
  Gertrude
    King Ref mr, 1688
  Henrietta
    NY Ref Ch mr, 1646
  Hilda
    NY Ref Ch mr, 1669
  Janet
    NY Ref Ch mr, 1671
  Joanna
    NY Ref Ch mr, 1686
  Josina
    Alb Ref mr, 1689
  Lavinia
    NY Ref Ch mr, 1693
  Margaret
    NY Ref Ch mr, 1695
  Margaret (d)
    NY Ref Ch mr, 1669
  Maria
    NY Ref Ch mr, 1673
  Mathilda
    Fltb Ref mr, 1690
    NY Ref Ch mr, 1685
  Susan
    NY Ref Ch mr, 1644
Evert (d)
  Anna
    NY Ref Ch mr, 1663
  Bridget
    NY Ref Ch mr, 1678
  Cornelia
    NY Ref Ch mr, 1681
  Janet
    NY Ref Ch mr, 1698

F

Felix (d)
  Maria
    NY Ref Ch mr, 1645
Francis
  Adriana
    Alb Ref mr, 1688
  Alida
    NY Ref Ch mr, 1665

  Alida (d)
    NY Ref Ch mr, 1675
  Anna
    NY Ref Ch mr, 1675, 1691,
    1695
  Anna (d)
    NY Ref Ch mr, 1683
  Barbara (d)
    NY Ref Ch mr, 1691
  Catherine
    NY Ref Ch mr, 1657, 1659,
    1679, 1697
  Dorothy
    NY Ref Ch mr, 1688
  Elizabeth
    NY Ref Ch mr, 1664, 1697
  Elsie
    Alb Ref mr, 1689
  Gertrude
    NY Ref Ch mr, 1661, 1685
  Gertrude (d)
    NY Ref Ch mr, 1692
  Helena
    NY Ref Ch mr, 1683
  Isabel
    NY Ref Ch mr, 1670
  Janet
    Hack Ref mr, 1696
    NY Ref Ch mr, 1659, 1685
  Leonora (d)
    NY Ref Ch mr, 1685
  Lucretia
    NY Ref Ch mr, 1646, 1680
  Margaret
    Bkln Ref mr, 1661
    NY Ref Ch mr, 1692
  Maria
    Berg Ref mr, 1690
  Maria (d)
    NY Ref Ch mr, 1697
  Palassa
    NY Ref Ch mr, 1642
  Rebecca
    NY Ref Ch mr, 1683
  Rose
    NY Ref Ch mr, 1656
  Walburg
    NY Ref Ch mr, 1660

(d) = deceased at time the
spouse remarried

Francis (d)

Anna
  Alb Ref mr, 1687, 1692
  NY Ref Ch mr, 1642, 1697
Catherine
  NY Ref Ch mr, 1679
Dorothy
  NY Ref Ch mr, 1694
Elizabeth
  Fltb Ref mr, 1679
Emma
  NY Ref Ch mr, 1672
Gertrude
  NY Ref Ch mr, 1665
Isabel
  NY Ref Ch mr, 1684
Maria
  NY Ref Ch mr, 1670
Palassa
  NY Ref Ch mr, 1642
Sophia
  Alb Ref mr, 1697

Fred

Anna
  NY Ref Ch mr, 1659
Apollonia (d)
  NY Ref Ch mr, 1663
Catherine
  Berg Ref mr, 1672
  NY Ref Ch mr, 1657, 1692
Christina (d)
  NY Ref Ch mr, 1657
Dina
  Fltb Ref mr, 1681
Elizabeth
  King Ref mr, 1681
Engel
  King Ref mr, 1666
Hester
  NY Ref Ch mr, 1677
Lea
  Fltb Ref mr, 1687
Margaret
  Alb Ref mr, 1692
  NY Ref Ch mr, 1656, 1662
Margaret (d)
  NY Ref Ch mr, 1692

Maria
  NY Ref Ch mr, 1663

G

Gabriel

Eunice
  NY Ref Ch mr, 1657
Gertrude
  Fltb Ref mr, 1692
Janet
  NY Ref Ch mr, 1658
Judith
  NY Ref Ch mr, 1674
Maria
  NY Ref Ch mr, 1699

Galeyn

Henrietta
  NY Ref Ch mr, 1668

Garret

Agnes
  Alb Ref mr, 1698
  Berg Ref mr, 1681
Alida
  Alb Ref mr, 1684
  NY Ref Ch mr, 1651
Alida (d)
  NY Ref Ch mr, 1659
Anna
  Fltb Ref mr, 1687
  NY Ref Ch mr, 1665
Barbara
  Alb Ref mr, 1696
Bernadine (d)
  NY Ref Ch mr, 1683
Bridget
  Alb Ref mr, 1687
Catherine
  Alb Ref mr, 1690, 1692
  Berg Ref mr, 1691
  Fltb Ref mr, 1689
  NY Ref Ch mr, 1659, 1685, 1689
Catherine (d)
  NY Ref Ch mr, 1697
Christina
  Fltb Ref mr, 1683
Cornelia
  Fltb Ref mr, 1682, 1691

Deborah
  NY Ref Ch mr, 1697
Dorothy
  NY Ref Ch mr, 1696
Elizabeth
  Alb Ref mr, 1693
  NY Ref Ch mr, 1659, 1690
Elsie
  NY Ref Ch mr, 1693
Gertrude
  King Ref mr, 1696
  NY Ref Ch mr, 1647, 1670
Harmina
  NY Ref Ch mr, 1654, 1664
Harmina (d)
  King Ref mr, 1696
Henrietta
  NY Ref Ch mr, 1663
Ida (d)
  NY Ref Ch mr, 1659
Isabel
  Berg Ref mr, 1692
  NY Ref Ch mr, 1673
Janet
  Fltb Ref mr, 1682, 1685, 1692
  NY Ref Ch mr, 1693
Janet (d)
  NY Ref Ch mr, 1693
Jemima
  King Ref mr, 1668
Joanna
  Fltb Ref mr, 1684
Josina
  NY Ref Ch mr, 1679
Lavinia
  NY Ref Ch mr, 1680
Magdalena
  Fltb Ref mr, 1677
  King Ref mr, 1684, 1692
  NY Ref Ch mr, 1659, 1693
Margaret
  King Ref mr, 1685
Maria
  Alb Ref mr, 1689
  NY Ref Ch mr, 1646, 1683, 1698

Maria (d)
  NY Ref Ch mr, 1679
Nelly
  Bkln Ref mr, 1661
  NY Ref Ch mr, 1682
Patricia
  NY Ref Ch mr, 1654
Reyntje (d)
  Alb Ref mr, 1693
Sarah
  Alb Ref mr, 1694
  NY Ref Ch mr, 1692, 1698
Susan
  NY Ref Ch mr, 1681
Vroutje
  Berg Ref mr, 1684
  Hack Ref mr, 1696
  NY Ref Ch mr, 1684
Vroutje (d)
  Berg Ref mr, 1691
Wilhelmina
  Fltb Ref mr, 1685
Garret (d)
Adriana
  Alb Ref mr, 1692
Alida
  Alb Ref mr, 1689
  King Ref mr, 1684
  NY Ref Ch mr, 1645, 1659
Elizabeth
  NY Ref Ch mr, 1664
Gertrude
  NY Ref Ch mr, 1643
Hester
  NY Ref Ch mr, 1665
Hilda
  NY Ref Ch mr, 1669
Jemima
  Berg Ref mr, 1672
Josina
  NY Ref Ch mr, 1685
Lavinia
  NY Ref Ch mr, 1693
Magdalena
  King Ref mr, 1696
George
Barbara
  NY Ref Ch mr, 1656

Elizabeth
  Alb Ref mr, 1691
  NY Ref Ch mr, 1693
Isabel
  NY Ref Ch mr, 1684
Margaret
  NY Ref Ch mr, 1688
Maria (d)
  Alb Ref mr, 1691
Rebecca
  NY Ref Ch mr, 1647
Vroutje
  NY Ref Ch mr, 1692
George (d)
Gertrude
  NY Ref Ch mr, 1641
Gerald
Adriana
  Alb Ref mr, 1692
Anna (d)
  Alb Ref mr, 1692
Gerbrant
Maria
  Berg Ref mr, 1674
Gerlach
Elizabeth
  NY Ref Ch mr, 1654
Gideon
Agnes (d)
  NY Ref Ch mr, 1683
Bernadine
  NY Ref Ch mr, 1683
Gilbert
Alida (d)
  NY Ref Ch mr, 1659
Catherine
  NY Ref Ch mr, 1643
Elizabeth
  NY Ref Ch mr, 1655
Janet
  Fltb Ref mr, 1689
  NY Ref Ch mr, 1688
Magdalena
  NY Ref Ch mr, 1659
Margaret
  King Ref mr, 1695
Nelly
  NY Ref Ch mr, 1659

Giles
Elizabeth
  Alb Ref mr, 1699
  Schn Ref mr, 1699
Elsie
  NY Ref Ch mr, 1642
Hilda
  NY Ref Ch mr, 1689
Maria
  NY Ref Ch mr, 1680
Rachel
  Alb Ref mr, 1695
Giles (d)
Henrietta
  NY Ref Ch mr, 1685
Godfrey
Elizabeth
  NY Ref Ch mr, 1664
Godwin (d)
Anna
  NY Ref Ch mr, 1685
Govert
Maria
  NY Ref Ch mr, 1649
Gowing (d)
Maria
  NY Ref Ch mr, 1699
Gregory
Frances
  NY Ref Ch mr, 1642
Gustave
Nicole
  NY Ref Ch mr, 1689
Priscilla (d)
  NY Ref Ch mr, 1689

H
Hacke
Anna
  NY Ref Ch mr, 1653
Hendrick
Adriana
  Fltb Ref mr, 1685
Agnes
  NY Ref Ch mr, 1689
Alida
  King Ref mr, 1664

(d) = deceased at time the
spouse remarried

Groom/Bride Pairs Directory

Hendrick (cont.)

Alida (d)
  NY Ref Ch mr, 1691

Anna
  Alb Ref mr, 1695
  Fltb Ref mr, 1679, 1680
  King Ref mr, 1663, 1684,
  1696, 1697
  NY Ref Ch mr, 1654, 1660,
  1677, 1679, **1680, 1686**

Anna (d)
  Alb Ref mr, 1688

Catherine
  Alb Ref mr, 1684, 1688,
  1695
  Fltb Ref mr, 1686, 1687
  King NYGB, 1672
  NY Ref Ch mr, 1652, 1660,
  1684, 1689, **1693, 1699**

Cecilia
  NY Ref Ch mr, 1661

Christina
  NY Ref Ch mr, 1659

Cornelia
  Alb Ref mr, 1685, 1698

Deborah
  Alb Ref mr, 1692, 1694
  King Ref mr, 1679

Deborah (d)
  NY Ref Ch mr, 1675

Elizabeth
  NY Ref Ch mr, 1699

Elsie
  King Ref mr, 1666

Frances (d)
  NY Ref Ch mr, 1650

Geesje
  Berg Ref mr, 1666

Gerarda
  King Ref mr, 1685

Gertrude
  Fltb Ref mr, 1680
  King Ref mr, 1688
  NY Ref Ch mr, 1655, 1657
  1663

Gilberta (d)
  Alb Ref mr, 1695

Hester
  Fltb Ref mr, 1688

Janet
  Fltb Ref mr, 1680
  King Ref mr, 1679
  NY Ref Ch mr, 1664, 1692

Joanna
  NY Ref Ch mr, 1681, 1698

Lavinia
  NY Ref Ch mr, 1697

Magdalena
  Bkln Ref mr, 1662
  NY Ref Ch mr, 1649, 1652,
  1662, 1675, **1697**

Magdalena (d)
  NY Ref Ch mr, 1686

Margaret
  NY Ref Ch mr, 1660, 1662,
  1686, 1687

Maria
  Alb Ref mr, 1688, 1689,
  1692
  Berg Ref mr, 1678, 1679,
  1685
  Fltb Ref mr, 1679, 1690
  NY Ref Ch mr, 1642, 1650,
  1655, 1672, **1673, 1676,**
  1685, 1691, 1694,
  1698, 1699

Martha
  NY Ref Ch mr, 1696

Mathilda
  NY Ref Ch mr, 1673

Nelly
  Alb Ref mr, 1697
  Berg Ref mr, 1669
  Fltb Ref mr, 1679
  King Ref mr, 1676
  NY Ref Ch mr, 1669, 1674

Petronella
  NY Ref Ch mr, 1676

Rachel
  NY Ref Ch mr, 1656

     rah
     ef mr, 1686
     h mr, 1644, 1660,

Sophia
  NY Ref Ch mr, 1682, 1694

Sophia (d)
  NY Ref Ch mr, 1669

Susan
  NY Ref Ch mr, 1644

Volkje
  NY Ref Ch mr, 1655

Wilhelmina
  Fltb Ref mr, 1685

Hendrick (d)

Anna
  NY Ref Ch mr, 1692, 1695

Catherine
  NY Ref Ch mr, 1643, 1645,
  1689

Cecilia
  NY Ref Ch mr, 1664

Elsie
  King Ref mr, 1684
  NY Ref Ch mr, 1660

Gerarda
  King Ref mr, 1698

Gertrude
  NY Ref Ch mr, 1653, 1664

Helena
  NY Ref Ch mr, 1685

Ida
  Alb Ref mr, 1692

Luytje
  NY Ref Ch mr, 1672

Margaret
  NY Ref Ch mr, 1688

Maria
  Alb Ref mr, 1696
  NY Ref Ch mr, 1684

Nelly
  Alb Ref mr, 1695

Rachel
  NY Ref Ch mr, 1677

Sophia
  Alb Ref mr, 1692

Herbert

Maria
  Alb Ref mr, 1695

Herman

Agatha (d)
  NY Ref Ch mr, 1682

(d) = deceased at time the
spouse remarried

Groom/Bride Pairs Directory

Anna
  Berg Ref mr, 1668, 1690
  NY Ref Ch mr, 1668, 1681
Anna (d)
  Hack Ref mr, 1695
Bridget
  NY Ref Ch mr, 1682
Bridget (d)
  NY Ref Ch mr, 1688
Christina
  King Ref mr, 1682
Clara (d)
  NY Ref Ch mr, 1662
Cornelia
  Fltb Ref mr, 1682
Elizabeth
  NY Ref Ch mr, 1645
Eunice
  NY Ref Ch mr, 1688
Geesje
  NY Ref Ch mr, 1688
Gertrude
  Berg Ref mr, 1686
  Hack Ref mr, 1695
Janet
  Berg Ref mr, 1678
Lavinia
  NY Ref Ch mr, 1660
Lucretia
  NY Ref Ch mr, 1674
Magdalena
  NY Ref Ch mr, 1657, 1682
Margaret
  Alb Ref mr, 1691
  NY Ref Ch mr, 1654, 1686
Maria
  NY Ref Ch mr, 1650, 1662, 1676
Nelly
  Bkln Ref mr, 1695
Rachel
  King Ref mr, 1695
Wybrecht
  NY Ref Ch mr, 1679
Herman (d)
Anna
  NY Ref Ch mr, 1682

Gertrude
  NY Ref Ch mr, 1670
Margaret
  NY Ref Ch mr, 1660, 1691
Maria
  Alb Ref mr, 1695
Hessel
Elizabeth
  Berg Ref mr, 1690
  NY Ref Ch mr, 1690
Heyman
Maria
  NY Ref Ch mr, 1683
Hieronymus
Joanna
  NY Ref Ch mr, 1659
Nelly
  Fltb Ref mr, 1691
Rebecca
  Alb Ref mr, 1684
Susan
  NY Ref Ch mr, 1682
Hieronymus (d)
Susan
  NY Ref Ch mr, 1699
Hildebrand
Alida
  King Ref mr, 1688
Anna
  Alb Ref mr, 1689
Hubert
Henrietta
  King Ref mr, 1679
Janet
  Bkln Ref mr, 1662
  NY Ref Ch mr, 1662
Maria
  Alb Ref mr, 1693
  NY Ref Ch mr, 1656
Wilhelmina
  NY Ref Ch mr, 1679
Hugh
Anna (d)
  NY Ref Ch mr, 1643
Catherine
  NY Ref Ch mr, 1643
Elizabeth
  NY Ref Ch mr, 1696

Maria
  NPal Ref mr, 1690
Hugh (d)
Catherine
  NY Ref Ch mr, 1648
Humphrey
Anna
  King Ref mr, 1684

I

Ide
Anna
  NY Ref Ch mr, 1698
Hilda
  NY Ref Ch mr, 1652
Isabel
  NY Ref Ch mr, 1685
Increase
Gertrude
  Hack Ref mr, 1699
Isaac
Adriana
  Fltb Ref mr, 1677
Alida
  NY Ref Ch mr, 1689, 1690, 1693
Anna
  Alb Ref mr, 1686
  NY Ref Ch mr, 1686
Anna (d)
  NY Ref Ch mr, 1691
Catlintje
  NY Ref Ch mr, 1653, 1680
Catlintje (d)
  NY Ref Ch mr, 1675
Cornelia
  Berg Ref mr, 1690
  NY Ref Ch mr, 1674
Cornelia (d)
  NY Ref Ch mr, 1680
Dorothy (d)
  NY Ref Ch mr, 1679
Elizabeth
  NY Ref Ch mr, 1652, 1653, 1681
Elizabeth (d)
  NY Ref Ch mr, 1663

Isaac (cont.)

Gertrude
Fltb Ref mr, 1687

Harmina
NY Ref Ch mr, 1685, 1691

Hester
NY Ref Ch mr, 1696

Hester (d)
NY Ref Ch mr, 1695

Ida
Berg Ref mr, 1684

Janet
Alb Ref mr, 1698
NY Ref Ch mr, 1659, 1694, 1695

Lavinia
Fltb Ref mr, 1689

Margaret
NY Ref Ch mr, 1682

Maria
Alb Ref mr, 1689, 1696
Fltb Ref mr, 1687
King Ref mr, 1683
NPal Ref mr, 1683
NY Ref Ch mr, 1663, 1675, 1687, 1693

Maria (d)
Alb Ref mr, 1698

Martha
NY Ref Ch mr, 1697

Nelly
NY Ref Ch mr, 1690

Sarah
NY Ref Ch mr, 1641, 1684, 1686

Temperence
NY Ref Ch mr, 1679

Isaac (d)

Alida
NY Ref Ch mr, 1698

Catlintje
NY Ref Ch mr, 1697

Elizabeth
NY Ref Ch mr, 1680

Harmina
NY Ref Ch mr, 1694, 1697

J

Jacob

Adriana
King Ref mr, 1662

Alida
Berg Ref mr, 1675
NY Ref Ch mr, 1671, 1687, 1695

Alida (d)
Berg Ref mr, 1695
NY Ref Ch mr, 1684

Anna
Alb Ref mr, 1688, 1691, 1692
Bkln Ref mr, 1695
Fltb Ref mr, 1682, 1691
Hack Ref mr, 1699
King Ref mr, 1665, 1695
NY Ref Ch mr, 1659, 1661, 1674, 1682, **1685**, **1686**

Barbara (d)
Alb Ref mr, 1695

Catherine
Alb Ref mr, 1687
Fltb Ref mr, 1684
NY Ref Ch mr, 1657, 1679, 1685, 1695

Catherine (d)
Alb Ref mr, 1691, 1696
Hack Ref mr, 1699

Catlintje
King Ref mr, 1698
NY Ref Ch mr, 1663

Christina
NY Ref Ch mr, 1683

Cornelia
NY Ref Ch mr, 1647, 1653, 1672

Elizabeth
Bkln Ref mr, 1677
King Ref mr, 1689
NY Ref Ch mr, 1652, 1674, 1688, 1697

Elsie
Bkln Ref mr, 1677
NY Ref Ch mr, 1663

Eva

King Ref mr, 1698
NY Ref Ch mr, 1691, 1697

Gertrude
Alb Ref mr, 1688
Berg Ref mr, 1672
Fltb Ref mr, 1684, 1687
Hack Ref mr, 1697
King Ref mr, 1688
NY Ref Ch mr, 1678, 1688

Gertrude (d)
Berg Ref mr, 1672

Henrietta
NY Ref Ch mr, 1685

Hilda
NY Ref Ch mr, 1658

Ida
Alb Ref mr, 1693

Isabel
King Ref mr, 1678

Janet
Fltb Ref mr, 1683, 1684
King Ref mr, 1698
NY Ref Ch mr, 1650, 1678, 1687

Jemima
Alb Ref mr, 1694
Schn Ref mr, 1694

Lydia
NY Ref Ch mr, 1698

Magdalena
NY Ref Ch mr, 1655, 1657, 1677

Margaret
Alb Ref mr, 1691
Berg Ref mr, 1695
King Ref mr, 1667
NY Ref Ch mr, 1652, 1655, 1688, 1693, **1695**

Margaret (d)
NY Ref Ch mr, 1699

Maria
Alb Ref mr, 1696
Bkln Ref mr, 1690
Fltb Ref mr, 1679, 1685, 1687
NY Ref Ch mr, 1654, 1676,

1678, 1679, 1684, 1697,
1699
Nelly
  Hack Ref mr, 1699
  NY Ref Ch mr, 1655, 1692
Nelly (d)
  NY Ref Ch mr, 1661
Patricia
  Berg Ref mr, 1696
Rebecca
  NY Ref Ch mr, 1648
Ruth
  Berg Ref mr, 1692
  NY Ref Ch mr, 1693
Sarah
  Alb Ref mr, 1695
  Fltb Ref mr, 1694
  NY Ref Ch mr, 1664, 1699
Sophia
  Fltb Ref mr, 1678
  NY Ref Ch mr, 1666, 1678
Sophia (d)
  NY Ref Ch mr, 1677
Susan
  King Ref mr, 1698
Theodora
  King Ref mr, 1698
Vroutje (d)
  NY Ref Ch mr, 1657
Wybrecht
  Berg Ref mr, 1681
Jacob (d)
Catherine
  Alb Ref mr, 1696
  NY Ref Ch mr, 1657, 1668
Christina
  NY Ref Ch mr, 1659
Cornelia
  NY Ref Ch mr, 1653
Elizabeth
  Alb Ref mr, 1691
Eunice
  NY Ref Ch mr, 1687
Gertrude
  King Ref mr, 1661
Janet
  NY Ref Ch mr, 1695

Magdalena
  NY Ref Ch mr, 1675
Margaret
  NY Ref Ch mr, 1695
Maria
  Alb Ref mr, 1689
  NY Ref Ch mr, 1686
Sarah
  NY Ref Ch mr, 1664
Jacques
Anna
  Fltb Ref mr, 1680
  NY Ref Ch mr, 1689
Cornelia
  NY Ref Ch mr, 1692
Eva
  NY Ref Ch mr, 1683
Maria
  Bkln Ref mr, 1663
  Fltb Ref mr, 1685
Sarah
  Fltb Ref mr, 1680
Jacques (d)
Anna
  NY Ref Ch mr, 1652
Hester
  NY Ref Ch mr, 1640
Maria
  NY Ref Ch mr, 1663
James
Anna
  NY Ref Ch mr, 1659, 1694
Anna (d)
  NY Ref Ch mr, 1659
Bathsheba
  NY Ref Ch mr, 1683
Catherine
  NY Ref Ch mr, 1659
Dorothy
  NY Ref Ch mr, 1692
Elizabeth
  King Ref mr, 1696
  NY Ref Ch mr, 1685
Gertrude
  Alb Ref mr, 1699
Janet
  NY Ref Ch mr, 1689

Margaret
  NY Ref Ch mr, 1665
Maria
  NY Ref Ch mr, 1695
Martha
  Berg Ref mr, 1697
Rebecca
  NY Ref Ch mr, 1644
James (d)
Elizabeth
  King Ref mr, 1683
  NY Ref Ch mr, 1695
Janet
  NY Ref Ch mr, 1689
Margaret
  NY Ref Ch mr, 1665
Maria
  Berg Ref mr, 1686
Jeremiah
Catherine
  NY Ref Ch mr, 1664
Janet
  NY Ref Ch mr, 1686
Maria
  NY Ref Ch mr, 1662
Rachel
  Schn Ref mr, 1697
Jochem
Anna
  King Ref mr, 1689
Elizabeth
  King Ref mr, 1676
  NY Ref Ch mr, 1667
Maria
  Berg Ref mr, 1686
Petronella
  King Ref mr, 1679
Petronella (d)
  King Ref mr, 1689
Jochem (d)
Lena
  NY Ref Ch mr, 1654
Magdalena
  NY Ref Ch mr, 1659
Jonas
Catherine
  Alb Ref mr, 1696
  NY Ref Ch mr, 1664

(d) = deceased at time the
spouse remarried

Jonas (cont.)
  Eva
    NY Ref Ch mr, 1688
  Magdalena
    Alb Ref mr, 1683
    Magdalena (d)
    Alb Ref mr, 1696
  Priscilla
    NY Ref Ch mr, 1661
Jonas (d)
  Eva
    NY Ref Ch mr, 1698
Jonathan
  Catherine
    Alb Ref mr, 1696
    NY Ref Ch mr, 1679
  Catlintje
    Alb Ref mr, 1697
  Lavinia
    Fltb Ref mr, 1692
  Lea
    Alb Ref mr, 1693
  Maria
    Alb Ref mr, 1695
Joost
see also Joseph
  Catherine
    Bkln Ref mr, 1663
    NY Ref Ch mr, 1688
  Elizabeth
    King Ref mr, 1668
    NY Ref Ch mr, 1662, 1694
  Elizabeth (d)
    NY Ref Ch mr, 1681
  Maria
    NY Ref Ch mr, 1681
  Sarah
    King Ref mr, 1682
  Sophia
    King Ref mr, 1663
    NY Ref Ch mr, 1663
  Sophia (d)
    King Ref mr, 1668
Joost (d)
see also Joseph
  Magdalena
    Bkln Ref mr, 1695

Joris
  Adriana
    NY Ref Ch mr, 1682
  Anna
    Fltb Ref mr, 1690
    NY Ref Ch mr, 1691, 1695
  Catherine
    Fltb Ref mr, 1689
  Elizabeth
    NY Ref Ch mr, 1688
  Geesje
    NY Ref Ch mr, 1652
  Janet
    NY Ref Ch mr, 1674
  Magdalena
    NY Ref Ch mr, 1672
  Maria
    Bkln Ref mr, 1685
    King Ref mr, 1696
    NY Ref Ch mr, 1666
  Nelly
    Bkln Ref mr, 1695
  Sarah
    Fltb Ref mr, 1678
  Sophia
    Fltb Ref mr, 1684
  Susan
    NY Ref Ch mr, 1699
Joris (d)
  Joanna
    NY Ref Ch mr, 1681
  Magdalena
    NY Ref Ch mr, 1696
  Maria
    NY Ref Ch mr, 1692
Joseph
see also Joost
  Alida
    Fltb Ref mr, 1687
  Anna
    Fltb Ref mr, 1692
    NY Ref Ch mr, 1696
  Elizabeth
    Berg Ref mr, 1678
    Fltb Ref mr, 1681
  Jemima
    NY Ref Ch mr, 1650

  Margaret
    NY Ref Ch mr, 1695
  Maria
    NY Ref Ch mr, 1683
  Sophia
    Alb Ref mr, 1688
    Fltb Ref mr, 1677
Joseph (d)
see also Joost
  Janet
    Fltb Ref mr, 1687
  Maria
    Bkln Ref mr, 1685
Joshua
  Engel
    NY Ref Ch mr, 1695
Josiah
  Alida
    Fltb Ref mr, 1682
    NY Ref Ch mr, 1682
Josiah (d)
  Elizabeth
    NY Ref Ch mr, 1694
Jurian
  Adriana
    NY Ref Ch mr, 1693
  Agnes
    Alb Ref mr, 1686
  Anna
    Fltb Ref mr, 1684
    Hack Ref mr, 1699
  Catherine
    NY Ref Ch mr, 1645
  Frederica
    Berg Ref mr, 1667
  Geesje
    Berg Ref mr, 1690
    NY Ref Ch mr, 1695
  Geesje (d)
    Hack Ref mr, 1699
  Harmina
    NY Ref Ch mr, 1658
  Hester
    NY Ref Ch mr, 1673
  Maria
    Fltb Ref mr, 1679
    NY Ref Ch mr, 1652

Groom/Bride Pairs Directory

Jurian (d)
Janet
NY Ref Ch mr, 1654
Justus
Anna
NY Ref Ch mr, 1697
Vaerende?
NY Ref Ch mr, 1673
Justus (d)
Catherine
NY Ref Ch mr, 1697

K

Kier
Elizabeth
NY Ref Ch mr, 1668
Janet (d)
NY Ref Ch mr, 1668
Kilian
Anna
Alb Ref mr, 1686
Kilian (d)
Anna
Alb Ref mr, 1688

L

Lambert
Anna
Fltb Ref mr, 1688
Janet
Alb Ref mr, 1693
Lea
Alb Ref mr, 1697
Lena
Bkln Ref mr, 1661
NY Ref Ch mr, 1661
Margaret
NY Ref Ch mr, 1682
Maria
NY Ref Ch mr, 1690
Sarah
Bkln Ref mr, 1663
Lancaster
Catherine
NY Ref Ch mr, 1694

Lavinus
Eunice (d)
Alb Ref mr, 1699
Wilhelmina
Alb Ref mr, 1699
Lawrence
Alida
NY Ref Ch mr, 1678
Anna
NY Ref Ch mr, 1641, 1662,
1666, 1698
Catherine
NY Ref Ch mr, 1687
Cornelia
Alb Ref mr, 1687
King Ref mr, 1687
Hilda
NY Ref Ch mr, 1669
Janet
Alb Ref mr, 1699
NY Ref Ch mr, 1658
Joanna
NY Ref Ch mr, 1692
Kunigunda
NY Ref Ch mr, 1676
Letitia
NY Ref Ch mr, 1665
Margaret
Berg Ref mr, 1665
NY Ref Ch mr, 1676
Maria
NY Ref Ch mr, 1677
Sarah
NY Ref Ch mr, 1661, 1666
Lawrence (d)
Elizabeth
NY Ref Ch mr, 1659
Lucy
NY Ref Ch mr, 1641
Sarah
NY Ref Ch mr, 1685
Leins
Elizabeth
NY Ref Ch mr, 1694
Leo
Adriana
NY Ref Ch mr, 1698

Leonard
Christina
NY Ref Ch mr, 1678
Elizabeth
NY Ref Ch mr, 1688
Gertrude
NY Ref Ch mr, 1683
Janet
Alb Ref mr, 1688
Magdalena
NY Ref Ch mr, 1683
Leonard (d)
Phizithiaen
NY Ref Ch mr, 1642
Louis
Alida
NY Ref Ch mr, 1654
Anna
Hack Ref mr, 1697
Frances
Berg Ref mr, 1672
Gertrude
Berg Ref mr, 1679
Helena
NY Ref Ch mr, 1646
Maria
King Ref mr, 1697
Nelly
NY Ref Ch mr, 1650
Wackraet (d)
NY Ref Ch mr, 1646
Louis (d)
Alida
NY Ref Ch mr, 1654
Lubbert
Hilda
Berg Ref mr, 1679
Margaret (d)
NY Ref Ch mr, 1669
Sophia
NY Ref Ch mr, 1669
Lucas
Anna
King Ref mr, 1695
NY Ref Ch mr, 1657
Barbara
Fltb Ref mr, 1682

(d) = deceased at time the
spouse remarried

Lucas (cont.)
Catherine
    Alb Ref mr, 1691
Eva
    NY Ref Ch mr, 1655
Henrietta
    Alb Ref mr, 1686
Henrietta (d)
    Alb Ref mr, 1692
Janet
    Fltb Ref mr, 1689
Judith
    Alb Ref mr, 1692
Maria
    Alb Ref mr, 1689
    Berg Ref mr, 1690
    Fltb Ref mr, 1690
Rachel
    NY Ref Ch mr, 1683

Lucas (d)
Anna
    NY Ref Ch mr, 1666
Catherine
    NY Ref Ch mr, 1658
Maria
    Alb Ref mr, 1693

Ludwich
Elsie
    NY Ref Ch mr, 1699
Hilda
    NY Ref Ch mr, 1699
Hillary
    NY Ref Ch mr, 1660
Janet
    King Ref mr, 1682
Janet (d)
    NY Ref Ch mr, 1699
Maria
    King Ref mr, 1696

Ludwich (d)
Hillary
    NY Ref Ch mr, 1682

M

Manasse
Patricia
    Alb Ref mr, 1699

Mangold
Anna
    NY Ref Ch mr, 1692

Marcus
Anna
    NY Ref Ch mr, 1697
Eva
    NY Ref Ch mr, 1698
Hester
    Fltb Ref mr, 1692

Marcus (d)
Adriana
    King Ref mr, 1662
Elizabeth
    NY Ref Ch mr, 1659

Marinus
Elsie
    NY Ref Ch mr, 1670
Magdalena (d)
    NY Ref Ch mr, 1670

Marshall
Patricia
    Berg Ref mr, 1681

Martin
Anna
    Alb Ref mr, 1693
    Bkln Ref mr, 1663
    Fltb Ref mr, 1683
Catherine
    NY Ref Ch mr, 1695
Elizabeth
    Bkln Ref mr, 1663
    NY Ref Ch mr, 1663, 1682
Elizabeth (d)
    NY Ref Ch mr, 1664
Emma
    NY Ref Ch mr, 1664
Henrietta
    Bkln Ref mr, 1662
    NY Ref Ch mr, 1662
Jacobina (d)
    NY Ref Ch mr, 1695
Janet
    NY Ref Ch mr, 1658, 1671
Janet (d)
    Alb Ref mr, 1686
Judith
    NY Ref Ch mr, 1696

Lena
    NY Ref Ch mr, 1668
Magdalena
    NY Ref Ch mr, 1671
Margaret
    Berg Ref mr, 1694
    Hack Ref mr, 1697
Maria
    Fltb Ref mr, 1690
Maria (d)
    Alb Ref mr, 1693
Nelly
    Alb Ref mr, 1686, 1692
Nicole
    King Ref mr, 1662
Sophia
    Alb Ref mr, 1696
Susan
    Fltb Ref mr, 1686
    NY Ref Ch mr, 1660

Martin (d)
Elizabeth
    NY Ref Ch mr, 1654
Janet
    NY Ref Ch mr, 1670
Nelly
    Alb Ref mr, 1697

Matthew
Anna
    Berg Ref mr, 1670, 1683
    King Ref mr, 1695
    NY Ref Ch mr, 1656, 1683
Anna (d)
    Berg Ref mr, 1686
    NY Ref Ch mr, 1656, 1670
Catherine
    Berg Ref mr, 1686, 1688, 1692
    NY Ref Ch mr, 1655, 1692
Cornelia
    Alb Ref mr, 1685
Elizabeth
    NY Ref Ch mr, 1675
Elizabeth (d)
    NY Ref Ch mr, 1696
Elsie
    NY Ref Ch mr, 1650

Gertrude
    NY Ref Ch mr, 1686
Janet
    King Ref mr, 1679
    NY Ref Ch mr, 1679, 1695,
    1698
Joanna
    NY Ref Ch mr, 1670
Magdalena
    NY Ref Ch mr, 1696
Margaret
    King Ref mr, 1679
    NY Ref Ch mr, 1673
Maria
    King Ref mr, 1698
    NY Ref Ch mr, 1656
Sarah
    King Ref mr, 1697
Sophia
    Fltb Ref mr, 1692
Susan
    Alb Ref mr, 1698
Matthew (d)
Adriana
    NY Ref Ch mr, 1683
Maria
    Alb Ref mr, 1685
Maurice
Anna
    Fltb Ref mr, 1690
Maynard
Anna
    NY Ref Ch mr, 1659
Anna (d)
    NY Ref Ch mr, 1660
Catherine
    NY Ref Ch mr, 1656, 1660
Elizabeth
    Bkln Ref mr, 1664
    NY Ref Ch mr, 1664
Janet
    NY Ref Ch mr, 1681
Maria
    NY Ref Ch mr, 1660, 1694
Rachel
    NY Ref Ch mr, 1693

Maynard (d)
Deborah
    Alb Ref mr, 1690
Melchior
Adriana (d)
    Alb Ref mr, 1692
Bridget
    NY Ref Ch mr, 1678
Catherine
    Alb Ref mr, 1696
Elizabeth
    Alb Ref mr, 1692
Susan
    NY Ref Ch mr, 1674
Melchior (d)
Bridget
    NY Ref Ch mr, 1682
Melem
Elsie
    NY Ref Ch mr, 1644
Michael
Alida
    NY Ref Ch mr, 1660
Anna (d)
    NY Ref Ch mr, 1668
Catherine
    Berg Ref mr, 1668
    NY Ref Ch mr, 1668
Elizabeth
    NY Ref Ch mr, 1642
Helena
    NY Ref Ch mr, 1693
Janet
    NY Ref Ch mr, 1655, 1661
Maria
    Alb Ref mr, 1686
    Berg Ref mr, 1691
    NY Ref Ch mr, 1640, 1680,
    1693
Mathilda
    NY Ref Ch mr, 1690
Reyertje
    NY Ref Ch mr, 1699
Sarah
    NY Ref Ch mr, 1699
Michael (d)
Alida
    King Ref mr, 1664

Frances
    Berg Ref mr, 1685
Henrietta
    Bkln Ref mr, 1685
Mones
Magdalena
    Bkln Ref mr, 1663
    NY Ref Ch mr, 1663
Moses
Anna
    Alb Ref mr, 1697
Janet
    NY Ref Ch mr, 1694
Maria
    NY Ref Ch mr, 1695

N

Nanning
Alida
    Alb Ref mr, 1686
Nathan
Anna
    NY Ref Ch mr, 1664
Christina
    NY Ref Ch mr, 1688
Margaret
    NY Ref Ch mr, 1677
Maria
    NY Ref Ch mr, 1689
Nicasius
Anna
    Berg Ref mr, 1691
Catherine
    NY Ref Ch mr, 1655
Nicholas
Agatha (d)
    NY Ref Ch mr, 1647
Agnes
    NY Ref Ch mr, 1656
Alida
    NY Ref Ch mr, 1659
Anna
    Alb Ref mr, 1699
    Berg Ref mr, 1697
    Fltb Ref mr, 1692
    NY Ref Ch mr, 1656, 1657

(d) = deceased at time the
spouse remarried

Nicholas (cont.)

Anna (d)
  Berg Ref mr, 1698
  NY Ref Ch mr, 1670
Apollonia
  NY Ref Ch mr, 1659
Barbara
  Schn Ref mr, 1699
Bernadine
  Fltb Ref mr, 1684
  NY Ref Ch mr, 1684
Bridget
  NY Ref Ch mr, 1649
Catherine
  Fltb Ref mr, 1689
  NY Ref Ch mr, 1691
Catlintje
  NY Ref Ch mr, 1670
Cornelia
  King Ref mr, 1679
  NY Ref Ch mr, 1679
Deborah
  NY Ref Ch mr, 1694
Elizabeth
  Fltb Ref mr, 1685
  King Ref mr, 1681
  NY Ref Ch mr, 1681
Elsie
  Berg Ref mr, 1698
Frances
  Fltb Ref mr, 1692
Geesje
  NY Ref Ch mr, 1667
Geesje (d)
  NY Ref Ch mr, 1672
Gertrude
  NY Ref Ch mr, 1647, 1653
Helena
  Fltb Ref mr, 1683
Hilda
  NY Ref Ch mr, 1646, 1682
Isabel
  NY Ref Ch mr, 1695
Janet
  Fltb Ref mr, 1692
  King Ref mr, 1698
  NY Ref Ch mr, 1672

Janet (d)
  NY Ref Ch mr, 1659
Jemima
  Berg Ref mr, 1684
  Fltb Ref mr, 1684
Judith
  NY Ref Ch mr, 1666
Kunigunda
  NY Ref Ch mr, 1671
Lucretia
  NY Ref Ch mr, 1680
Lydia
  NY Ref Ch mr, 1655
Lydia (d)
  King Ref mr, 1689
Margaret
  NY Ref Ch mr, 1656, 1678
Maria
  Fltb Ref mr, 1684, 1686
  NY Ref Ch mr, 1655, 1661,
  1670, 1672, **1681, 1693**
Maria (d)
  King Ref mr, 1681
  NY Ref Ch mr, 1681
Mathilda
  Bkln Ref mr, 1662
Nelly (d)
  NY Ref Ch mr, 1656
Sarah
  King Ref mr, 1689
  NY Ref Ch mr, 1680
Susan
  NY Ref Ch mr, 1649, 1652,
  1658
Volkje
  NY Ref Ch mr, 1652
Wilhelmina
  NY Ref Ch mr, 1689

Nicholas (d)

Catherine
  NY Ref Ch mr, 1645
Engel
  King Ref mr, 1698
Lea
  Alb Ref mr, 1693
Magdalena
  NY Ref Ch mr, 1685

Margaret
  NY Ref Ch mr, 1656, 1687
Maria
  NY Ref Ch mr, 1699
Mathilda
  NY Ref Ch mr, 1665
Patricia
  NY Ref Ch mr, 1654

Niew

Catherine
  Fltb Ref mr, 1682

O

Oben

Gertrude
  NY Ref Ch mr, 1641

Oliver

Margaret
  NY Ref Ch mr, 1682

Oliver (d)

Hilda
  NY Ref Ch mr, 1689

Olof

Anna
  NY Ref Ch mr, 1642

Omie

Elsie
  Alb Ref mr, 1697

Onckel

Judith
  NY Ref Ch mr, 1694

Onckel (d)

Judith
  NY Ref Ch mr, 1696

Otto

Elsie
  NY Ref Ch mr, 1664
Engel
  NY Ref Ch mr, 1668
Margaret
  NY Ref Ch mr, 1693
Maria
  NY Ref Ch mr, 1667

Otto (d)

Maria
  NY Ref Ch mr, 1695

Groom/Bride Pairs Directory

Owen
  Elizabeth
    NY Ref Ch mr, 1694
Owen (d)
  Elizabeth
    NY Ref Ch mr, 1698

P

Patrick
  Sophia
    Alb Ref mr, 1697
Paul
  Alida
    NY Ref Ch mr, 1660
  Anna
    NY Ref Ch mr, 1695
  Antoinette
    NY Ref Ch mr, 1653
  Catherine
    NY Ref Ch mr, 1640, 1645,
    1658
  Cecilia
    NY Ref Ch mr, 1664
  Janet
    NY Ref Ch mr, 1695
  Maria
    NY Ref Ch mr, 1644, 1658,
    1686, 1688
  Nelly (d)
    NY Ref Ch mr, 1640
  Nicole
    Bkln Ref mr, 1662
    NY Ref Ch mr, 1662
  Sarah
    Bkln Ref mr, 1677
    NY Ref Ch mr, 1677
Paul (d)
  Anna
    NY Ref Ch mr, 1699
  Lavinia
    Berg Ref mr, 1687
  Maria
    Bkln Ref mr, 1664
    NY Ref Ch mr, 1664, 1687
  Sarah
    NY Ref Ch mr, 1691

Peek
  Maria
    NY Ref Ch mr, 1697
Peter
  Adriana
    Alb Ref mr, 1693
    NY Ref Ch mr, 1653
  Agnes
    NY Ref Ch mr, 1663
  Alida
    King Ref mr, 1665
    NY Ref Ch mr, 1643, 1665,
    1692, 1698
  Anna
    Fltb Ref mr, 1681, 1687
    NY Ref Ch mr, 1657, 1672,
    1695
  Barbara (d)
    NY Ref Ch mr, 1663
  Bathilda
    NY Ref Ch mr, 1677
  Beverly
    Fltb Ref mr, 1689
  Blandina
    NY Ref Ch mr, 1674
  Bridget
    NY Ref Ch mr, 1656
  Catherine
    Berg Ref mr, 1687
    Fltb Ref mr, 1679
    NY Ref Ch mr, 1642, 1696,
    1698
  Catherine (d)
    NY Ref Ch mr, 1657
  Christina
    Berg Ref mr, 1698
    NY Ref Ch mr, 1659
  Constance
    Berg Ref mr, 1688
  Cornelia
    Berg Ref mr, 1686
    NY Ref Ch mr, 1685, 1686,
    1696, 1697
  Deborah
    NY Ref Ch mr, 1663
  Elizabeth
    Berg Ref mr, 1685
    Bkln Ref mr, 1685

    King Ref mr, no date
    NY Ref Ch mr, 1647, 1664,
    1667, 1680, **1685**
  Elizabeth (d)
    NY Ref Ch mr, 1679, 1699
  Elsie
    NY Ref Ch mr, 1652, 1699
  Elsie (d)
    NY Ref Ch mr, 1644
  Engel
    NY Ref Ch mr, 1677
  Engel (d)
    Alb Ref mr, 1691
  Eva
    King Ref mr, 1697
    NY Ref Ch mr, 1649
  Frances (d)
    NY Ref Ch mr, 1659
  Gertrude
    NY Ref Ch mr, 1661, 1688
  Henrietta
    Berg Ref mr, 1670
    NY Ref Ch mr, 1680
  Henrietta (d)
    Alb Ref mr, 1688
  Hester
    NY Ref Ch mr, 1640, 1666,
    1684
  Hilda
    King Ref mr, 1696
    NY Ref Ch mr, 1674
  Hillary
    NY Ref Ch mr, 1682
  Isabel
    NY Ref Ch mr, 1646, 1681,
    1693
  Janet
    Alb Ref mr, 1688, 1698
    Fltb Ref mr, 1684
    King Ref mr, 1682, 1697
    NY Ref Ch mr, 1657, 1674,
    1678, 1683, **1698**
  Joanna
    Alb Ref mr, 1684
  Josina
    NY Ref Ch mr, 1669
  Judith
    NY Ref Ch mr, 1642

(d) = deceased at time the
spouse remarried

Peter (cont.)
  Lavinia
    Berg Ref mr, 1687
  Lydia
    NY Ref Ch mr, 1695
  Margaret
    Alb Ref mr, 1685
    Fltb Ref mr, 1684
    NY Ref Ch mr, 1659, 1661, 1687
  Maria
    Alb Ref mr, 1691
    Fltb Ref mr, 1684, 1686
    NY Ref Ch mr, 1649, 1655, 1657, 1663, 1664, 1687, 1691, 1699
  Martha
    NY Ref Ch mr, 1644
  Rachel
    NY Ref Ch mr, 1698, 1699
  Rebecca
    King Ref mr, 1679
    NY Ref Ch mr, 1689
  Sarah
    Fltb Ref mr, 1680
    NY Ref Ch mr, 1648, 1687, 1688
  Sophia
    Bkln Ref mr, 1663
    NY Ref Ch mr, 1686, 1697
  Susan
    Alb Ref mr, 1688
    NY Ref Ch mr, 1665, 1683
  Susan (d)
    NY Ref Ch mr, 1682, 1699
  Theodora
    Berg Ref mr, 1683
  Theodora (d)
    NY Ref Ch mr, 1657
  Wilhelmina
    NY Ref Ch mr, 1653
Peter (d)
  Anna
    Alb Ref mr, 1693
    NY Ref Ch mr, 1659, 1686
  Britten
    NY Ref Ch mr, 1666

  Catherine
    Bkln Ref mr, 1663
    NY Ref Ch mr, 1659
  Elizabeth
    NY Ref Ch mr, 1662
  Elsie
    NY Ref Ch mr, 1663
  Emma
    Alb Ref mr, 1697
  Engel
    NY Ref Ch mr, 1686
  Josina
    NY Ref Ch mr, 1679
  Margaret
    NY Ref Ch mr, 1662
  Maria
    NY Ref Ch mr, 1647, 1672
  Nelly
    King Ref mr, 1697
  Volkje
    Alb Ref mr, 1685
Philip
  Anna
    Alb Ref mr, 1692
    NY Ref Ch mr, 1694
  Catherine
    NY Ref Ch mr, 1675
  Elizabeth
    NY Ref Ch mr, 1687
  Gertrude
    NY Ref Ch mr, 1647
  Hilda
    NY Ref Ch mr, 1696
  Janet
    NY Ref Ch mr, 1658
  Margaret
    NY Ref Ch mr, 1671, 1676
  Maria
    Alb Ref mr, 1688
    NY Ref Ch mr, 1642, 1668
Philip (d)
  Margaret
    NY Ref Ch mr, 1675
  Maria
    NY Ref Ch mr, 1656, 1681
Pierre
  Elizabeth (d)
    Alb Ref mr, 1693

  Esther
    NPal Ref mr, 1692
  Henrietta
    Alb Ref mr, 1696
  Maria
    Alb Ref mr, 1693

Q

Quirinus
  Nelly
    Fltb Ref mr, 1683

R

Randolph
  Margaret
    Fltb Ref mr, 1684
  Martha
    Fltb Ref mr, 1684
Reinhard (d)
  Margaret
    NY Ref Ch mr, 1688
Rembrant
  Cornelia
    NY Ref Ch mr, 1682
Remmet
  Janet
    NY Ref Ch mr, 1642
Reyer
  Jemima
    NY Ref Ch mr, 1686
Rebecca
  NY Ref Ch mr, 1696
Reyner
  Elizabeth
    NY Ref Ch mr, 1674
  Elizabeth (d)
    NY Ref Ch mr, 1692
  Henrietta
    Berg Ref mr, 1698
    Hack Ref mr, 1699
  Janet
    Fltb Ref mr, 1687
    NY Ref Ch mr, 1687
  Maria
    NY Ref Ch mr, 1696
  Nicole
    NY Ref Ch mr, 1692

(d) = deceased at time the spouse remarried

Sarah
Alb Ref mr, 1699
Susan
NY Ref Ch mr, 1660
Theodora (d)
Berg Ref mr, 1698
Hack Ref mr, 1699
Reyner (d)
Catherine
Alb Ref mr, 1696
Constance
Berg Ref mr, 1688
Richard
Anna
NY Ref Ch mr, 1659
Catherine
Alb Ref mr, 1699
Emma
Alb Ref mr, 1697
Judith (d)
NY Ref Ch mr, 1659
Magdalena
King Ref mr, 1696
Maria
NY Ref Ch mr, 1687, 1690, 1696
Richard (d)
Dorothy
NY Ref Ch mr, 1692
Janet
Alb Ref mr, 1693
Maria
NY Ref Ch mr, 1650
Robert
Anna
NY Ref Ch mr, 1699
Catherine
NY Ref Ch mr, 1685
Cornelia
Alb Ref mr, 1689
Gertrude
Alb Ref mr, 1686
Grace
NY Ref Ch mr, 1689
Helena
NY Ref Ch mr, 1694
Jemima
NY Ref Ch mr, 1690

Margaret
Alb Ref mr, 1697
Maria
NY Ref Ch mr, 1683, 1695
Robert (d)
Eleanor
NY Ref Ch mr, 1687
Elizabeth
King Ref mr, 1696
Maria
NY Ref Ch mr, 1685
Roelof
Alida
King Ref mr, 1664
Anna (d)
Fltb Ref mr, 1688
NY Ref Ch mr, 1688
Catherine
Fltb Ref mr, 1681, 1688
NY Ref Ch mr, 1688
Eva (d)
Berg Ref mr, 1691
NY Ref Ch mr, 1691
Frances
Berg Ref mr, 1691
NY Ref Ch mr, 1691
Gertrude
Hack Ref mr, 1695
NY Ref Ch mr, 1643
Susan
Berg Ref mr, 1682
Ursula
Berg Ref mr, 1688
NY Ref Ch mr, 1688
Roelof (d)
Christina
NY Ref Ch mr, 1661
Gertrude
Berg Ref mr, 1672
Roger
Anna
Berg Ref mr, 1698
Catherine
NY Ref Ch mr, 1646
Elizabeth
NY Ref Ch mr, 1694
Gertrude
Fltb Ref mr, 1684

Lavinia
Alb Ref mr, 1692
Maria
NY Ref Ch mr, 1695
Martha (d)
NY Ref Ch mr, 1694
Nelly
Berg Ref mr, 1697
Roger (d)
Catherine
Alb Ref mr, 1695
Rowland
Janet
NY Ref Ch mr, 1640
Rupert
Sarah
NY Ref Ch mr, 1684

S

Sampson
Maria
NY Ref Ch mr, 1699
Samuel
Adriana
NY Ref Ch mr, 1691
Alida
Bkln Ref mr, 1695
Anna
King Ref mr, 1688
Barbara
Alb Ref mr, 1699
Catherine
NY Ref Ch mr, 1644
Catlintje
Bkln Ref mr, 1691
Fltb Ref mr, 1690
Cecilia
NY Ref Ch mr, 1699
Elizabeth
NY Ref Ch mr, 1659
Hester
NY Ref Ch mr, 1689
Janet
Fltb Ref mr, 1689
NY Ref Ch mr, 1655
Margaret
NY Ref Ch mr, 1696

(d) = deceased at time the spouse remarried

Samuel (cont.)
  Nelly
    NY Ref Ch mr, 1699
Samuel (d)
  Anna
    NY Ref Ch mr, 1656
  Elizabeth
    NY Ref Ch mr, 1682
Sander
see also Alexander
  Elsie
    Fltb Ref mr, 1682
Sander (d)
see also Alexander
  Anna
    Alb Ref mr, 1696
Sara
  Rebecca
    NY Ref Ch mr, 1642
Seger
  Janet
    NY Ref Ch mr, 1677
  Sophia
    NY Ref Ch mr, 1686
Seger (d)
  Sophia
    NY Ref Ch mr, 1694
Servis
  Gertrude
    NY Ref Ch mr, 1697
Severin
  Catherine
    NY Ref Ch mr, 1656
  Catherine (d)
    NY Ref Ch mr, 1671
  Margaret
    NY Ref Ch mr, 1671
Siebold
  Maria
    Berg Ref mr, 1678
  Susan
    NY Ref Ch mr, 1645
Siegbert
  Hilda
    NY Ref Ch mr, 1697
Siegmond
  Gertrude
    Bkln Ref mr, 1660

    NY Ref Ch mr, 1660
  Inga (d)
    NY Ref Ch mr, 1660
Simon
  Anna
    Berg Ref mr, 1675
    Fltb Ref mr, 1691
    King Ref mr, 1681
    NY Ref Ch mr, 1649, 1655,
    1656
  Catherine
    NY Ref Ch mr, 1686
  Eunice
    NY Ref Ch mr, 1686
  Janet
    Alb Ref mr, 1685
    NY Ref Ch mr, 1686
  Lavinia
    NY Ref Ch mr, 1661
  Maria
    Bkln Ref mr, 1663
    King Ref mr, 1683
    NY Ref Ch mr, 1647
  Nelly
    Alb Ref mr, 1692
  Nicole (d)
    NY Ref Ch mr, 1686
  Sophia
    NY Ref Ch mr, 1671
Simon (d)
  Anna
    NY Ref Ch mr, 1679
  Janet
    Alb Ref mr, 1692
  Wilhelmina
    Alb Ref mr, 1699
Solomon
  Alida
    Alb Ref mr, 1699
  Anna
    Alb Ref mr, 1686
  Judith
    NY Ref Ch mr, 1685
Solomon (d)
  Anna
    NY Ref Ch mr, 1664

Stephen
  Dorothy
    NY Ref Ch mr, 1642
  Elizabeth
    Alb Ref mr, 1699
  Engel
    King Ref mr, 1698
  Gertrude
    NY Ref Ch mr, 1671
  Maria
    NY Ref Ch mr, 1696
Stephen (d)
  Rose
    NY Ref Ch mr, 1656
Swan
  Christina
    NY Ref Ch mr, 1664
  Susan
    Fltb Ref mr, 1685
Sybout
  Maria
    NY Ref Ch mr, 1669
Sybrant (d)
  Elizabeth
    Alb Ref mr, 1686

T
Thaddius
  Anna
    Berg Ref mr, 1679
Theodore
  Anna
    Fltb Ref mr, 1677
Thomas
  Agnes
    Alb Ref mr, 1692
  Alida
    NY Ref Ch mr, 1695
  Anna
    Bkln Ref mr, 1662
    NY Ref Ch mr, 1641, 1692,
    1695
  Barbara (d)
    NY Ref Ch mr, 1659
  Catherine
    Alb Ref mr, 1689, 1699
    NY Ref Ch mr, 1682, 1686

Deborah
NY Ref Ch mr, 1684, 1691
Dorothy (d)
NY Ref Ch mr, 1687
Eleanor
NY Ref Ch mr, 1687
Elizabeth
NY Ref Ch mr, 1642
Elsie
NY Ref Ch mr, 1656
Elsie (d)
NY Ref Ch mr, 1664
Eva
NY Ref Ch mr, 1698
Frances
Berg Ref mr, 1685
Frances (d)
NY Ref Ch mr, 1698
Gertrude
Alb Ref mr, 1691
King Ref mr, 1698
NY Ref Ch mr, 1664
Harmina
Bkln Ref mr, 1680
Fltb Ref mr, 1680
NY Ref Ch mr, 1680, 1697
Harmina (d)
NY Ref Ch mr, 1691
Ida
NY Ref Ch mr, 1696
Janet
Berg Ref mr, 1691
NY Ref Ch mr, 1654, 1659
Janet (d)
NY Ref Ch mr, 1645, 1657,
1696
Margaret
NY Ref Ch mr, 1693, 1694
Maria
Alb Ref mr, 1692
Fltb Ref mr, 1692
King Ref mr, 1683
NY Ref Ch mr, 1645, 1663,
1666, 1692, 1694
Schn Ref mr, 1696
Nelly
NY Ref Ch mr, 1664

Rachel
NY Ref Ch mr, 1697
Rymerick
King NYGB, 1672
Sarah
Fltb Ref mr, 1692
NY Ref Ch mr, 1640, 1643
Susan
Hack Ref mr, 1697
Thomas (d)
Anna
NY Ref Ch mr, 1692
Deborah
NY Ref Ch mr, 1691, 1697
Elizabeth
NY Ref Ch mr, 1694
Elsie
NY Ref Ch mr, 1699
Helena
NY Ref Ch mr, 1646
Josina
NY Ref Ch mr, 1659
Laurentia
King Ref mr, 1695
Margaret
NY Ref Ch mr, 1694
Maria
NY Ref Ch mr, 1646
Nelly
NY Ref Ch mr, 1674
Sarah
NY Ref Ch mr, 1644, 1647
Timothy
Elizabeth
NY Ref Ch mr, 1681
Elizabeth (d)
NY Ref Ch mr, 1686
Gertrude
Hack Ref mr, 1699
Hester
NY Ref Ch mr, 1686
Margaret
NY Ref Ch mr, 1675
Tobias
Alida
NY Ref Ch mr, 1678
Alida (d)
NY Ref Ch mr, 1684

Anna
NY Ref Ch mr, 1684
Elizabeth
Fltb Ref mr, 1684
NY Ref Ch mr, 1684
Hilda
NY Ref Ch mr, 1655
Janet
NY Ref Ch mr, 1649
Tobias (d)
Janet
NY Ref Ch mr, 1659
Tunis
Anna
NY Ref Ch mr, 1681, 1685
Catherine
Alb Ref mr, 1694
Berg Ref mr, 1677, 1684
Bkln Ref mr, 1694
Clara
King Ref mr, 1696
Elizabeth
Alb Ref mr, 1693
NY Ref Ch mr, 1659
Elsie
NY Ref Ch mr, 1689
Geesje (d)
NY Ref Ch mr, 1689
Gertrude
Fltb Ref mr, 1687
NY Ref Ch mr, 1687, 1696
Helena
NY Ref Ch mr, 1680
Janet
Alb Ref mr, 1696
NY Ref Ch mr, 1677
Margaret (d)
NY Ref Ch mr, 1696
Maria
NY Ref Ch mr, 1642, 1675,
1690
Maria (d)
King Ref mr, 1696
Phebe
NY Ref Ch mr, 1640

(d) = deceased at time the
spouse remarried

Tunis (cont.)
  Sarah
    Alb Ref mr, 1696
    Fltb Ref mr, 1684
    King Ref mr, 1695
    NY Ref Ch mr, 1650, 1684,
    1696
  Sarah (d)
    Fltb Ref mr, 1687
    NY Ref Ch mr, 1687
  Sophia
    NY Ref Ch mr, 1679
  Susan
    Berg Ref mr, 1683
    NY Ref Ch mr, 1683
  Vroutje
    NY Ref Ch mr, 1689
  Wilhelmina
    King Ref mr, 1696
Tunis (d)
  Anna
    NY Ref Ch mr, 1691
  Elizabeth
    Alb Ref mr, 1699
  Ida
    NY Ref Ch mr, 1696
  Maria
    Alb Ref mr, 1692

U

Ulrich
  Eva
    NY Ref Ch mr, 1641
  Hester
    Hack Ref mr, 1698
Urban
  Maria
    NY Ref Ch mr, 1689

V

Valentine
  Maria
    NY Ref Ch mr, 1662
Victor
  Nicole
    NY Ref Ch mr, 1679

Vincent
  Adriana
    NY Ref Ch mr, 1684
  Magdalena
    Bkln Ref mr, 1695
Volkert
  Dorothy
    NY Ref Ch mr, 1650
  Janet
    Alb Ref mr, 1698
  Nelly
    Fltb Ref mr, 1680
  Sarah
    Fltb Ref mr, 1681
Volkert (d)
  Margaret
    NY Ref Ch mr, 1671

W

W.
  Eleanor
    King Ref mr, 1673
Waling
  Catherine
    Berg Ref mr, 1671
Walran
  Catherine
    King Ref mr, 1688
  Kunigunda
    NY Ref Ch mr, 1668
  Margaret
    King Ref mr, 1664
Walran (d)
  Kunigunda
    NY Ref Ch mr, 1671
Walter
  Anna
    NY Ref Ch mr, 1697
  Catherine
    Fltb Ref mr, 1689
    NY Ref Ch mr, 1668
  Cornelia
    Alb Ref mr, 1696
  Deborah
    Berg Ref mr, 1689

Elizabeth
    Alb Ref mr, 1691
    Fltb Ref mr, 1679
    NY Ref Ch mr, 1698
Elizabeth (d)
    Alb Ref mr, 1691
Helena
    NY Ref Ch mr, 1698
Janet
    Alb Ref mr, 1695
Joanna (d)
    Fltb Ref mr, 1689
Maria
    Fltb Ref mr, 1686
    NY Ref Ch mr, 1662
Maria (d)
    NY Ref Ch mr, 1698
Nelly
    Fltb Ref mr, 1683
Walter (d)
  Maria
    NY Ref Ch mr, 1679, 1689
Wendel
  Alida
    Berg Ref mr, 1692
Werner
  Anna
    Alb Ref mr, 1696
  Anna (d)
    NY Ref Ch mr, 1675, 1677
  Deborah
    NY Ref Ch mr, 1667
  Elizabeth
    NY Ref Ch mr, 1677
Wessel
  Catherine
    Alb Ref mr, 1684
  Gertrude
    NY Ref Ch mr, 1643
  Jemima
    King Ref mr, 1694
    NY Ref Ch mr, 1693
  Laurentia
    King Ref mr, 1695
  Maria
    NY Ref Ch mr, 1670
  Maria (d)
    King Ref mr, 1695

(d) = deceased at time the
spouse remarried

Groom/Bride Pairs Directory

Susan
  NY Ref Ch mr, 1692
William
  Adriana
    Fltb Ref mr, 1690
    NY Ref Ch mr, 1686
  Adriana (d)
    NY Ref Ch mr, 1682
  Alida
    Fltb Ref mr, 1679
    NY Ref Ch mr, 1644, 1658,
    1679
  Alida (d)
    NY Ref Ch mr, 1661
  Anna
    Alb Ref mr, 1687, 1688,
    1693
    Berg Ref mr, 1690
    Fltb Ref mr, 1684
    NY Ref Ch mr, 1644, 1664,
    1685, 1694
  Apollonia
    NY Ref Ch mr, 1664
  Beatrice
    NY Ref Ch mr, 1694
  Bridget (d)
    NY Ref Ch mr, 1664
  Catherine
    Alb Ref mr, 1695
    NY Ref Ch mr, 1647, 1678,
    1682
  Catherine (d)
    King Ref mr, 1698
  Catlintje
    NY Ref Ch mr, 1649, 1695
  Christina
    Bkln Ref mr, 1663
    NY Ref Ch mr, 1663, 1677
  Deborah
    NY Ref Ch mr, 1697, 1699
  Eliza
    NY Ref Ch mr, 1649
  Elizabeth
    Alb Ref mr, 1692
    Bkln Ref mr, 1695
    King Ref mr, 1683
    NY Ref Ch mr, 1675, 1682,
    1688, 1694, **1695**

Elizabeth (d)
    King Ref mr, 1698
  Elsie
    Fltb Ref mr, 1681
  Engel
    NY Ref Ch mr, 1671
  Gerarda
    King Ref mr, 1698
  Gertrude
    Hack Ref mr, 1699
    NY Ref Ch mr, 1660, 1666
  Hilda
    King Ref mr, 1698
    NY Ref Ch mr, 1692
  Janet
    Berg Ref mr, 1676
    King NYGB, 1672
    NY Ref Ch mr, 1675
  Janet (d)
    NY Ref Ch mr, 1676
  Josina
    Bkln Ref mr, 1661
    NY Ref Ch mr, 1661
  Judith (d)
    NY Ref Ch mr, 1658
  Lavinia
    King Ref mr, 1698
    NY Ref Ch mr, 1659
  Lena
    NY Ref Ch mr, 1654
  Magdalena
    Hack Ref mr, 1697
    NY Ref Ch mr, 1693
  Margaret
    NY Ref Ch mr, 1663, 1672,
    1680
  Margaret (d)
    Bkln Ref mr, 1664
    NY Ref Ch mr, 1664, 1682,
    1685
  Maria
    Alb Ref mr, 1694
    Berg Ref mr, 1697
    Bkln Ref mr, 1664
    NY Ref Ch mr, 1642, 1664,
    1676, 1682, **1688, 1693,**
    1698, 1699

Martina
    Alb Ref mr, 1692
  Minnie
    NY Ref Ch mr, 1679
  Myra (d)
    Bkln Ref mr, 1695
  Patience
    NY Ref Ch mr, 1695
  Petronella
    NY Ref Ch mr, 1694
  Rachel
    Fltb Ref mr, 1692
    NY Ref Ch mr, 1686
  Sarah
    Hack Ref mr, 1696
    NY Ref Ch mr, 1656
  Sarah (d)
    Alb Ref mr, 1693
  Seyke
    Alb Ref mr, 1690
  Sophia
    Alb Ref mr, 1697
    Fltb Ref mr, 1690
    NY Ref Ch mr, 1674
  Susan
    NY Ref Ch mr, 1643, 1699
William (d)
  Anna
    NY Ref Ch mr, 1641, 1686,
    1687, 1690
  Catherine
    Fltb Ref mr, 1689
  Elizabeth
    NY Ref Ch mr, 1694
  Harmina
    NY Ref Ch mr, 1654
  Janet
    NY Ref Ch mr, 1664
  Maria
    NY Ref Ch mr, 1644, 1645,
    1691
  Mattina
    NY Ref Ch mr, 1663
  Nelly
    King Ref mr, 1664
  Sarah
    NY Ref Ch mr, 1690

(d) = deceased at time the
spouse remarried

William (d) (cont.)
  Sophia
    NY Ref Ch mr, 1697
  Susan
    NY Ref Ch mr, 1644
Wolfert
  Margaret
    NY Ref Ch mr, 1697
  Maria
    NY Ref Ch mr, 1692
Wolfgang
  Elsie
    NY Ref Ch mr, 1660
Wyatt
  Janet
    NY Ref Ch mr, 1678
Wynant
  Anna
    Bkln Ref mr, 1661
Wynant (d)
  Elizabeth
    NY Ref Ch mr, 1692

Z

Zachariah
  Alida
    NY Ref Ch mr, 1685
  Catherine
    NY Ref Ch mr, 1696
  Maria
    NY Ref Ch mr, 1693
Zachariah (d)
  Alida
    NY Ref Ch mr, 1695

Table 3D
Bride/Groom Pairs Directory

A

Abigail
  Anke
    NY Ref Ch mr, 1661
  Cornelius
    NY Ref Ch mr, 1682
Abigail (d)
  Adrian
    NY Ref Ch mr, 1672
  Cornelius
    NY Ref Ch mr, 1685
Adriana
  Albert
    NY Ref Ch mr, 1656
  Ambrose (d)
    NY Ref Ch mr, 1691
  Andrew
    Alb Ref mr, 1697
  Arnold
    NY Ref Ch mr, 1669
  Bartholomew
    Alb Ref mr, 1699
  Conrad
    Alb Ref mr, 1693
  Cornelius
    Alb Ref mr, 1689
    Fltb Ref mr, 1683
    NY Ref Ch mr, 1683
  Cornelius (d)
    Alb Ref mr, 1693
    NY Ref Ch mr, 1656
  Dirk
    NY Ref Ch mr, 1650, 1693
  Francis
    Alb Ref mr, 1688
  Garret (d)
    Alb Ref mr, 1692
  Gerald
    Alb Ref mr, 1692
  Hendrick
    Fltb Ref mr, 1685
  Isaac
    Fltb Ref mr, 1677
  Jacob
    King Ref mr, 1662

  Joris
    NY Ref Ch mr, 1682
  Jurian
    NY Ref Ch mr, 1693
  Leo
    NY Ref Ch mr, 1698
  Marcus (d)
    King Ref mr, 1662
  Matthew (d)
    NY Ref Ch mr, 1683
  Peter
    Alb Ref mr, 1693
    NY Ref Ch mr, 1653
  Samuel
    NY Ref Ch mr, 1691
  Vincent
    NY Ref Ch mr, 1684
  William
    Fltb Ref mr, 1690
    NY Ref Ch mr, 1686
Adriana (d)
  Arnold
    NY Ref Ch mr, 1675
  Melchior
    Alb Ref mr, 1692
  William
    NY Ref Ch mr, 1682
Agatha
  Abraham
    NPal Ref mr, 1694
    NY Ref Ch mr, 1647
  Barent
    NY Ref Ch mr, 1657
  Bartholomew
    Alb Ref mr, 1698
  Cornelius
    Fltb Ref mr, 1683
    Schn Ref mr, 1699
  Dirk
    NY Ref Ch mr, 1650
Agatha (d)
  Herman
    NY Ref Ch mr, 1682
  Nicholas
    NY Ref Ch mr, 1647

Agnes
  Adrian
    NY Ref Ch mr, 1660
  Adrian (d)
    NY Ref Ch mr, 1663
  Andrew (d)
    NY Ref Ch mr, 1682
  Arent (d)
    NY Ref Ch mr, 1647
  Caspar
    NY Ref Ch mr, 1699
  Christian
    NY Ref Ch mr, 1693
  Garret
    Alb Ref mr, 1698
    Berg Ref mr, 1681
  Hendrick
    NY Ref Ch mr, 1689
  Jurian
    Alb Ref mr, 1686
  Nicholas
    NY Ref Ch mr, 1656
  Peter
    NY Ref Ch mr, 1663
  Thomas
    Alb Ref mr, 1692
Agnes (d)
  Andrew
    NY Ref Ch mr, 1656
  Cornelius
    NY Ref Ch mr, 1692
  Gideon
    NY Ref Ch mr, 1683
Alida
  Abraham
    Berg Ref mr, 1683
    Fltb Ref mr, 1683
    NY Ref Ch mr, 1683
  Aert
    King Ref mr, 1684, 1695
  Aert (d)
    King Ref mr, 1698
  Albert
    NY Ref Ch mr, 1645

(d) = deceased at time the
spouse remarried

Alida (cont.)

Albert (d)
King Ref mr, 1665
Arent
King Ref mr, 1687
Barent
King Ref mr, 1698
Bastian
Berg Ref mr, 1688
Bernard
NY Ref Ch mr, 1669
Cornelius
Berg Ref mr, 1681
Fltb Ref mr, 1681, 1682,
1687
NY Ref Ch mr, 1645
Cornelius (d)
NY Ref Ch mr, 1644
Francis
NY Ref Ch mr, 1665
Garret
Alb Ref mr, 1684
NY Ref Ch mr, 1651
Garret (d)
Alb Ref mr, 1689
King Ref mr, 1684
NY Ref Ch mr, 1645, 1659
Hendrick
King Ref mr, 1664
Hildebrand
King Ref mr, 1688
Isaac
NY Ref Ch mr, 1689, 1690,
1693
Isaac (d)
NY Ref Ch mr, 1698
Jacob
Berg Ref mr, 1675
NY Ref Ch mr, 1671, 1687,
1695
Joseph
Fltb Ref mr, 1687
Josiah
Fltb Ref mr, 1682
NY Ref Ch mr, 1682
Lawrence
NY Ref Ch mr, 1678

Louis
NY Ref Ch mr, 1654
Louis (d)
NY Ref Ch mr, 1654
Michael
NY Ref Ch mr, 1660
Michael (d)
King Ref mr, 1664
Nanning
Alb Ref mr, 1686
Nicholas
NY Ref Ch mr, 1659
Paul
NY Ref Ch mr, 1660
Peter
King Ref mr, 1665
NY Ref Ch mr, 1643, 1665,
1692, 1698
Roelof
King Ref mr, 1664
Samuel
Bkln Ref mr, 1695
Solomon
Alb Ref mr, 1699
Thomas
NY Ref Ch mr, 1695
Tobias
NY Ref Ch mr, 1678
Wendel
Berg Ref mr, 1692
William
Fltb Ref mr, 1679
NY Ref Ch mr, 1644, 1658,
1679
Zachariah
NY Ref Ch mr, 1685
Zachariah (d)
NY Ref Ch mr, 1695
Alida (d)
Albert
NY Ref Ch mr, 1683
Francis
NY Ref Ch mr, 1675
Garret
NY Ref Ch mr, 1659
Gilbert
NY Ref Ch mr, 1659

Hendrick
NY Ref Ch mr, 1691
Jacob
Berg Ref mr, 1695
NY Ref Ch mr, 1684
Tobias
NY Ref Ch mr, 1684
William
NY Ref Ch mr, 1661
Anna
Abel (d)
NY Ref Ch mr, 1685
Abraham
Alb Ref mr, 1696
NY Ref Ch mr, 1692, 1695,
1698
Schn Ref mr, 1696
Adam (d)
Alb Ref mr, 1691
Adrian
NY Ref Ch mr, 1690
Aert (d)
King Ref mr, 1665
Andrew
NY Ref Ch mr, 1642, 1660,
1674, 1684
Andrew (d)
NY Ref Ch mr, 1664
Anthony
NY Ref Ch mr, 1653
Anthony (d)
Alb Ref mr, 1689
Arent
Bkln Ref mr, 1662
NY Ref Ch mr, 1694
August
NY Ref Ch mr, 1666, 1697
August (d)
NY Ref Ch mr, 1691
Azariah
NY Ref Ch mr, 1690
Barent
NY Ref Ch mr, 1652, 1664
Bastian
NY Ref Ch mr, 1689
Benjamin
Alb Ref mr, 1693
NY Ref Ch mr, 1699

Carl
  Alb Ref mr, 1688
Caspar
  NY Ref Ch mr, 1682
Christian
  NY Ref Ch mr, 1665
Clement
  NY Ref Ch mr, 1680
Conrad
  NY Ref Ch mr, 1682
Cornelius
  Bkln Ref mr, 1695
  NY Ref Ch mr, 1659, 1675,
  1680, 1689
Cornelius (d)
  NY Ref Ch mr, 1661, 1686
Daniel
  Alb Ref mr, 1696
  NY Ref Ch mr, 1686
David
  Berg Ref mr, 1692
Dirk
  Alb Ref mr, 1686
  Bkln Ref mr, 1662
  King Ref mr, 1685
  NY Ref Ch mr, 1654, 1663,
  1664
Dirk (d)
  Fltb Ref mr, 1679
Egbert
  King Ref mr, 1684
  NY Ref Ch mr, 1639
Egmont
  NY Ref Ch mr, 1642
Elias (d)
  NY Ref Ch mr, 1686
Evert
  Alb Ref mr, 1688
Evert (d)
  NY Ref Ch mr, 1663
Francis
  NY Ref Ch mr, 1675, 1691,
  1695
Francis (d)
  Alb Ref mr, 1687, 1692
  NY Ref Ch mr, 1642, 1697
Fred
  NY Ref Ch mr, 1659

Garret
  Fltb Ref mr, 1687
  NY Ref Ch mr, 1665
Godwin (d)
  NY Ref Ch mr, 1685
Hacke
  NY Ref Ch mr, 1653
Hendrick
  Alb Ref mr, 1695
  Fltb Ref mr, 1679, 1680
  King Ref mr, 1663, 1684,
  1696, 1697
  NY Ref Ch mr, 1654, 1660,
  1677, 1679, 1680, 1686
Hendrick (d)
  NY Ref Ch mr, 1692, 1695
Herman
  Berg Ref mr, 1668, 1690
  NY Ref Ch mr, 1668, 1681
Herman (d)
  NY Ref Ch mr, 1682
Hildebrand
  Alb Ref mr, 1689
Humphrey
  King Ref mr, 1684
Ide
  NY Ref Ch mr, 1698
Isaac
  Alb Ref mr, 1686
  NY Ref Ch mr, 1686
Jacob
  Alb Ref mr, 1688, 1691,
  1692
  Bkln Ref mr, 1695
  Fltb Ref mr, 1682, 1691
  Hack Ref mr, 1699
  King Ref mr, 1665, 1695
  NY Ref Ch mr, 1659, 1661,
  1674, 1682, 1685, 1686
Jacques
  Fltb Ref mr, 1680
  NY Ref Ch mr, 1689
Jacques (d)
  NY Ref Ch mr, 1652
James
  NY Ref Ch mr, 1659, 1694
Jochem
  King Ref mr, 1689

Joris
  Fltb Ref mr, 1690
  NY Ref Ch mr, 1691, 1695
Joseph
  Fltb Ref mr, 1692
  NY Ref Ch mr, 1696
Jurian
  Fltb Ref mr, 1684
  Hack Ref mr, 1699
Justus
  NY Ref Ch mr, 1697
Kilian
  Alb Ref mr, 1686
Kilian (d)
  Alb Ref mr, 1688
Lambert
  Fltb Ref mr, 1688
Lawrence
  NY Ref Ch mr, 1641, 1662,
  1666, 1698
Louis
  Hack Ref mr, 1697
Lucas
  King Ref mr, 1695
  NY Ref Ch mr, 1657
Lucas (d)
  NY Ref Ch mr, 1666
Mangold
  NY Ref Ch mr, 1692
Marcus
  NY Ref Ch mr, 1697
Martin
  Alb Ref mr, 1693
  Bkln Ref mr, 1663
  Fltb Ref mr, 1683
Matthew
  Berg Ref mr, 1670, 1683
  King Ref mr, 1695
  NY Ref Ch mr, 1656, 1683
Maurice
  Fltb Ref mr, 1690
Maynard
  NY Ref Ch mr, 1659
Moses
  Alb Ref mr, 1697
Nathan
  NY Ref Ch mr, 1664

(d) = deceased at time the
spouse remarried

Anna (cont.)
  Nicasius
    Berg Ref mr, 1691
  Nicholas
    Alb Ref mr, 1699
    Berg Ref mr, 1697
    Fltb Ref mr, 1692
    NY Ref Ch mr, 1656, 1657
  Olof
    NY Ref Ch mr, 1642
  Paul
    NY Ref Ch mr, 1695
  Paul (d)
    NY Ref Ch mr, 1699
  Peter
    Fltb Ref mr, 1681, 1687
    NY Ref Ch mr, 1657, 1672,
    1695
  Peter (d)
    Alb Ref mr, 1693
    NY Ref Ch mr, 1659, 1686
  Philip
    Alb Ref mr, 1692
    NY Ref Ch mr, 1694
  Richard
    NY Ref Ch mr, 1659
  Robert
    NY Ref Ch mr, 1699
  Roger
    Berg Ref mr, 1698
  Samuel
    King Ref mr, 1688
  Samuel (d)
    NY Ref Ch mr, 1656
  Sander (d)
    Alb Ref mr, 1696
  Simon
    Berg Ref mr, 1675
    Fltb Ref mr, 1691
    King Ref mr, 1681
    NY Ref Ch mr, 1649, 1655,
    1656
  Simon (d)
    NY Ref Ch mr, 1679
  Solomon
    Alb Ref mr, 1686
  Solomon (d)
    NY Ref Ch mr, 1664

Thaddius
    Berg Ref mr, 1679
  Theodore
    Fltb Ref mr, 1677
  Thomas
    Bkln Ref mr, 1662
    NY Ref Ch mr, 1641, 1692,
    1695
  Thomas (d)
    NY Ref Ch mr, 1692
  Tobias
    NY Ref Ch mr, 1684
  Tunis
    NY Ref Ch mr, 1681, 1685
  Tunis (d)
    NY Ref Ch mr, 1691
  Walter
    NY Ref Ch mr, 1697
  Werner
    Alb Ref mr, 1696
  William
    Alb Ref mr, 1687, 1688,
    1693
    Berg Ref mr, 1690
    Fltb Ref mr, 1684
    NY Ref Ch mr, 1644, 1664,
    1685, 1694
  William (d)
    NY Ref Ch mr, 1641, 1686,
    1687, 1690
  Wynant
    Bkln Ref mr, 1661
Anna (d)
  Anke
    NY Ref Ch mr, 1661
  Cornelius
    Alb Ref mr, 1689
  Dirk
    NY Ref Ch mr, 1691
  Francis
    NY Ref Ch mr, 1683
  Gerald
    Alb Ref mr, 1692
  Hendrick
    Alb Ref mr, 1688
  Herman
    Hack Ref mr, 1695

Hugh
    NY Ref Ch mr, 1643
  Isaac
    NY Ref Ch mr, 1691
  James
    NY Ref Ch mr, 1659
  Matthew
    Berg Ref mr, 1686
    NY Ref Ch mr, 1656, 1670
  Maynard
    NY Ref Ch mr, 1660
  Michael
    NY Ref Ch mr, 1668
  Nicholas
    Berg Ref mr, 1698
    NY Ref Ch mr, 1670
  Roelof
    Fltb Ref mr, 1688
    NY Ref Ch mr, 1688
  Werner
    NY Ref Ch mr, 1675, 1677
Antoinette
  Paul
    NY Ref Ch mr, 1653
Apollonia
  Conrad
    Hack Ref mr, 1698
  Cornelius (d)
    NY Ref Ch mr, 1659
  Nicholas
    NY Ref Ch mr, 1659
  William
    NY Ref Ch mr, 1664
Apollonia (d)
  Fred
    NY Ref Ch mr, 1663

B

Barbara
  Cornelius
    King Ref mr, 1688
  Garret
    Alb Ref mr, 1696
  George
    NY Ref Ch mr, 1656
  Lucas
    Fltb Ref mr, 1682

Nicholas
Schn Ref mr, 1699
Samuel
Alb Ref mr, 1699
Barbara (d)
Francis
NY Ref Ch mr, 1691
Jacob
Alb Ref mr, 1695
Peter
NY Ref Ch mr, 1663
Thomas
NY Ref Ch mr, 1659
Bathilda
Peter
NY Ref Ch mr, 1677
Bathsheba
James
NY Ref Ch mr, 1683
Beatrice
William
NY Ref Ch mr, 1694
Bernadine
Benjamin
Alb Ref mr, 1688
Cornelius
NY Ref Ch mr, 1661
Gideon
NY Ref Ch mr, 1683
Nicholas
Fltb Ref mr, 1684
NY Ref Ch mr, 1684
Bernadine (d)
Garret
NY Ref Ch mr, 1683
Beverly
Peter
Fltb Ref mr, 1689
Blandina
Peter
NY Ref Ch mr, 1674
Bridget
Evert
NY Ref Ch mr, 1670
Evert (d)
NY Ref Ch mr, 1678
Garret
Alb Ref mr, 1687

Herman
NY Ref Ch mr, 1682
Melchior
NY Ref Ch mr, 1678
Melchior (d)
NY Ref Ch mr, 1682
Nicholas
NY Ref Ch mr, 1649
Peter
NY Ref Ch mr, 1656
Bridget (d)
Herman
NY Ref Ch mr, 1688
William
NY Ref Ch mr, 1664
Britten
Peter (d)
NY Ref Ch mr, 1666

C

Catherine
Abel
Berg Ref mr, 1696
Abraham
Alb Ref mr, 1689
NY Ref Ch mr, 1659
Adrian
Alb Ref mr, 1699
Berg Ref mr, 1672, 1677
NY Ref Ch mr, 1673
Adrian (d)
Berg Ref mr, 1691
Aert
Berg Ref mr, 1692
NY Ref Ch mr, 1692
Albert
NY Ref Ch mr, 1648, 1685
Anthony
Alb Ref mr, 1692
Anthony (d)
NY Ref Ch mr, 1659
Arent (d)
NY Ref Ch mr, 1656
August
Alb Ref mr, 1699

Barent
Alb Ref mr, 1699
Fltb Ref mr, 1684
NY Ref Ch mr, 1662
Schn Ref mr, 1699
Caspar
Berg Ref mr, 1671
NY Ref Ch mr, 1696
Charles
Berg Ref mr, 1678
Christian
NY Ref Ch mr, 1657
Christopher
NY Ref Ch mr, 1660, 1661
Christopher (d)
Fltb Ref mr, 1688
NY Ref Ch mr, 1688
Conrad
Alb Ref mr, 1688
Cornelius
Bkln Ref mr, 1685
Fltb Ref mr, 1685
NY Ref Ch mr, 1659, 1693
Cornelius (d)
Alb Ref mr, 1692
NY Ref Ch mr, 1657
Daniel
NY Ref Ch mr, 1661
Daniel (d)
Fltb Ref mr, 1679
David
NY Ref Ch mr, 1668
Dietrich
Fltb Ref mr, 1678
Dirk
Berg Ref mr, 1698
King Ref mr, 1662, 1695
Dirk (d)
NY Ref Ch mr, 1657
Douw
Fltb Ref mr, 1688
Elias (d)
Alb Ref mr, 1695
Evert
NY Ref Ch mr, 1690
Francis
NY Ref Ch mr, 1657, 1659,
1679, 1697

Catherine (cont.)

Francis (d)
NY Ref Ch mr, 1679

Fred
Berg Ref mr, 1672
NY Ref Ch mr, 1657, 1692

Garret
Alb Ref mr, 1690, 1692
Berg Ref mr, 1691
Fltb Ref mr, 1689
NY Ref Ch mr, 1659, 1685,
1689

Gilbert
NY Ref Ch mr, 1643

Hendrick
Alb Ref mr, 1684, 1688,
1695
Fltb Ref mr, 1686, 1687
King NYGB, 1672
NY Ref Ch mr, 1652, 1660,
1684, 1689, 1693, 1699

Hendrick (d)
NY Ref Ch mr, 1643, 1645,
1689

Hugh
NY Ref Ch mr, 1643

Hugh (d)
NY Ref Ch mr, 1648

Jacob
Alb Ref mr, 1687
Fltb Ref mr, 1684
NY Ref Ch mr, 1657, 1679,
1685, 1695

Jacob (d)
Alb Ref mr, 1696
NY Ref Ch mr, 1657, 1668

James
NY Ref Ch mr, 1659

Jeremiah
NY Ref Ch mr, 1664

Jonas
Alb Ref mr, 1696
NY Ref Ch mr, 1664

Jonathan
Alb Ref mr, 1696
NY Ref Ch mr, 1679

Joost
Bkln Ref mr, 1663
NY Ref Ch mr, 1688

Joris
Fltb Ref mr, 1689

Jurian
NY Ref Ch mr, 1645

Justus (d)
NY Ref Ch mr, 1697

Lancaster
NY Ref Ch mr, 1694

Lawrence
NY Ref Ch mr, 1687

Lucas
Alb Ref mr, 1691

Lucas (d)
NY Ref Ch mr, 1658

Martin
NY Ref Ch mr, 1695

Matthew
Berg Ref mr, 1686, 1688,
1692
NY Ref Ch mr, 1655, 1692

Maynard
NY Ref Ch mr, 1656, 1660

Melchior
Alb Ref mr, 1696

Michael
Berg Ref mr, 1668
NY Ref Ch mr, 1668

Nicasius
NY Ref Ch mr, 1655

Nicholas
Fltb Ref mr, 1689
NY Ref Ch mr, 1691

Nicholas (d)
NY Ref Ch mr, 1645

Niew
Fltb Ref mr, 1682

Paul
NY Ref Ch mr, 1640, 1645,
1658

Peter
Berg Ref mr, 1687
Fltb Ref mr, 1679
NY Ref Ch mr, 1642, 1696,
1698

Peter (d)
Bkln Ref mr, 1663
NY Ref Ch mr, 1659

Philip
NY Ref Ch mr, 1675

Reyner (d)
Alb Ref mr, 1696

Richard
Alb Ref mr, 1699

Robert
NY Ref Ch mr, 1685

Roelof
Fltb Ref mr, 1681, 1688
NY Ref Ch mr, 1688

Roger
NY Ref Ch mr, 1646

Roger (d)
Alb Ref mr, 1695

Samuel
NY Ref Ch mr, 1644

Severin
NY Ref Ch mr, 1656

Simon
NY Ref Ch mr, 1686

Thomas
Alb Ref mr, 1689, 1699
NY Ref Ch mr, 1682, 1686

Tunis
Alb Ref mr, 1694
Berg Ref mr, 1677, 1684
Bkln Ref mr, 1694

Waling
Berg Ref mr, 1671

Walran
King Ref mr, 1688

Walter
Fltb Ref mr, 1689
NY Ref Ch mr, 1668

Wessel
Alb Ref mr, 1684

William
Alb Ref mr, 1695
NY Ref Ch mr, 1647, 1678,
1682

William (d)
Fltb Ref mr, 1689

Zachariah
  NY Ref Ch mr, 1696
Catherine (d)
  Cornelius
    King Ref mr, 1684
    NY Ref Ch mr, 1683
  Garret
    NY Ref Ch mr, 1697
  Jacob
    Alb Ref mr, 1691, 1696
    Hack Ref mr, 1699
  Peter
    NY Ref Ch mr, 1657
  Severin
    NY Ref Ch mr, 1671
  William
    King Ref mr, 1698
Catlintje
  Abraham
    NY Ref Ch mr, 1694, 1697
  Albert
    Fltb Ref mr, 1689
  Barent
    Berg Ref mr, 1698
  Charles
    NY Ref Ch mr, 1652
  Christopher
    NY Ref Ch mr, 1697
  Cosine
    NY Ref Ch mr, 1699
  David
    NY Ref Ch mr, 1657
  Dirk
    NY Ref Ch mr, 1669
  Elias
    NY Ref Ch mr, 1671
  Isaac
    NY Ref Ch mr, 1653, 1680
  Isaac (d)
    NY Ref Ch mr, 1697
  Jacob
    King Ref mr, 1698
    NY Ref Ch mr, 1663
  Jonathan
    Alb Ref mr, 1697
  Nicholas
    NY Ref Ch mr, 1670

Samuel
  Bkln Ref mr, 1691
  Fltb Ref mr, 1690
William
  NY Ref Ch mr, 1649, 1695
Catlintje (d)
  Anthony
    NY Ref Ch mr, 1641
  Isaac
    NY Ref Ch mr, 1675
Cecilia
  Abraham
    King Ref mr, 1682
  Hendrick
    NY Ref Ch mr, 1661
  Hendrick (d)
    NY Ref Ch mr, 1664
  Paul
    NY Ref Ch mr, 1664
  Samuel
    NY Ref Ch mr, 1699
Charity
  Evert
    King Ref mr, 1697
Christina
  Arent
    NY Ref Ch mr, 1665
  Barent
    NY Ref Ch mr, 1641, 1675
  Christian
    NY Ref Ch mr, 1657
  Cornelius
    NY Ref Ch mr, 1646, 1655,
    1678
  Cornelius (d)
    NY Ref Ch mr, 1681
  Daniel
    Fltb Ref mr, 1681
    NY Ref Ch mr, 1681
  David
    NY Ref Ch mr, 1659, 1696
  Emanuel
    NY Ref Ch mr, 1644
  Garret
    Fltb Ref mr, 1683
  Hendrick
    NY Ref Ch mr, 1659

Herman
  King Ref mr, 1682
Jacob
  NY Ref Ch mr, 1683
Jacob (d)
  NY Ref Ch mr, 1659
Leonard
  NY Ref Ch mr, 1678
Nathan
  NY Ref Ch mr, 1688
Peter
  Berg Ref mr, 1698
  NY Ref Ch mr, 1659
Roelof (d)
  NY Ref Ch mr, 1661
Swan
  NY Ref Ch mr, 1664
William
  Bkln Ref mr, 1663
  NY Ref Ch mr, 1663, 1677
Christina (d)
  Arent
    NY Ref Ch mr, 1685
  Fred
    NY Ref Ch mr, 1657
Clara
  Cornelius
    Alb Ref mr, 1696
  Tunis
    King Ref mr, 1696
Clara (d)
  Herman
    NY Ref Ch mr, 1662
Constance
  Peter
    Berg Ref mr, 1688
  Reyner (d)
    Berg Ref mr, 1688
Cornelia
  Abraham
    Fltb Ref mr, 1692
    NY Ref Ch mr, 1681
  Andrew
    NY Ref Ch mr, 1695
  Bartholomew
    Alb Ref mr, 1686
  Benjamin
    NY Ref Ch mr, 1693

Cornelia (cont.)

Cornelius
King Ref mr, 1685
NY Ref Ch mr, 1688

David
King Ref mr, 1689

Elias
Hack Ref mr, 1697
NY Ref Ch mr, 1672

Elias (d)
NY Ref Ch mr, 1692

Engelbert
NY Ref Ch mr, 1678

Evert (d)
NY Ref Ch mr, 1681

Garret
Fltb Ref mr, 1682, 1691

Hendrick
Alb Ref mr, 1685, 1698

Herman
Fltb Ref mr, 1682

Isaac
Berg Ref mr, 1690
NY Ref Ch mr, 1674

Jacob
NY Ref Ch mr, 1647, 1653, 1672

Jacob (d)
NY Ref Ch mr, 1653

Jacques
NY Ref Ch mr, 1692

Lawrence
Alb Ref mr, 1687
King Ref mr, 1687

Matthew
Alb Ref mr, 1685

Nicholas
King Ref mr, 1679
NY Ref Ch mr, 1679

Peter
Berg Ref mr, 1686
NY Ref Ch mr, 1685, 1686, 1696, 1697

Rembrant
NY Ref Ch mr, 1682

Robert
Alb Ref mr, 1689

Walter
Alb Ref mr, 1696

Cornelia (d)

Isaac
NY Ref Ch mr, 1680

D

Deborah

Arent
NY Ref Ch mr, 1678

Barent
NY Ref Ch mr, 1690

Daniel
Alb Ref mr, 1695

Garret
NY Ref Ch mr, 1697

Hendrick
Alb Ref mr, 1692, 1694
King Ref mr, 1679

Maynard (d)
Alb Ref mr, 1690

Nicholas
NY Ref Ch mr, 1694

Peter
NY Ref Ch mr, 1663

Thomas
NY Ref Ch mr, 1684, 1691

Thomas (d)
NY Ref Ch mr, 1691, 1697

Walter
Berg Ref mr, 1689

Werner
NY Ref Ch mr, 1667

William
NY Ref Ch mr, 1697, 1699

Deborah (d)

Hendrick
NY Ref Ch mr, 1675

Dina

Anthony
NY Ref Ch mr, 1695

Fred
Fltb Ref mr, 1681

Dorothy

Dominic
NY Ref Ch mr, 1694

Emanuel
NY Ref Ch mr, 1653

Francis
NY Ref Ch mr, 1688

Francis (d)
NY Ref Ch mr, 1694

Garret
NY Ref Ch mr, 1696

James
NY Ref Ch mr, 1692

Richard (d)
NY Ref Ch mr, 1692

Stephen
NY Ref Ch mr, 1642

Volkert
NY Ref Ch mr, 1650

Dorothy (d)

Caspar
NY Ref Ch mr, 1652

Emanuel
NY Ref Ch mr, 1689

Isaac
NY Ref Ch mr, 1679

Thomas
NY Ref Ch mr, 1687

E

Eleanor

Bartel
Berg Ref mr, 1695

Robert (d)
NY Ref Ch mr, 1687

Thomas
NY Ref Ch mr, 1687

W.
King Ref mr, 1673

Eliza

William
NY Ref Ch mr, 1649

Elizabeth

Abraham
NY Ref Ch mr, 1690

Abraham (d)
Alb Ref mr, 1692
NY Ref Ch mr, 1685

Adrian
NY Ref Ch mr, 1679

Albert (d)
NY Ref Ch mr, 1659

Bride/Groom Pairs Directory

Alexander
NY Ref Ch mr, 1688
Andrew
NY Ref Ch mr, 1690
Anthony
Alb Ref mr, 1698
Fltb Ref mr, 1684
King Ref mr, 1696
NY Ref Ch mr, 1696
Anthony (d)
Bkln Ref mr, 1695
Arent
King Ref mr, 1686
NY Ref Ch mr, 1685
Barne (d)
NY Ref Ch mr, 1645
Benoni
Alb Ref mr, 1686
Bernard
NY Ref Ch mr, 1688
Brayer (d)
NY Ref Ch mr, 1697
Bruno
Fltb Ref mr, 1682
King Ref mr, 1682
Carl
Fltb Ref mr, 1680
Caspar
NY Ref Ch mr, 1687
Cornelius
NY Ref Ch mr, 1692
Cornelius (d)
Alb Ref mr, 1691
Daniel
Alb Ref mr, 1696, 1697
David
NY Ref Ch mr, 1689
Dionysius
Fltb Ref mr, 1682
Dirk
Berg Ref mr, 1672
Fltb Ref mr, 1684
NY Ref Ch mr, 1657, 1672,
1684, 1698
Dirk (d)
NY Ref Ch mr, 1688
Edward
Berg Ref mr, 1684

Elias
NY Ref Ch mr, 1678
Elsy
NY Ref Ch mr, 1697
Ephraim
NY Ref Ch mr, 1679
Ephraim (d)
NY Ref Ch mr, 1692
Evert
Alb Ref mr, 1686
Francis
NY Ref Ch mr, 1664, 1697
Francis (d)
Fltb Ref mr, 1679
Fred
King Ref mr, 1681
Garret
Alb Ref mr, 1693
NY Ref Ch mr, 1659, 1690
Garret (d)
NY Ref Ch mr, 1664
George
Alb Ref mr, 1691
NY Ref Ch mr, 1693
Gerlach
NY Ref Ch mr, 1654
Gilbert
NY Ref Ch mr, 1655
Giles
Alb Ref mr, 1699
Schn Ref mr, 1699
Godfrey
NY Ref Ch mr, 1664
Hendrick
NY Ref Ch mr, 1699
Herman
NY Ref Ch mr, 1645
Hessel
Berg Ref mr, 1690
NY Ref Ch mr, 1690
Hugh
NY Ref Ch mr, 1696
Isaac
NY Ref Ch mr, 1652, 1653,
1681
Isaac (d)
NY Ref Ch mr, 1680

Jacob
Bkln Ref mr, 1677
King Ref mr, 1689
NY Ref Ch mr, 1652, 1674,
1688, 1697
Jacob (d)
Alb Ref mr, 1691
James
King Ref mr, 1696
NY Ref Ch mr, 1685
James (d)
King Ref mr, 1683
NY Ref Ch mr, 1695
Jochem
King Ref mr, 1676
NY Ref Ch mr, 1667
Joost
King Ref mr, 1668
NY Ref Ch mr, 1662, 1694
Joris
NY Ref Ch mr, 1688
Joseph
Berg Ref mr, 1678
Fltb Ref mr, 1681
Josiah (d)
NY Ref Ch mr, 1694
Kier
NY Ref Ch mr, 1668
Lawrence (d)
NY Ref Ch mr, 1659
Leins
NY Ref Ch mr, 1694
Leonard
NY Ref Ch mr, 1688
Marcus (d)
NY Ref Ch mr, 1659
Martin
Bkln Ref mr, 1663
NY Ref Ch mr, 1663, 1682
Martin (d)
NY Ref Ch mr, 1654
Matthew
NY Ref Ch mr, 1675
Maynard
Bkln Ref mr, 1664
NY Ref Ch mr, 1664
Melchior
Alb Ref mr, 1692

(d) = deceased at time the
spouse remarried

Elizabeth (cont.)

Michael
NY Ref Ch mr, 1642

Nicholas
Fltb Ref mr, 1685
King Ref mr, 1681
NY Ref Ch mr, 1681

Owen
NY Ref Ch mr, 1694

Owen (d)
NY Ref Ch mr, 1698

Peter
Berg Ref mr, 1685
Bkln Ref mr, 1685
King Ref mr, no date
NY Ref Ch mr, 1647, 1664,
1667, 1680, 1685

Peter (d)
NY Ref Ch mr, 1662

Philip
NY Ref Ch mr, 1687

Reyner
NY Ref Ch mr, 1674

Robert (d)
King Ref mr, 1696

Roger
NY Ref Ch mr, 1694

Samuel
NY Ref Ch mr, 1659

Samuel (d)
NY Ref Ch mr, 1682

Stephen
Alb Ref mr, 1699

Sybrant (d)
Alb Ref mr, 1686

Thomas
NY Ref Ch mr, 1642

Thomas (d)
NY Ref Ch mr, 1694

Timothy
NY Ref Ch mr, 1681

Tobias
Fltb Ref mr, 1684
NY Ref Ch mr, 1684

Tunis
Alb Ref mr, 1693
NY Ref Ch mr, 1659

Tunis (d)
Alb Ref mr, 1699

Walter
Alb Ref mr, 1691
Fltb Ref mr, 1679
NY Ref Ch mr, 1698

Werner
NY Ref Ch mr, 1677

William
Alb Ref mr, 1692
Bkln Ref mr, 1695
King Ref mr, 1683
NY Ref Ch mr, 1675, 1682,
1688, 1694, 1695

William (d)
NY Ref Ch mr, 1694

Wynant (d)
NY Ref Ch mr, 1692

Elizabeth (d)

Arent
NY Ref Ch mr, 1695

Cornelius
NY Ref Ch mr, 1659

Dirk
NY Ref Ch mr, 1672

Enoch
NY Ref Ch mr, 1699

Isaac
NY Ref Ch mr, 1663

Joost
NY Ref Ch mr, 1681

Martin
NY Ref Ch mr, 1664

Matthew
NY Ref Ch mr, 1696

Peter
NY Ref Ch mr, 1679, 1699

Pierre
Alb Ref mr, 1693

Reyner
NY Ref Ch mr, 1692

Timothy
NY Ref Ch mr, 1686

Walter
Alb Ref mr, 1691

William
King Ref mr, 1698

Elpkin

Albert
NY Ref Ch mr, 1652

David (d)
NY Ref Ch mr, 1652

Elsie

Abraham
Alb Ref mr, 1696

Adam (d)
NY Ref Ch mr, 1670

Adrian
NY Ref Ch mr, 1643

Albert
NY Ref Ch mr, 1668

Albert (d)
NY Ref Ch mr, 1664

Andrew
Alb Ref mr, 1697

Barent
NY Ref Ch mr, 1654

Barent (d)
NY Ref Ch mr, 1656

Benjamin
NY Ref Ch mr, 1671

Bernard
NY Ref Ch mr, 1698

Cornelius
King Ref mr, 1684, 1695

David
Alb Ref mr, 1694

Didlove
NY Ref Ch mr, 1680

Didlove (d)
NY Ref Ch mr, 1689

Edward
Berg Ref mr, 1688
NY Ref Ch mr, 1688

Egbert
NY Ref Ch mr, 1678

Evert
NY Ref Ch mr, 1657

Francis
Alb Ref mr, 1689

Garret
NY Ref Ch mr, 1693

Giles
NY Ref Ch mr, 1642

Hendrick
    King Ref mr, 1666
Hendrick (d)
    King Ref mr, 1684
    NY Ref Ch mr, 1660
Jacob
    Bkln Ref mr, 1677
    NY Ref Ch mr, 1663
Ludwich
    NY Ref Ch mr, 1699
Marinus
    NY Ref Ch mr, 1670
Matthew
    NY Ref Ch mr, 1650
Melem
    NY Ref Ch mr, 1644
Nicholas
    Berg Ref mr, 1698
Omie
    Alb Ref mr, 1697
Otto
    NY Ref Ch mr, 1664
Peter
    NY Ref Ch mr, 1652, 1699
Peter (d)
    NY Ref Ch mr, 1663
Sander
    Fltb Ref mr, 1682
Thomas
    NY Ref Ch mr, 1656
Thomas (d)
    NY Ref Ch mr, 1699
Tunis
    NY Ref Ch mr, 1689
William
    Fltb Ref mr, 1681
Wolfgang
    NY Ref Ch mr, 1660
Elsie (d)
Peter
    NY Ref Ch mr, 1644
Thomas
    NY Ref Ch mr, 1664
Emma
Dirk
    NY Ref Ch mr, 1672
Francis (d)
    NY Ref Ch mr, 1672

Martin
    NY Ref Ch mr, 1664
Peter (d)
    Alb Ref mr, 1697
Richard
    Alb Ref mr, 1697
Engel
Benjamin
    Alb Ref mr, 1692
Burger
    NY Ref Ch mr, 1639
Christian
    NY Ref Ch mr, 1658
Daniel
    Berg Ref mr, 1692
Deliverance
    NY Ref Ch mr, 1695
Egbert
    NY Ref Ch mr, 1641
Fred
    King Ref mr, 1666
Joshua
    NY Ref Ch mr, 1695
Nicholas (d)
    King Ref mr, 1698
Otto
    NY Ref Ch mr, 1668
Peter
    NY Ref Ch mr, 1677
Peter (d)
    NY Ref Ch mr, 1686
Stephen
    King Ref mr, 1698
William
    NY Ref Ch mr, 1671
Engel (d)
Anthony
    Alb Ref mr, 1684
Peter
    Alb Ref mr, 1691
Esther
Pierre
    NPal Ref mr, 1692
Eunice
Cornelius (d)
    NY Ref Ch mr, 1686
Dietrich (d)
    NY Ref Ch mr, 1657

Gabriel
    NY Ref Ch mr, 1657
Herman
    NY Ref Ch mr, 1688
Jacob (d)
    NY Ref Ch mr, 1687
Simon
    NY Ref Ch mr, 1686
Eunice (d)
Lavinus
    Alb Ref mr, 1699
Eva
Cornelius
    King Ref mr, 1696
    NY Ref Ch mr, 1661, 1696
Dirk
    NY Ref Ch mr, 1675
Jacob
    King Ref mr, 1698
    NY Ref Ch mr, 1691, 1697
Jacques
    NY Ref Ch mr, 1683
Jonas
    NY Ref Ch mr, 1688
Jonas (d)
    NY Ref Ch mr, 1698
Lucas
    NY Ref Ch mr, 1655
Marcus
    NY Ref Ch mr, 1698
Peter
    King Ref mr, 1697
    NY Ref Ch mr, 1649
Thomas
    NY Ref Ch mr, 1698
Ulrich
    NY Ref Ch mr, 1641
Eva (d)
Roelof
    Berg Ref mr, 1691
    NY Ref Ch mr, 1691

F

Frances
Abraham
    NY Ref Ch mr, 1656

(d) = deceased at time the
spouse remarried

Bride/Groom Pairs Directory

Frances (cont.)
Abraham (d)
  Berg Ref mr, 1691
Anthony
  NY Ref Ch mr, 1644
Dominic
  NY Ref Ch mr, 1652
Gregory
  NY Ref Ch mr, 1642
Louis
  Berg Ref mr, 1672
Michael (d)
  Berg Ref mr, 1685
Nicholas
  Fltb Ref mr, 1692
Roelof
  Berg Ref mr, 1691
  NY Ref Ch mr, 1691
Thomas
  Berg Ref mr, 1685
Frances (d)
Abraham
  NY Ref Ch mr, 1691
Hendrick
  NY Ref Ch mr, 1650
Peter
  NY Ref Ch mr, 1659
Thomas
  NY Ref Ch mr, 1698
Frederica
Jurian
  Berg Ref mr, 1667

G

Geesje
Abraham
  Alb Ref mr, 1687
Bruyn
  NY Ref Ch mr, 1681
Bruyn (d)
  NY Ref Ch mr, 1688
Caspar (d)
  NY Ref Ch mr, 1652
Conrad
  Alb Ref mr, 1697
Daniel
  Hack Ref mr, 1696

Dirk
  NY Ref Ch mr, 1658, 1667
Hendrick
  Berg Ref mr, 1666
Herman
  NY Ref Ch mr, 1688
Joris
  NY Ref Ch mr, 1652
Jurian
  Berg Ref mr, 1690
  NY Ref Ch mr, 1695
Nicholas
  NY Ref Ch mr, 1667
Geesje (d)
Jurian
  Hack Ref mr, 1699
Nicholas
  NY Ref Ch mr, 1672
Tunis
  NY Ref Ch mr, 1689
Gerarda
Ditmar
  Bkln Ref mr, 1664
  NY Ref Ch mr, 1664
Hendrick
  King Ref mr, 1685
Hendrick (d)
  King Ref mr, 1698
William
  King Ref mr, 1698
Gertrude
Abel (d)
  NY Ref Ch mr, 1647
Abraham
  Alb Ref mr, 1691
  Bkln Ref mr, 1695
  Fltb Ref mr, 1690
  NY Ref Ch mr, 1642, 1693,
  1696
Aelst
  NY Ref Ch mr, 1695
Aert
  Berg Ref mr, 1695
  King Ref mr, 1661
Andrew
  NY Ref Ch mr, 1672
Andrew (d)
  NY Ref Ch mr, 1660

Anthony
  Alb Ref mr, 1684
Arent
  Alb Ref mr, 1688
Barent
  Alb Ref mr, 1687
Bartel (d)
  NY Ref Ch mr, 1666
Bartholomew
  NY Ref Ch mr, 1688
Caspar
  NY Ref Ch mr, 1664
Christian
  NY Ref Ch mr, 1668
Christopher
  Fltb Ref mr, 1678
Cornelius
  Fltb Ref mr, 1678
  NY Ref Ch mr, 1665
Cornelius (d)
  NY Ref Ch mr, 1671
Dirk
  NY Ref Ch mr, 1659, 1660
Dirk (d)
  NY Ref Ch mr, 1687
Edward
  Berg Ref mr, 1681
  NY Ref Ch mr, 1681
Egbert
  NY Ref Ch mr, 1662
Evert
  King Ref mr, 1688
Francis
  NY Ref Ch mr, 1661, 1685
Francis (d)
  NY Ref Ch mr, 1665
Gabriel
  Fltb Ref mr, 1692
Garret
  King Ref mr, 1696
  NY Ref Ch mr, 1647, 1670
Garret (d)
  NY Ref Ch mr, 1643
George (d)
  NY Ref Ch mr, 1641
Hendrick
  Fltb Ref mr, 1680
  King Ref mr, 1688

NY Ref Ch mr, 1655, 1657, 1663
Hendrick (d)
NY Ref Ch mr, 1653, 1664
Herman
Berg Ref mr, 1686
Hack Ref mr, 1695
Herman (d)
NY Ref Ch mr, 1670
Increase
Hack Ref mr, 1699
Isaac
Fltb Ref mr, 1687
Jacob
Alb Ref mr, 1688
Berg Ref mr, 1672
Fltb Ref mr, 1684, 1687
Hack Ref mr, 1697
King Ref mr, 1688
NY Ref Ch mr, 1678, 1688
Jacob (d)
King Ref mr, 1661
James
Alb Ref mr, 1699
Leonard
NY Ref Ch mr, 1683
Louis
Berg Ref mr, 1679
Matthew
NY Ref Ch mr, 1686
Nicholas
NY Ref Ch mr, 1647, 1653
Oben
NY Ref Ch mr, 1641
Peter
NY Ref Ch mr, 1661, 1688
Philip
NY Ref Ch mr, 1647
Robert
Alb Ref mr, 1686
Roelof
Hack Ref mr, 1695
NY Ref Ch mr, 1643
Roelof (d)
Berg Ref mr, 1672
Roger
Fltb Ref mr, 1684

Servis
NY Ref Ch mr, 1697
Siegmond
Bkln Ref mr, 1660
NY Ref Ch mr, 1660
Stephen
NY Ref Ch mr, 1671
Thomas
Alb Ref mr, 1691
King Ref mr, 1698
NY Ref Ch mr, 1664
Timothy
Hack Ref mr, 1699
Tunis
Fltb Ref mr, 1687
NY Ref Ch mr, 1687, 1696
Wessel
NY Ref Ch mr, 1643
William
Hack Ref mr, 1699
NY Ref Ch mr, 1660, 1666
Gertrude (d)
Aert
King Ref mr, 1682, 1684
Arent
NY Ref Ch mr, 1665
Barent
NY Ref Ch mr, 1671
Francis
NY Ref Ch mr, 1692
Jacob
Berg Ref mr, 1672
Gilberta
Arent
NY Ref Ch mr, 1660
Gilberta (d)
Arent
NY Ref Ch mr, 1679
Hendrick
Alb Ref mr, 1695
Grace
Robert
NY Ref Ch mr, 1689

H

Harmina
Abraham
NY Ref Ch mr, 1694

Bartel
NY Ref Ch mr, 1662
Egbert (d)
NY Ref Ch mr, 1664
Garret
NY Ref Ch mr, 1654, 1664
Isaac
NY Ref Ch mr, 1685, 1691
Isaac (d)
NY Ref Ch mr, 1694, 1697
Jurian
NY Ref Ch mr, 1658
Thomas
Bkln Ref mr, 1680
Fltb Ref mr, 1680
NY Ref Ch mr, 1680, 1697
William (d)
NY Ref Ch mr, 1654
Harmina (d)
Garret
King Ref mr, 1696
Thomas
NY Ref Ch mr, 1691
Helena
Abraham
NY Ref Ch mr, 1685
Arent
NY Ref Ch mr, 1695
Carl
NY Ref Ch mr, 1648
Daniel
NY Ref Ch mr, 1696
David
Fltb Ref mr, 1681
NY Ref Ch mr, 1681, 1691
Dionysius
Fltb Ref mr, 1685
Edward
NY Ref Ch mr, 1692
Francis
NY Ref Ch mr, 1683
Hendrick (d)
NY Ref Ch mr, 1685
Louis
NY Ref Ch mr, 1646
Michael
NY Ref Ch mr, 1693

Helena (cont.)

Nicholas
Fltb Ref mr, 1683
Robert
NY Ref Ch mr, 1694
Thomas (d)
NY Ref Ch mr, 1646
Tunis
NY Ref Ch mr, 1680
Walter
NY Ref Ch mr, 1698

Helena (d)

David
NY Ref Ch mr, 1699

Henrietta

Aldert
NY Ref Ch mr, 1656
Andrew
Fltb Ref mr, 1690
Anthony
NY Ref Ch mr, 1698
Cornelius (d)
Berg Ref mr, 1698
Dirk
NY Ref Ch mr, 1691
Evert
NY Ref Ch mr, 1646
Galeyn
NY Ref Ch mr, 1668
Garret
NY Ref Ch mr, 1663
Giles (d)
NY Ref Ch mr, 1685
Hubert
King Ref mr, 1679
Jacob
NY Ref Ch mr, 1685
Lucas
Alb Ref mr, 1686
Martin
Bkln Ref mr, 1662
NY Ref Ch mr, 1662
Michael (d)
Bkln Ref mr, 1685
Peter
Berg Ref mr, 1670
NY Ref Ch mr, 1680

Pierre
Alb Ref mr, 1696
Reyner
Berg Ref mr, 1698
Hack Ref mr, 1699

Henrietta (d)

Cornelius
Hack Ref mr, 1699
Lucas
Alb Ref mr, 1692
Peter
Alb Ref mr, 1688

Hester

Abraham
Alb Ref mr, 1699
NY Ref Ch mr, 1697
Schn Ref mr, 1699
Albert
Hack Ref mr, 1695
Arent
NY Ref Ch mr, 1690
Claude (d)
NY Ref Ch mr, 1687
Dirk
Berg Ref mr, 1681
Fred
NY Ref Ch mr, 1677
Garret (d)
NY Ref Ch mr, 1665
Hendrick
Fltb Ref mr, 1688
Isaac
NY Ref Ch mr, 1696
Jacques (d)
NY Ref Ch mr, 1640
Jurian
NY Ref Ch mr, 1673
Marcus
Fltb Ref mr, 1692
Peter
NY Ref Ch mr, 1640, 1666, 1684
Samuel
NY Ref Ch mr, 1689
Timothy
NY Ref Ch mr, 1686
Ulrich
Hack Ref mr, 1698

Hester (d)

Isaac
NY Ref Ch mr, 1695

Hilda

Albert
King Ref mr, 1664
Andrew (d)
King Ref mr, 1664
Arent
Fltb Ref mr, 1677
Barent
Fltb Ref mr, 1692
Cornelius
NY Ref Ch mr, 1654, 1657
Evert
NY Ref Ch mr, 1669
Garret (d)
NY Ref Ch mr, 1669
Giles
NY Ref Ch mr, 1689
Ide
NY Ref Ch mr, 1652
Jacob
NY Ref Ch mr, 1658
Lawrence
NY Ref Ch mr, 1669
Lubbert
Berg Ref mr, 1679
Ludwich
NY Ref Ch mr, 1699
Nicholas
NY Ref Ch mr, 1646, 1682
Oliver (d)
NY Ref Ch mr, 1689
Peter
King Ref mr, 1696
NY Ref Ch mr, 1674
Philip
NY Ref Ch mr, 1696
Siegbert
NY Ref Ch mr, 1697
Tobias
NY Ref Ch mr, 1655
William
King Ref mr, 1698
NY Ref Ch mr, 1692

Hilda (d)
  Albert
    NY Ref Ch mr, 1652
Hillary
  Ludwich
    NY Ref Ch mr, 1660
  Ludwich (d)
    NY Ref Ch mr, 1682
  Peter
    NY Ref Ch mr, 1682

I

Ida
  Andrew
    Alb Ref mr, 1692
  Dirk (d)
    Alb Ref mr, 1693
  Hendrick (d)
    Alb Ref mr, 1692
  Isaac
    Berg Ref mr, 1684
  Jacob
    Alb Ref mr, 1693
  Thomas
    NY Ref Ch mr, 1696
  Tunis (d)
    NY Ref Ch mr, 1696
Ida (d)
  Garret
    NY Ref Ch mr, 1659
Inga (d)
  Siegmond
    NY Ref Ch mr, 1660
Isabel
  Adrian
    NY Ref Ch mr, 1685
  Albert
    NY Ref Ch mr, 1699
  Anthony
    NY Ref Ch mr, 1697
  Arent
    NY Ref Ch mr, 1660
  Arent (d)
    NY Ref Ch mr, 1685
  Bastian
    NY Ref Ch mr, 1646

Conrad
    NY Ref Ch mr, 1675
Francis
    NY Ref Ch mr, 1670
Francis (d)
    NY Ref Ch mr, 1684
Garret
    Berg Ref mr, 1692
    NY Ref Ch mr, 1673
George
    NY Ref Ch mr, 1684
Ide
    NY Ref Ch mr, 1685
Jacob
    King Ref mr, 1678
Nicholas
    NY Ref Ch mr, 1695
Peter
    NY Ref Ch mr, 1646, 1681,
    1693
Isabel (d)
  Cornelius
    NY Ref Ch mr, 1662

J

Jacobina (d)
  Martin
    NY Ref Ch mr, 1695
Janet
  Adam
    NY Ref Ch mr, 1647
  Adam (d)
    NY Ref Ch mr, 1659
  Aert
    King Ref mr, 1682
  Albert
    NY Ref Ch mr, 1679
  Alexander
    Fltb Ref mr, 1690
  Andrew
    Fltb Ref mr, 1692
    King Ref mr, 1682
  Anthony
    Berg Ref mr, 1692
    King Ref mr, 1667
  Arent
    Alb Ref mr, 1684
    NY Ref Ch mr, 1665

Arnold
    NY Ref Ch mr, 1675
August
    NY Ref Ch mr, 1651
Barent
    NY Ref Ch mr, 1687
Caspar
    NY Ref Ch mr, 1652, 1695
Christopher
    Berg Ref mr, 1684
Conrad
    NY Ref Ch mr, 1678
Cornelius
    King Ref mr, 1684, no date
    NY Ref Ch mr, 1696
Dirk
    King Ref mr, 1698
    NY Ref Ch mr, 1641, 1670
Edward (d)
    NY Ref Ch mr, 1645
Elken
    NY Ref Ch mr, 1647
Evert
    NY Ref Ch mr, 1671
Evert (d)
    NY Ref Ch mr, 1698
Francis
    Hack Ref mr, 1696
    NY Ref Ch mr, 1659, 1685
Gabriel
    NY Ref Ch mr, 1658
Garret
    Fltb Ref mr, 1682, 1685,
    1692
    NY Ref Ch mr, 1693
Gilbert
    Fltb Ref mr, 1689
    NY Ref Ch mr, 1688
Hendrick
    Fltb Ref mr, 1680
    King Ref mr, 1679
    NY Ref Ch mr, 1664, 1692
Herman
    Berg Ref mr, 1678
Hubert
    Bkln Ref mr, 1662
    NY Ref Ch mr, 1662

(d) = deceased at time the
spouse remarried

Janet (cont.)

Isaac
Alb Ref mr, 1698
NY Ref Ch mr, 1659, 1694,
1695
Jacob
Fltb Ref mr, 1683, 1684
King Ref mr, 1698
NY Ref Ch mr, 1650, 1678,
1687
Jacob (d)
NY Ref Ch mr, 1695
James
NY Ref Ch mr, 1689
James (d)
NY Ref Ch mr, 1689
Jeremiah
NY Ref Ch mr, 1686
Joris
NY Ref Ch mr, 1674
Joseph (d)
Fltb Ref mr, 1687
Jurian (d)
NY Ref Ch mr, 1654
Lambert
Alb Ref mr, 1693
Lawrence
Alb Ref mr, 1699
NY Ref Ch mr, 1658
Leonard
Alb Ref mr, 1688
Lucas
Fltb Ref mr, 1689
Ludwich
King Ref mr, 1682
Martin
NY Ref Ch mr, 1658, 1671
Martin (d)
NY Ref Ch mr, 1670
Matthew
King Ref mr, 1679
NY Ref Ch mr, 1679, 1695,
1698
Maynard
NY Ref Ch mr, 1681
Michael
NY Ref Ch mr, 1655, 1661

Moses
NY Ref Ch mr, 1694
Nicholas
Fltb Ref mr, 1692
King Ref mr, 1698
NY Ref Ch mr, 1672
Paul
NY Ref Ch mr, 1695
Peter
Alb Ref mr, 1688, 1698
Fltb Ref mr, 1684
King Ref mr, 1682, 1697
NY Ref Ch mr, 1657, 1674,
1678, 1683, 1698
Philip
NY Ref Ch mr, 1658
Remmet
NY Ref Ch mr, 1642
Reyner
Fltb Ref mr, 1687
NY Ref Ch mr, 1687
Richard (d)
Alb Ref mr, 1693
Rowland
NY Ref Ch mr, 1640
Samuel
Fltb Ref mr, 1689
NY Ref Ch mr, 1655
Seger
NY Ref Ch mr, 1677
Simon
Alb Ref mr, 1685
NY Ref Ch mr, 1686
Simon (d)
Alb Ref mr, 1692
Thomas
Berg Ref mr, 1691
NY Ref Ch mr, 1654, 1659
Tobias
NY Ref Ch mr, 1649
Tobias (d)
NY Ref Ch mr, 1659
Tunis
Alb Ref mr, 1696
NY Ref Ch mr, 1677
Volkert
Alb Ref mr, 1698

Walter
Alb Ref mr, 1695
William
Berg Ref mr, 1676
King NYGB, 1672
NY Ref Ch mr, 1675
William (d)
NY Ref Ch mr, 1664
Wyatt
NY Ref Ch mr, 1678
Janet (d)
Caspar
NY Ref Ch mr, 1685
Christopher
Berg Ref mr, 1698
Dirk
NY Ref Ch mr, 1659
Garret
NY Ref Ch mr, 1693
Kier
NY Ref Ch mr, 1668
Ludwich
NY Ref Ch mr, 1699
Martin
Alb Ref mr, 1686
Nicholas
NY Ref Ch mr, 1659
Thomas
NY Ref Ch mr, 1645, 1657,
1696
William
NY Ref Ch mr, 1676
Jemima
Abraham
Alb Ref mr, 1697
NY Ref Ch mr, 1662, 1691
Andrew
NY Ref Ch mr, 1698
Garret
King Ref mr, 1668
Garret (d)
Berg Ref mr, 1672
Jacob
Alb Ref mr, 1694
Schn Ref mr, 1694
Joseph
NY Ref Ch mr, 1650

Nicholas
  Berg Ref mr, 1684
  Fltb Ref mr, 1684
Reyer
  NY Ref Ch mr, 1686
Robert
  NY Ref Ch mr, 1690
Wessel
  King Ref mr, 1694
  NY Ref Ch mr, 1693
Joanna
Andrew
  Berg Ref mr, 1688
Barent
  NY Ref Ch mr, 1686
Barent (d)
  NY Ref Ch mr, 1694
Cornelius
  Bkln Ref mr, 1696
David
  Alb Ref mr, 1695
Evert
  NY Ref Ch mr, 1686
Garret
  Fltb Ref mr, 1684
Hendrick
  NY Ref Ch mr, 1681, 1698
Hieronymus
  NY Ref Ch mr, 1659
Joris (d)
  NY Ref Ch mr, 1681
Lawrence
  NY Ref Ch mr, 1692
Matthew
  NY Ref Ch mr, 1670
Peter
  Alb Ref mr, 1684
Joanna (d)
Walter
  Fltb Ref mr, 1689
Josina
Anthony
  NY Ref Ch mr, 1685
Cornelius
  NY Ref Ch mr, 1659
Evert
  Alb Ref mr, 1689

Garret
  NY Ref Ch mr, 1679
Garret (d)
  NY Ref Ch mr, 1685
Peter
  NY Ref Ch mr, 1669
Peter (d)
  NY Ref Ch mr, 1679
Thomas (d)
  NY Ref Ch mr, 1659
William
  Bkln Ref mr, 1661
  NY Ref Ch mr, 1661
Judith
Aegeus
  NY Ref Ch mr, 1663
Gabriel
  NY Ref Ch mr, 1674
Lucas
  Alb Ref mr, 1692
Martin
  NY Ref Ch mr, 1696
Nicholas
  NY Ref Ch mr, 1666
Onckel
  NY Ref Ch mr, 1694
Onckel (d)
  NY Ref Ch mr, 1696
Peter
  NY Ref Ch mr, 1642
Solomon
  NY Ref Ch mr, 1685
Judith (d)
Adrian
  NY Ref Ch mr, 1663
Richard
  NY Ref Ch mr, 1659
William
  NY Ref Ch mr, 1658
Julia
Albert
  Fltb Ref mr, 1681

K

Kunigunda
Lawrence
  NY Ref Ch mr, 1676

Nicholas
  NY Ref Ch mr, 1671
Walran
  NY Ref Ch mr, 1668
Walran (d)
  NY Ref Ch mr, 1671

L

Lambertina
Andrew
  NY Ref Ch mr, 1652
Laurentia
Thomas (d)
  King Ref mr, 1695
Wessel
  King Ref mr, 1695
Lavinia
Aert (d)
  NY Ref Ch mr, 1662
Benjamin
  Fltb Ref mr, 1688
Caspar
  NY Ref Ch mr, 1693
Cornelius
  NY Ref Ch mr, 1662
Evert
  NY Ref Ch mr, 1693
Garret
  NY Ref Ch mr, 1680
Garret (d)
  NY Ref Ch mr, 1693
Hendrick
  NY Ref Ch mr, 1697
Herman
  NY Ref Ch mr, 1660
Isaac
  Fltb Ref mr, 1689
Jonathan
  Fltb Ref mr, 1692
Paul (d)
  Berg Ref mr, 1687
Peter
  Berg Ref mr, 1687
Roger
  Alb Ref mr, 1692
Simon
  NY Ref Ch mr, 1661

(d) = deceased at time the
spouse remarried

Lavinia (cont.)
William
King Ref mr, 1698
NY Ref Ch mr, 1659
Lavinia (d)
Dirk
NY Ref Ch mr, 1663
Lea
Fred
Fltb Ref mr, 1687
Jonathan
Alb Ref mr, 1693
Lambert
Alb Ref mr, 1697
Nicholas (d)
Alb Ref mr, 1693
Lena
Arent (d)
NY Ref Ch mr, 1661
Jochem (d)
NY Ref Ch mr, 1654
Lambert
Bkln Ref mr, 1661
NY Ref Ch mr, 1661
Martin
NY Ref Ch mr, 1668
William
NY Ref Ch mr, 1654
Leonora (d)
Francis
NY Ref Ch mr, 1685
Letitia
David
NY Ref Ch mr, 1658
Lawrence
NY Ref Ch mr, 1665
Lievyntie
Cornelius
NY Ref Ch mr, 1673
Lucretia
Francis
NY Ref Ch mr, 1646, 1680
Herman
NY Ref Ch mr, 1674
Nicholas
NY Ref Ch mr, 1680

Lucy
Anthony
NY Ref Ch mr, 1641
Lawrence (d)
NY Ref Ch mr, 1641
Luytje
Adrian
NY Ref Ch mr, 1672
Hendrick (d)
NY Ref Ch mr, 1672
Lydia
Amos (d)
NY Ref Ch mr, 1687
Jacob
NY Ref Ch mr, 1698
Nicholas
NY Ref Ch mr, 1655
Peter
NY Ref Ch mr, 1695

Lydia (d)
Nicholas
King Ref mr, 1689

M
Magdalena
Adam
NY Ref Ch mr, 1645, 1661
Adam (d)
NY Ref Ch mr, 1663
Albert
Berg Ref mr, 1676
Anthony (d)
NY Ref Ch mr, 1659
Caspar
NY Ref Ch mr, 1685
Cornelius
Berg Ref mr, 1677
Bkln Ref mr, 1691
Hack Ref mr, 1699
NY Ref Ch mr, 1652
Cornelius (d)
NY Ref Ch mr, 1657, 1683
Dirk
King Ref mr, 1692
Dominic
Fltb Ref mr, 1689

Garret
Fltb Ref mr, 1677
King Ref mr, 1684, 1692
NY Ref Ch mr, 1659, 1693
Garret (d)
King Ref mr, 1696
Gilbert
NY Ref Ch mr, 1659
Hendrick
Bkln Ref mr, 1662
NY Ref Ch mr, 1649, 1652,
1662, 1675, 1697
Herman
NY Ref Ch mr, 1657, 1682
Jacob
NY Ref Ch mr, 1655, 1657,
1677
Jacob (d)
NY Ref Ch mr, 1675
Jochem (d)
NY Ref Ch mr, 1659
Jonas
Alb Ref mr, 1683
Joost (d)
Bkln Ref mr, 1695
Joris
NY Ref Ch mr, 1672
Joris (d)
NY Ref Ch mr, 1696
Leonard
NY Ref Ch mr, 1683
Martin
NY Ref Ch mr, 1671
Matthew
NY Ref Ch mr, 1696
Mones
Bkln Ref mr, 1663
NY Ref Ch mr, 1663
Nicholas (d)
NY Ref Ch mr, 1685
Richard
King Ref mr, 1696
Vincent
Bkln Ref mr, 1695
William
Hack Ref mr, 1697
NY Ref Ch mr, 1693

Bride/Groom Pairs Directory

Magdalena (d)
  Hendrick
    NY Ref Ch mr, 1686
  Jonas
    Alb Ref mr, 1696
  Marinus
    NY Ref Ch mr, 1670
Margaret
  Abraham
    Berg Ref mr, 1698
    NY Ref Ch mr, 1681, 1691,
    1698
  Adam
    Alb Ref mr, 1697
  Adrian
    NY Ref Ch mr, 1656
  Adrian (d)
    NY Ref Ch mr, 1664
  Albert
    Fltb Ref mr, 1683
    NY Ref Ch mr, 1666
  Albert (d)
    NY Ref Ch mr, 1672
  Andrew
    NY Ref Ch mr, 1666
  Barent
    NY Ref Ch mr, 1658, 1660
  Charles
    Fltb Ref mr, 1687
  Cornelius
    King Ref mr, 1698
    NY Ref Ch mr, 1658, 1672,
    1695
  Cornelius (d)
    NY Ref Ch mr, 1686
  Daniel
    NY Ref Ch mr, 1685
  Elias
    NY Ref Ch mr, 1665
  Enoch
    Berg Ref mr, 1691
    NY Ref Ch mr, 1691
  Evert
    NY Ref Ch mr, 1695
  Francis
    Bkln Ref mr, 1661
    NY Ref Ch mr, 1692

Fred
    Alb Ref mr, 1692
    NY Ref Ch mr, 1656, 1662
  Garret
    King Ref mr, 1685
  George
    NY Ref Ch mr, 1688
  Gilbert
    King Ref mr, 1695
  Hendrick
    NY Ref Ch mr, 1660, 1662,
    1686, 1687
  Hendrick (d)
    NY Ref Ch mr, 1688
  Herman
    Alb Ref mr, 1691
    NY Ref Ch mr, 1654, 1686
  Herman (d)
    NY Ref Ch mr, 1660, 1691
  Isaac
    NY Ref Ch mr, 1682
  Jacob
    Alb Ref mr, 1691
    Berg Ref mr, 1695
    King Ref mr, 1667
    NY Ref Ch mr, 1652, 1655,
    1688, 1693, 1695
  Jacob (d)
    NY Ref Ch mr, 1695
  James
    NY Ref Ch mr, 1665
  James (d)
    NY Ref Ch mr, 1665
  Joseph
    NY Ref Ch mr, 1695
  Lambert
    NY Ref Ch mr, 1682
  Lawrence
    Berg Ref mr, 1665
    NY Ref Ch mr, 1676
  Martin
    Berg Ref mr, 1694
    Hack Ref mr, 1697
  Matthew
    King Ref mr, 1679
    NY Ref Ch mr, 1673
  Nathan
    NY Ref Ch mr, 1677

Nicholas
    NY Ref Ch mr, 1656, 1678
  Nicholas (d)
    NY Ref Ch mr, 1656, 1687
  Oliver
    NY Ref Ch mr, 1682
  Otto
    NY Ref Ch mr, 1693
  Peter
    Alb Ref mr, 1685
    Fltb Ref mr, 1684
    NY Ref Ch mr, 1659, 1661,
    1687
  Peter (d)
    NY Ref Ch mr, 1662
  Philip
    NY Ref Ch mr, 1671, 1676
  Philip (d)
    NY Ref Ch mr, 1675
  Randolph
    Fltb Ref mr, 1684
  Reinhard (d)
    NY Ref Ch mr, 1688
  Robert
    Alb Ref mr, 1697
  Samuel
    NY Ref Ch mr, 1696
  Severin
    NY Ref Ch mr, 1671
  Thomas
    NY Ref Ch mr, 1693, 1694
  Thomas (d)
    NY Ref Ch mr, 1694
  Timothy
    NY Ref Ch mr, 1675
  Volkert (d)
    NY Ref Ch mr, 1671
  Walran
    King Ref mr, 1664
  William
    NY Ref Ch mr, 1663, 1672,
    1680
  Wolfert
    NY Ref Ch mr, 1697
Margaret (d)
  Adam
    Alb Ref mr, 1697

(d) = deceased at time the
spouse remarried

Margaret (d) (cont.)

Adrian
  NY Ref Ch mr, 1643
Evert
  NY Ref Ch mr, 1669
Fred
  NY Ref Ch mr, 1692
Jacob
  NY Ref Ch mr, 1699
Lubbert
  NY Ref Ch mr, 1669
Tunis
  NY Ref Ch mr, 1696
William
  Bkln Ref mr, 1664
  NY Ref Ch mr, 1664, 1682,
  1685

Maria

Abraham
  Alb Ref mr, 1694, 1698
  King Ref mr, 1676
  NY Ref Ch mr, 1684
Adam
  Fltb Ref mr, 1690
Adolf
  NY Ref Ch mr, 1671
Adrian
  Berg Ref mr, 1686
  NY Ref Ch mr, 1645
Albert
  Alb Ref mr, 1693
  NY Ref Ch mr, 1641
  Schn Ref mr, 1699
Alexander
  NY Ref Ch mr, 1663
Ambrose
  NY Ref Ch mr, 1644
Andrew
  Fltb Ref mr, 1683
  NY Ref Ch mr, 1655, 1656,
  1688, 1689
Andrew (d)
  Fltb Ref mr, 1687
  NY Ref Ch mr, 1662
Anthony
  Fltb Ref mr, 1682
  NY Ref Ch mr, 1654, 1672

Arent
  Alb Ref mr, 1686, 1698
  King NYGB, 1670
  NY Ref Ch mr, 1679, 1695
Baltus
  NY Ref Ch mr, 1664
Barent
  NY Ref Ch mr, 1671, 1686
Bastian
  NY Ref Ch mr, 1659, 1680
Benjamin
  NY Ref Ch mr, 1693
Bernard
  NY Ref Ch mr, 1687
Bouwen
  NY Ref Ch mr, 1674
Carl
  Fltb Ref mr, 1691
  NY Ref Ch mr, 1675
Charles
  King Ref mr, 1693
Christopher
  NY Ref Ch mr, 1656
Christopher (d)
  NY Ref Ch mr, 1671
Cornelius
  Alb Ref mr, 1689, 1695
  Fltb Ref mr, 1691
  Hack Ref mr, 1696
  King Ref mr, 1685
  NY Ref Ch mr, 1658, 1665,
  1666, 1677, 1680, 1685,
  1688, 1694
Cornelius (d)
  NY Ref Ch mr, 1663
Daniel
  Schn Ref mr, 1696
David
  NY Ref Ch mr, 1692, 1699
Dionysius
  Fltb Ref mr, 1691
Dirk
  Fltb Ref mr, 1691
  NY Ref Ch mr, 1646, 1660,
  1687
Dirk (d)
  NY Ref Ch mr, 1695

Dominic (d)
  NY Ref Ch mr, 1689
Douw
  Alb Ref mr, 1685
Edward
  Alb Ref mr, 1699
Elias
  NY Ref Ch mr, 1674
Emanuel
  NY Ref Ch mr, 1671, 1689
Enoch
  NY Ref Ch mr, 1699
Evert
  NY Ref Ch mr, 1673
Felix (d)
  NY Ref Ch mr, 1645
Francis
  Berg Ref mr, 1690
Francis (d)
  NY Ref Ch mr, 1670
Fred
  NY Ref Ch mr, 1663
Gabriel
  NY Ref Ch mr, 1699
Garret
  Alb Ref mr, 1689
  NY Ref Ch mr, 1646, 1683,
  1698
Gerbrant
  Berg Ref mr, 1674
Giles
  NY Ref Ch mr, 1680
Govert
  NY Ref Ch mr, 1649
Gowing (d)
  NY Ref Ch mr, 1699
Hendrick
  Alb Ref mr, 1688, 1689,
  1692
  Berg Ref mr, 1678, 1679,
  1685
  Fltb Ref mr, 1679, 1690
  NY Ref Ch mr, 1642, 1650,
  1655, 1672, 1673, 1676,
  1685, 1691, 1694, 1698,
  1699

Hendrick (d)
  Alb Ref mr, 1696
  NY Ref Ch mr, 1684
Herbert
  Alb Ref mr, 1695
Herman
  NY Ref Ch mr, 1650, 1662,
  1676
Herman (d)
  Alb Ref mr, 1695
Heyman
  NY Ref Ch mr, 1683
Hubert
  Alb Ref mr, 1693
  NY Ref Ch mr, 1656
Hugh
  NPal Ref mr, 1690
Isaac
  Alb Ref mr, 1689, 1696
  Fltb Ref mr, 1687
  King Ref mr, 1683
  NPal Ref mr, 1683
  NY Ref Ch mr, 1663, 1675,
  1687, 1693
Jacob
  Alb Ref mr, 1696
  Bkln Ref mr, 1690
  Fltb Ref mr, 1679, 1685,
  1687
  NY Ref Ch mr, 1654, 1676,
  1678, 1679, 1684, 1697,
  1699
Jacob (d)
  Alb Ref mr, 1689
  NY Ref Ch mr, 1686
Jacques
  Bkln Ref mr, 1663
  Fltb Ref mr, 1685
Jacques (d)
  NY Ref Ch mr, 1663
James
  NY Ref Ch mr, 1695
James (d)
  Berg Ref mr, 1686
Jeremiah
  NY Ref Ch mr, 1662
Jochem
  Berg Ref mr, 1686

Jonathan
  Alb Ref mr, 1695
Joost
  NY Ref Ch mr, 1681
Joris
  Bkln Ref mr, 1685
  King Ref mr, 1696
  NY Ref Ch mr, 1666
Joris (d)
  NY Ref Ch mr, 1692
Joseph
  NY Ref Ch mr, 1683
Joseph (d)
  Bkln Ref mr, 1685
Jurian
  Fltb Ref mr, 1679
  NY Ref Ch mr, 1652
Lambert
  NY Ref Ch mr, 1690
Lawrence
  NY Ref Ch mr, 1677
Louis
  King Ref mr, 1697
Lucas
  Alb Ref mr, 1689
  Berg Ref mr, 1690
  Fltb Ref mr, 1690
Lucas (d)
  Alb Ref mr, 1693
Ludwich
  King Ref mr, 1696
Martin
  Fltb Ref mr, 1690
Matthew
  King Ref mr, 1698
  NY Ref Ch mr, 1656
Matthew (d)
  Alb Ref mr, 1685
Maynard
  NY Ref Ch mr, 1660, 1694
Michael
  Alb Ref mr, 1686
  Berg Ref mr, 1691
  NY Ref Ch mr, 1640, 1680,
  1693
Moses
  NY Ref Ch mr, 1695

Nathan
  NY Ref Ch mr, 1689
Nicholas
  Fltb Ref mr, 1684, 1686
  NY Ref Ch mr, 1655, 1661,
  1670, 1672, 1681, 1693
Nicholas (d)
  NY Ref Ch mr, 1699
Otto
  NY Ref Ch mr, 1667
Otto (d)
  NY Ref Ch mr, 1695
Paul
  NY Ref Ch mr, 1644, 1658,
  1686, 1688
Paul (d)
  Bkln Ref mr, 1664
  NY Ref Ch mr, 1664, 1687
Peek
  NY Ref Ch mr, 1697
Peter
  Alb Ref mr, 1691
  Fltb Ref mr, 1684, 1686
  NY Ref Ch mr, 1649, 1655,
  1657, 1663, 1664, 1687,
  1691, 1699
Peter (d)
  NY Ref Ch mr, 1647, 1672
Philip
  Alb Ref mr, 1688
  NY Ref Ch mr, 1642, 1668
Philip (d)
  NY Ref Ch mr, 1656, 1681
Pierre
  Alb Ref mr, 1693
Reyner
  NY Ref Ch mr, 1696
Richard
  NY Ref Ch mr, 1687, 1690,
  1696
Richard (d)
  NY Ref Ch mr, 1650
Robert
  NY Ref Ch mr, 1683, 1695
Robert (d)
  NY Ref Ch mr, 1685
Roger
  NY Ref Ch mr, 1695

(d) = deceased at time the
spouse remarried

Maria (cont.)

Sampson
  NY Ref Ch mr, 1699
Siebold
  Berg Ref mr, 1678
Simon
  Bkln Ref mr, 1663
  King Ref mr, 1683
  NY Ref Ch mr, 1647
Stephen
  NY Ref Ch mr, 1696
Sybout
  NY Ref Ch mr, 1669
Thomas
  Alb Ref mr, 1692
  Fltb Ref mr, 1692
  King Ref mr, 1683
  NY Ref Ch mr, 1645, 1663,
    1666, 1692, 1694
  Schn Ref mr, 1696
Thomas (d)
  NY Ref Ch mr, 1646
Tunis
  NY Ref Ch mr, 1642, 1675,
    1690
Tunis (d)
  Alb Ref mr, 1692
Urban
  NY Ref Ch mr, 1689
Valentine
  NY Ref Ch mr, 1662
Walter
  Fltb Ref mr, 1686
  NY Ref Ch mr, 1662
Walter (d)
  NY Ref Ch mr, 1679, 1689
Wessel
  NY Ref Ch mr, 1670
William
  Alb Ref mr, 1694
  Berg Ref mr, 1697
  Bkln Ref mr, 1664
  NY Ref Ch mr, 1642, 1664,
    1676, 1682, 1688, 1693,
    1698, 1699
William (d)
  NY Ref Ch mr, 1644, 1645,
    1691

Wolfert
  NY Ref Ch mr, 1692
Zachariah
  NY Ref Ch mr, 1693

Maria (d)

Abraham
  NY Ref Ch mr, 1663
Adrian
  Alb Ref mr, 1685
  NY Ref Ch mr, 1679
Anthony
  NY Ref Ch mr, 1685
Conrad
  NY Ref Ch mr, 1682
Cornelius
  NY Ref Ch mr, 1693
Daniel
  NY Ref Ch mr, 1685
Francis
  NY Ref Ch mr, 1697
Garret
  NY Ref Ch mr, 1679
George
  Alb Ref mr, 1691
Isaac
  Alb Ref mr, 1698
Martin
  Alb Ref mr, 1693
Nicholas
  King Ref mr, 1681
  NY Ref Ch mr, 1681
Tunis
  King Ref mr, 1696
Walter
  NY Ref Ch mr, 1698
Wessel
  King Ref mr, 1695

Martha

Hendrick
  NY Ref Ch mr, 1696
Isaac
  NY Ref Ch mr, 1697
James
  Berg Ref mr, 1697
Peter
  NY Ref Ch mr, 1644
Randolph
  Fltb Ref mr, 1684

Martha (d)

Roger
  NY Ref Ch mr, 1694

Martina

William
  Alb Ref mr, 1692

Mathilda

Abraham
  NY Ref Ch mr, 1656
Adam
  Alb Ref mr, 1690
Cornelius
  Berg Ref mr, 1681
  NY Ref Ch mr, 1665
Evert
  Fltb Ref mr, 1690
  NY Ref Ch mr, 1685
Hendrick
  NY Ref Ch mr, 1673
Michael
  NY Ref Ch mr, 1690
Nicholas
  Bkln Ref mr, 1662
Nicholas (d)
  NY Ref Ch mr, 1665

Mattina

Adrian
  NY Ref Ch mr, 1663
Arent
  Bkln Ref mr, 1663
William (d)
  NY Ref Ch mr, 1663

Minnie

Albert
  Fltb Ref mr, 1684
William
  NY Ref Ch mr, 1679

Myra (d)

William
  Bkln Ref mr, 1695

N

Nelly
  Adam
    NY Ref Ch mr, 1660
  Adam (d)
    NY Ref Ch mr, 1676

(d) = deceased at time the
spouse remarried

338

Adrian
Fltb Ref mr, 1686
Aert
Fltb Ref mr, 1686
NY Ref Ch mr, 1686
Albert
King Ref mr, 1664
Azariah
NY Ref Ch mr, 1676
Cornelius
Fltb Ref mr, 1687
King Ref mr, 1667
NY Ref Ch mr, 1662
Daniel
Fltb Ref mr, 1685
Garret
Bkln Ref mr, 1661
NY Ref Ch mr, 1682
Gilbert
NY Ref Ch mr, 1659
Hendrick
Alb Ref mr, 1697
Berg Ref mr, 1669
Fltb Ref mr, 1679
King Ref mr, 1676
NY Ref Ch mr, 1669, 1674
Hendrick (d)
Alb Ref mr, 1695
Herman
Bkln Ref mr, 1695
Hieronymus
Fltb Ref mr, 1691
Isaac
NY Ref Ch mr, 1690
Jacob
Hack Ref mr, 1699
NY Ref Ch mr, 1655, 1692
Joris
Bkln Ref mr, 1695
Louis
NY Ref Ch mr, 1650
Martin
Alb Ref mr, 1686, 1692
Martin (d)
Alb Ref mr, 1697
Peter (d)
King Ref mr, 1697

Quirinus
Fltb Ref mr, 1683
Roger
Berg Ref mr, 1697
Samuel
NY Ref Ch mr, 1699
Simon
Alb Ref mr, 1692
Thomas
NY Ref Ch mr, 1664
Thomas (d)
NY Ref Ch mr, 1674
Volkert
Fltb Ref mr, 1680
Walter
Fltb Ref mr, 1683
William (d)
King Ref mr, 1664
Nelly (d)
Cornelius
NY Ref Ch mr, 1678
Jacob
NY Ref Ch mr, 1661
Nicholas
NY Ref Ch mr, 1656
Paul
NY Ref Ch mr, 1640
Nicole
Cornelius
NY Ref Ch mr, 1642
Cornelius (d)
King Ref mr, 1662
Gustave
NY Ref Ch mr, 1689
Martin
King Ref mr, 1662
Paul
Bkln Ref mr, 1662
NY Ref Ch mr, 1662
Reyner
NY Ref Ch mr, 1692
Victor
NY Ref Ch mr, 1679
Nicole (d)
Cornelius
NY Ref Ch mr, 1659
Simon
NY Ref Ch mr, 1686

P

Palassa
Francis
NY Ref Ch mr, 1642
Francis (d)
NY Ref Ch mr, 1642
Patience
Andrew
Berg Ref mr, 1668
William
NY Ref Ch mr, 1695
Patricia
Christian
Fltb Ref mr, 1689
Garret
NY Ref Ch mr, 1654
Jacob
Berg Ref mr, 1696
Manasse
Alb Ref mr, 1699
Marshall
Berg Ref mr, 1681
Nicholas (d)
NY Ref Ch mr, 1654
Petronella
Albert
NY Ref Ch mr, 1688
Aldert
King Ref mr, 1696
Christian
NY Ref Ch mr, 1692
Hendrick
NY Ref Ch mr, 1676
Jochem
King Ref mr, 1679
William
NY Ref Ch mr, 1694
Petronella (d)
Jochem
King Ref mr, 1689
Phebe
Tunis
NY Ref Ch mr, 1640
Phizithiaen
Emanuel
NY Ref Ch mr, 1642
Leonard (d)
NY Ref Ch mr, 1642

(d) = deceased at time the
spouse remarried

Priscilla
  Jonas
    NY Ref Ch mr, 1661
Priscilla (d)
  Gustave
    NY Ref Ch mr, 1689

R

Rachel
  Abraham
    Tary Ref mr, 1698
  Aldert
    King Ref mr, 1698
  Arent (d)
    King Ref mr, 1698
  David
    NY Ref Ch mr, 1675, 1694
  Dennis
    NY Ref Ch mr, 1696
  Dirk
    Alb Ref mr, 1687
    NY Ref Ch mr, 1677, 1679
  Giles
    Alb Ref mr, 1695
  Hendrick
    NY Ref Ch mr, 1656
  Hendrick (d)
    NY Ref Ch mr, 1677
  Herman
    King Ref mr, 1695
  Jeremiah
    Schn Ref mr, 1697
  Lucas
    NY Ref Ch mr, 1683
  Maynard
    NY Ref Ch mr, 1693
  Peter
    NY Ref Ch mr, 1698, 1699
  Thomas
    NY Ref Ch mr, 1697
  William
    Fltb Ref mr, 1692
    NY Ref Ch mr, 1686
Rebecca
  Abraham
    NY Ref Ch mr, 1689

Arent
  Bkln Ref mr, 1662
Dominic
  Alb Ref mr, 1699
Francis
  NY Ref Ch mr, 1683
George
  NY Ref Ch mr, 1647
Hieronymus
  Alb Ref mr, 1684
Jacob
  NY Ref Ch mr, 1648
James
  NY Ref Ch mr, 1644
Peter
  King Ref mr, 1679
  NY Ref Ch mr, 1689
Reyer
  NY Ref Ch mr, 1696
Sara
  NY Ref Ch mr, 1642
Reyertje
  Michael
    NY Ref Ch mr, 1699
Reyntje (d)
  Garret
    Alb Ref mr, 1693
Rose
  Francis
    NY Ref Ch mr, 1656
  Stephen (d)
    NY Ref Ch mr, 1656
Ruth
  Anthony
    King Ref mr, 1683
  Jacob
    Berg Ref mr, 1692
    NY Ref Ch mr, 1693
Rymerick
  Thomas
    King NYGB, 1672

S

Sarah
  Abraham
    NY Ref Ch mr, 1695

Albert
  Fltb Ref mr, 1683
  NY Ref Ch mr, 1683
Aldert
  NY Ref Ch mr, 1656
Arent
  King Ref mr, 1698
  NY Ref Ch mr, 1680
Azariah
  Alb Ref mr, 1697
Barent
  NY Ref Ch mr, 1685
Benjamin
  NY Ref Ch mr, 1670
Carl
  NY Ref Ch mr, 1647
Christopher
  Berg Ref mr, 1698
Cornelius
  Bkln Ref mr, 1686
  NY Ref Ch mr, 1669, 1684
Cornelius (d)
  NY Ref Ch mr, 1683
Daniel
  NY Ref Ch mr, 1673, 1674
David
  Hack Ref mr, 1697
Edward
  NY Ref Ch mr, 1674
Edward (d)
  NY Ref Ch mr, 1689
Garret
  Alb Ref mr, 1694
  NY Ref Ch mr, 1692, 1698
Hendrick
  Alb Ref mr, 1686
  NY Ref Ch mr, 1644, 1660,
    1686, 1689
Isaac
  NY Ref Ch mr, 1641, 1684,
    1686
Jacob
  Alb Ref mr, 1695
  Fltb Ref mr, 1694
  NY Ref Ch mr, 1664, 1699
Jacob (d)
  NY Ref Ch mr, 1664

Jacques
  Fltb Ref mr, 1680
Joost
  King Ref mr, 1682
Joris
  Fltb Ref mr, 1678
Lambert
  Bkln Ref mr, 1663
Lawrence
  NY Ref Ch mr, 1661, 1666
Lawrence (d)
  NY Ref Ch mr, 1685
Matthew
  King Ref mr, 1697
Michael
  NY Ref Ch mr, 1699
Nicholas
  King Ref mr, 1689
  NY Ref Ch mr, 1680
Paul
  Bkln Ref mr, 1677
  NY Ref Ch mr, 1677
Paul (d)
  NY Ref Ch mr, 1691
Peter
  Fltb Ref mr, 1680
  NY Ref Ch mr, 1648, 1687, 1688
Reyner
  Alb Ref mr, 1699
Rupert
  NY Ref Ch mr, 1684
Thomas
  Fltb Ref mr, 1692
  NY Ref Ch mr, 1640, 1643
Thomas (d)
  NY Ref Ch mr, 1644, 1647
Tunis
  Alb Ref mr, 1696
  Fltb Ref mr, 1684
  King Ref mr, 1695
  NY Ref Ch mr, 1650, 1684, 1696
Volkert
  Fltb Ref mr, 1681
William
  Hack Ref mr, 1696
  NY Ref Ch mr, 1656

William (d)
  NY Ref Ch mr, 1690
Sarah (d)
Arent
  NY Ref Ch mr, 1690
Tunis
  Fltb Ref mr, 1687
  NY Ref Ch mr, 1687
William
  Alb Ref mr, 1693
Seyke
William
  Alb Ref mr, 1690
Sophia
Abraham
  Berg Ref mr, 1691
Andrew
  NY Ref Ch mr, 1671
Barent
  NY Ref Ch mr, 1658
Benjamin
  Alb Ref mr, 1699
  NY Ref Ch mr, 1697
Cornelius
  Berg Ref mr, 1685
Dirk
  Alb Ref mr, 1687
  Berg Ref mr, 1698
  NY Ref Ch mr, 1695
Francis (d)
  Alb Ref mr, 1697
Hendrick
  NY Ref Ch mr, 1682, 1694
Hendrick (d)
  Alb Ref mr, 1692
Jacob
  Fltb Ref mr, 1678
  NY Ref Ch mr, 1666, 1678
Joost
  King Ref mr, 1663
  NY Ref Ch mr, 1663
Joris
  Fltb Ref mr, 1684
Joseph
  Alb Ref mr, 1688
  Fltb Ref mr, 1677
Lubbert
  NY Ref Ch mr, 1669

Martin
  Alb Ref mr, 1696
Matthew
  Fltb Ref mr, 1692
Patrick
  Alb Ref mr, 1697
Peter
  Bkln Ref mr, 1663
  NY Ref Ch mr, 1686, 1697
Seger
  NY Ref Ch mr, 1686
Seger (d)
  NY Ref Ch mr, 1694
Simon
  NY Ref Ch mr, 1671
Tunis
  NY Ref Ch mr, 1679
William
  Alb Ref mr, 1697
  Fltb Ref mr, 1690
  NY Ref Ch mr, 1674
William (d)
  NY Ref Ch mr, 1697
Sophia (d)
Hendrick
  NY Ref Ch mr, 1669
Jacob
  NY Ref Ch mr, 1677
Joost
  King Ref mr, 1668
Susan
Aert (d)
  NY Ref Ch mr, 1645
Arent
  NY Ref Ch mr, 1673
Cornelius
  Alb Ref mr, 1693
Evert
  NY Ref Ch mr, 1644
Garret
  NY Ref Ch mr, 1681
Hendrick
  NY Ref Ch mr, 1644
Hieronymus
  NY Ref Ch mr, 1682
Hieronymus (d)
  NY Ref Ch mr, 1699

(d) = deceased at time the
spouse remarried

Susan (cont.)

Jacob
King Ref mr, 1698
Joris
NY Ref Ch mr, 1699
Martin
Fltb Ref mr, 1686
NY Ref Ch mr, 1660
Matthew
Alb Ref mr, 1698
Melchior
NY Ref Ch mr, 1674
Nicholas
NY Ref Ch mr, 1649, 1652, 1658
Peter
Alb Ref mr, 1688
NY Ref Ch mr, 1665, 1683
Reyner
NY Ref Ch mr, 1660
Roelof
Berg Ref mr, 1682
Siebold
NY Ref Ch mr, 1645
Swan
Fltb Ref mr, 1685
Thomas
Hack Ref mr, 1697
Tunis
Berg Ref mr, 1683
NY Ref Ch mr, 1683
Wessel
NY Ref Ch mr, 1692
William
NY Ref Ch mr, 1643, 1699
William (d)
NY Ref Ch mr, 1644

Susan (d)

Adrian
NY Ref Ch mr, 1685
Arent
NY Ref Ch mr, 1678
Caspar
NY Ref Ch mr, 1682
Peter
NY Ref Ch mr, 1682, 1699

T

Temperence

Isaac
NY Ref Ch mr, 1679

Theodora

Daniel
Alb Ref mr, 1698
Enoch
Berg Ref mr, 1670
NY Ref Ch mr, 1670
Jacob
King Ref mr, 1698
Peter
Berg Ref mr, 1683

Theodora (d)

Dirk
NY Ref Ch mr, 1670
Enoch
Berg Ref mr, 1691
NY Ref Ch mr, 1691
Peter
NY Ref Ch mr, 1657
Reyner
Berg Ref mr, 1698
Hack Ref mr, 1699

U

Ursula

Dirk
NY Ref Ch mr, 1674
Roelof
Berg Ref mr, 1688
NY Ref Ch mr, 1688

Ursula (d)

Barent
NY Ref Ch mr, 1660

V

Vaerende?

Justus
NY Ref Ch mr, 1673

Volkje

Adrian
Alb Ref mr, 1685
Hendrick
NY Ref Ch mr, 1655

Nicholas
NY Ref Ch mr, 1652
Peter (d)
Alb Ref mr, 1685

Vroutje

Abraham
NY Ref Ch mr, 1689
Andrew
Berg Ref mr, 1671
Garret
Berg Ref mr, 1684
Hack Ref mr, 1696
NY Ref Ch mr, 1684   *
George
NY Ref Ch mr, 1692
Tunis
NY Ref Ch mr, 1689

Vroutje (d)

Garret
Berg Ref mr, 1691
Jacob
NY Ref Ch mr, 1657

W

Wackraet (d)

Louis
NY Ref Ch mr, 1646

Walburg

Francis
NY Ref Ch mr, 1660

Wilhelmina

Albert (d)
King Ref mr, 1668
Anthony
Alb Ref mr, 1685
Bartholomew (d)
NY Ref Ch mr, 1680
Cornelius
NY Ref Ch mr, 1658, 1693
Garret
Fltb Ref mr, 1685
Hendrick
Fltb Ref mr, 1685
Hubert
NY Ref Ch mr, 1679
Lavinus
Alb Ref mr, 1699

Nicholas
> NY Ref Ch mr, 1689

Peter
> NY Ref Ch mr, 1653

Simon (d)
> Alb Ref mr, 1699

Tunis
> King Ref mr, 1696

Wits

Andrew
> NY Ref Ch mr, 1655

Wybrecht

Herman
> NY Ref Ch mr, 1679

Jacob
> Berg Ref mr, 1681

Wybrecht (d)

Dirk
> NY Ref Ch mr, 1677

(d) = deceased at time the
spouse remarried